Dimensions in modern management

Page 302 is power → INFLUING

Dimensions in modern management

Second edition

Patrick E. Connor
Oregon State University

With the collaboration of
Theo Haimann Saint Louis University
William G. Scott University of Washington

Houghton Mifflin Company Boston
Dallas   Geneva, Illinois   Hopewell, New Jersey
Palo Alto   London

Printed in the U.S.A.
Library of Congress Catalog Card Number: 77-75692
ISBN: 0-395-25515-5

To Sara, Michael, Kristen, and Frank

Contents

Preface xiii

Introduction: Management and the organization 1

  1 The concept of formal organization 2
Peter M. Blau and W. Richard Scott
  2 What is management? 7
American Institute of Management

Part I The managerial perspective 13

  3 The management theory jungle 14
Harold Koontz
  4 The contingency theory of management: A path out of the jungle 29
Fred Luthans
  5 Hanging together: Mazda and the establishment 37
Norman Pearlstine

Part II Planning 41

II/A Setting objectives
  6 Setting goals in management by objectives 42
Henry L. Tosi, John R. Rizzo, and Stephen J. Carroll

II/B Planning
  7 Does GE really plan better? 57
Richard Zoglin

II/C Forecasting
  8 Elements of forecasting 64
James W. Redfield

9 A think tank that helps companies plan: Project Aware uses Delphi forecasting to predict the 1980s 81
Business Week

II/D Planning: An application
10 Urban planning: Ripe for systems analysis 85
Jerry L. Pollak and Martin I. Taft

Part III Organizing 93

III/A The span of management
11 Making theory operational: The span of management 95
Harold Koontz

III/B Authority
12 The three types of legitimate rule 110
Max Weber

III/C Centralization vs. decentralization
13 The centralization vs. decentralization issue: Arguments, alternatives, and guidelines 121
George Glaser

III/D Line and staff
14 Line and staff: An obsolete concept? 134
Hall H. Logan

III/E Coordinating
15 A review of vertical and lateral relations: A new perspective for managers 141
James L. Hall and Joel K. Leidecker
16 Committee management: Guidelines from social science research 149
A. C. Filley

III/F Organizational design
17 Principles of organization 163
S. Avery Raube
18 Organizational realities 171
Rocco Carzo, Jr.
19 Frankly speaking 184
Phil Frank
20 Is there a best way to organize a business enterprise? 184
Y. K. Shetty
21 People, productivity, and organizational structure 191
Joel E. Ross and Robert G. Murdick

III/G   Organizing: Applications

22 A goal approach to organizational design   201
Patrick E. Connor and Stefan D. Bloomfield

23 Organization and management techniques in the federal government   212
Forest W. Horton, Jr.

24 Government Simplication Department   225
The Wall Street Journal

Part IV   Staffing   227

IV/A   Identifying managerial competence

25 More concerns use "assessment centers" to gauge employees' Managerial abilities   228
James C. Hyatt

26 Affirmative action program: It's realities and challenges   231
Gopal C. Pati and Patrick E. Fahey

IV/B   Developing managerial skills

27 Management development as process of influence   243
Edgar H. Schein

28 An additional thought on management development: A note from the Editor   260
Patrick E. Connor

IV/C   Appraising managerial performance

29 Making performance appraisal relevant   262
Winston Oberg

30 Measuring managers by results   273
Dale D. McConkey

IV/D   Rewarding the manager

31 Executive fringe benefit: Cold cash   282
Roger Ricklefs

32 Executive Rewards   285
The New Yorker

33 What is an executive worth?   286
Arch Patton

Part V   Influencing   301

V/A   Influence and leadership

34 The bases of social power   302
John R. P. French, Jr., and Bertram Raven

35 How to choose a leadership pattern 311
Robert Tannenbaum and Warren H. Schmidt

36 Retrospective commentary 323
Robert Tannenbaum and Warren H. Schmidt

37 How do you make leaders more effective? New answers to an old puzzle 327
Fred E. Fiedler

38 The golden rule 344
Brent Parker and Johnny Hart

V/B Motivation

39 That urge to achieve 345
David C. McClelland

40 The motivation-hygiene concept and problems of manpower 353
Frederick Herzberg

41 Facts and fictions about working women explored; several stereotypes prove false in national study 360
Institute for Social Research

42 Beyond Theory Y 363
John J. Morse and Jay W. Lorsch

43 The jackpot 374
Anonymous

44 Motivation on Fiji 375
Reuters News Service

V/C Influencing: Organizational implications

45 Non-formal aspects of the organization 376
John M. Pfiffner and Frank P. Sherwood

46 The satisfaction-performance controversy: New developments and their implications 384
Charles N. Greene

47 A situational change typology 397
Robin Stuart-Kotzé

48 Workers can set their own wages—responsibly 405
Edward E. Lawler

Part VI Controlling 411

49 The many dimensions of control 412
Leonard Sayles

50 Human resource accounting in industry 422
R. Lee Brummet, William C. Pyle, and Eric G. Famholtz

51 Break-even charts 437
Earl P. Strong and Robert D. Smith

52 Some behavioral implications and budgeting systems 440
William Daugherty and Donald Harvey

Part VII Linking processes 447

VII/A Decision making
   53 Making effective decisions 448
      Alan J. Rowe
   54 Administrative decision making 456
      Herbert A Simon
   55 Techniques of operations research 463
      William G. Browne

VII/B Communicating
   56 Barriers and gateways to communication 473
      Carl R. Rogers and F. M. Roethlisberger
   57 Stimulating upward communication 483
      Earl G. Planty and William Machaver
   58 Ten Commandments of good communication 489
      American Management Association

Conclusion 493

Conclusion/A Managing social responsibilities
   59 Can business afford to ignore social responsibilities? 494
      Keith Davis
   60 The hazards of corporate responsibility 502
      Gilbert Burck
   61 The small society 512
      Morrie Brickman
   62 Feeding 3rd-world babies 512
      Philip West

Conclusion/B Organizational effectiveness
   63 How to evaluate a firm 515
      Robert B. Buchele

Conclusion/C Managing in the future
   64 The coming death of bureaucracy 535
      Warren G. Bennis
   65 The third sector and domestic missions 544
      Amitai Etzioni
   66 The manager of the future 560
      John F. Mee

Conclusion/D A final thought
   67 On technological progress 571
      John D. MacDonald
   68 See what we mean? 572
      George A. Krimsky

Preface

The principal objective of this volume is to provide a framework of selected readings to assist in understanding one of the most important tasks in our modern society: managing large organizations. This objective is facilitated by the two major subgoals of the book: first, the anthology has been compiled in order to provide the reader—whether student, practitioner, or teacher of management—with a collection of readings that is comprehensive in its coverage of the management field; second, the readings have been selected to broaden and deepen the understanding of management that the reader should gain from studying current textbooks in the field.

An anthology such as this is necessary because management is one of the most complex and important fields in the modern university. Its complexity, as well as its unsettled nature, stems in part from the variety of disciplines upon which it is founded; sociology, psychology, political science, engineering, economics, mathematics, and anthropology are only several of the fields involved. Not surprisingly, this variety often produces disagreements as to the very meaning of management and therefore differing opinions on the procedures a successful manager should follow.

The complexity of the field does not exist simply because of a lack of agreement among various scholars, however. As with medicine, management is a practical art, and as we shall see in this book, its practice is affected by a variety of factors. The managerial function is determined, first, by the organization's structure—its goals, the distribution of power and authority, and its technology and communications systems; second, by the needs, aspirations, and roles of its members; and third, by the impact of the environment on the organization. Because the specific ways in which these factors affect the manager are varied, the study of management becomes even more complex.

The importance of studying management is rooted in the fact that "management" per se is a modern institution, unique to our times. Peter F. Drucker has described the growth of management as a potent force in our society:

The emergence of management as an essential, a distant, and a leading institution is a pivotal event in social history. Rarely, if ever, has a new basic institution, a new leading group, emerged as fast as has management since the turn of this century. Rarely in human history has a new institution proven indispensable so quickly; and even less often has a new institution arrived with so little opposition, so little disturbance, so little controversy. [1]

As I have stated, the chief objective of this book is to further the understanding of this discipline called management. These readings are introduced by two selections, the first describing the area in which the manager operates—that is, the formal organization—and the second discussing what "management" means. Part I continues our introductory treatment by examining the two principal perspectives that shape managers' thinking: contingency and open systems.

Part II deals with the initial managerial task, planning. The selections range from a description of management by objectives (MBO) to the forecasting and planning processes themselves, concluding with an example of planning in the public sector.

Part III presents a wide-ranging discussion of the manager's organizing task; selections vary from statements of some classical principles to a description of the most recent idea in this area: organizational design. The section concludes with three examples.

Part IV begins the explicit acknowledgment that organizations are composed of people; it is therefore one of the principal tasks of a manager to ensure that the organization continues to enjoy good management so that employees will respond favorably. Part V deals specifically with the human aspects of the organizational membership: bases of influence, needs, motivation, and leadership processes.

Part VI presents some ways in which managers measure and monitor performance; the coverage ranges from a discussion of budgets to comprehensive ideas about overall organizational control.

Part VII provides discussions of two fundamental processes, decision making and communicating, that "link" the basic managerial functions discussed above.

The book concludes with an examination of three major issues facing modern managers: social responsibility, overall organizational effectiveness, and the future. The last two items in the volume are intended as thought-starters.

In general, I hope that this series of selections will serve as a stimulus to the reader. Although it is impossible to cover every aspect of every topic in the field, this book attempts to encourage the reader to explore further the institution we call management.

The astute reader will no doubt notice that many of the articles contained in this volume reflect an attitude toward social roles that some might label "sexist." The student should note that the articles subject to this criticism were written many years ago and will recognize the valuable and enduring contribution that they make to the professional literature. In their more current writings, however, the authors of these articles strive to reflect

[1] Peter F. Drucker, *The Practice of Management* (New York: Harper & Row, 1954), pp. 3–4.

a sensitivity in this area that befits their stature as scholars and educators and that is in line with contemporary standards.

My revision of this book has benefited from suggestions made by many people. Detailed analyses and reviews of the manuscript were prepared by Professor Arnold C. Cooper, of Purdue University; Professor David E. Blevins, of The University of Mississippi; and Mr. James Gatza, CPCU, of The American Institute for Property and Liability Underwriters. The ideas and comments of these people helped me to prepare this book.

These prefatory remarks would be incomplete without acknowledgments of appreciation to a number of people: Chief among these are my wife and family, to whom this volume is dedicated, and to Bill Scott, Theo Haimann, and Doug Simpson, whose assistance continues to be valuable and stimulating. I am also indebted to my colleague Craig Lundberg, who came to my aid at a couple of crucial points. In addition, I gratefully acknowledge the cooperation of the publishers and authors of the selections in permitting the reprinting of their articles. Elizabeth Marie Smith's cheerful and skilled assistance, especially with the organizing necessary to accomplish the editing of this volume, was invaluable. Finally, I appreciate the contribution by a Portland FM radio station toward helping to mitigate some of the more onerous aspects of such a project as this.

P.E.C.

Introduction

Management and the organization

We are born in organizations, educated by organizations, and most of us spend much of our lives working for organizations. We spend much of our leisure time paying, playing, and praying in organizations. Most of us will die in an organization, and when the time comes for burial, the largest organization of all—the state—must grant official permission.
    Amitai Etzioni

Management is a process by which human and nonhuman resources are coordinated to accomplish a set of objectives. In contemporary Western society, this process ordinarily occurs within the framework of the formal organization. A helpful definition of formal organizations is offered by W. Richard Scott, a sociologist specializing in organizations:

organizations are defined as collectivities . . . for the pursuit of relatively specific objectives on a more or less continuous basis. In addition, formal organizations are characterized by relatively fixed boundaries, a normative order, authority ranks, a communication system, and an incentive system which enables various types of participants to work together in the pursuit of common goals.[1]

A more comprehensive description of the formal organization is given in the first selection in this book by Blau and Scott.
    The second selection, presented by The American Institute of Management, informs us that the manager's role is fairly complex. That role furthermore, is undergoing significant changes.
    In general, our understanding of modern management is enhanced if we remember the fundamental managing process: *managers* perform basic *management functions* (of planning, organizing, staffing, influencing, and controlling), which are facilitated by the fundamental *linking processes* of decision making and communicating, to achieve the basic *managerial purpose* of organizational effectiveness.

[1] W. Richard Scott, "Theory of Organizations" in *Handbook of Modern Sociology*, ed. Robert E. L. Faris (Chicago: Rand McNally, 1964), p. 488.

1

1 The concept of formal organization
Peter M. Blau and W. Richard Scott

Social organization and formal organizations

Although a wide variety of organizations exists, when we speak of an organization it is generally quite clear what we mean and what we do not mean by this term. We may refer to the American Medical Association as an organization, or to a college fraternity; to the Bureau of Internal Revenue, or to a union; to General Motors, or to a church; to the Daughters of the American Revolution, or to an army. But we would not call a family an organization, nor would we so designate a friendship clique, or a community, or an economic market, or the political institutions of a society. What is the specific and differentiating criterion implicit in our intuitive distinction of organizations from other kinds of social groupings or institutions? It has something to do with how human conduct becomes socially organized, but it is not, as one might first suspect, whether or not social controls order and organize the conduct of individuals, since such social controls operate in both types of circumstances.

Before specifying what is meant by formal organization, let us clarify the general concept of social organization. "Social organization" refers to the ways in which human conduct becomes socially organized, that is, to the observed regularities in the behavior of people that are due to the social conditions in which they find themselves rather than to their physiological or psychological characteristics as individuals. The many social conditions that influence the conduct of people can be divided into two main types, which constitute the two basic aspects of social organizations: (1) the structure of social relations in a group or larger collectivity of people, and (2) the shared beliefs and orientations that unite the members of the collectivity and guide their conduct.

The conception of structure or system implies that the component units stand in some relation to one another and, as the popular expression "The whole is greater than the sum of its parts" suggests, that the relations between units add new elements to the situation.[1] This aphorism, like so many others, is a half-truth. The sum of fifteen apples, for example, is no more than fifteen times one apple. But a block of ice is more than the sum of the atoms of hydrogen and oxygen that compose it. In the case of the apples, there exist no linkages or relations between the units comprising the whole. In the case of the ice, however, specific connections have been

Source: From Peter M. Blau and W. Richard Scott, *Formal Organizations: A Comparative Approach* (New York: Intext Educational Publishers, 1962), pp. 2–8.
[1] For a discussion of some of the issues raised by this assertion, see Ernest Nagel, "On the Statement 'The Whole is More Than the Sum of Its Parts'," Paul F. Lazarsfeld and Morris Rosenberg (eds.). *The Language of Social Research,* Glencoe, Ill.: Free Press, 1955, pp. 519–527.

formed between H and O atoms and among H_2O molecules that distinguish ice from hydrogen and oxygen, on the one hand, and from water, on the other. Similarly, a busload of passengers does not constitute a group, since no social relations unify individuals into a common structure.[2] But a busload of club members on a Sunday outing is a group, because a network of social relations links the members into a social structure, a structure which is an emergent characteristic of the collectivity that cannot be reduced to the attributes of its individual members. In short, a network of social relations transforms an aggregate of individuals into a group (or an aggregate of groups into a larger social structure), and the group is more than the sum of the individuals composing it since the structure of social relations is an emergent element that influences the conduct of individuals.

To indicate the nature of social relations, we can briefly dissect this concept. Social relations involve, first, patterns of social interaction: the frequency and duration of the contacts between people, the tendency to initiate these contacts, the direction of influence between persons, the degree of cooperation, and so forth. Second, social relations entail people's sentiments to one another, such as feelings of attraction, respect, and hostility. The differential distribution of social relations in a group, finally, defines its status structure. Each member's status in the group depends on his relations with the others—their sentiments toward and interaction with him. As a result, integrated members become differentiated from isolates, those who are widely respected from those who are not highly regarded, and leaders from followers. In addition to these relations between individuals within groups, relations also develop between groups, relations that are a source of still another aspect of social status, since the standing of the group in the larger social system becomes part of the status of any of its members. An obvious example is the significance that membership in an ethnic minority, say, Puerto Rican, has for an individual's social status.

The networks of social relations between individuals and groups, and the status structure defined by them, constitute the core of the social organization of a collectivity, but not the whole of it. The other main dimension of social organization is a system of shared beliefs and orientations, which serve as standards for human conduct. In the course of social interaction common notions arise as to how people should act and interact and what objectives are worthy of attainment. First, common values crystallize, values that govern the goals for which men strive—their ideals and their ideas of what is desirable—such as our belief in democracy or the importance financial success assumes in our thinking. Second, social norms develop—that is, common expectations concerning how people ought to behave—and social sanctions are used to discourage violations of these norms. These socially sanctioned rules of conduct vary in significance from moral principles or mores, as Sumner calls them, to mere customs or folkways. If values define the ends of human conduct, norms distinguish behavior that is a legitimate

---

[2] A purist may, concededly, point out that all individuals share the role of passenger and so are subject to certain generalized norms, courtesy for example.

means for achieving these ends from behavior that is illegitimate. Finally, aside from the norms to which everybody is expected to conform, differential role expectations also emerge, expectations that become associated with various social positions. Only women in our society are expected to wear skirts, for example. Or, the respected leader of a group is expected to make suggestions and the other members will turn to him in times of difficulties, whereas group members who have not earned the respect of others are expected to refrain from making suggestions and generally to participate little in group discussions.

These two dimensions of social organization—the networks of social relations and the shared orientations—are often referred to as the social structure and the culture, respectively.[3] Every society has a complex social structure and a complex culture, and every community within a society can be characterized by these two dimensions of social organization, and so can every group within a community (except that the specific term "culture" is reserved for the largest social systems). The prevailing cultural standards and the structure of social relations serve to organize human conduct in the collectivity. As people conform more or less closely to the expectations of their fellows, and as the degree of their conformity in turn influences their relations with others and their social status, and as their status in further turn affects their inclinations to adhere to social norms and their chances to achieve valued objectives, their patterns of behavior become socially organized.

In contrast to the social organization that emerges whenever men are living together, there are organizations that have been deliberately established for a certain purpose.[4] If the accomplishment of an objective requires collective effort, men set up an organization designed to coordinate the activities of many persons and to furnish incentives for others to join them for this purpose. For example, business concerns are established in order to produce goods that can be sold for a profit, and workers organize unions in order to increase their bargaining power with employers. In these cases, the goals to be achieved, the rules the members of the organization are expected to follow, and the status structure that defines the relations between them (the organizational chart) have not spontaneously emerged in the course of social interaction but have been consciously designed a priori to anticipate and guide interaction and activities. Since the distinctive characteristic of these organizations is that they have been formally established for the explicit purpose of achieving certain goals, the term "formal organizations" is used to designate them. And this formal establishment for explicit purpose is the criterion that distinguishes our subject matter from the study of social organization in general.

[3] See the recent discussion of these concepts by Kroeber and Parsons, who conclude by defining culture as "transmitted and created content and patterns of values, ideas, and other symbolic-meaningful systems" and social structure or system as "the specifically relational system of interaction among individuals and collectivities." A. L. Kroeber and Talcott Parsons, "The Concepts of Culture and of the Social System," *American Sociological Review,* 23 (1958), p. 583.

[4] Sumner makes this distinction between, in his terms, "crescive" and "enacted" social institutions. William Graham Sumner, *Folkways,* Boston: Ginn, 1907, p. 54.

Formal organization and informal organization

The fact that an organization has been formally established, however, does not mean that all activities and interactions of its members conform strictly to the official blueprint. Regardless of the time and effort devoted by management to designing a rational organization chart and elaborate procedure manuals, this official plan can never completely determine the conduct and social relations of the organization's members. Stephen Vincent Benét illustrates this limitation when he contrasts the military blueprint with military action:

If you take a flat map
And move wooden blocks upon it strategically,
The thing looks well, the blocks behave as they should.
The science of war is moving live men like blocks.
And getting the blocks into place at a fixed moment.
But it takes time to mold your men into blocks
And flat maps turn into country where creeks and gullies
Hamper your wooden squares. They stick in the brush,
They are tired and rest, they straggle after ripe blackberries,
And you cannot lift them up in your hand and move them.[5]

In every formal organization there arise informal organizations. The constituent groups of the organization, like all groups, develop their own practices, values, norms, and social relations as their members live and work together. The roots of these informal systems are embedded in the formal organization itself and nurtured by the very formality of its arrangements. Official rules must be general to have sufficient scope to cover the multitude of situations that may arise. But the application of these general rules to particular cases often poses problems of judgment, and informal practices tend to emerge that provide solutions for these problems. Decisions not anticipated by official regulations must frequently be made, particularly in times of change, and here again unofficial practices are likely to furnish guides for decisions long before the formal rules have been adapted to the changing circumstances. Moreover, unofficial norms are apt to develop that regulate performance and productivity. Finally, complex networks of social relations and informal status structures emerge, within groups and between them, which are influenced by many factors besides the organizational chart, for example by the background characteristics of various persons, their abilities, their willingness to help others, and their conformity to group norms. But to say that these informal structures are not completely determined by the formal institution is not to say that they are entirely independent of it. For informal organizations develop in response to the opportunities created and the problems posed by their environment, and the formal organization constitutes the immediate environment of the groups within it.

[5] From *John Brown's Body.* Holt, Rinehart & Winston, Inc. Copyright, 1927, 1928, by Stephen Vincent Benét. Copyright renewed, 1955, 1956, by Rosemary Carr Benét.

When we speak of formal organizations in this book, we do not mean to imply that attention is confined to formally instituted patterns; quite the contrary. It is impossible to understand the nature of a formal organization without investigating the networks of informal relations and the unofficial norms as well as the formal hierarchy of authority and the official body of rules, since the formally instituted and the informally emerging patterns are inextricably intertwined. The distinction between the formal and the informal aspects of organizational life is only an analytical one and should not be reified; there is only one actual organization. Note also that one does not speak of the informal organization of a family or of a community. The term "informal organization" does not refer to all types of emergent patterns of social life but only to those that evolve within the framework of a formally established organization. Excluded from our purview are social institutions that have evolved without explicit design; included are the informally emerging as well as the formally instituted patterns within formally established organizations.

The decision of the members of a group to formalize their endeavors and relations by setting up a specific organization, say, a social and athletic club, is not fortuitous. If a group is small enough for all members to be in direct social contact, and if it has no objectives that require coordination of activities, there is little need for explicit procedures or a formal division of labor. But the larger the group and the more complex the task it seeks to accomplish, the greater are the pressures to become explicitly organized.[6] Once a group of boys who merely used to hang around a drugstore decide to participate in the local baseball league, they must organize a team. And the complex coordination of millions of soldiers with thousands of specialized duties in a modern army requires extensive formalized procedures and a clear-cut authority structure.

Since formal organizations are often very large and complex, some authors refer to them as "large-scale" or as "complex" organizations. But we have eschewed these terms as misleading in two respects. First, organizations vary in size and complexity, and using these variables as defining criteria would result in such odd expressions as "a small large-scale organization" or "a very complex complex organization." Second, although formal organizations often become very large and complex, their size and complexity do not rival those of the social organization of a modern society, which includes such organizations and their relations with one another in addition to other nonorganizational patterns. (Perhaps the complexity of formal organizations is so much emphasized because it is man-made whereas the complexity of societal organization has slowly emerged, just as the complexity of modern computers is more impressive than that of the human brain. Complexity by design may be more conspicuous than complexity by growth or evolution.)

The term "bureaucratic organization," which also is often used, calls attention to the fact that organizations generally possess some sort of

---

[6] For a discussion of size and its varied effects on the characteristics of social organization, see Theodore Caplow, "Organizational Size," *Administrative Science Quarterly,* 1 (1957), pp. 484–505.

administrative machinery. In an organization that has been formally established, a specialized administrative staff usually exists that is responsible for maintaining the organization as a going concern and for coordinating the activities of its members. Large and complex organizations require an especially elaborate administrative apparatus. In a large factory, for example, there is not only an industrial work force directly engaged in production but also an administration composed of executive, supervisory, clerical, and other staff personnel. The case of a government agency is more complicated, because such an agency is part of the administrative arm of the nation. The entire personnel of, say, a law-enforcement agency is engaged in administration, but administration of different kinds; whereas operating officials administer the law and thereby help maintain social order in the society, their superiors and the auxiliary staff administer agency procedures and help maintain the organization itself.

One aspect of bureaucratization that has received much attention is the elaboration of detailed rules and regulations that the members of the organization are expected to faithfully follow. Rigid enforcement of the minutiae of extensive official procedures often impedes effective operations. Colloquially, the term "bureaucracy" connotes such rule-encumbered inefficiency. In sociology, however, the term is used neutrally to refer to the administrative aspects of organizations. If bureaucratization is defined as the amount of effort devoted to maintaining the organization rather than to directly achieving its objectives, all formal organizations have at least a minimum of bureaucracy—even if this bureaucracy involves no more than a secretary-treasurer who collects dues. But wide variations have been found in the degree of bureaucratization in organizations, as indicated by the amount of effort devoted to administrative problems, the proportion of administrative personnel, the hierarchical character of the organization, or the strict enforcement of administrative procedures and rigid compliance with them.

---

2 What is management?
American Institute of Management

The American Institute of Management, like other students in this field, recognizes that management is a branch of the so-called behavioral sciences, subject to observation, analysis, and theoretical formulation in much the same way as sociology, psychology, and economics.

The systematic study of management is still too young to have devised any general unifying theory of management behavior. The Institute has

Source: From "What Is Management?" American Institute of Management, Inc., 1959, pp. 2–6. © 1959 by American Management Association, Inc.

been concerned by the lack of an adequate intellectual framework from which such a theory might arise. Semantic vagueness, unfortunately, characterizes the entire field. Indeed, the word *management* itself is so inadequately defined as to form a major obstacle to serious study. The boundaries of the term are too vague, and it includes too many different levels and types of activity. It is used to designate either a group of functions or the personnel who carry them out; to describe either an organization's official hierarchy or the activities of the men who compose it; to provide an antonym to either *labor* or *ownership.* Yet in spite of the confusion, everyone has a general (even if uneven and diffuse) idea of the broad range of phenomena to which the word refers.

A practical businessman or working executive may call this problem "academic" and "theoretical"—as it is. Nonetheless it is extremely important. There is an old, cynical saying among physicists and mathematicians that "A practical man is a man who does what he does without knowing why he does it." The saying is unfair. While the practical man's prime interest may not be in the *why*, and while he may have empirical insights that have not yet been accounted for in the theories, he wants to know "why" just the same. This is as true of practical managers as it is of practical technological men. And if practitioners and students of management are ever to get at the *why's* of their profession, they have to face and begin to solve the initial problem of what they understand the word *management* to mean.

The Institute here offers its members and readers the description of management that appears below as a modest contribution—admittedly tentative and preliminary—toward the first elements of a unified theory of management. It records the conclusion of the Institute's management auditors, gained during a number of years of studying excellently managed enterprises, that the definition of management must relate two major areas of function: the systematic analysis of values and the scientific establishment of casual relations.

Toward a general theory of the management process

Management is the art of bringing ends and means together—the art of purposeful action.

Essentially, it is a process—a process that usually contains three elements: the selection of a goal, the initiation of planned actions to reach it, and continuous review of the effectiveness of the actions and the value of the goal.

Management does not deal with human and material resources alone. It deals also with problems of morals, ethics, and ideals—because ends are determined by values (that is, preferences) and because means must be morally acceptable. It deals with problems of prediction—because its chosen means necessarily operate under conditions unknown when plans are made. It deals with problems of scientific truth—because it must assume an objectively verifiable cause-and-effect relation between the means selected and the ends desired.

Selection and clarification of ends is the first task in management. Commonly, goals are selected through a process of weighing the relative attractiveness of several possible ones against the supposed relative availability of the means of achieving each one. Both the ends and the means derive from the whole physical, social, and cultural environment of the undertaking. Hence management includes study of that environment.

Since practically no undertaking is ever carried on for a single purpose, management must rank its several ends in order to get a basis for distributing effort among them according to their relative importance.

Most major goals can be achieved only by breaking them down into subsidiary goals each of which is regarded as a means to the larger goal. Each intermediate goal in turn may have to be resolved into still further subsidiary goals on a lower level of subordination. The process continues down to the goals of the simplest activities employed as means. Some of the intermediate or enabling goals can be pursued simultaneously and independently of each other. Others must be achieved in sequence. Such a system of resolution leads to plans and time schedules for action. It is necessary in all enterprises, even those of individuals, though most people make such breakdowns unconsciously and as they go along.

The selection of goals and methods must take into account society's insistence that certain social and cultural ends and ideals be considered paramount over any undertaking's particular ends and methods. These general ideals must be held dominant even though it may be impossible to find anywhere a specific and accepted formulation of them.

Any undertaking by more than one person requires some sort of organization—that is, agreement on the division of functions and allocation of responsibility and resources. The resolution of major ends into enabling ones shapes this organization, with each principal group of enabling ends assigned to a major department. Within a department the diffusion of tasks continues with the successive delegations of responsibility to its various bureaus. Several patterns of organization have been developed around different principles of task allocation.

Whenever an undertaking involves two or more persons, one of them commonly assumes leadership. He supplies direction based on the original selections of ends and means, and bears the senior responsibility for success. He is responsible for deciding whether modifications are necessary. As head, he is also responsible for obtaining the cooperation of the other participants, assigning their tasks, and delegating such responsibilities as may be required. The other participants include any person whatever whose contribution is necessary to the success of the undertaking.

Now, each participant has his own personal ends. His contribution can be gotten only if he feels that making it can help him attain them. Hence a major task of the head of an undertaking and of his subordinates (each within his own field) is to blend these personal ends into the main purposes of the undertaking. The means of doing this range widely from brazen threats to subtle implicit promises. Commonly they consist of some sort of *quid pro quo*, in either an explicit or an implicit contract. (For the health of the organization, the *quid pro quo* should be no more—insofar as it is drawn from scarce resources—than is required to obtain the desired contribution.) To discharge their responsibility for getting cooperation, managers require a high degree of insight into human motives and needs, and sensitive skill in using it.

Communication is one of management's major tasks. Managers must enlist participants, assign duties, and allocate resources; and they must receive back information about the progress of subordinate tasks. These are problems of internal communication. The organization's structure provides the channels along which such communication flows, vertically and horizontally, so that responsible persons get regular and timely information on which to decide and act. There must also be external communication between the personnel of the undertaking and important outsiders—suppliers, customers, the public, and so on. Communication is an important means which becomes an enabling end, to be attained by the same processes of management as any other.

Every enterprise employs as means some kind of scarce resources—money, time, talent, labor, land and the natural resources it affords, or partly processed raw materials. It is a major task of management to obtain and allocate these scarce resources and to husband them so that they are available in proper quantity and quality wherever and whenever they are needed in the enterprise. To obtain them management must offer a return to suppliers. It may be tangible or intangible; it may be in material form or it may be in emotional, intellectual, or spiritual satisfaction. But the actual returns and the prospect of future returns must be sufficient to give the undertaking adequate access to the necessary supplies.

Progress toward the various enabling ends is usually uneven. The individuals responsible for attaining them may lack capacity, fail in devotion to duty, or put their own private ends ahead of those of the enterprise. Plans go wrong, unforeseen conditions emerge, some plans work better than expected. The result is that schedules get out of step. Management must keep itself informed of developments throughout its enterprise, must exert control and supervision over use of resources and performance, and must insure that all intermediate outcomes make their proper timely contribution to principal ends.

Ordinarily, most of the major and enabling ends of an enterprise can be reached, at least hypothetically, by a wide variety of means. From among those that are acceptable in the social environment, management's first responsibility is to select for each end, whatever its level, a set that is *effective.* That is, the means must lead verifiably to the achievement of the desired particular end. (Means applied to irrelevant or unintended ends—"boondoggling"—are futile and wasteful.)

After management has attained effectiveness, it then seeks *efficiency*—attainment of the chosen end with minimum expenditure of scarce resources. The quest for efficiencies calls for continuous study and analysis of existing means, and the search for others that may prove better.

Whatever means are used, they almost always produce results in addition to those intended. Such additional, irrelevant, often unforeseen "by-product" results may be either desirable or undesirable, in their effects on the principal goals. If they turn out to be desirable, they may inspire re-thinking and modification of the principal goals. If they run counter either to the undertaking's major ends or to the ends and ideals approved by society, they may force a change of means. Effective, efficient management strives to reduce the harmful effects of such by-products, and get the maximum net contribution of means to major ends. This may be a matter of survival, for though society is often slow in reacting to disapproved by-products of an activity, in the long run it tolerates few undertakings that persist in using methods that are more harmful than beneficial.

Management confronts a situation that often changes in fundamentals and is always changing in details. The desirability of an end itself may change. New means of achieving it may appear. New information about causal relations may emerge. Public opinion of the moral acceptability of a given end or means may change with alterations in society and culture. The personal goals of participating individuals may shift, and indeed, usually do shift as they grow older.

Management must be prepared to meet these changes. It continually needs the latest and best information about its total environment in all its aspects. It investigates the causes of past changes, and tries to appraise the forces that may produce other changes. It needs new ideas with which to initiate its own changes. Using this information, it continually reassesses the ends and means it has adopted, and revises them as it finds necessary. Research, review, and reassessment are important tasks of management.

In reassessing its ends and means, management bears in mind that it can choose either to pursue the existing ends, modify them, or abandon them permanently or temporarily—as for example, in the face of conditions that impose a new overriding end: the survival of the enterprise as an organized entity. In making changes, it must be mindful of the moral commitments it has already made, and of the moral conflicts that may arise. Management recognizes that these commitments have created claims upon it, and that if such claims are to be modified in favor of new arrangements, it must give fair return. To settle these claims and arbitrate conflicts, management requires a high sense of ethics and morality.

Many of the situations and problems about which management must make decisions fall into patterns that recur again and again. Some of these recurrences can be anticipated, and management can and does work out in advance uniform decisions for dealing with them. Successful past decisions dealing with them can be identified, and serve as precedents for future ones. From these two sources—solutions set up in advance of anticipated recurring problems, and precedents based on past experience with them—emerge policies. Policies are a device for obtaining efficiency and consistency, for they provide uniform ready-made answers, and save managers the trouble of completely re-thinking a recurring problem every time it appears. Policy-making is commonly regarded as one of the major functions of the higher echelons of management, as indeed it is, but all levels really share in it.

In all these matters of review, supervision, control, change, decision making, and policy making, management is continually confronted with questions of *authority* as well as of fact and morality.

Fundamentally, authority is granted by the subordinate, just as government is said to exist by consent of the governed. It lies in the subordinate's continued acceptance of the goals of the undertaking as being in harmony with his own. The moment he refuses this acceptance, the authority of the enterprise over him ceases. Authority lies in the goal, not in the individual at the head. But in practice, it must correspond to responsibility. Since the highest responsibility for the enterprise belongs to its head, and the next highest to his immediate subordinates, and since these people are *ex officio* the foci of information, all those who accept the authority of the undertaking must agree that the officers should decide what its welfare requires and should exercise its authority.

Of management's total activity, the greatest portion must be devoted to deciding what intermediate ends must be pursued to reach the main goals, and then to selecting, activating, supervising, and coordinating the means for achieving those intermediate ends. This corresponds to the common experience of managers that their most frequent problems are, "What should be done?" and "What is the best way to do it?" The next largest portion of time goes to deciding how to reconcile conflicting moral claims.

In summary, management is the art of

- selecting certain ends from those available;
- making the selection with due allowance for the nature of the field of action and for the means it can be made to afford;
- resolving the chosen ends into elements achievable separately and contributing to the main ends and arranging them in plans;
- enlisting assistance by relating the ends of the enterprise to the private ends of cooperating individuals;
- creating an organization by delegating responsibility for the various elements;
- supervising, controlling, and coordinating activity to obtain effectiveness with efficiency;
- minimizing unwanted effects of the means employed;
- providing for adequate internal and external communication;
- providing and husbanding the scarce resources required;
- obtaining new and additional information and ideas;
- reviewing, reassessing, and adjusting continually the ends, the means, and the performance with constant alertness to changing conditions;
- discharging moral claims on the enterprise and resolving moral conflicts; and
- doing all this in ways consistent with realization of the larger goals of human life.

Part I

The managerial perspective

We often think that when we have completed our study of one we know all about two, because "two" is "one and one." We forget that we have still to make a study of "and."
Sir Arthur Eddington

Managers have a variety of ideas, forces, institutions, and situations with which they must deal. This variety contributes to their sometimes unique perspective on the managerial role.

In the first selection, Harold Koontz describes the complex combination of ideas, concepts, issues, and theories that abound in the field of management. Although the classification scheme that Professor Koontz offers is by no means the only approach that can be taken, it does provide considerable insight into modern management thought.

The second selection contains a discussion of the situational nature of the manager's job. In this article, the author suggests a way to reconcile the kinds of difficulties identified by Koontz.

In the third selection the *Wall Street Journal* reports an interesting situation: The organization's environment, at least for Mazda, is not always the hostile jungle portrayed by many people.

3 The management theory jungle
Harold Koontz

Although students of management would readily agree that there have been problems of management since the dawn of organized life, most would also agree that systematic examination of management, with few exceptions, is the product of the present century and more especially of the past two decades. Moreover, until recent years almost all of those who have attempted to analyze the management process and look for some theoretical underpinnings to help improve research, teaching, and practice were alert and perceptive practitioners of the art who reflected on many ways of experience. Thus, at least in looking at *general* management as an intellectually based art, the earliest meaningful writing came from such experienced practitioners as Fayol, Mooney, Alvin Brown, Sheldon, Barnard, and Urwick. Certainly not even the most academic worshipper of empirical research can overlook the empiricism involved in distilling fundamentals from decades of experience by such discerning practitioners as these. Admittedly done without questionnaires, controlled interviews, or mathematics, observations by such men can hardly be accurately regarded as *a priori* or "armchair."

The noteworthy absence of academic writing and research in the formative years of modern management theory is now more than atoned for by a deluge of research and writing from the academic halls. What is interesting and perhaps nothing more than a sign of the unsophisticated adolescence of management theory is how the current flood has brought with it a wave of great differences and apparent confusion. From the orderly analysis of management at the shop-room level by Frederick Taylor and the reflective distillation of experience from the general management point of view by Henri Fayol, we now see these and other early beginnings overgrown and entangled by a jungle of approaches and approachers to management theory.

There are the behavioralists, born of the Hawthorne experiments and the awakened interest in human relations during the 1930's and 1940's, who see management as a complex of interpersonal relationships and the basis of management theory the tentative tenets of the new and undeveloped science of psychology. There are also those who see management theory as simply a manifestation of the institutional and cultural aspects of sociology. Still others, observing that the central core of management is decision making, branch in all directions from this core to encompass everything in organization life. Then, there are mathematicians who think of management primarily as an exercise in logical relationships expressed in symbols and the omnipresent and ever revered model. But the entanglement of growth reaches its ultimate when the study of management is regarded as a study of one of a number of systems and subsystems, with an understandable

Source: From *Academy of Management Journal,* Vol. 4, No. 3 (December 1961), pp. 174–188.

tendency for the researcher to be dissatisfied until he has encompassed the entire physical and cultural universe as a management system.

With the recent discovery of an ages-old problem area by social, physical, and biological scientists, and with the supersonic increase in interest by all types of enterprise managers, the apparent impenetrability of the present thicket which we call management theory is not difficult to comprehend. One can hardly be surprised that psychologists, sociologists, anthropologists, sociometricists, economists, mathematicians, physicists, biologists, political scientists, business administration scholars, and even practicing managers, should hop on this interesting, challenging, and profitable band wagon.

This welling of interest from every academic and practicing corner should not upset anyone concerned with seeing the frontiers of knowledge pushed back and the intellectual base of practice broadened. But what is rather upsetting to the practitioner and the observer, who sees great social potential from improved management, is that the variety of approaches to management theory has led to a kind of confused and destructive jungle warfare. Particularly among academic disciplines and their disciples, the primary interests of many would-be cult leaders seem to be to carve out a distinct (and hence "original") approach to management. And to defend this originality, and thereby gain a place in posterity (or at least to gain a publication which will justify academic status or promotion), it seems to have become too much the current style to downgrade, and sometimes misrepresent, what anyone else has said, or thought, or done.

In order to cut through this jungle and bring to light some of the issues and problems involved in the present management theory area so that the tremendous interest, intelligence, and research results may become more meaningful, it is my purpose here to classify the various "schools" of management theory, to identify briefly what I believe to be the major source of differences, and to offer some suggestions for disentangling the jungle. It is hoped that a movement for clarification can be started so at least we in the field will not be a group of blind men identifying the same elephant with our widely varying and sometimes viciously argumentative theses.

The major "schools" of management theory

In attempting to classify the major schools of management theory into six main groups, I am aware that I may overlook certain approaches and cannot deal with all the nuances of each approach. But it does seem that most of the approaches to management theory can be classified in one of these so-called "schools."

The management process school

This approach to management theory perceives management as a process of getting things done through and with people operating in organized groups. It aims to analyze the process, to establish a conceptual framework for it, to identify principles underlying it, and to build up a theory of management from them. It regards management as a universal process, regardless of the type of enterprise, or the level in a given enterprise, although recognizing, obviously, that the environment of management differs widely between enterprises and levels. It looks upon management theory as a way of organizing experience so that practice can be improved through research, empirical testing of principles, and teaching of fundamentals involved in the management process.[1]

Often referred to, especially by its critics, as the "traditional" or "universalist" school, this school can be said to have been fathered by Henri Fayol, although many of his offspring did not know of their parent, since Fayol's work was eclipsed by the bright light of his contemporary, Frederick Taylor, and clouded by the lack of a widely available English translation until 1949. Other than Fayol, most of the early contributors to this school dealt only with the organization portion of the management process, largely because of their greater experience with this facet of management and the simple fact that planning and control, as well as the function of staffing, were given little attention by managers before 1940.

This school bases its approach to management theory on several fundamental beliefs:

1 that managing is a process and can best be dissected intellectually by analyzing the functions of the manager;
2 that long experience with management in a variety of enterprise situations can be grounds for distillation of certain fundamental truths or generalizations—usually referred to as principles—which have a clarifying and predictive value in the understanding and improvement of managing;
3 that these fundamental truths can become focal points for useful research both to ascertain their validity and to improve their meaning and applicability in practice;
4 that such truths can furnish elements, at least until disproved, and certainly until sharpened, of a useful theory of management;
5 that managing is an art, but one like medicine or engineering, which can be improved by reliance on the light and understanding of principles;
6 that principles in management, like principles in the biological and physical sciences, are nonetheless true even if a prescribed treatment or design by a practitioner in a given case situation chooses to ignore a principle and the costs involved, or attempts to do something else to offset the costs incurred

---

[1] It is interesting that one of the scholars strongly oriented to human relations and behavioral approaches to management has recently noted that "theory can be viewed as a way of organizing experience" and that "once initial sense is made out of experimental environment, the way is cleared for an even more adequate organization of this experience." See Robert Dubin in "Psyche, Sensitivity, and Social Structure," critical comment in Robert Tannenbaum, I. R. Weschler, and Fred Massarik, *Leadership and Organization: A Behaviorial Science Approach* (New York: McGraw-Hill Book Co., 1961), p. 401.

(this is, of course, not new in medicine, engineering, or any other art, for art is the creative task of compromising fundamentals to attain a desired result); and

7 that, while the totality of culture and of the physical and biological universe has varying effects on the manager's environment and subjects, as indeed they do in every other field of science and art, the theory of management does not need to encompass the field of all knowledge in order for it to serve as a scientific or theoretical foundation.

The basic approach of this school, then, is to look, first, to the functions of managers. As a second step in this approach, many of us have taken the functions of managers and further dissected them by distilling what we see as fundamental truths in the understandably complicated practice of management. I have found it useful to classify my analysis of these functions around the essentials involved in the following questions:

1 What is the nature of the function?
2 What is the purpose of the function?
3 What explains the structure of the function?
4 What explains the process of the function?

Perhaps there are other more useful approaches, but I have found that I can place everything pertaining to management (even some of the rather remote research and concepts) in this framework.

Also, purely to make the area of management theory intellectually manageable, those who subscribe to this school do not usually attempt to include in the theory the entire areas of sociology, economics, biology, psychology, physics, chemistry, or others. This is done not because these other areas of knowledge are unimportant and have no bearing on management, but merely because no real progress has ever been made in science or art without significant partitioning of knowledge. Yet, anyone would be foolish not to realize that a function which deals with people in their various activities of producing and marketing anything from money to religion and education is [not] completely independent of the physical, biological, and cultural universe in which we live. And, are there not such relationships in other "compartments" of knowledge and theory?

The empirical school

A second approach to management I refer to as the "empirical" school. In this, I include those scholars who identify management as a study of experience, sometimes with intent to draw generalizations but usually merely as a means of teaching experience and transferring it to the practitioner or student. Typical of this school are those who see management or "policy" as the study and analysis of cases and those with such approaches as Ernest Dale's "comparative approach."[2]

This approach seems to be based upon the premise that, if we study the experience of successful managers, or the mistakes made in management, or if we attempt to solve management problems, we will somehow understand and learn to apply the most effective kinds of management techniques. This approach, as often applied, assumes that, by finding out what worked or did not work in individual circumstances, the student or the practitioner will be able to do the same in comparable situations.

No one can deny the importance of studying experience through such study, or of analyzing the "how-it-was-done" of management. But management, unlike law, is not a science based on precedent, and situations in the future exactly comparable to the past are exceedingly unlikely to occur. Indeed, there is a positive danger of relying too much on past experience and on undistilled history of managerial problem-solving for the simple reason that a technique or approach found "right" in the past may not fit a situation of the future.

Those advocating the empirical approach are likely to say that what they really do in analyzing cases or history is to draw from certain generalizations which can be applied as useful guides to thought or action in future case situations. As a matter of fact, Ernest Dale, after claiming to find "so little practical value" from the principles enunciated by the "universalists," curiously drew certain "generalizations" or "criteria" from his valuable study of a number of great practitioners of management.[3] There is some question as to whether Dale's "comparative" approach is not really the same as the "universalist" approach he decries, except with a different distiller of basic truths.

By the emphasis of the empirical school on study of experience, it does appear that the research and thought so engendered may assist in hastening the day for verification of principles. It is also possible that the proponents of this school may come up with a more useful framework of principles than that of the management process school. But, to the extent that the empirical school draws generalizations from its research, and it would seem to be a necessity to do so unless its members are satisfied to exchange meaningless and structureless experience, this approach tends to be and do the same as the management process school.

The human behavior school

This approach to the analysis of management is based on the central thesis that, since managing involves getting things done with and through people, the study of management must be centered on interpersonal relations. Variously called the "human relations," "leadership," or "behavioral sciences"

[2] *The Great Organizers* (New York: McGraw-Hill Book Co., 1960), pp. 11–28.
[3] *Ibid.,* pp. 11, 26–28, 62–68.

approach, this school brings to bear "existing and newly developed theories, methods, and techniques of the relevant social sciences upon the study of inter- and intrapersonal phenomena, ranging fully from the personality dynamics of individuals at one extreme to the relations of cultures at the other."[4] In other words, this school concentrates on the "people" part of management and rests on the principle that, where people work together as groups in order to accomplish objectives, "people should understand people."

The scholars in this school have a heavy orientation to psychology and social psychology. Their primary focus is the individual as a socio-psychological being and what motivates him. The members of this school vary from those who see it as a portion of the manager's job, a tool to help him understand and get the best from people by meeting their needs and responding to their motivations to those who see the psychological behavior of individuals and groups as the total of management.

In this school are those who emphasize human relations as an art that the manager should advantageously understand and practice. There are those who focus attention on the manager as a leader and sometimes equate management to leadership, thus, in effect, tending to treat all group activities as "managed" situations. There are those who see the study of group dynamics and interpersonal relationships as simply a study of socio-psychological relationships and seem, therefore, merely to be attaching the term "management" to the field of social psychology.

That management must deal with human behavior can hardly be denied. That the study of human interactions, whether in the environment of management or in unmanaged situations, is important and useful one could not dispute. And it would be a serious mistake to regard good leadership as unimportant to good managership. But whether the field of human behavior is the equivalent of the field of management is quite another thing. Perhaps it is like calling the study of the human body the field of cardiology.

The social system school

Closely related to the human behavior school and often confused or intertwined with it is one which might be labeled the social system school. This includes those researchers who look upon management as a social system, that is, a system of cultural interrelationships. Sometimes, as in the case of March and Simon,[5] the system is limited to formal organizations, using the term "organization" as equivalent to enterprise, rather than the authority-activity concept used most often in management. In other cases, the approach is not to distinguish the formal organization, but rather to encompass any kind of system of human relationships.

[4] R. Tannenbaum, I. R. Weschler, and F. Massarik, *Leadership and Organization* (New York: McGraw-Hill Book Co., 1961), p. 9.
[5] *Organizations* (New York: John Wiley & Sons, Inc., 1958).

Heavily sociological in flavor, this approach to management does essentially what any study of sociology does. It identifies the nature of the cultural relationships of various social groups and attempts to show these as a related, and usually an integrated, system.

Perhaps the spiritual father of this ardent and vocal school of management theorists is Chester Barnard.[6] In searching for an answer to fundamental explanations underlying the managing process, this thoughtful business executive developed a theory of cooperation grounded in the needs of the individual to solve, through cooperation, the biological, physical, and social limitations of himself and his environment. Barnard then carved from the total of cooperative systems so engendered one set of interrelationships which he defines as "formal organization." His formal organization concept, quite unlike that usually held by management practitioners, is any cooperative system in which there are persons able to communicate with each other and who are willing to contribute action toward a conscious common purpose.

The Barnard concept of cooperative systems pervades the work of many contributors to the social system school of management. For example, Herbert Simon at one time defined the subject of organization theory and the nature of human organizations as "systems of interdependent activity, encompassing at least several primary groups and usually characterized, at the level of consciousness of participants, by a high degree of rational direction of behavior toward ends that are objects of common knowledge."[7] Simon and others have subsequently seemed to have expanded this concept of social systems to include any cooperative and purposeful group interrelationship or behavior.

This school has made many noteworthy contributions to management. The recognition of organized enterprise as a social organism, subject to all the pressures and conflicts of the cultural environment, has been helpful to the management theorist and the practitioner alike. Among some of the more helpful aspects are the awareness of the institutional foundations of organization authority, the influence of informal organization, and such social factors as those Wight Bakke has called the "bonds of organization."[8] Likewise, many of Barnard's helpful insights, such as his economy of incentives and his theory of opportunism, have brought the power of sociological understanding into the realm of management practice.

Basic sociology, analysis of concepts of social behavior, and the study

[6] *The Functions of the Executive* (Cambridge, Mass.: Harvard University Press, 1938).
[7] "Comments on the Theory of Organizations," 46 *American Political Science Review,* No. 4 (December, 1952), p. 1130.
[8] *Bonds of Organization* (New York: Harper & Brothers, 1950). These "bonds" or "devices" of organization are identified by Bakke as (1) the functional specifications system (a system of teamwork arising from job specifications, and arrangements for association): (2) the status system (a vertical hierarchy of authority): (3) the communications system; (4) the reward and penalty system; and (5) the organization charter (ideas and means which give character and individuality to the organization, or enterprise).

of group behavior in the framework of social systems do have great value in the field of management. But one may well ask the question whether this is management. Is the field of management coterminous with the field of sociology? Or is sociology an important underpinning like language, psychology, physiology, mathematics, and other fields of knowledge? Must management be defined in terms of the universe of knowledge?

The decision theory school

Another approach to management theory, undertaken by a growing and scholarly group, might be referred to as the decision theory school. This group concentrates on rational approach to decision—the selection from among possible alternatives of a course of action or of an idea. The approach of this school may be to deal with the decision itself, or to the persons or organizational group making the decision, or to an analysis of the decision process. Some limit themselves fairly much to the economic rationale of the decision, while others regard anything which happens in an enterprise the subject of their analysis, and still others expand decision theory to cover the psychological and sociological aspect and environment of decisions and decision-makers.

The decision-making school is apparently an outgrowth of the theory of consumer's choice with which economists have been concerned since the days of Jeremy Bentham early in the nineteenth century. It has arisen out of such economic problems and analyses as utility maximization, indifference curves, marginal utility, and economic behavior under risks and uncertainties. It is, therefore, no surprise that one finds most of the members of this school to be economic theorists. It is likewise no surprise to find the content of this school to be heavily oriented to model construction and mathematics.

The decision theory school has tended to expand its horizon considerably beyond the process of evaluating alternatives. That point has become for many only a springboard for examination of the entire sphere of human activity, including the nature of the organization structure, psychological and social reactions of individuals and groups, the development of basic information for decisions, an analysis of values and particularly value considerations with respect to goals, communications networks, and incentives. As one would expect, when the decision theorists study the small, but central, area of decision *making*, they are led by this keyhole look at management to consider the entire field of enterprise operation and its environment. The result is that decision theory becomes no longer a neat and narrow concentration on decision, but rather a broad view of the enterprise as a social system.

There are those who believe that, since management is characterized by its concentration on decisions, the future development of management theory will tend to use the decision as its central focus and the rest of management theory will be hung on this structural center. This may occur and certainly the study of the decision, the decision process, and the decision maker can be extended to cover the entire field of management as anyone might conceive it. Nevertheless, one wonders whether this focus cannot also be used to build around it the entire area of human knowledge. For, as most decision theorists recognize, the problem of choice is individual, as well as organizational, and most of what has been said that is pure decision theory can be applied to the existence and thinking of a Robinson Crusoe.

The mathematical school

Although mathematical methods can be used by any school of management theory, and have been, I have chosen to group under a school those theorists who see management as a system of mathematical models and processes. Perhaps the most widely known group I arbitrarily so lump are the operations researchers or operations analysts, who have sometimes anointed themselves with the rather pretentious name of "management scientists." The abiding belief of this group is that, if management, or organization, or planning, or decision making is a logical process, it can be expressed in terms of mathematical symbols and relationships. The central approach of this school is the model, for it is through these devices that the problem is expressed in its basic relationships and in terms of selected goals or objectives.

There can be no doubt of the great usefulness of mathematical approaches to any field of inquiry. It forces upon the researcher the definition of a problem or problem area, it conveniently allows the insertion of symbols for unknown data, and its logical methodology, developed by years of scientific application and abstraction, furnishes a powerful tool for solving or simplifying complex phenomena.

But it is hard to see mathematics as a truly separate school of management theory, anymore than it is a separate "school" in physics, chemistry, engineering, or medicine. I only deal with it here as such because there has appeared to have developed a kind of cult around mathematical analysts who have subsumed to themselves the area of management.

In pointing out that mathematics is a tool, rather than a school, it is not my intention to underestimate the impact of mathematics on the science and practice of management. By bringing to this immensely important and complex field the tools and techniques of the physical sciences, the mathematicians have already made an immense contribution to orderly thinking. They have forced on people in management the means and desirability of seeing many problems more clearly, they have pressed on scholars and practitioners the need for establishing goals and measures of effectiveness, they have been extremely helpful in getting the management area seen as a logical system of relationships, and they have caused people in management to review and occasionally reorganize information sources and systems so that mathematics can be given sensible quantitative meaning. But with all this meaningful contribution and the greater sharpness and sophistication of planning which is resulting, I cannot see that mathematics is management theory any more than it is astronomy.

The major sources of mental entanglement in the jungle

In outlining the various schools, or approaches, of management theory, it becomes clear that these intellectual cults are not drawing greatly different inferences from the physical and cultural environment surrounding us. Why, then, have there been so many differences between them and why such a struggle, particularly among our academic brethren to obtain a place in the sun by denying the approaches of others? Like the widely differing and often contentious denominations of the Christian religion, all have essentially the same goals and deal with essentially the same world.

While there are many sources of the mental entanglement in the management theory jungle, the major ones are the following:

The semantics jungle

As it so often true when intelligent men argue about basic problems, some of the trouble lies in the meaning of key words. The semantics problem is particularly severe in the field of management. There is even a difference in the meaning of the word "management." Most people would agree that it means getting things done through and with people, but is it people in formal organizations, or in all group activities? Is it governing, leading, or teaching?

Perhaps the greatest single semantics confusion lies in the word "organization." Most members of the management process school use it to define the activity-authority structure of an enterprise and certainly most practitioners believe that they are "organizing" when they establish a framework of activity groupings and authority relationships. In this case, organization represents the formal framework within an enterprise that furnishes the environment in which people perform. Yet a large number of "organization" theorists conceive of organization as the sum total of human relationships in any group activity; they thus seem to make it equivalent to *social* structure. And some use "organization" to mean "enterprise."

If the meaning of organization cannot be clarified and a standard use of the term adopted by management theorists, understanding and criticism should not be based on this difference. It hardly seems to me to be accurate for March and Simon, for example, to criticize the organization theories of the management process, or "universalist," school for not considering the management planning function as part of organizing, when they have chosen to treat it separately. Nor should those who choose to treat the training, selecting, guiding or leading of people under staffing and direction be criticised for a tendency to "view the employee as an inert instrument" or a "given rather than a variable."[9] Such accusations, proceeding from false premises, are clearly erroneous.

Other semantic entanglements might be mentioned. By some, decision making is regarded as a process of choosing from among alternatives; by others, the total managerial task and environment. Leadership is often made synonymous with managership and is analytically separated by others. Communications may mean everything from a written or oral report to a vast network of formal and informal relationships. Human relations to some implies a psychiatric manipulation of people, but to others the study and art of understanding people and interpersonal relationships.

Differences in definition of management as a body of knowledge

As was indicated in the discussion of semantics, "management" has far from a standard meaning, although most agree that it at least involves getting things done through and with people. But, does it mean the dealing with all human relationships? Is a street peddler a manager? Is a parent a manager? Is a leader of a disorganized mob a manager? Does the field of management equal the fields of sociology and social psychology combined? Is it the equivalent of the entire system of social relationships?

While I recognize that sharp lines cannot be drawn in management any more than they are in medicine or engineering, there surely can be a sharper distinction drawn than at present. With the plethora of management writing and experts, calling almost everything under the sun "management," can one expect management theory to be regarded as very useful or scientific to the practitioner?

The *a priori* assumption

Confusion in management theory has also been heightened by the tendency for many newcomers in the field to cast aside significant observations and analyses of the past on the grounds that they are *a priori* in nature. This is an often-met accusation made by those who wish to cast aside the work of Fayol, Mooney, Brown, Urwick, Gulick, and others who are branded as "universalists." To make the assumption that the distilled experiences of men such as these represent *a priori* reasoning is to forget that experience in and with managing is empirical. While the conclusions of perceptive and experienced practitioners of the art of management are not infallible, they represent an experience which is certainly real and not "armchair." No one could

[9] March, J. G., and H. A. Simon, *Organizations* (New York: John Wiley & Sons, Inc., 1958), pp. 29–33.

deny, I feel sure, that the ultimate test of accuracy of management theory must be practice and management theory and science must be developed from reality.

The misunderstanding of principles

Those who feel that they gain caste or a clean slate for advancing a particular notion or approach often delight in casting away anything which smacks of management principles. Some have referred to them as platitudes, forgetting that a platitude is still a truism and a truth does not become worthless because it is familiar. (As Robert Frost has written, "Most of the changes we think we see in life are merely truths going in or out of favor.") Others cast away principles of Fayol and other practitioners, only to draw apparently different generalizations from their study of management; but many of the generalizations so discovered are often the same fundamental truths in different words that certain criticized "universalists" have discovered.

One of the favorite tricks of the managerial theory trade is to disprove a whole framework of principles by reference to one principle which the observer sees disregarded in practice. Thus, many critics of the universalists point to the well-known cases of dual subordination in organized enterprise, coming to the erroneous conclusion that there is no substance to the principle of unity of command. But this does not prove that there is no cost to the enterprise by designing around, or disregarding, the principle of unity of command; nor does it prove that there were not other advantages which offset the costs, as there often are in cases of establishing functional authorities in organization.

Perhaps the almost hackneyed stand-by for those who would disprove the validity of all principles by referring to a single one is the misunderstanding around the principle of span of management (or span of control). The usual source of authority quoted by those who criticize is Sir Ian Hamilton, who never intended to state a universal principle, but rather to make a personal observation in a book of reflections on his Army experience, and who did say, offhand, that he found it wise to limit his span to 3 to 6 subordinates. No modern universalist relies on this single observation, and, indeed, few can or will state an absolute or universal numerical ceiling. Since Sir Ian was not a management theorist and did not intend to be, let us hope that the ghost of his innocent remark may be laid to deserved rest!

What concerns those who feel that a recognition of fundamental truths, or generalizations, may help in the diagnosis and study of management, and who know from managerial experience that such truths or principles do serve an extremely valuable use, is the tendency for some researchers to prove the wrong things through either misstatement or misapplication of principles. A classic case of such misunderstanding and misapplication is in Chris Argyris' interesting book on *Personality and Organization.*[10]

[10] New York: Harper & Brothers, 1957.

This author, who in this book and his other works has made many noteworthy contributions to management, concludes that "formal organization principles make demands on relatively healthy individuals that are incongruent with their needs," and that "frustration, conflict, failure, and short-time perspective are predicted as results of this basic incongruency."[11] This startling conclusion—the exact opposite of what "good" formal organization based on "sound" organization principles should cause — is explained when one notes that, of four "principles" Argyris quotes, one is not an organization principle at all but the economic principle of specialization and three other "principles" are quoted incorrectly.[12] With such a postulate, and with no attempt to recognize, correctly or incorrectly, any other organization and management principles, Argyris has simply proved that wrong principles badly applied will lead to frustration; and every management practitioner knows this to be true!

The inability or unwillingness of management theorists to understand each other

What has been said above leads one to the conclusion that much of the management theory jungle is caused by the unwillingness or inability of the management theorists to understand each other. Doubting that it is inability, because one must assume that a person interested in management theory is able to comprehend, at least in concept and framework, the approaches of the various "schools," I can only come to the conclusion that the roadblock to understanding is unwillingness.

Perhaps this unwillingness comes from the professional "walls" developed by learned disciplines. Perhaps the unwillingness stems from a fear that someone or some new discovery will encroach on professional and academic status. Perhaps it is fear of professional or intellectual obsolescence. But whatever the cause, it seems that these walls will not be torn down until it is realized that they exist, until all cultists are willing to look at the approach and content of other schools, and until, through exchange and understanding of ideas, some order may be brought from the present chaos.

Disentangling the management theory jungle

It is important that steps be taken to disentangle the management theory jungle. Perhaps, it is too soon and we must expect more years of wandering through a thicket of approaches, semantics, thrusts, and counter-thrusts. But in any field as important to society where the many blunders of an unscientifically based managerial art can be so costly, I hope that this will not be long.

[11] *Ibid.*, p. 74.
[12] *Ibid.*, pp. 58–66.

There do appear to be some things that can be done. Clearly, meeting what I see to be the major sources of the entanglement should remove much of it. The following considerations are important:

1 *The need for definition of a body of knowledge*   Certainly, if a field of knowledge is not to get bogged down in a quagmire of misunderstandings, the first need is for definition of the field. Not that it need be defined in sharp, detailed, and inflexible lines, but rather along lines which will give it fairly specific content. Because management is reality, life, practice, my suggestion would be that it be defined in the light of the able and discerning practitioner's frame of reference. A science unrelated to the art for which it is to serve is not likely to be a very productive one.

Although the study of managements in various enterprises, in various countries, and at various levels made by many persons, including myself, may neither be representative nor adequate, I have come to the conclusion that management is the art of getting things done through and with people in *formally organized groups,* the art of creating an environment in such an organized group where people can perform as individuals and yet cooperate toward attainment of group goals, the art of removing blocks to such performance, the art of optimizing efficiency in effectively reaching goals. If this kind of definition of the field is unsatisfactory, I suggest at least an agreement that the area should be defined to reflect the field of the practitioner and that further research and study of practice be done to this end.

In defining the field, too, it seems to me imperative to draw some limits for purposes of analysis and research. If we are to call the entire cultural, biological, and physical universe the field of management, we can no more make progress than could have been done if chemistry or geology had not carved out a fairly specific area and had, instead, studied all knowledge.

In defining the body of knowledge, too, care must be taken to distinguish between tools and content. Thus mathematics, operations research, accounting, economic theory, sociometry, and psychology, to mention a few, are significant *tools* of management but are not, in themselves, a part of the *content* of the field. This is not to mean that they are unimportant or that the practicing manager should not have them available to him, nor does it mean that they may not be the means of pushing back the frontiers of knowledge of management. But they should not be confused with the basic content of the field.

This is not to say that fruitful study should not continue on the underlying disciplines affecting management. Certainly knowledge of sociology, social systems, psychology, economics, political science, mathematics, and other areas, pointed toward contributing to the field of management, should be continued and encouraged. And significant findings in these and other fields of knowledge might well cast important light on, or change concepts in, the field of management. This has certainly happened in other sciences and in every other art based upon significant science.

2 *Integration of management and other disciplines*   If recognition of the proper content of the field were made, I believe that the present crossfire of

misunderstanding might tend to disappear. Management would be regarded as a specific discipline and other disciplines would be looked upon as important bases of the field. Under these circumstances, the allied and underlying disciplines would be welcomed by the business and public administration schools, as well as by practitioners, as loyal helpful associates. Integration of management and other disciplines would then not be difficult.

3 *The clarification of management semantics*   While I would expect the need for clarification and uniformity of management semantics would largely be satisfied by definition of the field as a body of knowledge, semantics problems might require more special attention. There are not too many places where semantics are important enough to cause difficulty. Here again, I would suggest the adoption of the semantics of the intelligent practitioners, unless words are used by them so inexactly as to require special clarification. At least, we should not complicate an already complex field by developing a scientific or academic jargon which would build a language barrier between the theorist and the practitioner.

Perhaps the most expeditious way out of this problem is to establish a commission representing academic societies immediately concerned and associations of practicing managers. This would not seem to be difficult to do. And even if it were, the results would be worth the efforts.

4 *Willingness to distill and test fundamentals*   Certainly, the test of maturity and usefulness of a science is the sharpness and validity of the principles underlying it. No science, now regarded as mature, started out with a complete statement of incontrovertibly valid principles. Even the oldest sciences, such as physics, keep revising their underlying laws and discovering new principles. Yet any science has proceeded, and more than that has been useful, for centuries on the basis of generalizations, some laws, some principles, and some hypotheses.

One of the understandable sources of inferiority of the social sciences is the recognition that they are inexact sciences. On the other hand, even the so-called exact sciences are subject to a great deal of inexactness, have principles which are not completely proved, and use art in the design of practical systems and components. The often-encountered defeatist attitude of the social sciences, of which management is one, overlooks the fact that management may be explained, practice may be improved, and the goals of research may be more meaningful if we encourage attempts at perceptive distillation of experience by stating principles (for generalizations) and placing them in a logical framework. As two scientists recently said on this subject:

The reason for this defeatist point of view regarding the social sciences may be traceable to a basic misunderstanding of the nature of scientific endeavor. What matters is not whether or to what extent inexactitudes in procedures and predictive capability can eventually be removed . . . : rather it is objectivity, i.e., the intersubjectivity of findings independent of any one person's intuitive judgment, which distinguishes science from intuitive guesswork however brilliant. . . . But once a new fact or a new idea has been conjectured, no matter how intuitive a foundation, it must be capable of objective test and confirmation by anyone. And it is this crucial standard of scientific objectivity rather than any purported criterion of exactitude to which the social sciences must conform.[13]

In approaching the clarification of management theory, then, we should not forget a few criteria:

1 The theory should deal with an area of knowledge and inquiry that is "manageable"; no great advances in knowledge were made so long as man contemplated the whole universe;
2 The theory should be *useful* in improving practice and the task and person of the practitioner should not be overlooked;
3 The theory should not be lost in semantics, especially useless jargon not understandable to the practitioner;
4 The theory should give direction and efficiency to research and teaching and
5 The theory must recognize that it is a part of a larger universe of knowledge and theory.

[13] Helmer, O., and N. Rescher, "On the Epistemology of the Inexact Sciences," (Santa Monica, California: The Rand Corporation, P-1513, 1958), pp. 4–5.

---

4 The contingency theory of management: A path out of the jungle
Fred Luthans

Over a decade ago Harold Koontz wrote about the existing management theory jungle in which he identified six different theoretical schools of thought.[1] Although Koontz wrote the article to defend the process approach, his efforts have turned out to be a losing battle. The traditional management process has failed to unify management theory.

Today a jungle of management theories still exists, but there are some clearly identifiable paths that seem to be leading out of the jungle. The purpose of this article is to identify the paths and trace them through the jungle and beyond. The figure accompanying this article can be used as a guide to

Source: From *Business Horizons* (June 1973), pp. 67–72. Copyright © 1973 by the Foundation for the School of Business at Indiana University. Reprinted with permission.
[1] The six schools identified by Koontz were the management process, empirical, human behavior, social system, decision theory, and mathematical schools. Harold Koontz, *Academy of Management Journal* (December 1961), pp. 174–88.

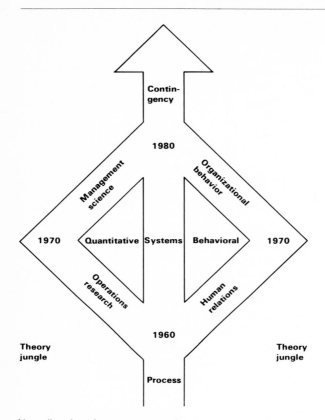

New directions in management theory

the discussion; it shows that the path leading up to the current jungle was the process approach. Other names applied to this path were classical, traditional, universal, operational, and functional.

The starting point for this process approach can be traced to the work of Henri Fayol. In 1916, he identified the universal functions of management as planning, organizing, commanding, coordinating, and controlling. He also described some universal principles of management such as unity of command and equal authority and responsibility. Unfortunately, Fayol's work on the functions and principles of management did not become part of the mainstream of management theory in this country until the 1950s. Since that time, there have been many other process theorists, but they have not added much to Fayol's original conception of management theory.[2]

[2] Probably the most widely recognized standard bearers of the process approach in modern times are Harold Koontz and Cyril O'Donnell, authors of *Principles of Management* (New York: McGraw-Hill Book Company, 1972). The book, which came out in 1955, is in its fifth edition.

Much of the terminology has been changed; for example, Fayol's commanding is now known as directing or leading. Also the meanings of Fayol's functions have become broader; for example, planning now incorporates communication, motivation, and leadership. The principles have also changed in terminology and number. Yet, despite these changes, the universality assumption is still made, and the process approach as a theoretical base for management remains basically the same as that given by Fayol over fifty years ago.

The process approach has undoubtedly had some unjustifiable criticism over the years. However, it is also true that it was not strong enough to weather the storm of protest in recent years. This approach became overgrown and entangled by other theoretical approaches. By 1960 the process path had been completely overrun, and two separate paths emerged in opposite directions. These new paths became known as the quantitative and behavioral approaches to management.

The new paths

Quantitative approach

The quantitative approach has its roots in the scientific management movement that actually predates the process approach. However, as a major thrust in management theory, the quantitative approach really got under way about 1960. This new approach made a clean break from the traditional process orientation of management.

During the 1960s the quantitative approach was characterized by the techniques of operations research. Various mathematical models were developed to solve decisional problems. However, it soon became apparent that, although OR techniques were effective tools for management decision making, this approach fell short of providing a theoretical base for management as a whole.

Starting in about 1970, the quantitative approach turned away from emphasis on narrow operations research techniques toward a broader perspective of management science. The management science approach incorporates quantitative decision techniques and model building as in the OR approach, but it also incorporates computerized information systems and operations management. This latter emphasis in the quantitative approach marked the return toward a more broadly based management theory.

Behavioral approach

At about the same time the quantitative approach broke off from the process base, the behavioral approach struck out on its own. At first the behavioral path was characterized by human relations. Simplistic assumptions

were made about human beings, and equally simplistic solutions to behavioral problems were offered. The human relations movement in the
1960s searched for ways to improve morale, which was assumed would
lead to increases in productivity. This approach certainly did no harm, but it
also produced few, if any, results.

Around 1970, about the same time the quantitative approach moved
from emphasis on narrow operations research to a broad management science perspective, the behavioral approach had a parallel development. This
path veered toward a more broadly based organizational behavior approach,
and now relies heavily on the behavioral sciences and makes more complex
assumptions. More direct attention is devoted to organization theory and organization development. Organizational behavior is the result of the interaction between the human being and the formal organization.

Systems approach

While the quantitative and behavioral approaches were going their separate
ways, a new trend appeared—the systems approach. During the 1960s to
the present, it took up where the process approach left off in unifying management theory.

As a specific, theoretical approach, systems can be traced back to the
natural and physical sciences nearly a quarter of a century ago. The application to management has been more recent. The systems approach—
physical, biological, or managerial—stresses the interrelatedness and interdependency of the parts to the whole. Systems has served as a magnet to
attract the quantitative and behavioral approaches to management.

At the present time, both the management science and organizational
behavior detours are heading back toward the main path of systems. In
management science, the new emphasis on computer applications and operations management techniques are systems based. The same holds true
for organizational behavior. The formal organization is viewed as a system
consisting of structure, processes, and technology, and the human being is
conceived of as a system containing a biological-physiological structure,
psychological processes, and a personality.[3]

Whether systems will actually unify the quantitative and behavioral approaches to management only time will tell. To date, the quantitative, behavioral, and systems approaches are clear but distinctly separate paths
through the jungle. However, as indicated by the figure, both the behavioral
and quantitative paths are headed toward the systems path. If the three approaches do come together in the next ten years, then the results may be
something entirely different. This something that is different from the sum
of the parts is referred to in the figure as the contingency theory of management.

[3] Fred Luthans, *Organizational Behavior* (New York: McGraw-Hill Book Company, 1973).

Contingency theory

The beginning of a path called contingency or sometimes situational is just starting to emerge.[4] The figure indicates that by 1980 this path may be the one that leads management out of the existing jungle of theories. The pressure leading to a contingency theory has largely come from people who are actually practicing management.

For the past fifteen years, scholars, consultants, and practicing managers have attempted to apply either quantitative or behavioral approaches, depending on their orientation, to all situations. The performance results of this universalist assumption were generally disappointing. Certain quantitative approaches worked in some situations with some types of problems but not in others. The same was true for behavioral approaches. For example, job enrichment seemed to work well with skilled technicians but not unskilled machine operators.[5]

Two of the difficulties encountered in practice were that the quantitative people could not overcome behavioral problems and the behavioral people could not overcome operations problems adaptable to quantitative solutions. In the 1970s it is becoming more and more apparent that neither the quantitative nor behavioral approaches have all the answers for all situations.

Many of today's management theorists believe that a systems-based theory can solve the quantitative/behavioral dilemma. The December 1972 issue of *Academy of Management Journal* was entirely devoted to general systems theory (GST) applied to management. The authors weighed the pros and cons of whether GST can unify management. The majority concluded that the systems approach is appealing and has a great deal of future potential, but is as yet incomplete. The open, as opposed to closed, systems view is able to cope better with the increased complexity and environmental influence facing today's managers. Systems concepts such as entropy (a system will become disorganized over time) and equifinality (a system can reach the same final state from different paths of development) are quite applicable to the present managerial situation.

Despite the advances made in general systems development and the trend for both the quantitative and behavioral approaches to move toward a systems base, a contingency path seems better suited to lead management out of the present theory jungle. Kast and Rosenzweig, who are closely associated with the systems approach, support this view, at least for the present. They call for a contingency approach, a mid-range concept that falls somewhere between "simplistic, specific principles" and "complex, vague notions."

---

[4] For example see Robert J. Mockler, "Situational Theory of Management," *Harvard Business Review* (May–June 1971), pp. 146–55, and Fremont E. Kast and James E. Rosenzweig, *Contingency Views of Organization and Management* (Chicago: Science Research Associates, Inc., 1973).

[5] William E. Reif and Fred Luthans, "Does Job Enrichment Really Pay Off?" *California Management Review* (Fall 1972), pp. 30–37.

The contingency approach "recognizes the complexity involved in managing modern organizations but uses patterns of relationships and/or configurations of subsystems in order to facilitate improved practice."[6] Important breakthroughs in various subsystems of management (organization design, leadership, behavior change, and operations) have already demonstrated the value of the contingency approach.

Current contingency approaches

Pigors and Myers have been associated with a situational approach to personnel management for the past twenty-five years. However, the work of Joan Woodward in the 1950s marks the beginning of a situational approach to organization and to management in general. She clearly showed in the British companies studied that organization structure and human relationships were largely a function of the existing technological situation. Armed with this and supporting follow-up evidence, some organizational theorists such as Lawrence and Lorsch began to call for contingency models of organizational structure.[7]

Organization designs

The contingency approach to organization design starts with the premise that there is no single design that is the best for all situations. The classical approach was to say that a bureaucratic design would lead to maximum efficiency under any circumstances. The neoclassical theorists pushed decentralization for all conditions. It is inferred that even the modern free-form systems and matrix designs have universal applicability. In practice, the classical, neoclassical, or modern structural designs did not hold up under all situations.

For example, bureaucracy was not able to cope with a highly dynamic situation; decentralization did not work well in a highly cybernated situation; and the free-form, matrix designs were not adaptable to a situation demanding cutbacks and stability. Even Warren Bennis, who has been a leading advocate of discarding classical, bureaucratically organized structures and replacing them with modern free-form, behaviorally oriented structures, has

---

[6] Fremont E. Kast and James E. Rosenzweig, "General Systems Theory: Applications for Organization and Management," *Academy of Management Journal* (December 1972), p. 463.

[7] Joan Woodward, *Industrial Organization* (London: Oxford University Press, 1965). Follow-up evidence from William L. Zwerman, *New Perspectives on Organization Theory* (Westport, Conn.: Greenwood Publishing Corporation, 1970). For examples of support for contingency models see Paul R. Lawrence and Jay W. Lorsch, "Differentiation and Integration in Complex Organizations," *Administrative Science Quarterly* (June 1967), pp. 1–47, and, more recently, Y. K. Shetty and Howard M. Carlisle, "A Contingency Model of Organization Design," *California Management Review* (Fall 1972), pp. 38–45.

recently retrenched. Ironically, because of his actual experience as a practitioner, he now admits that bureaucratic structures may be appropriate in certain situations.[8]

The contingency designs are conditional in nature. The bureaucracy may work best in a stable situation and the free form in a dynamic situation. Technology, economic and social conditions, and human resources are some of the variables that must be considered in a contingent organization design.

Model of leadership

More has probably been written about leadership than any other single topic. Although all this attention has been devoted to it, for years research was not able to come up with any concrete results. Most often the leader and his traits were examined. Recently, the work of Fred Fiedler, who emphasizes the importance that the situation has in leadership effectiveness, has produced a significant breakthrough. Based on years of empirical research, Fiedler was able to develop a contingency model of leadership effectiveness.

In simple terms, the model states that a task-directed leader is most effective in moderately favorable and moderately unfavorable situations.[9] Of special interest, however, is his ability to classify situations according to the three dimensions of position power, acceptance by subordinates, and task definition. This type of classification is the necessary goal of any contingency approach.

Model of behavioral change

Although not generally recognized in a managerial context, the contingency approach has been widely applied to behavioral change in mental health and education. Based on the principles of operant conditioning, this approach assumes that behavior depends on its consequences. Therefore, to change a person's behavior, he must be able to perceive a contingent relationship between his behavior and the consequence of that behavior. This contingent relationship, once established, will affect the frequency of subsequent behavior.

The author is currently directing a major field research program that is using this contingency concept. The approach is called Organizational Behavior Modification (O. B. Mod.). It can be used to train industrial supervisors through a process method of instruction to be contingency managers of their workers. Preliminary results of this program are very encouraging.[10]

[8] Warren Bennis, "Who Sank the Yellow Submarine?" *Psychology Today* (November 1972), pp. 112–20.
[9] Fred Fiedler, A Theory of Leadership Effectiveness (New York: McGraw-Hill Book Company, 1967).
[10] Fred Luthans, Robert Ottemann, and David Lyman are currently in the process of writing the study in monograph form. Published results may be available in late 1973 or 1974.

The study has demonstrated that when first-line supervisors apply O. B. Mod. techniques to their subordinates, desirable job behaviors leading to improved performance can be accelerated through the use of reinforcement and undesirable behaviors can be decelerated through the use of punishment.

However, the key to the success of the approach depends upon the worker's ability to perceive the contingency that if he behaves a certain way, then his behavior will result in a certain consequence. The if-then contingency pattern used in O. B. Mod. is similar to the contingency approaches used in organizational design and leadership style.

Approaches in the quantitative area

Although the examples so far are primarily drawn from organizational behavior, the quantitative areas have also begun to use contingency approaches. Operations research itself is actually based on a situational premise. The starting point in developing any OR model is to account for the situational givens. However, as OR was applied through the years this premise was often abused. Questionable initial assumptions which were often totally divorced from reality were cranked into OR models. However, in recent years with the development of a broader management science approach, more attention is being given to situational factors. Recent books in the management science area have begun to use a situational framework. For example, Stanley Young states that:

We must know under what conditions it is advisable to move from Linear Programming to rule of thumb and then back to Linear Programming. There is an over-concern with single decision rule, and we must learn how to use different combinations of rules under a variety of operating conditions.[11]

This article suggests that a contingency approach may be the path out of the existing theoretical jungle in management. The process path was split by the behavioral and quantitative paths. However, neither of these approaches by itself seems capable of leading management out of the jungle. Currently, the systems path seems to be drawing them together toward a unified theoretical development, but by the time the juncture is reached in the future, something may emerge which differs from the sum of the parts. This outcome is predicted to be the contingency theory of management.

The successful contingency approaches in the behavioral and quantitative areas which are beginning to surface are evidence of the potential that a

[11] Stanley D. Young, "Organization as a Total System," in Fred Luthans, ed., *Contemporary Readings in Organizational Behavior* (New York: McGraw-Hill Book Company, 1972), p. 109. For other examples see David W. Miller, and Martin K. Starr, *Executive Decisions and Operations Research* (Englewood Cliffs, N.J.: Prentice-Hall, 1970) and Thomas R. Prince, *Information Systems for Management Planning and Control* (Homewood, Ill.: Richard D. Irwin, Inc., 1970).

contingency theory may have for leading management out of the theory jungle. The overall goal of a contingency theory of management would be to match quantitative, behavioral, and systems approaches with appropriate situational factors.

Although this goal would be difficult to reach, the contingency theory could serve as an effective framework for development. Fiedler's work proves that it is possible. His contingency model could serve as a prototype. The challenge for the future is to develop a contingency theory for management as a whole.

5 Hanging together: Mazda and the establishment
Norman Pearlstine

Toyo Kogyo Co., developer of the rotary-engine Mazda and Japan's No. 3 auto maker, has its back to the wall. Slack sales and swollen inventories have created a serious cash shortage. An American company in this shape might fold or go into receivership. Certainly it would lay off many workers. Any government assistance would come only after prolonged congressional debate over federal giveaways and the free enterprise system.

Things work differently in Japan. Toyo Kogyo's problems have promoted the biggest corporate rescue in recent Japanese history. That unusual combination of business and government interests colloquially called "Japan Inc." is giving Toyo Kogyo a lot of tender, loving care in the form of experienced management advice, loans, special tax breaks and big fleet-size purchases of Toyo Kogyo's slow-selling cars.

Employing about 35,000 workers, Toyo Kogyo is Hiroshima's largest employer. Another 250,000 people, including workers' families and employes at hundreds of subsidiaries and suppliers, depend on the company for a living. "If the worst befell Toyo Kogyo," a Japanese magazine asserts, "it would be like a second atomic bomb for Hiroshima."

It helps to be in

The incestuous relationships among most big Japanese firms are such that the collapse of one could touch off the collapse of others. "If it were just a question of a big manufacturer going belly up, you would send a guy in and liquidate it," says James C. Abegglen, head of the Boston Consulting Group's Tokyo office and a specialist in Japanese business. "The real concern is that much more than Toyo Kogyo is at stake."

Still, Japan Inc. isn't monolithic. Personalities often clash. Disputes simmer over the amount of aid Toyo Kogyo needs and who should offer it. Nevertheless, the rescue sharply contrasts with the abandonment last year of Nihon Netsugaku Co., a large maker of air conditioners. This firm's failure didn't imperil other companies. Nor was Nihon Netsugaku an established member of the corporate hierarchy; so Japan Inc. wasn't much concerned.

Toyo Kogyo's troubles began in late 1973. Through the 1960s and early 1970s, it had grown from a small truck-maker into an integrated auto manufacturer with yearly sales exceeding $1.6 billion. Its powerful little rotary engine doesn't pollute the air as much as conventional engines. But the engine consumes more gasoline than piston engines of similar size. When fuel prices rose sharply, would-be Mazda buyers soured on the car.

Toyo Kogyo's management, headed by Kohei Matsuda, 53-year-old grandson of the firm's founder, was slow to grasp the dimensions of the problem. Mr. Matsuda balked at suggestions from Sumitomo Bank that he cut output and forgo 1975-model exports to the U.S. so that 1974 models could be cleared from dealer showrooms. Sumitomo Bank and its affiliate, Sumitomo Trust Co., are major Toyo Kogyo shareholders, and they have lent the company more than $400 million—more than the two banks' combined capital of $319 million.

The Sumitomo connection

Mr. Matsuda's belief that sales soon would pick up was proved wrong. Toyo Kogyo's net income fell by 66% in the six months ended Oct. 31, 1974. By mid-December, inventories had risen to some 160,000 vehicles, or about 60% above their normal level. Humbled, Mr. Matsuda became more amenable to outside advice. With this change in attitude, the rescue began in earnest.

By his own admission, Mr. Matsuda lacks the "high-level connections" with key business and government leaders that his troubled firm needs. But Shozo Hotta, the wizened, 76-year-old chairman of Sumitomo Bank, is one of the in-group's most eminent members, and he is filling some of Mr. Matsuda's leadership gaps.

Though Mr. Hotta won't talk to outsiders about Toyo Kogyo, people who understand his thinking say that he decided about four months ago that the company's lack of cash should be tackled first. Sumitomo alone couldn't provide all of it. So Mr. Hotta began a campaign to interest others. He had Sumitomo buy hundreds of Mazdas for its own fleet. Sumitomo ordered officials at its 191 branches to steer bank customers to Mazda dealers. Mr. Hotta, in meetings with bankers and businessmen, talked up Toyo Kogyo and, a banker recalls, "he stressed that Hiroshima's prosperity depended on a healthy Toyo Kogyo and that the rotary engine was needed to save Japan from pollution."

A little arm-twisting

C. Itoh & Co., Japan's fourth largest trading firm, with yearly sales of $17.4 billion, never had shown much interest in distributing Mazdas abroad. The firm has close ties with General Motors Corp. and Isuzu Motors Co., GM's Japanese affiliate, and was less than eager to help the competition.

But Mr. Hotta had the power to try a little arm-twisting, and he did. His Sumitomo Bank had lent C. Itoh some $375 million, and Sumitomo holds about 9% of C. Itoh's outstanding shares. When Sumitomo made a formal request that C. Itoh start distributing Mazdas in the eastern United States, it was a proposition that C. Itoh couldn't refuse.

Next, Shigeo Nagano, 74-year-old head of the Japan Chamber of Commerce and Industry, agreed to become Toyo Kogyo's "supreme adviser and counselor." If anything, Mr. Nagano is even more eminent than Mr. Hotta. He is an old friend of the Matsuda family. He also is a director and former chairman of Nippon Steel, of which Sumitomo Bank is a major lender and sixth-largest shareholder. Nippon Steel, in turn, is Toyo Kogyo's largest supplier and Sumitomo Bank's fifth-largest shareholder.

Meanwhile, Nippon Steel's sales executives talked with executives of Toyota Motor Co. and Nissan Motor Co., Toyo Kogyo's main competitors. Their aim: to get assurance that the competitors, also big customers of Nippon Steel, wouldn't frown on Mr. Nagano's participation in the effort to rescue their rival. The competitors gave their approval.

Mr. Nagano has tried to minimize his role in Toyo Kogyo. Others scoff at his self-depreciation. "Mr. Nagano has a quasi-official position in Japanese society," says Boston Consulting's Mr. Abegglen. Says Robert Ballon, chairman of the Socio-Economic Institute at Tokyo's Sophia University and an analyst of Japanese business: "Nagano's coming in means that all of Japan is standing behind Toyo Kogyo."

In any case, Sumitomo Bank soon was able to interest more than 50 other banks in getting together on a $119 million stop-gap loan for Toyo Kogyo. The money is needed to float Toyo Kogyo through next month. Bankers concerned over the size of the company's total bank debt—now exceeding $1.12 billion—have been reassured by the aura of solvency and stability that Mr. Nagano and his close associates exude.

Even some Sumitomo-affiliated firms were reluctant to join the rescue effort, because they have close ties of their own with some of Toyo Kogyo's competitors. But at a meeting last month, the Hakusui Kai ("White Water Club"), a policy-planning council of the heads of the Sumitomo group's 16 largest companies, agreed to help Toyo Kogyo in any way it could. An official says: "Once Mr. Nagano, who isn't part of Sumitomo, accepted Mr. Hotta's request for help, none of us could refuse a similar plea."

Boosterism and tax cuts

In the U. S., of course, almost any one of all these gestures would arouse the suspicion of the Justice Department's antitrust division. In Japan, it's

almost universally agreed that anything to further the national economy deserves broad-based support. That attitude was forged during the 19th century by the leaders of the Meiji Restoration, a modern-minded group that
reestablished the emperor as ruler of a unified nation and ended 250 years
of feudalism. The attitude has been refined over 100 years of cooperation
among businessmen, bureaucrats and politicians.

Consequently, the effort to save Toyo Kogyo has drawn in many
people outside the most prestigious corporate suites. In Hiroshima, seven
businessmen have formed an association called Kyoshin Kai ("Home Heart
Group") to promote Mazda sales. It has five full-time employes who try to
arrange purchases of Mazdas by fleet operators and individual government
and business officials. Partly because of this promotion, Toyo Kogyo's share
of the Hiroshima car market jumped to 34% in February from its normal
level of slightly more than 20%.

Hiroshima officials have enacted an anti-pollution measure that reduces a local tax on Mazdas by 50% and raises a tax on many competitive
cars by 10%. Hiroshima politicians in the national legislature are pushing for
similar tax treatment nationwide. Mr. Nagano's nephew, Itsuo Nagano, is an
important national politician. In the bureaucracy, the trade and industry
ministry has started giving subsidies and low-cost loans to some Toyo
Kogyo subcontractors.

Is merger a last resort?

Toyo Kogyo itself has turned 1,100 clerical workers into instant salesmen,
working in dealer showrooms. It has cut its planned output for 1975 to
about 640,000 vehicles from 740,000 in 1974 and in 1973. Production workers have been laid off for two or three days a month, with 70% of their
usual pay, since January.

Mr. Matsuda, Toyo Kogyo's chief executive, has conceded that only a
fraction of the cars he wanted to export to the U. S. actually should cross
the Pacific.

Toyo Kogyo has persuaded many suppliers to wait a while to get paid.
It gave its usual year-end, lump-sum bonus to union workers in three
monthly installments. It canceled management raises. It sold its office building in Tokyo, and it plans to sell a building in Osaka to a real-estate firm controlled by the Sumitomo group. Toyo Kogyo also is selling some undeveloped land and its interests in some Sumitomo group companies.

All of this, Mr. Matsuda thinks, will bail out his company. "I expect our
crisis will last through October this year," he says. If it lingers, the company's outside supporters may promote a merger with another company—
perhaps Toyota or Nissan. These firms now profess little interest in taking
over Toyo Kogyo. But most people here think that if there is no other way to
save it, somebody will be persuaded to absorb it. That's the way Japan Inc.
works.

Part II

Planning

No amount of sophistication is going to allay the fact that all your knowledge is about the past and all your decisions are about the future.
Ian H. Wilson

Management scholars and practitioners traditionally have identified five major functions as the framework of the managerial process: planning, organizing, staffing, influencing, and controlling. Although the latter four will be treated in subsequent sections, it is worth pointing out that their discussion is preceded by a review of that function which forms the antecedent of all the others: planning. Ultimate success is largely dependent on the process by which managers identify alternative courses of action, assess their probable outcomes, and determine the path by which to achieve their goals. In short, success depends on sound planning.

In the first selection of this Part, Tosi, Rizzo, and Carroll argue persuasively that in order to plan—indeed, manage—intelligently, managers must first identify their objectives.

The remaining selections deal with the execution of planning and discuss various aspects of the process. Zoglin reports an interesting interview with General Electric's chief planner; Redfield discusses the essential components of effective forecasting; and *Business Week* describes a specific device to assist managers in their forecasting task. Finally, Pollak and Taft give us an example of planning in the public sector. Taken together, these selections provide a comprehensive view of planning—what it involves and what it implies.

II/A
Setting objectives

---

6 Setting goals in management by objectives
Henry L. Tosi, John R. Rizzo, and Stephen J. Carroll

Management by objectives (MBO) is a process in which members of complex organizations, working in conjunction with one another, identify common goals and coordinate their efforts toward achieving them. It emphasizes the future and change, since an objective or goal is an end state, or a condition to be achieved or have in effect at some future time. The emphasis is on where the organization is going—the what and the how of its intended accomplishments. Objectives can be thought of as statements of purpose and direction, formalized into a system of management. They may be long-range or short-range. They may be general, to provide direction to an entire organization, or they may be highly specific to provide detailed direction for a given individual.

One purpose of MBO is to facilitate the derivation of specific from general objectives, seeing to it that objectives at all levels in the organization are meaningfully located structurally and linked to each other. Sets of objectives for an organizational unit are the bases which determine its activities. A set of objectives for an individual determines his job, and can be thought of as a different way to provide a job description. Once objectives are determined and assumed by organizational units and by individuals, it is possible to work out the means or performance required for accomplishing the objectives. Methods of achieving objectives, resources required, timing, interactions with others, control, and evaluation must have continuing attention.

Objectives may or may not require change

The goal or end-state may be one of insuring that no change occurs—for example, an important recurring organizational operation. However, the em-

Source: © 1970, by The Regents of the University of California. Reprinted from *California Management Review,* Vol. 12, No. 4, pp. 70–78, by permission of the Regents.

phasis still remains on change and the future, and "no change" conditions can be thought of as making finer change discriminations in the management process. However, MBO is deemed most appropriate in situations where activities tend not to be recurring or repetitious, where change toward new or improved conditions is sought. Typically, these would be innovative endeavors, problem-solving situations, improvements, and personal development.

Objectives may originate at any point in the organization structure

Quite naturally, they should be derived from the general purposes of the organization, and consistent with its philosophy, policies, and plans. It is beyond the scope of this paper to discuss the details of policy formulation and planning. Rather, it is recognized that these activities take place and that the setting of objectives can, and often does, occur in concern and consonance with them. For example, plans can specify the phasing and timing of organizational operations, out of which are derived objectives for those involved in implementing them. Objectives are not considered as substitutes for plans, but rather as a basis for developing them. Stating objectives accomplishes the following:

1 Document expectations in superior-subordinate relationship regarding what is to be done and the level of attainment for the period covered by the goal.
2 Provide members with a firmer base for developing and integrating plans and personal and departmental activity.
3 Serve as the basis for feedback and evaluation of subordinates' performance.
4 Provide for coordination and timing of individual and unit activities.
5 Draw attention to the need for control of key organizational functions.
6 Provide a basis for work-related rewards as opposed to personality-based systems.
7 Emphasize change, improvement, and growth of the organization and the individual.

Objectives as means-end distinctions

The formulation of objectives throughout an organization represents a kind of means-end analysis, which is an attempt to factor general requirements into specific activities. Means-end analysis starts "with the general goal to be achieved, (2) discovering a set of means, very generally specified, for accomplishing this goal, (3) taking each of these means, in turn, as a new sub-goal and discovering a more detailed set of means for achieving it, etc."[1]

[1] J. March and H. Simon, *Organizations*. New York: Wiley, 1958, p. 191.

MBO is predicated on this concept. It is assumed that a means-end analysis can occur with a degree of precision and accuracy. The end represents a condition or situation that is desired, a purpose to be achieved. Here, the concept of *end* is equated with *goal* or *objective*. Objectives may represent required inputs to other sectors of the organization. They may be specific achievement levels, such as product costs, sales volume and so on. They may also be completed projects. For instance, the market research department may seek to complete a sales forecast by a particular date so the production facilities may be properly coordinated with market demands. Objectives, or end states, are attained through the performance of some activity. These activities are the *means* to achieve the *end*. It is important to distinguish between ends and means in the use of the "objectives approach" since there are implications for measurement and assessment which will be discussed later in the paper.

It is obvious that a malfunction or break in such a process may lead to major problems in implementing management by objectives. It is for this reason that commitment, effort, support, and use by top management is critical at all levels to obtain consensus of objectives, cooperation in achievement, and the use of objectives as criteria for evaluation. But there are some problems in doing this. This paper is directed toward these: stating objectives, areas they should cover, the question of measurement, as well as some suggestions for dealing with them.

The objective

The objectives for any position should reflect the means-end distinction discussed earlier. The first critical phase of objectives-setting is the statement which describes the end state sought. It should be:

- Clear, concise and unambiguous.
- Accurate in terms of the true end-state or condition sought.
- Consistent with policies, procedures, and plans as they apply to the unit.
- Within the competence of the man, or represent a reasonable learning and developmental experience for him.
- Interesting, motivating, and/or challenging whenever possible.

Some examples of goal statements might be written as: increase sales by 10 percent; reduce manufacturing costs by 5 percent; reduce customer complaints; increase sales by 5 percent by December 1; increase quality within a 5 percent increase in production control costs; develop understanding and implementation of computer techniques among subordinates.

Notice that these goal statements have at least two key components. First, each clearly suggests an *area of activity* in which accomplishment occurs. Second, some clearly specify a level of achievement, the quantity or deadlines to be met. We will refer to the desired level of achievement as *performance level.* The need for this distinction is obvious. It indicates the evaluation criterion by specifying the *level* or the condition which should exist. This has clear implications for both measurement and appraisal. Before discussing these implications, however, a more detailed examination of the scope and types of objectives in the MBO process is required.

Scope and type of objectives

It would be difficult to conceive of developing objectives for a manager which would cover each and every area of responsibility. The structure of most jobs is simply too complex. Yet once objectives are set for a position, they should comprise the major description of the job, and their achievement in light of what is known about total job requirements should be assessed. A sense of interference or conflict between objectives and other job requirements should be prevented.

Two major types of objectives may be delineated: *performance* objectives and *personal development* objectives.[2] *Performance objectives* refer mainly to those goals and activities that relate to the individual's position assignment. *Personal development* goals have to do with increasing the individual's skills, competence, or potential. Delineating types of objectives in this manner, more importantly, allows for an assessment of how MBO is being used and what emphases are deriving from it. For instance:

- Once all objectives are set for a person, a basis exists to ensure that there is a "balance" of different types, that he is problem solving, developing and maintaining critical functions.
- Some estimates can be made regarding the importance of objectives and consequences of failure to achieve them. For example, a man who fails on a difficult creative objective should not be evaluated the same as one who fails to maintain a critical recurring operation.

Performance objectives

This type is derived directly from the job assignment, from the major areas of responsibility and activity of the individual that he must sustain or manage. Among them would be the maintenance of recurring or routine activities, the solving of problems, or the creation of innovative ideas, products, services, and the like. Some of these may take on the form of special activities or projects not normally part of the job. That is, even though they are part of the normal job requirements, they are goals which may take on special importance for a number of reasons—emergencies, changes in priorities, or simply management decisions.

[2] These categories are similar to those proposed by Odiorne. See his *Management by Objectives.* New York: Pitman, 1964, especially Chapters 7, 8, & 9.

A special activity for one position may be routine for another: A special project goal for a lower-level manager might be a routine goal for his boss. Developing a computer-based information system for personnel records may be a highly creative objective for the personnel department, yet should probably be considered a routine goal for a systems analysis group.

Discretionary areas and other problems

By its very nature, organization imposes restrictions on individuals. The structure of an organization defines legitimate areas of influence and decision making for an individual. Specialization and definition of function tend to limit decisions and activities to those defined for the incumbent.

If the objectives process is intended to, and does, facilitate subordinate participation and involvement, we must recognize the implicit nature of power. A lower-level manager cannot *legitimately* influence goal levels and action plans in areas in which he has no discretion, unless he has the *approval of his superior.* Therefore, it is necessary to spell out areas in which the subordinate has some latitude so that he knows what his decision limits are. Otherwise he may be misled into believing that he can participate in departmental and organizational decisions which have been defined, either procedurally or by managerial fiat, as being outside his discretion area. When you expect to participate and then cannot, negative consequences may occur. It is for this reason that it is important to determine and *communicate to the subordinate* what these discretion areas are.

One way to define discretion areas is to determine whether an individual should influence means or ends. If the activity operates primarily across the boundaries of the organization and is affected by conditions beyond its control, then the individual charged with performing it may be in a better position to determine both the goals (or ends) and the most appropriate manner to achieve them. For instance, the marketing executives in constant touch with the external environment are in a better position to determine possible sales penetration and programs than others in the organization. However, not having discretion over goal levels should not preclude involvement in goal setting. Here the MBO process should focus on developing the best *means* (later called action plans) for goal attainment.

High levels of skill and technology required in a particular function may make the specialist better able than a nontechnical person to assess what can be done in a technical field. Thus, he should be involved in determining goal levels, as well as in carrying out activities. This is not to suggest that organizational constraints and requirements be entirely removed. Budget limitations, sales quotas, and production requirements are boundaries or restrictions which may not be removed but may have to be made more flexible.

If performance levels are set, for any reason, at higher organization levels, then there is little option but to focus on the determination of the ''best'' activities to achieve these levels. Internal definition of goal levels will most probably be for activities which function primarily within the boundaries of the organization. The assumption, of course, is that the one defining the objective, or level, is either competent to do so or must because of its critical importance.

An important limitation on discretion is organization level. The lower the organizational level, the more and more narrow the zone of a manager's discretion. That is, the manager at the lower levels is responsible for fewer, more specific, and more measurable activities and can commit smaller quantities of resources than those at higher levels.[3]

Another factor which causes variation in the discretion range for a particular job is the changing competency levels of the incumbent. A person learning a job may need more guidance from the superior. However, as his skills increase, the superior may spend less time since the subordinate can capably handle more activities and make more decisions. The objectives approach, incidentally, may help the superior make assessments of the subordinate's competence to expand the decision area. As a subordinate becomes more successful in achieving goals, additional and more challenging goals within the parameters of the job could be added. When the incumbent can perform these adequately, then consideration should be given to possible promotion and transfer.

What about those decision areas beyond the discretion limits? We are not suggesting that the subordinate should have no part in these decisions. His role may be contributing information and assistance, such as providing inputs to the decision-making process of the superior, which the superior may choose to accept or reject. But this type of activity must be differentiated from *goal setting participation,* in which the individual *has something to say about the final shape and form* of the goals and activities. However, discretion boundaries are not rigid. While a particular decision may fall within the discretion range under normal circumstances, emergencies might develop which would result in the decision being made by the boss. These conditions cannot be foreseen, and consequently not planned for.

Personal development objectives

First, it is important to stress that these must be based on problems or deficiencies, current or anticipated, in areas such as improvements in technical skills or interpersonal problems. They may also be directed at developing one for movement within the organization. The critical nature of these objectives lies in their potential as means to combat obsolescence under a rapid expansion of knowledge, to prepare people for increased responsibility, and to overcome problems in organizational interactions.

Setting development goals is probably more difficult than setting performance goals, since they are personal in nature and, as such, must be

[3] H. Tosi and S. Carroll, "Some Structural Factors Related to Goal Influence in the Management by Objectives Process," *Business Topics* (Spring 1969), 45–50.

handled with care and tact. This difficulty may be avoided by simply not setting them. It could be argued that they should be avoided since they are an
intrusion into the individual's privacy by the boss or the organization. However, when perceived personal limitations hinder effective performance, the
problem must be treated.

Thus, if at any time the superior believes an individual's limitations
stand clearly in the way of the unit's goal achievement, it should be made
known to the individual. He may not be aware that he is creating problems
and would gladly change—if he knew. Many technically competent people
have been relieved from positions because of human problems they ostensibly create. Many might have been retained had they only known that problems existed or were developing.

Personal development objectives should be a basic part of the MBO
program, *when there is a need for them.* But, if they are included only to
meet formal program requirements and are not problem-based, little value
will obtain. Then personal improvement goals will probably be general and
ambiguous, tenable only if the organization wishes to invest in "education
for education's sake." For other than a philosophical or value-based justification, personal development should attack deficiencies related to performance, containing specific action proposals for solving the problems. This may
be done in the following manner.

Pinpoint a problem area

Parties involved in goal setting should continually be alert to negative incidents resulting from personal incapacities. The boss is in a particularly important position for recognizing problems. When situations occur which he believes are due to either personal or technical limitations, he should be aware
of who was involved, and make some determination of the cause of these
problems. Other individuals in the unit may bring problems to the fore.
Those with whom an individual interacts may be in a reasonably good position to judge his technical competence or to determine when problems are
due to his behavior. If colleagues are continually complaining about another
person, additional investigation into the problem is warranted. Perhaps the
most important source of these negative incidents is the subordinate himself. He may be very aware of problems in which he is involved and by discussing them may determine those in which he has been the primary cause.

These negative incidents should be relatively significant in effect and
frequency and not simply a single event that has caused some notice to be
taken. This does not mean, however, that an important incident which occurs one time should be overlooked if it suggests serious deficiencies.

There are at least three areas in which personal development objectives should be set.

- *Improve interpersonal relations*   Inability to maintain reasonably effective
working relationships may be due to a person's lack of awareness or his inability to cooperate. This may arise from personality deficiencies or simple

lack of awareness of his impact upon others. He may be unable to recognize that he is precipitating problems.

- *Improve current skills*   A manager may be, for instance, unable to prepare a budget or to engage in research because he has not had adequate training in these areas or because his training is not up to date. His general performance may be acceptable, but his skills should be improved.
- *Prepare for advancement*   Another possibility covers either technical or human skills required for different or higher level positions. These are truly developmental goals which focus on preparation for advancement. There are many ways in which they may be achieved. In some cases the individual may be given advanced work assignments; in others, they may be achieved by exposure in training situations to new concepts. In any event, they represent a *potential* problem area.

Assess the causes of the problem

Once it has been established that a problem exists, the cause needs to be determined. Causes should be sought jointly, a result of investigation and discussion by both the superior and subordinate after both have thought of possible causes.

The possible causes of problems may be grouped into three general categories:

- *Procedures and structure*   The structure of the organization itself may induce disturbances. Interpersonal conflict may develop because of the interdependence of work activities. For instance, if formal requirements cause a delay in information transmission, those who need it may develop negative attitudes and feelings.
- *Others with whom an individual must work*   Problems with subordinates or managerial peers of the goal setter may be caused by personality incompatibility or lack of certain technical skills. While this may represent an important cause of problems, it is too easy to blame negative incidents on others.
- *The person himself*   The *individual* may have habits and characteristics which are not congruent with those of subordinates or colleagues.Or, he may lack the technical skills requisite to carry out certain responsibilities.

Attempting to define problems and causes facilitates converting development objectives into achievable goals. Like other objectives, they can be general (attend a sensitivity training course or role playing seminar), or more specific (attend XYZ course in financial planning, use PERT techniques on Project X).

Self-improvement goals may be designed to improve current performance, or may be specifically intended to develop skills required at higher levels, or in different jobs (where it may be impossible to describe the end state of affairs to be achieved because success can be determined only in the future, or in other positions).

For development objectives it is necessary simply to rely upon the determination that the action plan has been carried out and that the individual has learned something. Suppose, for instance, that a development goal for an engineer destined to be a supervisor read as follows: "To meet with members of the financial, marketing, and production groups in order to learn how product release schedules affect their areas." Currently, he may have to know little about this since he may now have little impact on product release schedules. The question is, "How do you know that the activity produced the desired learning?" You don't. At some point in time, the superior, who presumably has some knowledge in the goal area, should discuss the results of the meeting with the subordinate, emphasizing particularly the important points that should have been learned. If this is done the subordinate will have the learning experience of the meeting and the reinforcement from discussion.

There is obviously no way to determine if these activities will improve the current, or future, performance of the manager. Managerial judgment is important here. We must simply assume that the superior is able to work with the subordinate to define activities of value in future work assignments.

Finally, it should be clear that performance and development objectives may well be derived from and related to management training and development efforts. These efforts must account for current organizational problems and future needs, and treat development as an integrated organization-wide effort. MBO should therefore be integrally tied to them.

Performance required: The action plan

Some of the problems inherent in MBO can be overcome by stating and discussing the specifics of the performance required to accomplish an objective. Earlier, the differentiation of means and ends was stressed. The goal statements reflected the ends: here, the performance or "action plan" refers to the means to accomplish an objective. It describes the manner in which it is to be attained. These means reflect alternatives which lead to the desired end and performance level.

The action plan may be brief statements, but it should summarize what is to be done. The action plan for a complex activity should be broken down into major subprograms and should represent the "best" alternative, of possibly many, which would achieve the goal level. The action plan provides an initial basis for a total action program for the individual or department. These action plans might be stated in the following manner:

- *For the sales increase*   develop more penetration in a particular market area by increasing the number of calls to dealers there.
- *For the reduced manufacturing costs*   analyze the overtime activities and costs and schedule more work during regular hours.

Subordinates may base their own action plans on those developed by their manager, using his plan to guide their own roles in the unit's effort.

Thus, clear differentiation of means from ends can facilitate lower-level use of the objectives process.

Including both means and ends permits comparing performance with some criteria and determining if events occurred which are presumed to lead to a desired outcome. It is important to recognize the distinction between measuring an objective and determining if an event has occurred. If we are unable to quantify or specify the goal level adequately, then we simply *assume that the desired goal level will be achieved* if a particular event or set of activities takes place. For example, while it is very difficult to measure if a manager is developing the talents of subordinates by means of any hard criteria, we can determine if he has provided them with development opportunities. If they have participated in seminars, attended meetings, or gone off to school, it may be *assumed* that the development activity is being properly conducted.

Some further benefits and opportunities provided by adequate attention to an action plan are as follows:

1 Aids in search for better, more efficient methods of accomplishing the objective.
2 Provides an opportunity to test the feasibility of accomplishing the objectives as stated.
3 Develops a sounder basis to estimate time or cost required and deadline for accomplishment.
4 Examines the nature and degree of reliance on other people in the organization toward coordination and support needed.
5 Uncovers anticipated snags or barriers to accomplishment.
6 Determines resources (manpower, equipment, supplies, facilities) required to accomplish the objective.
7 Facilitates control if the performance is well specified and agreed upon; reporting need only occur when problems arise in implementing. This is a form of planning ahead; when plans are sufficiently complete, only deviations from it need be communicated.
8 Identifies areas in which the superior can provide support and assistance.
9 Facilitates the delegation process.

Determine coordinating requirements and contingencies

Successful achievement or failure of an objective may depend upon the contribution and performance of other individuals or departments. Therefore, since they may be extremely critical to successful performance, they must be considered.

Some contingencies apply to all objectives and need not be documented on each. For example, delays in the availability of resources, change in support or priorities from higher management, equipment failures, delayed information or approval, and the like, which are unplanned, should relieve some responsibility for objective accomplishment.

Other contingencies, specific to the objective, should be discussed.

Among these might be inadequate authority of the subordinate, lack of policy covering aspects of the objective, possible failure to gain others' cooperation, known delays in the system, and so on. Once these are uncovered, several actions are possible:

- Reexamination of the objective (e.g. alteration of a deadline) when and if the contingency occurs.
- Commitment of the superior to aid by overcoming or preventing the contingency.
- Revision of the performance required to accomplish the objective.
- Establishment of a new objective. If a contingency is serious enough, an objective aimed at overcoming the problem may be justified.

Measurement and appraisal

Management by objectives carried with it most of the familiar difficulties and complications of measurement and appraisal processes. Its emphasis on performance, as opposed to personality traits or criteria presumed related to performance, makes it potentially more effective. But this potential cannot be realized unless measurement and appraisal are reasonably valid, reliable, objective, and equitable.

Means, ends, and evaluation Performance evaluations should rarely be based only on whether or not the objective was accomplished, or on the sheer number accomplished. They should include:

1 Quantitative aspects. (Was cost reduced 5 percent as planned?)
2 Qualitative aspects. (Have good relations been established with Department X? Has an evaluation technique been established?)
3 Deadline considerations. (Was the deadline beaten? Was it met?)
4 Proper allocation of time to given objectives.
5 Type and difficulty of objectives.
6 Creativity in overcoming obstacles.
7 Additional objectives suggested or undertaken.
8 Efficient use of resources.
9 Use of good management practices in accomplishing objectives (cost reduction, delegation, good planning, etc.)
10 Coordinative and cooperative behavior; avoidance of conflict-inducing or unethical practices, etc.

Evaluation and measurement, therefore, require considering both means and ends, being concerned with both the objective (number, type, difficulty, etc.) and the means to its achievement (cost, cooperativeness, time consumed, etc.). Unless this is done, an important opportunity to communicate expectations, feedback performance results, and setting effective goals may be lost. It must be fully understood that evaluation has obvious links to action plans, as well as to desired end states.

Further consideration in measurement   Some goals lend themselves more easily than others to measurement—scrap rates, production costs, sales volume, and other "hard" measures. These measures pertain most to lower organizational levels and to areas such as production, marketing, or other major functional activities of the organization and least to most staff and specialist units. The measurement problem often can be reduced to finding the appropriate, agreed-upon criterion for each objective, realizing that some will apply to many situations while others are unique to a single objective.

We have already detailed the distinction between performance and personal development objectives. Another distinction relevant to the measurement problem is the difference between routine and special project objectives. Classifying objectives according to these types permits some important refinements in evaluation and control. By examining the nature of the mix of objectives for a set of positions it is possible to determine any or all of the following:

- The extent to which each individual has some personal development objectives.
- That sufficient problem-solving or innovative activities were forthcoming in units where they might be required.
- The priorities for performance or personal development objectives.

Routine objectives are basic to the job, a core part of the job description. How should they be measured? The most appropriate method for evaluating if an individual has achieved them is first to insure that he is aware of these activities and required levels. The manager must tell the subordinate—early in the relationship—what the activities of the job are and what the desired level of performance is. Evaluation should not occur after a period of service unless there has been previous discussion of criteria.

At the same time that the criteria are being specified, acceptable tolerance limits should be developed. Measurement of the routine should be a major part of the objectives process, yet it should be of most concern *when performance falls outside acceptable levels.* Essentially, we are proposing that minimum performance levels be set for routine activities. Therefore, evaluation of routine goals is *by exception,* or when these standards are not met. Naturally, the ability to manage by exception demands good plans or clear standards from which exceptions can be specified in advance. Odiorne cites the following example:

The paymaster, for example, may report that his routine duties cluster around getting the weekly payroll out every Friday. It is agreed that the measure of exception will be zero—in other words, the boss should expect no exceptions to the diligent performance of this routine duty. Thus, the failure any week to produce the payroll on Friday will be considered an exception that calls for explanation by the subordinate. If the cause were reasonably under his control or could have been averted by extra care or effort, the absence of the payroll will be considered a failure on the part of the subordinate. [4]

What about superior performance? When a subordinate frequently exceeds the performance levels, the manager should let him know that his outstanding performance has been noticed. Positive feedback should occur, especially to let the individual know when he is performing his major job responsibilities exceptionally well.

Generally, routine job responsibilities or goals are expressed as job standards, or other "hard" performance measures. Although appraisal and evaluation essentially compare performance to the standard, this may be relatively short sighted and suboptimal. Recall that the manager should also evaluate the activities or the manner in which performance was carried out. Often costs may be reduced by foregoing other expenditures, which may have negative long-run effects. There can be substantial distortions of behavior when only quantitative criteria are used in measurement.

Problem-solving, special project, or creative objectives are more difficult to quantify than the essentially routine. If the ends are truly creative, determining an adequate performance level may necessarily rely on intuitive judgment. Since innovation and invention are needed in their very formulation, we cannot generally measure results in these areas adequately, or directly. It is usually possible, however, to judge if an activity has been performed appropriately even though the ends, or the performance levels, are neither quantifiable nor measurable. Furthermore, constraints may be set on the activities. We can assess that they have occurred by some specific point in time or that a specific dollar amount has been expended. Thus, we are not only concerned with whether or not events have occurred, but also within some tolerance limit such as of target dates, budget constraints, or a quality assessment by the manager. It becomes possible under these conditions to establish review points, thus giving attention to the outcome of activities when they occur. Deliberations on these outcomes can serve to reevaluate both objectives and means. Thus changes are possible, and both flexibility and control are assured where they appear to be most needed— where predictions, plans, and standards could not be specified or articulated in advance.

Deadlines and budget constraints can be strictly specified in some cases and not in others. A great deal depends on:

- The importance of the objective.
- The ability to determine the time or costs required in performance.

[4] Odiorne, p. 104.

- Whether or not written plans or objectives of other people require coordinated completion dates.
- The amount of time and money the subordinate will spend on the particular objective under discussion.
- The predictability of problems or barriers to accomplishment.

Discussing these constraints allows greater understanding between superiors and subordinates and establishes their use in evaluation. Expectations become known; realities can be tested. Deadlines and costs should be viewed as "negotiable," and should be reasonably and rationally arrived at whenever possible. Deadlines especially should not be set simply to insure that action is initiated.

We wish to re-emphasize the importance of this criterion problem. A fundamental requirement for MBO is the development and use of sound criteria for evaluation, appraisal, and feedback. This is critical to achieve meaningful changes in behavior. "Hard" criteria must be used with extreme care. They are best viewed as ends or levels; they indicate nothing about attaining either. "Soft" criteria involve not a particular level of achievement, but determination that an event or condition has or has not occurred. These soft criteria are a vital and fundamental part of MBO. Without them, the approach cannot be well implemented.

To some managers, the development and communication of goals comes naturally. There are those who are able intuitively to determine and specify appropriate measures, criteria, goals, and the most satisfactory methods for achieving them. They innately sense what must be observed and measured and communicate this effectively to subordinates. This, of course, is the behavior which management by objectives seeks to develop and reinforce.

Summary

Research and experience strongly support the relationship between the degree of a subordinate's acceptance of the objectives approach and his perception of its support and reinforcement from top management.[5] Organization support is critical for two reasons.

Top management may be an important reference group for lower level managers. Ambitious employees are likely to emulate managerial behavior. They identify with the top management and act similarly. If top management uses a particular method of managing, lower level managers are likely to use it also.
Consistent factoring and communication of goals to lower organizational levels is necessary. The general objective of the organization must be

[5] H. Tosi and S. Carroll, "Managerial Reactions to Management by Objectives," *Academy of Management Journal* (December 1968), 415–426.

continually broken down into smaller and smaller units. The boss must learn what is expected, must communicate this to his subordinates, and must work with them to achieve these objectives. If this process breaks down at any point, then the whole approach is difficult to use.

Objectives must be written down for the entire organization, but the degree of detail and precision cannot easily be specified. This may be a matter for organizational policy and procedure, or it may be determined by mutual superior-subordinate agreement. However this is resolved, the varied aspects of objectives-setting should be attended to, discussed, and resolved as fully as possible to benefit from the MBO process.

Most important is that the approach must be intrinsically built into the job of managing. It must be related to other organizational processes and procedures, such as budgeting. It should be fundamentally incorporated into planning and development activities. It should be one of the major inputs to the performance appraisal and evaluation process. If not, it is likely that unless a manager intuitively uses this approach, it is easier to do other things. There are costs involved in MBO. There must be some value or pay-off which managers can recognize; otherwise they will view it as a waste of time.

---

7 Does GE really plan better?
Richard Zoglin

In 1967 a remarkable document, entitled "Our Future Business Environment," emerged from a newly formed unit at General Electric. The 65-page study attempted nothing less than a comprehensive prediction of what social and economic conditions would be like in the United States in the year 1980. The study was updated two years later, and refined in 1971 through the development of four "alternative world/U.S. scenarios," which attempted to consider the entire range of possibilities for change over the next ten years.

 The hand that guided the production of those reports belongs to Ian H. Wilson, a British-born Oxfordian [classics] who came to General Electric in 1954. He is now in charge of the company's Business Environment Research and Forecasting unit, which is widely regarded as one of the most sophisticated long-range planning operations in the nation. *MBA* Associate Editor Richard Zoglin spent a recent morning at GE's sprawling Bridgeport, Connecticut, headquarters to learn what Mr. Wilson thinks of his predictions today—and to find out what makes long-range planning tick at GE.

MBA What is the history of the long-range planning effort at General Electric?
Wilson It really began in 1967, when a business environment studies unit was established as part of the personnel and industrial relations section of the company. There is no real logic to its emerging in that part of the company, except that the type of policy analysis, trend analysis, and forecasting that we were set up to do was essentially people-oriented rather than economics-oriented or technology-oriented. The charter that evolved for this work was the identification and analysis of the long-term social, political, and, in a broad sense, economic trends influencing the corporation, with particular emphasis on their impact on personnel relations, management style,

Source: Reprinted by permission from *MBA/Masters in Business Administration,* magazine (November 1975), pp. 42–46.

organization of work, union relations—the sub-functions of the major component to which we were attached.

After three years, this work was transferred to the corporate strategic planning component at the corporate level. That is the one place where we try to take a holistic view of the corporation and of its relations with the market, the society, the government. It's a logical forum for making executive decisions based on the whole range of perspectives.

MBA   Did this change in focus reflect a belief that the long-range planning function was growing in importance?

Wilson   Yes, I think that is so. The major reorganization of the company that took place in 1970 focused on differentiating between the long-term planning and the policy-making function of the corporation, and the shorter-term administrative functions. Up until that time each one of the functional components had a long-term and a short-term responsibility. Well, one of the problems of assigning a combination of long-term and short-term responsibilities to any one component is that inevitably the firefighting tends to win out. And then to the extent that there was any long-range planning, it tended to be compartmentalized in each of the components. Furthermore, the planning horizons were too exclusively economic and technological and paid inadequate attention to the social and political domain, which we were then exploring and analyzing.

As a result of the reorganization, we differentiated at the corporate level between the long-term perspectives of the corporation, which were made the responsibility of a corporate executive staff, and the short-term, day-to-day running of the company, which was assigned to a corporate administrative staff. The impact of the reorganization on the operating components was to superimpose on the traditional organizational elements of departments, divisions, and groups a unit we called the Strategic Business Unit.

MBA   What does that unit study?

Wilson   In a general sense, we are looking at the longer-term social and political trends that have an impact on the corporation. But when we're dealing with a corporation as large and diverse and geographically scattered as General Electric, there are very few social and political trends that do not have some bearing on the planning function of the company. Obviously, we very quickly got into identifying the sort of trends that made for the developing movements of the time—the women's movement, minority rights movement, environmental movement, consumerism movement. As much as anything else, we tried to gauge the changing social values and expectations of corporate performance.

It sounds like a very nebulous area to be working in, and indeed it is. But looking back on the very first report that we put out in 1967, in which we made a number of predictions for the year 1980, it's striking that the "hits"—the things we guessed right on—mostly related to changing attitudes and values and behavior. What we went wide of the mark on were some of the more apparently solid, quantifiable things such as economic stabilization, unemployment, and so on.

MBA   In that report didn't you predict, for example, that unemployment by 1980 would remain at the 3.0 to 4.5 percent level?
Wilson   Yes, that was one of the statements that was made. I don't want to get off the hook on that one—after all, we did put it out—but essentially that first report was not our own thinking but the synthesis of what we had learned from other people. We did it within three or four months of being established, and therefore we had not had time to do any serious research on our own. That initial study was very largely to acquaint ourselves with what was going on in the field, to give ourselves a broad perspective and a way of arriving at some priorities for our future research. In 1974 I sent back the original report to most of the same experts we had consulted in 1967. About 75 specific trends were underscored, and we asked for their views as to whether they saw these trends as being of increasing, continuing, or diminishing significance over the next ten years. Of those 75 predictions, virtually all those that related to attitudes toward education, leisure, work, income, motivation, and participation tended to get strong votes of reaffirmation. But the areas where there was the greatest turning away from the forecast were exactly the economic ones. There was no longer a belief that we would be growing at 4 percent a year, no longer a belief that inflation at 3 percent was a realistic expectation, no longer a belief that we could hold unemployment to between 3 and 4.5 percent. And I ask myself now: Are we making the same mistake in mirror image? Are we again projecting the present into the indefinite future?

MBA   Isn't that the problem with all future planning—the fact that all we have to go on is the present and the past?
Wilson   Of course, no amount of sophisticated methodology is going to get you away from the crunch situation that all your knowledge is about the past and all your decisions are about the future. That's a problem that we're always going to be confronted with. I don't think, however, that one therefore adopts a counsel of despair and says that it is totally useless to try to project the future because we've had some dismal failures in the past. Who foresaw a quadrupling in the price of oil? The answer is, I think, no one. I think what one can say is that a more systematic and *continuous* attempt to try to project future trends, and the intellectual honesty to admit that we cannot project with certainty and therefore to talk about *alternative* futures, is going to be the way we'll have to go.

The concept of alternative futures is absolutely essential for planning. To say that we are now going to do more systematic forecasting and monitoring of trends, and will plan on the basis of those monitoring and forecasting efforts in a simplistic, uni-dimensional sense, would be to negate the value of the monitoring and forecasting. If, as forecasters, we tried to project, however sophisticatedly, *the* future—this is it, plan for that—we would, I think, be doing ourselves and the decision makers a profound disservice. If we have learned one lesson from the past eight to ten years, it is that the future is very difficult to predict; it is fraught with uncertainties, and we simply have got to learn to live with that.

MBA   What good, then, does it do to know of these "alternative" futures? In what way can a company act in the face of such uncertainty?

Wilson   Well, when you come to make decisions, you obviously have to make them on the basis of a future that, all things considered, you believe to be most probable. However, if you have been conscientious in trying to open your minds to some of the alternative possibilities, you will probably also begin to analyze the impact on your plans of these alternative possibilities and to institute some beginning system of contingency planning. What if the market doesn't grow at 20 percent per annum, but only comes in at 5 percent—what do I do then? What does this do to my plans? It's a way of hedging your bets. It's a way of getting, shall we say, anticipatory flexibility into the system. Even if you've discounted something—even if you say that on balance I think that controls on oil are going to be lifted, and we're going to plan for that—the fact that you've considered the alternative possibility means that if controls are, in fact, continued, you're no longer scrambling for a response. Some of the preliminary thinking, some of the preliminary staff work, has been done. The adjustment of plans and attitudes can be made that much more rapidly.

MBA   What specifically does the Strategic Business Unit do on an annual basis?

Wilson   We make inputs to an annual planning cycle as well as contribute to specialized ad hoc studies and task forces. In the first case, each planning year starts with a revised look at the long-term environmental horizon. By long-term, I am thinking of 10 to 15 years. By environmental, I mean all the aspects of that environment—social, political, marketing, competitive, technological, manpower, and so on. This is not to say that every year we produce a totally comprehensive view of the next 10 to 15 years. The first planning cycle that we engaged in, in 1971, we did indeed do that. The product was the depicting of four alternative world/U.S. scenarios.

MBA   What did those consist of?

Wilson   We produced what we termed a benchmark forecast, which was the most probable future that we could conceive of; a "momentum" forecast, which was based on a trend extrapolation; and two polar extremes, to which we assigned very low probability, one of which was very much sweetness and light—everything goes right in the world and domestically—and another that predicted doom and disaster—everything comes apart, confrontation on the international scene, conflict on the domestic social scene, economic disaster, and so on. The point in that exercise was really to introduce this idea of alternative futures, and to show the range of unthinkable possibilities, both on the plus side and on the minus side.

Since 1972, we have done really two things each year: a quick checklist up-dating of the whole environment—what are some of the things that have gone right or gone wrong in our forecast, what new things have come up on the horizon? And the other thing is zeroing in on particular areas. Those scenarios are so general that they're not a great deal of help to a planner. You can only contribute that help as you focus in on a particular area—like the whole question of energy. Where is the technology going? Where are the economics going? Where is national energy policy going? What impact are these going to have on the company's business? How much attention should we pay to energy conservation—is that going to be the wave of the future? What effect are public attitudes about nuclear power likely to have on our business, and how do we respond to it? When you get that sort of specific question, to which an answer is required and on which a decision would be based, then you can start to pull together your environmental analyses into a much tighter web, and much more useful data can flow from it.

At the moment, to give another example, I am at work on a broad look at the future of the consumer market. And I don't mean the next two years; I mean the next 25 years, contrasting it to the past 25. What will the attitudes of the new generation be? Will there be the same acquisitiveness? Will attitudes toward the purchase of durables be different? As it is now, status comes via possessions—whether you have one car, two cars, three cars, whether you have a Buick or a Cadillac. There is also an emphasis on novelty, gimmicks, add-on features. Well, we're pretty certain that those attitudes are in for substantial change. Not that people won't still want refrigerators, cars, and so on. But, one, they will take them more for granted—they won't be the status symbols they are now. And, two, people will pay more attention to functionality, serviceability, durability, rather than flashiness and gimmickry.

MBA   What is the purpose of predicting 25 years in advance? How does that affect what the company does now?
Wilson   It seems to me that you need to take that long a look ahead, because, for example, if you do conclude that there are going to be substantial changes in consumer values and consumer expectations in 1985 or 1990, you need to start planning and adjusting to that between 1975 and 1980. I would suggest that if you looked, particularly in this area, to a relatively short-time horizon, even seven or eight years, you might come up with a very distorted picture, because almost inevitably this is going to be a very turbulent time of adjustments to all sorts of problems. There will be adjustment to the fact that there may be a reversal in the historical downward trend in food as a percentage of budget; a reversal in the downward trend of energy cost in the consumer budget; a continuing increase in the cost of housing. A lot of these adjustments are going to take place, I think, in this next ten-year period.

My point is that if you concentrate on just the next seven to eight years, you might make the mistake of making decisions about what sort of businesses we should get into or out of based on an analysis of the immediate turbulence—of the adjustments consumers are making, struggling to readjust lifestyles and budget allocations—and not on where this new equation will come out when we move into relatively calmer waters. If you've adjusted yourself to the period of turbulence rather than to the new equation that may be coming out, you may very well have made the wrong decisions.

MBA   Why do you think General Electric has taken a lead in this kind of long-range forecasting?
Wilson   I think we had a number of things going for us in the style and characteristics of the company. For one thing, the fact that we had been a high technology company, used to making long-term commitments in the technology area, predisposed us to taking a longer-term view. Point two, a number of our businesses—such as power generation—were inevitably forced into taking long-range perspective. The third factor is that we had, perhaps more than most companies, sensed since World War II the impact of political change on the way the corporation does business. These three characteristics in the corporate style perhaps predisposed us toward acceptance of this expansion of our planning horizons and expansion of planning parameters.

MBA   Have you seen specific examples of cases where your long-range forecasting efforts have made the company respond more quickly to some changes that other companies may not have foreseen?
Wilson   I would say that our early studies of the minority rights and women's rights movement enabled us to get a bit of a jump on things. Our original 1967 study stated, for instance, that the major domestic social trend of the next decade would focus on what we termed the Negro-Urban problem. Although you might question the validity of that statement now, it did have the effect of saying to our management that the problem of minority relations was not merely a present occurrence—and you didn't need a study to tell you that things were happening in Newark and Detroit, as they were that summer—but was going to be of continuing significance and did demand long-term, systematic corporate planning to deal with the impact on the business. That obviated any possibility of thinking that once the riots did calm down, the problem would disappear. Having got that far, the problem was going to demand a heavy degree of corporate participation in the development of solutions. One impact of that was to help to crystallize a decision at the corporate level that we needed a special staff component to deal with equal opportunity and minority relations. That decision was made in 1968.

After that, we did a study of the future of minority relations over the next decade, and this detailed look gave us some insight as to the needed level of corporate long-term response. Back in 1968 and '69 I think it would be fair to say that corporate response to the minority and race problem was largely couched in terms of "hire and train the hard-core unemployed." Our analysis suggested that a simple corporate response of this kind was inevitably going to be inadequate over the long-term.

As a postscript, whereas we completed that exercise about the end of 1969, we started picking up some of the early signals about the women's rights movement, which was then starting to surface. We saw that we would be foolish to ignore this. We found that having gone through the exercise of analysis and systems design and consciousness raising on the minority front, it was, despite the differences between the two problems, relatively easier to deal with the sex discrimination problem. And I would say that, while on the minority front we were perhaps playing a game of catch-up—in other words, our analysis was trying to bring us up to where the trends were already—on the women's front we were able to get a little bit ahead of the game, as measured by the fact that our own internal guidelines for affirmative action were published a year before the government's. Even though that's only beating the game by a year, that's the sort of anticipation that we need to aim for.

MBA   Has top management shown increased receptivity to your work during the eight years you've been operating?
Wilson   I think the answer is unquestionably yes. We do have, institutionalized in the corporation, a strategic planning system, which mandates the inclusion of this new sort of data. Of course, breaking out of old modes of thinking, old parameters of data collection, is very difficult. We all have difficulty in making personal changes to new modes of thinking. But this is only to say that it will take time to implement this system satisfactorily. Changed actions, changed policies, and changed strategies will only emerge slowly.

I do think that, in a sense, the best hope for social change lies in the predominance of the younger generation, the fantastic numbers in the 25-34 age group that are coming upon us. They have been brought up wholly in a climate of changing trends and attitudes; they are much more comfortable operating in this mode, and they understand this type of world much better than the older generation, whose main conditioning was, if not in the Depression and the war, at least in the postwar period. And the postwar period has finally ended. That 1947–1973 stretch had a lot of continuity to it in terms of population growth, economic growth, affluence, the declining cost of energy, relatively stable inflation. But every one of those dimensions is changing now. Obviously the next 25 years are going to be substantially different. I think that future analysis will show that this period of 1973–1975 really did mark a watershed economically, as, I think, 1965–70 or 1967–71 marked a watershed socially. The break point is not sharp. But by now, it seems to me all the major dynamics and attitudes that characterized that postwar period have finally changed. And now finally we're into something new.

II/C
Forecasting

---

8 Elements of forecasting
James W. Redfield

The businessman who said, "I'd like a copy of next Thursday's newspaper," when he was asked what he'd like most in the world to have, expressed a universal wish. Who wouldn't like to know what is coming, particularly in business? Who wouldn't like to know what is going to happen in his business during the next year, or in the next five years—with the assurance of at least reasonable accuracy?

In business, a great deal of time and energy are spent in trying to figure out what is likely to happen next. It is always the first step in budgeting, scheduling, and planning; and every businessman does it at least to some extent, either consciously or subconsciously, either systematically or otherwise. There simply has to be some basis for setting up future financial, production, and sales requirements and objectives. However, although estimating future business by one means or another is an essential and regular practice, the way it is done often leaves much to be desired from the standpoint of the reliability and dependability of the resulting forecasts. Many executives, consequently, have only loose estimates to use as the basis for business planning—estimates that often reflect the sales manager's optimism, on the one hand, or the controller's or production manager's conservatism, on the other. In either case these estimates are likely to be highly subjective and, as a result, biased by the distinctly human tendencies toward caution, self-protection, or the desire to please.

As a matter of fact, also, many businessmen, even in large companies where forecasting is an organized staff function, tend to distrust formalized forecasting. They are inclined either to discount or reject it as a "crystal-ball" activity or, once having given it a trial, mistakenly to expect a great deal more from it than it is intended to achieve. This is not only unfortunate, but it is also unnecessary. Business forecasting, done properly on a formalized basis, minimizes overenthusiastic as well as unduly conservative estimates, and the results can be rational, realistic, and believable.

The purpose, here, is to throw some light on systematic business forecasting in the hope that this highly useful activity will be better understood and more widely used. Rather than focusing on statistical procedures, which do play an important part in certain of its phases, the approach will be to discuss in simple but down-to-earth terms: (1) what a formal business forecasting program can contribute to management, (2) how it should be carried out, and (3) what its inherent limitations are.

Accepting business forecasting

Let it be noted immediately that the value of establishing a formal forecasting program is not limited to the assistance it provides in future planning. There are a number of important subsidiary advantages that should not be overlooked. Some of them are likely to have far-reaching effects on the operation of the business and can lead to a better control over and evaluation of the key functions of the company.

Such corollary benefits come automatically, as a consequence of setting up a logical basis for looking ahead. These preparations (particularly if the activities involved are not already established as regular procedures in the company), while producing information needed for the forecast, are likely also to bring to light the lack of control information on certain operations of the business or the need for improving some of the existing control reports. Not least important are the opportunities a formal forecasting program presents for encouraging teamwork among the key executives and for allocating accountability for actual results where these differ from earlier estimates.

Add these advantages to the more immediate gains in the form of sounder procurement and production schedules, firmer budgets and appropriations for sales, advertising, and so forth, and it becomes plain common sense to approach the question of business forecasting with an open mind.

Actually, the crystal-ball tag has become attached to forecasting primarily because the process has not been fully understood. In particular, one limitation of forecasting has not been brought out into the open, recognized, and accepted: no one can foretell the future *exactly*, and all forecasting must include some elements of *guesswork*.

Once that fact is recognized, one can go on to ask himself, "Since no business can operate successfully without planning ahead, is it not sensible to make sure we obtain the best possible and most logical estimates of what will occur?" Certainly the best possible guess is infinitely better and more reliable than any substitute—including the "rule of thumb" or "feel" methods that are still used by many otherwise astute businessmen.

Guesswork being inescapable, the idea is simply to reduce the limits of error to a minimum. This can be done by following a procedure for combining mathematical analysis with the best business judgment available and then using the resulting estimates as the basis for future planning.

The forecasting procedure

The forecasting process itself is approached on the premise that a general understanding of what is done and of how sound future estimates can be obtained is prerequisite to a full utilization of this activity as a practical business tool.

There are four essential elements in the process. Whether the forecast is to cover a short period (of several months to a year) or a longer period, the steps are as follows:

1 *Developing the groundwork* That is, carrying out an orderly investigation of products, company, and industry, in order to determine generally how each of these has progressed in the past, separately and in relation to each other. In short, the aim is to build a structure on which future estimates can be based.

2 *Estimating future business* That is, following a clear-cut plan for working out future expectancies in the form of a *mutual* undertaking with key executives and, after future business has been estimated in accordance with the predetermined step-by-step procedure, issuing an official statement of the resultant forecast. The key executives, by mutually developing the forecast, automatically assume coresponsibility and individual accountability for such later deviations of actual from estimated results as may occur.

3 *Comparing actual with estimated results* That is, checking the attained with the anticipated status of the business periodically, and tracking down reasons for any major differences. The forecast provides bench marks for measuring unanticipated gains or losses. Once measured, the reasons for important variations can be investigated on the spot.

4 *Refining the forecast process* That is, once familiarity with estimating the future of the business is gained through practice, sharpening the approach and refining the procedure. One must be reasonably tolerant with early forecasts, recognizing that proficiency with a new tool is not acquired overnight, and at the same time insist on constant improvement as experience with the process is gained.

Each of these elements of the process is described below in some detail—(a) to show the part it plays in the development of the forecast and (b) to point out the subsidiary benefits which management can reasonably expect as by-products of proper forecasting procedure.

But, first, a word of warning: the accuracy and dependability of any forecast depend to a great extent on the care and analytical astuteness with which the early steps of the process are carried out. The results of the early steps become the foundation for later steps. Therefore, careful planning and a thorough job are essential. For example, the initial step, analyzing historical data, often is a lengthy operation. However, enough time must be allowed for its proper accomplishment. The common tendency of management to "hurry things along," particularly in the preparatory states of a project involving statistical analyses, should be curbed. Putting the pressure on at this point can only lead to hastily done and poorly planned work that is likely to distort the picture later on.

Developing the groundwork

The logical starting point is to find out everything possible about the past activities of the business and of the industry. A familiar principle is involved: that you cannot figure out where you are *going* unless you know where you *have been*.

Some of the questions about the business and industry for which answers will be wanted are presented below. Answers to such questions on the past and present situation will tell you where you have been going and will establish the basis for judging the future. In addition, unless this sort of historical analysis has already been carried out in a company, some highly interesting and pertinent information is likely to come to light that will contribute to an even better understanding of the business. This could well become subsidiary benefit No. 1.

In this initial step of the forecast process, it is wise to try to find out:

1 Did the trend of company sales return to its pre-1929 level, or did a new era at a different level set in after 1932?
2 What was the trend of the *company's* sales (by products, product lines, total, etc.) *before* and *after* World War II—through a sufficiently long period prior to the war for the trend to be significant? Has this trend been generally the same postwar as it was prewar, or has a significant change occurred?
3 What has been the trend of sales in the *industry* through the same periods?
4 Has the industry trend remained the same or has it, also, changed significantly?
5 What has been the relationship between the company trend and the industry trend? Has the company been losing or gaining ground in the industry; that is, has the company's share of the total market been increasing or decreasing?
6 Is there evidence that the market for the company's particular type of product is or may soon become saturated and, therefore, that the replacement market is likely to be the principal source of business in the future?
7 From an internal standpoint, how do the trends of the several product lines compare, one with the other? Have some shown consistent gains while others have dropped off? Have some gained more rapidly than others and consequently carried more than their share of the load?

Analyzing company historical records

Now, how does one get the answers to these questions? First of all, the old company records are brought out and appropriate tabulations made showing the company's monthly and yearly sales, by products and totals, for an extended period before World War II and for the postwar years. As many prewar years as possible should be included, even going back beyond the early 1930's. Comparing the general direction of sales prior to and after 1930–1932 and before and after World War II may be revealing. In any event, the longer the period studied, the better.

It is important at this stage to plan ahead, having in mind that later comparisons based on the historical data about to be developed can be valid only if the data are set forth in comparable terms. For example, unit sales prewar and postwar are likely to be capable of direct comparison. Dollars of sales prewar, however, are less likely to be comparable because selling prices probably have been increased. In the latter case, it would be necessary to devalue the postwar dollar figures using the prewar prices as the base in order to achieve comparability.

The chances are that the best procedure will be to tabulate the monthly and yearly sales of individual products or product lines in units, and thus avoid the necessity of reducing the more recent figures to a comparable dollar base. It will be possible later to convert units to dollars for budget purposes. When it comes to over-all company sales, however, perhaps the dollar basis will be better. Part of the process is comparing company sales over the period being studied with industry sales and other figures (to be discussed) for the same period, and these are most likely to be stated in dollars. The principal idea is to look ahead, now, to the future uses for the tabulations and thus avoid the need for redoing them later on.

Tabulating sales over the selected past period by month and year for each product or line separately will be helpful. In this way each product can be studied individually. A "total" sheet for over-all company sales should also be included in order to develop a picture of the past trend of the company as a whole. (Large columnar sheets are useful for such tabulations.)

Of course, the initial going may not be so smooth as one would like. For example, the company sales records may be buried deep in the archives and have to be "dug out." Again, record-keeping methods may have changed over the years; sales may be listed only in total and not by type of product; or cancellations of orders, returned goods, and the like may not be properly accounted for. Regret that the company's record keeping has not been all it should have been and realization that more accurate records are needed will naturally result in making improvements in the record-keeping methods—and this could be subsidiary benefit No. 2.

Developing information on the industry

Historical data on the industry as a whole are usually fairly easy to obtain. Dollar (and/or sometimes unit) figures for an increasing number of industries are being published or are available from the proper sources, now that managements are beginning to recognize the importance of having current figures on the industries they work in. One good source is the standard government publications of the Census Bureau, the Federal Reserve Board, the Department of Labor, or other government agencies; also, industry associations may have previous studies or may currently publish data that will be helpful. A little searching will probably turn up figures that can be tabulated on the same basis as the company figures and therefore can be used to good advantage.

Here, again, the important thing is to achieve comparability. Industry sales data which are later to be compared with company sales must be stated in the same terms—units or dollars—and they must cover all or the greater part of the same period of years selected for study.

It may happen, however, that only broad breakdowns of the industry figures are available from published sources. Though these may be used, it soon becomes obvious that finer breakdowns would be even more helpful, not only to the particular company but also to others in the same general field. Management may decide, therefore, to arouse interest among members of the industry association in having it, or some other impartial body, currently assemble and circulate more detailed industry information on a controlled basis. Setting up the mechanics for this exchange of industry information, if there is no provision for it now, certainly would lead to subsidiary benefit No. 3.

Developing information on competitors

Once company and industry figures have been whipped into shape for the forecast, the job of accumulating historical information on the company's chief competitors must be tackled. Of course, competitive data are not easy to obtain. Competitors are notoriously cagey about publishing their sales figures in convenient form for others' analysis. In fact, marketing analysis or field research is often needed to fill in this gap. But by digging in the right places much helpful information can be obtained.

For example, the company may be able to size up competitors fairly well through its own salesmen's knowledge of what goes on in their territories. A review of the salesmen's reports, particularly reports of business lost if they are available, and similar records will be helpful. In addition, it may be desirable to talk to the salesmen in person or send them a carefully worked-out questionnaire designed to get as many facts as possible about competitive activities. Questions such as these will be appropriate: "Are our competitors making any greater inroads on our customers than in the past?" "How does our company stand alongside our chief competitors in the market now and as compared with past years?" "What are competitors' plans as reflected in their field activities?"

Information of this sort, obtained from all corners of the market and from the men right on the ground, and boiled down to its essentials, can be of considerable help in providing an understanding of competitive activities and of the company's status in the trade. To be most meaningful, however, such a search for information should be thought through and carefully planned. If this is done first, then all of the salesmen will understand thoroughly what they are expected to do, will answer the same questions on the competitive and company situation, and will comment on the same aspects of the market; and, of utmost importance, the questions asked will go directly to the core of the situations being explored and will cover the subject completely.

Such a tussle with past company figures sharpens the attention to other operational weaknesses that may exist. Perhaps in talking to the salesmen, reviewing sales reports, and so on, areas of information on characteristics of the market or on competitive aspects wherein some, or maybe all, of the salesmen are weak may come to notice. Perhaps it will become clear that the salesmen would sell better if they knew more about these things. If such is the case, the decision may be made to look into ways of educating them as soon as the forecast project has been completed—subsidiary benefit No. 4.

(All along, the exploratory work is likely to touch upon activities of the business which are related to, even though they may not be specifically a part of, the forecasting project—activities which perhaps could, and should, be strengthened. Once these are brought to light, corrective measures can be applied promptly and systematically, whereas these activities might otherwise have continued to limp along. Thus, there may be possibilities all the way through for additional subsidiary benefits.)

The executives should be questioned too. One or several probably have wide acquaintance with and special knowledge of competitors. This suggests making a systematic effort to find out what information these men can add about the company's competition, about competitors' progress over the years, and about their future intentions. Even though a great deal of what will be contributed may already be known, pertinent bits of added information are very likely to come to light. Perhaps Company A, for instance, has a new product in mind that could hurt the company's sales if it is marketed; or Company B may be thinking of changing its method of distribution; and so on. All of this additional information adds to the detailed background.

In addition, during this questioning the executives obviously will want to know the "why" of the interrogation. This provides the opportunity to get *them* interested in the forecast project. They are going to be brought into the proceedings later on anyway, and this is a good time to get started. Let them have a brief "rundown" on the forecast project and on the way in which any information they can supply is to be used. A little "selling" of the forecast project now will help just that much toward obtaining the cooperation of all of these interested executives during the steps to come later.

Developing trends and relationships

By this time a lot of information on what the company and industry have done over the past years will have been assembled. Now the job is to find out what the various figures mean. There is nothing mysterious or difficult about this, and nothing basically complicated. What is necessary is merely knowing how to figure percentages and the like and being alert to detect relationships and trends. Native curiosity and good business judgment are two very useful aids at this stage.

The objective is to show how the sales of each product and of the company as a whole have varied throughout the period, but in such a way as to avoid the picture's being confused by individual monthly or annual variations.

Trends

For this purpose, company and industry trends are developed from the historical figures already assembled. These trends are part of the basic forecast structure, now beginning to shape up, on which the forecast itself will later be based. So long as they truly represent a broad past period, they will be highly useful as the starting point for working out the future estimates.

Once sales for each product and for the company as a whole have been tabulated by months and years for a period extending from, say, around 1920 up through the current year, it is a simple matter to plot these figures on separate cross-ruled charts. Then curves are drawn on these charts to represent the general direction taken by the plotted points and thus show the trends of individual product and company sales over the selected period of years.

A trend curve is nothing more than a simple way to show the predominant, over-all characteristics of a series of figures. Its principal advantages lie in its ability to reconcile the wide variations in magnitude that usually occur in untreated historical figures and in its facility for showing the net effect of these variations.

These curves can be drawn by hand, or they can be developed mathematically. The latter method, of course, is preferred, but freehand curves, if drawn carefully, will serve the purpose. Whether drawn freehand or computed mathematically, the curves will not pass through all of the plotted points but will take a "middle course" leaving about as many plotted points above as below the curve, thus in essence "averaging out" the variation in magnitude of the plotted points. The purpose, remember, is to show the *general* direction of sales. Exhibit I provides a rough—and admittedly oversimplified—illustration.

At this point we must take notice of a rather common objection. It is often said that trend curves are coldly impartial and will reflect unusual as well as usual conditions with equal unconcern. How, then, can historical trend curves be used as a valid basis for future estimates? The solution is simply to make sure, in developing them, that they represent *only* the *usual* conditions: (1) The monthly or yearly historical figures are examined to discover unusual variations; (2) the cause of these variations is located; (3) the original figures are corrected as required; and then (4) the trends are developed from the *corrected* data. Almost invariably unusual past conditions are reflected unmistakably by wide variations in the historical figures, and it

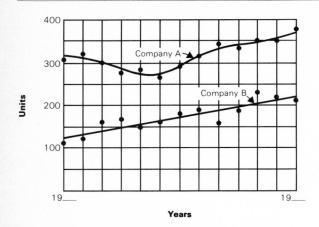

Exhibit I Trend curves for annual sales, in units, over a period of 13 years, of Company A (drawn freehand) and Company B (computed by the least square method)

is not difficult to identify and find explanations for these abnormalities in corollary company and other records or in the memories of company executives.

For example, suppose the sales curve for product "X" looks something like that in Exhibit II. Only the year 1936 is shown in order to illustrate the point. It is unmistakable that all was rational until July, when for no apparent reason the bottom dropped out. Such a variation would be patently atypical.

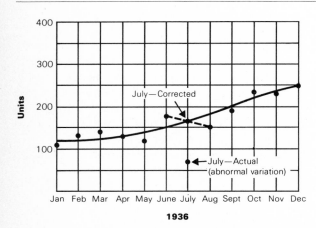

Exhibit II Trend curve of monthly sales, in units, 1936, showing abnormal variation for July and correction made on basis of previous and succeeding month

In the actual case from which this example was taken, it was found after considerable digging that someone way back there in 1936 had "charged off" a large number of backlogged orders that had been accumulating on the books and had reduced the record of July's sales accordingly. (Perhaps it should not have been done, but it was.) It is logical, therefore, to synthesize a July figure that conforms generally with the figures for the preceding and succeeding months. This correction is indicated by the dotted line. Other such unusual variations can be adjusted in the same way once the reasons have been ascertained.

Charts showing plotted sales and trends for each product or line, for the company, and for the industry should be set up, more or less as in Exhibit III. For this example two possible company situations have been hypothecated and their sales curves shown.

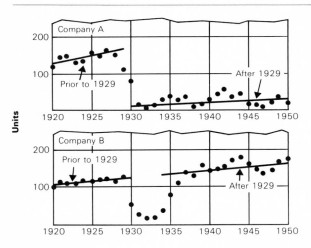

Exhibit III Trend curves of annual sales, in units, 1920 to 1950, showing radical change in Company A's level and recovery of Company B after 1929

Curve A is patterned after the sales curve of a large manufacturer in the midwest. Two points become apparent: (1) a decided drop in business occurred *prior* to the general business decline that followed 1929; and (2) the sales curve did not return to its previous level. In the actual case from which this example was taken it was found that the market for the products involved had become saturated along about 1927, and a decline in sales had already started by the time 1929 came along. Significantly, it was apparent that during the succeeding years a new "era" had set in. Since about 1932 replacement business had accounted for most of the company's sales. The entirely new and lower level of the sales curve did not necessarily reflect successful competitive inroads.

Curve B, on the other hand, reflects a less exciting situation. This sales curve shows that ground lost after 1929 has been regained and that the trend has been generally the same throughout the whole period.

Close examination of any company's charts will reveal similar or other equally interesting information about total company sales during the period before and after 1929 and the years before and after World War II.

Relationships

In addition to charting product, company, and industry sales and developing trend curves for these, it is desirable also to compute and tabulate percentages representing the relationship of each one to the other throughout the past period selected for study. In doing this, it is best to determine for each month and year: (1) the percent, or share, of the industry's sales accounted for by the company; and (2) the percent, or share, of total company sales accounted for by each of the products or lines. Then, the resulting percentage figures for each of these can be plotted on charts and trend curves developed for them.

These relationships and their trends tell their own very interesting stories. For example, examining this record of the share the company has obtained of the total market over the years will tell where the company has been heading *in relation to the industry*—that is, whether the business has increased at a greater rate than competition (which is always good to see) or whether it has been losing ground in the industry over the years. Although an increasing trend would reflect company progress compared with past years, one that has increased at a rate less than that of the industry would indicate that the competition has progressed even more rapidly. In other words, a company could have been gaining, on the one hand, and (without realizing it) losing, on the other. A little study along these lines can easily lead to subsidiary benefit No. 5.

It may appear desirable to examine the past sales of individual products or product lines the same way as total company and industry sales. Comparing the trends of the products' sales will show how successful each one has been *in relation to the others*. The fact may be uncovered that one or another of the products or lines, while showing some gains over the years, has actually lagged behind the others so far as its contribution to total company sales is concerned. To know such facts about the company's products or lines could be subsidiary benefit No. 6.

These percentage relationships and trends also will help later on in the forecast process in determining the share of industry sales that the company is likely to obtain, and the share of company sales that each product or line is likely to account for in the period ahead.

Short-term characteristics

The next step is to determine whether seasonal or other repetitive variations have been characteristic of the past sales of individual products, the company, or the industry. Preferably this is done mathematically, in order to obtain precise measures of whatever periodic swings in sales there may be.

However, the same results can be obtained roughly by visually comparing the charts. If up-surges or valleys occur every year during the same season or month, the percentage of the annual total that each month of the year characteristically accounts for can be figured out.

Such a measure of past seasonal, or similar, variations will help to make the forthcoming forecast realistic. Later on future annual sales will be estimated without regard to these periodic increases or decreases, and then the annual expectancy can be distributed over the months of the year in accordance with the characteristic monthly proportions.

A national index

Finally, it is necessary to have a series of figures representing activities up to the present in some broad segment of the national economy—a series whose trend over the past period being studied closely approximates the trend of the industry.

Nationally published indexes on production or on the financial aspects of the nation's industrial activity are commonly used for this purpose, and there are often several to choose from among the many now compiled by various governmental agencies. Here the personnel of the local Federal Reserve or Department of Commerce field office should be consulted; these people are universally helpful and cooperative and are qualified to suggest still other sources.

Reflecting, as they do, activities for large segments of the nation's total economy, such indexes are not likely to be affected materially by activities within most single businesses or industries. Moreover, they will tend to maintain a relatively even course over the years, except in the event of drastic economic changes. Because this sort of index is relatively stable, the trend of the selected national series, developed for the past years and up to the present and extended out through the future period of the forecast, is particularly useful as the backbone of the forecast structure being built.

Progress to this point

Most of the preliminary work has now been done. The past activities of the individual products, of the company, and of the industry have been "boiled down"; and a related national index has been found and adapted. As a result, these things can now be seen:

1 *Trends*   That is, where the individual products, the company, the industry, and a related large segment of the national economy are heading, as of today;
2 *Relationships*   That is, how the company's progress has compared with that of the industry, and how the individual products or lines have fared in relation to each other;

3 *Inherent characteristics* That is, whatever seasonal variations are characteristic of the company and the industry.

In addition, certain of the control aspects of the business have had a
close scrutiny. Possible improvements in these and in other control and reporting activities, particularly those that heretofore have been conducted too
loosely to be relied upon as the basis for future planning, have probably
been considered, if not actually initiated.

As far as the groundwork of the project is concerned, all that remains
now is to extend (on the chart) the trend curve of the selected national
index out through the future period to be forecast, and to extend the trend
curve of the industry out through the same period in such a way as to parallel the national index curve.

Estimating future business

Actually working out the forecast from this point on should be a mutual undertaking participated in by all of the company's key executives whose
knowledge and experience qualify them to contribute opinions on the future
of the company and the industry.

In the first place, each of the key executives has a definite stake in the
company's progress. Each one, therefore, not only should contribute to the
best of his ability toward planning for its future, but also should be placed in
a position of joint accountability for the accuracy of the estimates on which
these plans are to be based. In the second place, a group approach avoids
the mistake of placing the whole responsibility for the forecast on one head.
Too often the findings of that one executive about the future of the business
become the target of the remaining executives or provide them with a
ready-made defensive position when future sales do not stack up with what
was expected. Unless they are brought into it, these other executives, not
having contributed to the forecast, can (and will) deny with impunity any responsibility and accountability for deviations of actual from forecast results.

Developing the forecast plan

The next step, therefore, is to bring the best brains available in the company
to bear on the forecast problem. This requires planning and a spelled-out
approach. These men should do some concentrated thinking about the forecast, but they are also going to be busy with other problems. The easier it is
made for them to grasp and understand the forecast aims and procedures,
and their individual reponsibilities in connection with the project the better
chance there will be of getting their full cooperation.

Accordingly, the forecast program should be described briefly in writing, and the plan circulated among the key executives. This write-up should
have the overt approval of the chief executive and should explain the pur-

pose of the forecast project, stating what it is intended specifically to do. Above all, it should stress the cooperative part and responsibilities the key executives are to have in it. This description should also cover the mechanics of the process and should include charts and tables as required.

These points should be made and emphasized:

1 That the trend curves, the percentage relationships, and the charted historical characteristics of the business and industry, while revealing past activities, are also capable of indicating what is *likely* to happen in the future, *"all other things being equal"*;
2 That the best collective judgment and knowledge of the company's executives with respect to the business and industry is now to be called into action in order to form a *composite company opinion* on (a) whether all things *will* be "equal" in the future period as compared with the past period or (b) whether things will be different; and, if different, in what ways and to what extent.

The stage is set in this way so that the forecast will be the product of: (1) precise mathematical or at least reasonably accurate measures of known facts—measures that are both objective and impersonal; and (2) a consensus of considered executive judgment—judgment that is based on a variety of experience in the business and the industry. The stage is also set so that a group executive meeting (or meetings, if necessary) may be held for working out the forecast, and so that executives included can come in fully prepared for the discussions.

Working out the forecast

In the executive meeting the forecast should be worked out systematically. The chief executive of the company, or another executive of adequate standing, should direct this activity. Strong leadership will be desirable because differences of opinion will need ironing out; overoptimistic and overpessimistic opinions will have to be reconciled; and a clear, hardheaded, and realistic view of the company's future must be maintained throughout. The actual working out involves two steps:

1 Determining how much business there is likely to be for the *industry* as a whole during the forecast period by (a) observing the out-and-out mechanical extensions of the past trends of the industry and of the related national index through the forecast period, and (b) adjusting this rough industry forecast upwards or downwards until it conforms with the executive group's consensus of opinion of anticipated general business conditions and the future outlook for the industry.
2 Reaching a consensus of realistic opinions concerning the trends which the company's own total business and its several products or lines are likely to take during the forecast period, based on considerations of (a) the products'

and the company's past trends as shown on the charts; (b) the trends which, it is anticipated, the products, the company, and the industry will follow; and (c) the share of the industry's total business that the company has obtained in the past and is likely to obtain in the future.

These joint opinions, obviously, should take into consideration the company's own plans and what is known of competitors' plans for the future. Any unusual internal conditions of backlog, shortage of materials, and the like which threaten to affect the forecast should also be considered.

Applying the forecast

It is a simple matter to translate this consensus of executive opinion into formal chart form showing the anticipated trends of the industry, of the company, and of the individual company products or lines throughout the forecast period. At this point the company forecasts should be adjusted according to whatever predetermined seasonal or similar variations may have been characteristic of the business in the past.

It is now time to write up a brief, final statement of the official company forecast, including a full description of the assumptions on which the forecast was based. Here is an example of the way it might go:

In the official opinion of the company, the trend of general business, of the industry, and of the company is expected to continue to rise [or to decline, as the case may be]. The company's plans for expanding its distribution are to be implemented shortly and are expected to produce x% of additional business. On the other hand, new [or improved] competitive products, now about ready for the market, are expected to account for a loss of y% of the company's business during the forecast period. On the basis of these assumptions, such-and-such an amount of business is forecast for each product and for the company during the forecast period.

In such a forecast, developed mutually by all of the key executives of the company from a sound base of historical facts, no one executive opinion is likely to be predominant, and each participant has had free opportunity to contribute his opinions. It follows, then, that each of these executives can be expected to accept the forecast, without personal reservation, as the basis for planning his own segment of company operations. Consequently, the controller, sales manager, advertising manager, production chief, and any other of these executives can plan his respective operation with the assurance that management *as a whole* has taken into full account all major contingencies that can reasonably be anticipated.

Using an official forecast like this as the starting point for company planning is likely to produce another important subsidiary benefit. Inasmuch as the group method of developing the forecast discourages individual hedging with an eye to a later accounting and particularly because it provides a mutually developed starting point for planning, certain executives begin to operate more from an aggressive and less from a defensive position with respect to their own segments of the company's operations.

Comparing actual with estimated results

It would be a mistake to drop the forecast project at this point. To regard any business forecast as static and unchanging and, once having worked it out, to file it away and forget it, or, on the other hand, to accept it without a further look as the year proceeds, is the surest possible road to disappointment. Disappointments need not occur, however, if the forecast is looked on not only as the very best estimate possible at the time of its inception but also as a means of bringing to light, throughout the entire forecast period, any major variations from what has been forecast when and as such variations occur.

To avoid disappointment, and to use the forecast for all it is worth, arrangements must be made to compare actual with anticipated sales results periodically. It must be understood that minor variations from the forecast are bound to occur; so, as the months (or weeks or quarters) unfold, no one should worry about small interim swings. But major variations and also lesser deviations which begin consistently to repeat should be scrutinized closely.

These are the danger signals. As soon as a significant variation appears, and regardless of whether the actual performance is greater or less than was expected, it is important to try to determine what lies behind the difference.

Tracking down causes for variations

Suppose actual sales results are appreciably less than were forecast. The immediate reaction is: "Let's get to the bottom of this." The first move is to call in the sales manager and ask him why sales, apparently, have gone sour. Things begin to happen! Developing the forecast has accustomed executives to looking at sales results from the vantage point of specific measurements; so now they want facts.

Probably one of these two situations will be revealed:

1 If the sales control and analysis function is operating properly, it is probable that the sales manager has anticipated this action and has taken steps to find out why sales have slipped. In that case he will already have analyzed current reports and identified the sales territories, the products, or the product lines that are responsible. Perhaps he already has made a move to find out directly from the field what is happening.
2 On the other hand, perhaps what develops is that the sales control and analysis function needs strengthening; that current analysis of sales is not

being carried out effectively; and that, as a result, it is proving difficult to isolate the specific reasons for the decline promptly enough to take effective remedial action.

In cases such as the former, it is usually easy to provide a logical follow-through—that is, to establish the facts and take direct and speedy action on the adverse situation. In the latter case, the need for establishing adequate sales controls or for improving the present function becomes apparent, and the required steps for improvement can be taken. Subsidiary benefits of the forecast project like this may continue to crop up.

It might be, for example, that as various problems of this nature arise, more information is needed, say on markets or distribution methods than is regularly available in the company. A detailed study of these factors may be highly desirable. In that case, the market research department can be put to work on this specific project. Or, if no formal market research function is established in the company, expert assistance can be obtained from the outside either on a project basis or to aid in establishing a permanent market research activity within the company.

Adjusting the forecast

Perhaps the reasons found for a major deviation from the forecast may strongly indicate that a new situation has developed that could not reasonably have been foreseen. Competitive activity may have changed radically; or there may have been some other serious alteration of the basic assumptions of the initial forecast. In that case, either the company's competitive tactics must be altered so as to counteract the change; or, if that is not possible, the forecast must be adjusted to conformity with this new situation. Significant variations of actual from forecast results, like these, can happen at any time and must be taken care of "on the spot."

It would be foolhardy, however, to limit re-examination of the forecast to the times when these danger signals appear. If it is to reflect accurately company and industry-wide influences and activities—which are always changing and are never static—the forecast, perforce, must be periodically rechecked and, if necessary, adjusted. Company plans may change, not necessarily radically but enough to have an effect on future expectancies; the trend of the industry or the national economy may shift. Of particular importance is the fact that conditions affecting the forecast in the third or fourth quarter of a year can be foreseen and evaluated with much greater accuracy at the beginnings of these quarters than at the beginning of the year, the time the initial forecast ordinarily is completed.

It should be a regular and unchanging procedure in the company at the beginning of each quarter (1) to restudy the principal measurable factors affecting the forecast and to re-evaluate the extent of their change since the last recheck, and (2) to assemble the executive group as was done for the initial forecast and mutually re-affirm or adjust the forecast as it will apply to the period then ahead. This should be done in the light of whatever changes may have occurred in the measurable factors and on the basis of the then current opinions of the executives. If a change in the forecast seems indicated, it is also advisable to repeat the procedure used initially of issuing a new official forecast statement showing and explaining the changes.

Refining the forecast process

The foregoing description of the forecasting process undoubtedly is something of an oversimplification. The primary objective, however, has been to point up the basic principles, procedures, and benefits that are involved. Some difficult problems are bound to be encountered; and, particularly at first, mistakes may be made. But it should be realized that forecasting, like anything else, gets better and more accurate with practice. One can learn only by experience how to gauge with accuracy the sensitivity of products and industry to changing company, industry and economic conditions.

With learning will come more and more precise evaluations of the extent to which products, company, and industry are likely to react to various stimuli. Moreover, the method adopted initially for developing a forecast almost invariably is subject to some later refinements of application to the particular characteristics of the business, based on experience gained with the selected method in actual use.

For these reasons a certain latitude should be allowed the forecast when evaluating its effectiveness during its early years in the company—but not to the extent of being complacent. There is always opportunity to improve not only the mathematical but also the judgment aspects of the forecast method in use. In that way it will become more and more helpful, in fact more and more indispensable.

9 A think tank that helps companies plan: Project Aware uses Delphi forecasting to predict the 1980s
Business Week

Four big companies—Du Pont, Scott Paper, Lever Bros., and Monsanto—are getting a peek at the 1980s this month. The four are backers of Project Aware, a unique attempt to predict long-range changes in the social, economic, and technological environment that the companies will face in the next decade. The first results, released this week by a tiny but prestigious California think tank called the Institute for the Future, outline a world of utopian dreams and Orwellian nightmares:

The quality of life

It is likely to decline as measured by such trends as urban decay, the depersonalization of daily activities, and distrust of major institutions. And though America's economic standard of living will continue to climb, expectations of citizens will outrun the economy's ability to fulfill them.

What's likely to happen by 1985

Event	Percent probability
Many chemical pesticides phased out	95%
National health insurance enacted	90
Spending on environmental quality exceeds 6% of GNP	90
Insect hormones widely used as pesticides	80
Community review of factory locations	80
Substantial understanding of baldness and skin wrinkling	40
A modest (3%) value-added tax passed	40
Wide use of computers in elementary schools	25
Development of cold vaccines	20
Autos banned in central areas of at least seven cities	20
Breeder reactors banned for safety reasons	20

Data: Institute for the Future

The energy crisis

It will probably be resolved by market forces as rising prices change energy use and spur development of new energy sources. But ecological degradation may drive environmental spending up to 12% of national income after 1980.

Worker discontent

It will intensify, despite improvements in working conditions and efforts to mechanize routine work. Nevertheless, changes in manufacturing methods and job enrichment programs could increase worker productivity by as much as 50% in the next 10 years.

Business procedures

They probably will not change much in the next decade or so. After about 1985, however, the costs of computer entry, storage, and access will fall below the cost of paper files, and the use of paper in the average office will fall dramatically.

Just how useful these and other prophecies (table) will be is still uncertain. "If it does nothing more than highlight one key trend we need to be aware of, it will be worthwhile," says Monsanto's J. Kenneth Craver.

Project Aware, which costs each of its sponsors $40,000 per year for three years, is the latest and most ambitious product of the Institute for the Future. Founded five years ago by a small group of scientists from Rand Corp. and Stanford Research Institute, the nonprofit IFF has only 15 professionals and a $600,000 budget. But it has emerged as a leading practitioner of a forecasting technique known as Delphi, which was used in Project Aware. "We've probably done more Delphis than any other organization," says Roy Amara, the soft-spoken engineering Ph.D. who is president of IFF.

Techniques

Developed at Rand by Olaf Helmer and Norman Dalkey, Delphi relies on a panel of experts who answer elaborate questionnaires. Their answers are summarized, and the questioning is repeated until the oracles reach a consensus on future trends. The method gained wide attention in 1964, when Rand used it to forecast a variety of technological events, including a manned lunar landing by 1970. Helmer left Rand in 1968 and launched IFF to apply the Delphi technique to business and government.

Delphi, of course, is only one of many exotic forecasting methods that have evolved in the last decade. Other "futures research" often features the sort of scenarios made famous by Herman Kahn of the Hudson Institute or the complex mathematical models developed by MIT's Jay Forrester and Dennis Meadows as the basis for the chilling forecasts in *The Limits to Growth* (BW—Mar. 11, 1972). Actually, Amara points out, the methods overlap. "If Forrester and Meadows had used experts to determine their key coefficients," he says, "their model would have been richer. You could take their findings and spin scenarios from them. And there is a lot of math in the experts' contributions to a Delphi study."

Whatever the method, forecasting holds obvious promise for business, and IFF has had corporate support from its inception. IFF does about a third of its work for private industry, most of it in technological and industrial forecasting. "A Delphi study tells you what ballpark you're playing in," comments Frederick Meyers, manager of corporate process development for Owens-Corning Fiberglas Corp.

The institute has done two projects for Owens-Corning, one on the future of residential housing and another on plastics. "Acceptance of the studies was mixed," Meyers admits. "Some of our managers thought it might be witchcraft, and others thought the experts' opinions were no better than their own." But Owens-Corning was impressed enough to incorporate Delphi techniques into its corporate planning and now runs its own Delphi every year. Many other companies also use Delphi methods, and a number of consultants, including a profit making spinoff of IFF called The Futures Group, have sprung up.

Problems

But the Delphi technique has several shortcomings. "With mailed questionnaires," says Amara, "there can be enormous delays between rounds. The experts often forget what excited them the first time around." Then, too, the usual Delphi study makes little effort to rank the experts by either their knowledge or their ability to predict. "If the real expert is outnumbered," Amara acknowledges, "the Delphi may force a consensus that is not supported by the evidence."

Overcoming such problems is the task of a group of mathematicians, engineers, and social scientists who work in IFF's comfortable, modern offices in an industrial park near the Stanford campus. They are now concentrating on ways to computerize the Delphi study. With a grant from the National Science Foundation, IFF has programmed a computer network that allows experts across the country to tackle a Delphi problem simultaneously. "The computer lets us run a study quickly," Amara says, "and it produces more disciplined answers." Eventually, IFF hopes the computer will participate in the study by seeking responses and organizing data.

IFF is also breaking new ground in organizing conventional Delphi studies. Normally, most Delphis are limited to a handful of issues, but the 70 experts who participated in Aware took on 75 widely divergent subjects. "In effect," says Amara, "we did 75 mini-Delphis." IFF also took unusual pains to uncover the issues of most interest to the client companies. "We asked top executives to suppose they had five minutes with a clairvoyant," says Andrew J. Lipinski, the senior investigator for Project Aware. "When they stopped asking who would be President in 1985, we began getting a useful idea about their concerns."

The results of Project Aware's first year are summarized in a 150-page volume backed up by stacks of raw data. While the study abounds with intriguing forecasts, it mainly isolates trends and describes the influences that may shape them. "We weren't looking for a crystal ball," Lipinski says. "The future is a very foggy environment, with things looming out of the fog as we move through it. We are trying to draw a rough map so that somebody can put a spotlight on the important obstacles."

II/D
Planning: An application

10 Urban planning: Ripe for systems analysis
Jerry L. Pollak and Martin I. Taft

Although considerable work has been done on the analysis of transportation, communication, production, law enforcement, resource management, and educational systems, these are but subsystems of the typical urban system. The systems analyst is faced with a complex total system which poses some unique problems. Some of these major problems are:

1 There is no general understanding of what the significant problems are in urban planning.
2 Responsibility and authority are diffused among many planning organizations hindering good communications and cooperation.
3 Independent and reliable criteria for evaluating alternative solutions are hard to establish because of the conflicting interests of the various organizations.
4 Much demographic and other statistical data is in existence but it is often not available when needed.
5 The relationships between variable segments of urban systems are hard to define because of the long periods of time and extraordinarily large sums of money required for testing and verification.
6 Simulation models for urban systems tend to be so large and complex that few organizations have the resources for their development and maintenance. There is also a shortage of trained people who can effectively utilize such models and interpret the results to others.
7 There are as yet no generalized approaches to systematic planning which have found wide acceptance among all interested parties.

The following is an overview of the analytical tools and areas in which systems development work must be done.

Source: Reprinted by permission from *Journal of Systems Management,* 22, No. 1 (January 1971), pp. 12–17.

A general problem-solving model

The process of solving any type of problem may be shown by means of the spiral model (Figure 1). The solution of the problem lies somewhere on the axis of the spiral. The process of solving the problem involves proceeding along the spiral path toward a solution. The solution axis is also a "time" axis. As the spiral converges on the axis in an exponential manner, the ideal solution occurs at an infinite time in the future. Thus, the ideal solution can be reached, providing that the resources and time do not run out. In the real world, one works with limited amounts of money, time, and other resources. So the model indicates that there are "diminishing returns" in the refinement of the solution. Initially great progress is made toward the solution but with each succeeding loop the improvements become smaller and smaller. At some point, it becomes more prudent to allocate resources to a new problem rather than to try to refine the present solution another few percentage points.

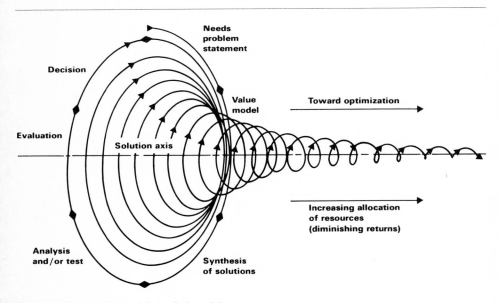

Figure 1 The problem-solving spiral model

The structure of the problem-solving process is often called the "morphology" of the process with every loop of the spiral being characterized by a number of distinct steps. These steps, or activities, are depicted in Figure 2 and are commonly called the "anatomy" of the problem-solving process. Although activities may be traversed in a sequential manner (as

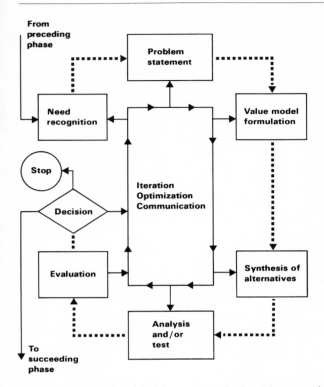

Figure 2 A general model of the anatomy (horizontal structure) of the problem-solving process

shown by the double-lined arrows), it is possible to proceed from any activity to any other activity at any instant in time. The single lines in the diagram indicate some of the alternative paths that may be taken between activities.

The systems design procedure

Figure 3 represents a highly aggregated schematic of the processes involved in the design or redesign of socio-economic systems. This design procedure is an out-growth of well-established methodologies in the engineering design of complex physical systems. If the system must be designed in its entirety, then the starting point may be as shown in Figure 3. However, in the modification or in the redesign of an existing system, it is possible to start at any other point in the loop.

In defining the objective functions of the urban system (Step 3) one could maximize the economic value of land in a given sub-section, in relation

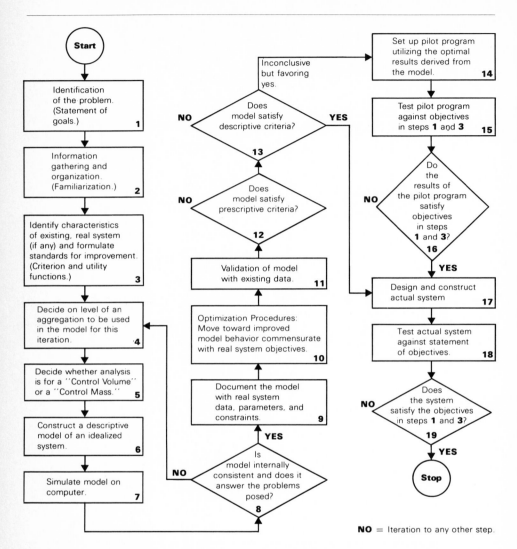

Figure 3 Generalized systems design procedure: a schematic representation of the iterative process

to the availability of manpower, financial capability of local industry, time and budget allocated for planning, and so forth. Or, for some other problem, given the planning of a low-income neighborhood, the analyst may attempt to minimize the average walking distance covered by the local residents in their everyday activities, such as shopping, schooling, and recreation.

The problem of defining the objective functions is a very difficult one, especially at the beginning of an analysis. This is often due to the lack of the pertinent information. However, tentative generalizations can be made and be refined as the analysis proceeds. The usual procedure is to find one single major objective and optimize its subject to a series of lesser constraints.

The descriptive model of the system usually consists of a series of generalized block and flow diagrams (Step 6). The block diagrams delineate the control volumes that will be used in the analysis. Each control volume usually represents a subsystem of the entire system; in this case the entire system may be a city and subsystems may be a residential neighborhood, industrial parks, shopping centers, civic monuments, municipal parks, and other kinds of operational entities within the city.

The control volumes represent highly aggregated levels of the system. The control volumes or subsystems measure and control the quantities of people, automobiles, raw materials, and so forth which enter or leave these subsystems, over finite periods of time. Flow diagrams are used to show all of the flows and their interrelationships.

Once the total picture in terms of control volumes is reached, the analyst has an initial concept of all the interrelationships, the questions as to whether the properties of the various flows can be measured in such a way to determine whether the system is achieving its objectives. At this point, chances are that measurement of the quantities which are necessary for the kind of analysis outlined will be unavailable. Therefore, the system switches to a Control Mass Analysis by observing the interactions of a single citizen or a group of citizens within the environment. Theoretically, the answers gained from Control Mass Analysis should be identical to those received from a Control Volumes Analysis. However, the difference in perspective gives a great deal more information and ability to measure things. Ability, for instance, to measure income levels, employment opportunities, average walking or riding distances, or accessibility of recreative facilities.

If the measurements enable the analyst to set up standards for achieving the objective functions, then he would proceed to the next step in the systems analysis. If not, he returns to the Control Volumes Analysis and deaggregates. The deaggregation process involves breaking down into more and more elemental components each of the subsystems that have already been delineated. Having reached a level of aggregation at which the variables in question cannot only be quantified but also measured, the analyst is now in the position to develop a mathematical or a computer-based model of the system.

Program planning and evaluation model

The solution of a given problem (Figure 4) begins with a recognition of a need which must be satisfied. There may be a need for new policies, new procedures, replacement of roads or sewers, improved information, or more money. The "need statement" recognizes the problem. The problem definition involves stating what the problem is, who will do it, when it must be completed, and the resources to be allocated to the solution of the problem.

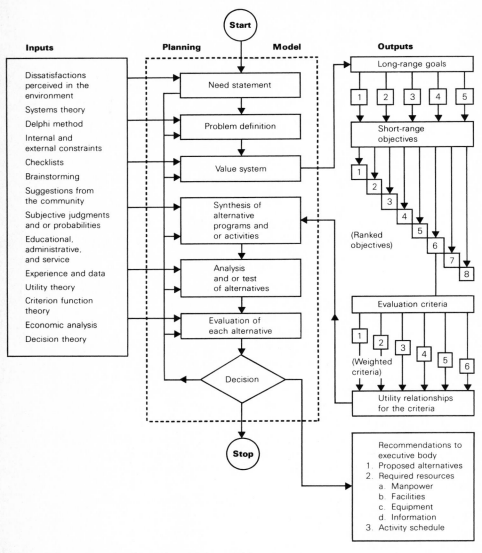

Figure 4 A program planning and evaluation model

The next step, namely the specification of a value system, is often left largely to the imagination.

The long-range goals represent the "directions"; the short-range objectives represent specific steps that must be taken in order to move in the directions of the goals. Usually it is possible to write the objectives in their relative order of importance with respect to achieving the goals. An objective is an activity, a task, or a project which must be completed within a given amount of time with a given set of resources such as manpower facilities, equipment, and information. Some objectives may be achieved sequentially through time while others may be achieved simultaneously or in parallel with each other. The objectives may be thought of as milestones against which progress toward the goals can be measured.

It is important to develop a set of evaluation criteria for each of the short-range objectives. Criteria, such as cost, effectiveness, reliability, attractiveness, and so forth, make it possible to evaluate the relative merits or value of each of the potential solutions to the problem. Since not all of the criteria are equally important in terms of the goals and objectives of the problem solver, they must be weighed relative to each other. For instance, the utility of a freeway may vary inversely as to its costs but directly as to its effectiveness. Furthermore, the relationships between utility and the criteria are usually nonlinear. It is essential to develop such utility relationships and to make them explicit.

Once the value system has been established it is then desirable to consider as many alternative solutions to the problem as possible. The usual tendency is to select one alternative solution and then proceed to carry it out after much work. If this solution proves to be inadequate, another one is attempted. Such a procedure is usually very inefficient. It is suggested that many different alternatives be considered and the ones that are most obviously the least compatible with the long-range goals, objectives, constraints, and available resources be rejected. Thus it is possible to reduce a large number of alternatives to a small number of realistic ones. Each of these potential solutions may then be analyzed or tested to determine its properties. The important properties are those represented by the evaluation criteria. A rating for each criterion may be obtained by computation, empirical testing, or by utilizing the subjective judgments of one or more individuals.

The evaluation phase of this problem-solving model involves converting each of the ratings into a corresponding utility number and summing[1] all of the utility numbers for a given alternative solution to obtain its total utility to the problem solver. The relative overall utilities of the various solutions may then be compared and the alternative having the highest utility may be selected. In some problems, resources are allocated in direct proportion to the utility of the given project, program or activity.

In Figure 4 it can be seen that the decision-making process offers three major alternatives. First, it is possible that more information is needed before continuing on to another phase of the problem or to another problem, resulting in an iteration to any of the preceding steps. On the other hand, the analyst may decide that all of the work done so far has led to unacceptable alternatives and that the project should be ended. Hence, "stop."

Finally, the analyst may consider that the problem under consideration has been satisfactorily solved, and would submit a set of recommendations to some higher authority or make the required decision. This above set of

[1] This procedure requires that the criteria selected be relatively independent of each other. To the extent that they are independent, the additivity concept holds; otherwise it must be considered as a good first approximation.

recommendations typically includes a set of conclusions regarding the alternative solutions that were considered, a detailed projection of the resources required to implement the recommended solution, and a tentative schedule of forthcoming activities.

Conclusion

It has been shown that some of the existing problem-solving models of systems analysis can be readily applied in the field of urban planning. What is urgently needed is an intensive continuous dialogue between systems analysts, operations researchers, computer technologists, political scientists, sociologists, economists, architects, educators, and urban planners. Such a dialogue is already occurring on large-scale urban projects, but day-to-day interaction between professionals in diverse fields is yet to come.

Part III

Organizing

The reason why people organize is always the same: to ensure that individual efforts are directed towards a common purpose and that they support each other.
Lyndall F. Urwick

Although planning is the forerunner to effective management, the formal organizational structure provides the framework within which the management process occurs. As noted earlier, this book is concerned with management as it is practiced within the context of the formal organization; organizing is the administrative function that provides this context. Broadly speaking, organizing is concerned with the formal structure of the organization (non-formal aspects of the organization are discussed in Part V). Organization identifies the official distribution of authority in the organization and, concomitantly, establishes formal roles for the organizational members.

Historically, thoughts on organizing were focused on formulas for proper structural arrangements. The past several years have produced new insights: the old formulas have been found inadequate because of their inability to deal with or explain the complexities of large organizations. The Hawthorne researchers and their successors, for example, found that their observations of worker behavior were not explained by traditional principles.[1] More recently, managers in research and development firms have discovered that the conventional ways of organizing have been simply inadequate in the electronic age. Still more recently, a number of researchers have suggested that none of it matters: the dominant technology of the organization may be the determining factor in proper organizing.

Part III begins with two basic concepts underlying the organizing function: span of management and authority. Next, Glaser and Logan present discussions of centralization and line-staff relationships. The subsequent two

[1] F. J. Roethlisberger and William J. Dickson, *Management and the Worker* (Cambridge, Mass: Harvard University Press, 1956).

articles, by Hall and Leidecker and by Filley, concern two different aspects of a critical managerial task, coordination.

The next set of articles deals with the operational character of organizing: organizational design. These items range from a defense and criticism of traditional organizing principles to two descriptions of organizational design in the public sector. The section concludes with a statement depicting the incredibly complex—not to say mind-boggling—task of organizational restructuring.

III/A
The span of management

11 Making theory operational: The span of management
Harold Koontz

One of the most striking phenomena of the latter half of the twentieth century is the belated search for a science of management. Not that the importance of effective group operation had theretofore gone unnoticed. One finds references to the problem in the Old Testament of the Bible, in the early Egyptian papyri extending back to 1300 B.C., in Confucius's parables, and in the writing of the early Greek philosophers. But the real awakening to the possibility that there might be an underlying science of managing is largely ascribable to the pioneering writings of the French industrialist Henri Fayol and the American engineer Frederick Taylor shortly after the turn of the twentieth century. Since World War II these slow beginnings have developed into a crescendo of thought, speculation, theory, research, trials and errors, and new techniques.

Despite the current interest in effective and efficient managing, management may be thought of as a science groping for useful knowledge. Managing is an art—but so is medicine, engineering, and baseball. Every art is made better if underlying it is a science—organized knowledge. Likewise, science has more practical meaning, if it has been structured around principles—significant predictive explanations of fundamental relationships.

What has been lacking in many areas of management theory is the means of translating available understanding into the most useful tools for the practitioner. While distilled management knowledge, summarized in concepts and principles, has already been found valuable as a guideline for practicing managers, it would be more useful if it could be translated into quantitatively or qualitatively verifiable tools.

To some extent this has been done. One of the major contributions of the mathematicians and systems theorists has been to bring the approaches

Source: Reprinted by permission from *The Journal of Management Studies* (October 1966), pp. 229–243.

of the physical sciences into the field of management. This has sharpened the understanding and techniques of management planning and control through the application of such techniques as operations research and critical path networks (PERT). Also, a major breakthrough in making managing subject to verifiable measures has taken place with the recently developed "results" approach to management appraisal. There are other, but still relatively few, techniques by which principles have been applied in a scientific way.

In the area of organizing—establishing an intentional structure of roles so that people can work effectively and efficiently together in groups—one has seen rather little development beyond the principles distilled from experience by such practitioners as Fayol, Alvin Brown, or Urwick. To be sure, the behavioralists have made progress in finding out some of the "people" problems in formally organized enterprise, but their researches still have not shed much light on what to do to establish a structural environment for performance.

One of the organizational areas which has been recognized as a difficult one at least since the time Moses organized to bring the children of Israel to the Promised Land[1] is that of the span of management.[2] The question of how many persons a manager should have reporting to him has long plagued managers. Yet, little progress has been made in answering this apparently simple question. However, as indicated by one company's approach to this question, referred to below, there is indication that progress can be made. This and other approaches may be crude and suffer from inexactness. They must, therefore, be used with care and judgment. But if they offer means for the manager to reach better answers than through intuition and trial-and-error, the gains are such that they are unquestionably justified.

The span of management: A practical problem needing clarification

In looking over the literature, research, and programs of management, one cannot help but be impressed with the lack of real light cast on the question of span of management. This is particularly so when one notes the long concern over proper delegation of authority, over the need for having a work environment where people can perform, and over the impact of organization structure on the individual.[3] It is also surprising when only simple arithmetic

[1] In Exodus 18: 17–26 his father-in-law advised Moses to delegate and establish "rulers of thousands, and rulers of hundreds, rulers of fifties, and rulers of ten" so that these leaders could share the burdens of administration.

[2] In much of the literature of management, this is referred to as the "span of control." The writer and his co-author, Cyril O'Donnell have preferred since 1955 to use the term of "span of management" as being more descriptive. See *Principles of Management* (New York: McGraw-Hill, 1955), p. 83. Other later writers have "coined" this phrase. See G. G. Fisch, "Stretching the Span of Management," *Harvard Business Review,* Vol. 41, No. 5 (September–October, 1953), pp. 74–85.

[3] See, among many others, the excellent work of Chris Argyris, reported most recently in his *Integrating the Individual and the Organization* (New York: John Wiley and Sons, Inc., 1964).

will show that the difference between an average managerial span of, say four, and one of eight in a company of 4,000 non-managerial employees can make a difference of two entire levels of management and of nearly 800 managers!

Narrow spans cost money for salaries, fringes, space and other support. Perhaps even greater than the money cost is the cost of longer lines of communications, not only from the top down but from the bottom up. And these communications are significant in terms of plans made and transmitted, delegations made clear and effective, performance being known and evaluated, and control information being available and interpreted. In other words, organizational communication is far more complex than simply the ability to speak and be understood. Organization structure constitutes a decision-making communications network. Its task is to show the way, with respect to information that must be processed in the making of decisions, to whom one must communicate on what.

On the other hand, too wide a span of management may likewise be dangerous. The overburdened manager unable to arrive at and communicate decisions, with inadequate time and energy to select and appraise and teach his subordinates, and with too little time to plan and see that plans succeed may be the source of as much cost and frustration as the manager with too narrow a span.

The "classical" position on span of management

Early theorists, generally placed in a school referred to as "classical," had only their experience or that of companies and managers they had observed to draw upon. Perhaps the most widely quoted authority on the span of management has been the eminent management consultant and scholar Lyndall F. Urwick. Reflecting on his experience and opportunities for astute observation, Urwick concluded that "no superior can supervise directly the work of more than five, or, at the most, six subordinates *whose work interlocks*."[4] Placing heavy emphasis on the element of interlocking, Urwick readily admitted that the span may be much wider where the work of subordinates is not closely interrelated and managerial coordination is not required, or where a manager is well supported by staff, or where the requirements of leadership and morale do not require close and frequent face-to-face communication between the manager and his subordinates.

Other early writers on management advocate various spans. As summarized by one scholar,[5] these "classical" writers appeared to advocate a span of control of from three to seven or eight persons at the higher levels of organization and a span of up to twenty or thirty persons at the lowest echelon.

It is interesting that the so-called "classical" point of view is borne out

[4] "The Manager's Span of Control," *Harvard Business Review,* Vol. 34, No. 3 (May–June, 1956), p. 41.
[5] Healey, J. H., *Executive Coordination and Control* (Columbus, Ohio: Ohio State University, 1956). See discussion on this point, pp. 11–15.

in practice more often than is usually suspected. After extensive research on this point Healey found in a study of 620 industrial plants in Ohio that in 93.7 per cent of main plants and 84.2 per cent of the branch plants, the top executive had less than nine immediate subordinates and almost as high a percentage (76.3 per cent for main-plant executives and 70.3 per cent of branch plant managers) had from three through eight.

Substantially similar results were found by Dale in his study of 141 companies in 1951.[6] While he observed variations from one to twenty-four subordinates of chief executives in the companies, Dale found a median between eight and nine for the large companies and six to seven in the medium-sized companies. Comparable results were found by White in 1963 in a study of sixty-six companies.[7] In a much more narrowly based study, using a random sample, Fisch, on the other hand, discovered a tendency among very large [companies] (over $1 billion of sales) for a span of management at the top of more than twelve, with the span tending to be smaller as company size decreases.[8]

In a very real sense, none of these studies is truly indicative of the span of management actually practiced. For one thing, they only measure the span at the top of an enterprise. This is hardly typical of what the span may be throughout the enterprise, particularly since every organizer has experienced the tremendous pressure for a large number of functions of a business to report to the top executive. It is probable that the span below the top executive is much narrower. Indeed analysis of more than 200 companies of all sizes made by the author discloses a much narrower span in the middle levels of management than at the top.

In addition, the fact that apparently well managed companies have, as between them, and certainly within them, widely varying spans indicates that merely counting what is actually done is not enough to establish what a span *ought* to be. And this is true even if it could be assumed that, through trial and error, each company had reached an optimum span. It may only prove that underlying conditions vary.

The "revisionist" or "operational" school position on span of management

More recent management theorists have taken the position that there are too many variables in a management situation to conclude that there is any particular number of subordinates which a manager can effectively super-

---

[6] Dale, E., *Planning and Developing the Company Organization* Res. Rep. No. 20 (New York: American Management Association, 1952), pp. 57–59.

[7] White, K. K., *Understanding the Company Organization Chart* (New York: American Management Association, 1963), pp. 60–61.

[8] Fisch, G. G., "Stretching the Span of Management," *Harvard Business Review,* Vol. 41, No. 5 (September–October, 1962), pp. 80–81.

vise.[9] It is concluded that there is a limit to the number of subordinates a manager may effectively supervise but the exact number will depend upon underlying factors, all of which affect the time requirements of managing.

In other words, the predominant current view is to look for the causes of limited span in individual situations, rather than to assume there is a given numerical limit generally applicable to all. If one can look at what it is that consumes the time of a manager in his handling of his superior-subordinate relationships and also ascertain what devices can be used to reduce these time pressures, the analyst has an approach helpful in determining the optimum span in individual cases. He also has a powerful tool to find out what can be done to extend the span without destroying effective supervision. There can be no argument that the costs of levels and supervision are such as to make it highly desirable for every individual manager to have as many subordinates as he can *effectively* supervise.

Identifying the underlying factors

As a general proposition, the more subordinates an individual manager has, the greater the complexity of superior-subordinate relationships. That these can become astronomical is indicated by Graicunas' formula which discloses eighteen different human relationship situations existing when a manager has three subordinates, rising to 2,376 with nine subordinates, and 24,708 with twelve.[10]

What is more significant than the complexity and number of individual human relationship situations is their frequency and severity. In other words, how often do they occur and take the time of the superior, and, when they occur, how much of his time do they take? Certainly, time, itself, is the most limiting factor of all in the managerial task.

Looking at these underlying factors, the principal ones appear to be the following:

1 *Training required or possessed by subordinates*   The more a job requires training, the more training a subordinate must possess; the better trained a subordinate is, in relation to his job requirements, the less of a manager's time must be spent in teaching, in clarifying duties and desired results, and in correcting mistakes.

---

[9] See, for example, Koontz, H. and O'Donnell, C., *Principles of Management,* 3rd ed. (New York: McGraw-Hill, 1964), p. 229; also see Stieglitz, H., *Corporate Organization Structures,* Studies in Personnel Policy No. 183 (New York: National Industrial Conference Board, 1961), p. 8.

[10] Although his formula is little more than an arithmetic truism, V. A. Graicunas found that the complexity of superior-subordinate relationships is given by the formula $n(2^n/2 + n - 1)$ where n equals the number of subordinates. See his "Relationship in Organization" in L. Gulick and L. Urwick (eds.) *Papers on the Science of Administration* (New York: Institute of Public Administration, 1937), pp. 181–87.

2 *Clarity of authority delegations* The greater the clarity of authority delegations (note: *clarity,* not detail), the less time of the manager needs to be taken in explaining a task, making decisions that the subordinate should make, and explaining to others what the subordinate's responsibilities are.

3 *Clarity of plans* If plans (and particularly that part of plans encompassed in goals and policies) are clear (again, not necessarily detailed), the subordinate can proceed with his task, knowing where he is going and what is expected of him without continual checking with his superior; nor need the superior continually look over his subordinate's shoulder.

4 *Dynamics of a plan* Understandably, if a company or a given plan is subject to a high rate of change, it is more difficult to keep plans up-to-date and clear and to maintain meaningful delegations; in this case, much more of a manager's time will be taken in supervision than where things move more slowly.

5 *Extent to which adequate controls are available* Since a manager delegates none of his responsibility when he assigns a task to a subordinate and delegates authority to do it, he must necessarily make sure that task is being done and the authority is being used properly. This means control. The more effective his control devices, the less time he will be forced to spend to make sure that plans succeed.

6 *The quality of communications techniques* An executive's task involves heavy time demands in communicating plans and instructions, teaching and interpreting delegations, and receiving information with respect to problems and progress against plans. Clearly, the more effective communications techniques are in making sure that information is transmitted accurately and quickly, the less time must be spent on communications, and, other things being equal, the wider a span of management he can handle.

7 *Amount of personal contact needed* All managerial positions require a certain amount of face-to-face relationships. Many situations can be handled by written reports, others by special communications techniques not involving personal contact, but many require the manager spending time with people. Moreover, even where a matter might be handled without personal contact, situations of delicacy, cases where a "feel" of attitudes is necessary, and instances where simply the presence of a superior lends weight to a problem solution or a responsibility are among the many that make face-to-face relationships wise and necessary. Almost invariably these are time consuming.

While other factors might be noted, it has seemed that these are the principal ones which bear on the frequency and time severity of human relationship situations. It becomes readily apparent that, if a manager can solve the time demands involved in these, and still do an effective job of supervision, he should be able to handle a larger number of subordinates than otherwise.

Furthermore, the more a manager can have effective staff or line assistance to take over these time burdens, the more subordinates he should be able to manage. Note that the emphasis is upon "effective" assistance.

There have been too many instances where an overburdened manager has tried to lower his load by use of staff or line assistants, only to find he then spends more of his time with them or in undoing the problems and frictions they cause.

The problem of balance

It can readily be seen that the span of management problem, like most in life, raises a difficult question of balance. In general, the narrower the span, the more complete the supervision can be, although there are many cases of very narrow spans where the superior, having too little to do, tends to over-supervise his subordinates. On the other hand, the narrower the span, the more the cost in terms of supervision and communications difficulties.

The exact optimum balance in any given situation depends upon underlying factors such as those outlined above. One thing is certain. The subordinate who cannot reach his superior when he must, or the superior who does not have time to guide his subordinate and remove obstacles to performance are just as much a source of cost and loss of morale and effectiveness as the problem of too much supervision and too many levels.

Need for objective standards

In the case of the span of management, as in virtually every area of managing, there is an urgent need for objective standards. Even though one may identify accurately the underlying factors that determine the span, it is hardly possible to arrive at an optimum span until these factors can be given some degree of verifiable meaning.

This is necessary for determining the right span. It is also necessary if a superior is to find out whether a given technique, such as staff assistance, authority delegation, or special reports, is really helping or hindering him in the solution of the span of management. It may be too early to expect truly objective and verifiable measures of such factors as those involved in the span of management. It may be that such measures as can be used are crude. But it is reasonable to suspect that, if more effort were spent in finding methods of objectively verifying, progress might be made in management effectiveness comparable to the switch to verifiable planned results as the primary means of appraising managerial performance.

Quantifying the underlying factors: The Lockheed program

One of the pioneering programs undertaken by an American company to give sharper meaning to the factors underlying the span of management was that introduced several years ago by the Lockheed Missiles and Space Company.[11] Although carried on as an experimental program and not presented here as a case of a completely proved approach to management problems, the originality and intelligence used by the company are admirable and could well show a way toward better seeing and solving span of management and other managerial problems.

Lockheed's diagnosis of its span problem

As many companies have discovered when they examine their organization structure, Lockheed found that the spans of management at the middle management level appeared to be too narrow. The span of the upper and top general manager and director level ranged from five to ten; the average spans of the first line supervisors ranged from fifteen to eighteen; but the spans of the middle management[12] averaged only 3.2, and ranged from 2.9 to 3.4.

As one might suspect, the analysis also disclosed that there were apparently too many levels of supervision. Surveys made in portions of the organization indicated that, in this company of some 4,000 persons, there were two levels of supervisors, four levels of managers, and a director, or seven levels in all. If direct line assistants were included as levels, these, in some cases, increased the total to eleven.

In examining the problem further, and feeling that a middle manager is better off if he does not have idle time to worry about his subordinates, the company observed that the narrow spans and excessive levels at the middle management level were apparently causing the following problems:

1 *Decrease in initiative and morale*   There was a tendency not to delegate real authority, particularly at the first and second lines of supervision. This caused problems of accomplishing tasks and thwarted a feeling of accomplishment by many of these supervisors.
2 *High costs*   Narrow spans and added levels were increasing costs through multiplying supervisors, secretaries, space and service requirements.
3 *Delay in decisions*   A major problem encountered was delay in decisions in a company whose fast growth and highly dynamic product line required quick action. The added levels caused managers to review actions of levels

---

[11] For this section of the paper, the author is indebted to D. L. Harris who undertook extensive research of this program. Mr. Harris, in turn, received valuable assistance from Richard C. Anderson, Manager of Organization Analysis of the Company, who made available much of the data used in this paper. Likewise, the author is grateful to Herschel Brown, Executive Vice-President of the Company for permission to use Company records. The Lockheed program has been briefly reported in Harold Stieglitz, "Optimizing Span of Control," *Management Record,* Vol. 24, No. 9 (September, 1962), pp. 25–29 and in C. W. Barkdull, "Span of Control—A Method of Evaluation," *Michigan Business Review,* Vol. 15, No. 3 (May, 1963), pp. 25–32.
[12] Defined as all managers, except for department directors and general managers, having supervisory personnel reporting to them.

below, causing delays, and in many cases implementing action was made more difficult because instructions had to be transmitted through many levels.
4 *Decrease in opportunities for self-development*   The narrow spans at the middle management level limited managers to fewer activities and deprived them of the broadening knowledge of supervising related activities.
5 *Over-management*   It was also found that managers were spending excessive time in reviewing and directing their subordinates in greater detail than necessary.

It became apparent that, if only the middle management group of the company where the span seemed obviously narrow were changed, significant reduction in levels could be attained. Starting with an average span of three at the middle management level, and with no other changes in first level or top level spans, it was calculated that an average span of four would reduce needed levels from six to five and total middle management employees in a major area of the company from 302 to 268. With a further widening of the span to six, the number of levels could be reduced to four and only 241 middle management employees would be required.

Critical variables underlying the span of management

If the span of management problem was to be approached intelligently, it was recognized that the underlying critical variables which determined the span would have to be examined. The analysts studied the inherent functions of each job and the actual activities needing direction in order to ascertain the complexity of managerial relationships. This analysis yielded seven factors which appeared to be closely related to an effective span of management or indicative in selecting an optimum span.
Although the underlying factors disclosed by the Company's study are somewhat different from those outlined above as being generally applicable, it is interesting how fundamentally similar they are. Those that were determined to be most indicative were the following:

1 *Similarity of functions*   This factor refers to the degree to which functions performed by the various components or personnel reporting to a manager are alike or different. Its importance evolves from the fact that, as functions decrease in degree of variability, fewer factors and interrelationships must be kept in mind by the supervisor and the greater the number of persons he can effectively supervise.
2 *Geographic contiguity*   This factor refers to physical locations of units and personnel. The greater the geographic separation, the greater the difficulty in administration because of problems of communications.
3 *Complexity of functions*   This factor refers to the nature of the tasks done and involves a determination of the degree of difficulty in performing satisfactorily. Although admittedly a very difficult factor to measure objectively,

Lockheed found that there was a high degree of coordination between what was generally believed to be complexity and the salary of a job.

4 *Direction and Control* In identifying this factor, the analysts had in mind the nature of personnel reporting directly to a superior, the amount of training required, the extent to which authority can be delegated, and the personal attention needed.

5 *Coordination* This related to time requirements for keeping an organizational unit keyed in with other divisional or company-wide activities.

6 *Planning* This factor refers to the importance, complexity, and time requirements necessary to review goals, programs, and budgets, with particular emphasis on whether these planning functions are actually being performed by the manager or by others and whether the planning must be done on a continuing basis or merely once a year when budgets are approved.

7 *Organizational assistance* This has to do with the extent and nature of assistance received from direct line assistants, assistants to, staff, or other personnel having planning, administrative, and control responsibilities.

The impact of the above factors on the span of management is easily perceived. The more similar the functions, the closer the geographic contiguity, and the more organizational assistance a manager has, the more people it might be expected that he could effectively supervise. The more complex functions are, the greater the need for direction, control and coordination, and the more difficult the planning, the fewer persons a manager might be expected to supervise. It will be noted, also, that the factors used by Lockheed, in general, deal with the same underlying variables as those outlined earlier in this paper.

Determining degrees of supervisory burden within span factors

Excluding the factor of the influence of organizational assistance, other span factors were spread over a spectrum of five degrees of difficulty, from the easiest situation (from the standpoint of span) to the most difficult. These were then assembled in a matrix as shown in Table I. As will be noted presently, the element of organizational assistance was conceived of as a multiplier which reduced the span values derived from the other factors.

Determining a value for these other span factors was, as might be expected, a difficult task. After analysis of 150 cases at the middle management and director levels, to determine the span used and the underlying factors, preliminary weighting[s] of the various factors were developed. These, in turn were checked against a number of comparative cases, with reference as a standard to those units regarded as well-managed. The weightings for each degree of difficulty of the six primary variables so derived are shown in Table I.

Table I Degrees of supervisory burden within span factors. Numbers show relative weighting

Span factor					
Similarity of functions	Identical	Essentially alike	Similar	Inherently different	Funda- mentally distinct
	1	2	3	4	5
Geographic contiguity	All together	All in one building	Separate building, 1 plant location	Separate locations, 1 geographic area	Dispersed geographic areas
	1	2	3	4	5
Complexity of functions	Simple repetitive	Routine	Same complexity	Complex, varied	Highly complex, varied
	2	4	6	8	10
Direction and control	Minimum supervision and training	Limited supervision	Moderate periodic supervision	Frequent continuing supervision	Constant close super- vision
	3	6	9	12	15
Coordina- tion	Minimum relation with others	Relation- ships limited to defined courses	Moderate relation- ships easily controlled	Considerable close relationship	Extensive mutual non- recurring relation- ships
	2	4	6	8	10
Planning	Minimum scope and complexity	Limited scope and complexity	Moderate scope and complexity	Considerable effort required; guided only by broad policies	Extensive effort required; areas and policies not charted
	2	4	6	8	10

To illustrate the way these burdens were analysed, a few examples may be noted:

Complexity of functions   (1) Simple repetitive duties which require little training (less than six months) and which follow simple well-defined rules, and procedures. Examples would include typing, stock handling, mailing, simple assembly (generally in hourly grades 13–17 and professional grades 1–3). (2) Extremely complex duties which involve a wide variety of tasks and which require long training and experience (8–10 years). Abstract or creative thinking and/or necessity for consideration of many factors in arriving at courses of action would be typical. Examples: research scientist, engineer- ing development (salary, grades 18–20, professional grades 7–10).

Direction and control Constant close daily supervision, instruction, and control. The closeness of the supervision could be the result of the type of work which requires constant attention from supervision, such as very important and costly experiments, or it could be a result of the type of employees whose knowledge and skills are such that continual careful instruction and direction are required . . . typically, where regular rules, guides, or procedures for subordinates' conduct would be difficult or impossible to prepare.

The supervisory index

After weighting the six primary span factors, the analysts undertook the development of a supervisory index. Admitting to a bias toward widening the span of management, the analysts used as a standard the cases of wider spans, which were generally considered to be effectively organized and managed, from a sample of 150 middle management positions. Against the standards and from the numbers derived by weighting the six underlying factors, the following supervisory indices were developed:

Table II Suggested supervisory index

Total span factor weightings	Suggested standard span
40–42	4–5
37–39	4–6
34–36	4–7
31–33	5–8
28–30	6–9
25–27	7–10
22–24	8–11

These indices, it was pointed out, were intended for middle managers only. However, upon the basis of their study the analysts concluded that the above data could be used for first line supervisors, by approximately doubling the span indicated above.

Correction for organizational assistance

In arriving at a correction for organizational assistance, the analysts differentiated between types of assistants, as shown in Table III. The multiplier factor value was determined again by reference to the 150 sample cases, with special emphasis, as standards, on those units with wider spans which were regarded as well organized and managed. In addition, these multipliers were checked through discussion with managers concerned. As can be seen, the more complete the organizational assistance, the lower the multiplier factor and the more a manager's initial supervisory index (not taking account the assistance) would be reduced downward.

Table III Adjustment to span index for organizational assistance

Type of organizational assistance provided	Multiplier factor
Direct line and staff activities	0.60
Direct line assistant (only)	0.70
Staff activities (administrative, planning *and* control functions)	0.75
Staff activities (administrative, planning *or* control functions)	0.85
Assistant to (limited duties)	0.95
For first line supervisors	
Number of leadmen	
1	0.85
2	0.70
3	0.55
4	0.40
5	0.25

Note: The numbers reduce total point values derived from Table I thus increasing the potential span of management.

Results under the plan

Although there were other variables that intervened after the program was instituted in 1962, such as a company austerity program in 1963, and even though the program was not applied throughout the company, there are clear indications that it did cause a widening of the span of management. It also led to a general reduction of one level of supervision.

In terms of costs and size of span, the following company-wide data indicate a significant change of span, particularly when it is realized that the program was not completely adopted and not too strongly pressed throughout the company:

	October 1961	January 1965
Total company personnel	25,846	23,236
Total managers[1]	672	575
Managerial ratio[2]	37.5	39.5
Total supervisory personnel	1,916	1,314
Supervisory ratio[3]	12.4	16.7
Supervisory cost per employee[4]	$19.77	$14.98
Average span of management	3.4	4.2

[1] All managerial personnel above the supervisory levels (supervisor is the title used at the lowest organizational level).
[2] Number of non-managerial personnel per manager.
[3] Number of non-supervisory personnel per supervisor.
[4] Ratio of weekly supervisory payroll to the total number of non-supervisory personnel.

In addition to those apparent above, it should be remembered that the dollar cost savings are actually greater than shown. During the period involved, there were, of course, considerable pay rate increases. Moreover, the above results do not portray betterment in morale, reduction in over-supervision, and improvement in delegation believed by many observers to have occurred.

Can quantification be meaningful?

Although the Lockheed case is used as a practical instance where a well-managed company used ingenuity in an attempt to wrestle quantitatively with one aspect of management, the question may be asked, is it meaningful? Does this kind of approach show a practical way to approach certain management problems which cannot be reduced to the elegance of a complex mathematical model and the niceties of objective data and 'answers'?

The dangers of pseudo-science

There is, of course, a risk in approaches like this of giving the sanctity of numbers to phenomena that cannot accurately be quantified. In giving numerical weights to underlying variables and developing indices on the basis of standards of what is regarded as "good," there is indeed grave danger of falling into the trap of making a thing seem important and right merely because it is in numerical form.

On the other hand, if one were to rule out all such exercises in life, he would have to abandon cost accounting—even accounting itself (for what is *real* depreciation?), job evaluation programs based on point systems, and even most university grades. The question is not so much whether the numbers are real and accurate and free from question. It is rather several things. In the first place, are the values assigned reasonable and therefore useful for comparison? Does the breakdown of a problem into its component parts and the assignment of a system of numerical values and indices help in the understanding and analysing of a problem? Do the people who use the data so derived realize the elements of inaccuracy and subjectivity underlying them and realize that they should be used as aids and guides and not as ironclad conclusive rules?

If the answers to these questions can be in the positive, as they can be in many areas of management, then such data should be used, at least until better information is available. And the dangers of pseudo-science tend to be more than offset by the advantages of greater visibility.

The test of results

If even crude methods give visibility and through doing so yield results, they can hardly be overlooked. In the Lockheed case, there is evidence that the system used did yield measurable results and that organization effectiveness was improved thereby.

Moreover, if problems such as those of the span of management are to wait until completely verifiable input data are available, those who must solve the realities of managing an enterprise would be deprived of much progress that can be made. Furthermore, if analysts and scholars of management are encouraged to search for data to give meaning to management problems, it is highly probable that more accurate and useful data can be developed. The approach of looking for answers to the span of management problem through analysis of the underlying contributing variables is certainly a step in the right direction. The additional attempt to give some quantitative meaning to these variables, even though crude by the objective standards of the more exact sciences, is a further significant step.

More experiments and studies should be made along these lines, not only with respect to the span of management, but in many other of the relatively unexplored areas of management. With the interest in managing which has risen in the past two decades and the examination of the management process by perceptive practitioners and those scholars who understand and deal with the realities of the managing art, we now have a reasonably operational understanding of the underlying variables in many aspects of managing. If there can be greater realization that, through effort and research, some progress can be made toward needed quantification of these variables, the usefulness of present management understanding can be greatly enhanced.

III/B
Authority

12 The three types of legitimate rule
Max Weber
Translated by Hans Gerth

Authority means the probability that a specific command will be obeyed. Such obedience may feed on diverse motives. It may be determined by sheer interest situation, hence by the compliant actor's calculation of expediency; by mere custom, that is, the actor's inarticulate habituation to routine behavior; or by mere affect, that is, purely personal devotion of the governed. A structure of power, however, if it were to rest on such foundations alone, would be relatively unstable.

As a rule both rulers and rules uphold the internalized power structure as "legitimate" by right, and usually the shattering of this belief in legitimacy has far-reaching ramifications.

There are but three clearcut grounds on which to base the belief in legitimate authority. Given pure types, each is connected with a fundamentally different sociological structure of executive staff and means of administration.

Source: Reprinted by permission from *Berkeley Journal of Sociology,* Vol. 4 (1953), pp. 1–11. Copyright 1953 by Hans H. Gerth. *BJS* editor's note: Weber's "Three Types of Legitimate Rule" appeared posthumously in the *Preussische Jahrbuecher* in 1922 (vol. 187, pp. 1–12). This exposition was not included in the first editions of *Wirtschaft und Gesellschaft (The Theory of Social and Economic Organization).* In 1949, however, Johannes Winckelmann proposed a reorganization of *Wirtschaft und Gesellschaft,* largely on the basis of Weber's original plan. (Johannes Winckelmann, "Max Weber's Opus Posthumum," *Zeitschrift fuer die gesamte Staatswissenschaft,* 1949, vol. 105, pp. 368–387.) He showed that the "Three Types of Legitimate Rule" is part of Weber's original manuscript and is necessary for the adequate understanding of his analysis of authority which appeared as the third part of *Wirtschaft und Gesellschaft* under the title "Types of Authority." The meaning of this part and its connection with the whole of the work was obscured by the omission of the separately published manuscript. In the 1956 edition of *Wirtschaft und Gesellschaft* (Tuebingen: J. C. B. Mohr, 1956), which was substantially revised by Wickelmann, "The Three Types of Legitimate Rule" appears as Section 2 of the "Sociology of Authority" (vol. 2, pp. 551–558); it precedes the sections on "Bureaucratic Authority," "Patriarchal and Patrimonial Authority," "Feudalism, Estates and Patrimonialism" and "Charismatic Authority and Its Transformation." These sections turn out to be elaborations of the section which is here published for the first time in English.

I.

Legal authority rests on enactment; its pure type is best represented by bureaucracy. The basic idea is that laws can be enacted and changed at pleasure by formally correct procedure. The governing body is either elected or appointed and constitutes as a whole and in all its sections rational organizations.

A heteronomous and heterocephalous sub-unit we shall call "public authorities" (Behörde). The administrative staff consists of officials appointed by the ruler; the law abiding people are members of the body politic ("Fellow citizens").

Obedience is not owed to anybody personally but to enacted rules and regulations which specify to whom and to what rule people owe obedience. The person in authority, too, obeys a rule when giving an order, namely "the law," or "rules and regulations" which represent abstract norms. The person in command typically is the "superior" within a functionally defined "competency" or "jurisdiction," and his right to govern is legitimized by enactment. Specialization sets limits with regard to functional purpose and required skill of the office incumbent.

The typical official is a trained specialist whose terms of employment are contractual and provide a fixed salary scaled by rank of office, not by amount of work, and the right to a pension according to fixed rules of advancement. His administration represents vocational work by virtue of impersonal duties of office; ideally the administrator proceeds *sine ira et studio,* not allowing personal motive or temper to influence conduct, free of arbitrariness and unpredictability, especially he proceeds "without regard to person," following rational rules with strict formality. And where rules fail he adheres to "functional" considerations of expediency. Dutiful obedience is channeled through a hierarchy of offices which subordinates lower to higher offices and provides a regular procedure for lodging complaints. Technically, operation rests on organizational discipline.

1 Naturally this type of "legal" rule comprises not only the modern structure of state and city government but likewise the power relations in private capitalist enterprise, in public corporations and voluntary associations of all sorts, provided that an extensive and hierarchically organized staff of functionaries exists. Modern political bodies merely represent the type preeminently. Authority of private capitalist organization is partially heteronomous, its order is partly prescribed by the state and it is completely heterocephalous as regards the machinery of coercion. Normally the courts and police take care of these functions. Private enterprise, however, is autonomous in its increasingly bureaucratic organization of management. The fact that, formally speaking, people enter into the power relationship *(Herrschaftsverband)* voluntarily and are likewise "free" to give notice does not affect the nature of private enterprise as a power structure since conditions of the labor market normally subject the employees to the code of the organization. Its sociological affinity to modern state authority will be clarified further in

the discussion of the economic bases of power and authority. The "contract" as constitutive for the relations of authority in capitalist enterprise makes this a preeminent type of "legal authority."

2 Technically, bureaucracy represents the purest type of legal authority. No structure of authority, however, is exclusively bureaucratic, to wit, is managed by contractually hired and appointed officials alone. That is quite impossible. The top positions of the body politic may be held by "monarchs" (hereditary charismatic rulers), or by popularly elected "presidents" (hence plebiscitarian charismatic rulers), or by parliamentary elected presidents. In the latter case the actual rulers are members of parliament or rather the leaders of the prevailing parliamentary parties. These leaders in turn may stand close to the type of charismatic leadership or to that of notabilities. More of this below.

Likewise the administrative staff is almost never exclusively bureaucratic, but usually notables and agents of interest groups participate in administration in manifold ways. This holds most of all for the so-called self government.

It is decisive that regular administrative work is predominantly and increasingly performed by bureaucratic forces. The historical development of the modern state is identical indeed with that of modern officialdom and bureaucratic organization (cf. below), just as the development of modern capitalism is identical with the increasing bureaucratization of economic enterprise. The part played by bureaucracy becomes bigger in all structures of power.

3 Bureaucracy does not represent the only type of legal authority. Other types comprise rotating office holders or office holders chosen by lot or popularly elected officers. Parliamentary and committee administration and all sorts of collegiate and administrative bodies are included under the type, if and when their competency rests on enacted rules, and if the use they make of their prerogative follows the type of legal administration. During the rise of the modern state collegiate bodies have made essential contributions to the development of legal authority, especially the concept of "public authorities" (Behörde) originated with them. On the other hand elected officialdom has played an important role in the prehistory of the modern civil service and still does so today in the democracies.

II.

Traditional authority rests on the belief in the sacredness of the social order and its prerogatives as existing of yore. Patriarchal authority represents its pure type. The body politic is based on communal relationships, the man in command is the "lord" ruling over obedient "subjects." People obey the lord personally since his dignity is hallowed by tradition; obedience rests on piety. Commands are substantively bound by tradition and the lord's inconsiderate violation of tradition would endanger the legitimacy of his personal rule, which rests merely upon the sacredness of tradition. The creation of new law opposite traditional norms is deemed impossible in principle. Actually this is done by way of "recognizing" a sentence as "valid of yore" (the *Weistum* of ancient Germanic law). Outside the norms of tradition, however, the lord's way in a given case is restricted only by sentiments of equity, hence by quite elastic bonds. Consequently the rule of the lord divides into a strictly tradition-bound sphere and one of free favor and arbitrariness where he rules at pleasure as sympathy or antipathy move him, following purely personal considerations subject especially to the influence of "good turns."

So far as principles are followed in administration and settlement of disputes, they rest on substantive considerations of ethical equity, justice, or utilitarian expediency, not on formal considerations characteristic of the rule of law. The lord's administrative staff proceeds in the same way. It consists of personally dependent men (members of the household or domestic officials), of relatives, of personal friends (favorites), or associates bound by personal allegiance (vassals, tributory princes). The bureaucratic concept of "competency" as a functionally delimited jurisdictional sphere is absent. The scope of the "legitimate" prerogatives of the individual servant is defined from case to case at the pleasure of the lord on whom the individual servant is completely dependent as regards his employment in more important or high ranking roles. Actually this depends largely on what the servant may dare do opposite the more or less docile subjects. Personal loyalty of the faithful servant, not functional duty of office and office discipline, control the interrelationship of the administrative staff.

One may, however, observe two characteristically different forms of positional relationships, the patriarchal structure and that of estates.

1 In the purely patriarchal structure of administration the servants are completely and personally dependent on the lord; they are either purely patrimonially recruited as slaves, bondsmen-serfs, eunuchs, or extra patrimonially as favorites and plebeians from among strata lacking all rights. Their administration is entirely heteronomous and heterocephalous; the administrators have no personal right to their office, there is neither merit selection nor status honor; the material means of administration are managed under, and on account of, the lord. Given the complete dependency of the administrative staff on the lord, there is no guarantee against the lord's arbitrariness which in this set-up can therefore have its greatest possible sway. Sultanistic rule represents the pure type. All genuine "despotism" was of this nature. Prerogatives are considered like ordinary property rights of the lord.
2 In the estate system the servants are not personal servants of the lord but independent men whose social position makes them presumably socially prominent. The lord, actually or according to the legitimacy fiction, bestows office on them by privilege or concession; or they have contractually, by purchase, tenancy or lease, acquired a title to their office which cannot be arbitrarily taken away from them; hence within limits, their administration is autocephalous and autonomous. Not the lord but they dispose over the material means of administration. This represents estate rule.

The competition of the officeholders for larger bailiwicks (and income) then determines the mutual delimitation of their actual bailiwicks and takes the place of "competency." Privilege often breaks through the hierarchic structure (*de non evocando, non apellando*). The category of "discipline" is absent. Tradition, privilege, feudal or patrimonial bonds of allegiance, status honor and "good will" regulate the web of interrelations. The power prerogatives of the lord hence are divided between the lord and the privileged administrative staff, and this division of powers among the estates brings about a high degree of stereotypy in the nature of administration.

Patriarchal rule (of the family father, sib chief, father of his people *(Landesvater)*) represents but the purest type of traditionalist rule. Any "authorities" who claim legitimacy successfully by virtue of mere habituation represent the most typical contrast, on the one hand, to the position of a contractually employed worker in business enterprise; on the other, to the way a faithful member of a religious community emotionally relates to a prophet. Actually the domestic group *(Hausverband)* is the nucleus of traditionalist power structures. The typical "officials" of the patrimonial and feudal state are domestic officers with originally purely domestic tasks (dapifer, chamberlain, marshall, cupbearer, seneschal, major domo).

The co-existence of the strictly tradition-bound and the free sphere of conduct is a common feature of all traditionalistic forms of authority. Within the free sphere, action of the lord or of his administrative staff must be bought or earned by personal relations. (This is one of the origins of the institution of fees.) It is decisive that formal law is absent and that substantive principles of administration and arbitration take its place. This likewise is a common feature of all traditionalist power structures and has far-reaching ramifications, especially for economic life.

The patriarch like the patrimonial ruler governs and decides according to the principles of "cadi justice": on the one hand decisions are strictly bound by tradition; however, where these fetters give leeway, decisions follow juristically informal and irrational considerations of equity and justice from case to case, also taking individual differences into account. All codifications and laws of patrimonial rulers embody the spirit of the so-called "welfare state." A combination of social ethical with social utilitarian principles prevails, breaking through all rigor of formal law.

The sociological distinction between the patriarchal power structure and that of the estates in traditionalist rule is fundamental for all states of the pre-bureaucratic epoch. (The contrast will become fully clear only in connection with its economic aspect, that is, with the separation of the administrative staff from the material means of administration or with their appropriation by the staff.) This has been historically decisive for the question whether and what status groups existed as champions of ideas and culture values.

Patrimonial dependents (slaves, bondsmen) as administrators are to be found throughout the mideastern Orient and in Egypt down to the time of the Mamelukes; they represent the most extreme and what would seem to be the most consistent type of the purely patriachal rule devoid of estates.

Plebeian freemen as administrators stand relatively close to rational official-dom. The administration by literati can vary greatly in accordance with their nature: typical is the contrast between Brahmins and Mandarins, and both in turn stand opposite Buddhist and Christian clerics—yet their administration always approximates the estate type of power structure.

The rule of estates is most clearly represented by aristocracy, in purest form by feudalism which puts in the place of the functional and rational duty of office the personal allegiance and the appeal to status honor of the enfeoffed.

In comparison to patriarchalism all estate rule, based upon more or less stable appropriation of administrative power, stands closer to legal authority as the guarantees surrounding the prerogatives of the priviledged assume the form of special "rights" (a result of the "division of power" among the estates). This rationale is absent in patriarchal structures, with their administration completely dependent on the lord's arbitrary sway. On the other hand the strict discipline and the lack of rights of the administrative staff within patriarchalism is more closely related to the discipline of legal authority than is the administration of estates, which is fragmented and stereotyped through the appropriation of the means of administration by the staff. Plebeians (used as jurists) in Europe's princely service have been pacemakers of the modern state.

III.

Charismatic authority rests on the affectual and personal devotion of the follower to the lord and his gifts of grace (charisma). They comprise especially magical abilities, revelations of heroism, power of the mind and of speech. The eternally new, the nonroutine, the unheard of and the emotional rapture from it are sources of personal devotion. The purest types are the rule of the prophet, the warrior hero, the great demagogue. The body politic consists in the communal relationship of a religious group or following. The person in command is typically the "leader"; he is obeyed by the "disciple." Obedience is given exclusively to the leader as a person, for the sake of his nonroutine qualities, not because of enacted position or traditional dignity. Therefore obedience is forthcoming only so long as people ascribe these qualities to him; that is, so long as his charisma is proven by evidence. His rule falls if he is "forsaken" by his god[1] or deprived of his heroic strength or

---

[1] Translator's note: This allusion to Jesus' death and its interpretation as a downfall of his charismatic authority come out more strongly in Weber's "Sociology of Charismatic Authority" (Charismatismus), *Wirtschaft und Gesellschaft,* in *From Max Weber: Essays in Sociology,* H. H. Gerth and C. Wright Mills, trs. (New York: Oxford University Press, 1946, p. 248). There Weber states: "by its very nature, the existence of charismatic authority is specifically unstable. The holder may forego his charisma; he may feel 'forsaken by his God,' as Jesus did on the cross; he may prove to his followers that 'virtue is gone out of him.' It is then that his mission is extinguished, and hope waits and searches for a new holder of charisma."

In his later work, *Ancient Judaism,* Hans H. Gerth and Don Martindale, trs.

if the masses lose faith in this leadership capacity. The administrative staff is selected according to charisma and personal devotion; hence selection does not consider special qualification (as in the case of the civil servant) nor rank and station (as in the case of administration by estates) nor domestic or other forms of personal dependency (as, in contrast to the above, holds for the patriarchal administrative staff). The rational concept of "competency" is lacking as is the status idea of "privilege." Decisive for the legitimation of the commissioned follower or disciple is alone the mission of the lord and his followers' personal charismatic qualification. The administration—so far as this word is adequate—lacks all orientation to rules and regulations whether enacted or traditional. Spontaneous revelation or creation, deed and example, decision from case to case, that is—at least measured against enacted orders—irrational decisions are characteristic of charismatic authority. It is not bound to tradition: "It is written but I say unto you" holds for the prophet. For the warrior hero the legitimate orders vanish opposite new creations by power of the sword; for the demagogue, by virtue of his annunciation or suggestion of revolutionary "natural law." The genuine form of charismatic justice and arbitration the lord or "sage" speaks the law and the (military or religious) following give it recognition which is obligatory, unless somebody raises a counter claim to charismatic validity. This case presents a struggle of leaders which in the last analysis can solely be decided by the confidence of the community; only one side can be right, the other side must be wrong and be obliged to make amends.

A The type of charismatic authority has first been developed brilliantly by R. Sohm in his *Kirchenrecht* for the early Christian community without his recognizing that it represents a type of authority. The term has since been used repeatedly without recognition of its bearing.

Early history shows alongside a few beginnings of "enacted" authority, which are by no means entirely absent, the division of all power relationships under tradition and charisma. Beside the "economic chief" (sachem) of the Indians, an essentially traditional figure, stands the charismatic warrior prince (corresponding to the Germanic "duke") with his following. Hunting and war campaigns, both demanding a leader of extraordinary personal endowments, are the secular, magic is the "sacred" place of charismatic leadership. Throughout the ages charismatic authority exercised by prophets and warrior princes has held sway over men. The charismatic politican—the "demagogue"—is the product of the occidental city state. In the city state of

---

(Glencoe, Ill.: The Free Press, 1952), p. 376, Weber reversed his position. He points out that "the words of the cross, 'My God, My God, why hast thou forsaken me' form the beginning of the twenty-second Psalm which from beginning to end elaborate Deutero-Isaiah's thesis of meekness and the prophecy of the Servant of God. If actually not first the Christian community but Jesus himself should have applied this verse to himself, this would certainly allow us to infer not intense despair and disappointment—a strangely frequent interpretation of the word—but on the contrary, messianic self-reliance in the sense of Deutero-Isaiah and the hopes expressed at the end of the Psalm."

Jerusalem he emerged only in religious costume as a prophet. The constitution of Athens, however, was completely cut out for his existence after the
innovations of Pericles and Ephialtes, since without the demagogue the
state machine would not function at all.

Charismatic authority rests on the "faith" in the prophet, on the "recognition" which the charismatic warrior hero, the hero of the street or the demagogue find personally, and this authority falls with him. Yet charismatic
authority does not derive from this recognition by the subjects. Rather the
reverse obtains: the charismatically legitimized leader considers faith in the
acknowledgement of his charisma obligatory and punishes their violation.
Charismatic authority is even one of the great revolutionary forces in history,
but in pure form it is thoroughly authoritarian and lordly in nature.

It should be understood that the term "charisma" is used here in a completely value-neutral sense. For the sociologist the manic seizure and rage
of the nordic berserk, the miracles and revelations of any pettifogging
prophecy, the demagogic talents of Cleon are just as much "charisma" as
the qualities of a Napoleon, Jesus, Pericles. Decisive for us is only whether
they were considered charismatics and whether they were effective, that is,
gained recognition. Here, "proof" is the basic prerequisite. The charismatic
lord has to prove his being sent "by the grace of God" by performing miracles and being successful in securing the good life for his following or subjects. Only as long as he can do so will he be recognized. If success fails
him, his authority falters. Wherever this charismatic concept of rule by the
grace of God has existed, it has had decisive ramifications. The Chinese
monarch's position was threatened as soon as drought, floods, military failure or other misfortune made it appear questionable whether he stood in
the grace of Heaven. Public self-impeachment and penance, in cases of
stubborn misfortune, removal and possible sacrifice threatened him. Certification by miracles was demanded of every prophet (the Zwickau people
demanded it still from Luther).

So far as the belief in legitimacy matters for the stability of basically
legal structures of authority, this stability rests mostly on mixed foundations.
Traditional habituation of "prestige" (charisma) fuses with the belief in formal legality which in the last analysis is also a matter of habit. The belief in
the legitimacy of authority is shattered alike through extraordinary misfor-
tunes whether this exacts unusual demands from the subjects in the light of
tradition, or destroys the prestige or violates the usual formal legal correctness. But with all structures of authority the obedience of the governed as a
stable condition depends above all on the availability of an administrative
staff and especially its continuous operation to maintain order and (directly or
indirectly) enforce submission to the rule. The term "organization" means to
guarantee the pattern of conduct which realizes the structure of authority.
The solidarity of its (ideal and material) interests with those of the lord is decisive for the all important loyalty of the staff to the lord. For the relation of
the lord to the executive staff it generally holds that the lord is the stronger
opposite the resisting individual because of the isolation of the individual
staff member and his solidarity with the lord. The lord is weak opposite the

staff members as a whole when they band themselves together, as has happened occasionally in the past and present. Deliberate agreement of the staff is requisite in order to frustrate the lord's action and rule through obstruction or deliberate counter action. Likewise the opposition requires an administrative staff of its own.

D Charismatic rule represents a specifically extraordinary and purely personal relationship. In the case of continued existence, however, at least when the personal representative of charisma is eliminated, the authority structure has the tendency to routinize. This is the case when the charisma is not extinguished at once but continues to exist in some form and the authority of the lord, hence, is transferred to successors. This routinization of charisma proceeds through:

1 Traditionalization of the orders. The authority of precedents takes the place of the charismatic leader's or his staff's charismatic creativity in law and administration. These precedents either protect the successors or are attributed to them.

2 The charismatic staff of disciples or followers changes into a legal or estate-like staff by taking over internal prerogatives or those appropriated by privilege (fiefs, prebends).

3 The meaning of charisma itself may undergo a change. Decisive in this is the way in which the problem of successorship is solved, which is a burning question for ideological and indeed often material reasons. This question can be solved in various ways: the merely passive tarrying for a new charismatically certified or qualified master usually gives way to an active search for a successor, especially if none readily appears and if any strong interests are vested in the continuity of the authority structure.

a) In this endeavor people may search for characteristic traits of the charismatic qualification. A rather pure type is represented by the search for a new Dalai Lama. The strictly personal, extraordinary character of the charisma thus is transformed into a regularly determinable quality.

b) People may use the lot, oracles, or other indicative techniques. Thus, the belief in the qualified charismatic shifts to a belief in the respective techniques.

c) People may designate the qualified charismatic leader:

(ca) The charismatic leader himself may do so. In this case we have successorship by designation, which occurs frequently among prophets and warlords. Therewith the belief in the personal legitimacy of charisma changes into the belief in the legitimate acquisition of power prerogatives by lawful and divine designation.

(cb) The charismatically qualified disciples or following may designate the successor and have the religious or military community accede to it by granting recognition. The conception of this procedure as a right to "elect" or "nominate" the successor is secondary. The modern concepts of election and nomination must be kept out of this. The original idea was not that of "voting" for an electoral candidate of one's choice but to determine and recognize the "right one," that is, the charismatically qualified master who has a call to successorship. A "wrong" election, hence, was an atonable wrong. The basic postulate was that unanimity must be attainable; lack of unanimity was error and weakness.

In any case belief then no longer was belief in the person *per se* but in the person of the master as "correctly" and "validly designated" (possibly enthroned) or otherwise inaugurated into power like into possession of a property object.

(cc) People may believe in "hereditary charisma" and think that the charismatic qualification is in the blood. This suggestive idea represents, first, the notion of a "hereditary right" in prerogatives. The idea has become dominant in the Occident only during the Middle Ages. Frequently charisma attaches only to the sib and its new depository must first be determined according to one of the aforementioned rules and methods (ca, cb, or cc). Where fixed rules exist with regard to the person, they are not homogeneous. Only in the medieval occident and in Japan the right to inherit the crown by primogeniture has clearly won out and has greatly contributed to the stability of supreme authority, as all other forms give rise to internal conflicts.

The belief then is no longer belief in the person *per se* but in the "legitimate" heir of the dynasty: the timely and extraordinary nature of charisma is strongly transformed in a traditionalist direction; the idea of the divine right of kings ruling by the grace of God has also changed its meaning completely. Now the lord reigns in his own right, not by virtue of "personal" charisma acknowledged by the subjects. The right to rule then is completely independent of personal qualities.

(cd) Charisma may be depersonalized as objectified into ritual. Then people believe that charisma is a magical quality which can be transferred or produced by a special kind of hierurgy, ointment, laying on of hands or other sacramental acts.

Then people no longer believe in the charismatic person but in the efficacy of the respective sacramental act. The claim to authority is completely independent of the charismatic's personal qualities, as is especially obvious in the Catholic principle of the *character indelebilis* of the priest.

(ce) The charismatic principle of legitimation, which is primarily authoritarian in meaning, may be re-interpreted in an anti-authoritarian direction. The empirical validity of charismatic rule rests on whether or not the person of the charismatic is recognized as qualified by the governed and has proven his charisma. According to the genuine conception of charisma, people owe this recognition to the legitimate pretender because of his quality. This relationship can, however, easily be reversed to mean that the free recognition of the part of the governed be the presupposition of legitimacy and its basis (democratic legitimacy). Then recognition becomes an "election" and the lord, legitimate by virtue of his own charisma, becomes the rule by grace of the ruled and the mandate. Designation by the following, acclamation by the (military or religious) community, and the plebiscite have historically often assumed the nature of an election by vote. Thus they have made the chosen lord or charismatic claims into an official of the governed whom they elect at their pleasure.

A comparable development can be observed in the transformation of the principle of charismatic law. Originally the military or religious community had to recognize the pronounced law. Thus the competition of possible diverse and contradictory laws might be decided by charismatic means, as a last resort by commitment of the community to the "right" law. This charismatic principle could easily change to the—legal—idea that the governed should freely determine the law to be enforced by freely expressing their will and intention, and that vote counting, hence, majority decision, be the legitimate means for so doing.

The difference between a chosen *leader* and an elected official then consists only in the meaning which the person elected, given his personal qualities, can and does attach to his behavior opposite the staff and the governed. The official will wholly behave as the mandatary of his master— here the voters. The leader will behave as solely responsible to himself. Hence as long as the leader can successfully claim their confidence, he will act as he sees fit (leader-democracy) and not as the official, who follows the expressed or presumed will of the voters as an imperative mandate.

III/C
Centralization vs. decentralization

13 The centralization vs. decentralization issue: Arguments, alternatives, and guidelines
George Glaser

The major organizational issues facing industrial management today in its use of computers are four:

1 Centralization versus decentralization of staff, equipment and authorities
2 Reporting relationship of the data processing manager
3 Internal organization of the data processing department
4 Procedures to be used for charging (or absorbing) data processing costs.

This paper deals only with the first—the most controversial—of these issues: centralization versus decentralization—an issue arising from disagreements about the degree (and form) of control that a company should exercise over data processing in its operating divisions* and staff functions.

The centralization vs. decentralization issue

The centralization issue is not a new one; it has been widely discussed and hotly debated in academic institutions, management literature, and in less formal arenas for years—long before those particular aspects relating to the use of computers in industry came to the fore. It is an issue of great importance for governments—particularly those that do extensive economic planning at the state or industry level for multiple dispersed production units.

Obviously, many of the traditional arguments for or against centralization boil down to matters of management style. Even though it is rather

Source: Reprinted, by permission from the author and the Association for Computing Machinery, Inc., from Data Base, 2 (Fall/Winter 1970), 1–7. © 1970 by the Association for Computing Machinery, Inc.
* The term "division(s)" will be used throughout to refer to an operating unit located at a distance from corporate headquarters.

difficult to *prove* whether, for example, a centralized purchasing function is intrinsically superior to a decentralized one, both alternatives have strong proponents. And to add to the confusion, styles change as the pendulum of management philosophy swings to and fro—it may be quite fashionable to be highly decentralized in one era and equally unfashionable only a few years later. Furthermore, at any one time, individual management styles inevitably will differ within an organization.

As a result, arguments often are charged with emotion, leading to incomplete or misleading analyses of the alleged economics of the alternatives. And because organizations (and the individuals who make them up) are characterized by a variety of styles, abilities, and needs, it is not possible to propose a "solution" that will apply in all situations. One can only suggest alternatives—and the questions that must be answered in deciding among them.

General rules are always dangerous (and often trite), but these seem to apply:

- The organizational approach to data processing should be consistent with the overall organizational approach of the company in which it functions. For example, a company that operates multiple manufacturing units, each in a separate geographic location, and that imposes strict profit and loss accountability on local managers would be expected to lean strongly toward decentralized data processing. Very few economies—and perhaps many difficulties —would await it if it attempted to centralize data processing in a single corporate location.
- It will be expensive (at least in the short term) and possibly disruptive to make any organizational change; therefore, no change should be introduced unless the projected benefits of transition are both large and concrete. In other words, a centralized organization that is functioning well should probably remain centralized (and vice versa).
- Reorganization may be a good idea, but only competent people and hard work can produce consistently good performance. If hiring practices have been sloppy and training programs nonexistent, then staff qualifications most likely are weak as a result—and, regardless of how a staff is organized, weak qualifications tend to lead to poorly designed systems.

Perhaps the most challenging "rule" of all: No organizational structure or policy will work unless accepted by the majority of people affected by it as logical, satisfactory, and workable.

The issue in data processing

When the issue of centralization versus decentralization of data processing arises, those who argue for centralization point out that the costs of data processing are large and that the economies of scale are very important. Those who argue for decentralization express primary concern for the level of data processing service available to users; they believe that the additional out-of-pocket costs typically associated with a decentralized operation are justified.

The issue is a serious one for most industrial enterprises. And it becomes critical (and particularly difficult to resolve) for organizations that manufacture products in multiple operating divisions in diverse locations. Additional complications arise when lines of control cross international boundaries because of differences in national practices and laws, and poor cross-boundary communications, both human and electrical. Still further complications—and some of the most difficult to deal with—are caused by acquisitions and mergers that result in the need to manage incompatible equipment, programming languages, data structures, systems, and people; these may complicate (or even preclude) the interchange of data and limit sharing of technical accomplishments.

Most industrial data processing departments would claim these two objectives: (1) the desire to utilize corporate computer assets efficiently and effectively, and (2) the desire to offer a high level of service of low cost in solving a wide range of user problems.

Unfortunately, these two objectives often are in direct conflict, for increased efficiency of computer hardware nearly always leads to reduced accessibility and degraded service for individual users. For example, consider the "efficiencies" bestowed upon users of data processing by developments in operating systems: operating systems have been designed to allow highly efficient use of very powerful computers; but this "efficiency" has made it necessary for all users (or their agents) to master a difficult job control language that contributes nothing directly to the solution of their problems.

Analyzing the pros and cons

When an analysis of the pros and cons of centralization (or decentralization) is undertaken, said analysis typically is performed by a corporate data processing staff whose sensitivity to the needs of individual users is dulled by its passion for working with the most exotic hardware available—a strong economic motive for résumé-conscious technicians. And typical users are no more rational in their counterarguments—they embrace the concepts of autonomy and economy with considerable fervor—perhaps, in the process, rejecting badly needed assistance from well-qualified professionals in the central organization. And although the users outnumber the central staff, the former usually are geographically dispersed, poorly organized, and poorly qualified (in a technical sense) to ensure themselves of an equal hearing in the debate. As a result, more often than not, the corporate staff wins and centralized control results. Let's examine the arguments used by both sides.

Arguments for centralization

Proponents of centralization cite the following grounds for their point:

1 *Company-wide consolidation of operating results* Divisional financial and operating data must be consolidated at the corporate level. Compatibility of systems design, coding schemes, and data formats facilitate this consolidation. And such compatibility can be achieved only by close centralized direction of hardware/software procurement and development efforts.

2 *Economies of scale* Economies of scale—as measured by purchase or rental costs—result when several small computers are replaced by a single large one. Other economies of scale result from consolidation of development staffs and reduction of duplicate development efforts. Because rental and personnel costs appear as identifiable expenditures on accounting reports, they present obvious targets for those charged with the responsibility for keeping costs low.

3 *Shortage of qualified data processing personnel* Qualified data processing personnel are scarce and, from all evidence at hand and the present economy notwithstanding, will continue to be so. They show less allegiance to their employer than to their technology. Turnover is high, as individuals move from company to company, boosting their salaries substantially in the process. Centralization reduces the impact of this phenomenon by permitting fewer staffs of larger size, thus reducing dependence on individuals and enhancing the company's ability to recruit and retain a well-qualified staff.

4 *Ease of control* It is easier for corporate executives to control individual divisions when reporting systems are uniform. Unique systems in operating divisions are regarded as an impediment to adequate control. Through centralization, the arguments run, uniformity can be enforced.

Arguments for decentralization

Proponents of decentralization argue the following points:

1 *Familiarity with local problems* To apply the computer intelligently to the solution of complex problems in complex environments, systems analysts and programmers must be thoroughly familiar with the problems in detail. This level of familiarity can best be achieved by individuals who are close (both physically and organizationally) to the problem to be solved and to those who want solutions, i.e., by locating development staffs at the site of the manufacturing plant, warehouse, or other functional operation.

2 *Rapid response to local processing needs* The need of local management for rapid processing turnaround on large volumes of data often requires that conputers be located in their immediate vicinity. This is particularly true in manufacturing operations, where production schedules, order booking, and shipping papers must be prepared and returned rapidly to the user organization for action. Currently available communications facilities are inadequate to allow dependence on a remote computer for such applications.

3 *Profit and loss responsibility*   Many industrial organizations have adopted a principle of decentralized responsibility for operating results; because the selection and implementation of computer application can play a vital role in actual profits and losses, these tasks should be decentralized as well.

Needless to say, a great many more arguments are heard on both sides, and heatedly defended (1).

Elements of the issue

The approach to centralization/decentralization can be made somewhat rational if the major elements of the issue are considered separately; these elements are:

1 Equipment
2 Staff
3 Decision authorities.

Equipment

The most obvious element of the centralization versus decentralization issue is the location and custody of computing and communications equipment. Because the range of equipment, size, and power is so great, many options are available. Individual manufacturing plants might have small computers, often dedicated to a particular process or product line. Large powerful computers might be located in corporate offices to serve a multitude of corporate needs and home-office-based users; medium-sized machines might be placed in one or more regional centers to serve a number of smaller users in a local area.

Uniformity of equipment configuration, compatibility of languages, and interchangeability of data and storage media are other aspects of the centralization/decentralization issue that are closely related to equipment. For example, to what extent must equipment configurations be identical so that common applications programs may be used in multiple locations?

Equipment issues are further complicated when more than one vendor has manufactured the equipment installed in various locations throughout a single company. This situation may have resulted from independent equipment selection decisions made at an earlier date; or from acquisitions or mergers where uniformity requirements did not exist or could not be foreseen; or when individual applications requirements lead to a deliberate choice of noncompatible equipment.

In most cases, there will be some requirement for the interchange of data and programs within the corporation. The requirements may be continuous or occasional; the cost of meeting them may be high or trivial.

Several trends in equipment design are well established—the cost of electronics assembly has gone down dramatically in recent years, making large-scale integration attractive economically. This, in turn, has led to the mini-computer—now introduced on a broad scale in a number of interesting applications. At the same time, telecommunications capability has improved dramatically, from both a device and a network point of view—although the latter seems to be lagging badly in some geographical areas. The net result of these developments will be even further decentralization of data processing personnel and widespread dispersion of equipment.

Why? First, the incentive to build very large machines because of manufacturing economies will no longer be present. Second, as equipment becomes smaller and more powerful, fewer economies of scale (based on physical factors such as space and air conditioning) will be available through consolidation of several small machines into one or more larger ones. Third, improved communications will facilitate consolidation of operating results between small machines at remote locations and a larger machine at corporation headquarters without requiring that large volumes of data be moved over long distances.

Large corporations are unlikely to centralize their data in a single file (or a small group of files)—although they may very well have highly developed data management standards and explicit controls over the content of data files throughout the corporation.

Unfortunately, the majority of centralization arguments are based on improving the *efficiency* of the equipment used in computer installation; but efficient installations do not necessarily house effective computers.

An efficient steam engine may indeed be a source of great pride to the thermodynamicist who designed it and to the caretaker who maintains it; but if it is impractical to move the mechanical energy from the steam engine to the location where it is needed, then the efficiency of the engine is a little value. Today, there are too many highly efficient computers that bring great satisfaction to *their* caretakers but do so at considerable cost to the organization that pays the rent for both. Furthermore, efficient use of equipment isn't as important (in the United States) as it once was; computer rental costs now comprise only 35 percent of the total costs of data processing (2). This is certainly not a trivial amount but, in most cases, it is less than the percentage of costs spent on data processing staff salaries.

Staff

Many people possessing a variety of skills are required to support a corporate data processing effort (3). Some of these individuals, by definition, must be located in the immediate vicinity of the machines, e.g., operators and maintenance personnel. Keypunch clerks and data preparation clerks have in the past been located near the computer room also, particularly when the volume of data to be handled was high. However, the introduction of keyboard-to-tape and keyboard-to-disc units has relieved the need for close proximity of these personnel to processing equipment.

Other developments in equipment have provided increased latitude in the location of systems analysts and programmers who no longer must be located in the immediate vicinity of major equipment. Conversational programming and remote job entry techniques now allow both analysts and programmers to be at a considerable distance from the computers on which their programs will be run.

Several arguments have been presented above that are used by either centralists or decentralists to influence the location of the technical development staff. One of these—the economies of scale expected from consolidation of development staffs—is based on a alleged synergistic effect (4). But a single large development staff is *not* necessarily more effective than several smaller ones. Manpower management and project assignments might be facilitated in the larger group, but any economies of direct labor may easily be offset by additional administrative (indirect) labor.

Parties arguing either side of the issue would no doubt agree that it is worthwhile to avoid duplication of effort. But it is not obvious that consolidation of development staffs is the best way to do so; bootleg developments are easy to disguise *if* that is the intent of the developer, whether developments are officially centralized or not. On the other hand, if he is motivated to disclose what he is doing and share his results, he can do so equally well in a decentralized organization.

Perhaps one of the more compelling arguments for staff centralization is that larger staffs are less susceptible to damage from high turnover. True—the loss of even one person who is a key man on a small staff can hurt badly. But turnover rates often are considerably lower in small installations, particularly when these are located in rural or semirural areas. Typically, it is the major cities and densely populated areas that have high turnover rates—primarily because of the multiple opportunities offered without relocating one's family. The counterargument is that large staffs with powerful centralized equipment and extensive training programs are alleged to be more attractive to recruits than are smaller staffs in remote locations. Fortunately, turnover rates (and their causes) and recruiting results can be analyzed quantitatively; they are among the few variables for which this is so.

The decentralist's argument that physical proximity to a problem may ease its solution assumes that qualified people are available. This assumption may not be justified—in fact, it is likely that a larger number of more highly qualified individuals would be members of a central staff than of any one (or all) local staffs. But the tradeoff between technical qualifications and familiarity with a problem can be a tough one to evaluate. A "local" analyst who is familiar with a problem but who lacks certain specialized knowledge may need to ask for help; and a highly qualified specialist who is not familiar with a problem may need to take particular pains to develop the knowledge and rapport at the local level that he will need eventually to solve it. But given the choice between the two, the local analyst often will be more successful because most of the *tough* problems are so defined for other than technical reasons.

A different kind of "problem knowledge" often is important—that knowledge bearing on the operational feasibility* of a particular application. Operational impediments to a successful implementation often are subtle and are never easy to overcome; but familiarity with "how things really work around here," i.e., with local personalities, politics, and mores, may be the key to doing so.

Whenever comparisons are being made between the advantages of a centralized versus decentralized staff, it is important (and difficult) to keep the comparisons equitable. If a poorly organized and poorly trained central staff is compared to small but elite decentralized staffs, the latter would surely win. Conversely, decentralization is not a very realistic alternative for the near term if there are only six analysts and programmers in the entire company.

What of the future? Two trends are working in favor of decentralized data processing staffs. First, the problem of scarcity of personnel—recently so severe—will not last indefinitely. Within 5 years, work loads in data processing will be much more stable and the influx of competent individuals from year to year will provide an adequate and stable work force. Companies will no longer centralize as a defensive measure. Second, as the use of data processing becomes more accepted and better understood by middle- and upper-level managers of operating units, they will insist that local data processing talent be available (and responsible) to them; systems analysis and programming will be as routine as plant maintenance and accounting.

In summary, the arguments based on staff—not equipment—considerations are the most important in nearly every case (6). Failure to recognize this can lead to organizational recommendations that, while intended to *cut* data processing costs, may lead to *higher* costs in the long run.

Decision authorities

The third and most complex aspect of the centralization versus decentralization issue is the assignment of decision authorities. Decision authorities can be grouped under five major headings:

1 *Direction setting*   Who establishes long-range data processing objectives and sets the level of effort?, e.g., funds.
2 *Project evaluation and selection*   On whose authority will projects be approved? Can approval authorities realistically be delegated, allowing lower level organization units to approve certain projects, while reserving control of large projects for higher authorities?
3 *Hardware and software selection*   Who approves new expansion of EDP hardware? On what basis are programming languages selected? To what extent should the use of multiple languages be restricted? Should responsibility

---

* Operational feasibility is a measure of how well the system will function within the operating policies, organization, and economic environment of the corporation (5).

for approving the *need* for equipment be separated from responsibility for approving the type and manufacturer? Should file structures and data definitions be standardized? Coding systems? Programming and documentation standards?

4 *Personnel assignment* Who approves staffing levels? How will major interfunctional or interdivisional projects be staffed? Who will lead such projects? How will development costs of such projects be allocated? How will salary levels be administered and career opportunities be provided?

5 *Use of outside services* Do users have the option when choosing the "source" of manpower for their development and operating needs? If so, under what circumstances will an individual user or department be allowed to contract for outside data processing services? Only for peak loads? Only where special expertise is required?

Questions like these arise every day in large corporations. It is impossible to provide answers that will apply in all situations; but it is imperative that responsibility for answering them be assigned unambiguously and that they be answered clearly and consistently when they arise.

Criteria for the decision

In attempting to decide between a centralized or decentralized policy (or some combination of the two), seven criteria should be considered:

1 *Minimum total cost* The total cost of system development, operations, and maintenance is one of the major selection criteria. But it is important to remember that not all costs are reported by the accounting system. For example, late inventory status reports may lead to poor purchasing decisions, or to the loss of a customer order; both have high costs but neither is likely to effect short-term accounting results.

2 *User satisfaction* Because this criterion is so difficult to quantify, it often receives inadequate consideration. Yet, it represents a fundamental issue in selecting a policy. Efficient computer operations that render poor service have a very high ratio of costs to benefits. This criterion is often difficult to quantify, but not that difficult to evaluate quantitatively. Dissatisfied users usually are quite vocal in their criticism; whether that criticism is fully justified in every case is a moot point. If users are generally unhappy, then odds are that their attitude is based on a real problem.

3 *Effective utilization of personnel* Because technical talents are scarce, their effective utilization is an important consideration. But it must not be assumed that effective utilization of personnel calls for consolidated development staffs; quite often, the reverse is true.

4 *The ability to attract and retain personnel* Certain technical personnel are attracted by installations of large complex computer equipment. Others,

equally skilled, prefer the independence that a smaller installation may offer. Some may prefer to work in a big city; others, in the country.

5 *Rational selection of development projects*   Where a number of projects are competing for limited resources, there must be a procedure that will allow rational selection among them. In some cases, this will have to be carried out at the corporate staff level; in others, selection might be the responsibility of the local plant manager or of a functional, e.g., manufacturing, executive.

6 *The opportunity to share common systems*   Companies with fairly uniform products and processes have attractive opportunities to share common systems, facilities, and staffs. Companies characterized by diversity may offer few such opportunities except for certain administrative applications such as personnel and asset accounting.

7 *Adaptability to changes in the technical and economic environment*   Since no one can anticipate all significant changes in technology or developments in industry or company structure, the organization must be sufficiently flexible to accommodate a variety of unforeseen future developments. At no time is this more evident than after a successful merger that results in two programming staffs—one of PL/1 (only) programmers and another of COBOL (only) programmers.

Additional factors influencing the decision

Additional factors—some of which may be unique to the situation—and many of which will be subjective—may play an important role in determining the appropriate degree of centralization.

One of these is the nature of the information flow among sub-units in the organization. If the volume of information is low and infrequent, manual consolidation of operating results may be best, thus reducing the need for centralized processing. If, on the other hand, large volumes of data must be consolidated quickly and frequently, then a centralized approach is indicated. Good examples of the latter case are airline reservations systems that rely completely on a single inventory of available seats.

The need of operating managers for rapid turnaround of operating information may transcend any economies that might be provided by sharing data processing facilities located at some distance (and time) from the local area.

The availability of reliable and inexpensive data communications will often dictate the degree of centralization possible. If communications are poor, the cost of moving data to (and results from) a major installation may be prohibitive. And even when the economics are favorable, provisions must be made for correcting data input errors. If it is necessary to contact the source of the original data, the resulting delays and costs may be unacceptable.

The current "state of the DP art" will heavily influence the centralization decision. A company that is introducing data processing for the first time may wisely elect to begin with a small group in a single location under tight managerial control. As the group expands and matures, it then may be desirable gradually to spin off (decentralize) small subgroups that, in time, will become self-sustaining and will operate independently of the parent organization.

To centralize, i.e., to collapse a number of existing decentralized operations into a single centralized one, is very difficult unless the work load in the decentralized units is heavily concentrated on a few applications that are identical from unit to unit. For example, successful consolidation of credit card processing centers is both possible and (often) attractive economically. But attempts to achieve economies by centralizing heterogeneous applications, currently running on different machines, programmed and operated by independent groups of people, will frequently meet with disastrous results. Unfortunately, there is a seductive but inevitably costly urge to "pull everything together, get it on a single machine, eliminate our operating problems, and cut our costs." The results often are disappointing.

Finally, the degree of uniformity of coding systems, managerial practices, and operating policies within the corporation can be a constraint. If there is little uniformity, centralization will produce relatively marginal benefits; in fact, centralization may be impractical *until* uniformity is achieved— usually a long and difficult process.

The alternatives

Although there are an infinite number of possible organizational structures that might be offered to deal with the issues discussed above, most existing structures are variations on four major alternatives:

1 *Centralized development and operations* All development efforts are performed by a centralized development staff; all computing and communications equipment is operated by a centralized organization. Neither staffs nor computers need be in a single location; for example, regional centers might be established under centralized control.
2 *Independent development and centralized operations* Individual users, based on their individual needs, employ development staffs; a centralized authority operates all computing and communications equipment.
3 *Independent development and operations under central coordination* Independent users employ their own development and operations staffs and operate their own equipment. Those that are too small to justify either staffs or equipment obtain services from other operating units within the company or from outside service bureaus. Central coordination is provided in terms of programming and documentation standards; authority over configuration, types and manufacturers of equipment; establishment of internal training programs, salary administration and career path planning; and responsibility for consistent and rational project evaluation and selection. In short, the central group controls the methods and processes by which data processing is

used, but is not responsible for the design and implementation of individual systems.

4 *Independent development and operations*   All aspects of data processing enjoy complete autonomy within the constraints of divisional accountability. If a corporate data processing staff and/or installation exists, its only function is to serve users at the corporate level in the same sense that divisional staffs serve divisional users.

In most situations, industrial companies choose alternatives 2 or 3 above, or compromise between them. Neither the completely centralized nor the completely decentralized mode of operation is found often in practice. Where complete centralization has been attempted, clandestine staffs and equipment installations are likely to develop. The reasons are simple: If a user has a problem and is determined to solve it, and if he cannot get an acceptable solution to his problem from the "legal" source of help, he will seek (and find) illegal sources.

Guidelines for allocating the tasks

Although no single set of rules will apply in all cases, the following general guidelines may be useful in deciding when to allocate tasks to a centralized staff as opposed to allocating them to divisions.

The *centralized* staff should be responsible for the following:

1 The work of the corporate office. These needs are "local" at the corporate level in the same sense that production scheduling is a local need in a manufacturing plant.
2 Company-wide functions, e.g., personnel, payroll, and certain other routine accounting applications.
3 Divisional work that does not require rapid turnaround and that can be done more economically on a centralized basis.
4 Work for small divisions that cannot justify facilities or staffs of their own. In this role, the central facility functions as a service bureau; geographically far-flung enterprises may find it appropriate to delegate some central "bureau" functions to one or more regional outposts.
5 Interdivision and interplant applications that are part of an integrated system where, for technical reasons, a single computer must process all data within the system. Certain order entry and inventory applications are of this nature.

Decentralized staffs should be responsible for:

1 Applications that depend on rapid turnaround, e.g., production scheduling.
2 All work for which there are no *compelling* reasons to centralize.

The underlying principle is that *work should be done locally whenever possible;* it should be done centrally only when the economics or some other performance requirement dictates so. This is the converse of the principle frequently applied that presumes that work should be done centrally unless special circumstances dictate otherwise.

In all cases there is a risk of spending too much money and of spending it unwisely; there is the threat of missed opportunities and of duplicated efforts; there is the danger of inappropriate equipment and unqualified staff. All must be considered in designing the organization that is appropriate for each environment.

In the long run, the computer's existence is justified only by its usefulness in solving problems—quickly, with minimum disruption to the fundamental operations of the business, and at the lowest feasible costs. To do so depends heavily on close working relationships with those who face the problems and whose valuable insight into their solution, whose ability to generate enthusiasm for the results, and whose dedication to make systems work are the *sine qua non* of success.

References

1 For a debate on this subject, see Martin B. Solomon, "Economies of Scale and Computer Personnel," *Datamation,* March 1970, pp. 107–110; Peter Berman, "A Vote Against Centralized Staff," *Datamation,* May 1970, pp. 289–290; Solomon, "Economies of Scale Defended," *Datamation,* June 1970, pp. 293–294; and Berman, "Decentralization Again," *Datamation,* October 15, 1970, pp. 141–142.

2 McKinsey & Company, Inc., *Unlocking the Computer's Profit Potential* (New York, 1968), pp. 7–10.

3 Enid Mumford and T. B. Ward, *Computers: Planning for People* (London, B. T. Batsford Ltd., 1968), pp. 70–78.

4 Solomon, "Economies of Scale and Computer Personnel," *Datamation,* March 1970, pp. 107–110.

5 George Glaser, "Are You Working on the Right Problem?", *Datamation,* June 1967, pp. 22–25.

6 Joseph Orlicky, *The Successful Computer System* (McGraw-Hill Book Company, 1969), p. 179.

III/D
Line and staff

14 Line and staff: An obsolete concept?
Hall H. Logan

The concept that all functions or departments of a business enterprise are either "line" or "staff" is now so firmly entrenched in management theory that any attempt to dislodge it may well seem doomed to failure. Yet it is certainly pertinent to ask, how applicable to business today is this seemingly immutable principle of organization? Does it really serve any practical purpose—other than to add further confusion to the already complex system of interlocking relationships through which any company of any size actually achieves its goals?

Under the line-staff concept, as we all know, line departments are those directly engaged in producing or selling the goods or services the enterprise exists to provide. All other activities are staff—a definition that inevitably relegates staff people to positions of secondary or ancillary importance in the organization. This either-or theory may have some relevance for a company in its earliest stage of development, when there is usually little difficulty in distinguishing the people who are really bringing home the bacon from those whose activities clearly fall into the category of overhead. But as the enterprise grows and its operations become more and more complex, the demarcation between line and staff functions becomes progressively fuzzier until, in the typical large corporation, it is no longer possible to state unequivocally just who is directly engaged in furthering its objectives and who is not.

To take a simple example, who sells more beer—the market research and advertising people or the driver salesman on the beer truck? There can be little dispute as to who is closer to the final product; but a concept of organization that revolves around this matter of direct involvement in the fabrication or sale of the product overlooks the vast amount of work that has to be done before any sales are consummated, as, for example, in the consumer industries. Nor does it recognize the skill and precision that go into the evolution of a product long before it reaches the production stage.

Source: Reprinted by permission of the publisher from *Personnel* (January/February 1966), 26–33. © 1966 by the Amercian Management Association, Inc.

134

What kind of label?

As an example of the latter, let's consider the case of a company operating under a prime or major secondary contract with the Department of Defense. In such companies, the responsibility for developing design concepts is usually assigned to the Advanced Design department. Once a concept has been sold, responsibility for designing the hardware then passes to the Product Design department. Next, it is up to the Tooling department to establish a manufacturing plan—determining the component breakdown, line stations, major fixtures, etc. This planning phase completed, Tooling then has the responsibility for designing and manufacturing all tools and fixtures.

What kind of departments are these? The orthodox would call them "staff," because they never get their hands on the salable article. The more liberal element would say, "Well, if the company's objectives say 'design, manufacture, and sell,' Product Design is a 'line' department. But Advanced Design? Now that's research—or is it? Well, probably they will have to be 'staff.' "

Such answers are attempts to explain organizational relationships on the basis of the type of work performed by each unit of the enterprise. But organizational relationships—the relationships that management establishes between departments, groups, and individuals, and the degree of responsibility and authority it assigns to these various organizational units to meet the needs of the situation—are not determined by type of work per se. While some functions do rather consistently possess a certain kind of authority, modern practice has tended to spread authority more widely, particularly among the skilled functions. The attempt to establish authority by type of function is totally at variance with the relationships that actually exist in the modern corporation.

Later, I shall give some examples of the wide variations that can exist in organizational relationships. At this point, though, I should like to outline a concept of formal organization that portrays what really goes on in business these days.

The aim of formal organization is to insure singleness of purpose. A company's success in attaining its goals depends upon the skill with which management functions and authority are divided and, probably more important, how the divisions are integrated into unified action. In practice, this boils down to first assigning responsibilities and then trying to insure, as far as possible, authority co-equal with these responsibilities.

Authority spelled out

Particularly at the lower echelons of the organizational structure, authority relationships must be well established and thoroughly understood because of the heavy travel over these paths. There must be a clear understanding of who is responsible for what, as well as the degree of this responsibility. Relationships at the top echelons, between corporate staffs and multiplant managers, generally require less explanation, and are expressed in broader terms.

Organizational relationships take three basic forms: line, functional, and staff. Each type achieves its purpose through the exercise of its own kind of authority. Let's take a closer look at these different forms of authority. Here, though, a preliminary definition is called for:

Authority is the right or power to issue commands and to discipline for violation: an accepted source of information. This definition must be firmly grasped if the three basic types of organizational relationships are to be clearly understood.

Line authority

This inheres in the relationship between superior and subordinate at any level. It is administrative authority, having the right and power to issue commands, to exact accountability, and to discipline for violations. Rarely, however, does it exist in a pure form. Over and above his line authority, a supervisor invariably has some degree of functional authority also. Line authority never crosses departmental lines horizontally, but is the scalar chain that, regardless of the type of work or function performed, links the lowest unskilled worker through successive echelons of supervision to the president.

Functional authority

This is the authority delegated by formal action of management to an "accepted source of information" or a specialist. Functional authority is the right and power of one department to issue orders or instructions to one, several, or all other departments in an enterprise, also with the right of accountability from the addressee. Functional authority is as binding as line authority, but it *does not carry the right to discipline for violation* (or even to threaten) in order to enforce compliance.

This authority to issue orders pertains to a single function, or to a limited number of functions in which the subject department is authorized to act. Functional authority should be formally established by agreement among the departments affected, preferably in written procedures that are approved by middle management and finally by the president, or at least by the manager who supervises all the departments concerned.

Functional authority also implies co-equality of responsibility. The department issuing the orders is responsible for the results of its directives, and thus shares in the total responsibility for other departmental tasks.

Functional authority is usually impersonal in nature. In larger companies, it takes the form of written orders, schedules, inspection reports, and the like. If, however, the individual exercising functional authority cannot, as I said, threaten, or take reprisals outside of his own department, where are the teeth? The prior agreement is the basis for the working relationship. Furthermore, the functional department usually issues periodic reports, or on an emergency basis if necessary, which go both to the supervisor directly concerned and to the next level of supervision above. This feedback permits each supervisor to evaluate the effectiveness of his performance in achieving prescribed targets or goals, and to take corrective action as required.

If management promotes a teamwork philosophy and the use of functional and staff organizations, employees will readily accept orders from authorized sources outside the linear chain of command. A supervisor will no more readily question or reject a functional order than he would one from his immediate superior. But if he honestly believes that he cannot carry out a particular order, he can and does question it, regardless of its origin.

A key difference

It is the right to reprimand that differentiates line from functional relationships and distinguishes today's organizational practices from Taylor's pure functional foremanship. Through functional authority, the benefits of functional specialization are attained while retaining unity of command—for each man, one person-to-person boss relationship.

Staff authority

This actually is a misnomer, for the person or department operating in a staff relationship has no authority to issue orders to other departments and no right to demand accountability. "Pure staff" personnel carry out their work through influence. Such relationships exist where the function is variable or intermittent in nature. For example, the industrial engineer may have the responsibility to develop better methods throughout the enterprise. It is usually deemed best to let the I.E. sell individual departments on the value of his proposals. However, in companies where centralized authority is a policy, the I.E. may have the authority to direct each department in how best to perform its work. In the latter situation, the I.E. would have functional authority. Here is one example of how different managements can establish different organizational relationships for what on their respective organizational charts might appear to be the same.

What should we call departments having line relationships, functional authority relationships, or staff relationships? In practice, because of their ambiguous meanings, the terms "line" and "staff" are rarely used to designate a department's exact relationship with other segments of the enterprise. In fact, as subsequent examples will show, departments do not operate with the same authority relationships in all phases of their work.

In their practical, day-to-day work, people are concerned only with how to carry out a particular job and who is involved in the process. In explaining the job to a new worker, the foreman does not say, "You are a line operator; I am a line man; the Production Control people are staff, and so are the Inspection and Process Control people." Most likely his remarks will go something like this: "You are responsible for making a good product, but to be certain that we have uniform quality and that all specifications are met, all parts must be approved by the inspector—that guy over there with the red vest. Orders and schedules come to us from Production Control. You have to make the exact quantity specified on the order and work according to the schedule. The required materials, tools, and engineering drawings are specified on the production order. You get these from the Production Control crib over there.

"And if the order calls for process instruction No. so-and-so, you'll find these instructions in this drawer, filed by number. They are prepared by the Process Control department and are like a part of the engineering design. You must follow them carefully. Now, if the tools won't produce a good part, come to me and we may have to call in the Tool Liaison man. Don't try to rework the tool yourself. That's Tooling's responsibility. . . ."

Fusing of operations

From the examples I have already cited, it should be clear that, in the modern corporation, the departments operating only through line relationships are by no means confined to the classic sales and production functions. Moreover, there are many functional departments whose activities cannot be reconciled with the proposition that production and sales are the only segments of the organization directly concerned with furthering its prime objectives. Let's consider some further examples bearing out these contentions.

We might begin by reconsidering the question I cited at the outset— the status of the Advanced Design department of a large defense contractor. Under the line-staff concept, this would be a staff department. Actually, in discharging its basic reponsibility it will operate through line relationships only. It is unlikely to have any functional relationships, though its members might be called upon for advice on certain projects from time to time.

Inspection provides an interesting example of how a particular function's authority relationships can change with the changing demands of the situation. In some companies, Inspection may not even exist as a separate function, each foreman being directly responsible for the quality of the work he supervises. As operations expand, management may, however, permit the foreman to add one or more inspectors and an assistant foreman to relieve him of routine inspection duties. While this group would approve or reject all items produced, it would report to the foreman and thus serve, in the formal sense, as a staff unit.

Later on, quality control may be so crucial to the continued success of the company's over-all operations that it becomes advisable to make it an independent operation. To insure the desired level of quality, Inspection, or

Quality Control as it might henceforth be termed, will then have to have functional authority. It will be directly accountable to the vice president of Manufacturing, or may even be independent of Manufacturing.

Accounting operates through all three types of authority. Usually, the accounting department has functional authority to prescribe the kind of input data it needs and to insure its timely collection or submission. But the ultimate purpose of both internal and external accounting reports is to inform the several levels of management, stockholders, and other interested parties of the results of the company's operations. This is an advisory function carried out through a staff relationship.

Wearing two hats

Payroll and Accounts Payable perform a basic function of the business through line relationships only, insofar as their output is concerned. Nevertheless, these units exercise functional authority in the collection of time cards, invoices, receiving reports, and other supporting data needed to carry out their responsibility.

Depending on general management policy, Purchasing can operate through line or staff relationships. Thus, if Purchasing is completely subordinate to Production—a purely clerical operation that makes no independent decisions—it will have a staff relationship with the production departments. However, these days, Purchasing is mostly centralized, particularly in larger companies. Though a good purchasing agent will work with the technical departments in selecting suppliers, the actual contractual negotiations, placing of purchase orders, and follow-up are his responsibilities, and are carried out through normal line relationships.

As I earlier pointed out, Industrial Engineering can operate through staff or functional relationships, again depending upon general management policy. Occasionally, Industrial Engineering will be told to "take over and get the job done," after it has sold a proposal to another department. Some experts hold that this is assuming line authority, but it is not the case because, in such a situation, the I.E. does not have full authority of reprimand; he cannot fire or suspend an employee. He will discuss any serious disciplinary problem with the worker's regular supervisor, but leave it to him to take the necessary action. In short, the I.E. has temporary functional authority.

Production Control is another function that can operate through staff or functional relationships. Thus, shop orders and schedules may be prepared by a production control group that reports to a superintendent. If all their work is subject to his formal approval, the clerks will have only staff authority even though most of their orders bypass the superintendent because of their routine nature. But a production control department that has clearly defined responsibilities, and reports to the works manager or the vice president of Manufacturing, will issue orders and schedules directly to first-line supervision. This is a functional authority at this lower level.

In most mass production industries, Tooling carries out its authority through line relationships. It does not advise the shop, nor does it exercise functional direction or authority over it. In fact, since the advent of the numerical control process, responsibility for the accuracy and quality of the final product rests essentially in the tooling function.

The tape instructions are prepared by the tooling programer. Theoretically, in any event, this reduces the shop operation to pushing a button on the console. If the man who pushes the button can be said to be "advancing the product," who, it must be asked, is more directly concerned with furthering the prime objectives of the business?

From the foregoing examples it is clear that the production and direct sales departments are not the only ones with line authority. There are a number of other departments that neither advise nor functionally direct other units, but operate solely through line relationships to discharge their responsibilities. Some of these are in the mainstream of the business—others are less so.

Then there are many other departments that exercise functional authority in their relations with other groups, thus diluting and sharing in the responsibility for the total activities and the end products of the latter units.

On the other hand, "pure staff" personnel are relatively few and staff-type departments relatively fewer still.

This presents an entirely different pattern and proportional mix of authority relationships from that of the line-staff concept, about which, incidentally, studies have indicated that 50 per cent of the total workforce in sample industries is engaged in staff work. (With present-day competition, can any enterprise afford the luxury of 50 per cent "planners" and 50 per cent "doers"?)

Regardless of what the theorists may say, in practice, as I have tried to show, working relationships are designed—or evolve—to meet the demands of the situation. In practice, also, the members of the enterprise pay little attention to "line" and "staff" labels. They are concerned only with the responsibility and authority of the persons with whom they associate in carrying out their jobs. As the situation was aptly summed up by one vice president, "We aren't aware of many staff people around here. Everybody has a job to do and does it, no matter what you call him."

III/E
Coordinating

---

15 A review of vertical and lateral relations: A new perspective for managers

James L. Hall and Joel K. Leidecker

Lateral, or horizontal, relations are a dimension of organizational behavior generally neglected by the "principles of management." These principles, set forth in traditional or classical management theory, focus on vertical, or superior-subordinate relationships. According to classical theory, the critical task of coordination will be accomplished solely by means of standard operating procedures and *vertical relations* (those between superiors and subordinates). The difficulty with this view is that several studies have shown that managers lack adequate control over task accomplishment when they limit themselves to vertical relations (1). These studies found that, in order to get the job done, many managers spend a considerable amount of their time, *ranging from one-third to over three-quarters,* in activities other than those dealing with superiors and subordinates. It is our position that lateral relations are necessary to accomplish effective coordination in the organization, and that the classical view of the manager's coordinative function is incomplete (2).

This article first describes the nature of lateral relations, pointing out the types of lateral relations that may occur, and then discusses some of the differences between the concept of classical theory and that of lateral relations. Finally, the importance of lateral relations to current concepts of the managerial role, such as "linking-pin," "integrator," and "boundary mediator," is noted.

The nature of lateral relations

Lateral relations are those that exist among departments of about the same rank in the organizational hierarchy. Their function is to improve coordination

Source: This article was prepared especially for this volume.

between various departments. This positive view of lateral relations contrasts with that of classical theory, which tends to look upon lateral activities as dysfunctional for organizational goals, reflecting personality conflicts, "empire building," "office politics," or "bureaucratic gamesmanship" (3).

Sayles (4) has developed the most extensive model to explain the concept of lateral relations. He classifies the manager's role as: (1) leader, (2) monitor or appraiser, and (3) participant in external work flows. The first two categories consist of vertical relations, while "external work flows" refers to lateral relations:

1 Unlike superior-subordinate relations, lateral contacts are between managers who occupy a roughly equivalent position in the organization's hierarchy; one is not the boss of the other. No clear-cut, established pattern exists, in which one of the parties is prepared to accept unequivocally the responsibility for initiating the other's actions. Substantial ambiguities exist in what the pattern of give and take should be.
2 The parties to the relationship, in all likelihood, work under different standards of performance or with differing, and often conflicting, objectives. Lateral, or external, relations, therefore, have more built-in conflicts than superior-subordinate relations.
3 As a direct result of (1) and (2), these external relationships typically involve more difficult and more lengthy contacts, which require more negotiations. These relationships tend to be uncomfortable and tension producing, calling for a high level of skill in human relations (5).

There are several patterns of lateral relations in Sayles's view: trading, work flow, service, advisory, audit, and stabilization. All have some common aspects, but each is sufficiently unique to warrant separate classification. The patterns are set forth schematically in Chart I.

Trading describes the manager's attempts to search for, and establish, contacts with other managers who may be of help to him or her, either as "buyers" of his or her services, or as "sellers" of useful resources. For example, the manager of graphic arts may try to convince the manager of marketing that graphic arts should do marketing's layout work. Trading may lead to work-flow or service relations.

Work-flow relations are those a manager engages in with other managers who either precede or follow him or her in sequential activities, such as assembling physical goods or developing a product (A → B → C). For example, A (marketing–product development) identifies a new market for a product. B (advertising) then creates a program to introduce the product, and finally C (graphic arts) does the layout and artwork. Any department may try to increase its control in the work-flow relationship by changing role boundaries (advertising takes over a function of graphic arts) or by changing position in the established pattern (advertising becomes involved in identifying consumer needs).

To illustrate *service* relations: an organization may decide to centralize certain activities (such as personnel, supplies, or purchasing) for economic

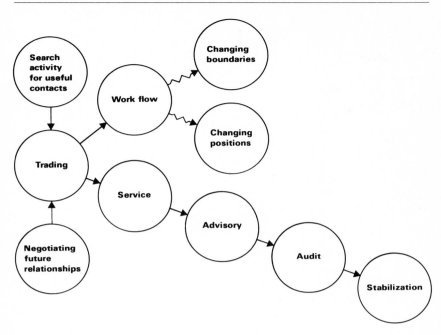

Chart I Types of lateral relations
Source: Derived from *Managerial Behavior,* by Leonard Sayles, pp. 58–73, 114.
Copyright 1964 by McGraw-Hill Book Company. Used with permission of McGraw-Hill
Book Company.

reasons and to provide specialized assistance. Forms of the service relationship that have been identified include advisory, auditing, and stabilization.

   Advisory (advising) is the primary form of the service relation. A service manager may try to maximize the efficient use of his or her service by initiating the flow of interaction. Rather than waiting for other managers to approach him or her, a service manager may approach those who are likely to
need or want his or her services and try to establish a working relationship
which will enable him to do a better job with less time pressure. However,
initiating interaction does not guarantee that the advice will be taken. Consequently, the manager may try to develop an audit or stabilization relationship to gain more control over the use of the services he or she provides.

   Auditing describes a relationship in which a service manager has the
right to evaluate the actions of others, increasing the probability that his or
her advice will be taken.

   The next logical step is *stabilization*. In this relationship, the service
manager's advice and *approval* must be obtained before activities are undertaken.

   To sum up, we have seen that studies of the managerial role reveal
that lateral relations, which take from one-third to over three-quarters of the

manager's time, are as important to successful task accomplishment as vertical relations are. We have also found that the manager who is under pressure to obtain scarce resources, or to ensure that resources are appropriately employed, can take a variety of actions to reduce his or her dependency on other managers. Lateral relations reflect the manager's recognition of interdependence with other managers and describe the manager's efforts to coordinate these interdependent activities more effectively. Various patterns of lateral relations have been identified, and the potential contribution of each pattern to the manager's control over his or her task has been described.

A comparative look at lateral relations

Recent comparative studies of organizations show that few concepts or principles are equally applicable to all organizations or industries. An interesting and logical question, then, is, "How prevalent are lateral relations?" For example, are they more important in some organizations than in others? The principal attempt to answer these questions was made in a study by Lawrence and Lorsch (7). They examined organizations in two different environments: (1) a stable environment with little change (the container industry) and (2) a rapidly changing environment (the food industry and the plastics industry). The investigators concluded that, despite the contrasting environments, lateral relations were equally important in the two industries. Although no significant difference appeared in the overall importance of lateral relations, different industries tended to stress lateral relations between different departments.

Another distinction between the two categories was that lateral relations tended to occur at higher levels in the organizations with stable environments. In organizations with rapidly changing environments, lateral relations tended to occur more frequently at lower levels of the organizational hierarchy. To some extent, this distinction seems to stem from the greater centralization of decision making that is possible in organizations with stale environments (8).

From this evidence, then, we are able to draw three tentative conclusions: (1) lateral relations are important to two broad organizational categories—organizations with relatively stable environments and organizations with rapidly changing environments; (2) the departments between which critical lateral relations develop will differ, depending on the environmental stability; and (3) the heirarchical level at which lateral relations occur most frequently also varies as a function of the environmental stability.

Implications of lateral relations for classical theory

The nature and importance of lateral relations are better understood when they are compared with the principles and assumptions of classical management theory. The first part of this section outlines those dimensions of the classical model that are challenged by the concept and reality of lateral relationships. The second describes dimensions that are common to both, but that may require the manager to use a different approach.

Challenges to the classical model (9)

Task accomplishment
According to classical doctrine, the work assignment is primarily accomplished by the manager and his or her subordinates. The prevalence of lateral relations, however, indicates that this assumption is not entirely correct. As we have seen, resources and services provided from outside the structural boundaries of the manager's position are necessary for the accomplishment of his or her task. The activities described by Sayles in his model as service, work flow, advisory, auditing, and stabilization relations all reflect time spent in task accomplishment that has very little to do with supervision of subordinates.

Unity of command
The principle of the unity of command implies that order and direction emanate from the superior to the subordinate. In fact, however, a manager operating in a horizontal work-flow pattern will receive many requests initiated by managers on the same level. In a stabilization relationship, for example, the line manager is not allowed to purchase material without prior approval by the purchasing department. The manager thus engages in activity that has been imposed on him or her from outside the normal, vertical, superior-subordinate relationship. Such requests will significantly affect his or her ability to accomplish the task described and defined by the vertical organization.

Authority and responsibility
Finally, a commonly heard prescription of classical theory is that authority must equal responsibility. In contrast, the essence of lateral relations is that the manager, in order to discharge his or her responsibilities effectively, must often interact with and depend upon individuals over whom he or she enjoys no formal authority.

Some dimensions in common that require different approaches (10)

Some dimensions are common to both vertical and lateral relations: (1) role legitimation, (2) mutual dependency, and (3) anticipation of role expectancies. However, it is likely that the approach to each dimension will differ significantly. An awareness of these differences will provide the manager with further insight into organizational behavior.

Role legitimation

Initiation of an activity, whether in lateral or in vertical relations, must be perceived by the manager as *legitimate* if it is to provide some basis for his or her acceptance. The traditional sources of legitimation are (1) positional power (organization structure), (2) competence of the individual, and (3) organizational requirements of the work situation. Vertical relationships seem to rely on (1) and to some extent (2), whereas lateral relationships concentrate on (2) and (3) as the basis of acceptance. The practical ramification of this distinction is that techniques and methods of initiating and directing activity in vertical relations will be inappropriate in lateral relations. In lateral relations, neither party generally possesses positional power over the other. The parties involved must therefore rely more extensively on establishing their competence if they expect their initiation of activities to be favorably recieved (legitimated).

Mutual dependency

Regardless of the relationship, whether vertical or lateral, some mutual dependency exists. However, the dependency in lateral relations is apt to differ in two ways from that in superior-subordinate relations. First the mutual dependency in lateral relations is likely to be more equal than in vertical relations.

Second, there will probably be several lines of lateral dependency, compared to the single superior-subordinate line in vertical relations. On a baseball team the manager-player relationship illustrates the inequality and single-line dimension of the vertical relationship. The interdependency of the players exemplifies the equality and multiline dimensions of the lateral relationship.

Anticipation of role expectancies

Because the subordinate has legitimated the authority of the superior (on a basis of demonstrated competence or positional power, for example), he or she tries to anticipate the actions and demands of the superior on whom he or she is dependent. Similarly, in lateral relations the manager tries to anticipate the actions and demands of those with whom he or she is interdependent in order to work more effectively. It is likely, however, that the *reasons* are different. The authors conjecture that the subordinate in a vertical relationship anticipates in order to gain favor with the superior, while the manager in a lateral relationship anticipates for the more impersonal reasons of improving his or her task effectiveness (11).

In this section we have described characteristics of lateral relations that lead one to question the applicability of certain classical management principles. This is not to say that traditional principles do not have merit. Rather, it implies that the effective manager, in addition to being familiar with classical management principles, must understand and be skilled in lateral relations. We stress that the manager must have a knowledge of lateral relations as well as of the vertical relations with which the classical model is concerned.

We have also identified three dimensions that are important in both vertical and lateral relations, but to which different approaches must be taken. Perhaps most important is the approach taken to role legitimation.

Lateral relations and current managerial concepts

In the preceding sections of this article, we have shown that an understanding of classical theory, with its focus on vertical relations, is inadequate for effective management performance. In particular, we have explored the nature and importance of lateral relations in order to provide greater insight into the complexity of the managerial role. The concept of lateral relations is incorporated in some of the stimulating thinking that is now evolving concerning effective management. This thinking recognizes that more effective means of achieving coordination must be found if the fruits of specialization are to be realized.

Linking pin

One approach has been to encourage the use of membership in more than one group or function (12). Likert describes such memberships as "linking pins," and suggests that they are important prerequisites to high performance.

The traditional organizational structure . . . consists of a man to man model of interaction, i.e., superior to subordinate.
A more effective approach, in contrast, uses an overlapping group form of structure with each work group linked to the rest of the organization by means of persons who are members of more than one group. These individuals who hold overlapping group memberships are called linking pins. (13)

Integrator

Whereas the linking pin seems to refer to a part-time role, Lawrence and Lorsch foresee the widespread use of a full-time position, which they entitle "the integrator":

one of the critical organizational innovations will be the establishment of management positions, and even formal departments, charged with the task of achieving (coordination). (14)

Lawrence and Lorsch indicate that the activities of the integrator would be similar to those now performed under such labels as "product manager," "project leader," and "task force chairman."

Boundary mediator

Another role, similar to those of the linking pin and the integrator, is that of the "boundary mediator" (15). The boundary mediator extends the coordination concept to coordination between the organization and its environment. In his or her role as a boundary mediator, a manager must interact with agents from the external environment and assimilate the results of this influence into the organization. For example, the plant manager might meet with local conservation groups to explore the company's impact on the local environment.

Summary

The manager's job is not an easy one. He or she finds, moreover, that the "book" is frequently amended, generally adding to the complexity of the managerial role. In the past, revisions generally have focused on how to make *vertical*, superior-subordinate relationships work better. For example, the manager has been required to develop a more sophisticated understanding of the relationship between subordinates' needs and performance. Recent revisions have underscored the importance of *lateral* relations. This article has reviewed the important aspects of lateral relations in an attempt to provide the manager with the perspective he or she needs for effective performance.

Notes

1 Charles R. Walker, Robert H. Guest, and Arthur N. Turner, *The Foreman on the Assembly Line* (Cambridge, Mass.: Harvard University Press, 1956); Leonard Sayles, *Managerial Behavior* (New York: McGraw-Hill, 1964); Henry A. Landsberger, "The Horizontal Dimension in Bureaucracy," *Administrative Science Quarterly* 6 (1961): 298–332.

2 For discussion of other criticisms of classical theory, see James G. March and Herbert A. Simon, *Organizations* (New York: John Wiley & Sons, 1958), Chapter 3; and Edgar H. Schein, *Organization Psychology* (Englewood Cliffs, N.J.: Prentice-Hall, 1965), Chapter 4.

3 Landsberger, p. 302; and George Strauss, "Tactics of Lateral Relationships: The Purchasing Agent," *Administrative Science Quarterly* 7 (1962): 161–186

4 Sayles, pp. 49–54.

5 Ibid., pp. 59–60.

6 For a review of comparative studies, see Raymond G. Hunt, "Technology and Organization," *Academy of Management Journal* (September 1970): 235–252.

7 Paul R. Lawrence and Jay W. Lorsch, *Organization and Environment* (Boston: Division of Research, Graduate School of Business Administration, Harvard University, 1967).

8 Ibid., p. 97.

9 This section is based on the work of Sayles, pp. 41–43.

10 This section is based on the work of Landsberger, pp. 308–311.

11 For an excellent discussion concerning the tendency of organizational members to defer to those with positional authority, see Robert Presthus, *The Organizational Society* (New York: Vintage Books, 1962), especially Chapter 4.

12 Rensis Likert, *The Human Organization* (New York: McGraw-Hill, 1967).

13 Ibid., p. 50.

14 Paul R. Lawrence and Jay W. Lorsch, "New Management Job: The Integrator," *Harvard Business Review* (November–December 1967): 142–151.

15 Keith Davis and Robert Blomstrom, *Business, Society and Environment: Social Power and Social Response* (New York: McGraw-Hill, 1971), pp. 76–77.

16 Committee management: Guidelines from social science research
A. C. Filley

The committee is one of the most maligned, yet most frequently employed forms of organization structure. Yet despite the criticisms, committees are a fact of organization life. For example, a recent survey of 1,200 respondents revealed that 94 percent of firms with more than 10,000 employees and 64 percent with less than 250 employees reported having formal committees.[1] And, a survey of organization practices in 620 Ohio manufacturing firms showed a similar positive relationship between committee use and plant size.[2] These studies clearly indicate that committees are one of management's important organizational tools.

My thesis is that committee effectiveness can be increased by applying social science findings to answer such questions as:

Source: © 1970 by the Regents of the University of California. Reprinted from *California Management Review,* volume XIII, number 1 (Fall 1970), pp. 13–21, by permission of the Regents.

1 Rollie Tillman, Jr., "Problems in Review: Committees on Trial," *Harvard Business Review,* 38 (May–June 1960), 6–12, 162–172. Firms with 1,001 to 10,000 reported 93 percent use; 250 to 1,000 reported 82 percent use.

2 J. H. Healey, *Executive Coordination and Control,* Monograph No. 78 (Columbus: Bureau of Business Research, The Ohio State University, 1956), p. 185.

- What functions do committees serve?
- What size should committees be?
- What is the appropriate style of leadership for committee chairmen?
- What mix of member characteristics makes for effective committee performance?

Committee purposes and functions

Committees are set up to pursue economy and efficiency within the enterprise. They do not create direct salable value, nor do they supervise operative employees who create such value.

The functions of the committee have been described by business executives as the exchange of views and information, recommending action, generating ideas, and making major decisions,[3] of which the first may well be the most common. After observing seventy-five conferences (which were also referred to as "committees"), Kriesberg concluded that most were concerned either with communicating information or with aiding an executive's decision process.[4] Executives said they called conferences to "sell" ideas rather than for group decision making itself. As long as the executive does not manipulate the group covertly, but benefits by its ideas and screening processes, this activity is probably quite legitimate, for members are allowed to influence and to participate, to some extent, in executive decision making.

Some committees also make specific operating decisions which commit individuals and organization units to prescribed goals and policies. Such is often the province of the general management committee composed of major executive officers. According to one survey, 30.3 percent of the respondents reported that their firms had such a committee and that the committees averaged 8.6 members and met 27 times per year.[5]

Several of the characteristics of committee organization have been the subject of authoritative opinion, or surveys of current practice, and lend themselves to evaluation through inferences from small-group research. Current practice and authoritative opinion are reviewed here, followed by more rigorous studies in which criteria of effectiveness are present. The specific focus is on committee size, membership, and chairmen.

Committee size

Current practice and opinion

The typical committee should be, and is, relatively small. Recommended sizes range from three to nine members, and surveys of actual practice sel-

[3] "Committees," *Management Review,* 46 (October 1957), 4–10; 75–78.
[4] M. Kriesberg, "Executives Evaluate Administrative Conferences," *Advanced Management,* 15 (March 1950), 15–17.
[5] Tillman, *op. cit.,* p. 12.

dom miss these prescriptions by much. Of the 1,658 committees recorded in the *Harvard Business Review* survey, the average membership was eight. When asked for their preference, the 79 percent who answered suggested an ideal committee size that averaged 4.6 members. Similarly, Kriesberg reported that, for the 75 conferences analyzed, there were typically five or six conferees in the meetings studied.[6]

Committees in the federal government tend to be larger than those in business. In the House of Representatives, Appropriations is the largest standing committee, with fifty members, and the Committee on Un-American Activities is smallest, with nine. Senate committees average thirteen members; the largest, also Appropriations, has twenty-three.[7] The problem of large committee size is overcome by the use of subcommittees and closed executive committee meetings. The larger committees seem to be more collections of subgroups than truly integrated operating units. In such cases, it would be interesting to know the size of the subcommittees.

Inferences from small-group research

The extent to which a number is "ideal" may be measured in part in terms of the effects that size has on socio-emotional relations among group members and thus the extent to which the group operates as an integrated whole, rather than as fragmented subunits. Another criterion is how size affects the quality of the group's decision and the time required to reach it. Several small experimental group studies have evaluated the effect of size on group process.

Variables related to changes in group size include the individual's capacity to "attend" to differing numbers of objects, the effect of group size on interpersonal relations and communication, its impact on problem-solving functions, and the "feelings" that group members have about proper group size and the nature of group performance. To be sure, the effects of these variables are interrelated.

Attention to the group
Each member in a committee attends both to the group as a whole and to each individual as a member of the group. There seem to be limits on a person's ability to perfrom both of these processes—limits which vary with the size of the group and the time available. For example, summarizing a study by Taves,[8] Hare[9] reports that "Experiments on estimating the number of dots in a visual field with very short-time exposures indicate individual subjects can report the exact number up to and including seven with great

---

[6] Kriesberg, *op. cit.,* p. 15.
[7] "The Committee System—Congress at Work," *Congressional Digest,* 34 (February 1955), 47–49; 64.
[8] E. H. Taves, "Two Mechanisms for the Perception of Visual Numerousness," *Archives of Psychology,* 37 (1941), 265.
[9] A. Paul Hare, *Handbook of Small Group Research,* (New York: The Free Press of Glencoe, 1962), p. 227.

confidence and practically no error, but above that number confidence and accuracy drop."

Perhaps for similar reasons, when two observers assessed leadership characteristics in problem-solving groups of college students, the raters reached maximum agreement in groups of six, rather than in two, four, eight, or twelve.[10]

The apparent limits on one's ability to attend both to the group and the individuals within it led Hare to conclude:

The coincidence of these findings suggests that the ability of the observing individual to perceive, keep track of, and judge each member separately in a social interaction situation may not extend much beyond the size of six or seven. If this is true, one would expect members of groups larger than that size to tend to think of other members in terms of subgroups, or "classes" of some kind, and to deal with members of subgroups other than their own by more stereotyped methods of response.[11]

Interpersonal relations and communication

Given a meeting lasting a fixed length of time, the opportunity for each individual to communicate is reduced, and the type of communication becomes differential among group members. Bales *et al.*[12] have shown that in groups of from three to eight members the proportion of infrequent contributors increases at a greater rate than that theoretically predicted from decreased opportunity to communicate. Similarly, in groups of from four to twelve, as reported by Stephen and Mishler,[13] size was related positively to the difference between participation initiated by the most active and the next most active person.

Increasing the group size seems to limit the extent to which individuals want to communicate, as well. For example, Gibb[14] studied idea productivity in forty-eight groups in eight size categories from 1 to 96. His results indicated that as group size increases a steadily increasing proportion of group members report feelings of threat and less willingness to initiate contributions. Similarly, Slater's[15] study of 24 groups of from two to seven men each working on a human relations problem indicated that members of the larger groups felt them to be disorderly and time-consuming, and complained that other members became too pushy, aggressive, and competitive.

[10] B. M. Bass, and F. M. Norton, "Group Size and Leaderless Discussions," *Journal of Applied Psychology,* 35 (1951), 397–400.

[11] Hare, *op. cit.,* p. 228.

[12] R. F. Bales, R. L. Strodtbeck, T. M. Mills, and M. E. Roseborough, "Channels of Communication in Small Groups," *American Sociological Review,* 16 (1951), 461–468.

[13] F. F. Stephen and E. G. Mishler, "The Distribution of Participation in Small Groups: An Exponential Approximation." *American Sociological Review,* 17 (1952), 598–608.

[14] J. R. Gibb, "The Effects of Group Size and of Threat Reduction Upon Creativity in a Problem-Solving Situation," *American Psychologist,* 6 (1951), 324. (Abstract)

[15] P. Slater, "Contrasting Correlates of Group Size," *Sociometry,* 21 (1958), 129–139.

Functions and conflict

An increase in group size seems to distort the pattern of communication and create stress in some group members, yet a decrease in group size also has dysfunctional effects. In the Slater study checklist responses by members rating smaller groups of 2, 3, or 4 were complimentary, rather than critical, as they had been for larger groups. Yet observer impressions were that small groups engaged in superficial discussion and avoided controversial subjects. Inferences from post hoc analysis suggested that small group members are too tense, passive, tactful, and constrained to work together in a satisfying manner. They are afraid of alienating others. Similar results have been reported in other studies regarding the inhibitions created by small group size, particularly in groups of two.[16]

Groups of three have the problem of an overpowerful majority, since two members can form a coalition against the unsupported third member. Four-member groups provide mutual support when two members oppose the other two, but such groups have higher rates of disagreement and antagonism than odd-numbered groups.[17]

The data reported above are not altogether consistent regarding the reasons for dysfunctional consequences of small groups. The "trying-too-hard-for-agreement" of the Slater study seems at odds with the conflict situations posed in the groups of three and four, yet both agree that for some reason tension is present.

Groups of five

While it is always dangerous to generalize about "ideal" numbers (or types, for that matter), there does appear to be logical and empirical support for groups of five members as a suitable size, if the necessary skills are possessed by the five members. In the Slater study, for example, none of the subjects felt that a group of five was too small or too large to carry out the assigned task, though they objected to the other sizes (two, three, four, six, and seven). Slater concluded:

Size five emerged clearly . . . as the size group which from the subjects' viewpoint was most effective in dealing with an intellectual task involving the collection and exchange of information about a situation, the coordination analysis, and evaluation of this information, and a group decision regarding the appropriate administrative action to be taken in the situation. . . . These findings suggest that maximal group satisfaction is achieved when the group is large enough so that the members feel able to express positive and negative feelings freely, and to make aggressive efforts toward problem solving even at the risk of antagonizing each other, yet small enough so that some regard will be shown for the feelings and needs of others; large

[16] R. F. Bales, and E. F. Borgotta, "Size of Group as a Factor in the Interaction Profile," in *Small Groups: Studies in Social Interaction,* A. P. Hare, E. F. Borgotta, and R. F. Bales, eds. (New York: Knopf, 1965, rev. ed.), pp. 495–512.

[17] *Ibid.,* p. 512.

enough so that the loss of a member could be tolerated, but small enough so that such a loss could not be altogether ignored.[18]

From this and other studies,[19] it appears that, excluding productivity measures, generally the optimum size of problem-solving groups is five. Considering group performance in terms of quality, speed, efficiency and productivity, the effect of size is less clear. Where problems are complex, relatively larger groups have been shown to produce better quality decisions. For example, in one study, groups of 12 or 13 produced higher quality decisions than groups of 6, 7, or 8.[20] Others have shown no differences among groups in the smaller size categories (2 to 7). Relatively smaller groups are often faster and more productive. For example, Hare found that groups of five take less time to make decisions than groups of 12.[21]

Several studies have also shown that larger groups are able to solve a greater variety of problems because of the variety of skills likely to increase with group size.[22] However, there is a point beyond which committee size should not increase because of diminishing returns. As group size increases coordination of the group tends to become difficult, and thus it becomes harder for members to reach consensus and to develop a spirit of teamwork and cohesiveness.

In general, it would appear that with respect to performance, a task which requires interaction, consensus and modification of opinion requires a relatively small group. On the other hand, where the task is one with clear criteria of correct performance, the addition of more members may increase group performance.

The chairman

Current practice and opinion

Most people probably serve on some type of committee in the process of participating in church, school, political, or social organizations and while in that capacity have observed the effect of the chairman on group progress. Where the chairman starts the meeting, for example, by saying, "Well, we all know each other here, so we'll dispense with any formality," the group flounders, until someone else takes a forceful, directive role.

If the committee is to be successful, it must have a chairman who

---

[18] Slater, *op. cit.,* 137–138.

[19] R. F. Bales, "In Conference," *Harvard Business Review,* 32 (March–April 1954), 44–50; also A. P. Hare, "A Study of Interaction and Consensus in Different Sized Groups," *American Sociological Review,* 17 (1952), 261–267.

[20] D. Fox, I. Lorge, P. Weltz, and K. Herrold, "Comparison of Decisions Written by Large and Small Groups," *American Psychologist,* 8 (1953), 351 (Abstract).

[21] A. Paul Hare, "Interaction and Consensus in Different Sized Groups," *American Sociological Review,* 17 (1952), 261–267.

[22] G. B. Watson, "Do Groups Think More Efficiently Than Individuals?" *Journal of Abnormal and Social Psychology,* 23 (1928), 328–336; Also D. J. Taylor and W. L. Faust, "Twenty Questions: Efficiency in Problem Solving as a Function of Size of Group," *Journal of Experimental Psychology,* 44 (1952), 360–368.

understands group process. He must know the objectives of the committee and understand the problems at hand. He should be able to vary decision strategies according to the nature of the task and the feelings of the group members. He needs the acceptance of the group members and their confidence in his personal integrity. And he needs the skill to resist needless debate and to defer discussion upon issues which are not pertinent or where the committee lacks the facts upon which to act.

Surveys of executive opinion support these impressions of the chairman's role. *The Harvard Business Review* survey stated that "The great majority (of the suggestions from survey respondents) lead to this conclusion: the problem is not so much committees in management as it is the management of committees." This comment by a partner in a large management consulting firm was cited as typical:

Properly used, committees can be most helpful to a company. Most of the criticism I have run into, while probably justified, deals with the way in which committees are run (or committee meetings are run) and not with the principle of working with committees. [23]

A chairman too loose in his control of committee processes is by no means the only difficulty encountered. Indeed, the chronic problem in the federal government has been the domination of committee processes by the chairman. This results from the way in which the chairman is typically selected: he is traditionally the member of the majority party having the longest uninterrupted service on the committee. The dangers in such domination have been described as follows:

If there is a piece of legislation that he does not like, he kills it by declining to schedule a hearing on it. He usually appoints no standing subcommittees and he arranges the special subcommittees in such a way that his personal preferences are taken into account. Often there is no regular agenda at the meetings of his committee—when and if it meets . . . they proceed with an atmosphere of apathy, with junior members, especially, feeling frustrated and left out, like first graders at a seventh grade party. [24]

Inferences from small group research

The exact nature of the chairman's role is further clarified when we turn to more rigorous studies on group leadership.

We shall confine our discussion here to leader roles and functions, using three approaches. First, we shall discuss the nature of task leadership in the group and the apparent reasons for this role. Then we shall view more specifically the different roles which the leader or leaders of the group may play. Finally, we shall consider the extent to which these more specific roles may be combined in a single individual.

[23] Tillman, *op. cit.,* p. 168.
[24] S. L. Udall, "Defense of the Seniority System," *New York Times Magazine* (January 13, 1957), 17.

Leader control

Studies of leadership in task-oriented, decision-making groups show a functional need for and, indeed, a member preference for directive influence by the chairman. The nature of this direction is illustrated in a study by Schlesinger, Jackson, and Butman.[25] The problem was to examine the influence process among leaders and members of small problem-solving groups when the designated leaders varied on the rated degree of control exerted. One hundred six members of twenty-three management committees participated in the study. As part of an initial investigation, committee members described in a questionnaire the amount of control and regulation which each member exercised when in the role of chairman. Each committee was then given a simulated but realistic problem for 1.5 hours, under controlled conditions and in the presence of three observers.

The questionnaire data showed that individuals seen as high in control were rated as more skillful chairmen and as more valuable contributors to the committee's work.

The study also demonstrated that leadership derives from group acceptance rather than from the unique acts of the chairman. "When the participants do not perceive the designated leader as satisfactorily performing the controlling functions, the participants increase their own attempts to influence their fellow members."[26] The acceptance of the leader was based upon task (good ideas) and chairmanship skills and had little to do with his personal popularity as a group member.

The importance of chairman control in committee action has been similarly demonstrated in several other studies.[27] In his study of 72 management conferences, for example, Berkowitz[28] found that a high degree of "leadership sharing" was related inversely to participant satisfaction and to a measure of output. The norms of these groups sanctioned a "take-charge" chairman. When the chairman failed to meet these expectations, he was rejected and both group satisfaction and group output suffered. These studies do not necessarily suggest that committees less concerned with task goals also prefer a directive chairman. Where the committees are composed of more socially oriented members, the preference for leader control may be less strong.[29]

---

[25] L. Schlesinger, J. M. Jackson, and J. Butman, "Leader-Member Interaction in Management Committees," *Journal of Abnormal and Social Psychology,* 61, No. 3 (1960), 360–364.

[26] *Ibid.,* p. 363.

[27] L. Berkowitz, "Sharing Leadership in Small Decision-Making Groups," *Journal of Abnormal and Social Psychology,* 48 (1953), 231–238; Also N. T. Fouriezos, M. L. Hutt, and H. Guetzkow, "Measurement of Self-Oriented Needs in Discussion Groups," *Journal of Abnormal and Social Psychology,* 45 (1950), 682–690; also H. P. Shelley, "Status Consensus, Leadership, and Satisfaction with the Group," *Journal of Social Psychology,* 51 (1960), 157–164.

[28] Berkowitz, *ibid.,* p. 237.

[29] R. C. Anderson, "Learning in Discussions: A Resume of the Authoritarian-Democratic Studies," *Harvard Education Review,* 29 (1959), 201–214.

Leadership roles

A second approach to understanding the leadership of committees is to investigate leadership roles in small groups. Pervading the research literature is a basic distinction between group activities directed to one or the other of two types of roles performed by leaders. They are defined by Benne and Sheats[30] as task roles, and as group-building and maintenance roles. Task roles are related to the direct accomplishment of group purpose, such as seeking information, initiating, evaluating, and seeking or giving opinion. The latter roles are concerned with group integration and solidarity through encouraging, harmonizing, compromising, and reducing conflict.

Several empirical investigations of leadership have demonstrated that both roles are usually performed within effective groups.[31] However, these roles are not always performed by the same person. Frequently one member is seen as the "task leader" and another as the "social leader" of the group.

Combined task and social roles

Can or should these roles be combined in a single leader? The prototypes of the formal and the informal leader which we inherit from classical management lore tend to lead to the conclusion that such a combination is somehow impossible or perhaps undesirable. The research literature occasionally supports this point of view as well.

There is much to be said for a combination of roles. Several studies have shown that outstanding leaders are those who possess both task and social orientations.[32] The study by Borgotta, Couch, and Bales illustrates the point. These researchers assigned leaders high on both characteristics to problem-solving groups. The eleven leaders whom they called "great men" were selected from 126 in an experiment on the basis of high task ability, individual assertiveness, and social acceptability. These men also retained their ratings as "great men" throughout a series of different problem-solving sessions. When led by "great men" the groups achieved a higher rate of suggestion and agreement, a lower rate of "showing tension," and higher rates of showing solidarity and tension release than comparable groups without "great men."

[30] K. D. Benne, and P. Sheats, "Functional Roles of Group Members," *Journal of Social Issues,* 4 (Spring 1948), 41–49.
[31] R. F. Bales, *Interaction Process Analysis* (Cambridge: Addison-Wesley, 1951); Also R. M. Stogdill and A. E. Coons (eds.), *Leader Behavior: Its Description and Measurement,* Monograph No. 88 (Columbus: Bureau of Business Research, The Ohio State University, 1957); Also A. W. Halpin, "The Leadership Behavior and Combat Performance of Airplane Commanders," *Journal of Abnormal and Social Psychology,* 49 (1954), 19–22.
[32] E. G. Borgotta, A. S. Couch, and R. F. Bales, "Some Findings Relevant to the Great Man Theory of Leadership," *American Sociological Review,* 19 (1954), 755–759; Also E. A. Fleishman, and E. G. Harris, "Patterns of Leadership Behavior Related to Employee Grievances and Turnover," *Personnel Psychology,* 15, No. 1 (1962), 43–56; Also Stogdill and Coons, *ibid.;* Also H. Oaklander and E. A. Fleishman, "Patterns of Leadership Related to Organizational Stress in Hospital Settings," *Administrative Science Quarterly,* 8 (March 1964), 520–532.

When viewed collectively two conclusions emerge from the above studies. Consistent with existing opinion, the leader who is somewhat assertive and who takes charge and controls group proceedings is performing a valid and necessary role. However, such task leadership is a necessary but not a sufficient condition for effective committee performance. Someone in the group must perform the role of group-builder and maintainer of social relations among the members. Ideally both roles should probably be performed by the designated chairman. When he does not have the necessary skills to perform both roles, he should be the task leader and someone else should perform the social leadership role. Effective committee performance requires both roles to be performed, by a single person or by complementary performance of two or more members.

Committee membership

The atmosphere of committee operations described in the classic literature is one where all members seem to be cooperating in the achievement of committee purpose. It is unclear, however, if cooperation is necessarily the best method of solving problems, or if competition among members or groups of members might not achieve more satisfactory results. Cooperation also seems to imply a sharing or homogeneity of values. To answer the question we must consider two related problems: the effects of cooperation or competition on committee effectiveness, and the effects of homogeneous or heterogeneous values on committee effectiveness.

Cooperation or competition

A number of studies have contrasted the impact of competition and cooperation on group satisfaction and productivity. In some cases the group is given a cooperative or competitive "treatment" through direction or incentive when it is established. In others, competition and cooperation are inferred from measures of groups in which members are operating primarily for personal interest, in contrast with groups in which members are more concerned with group needs. These studies show rather consistently that "group members who have been motivated to cooperate show more positive responses to each other, are more favorable in their perceptions, are more involved in the task, and have greater satisfaction with the task."[33]

The best known study regarding the effects of cooperation and competition was conducted by Deutsch[34] in ten experimental groups of college students, each containing five persons. Each group met for one three-hour period a week for six weeks, working on puzzles and human relations problems. Subjects completed a weekly and post-experimental questionnaire.

[33] Hare, *Handbook of Small Group Research, op. cit.,* p. 254.
[34] M. Deutsch, "The Effects of Cooperation and Competition Upon Group Process," in *Group Dynamics, Research and Theory,* D. Cartwright and A. Zander, eds. (New York: Harper and Row, 1953).

Observers also recorded interactions and completed over-all rating scales at the end of each problem.

In some groups, a cooperative atmosphere was established by instructing members that the group as a whole would be evaluated in comparison with four similar groups, and that each person's course grade would depend upon the performance of the group itself. In others, a competitive relationship was established by telling the members that each would receive a different grade, depending upon his relative contribution to the group's problem solutions.

The results, as summarized by Hare, show that:

Compared with the competitively organized groups, the cooperative groups had the following characteristics:

1 Stronger individual motivation to complete the group task and stronger feelings of obligation toward other members.
2 Greater division of labor both in content and frequency of interaction among members and greater coordination of effort.
3 More effective inter-member communication. More ideas were verbalized, members were more attentive to one another, and more accepting of and affected by each other's ideas. Members also rated themselves as having fewer difficulties in communicating and understanding others.
4 More friendliness was expressed in the discussion and members rated themselves higher on strength of desire to win the respect of one another. Members were also more satisfied with the group and its products.
5 More group productivity. Puzzles were solved faster and the recommendations produced for the human-relations problems were longer and qualitatively better. However, there were no significant differences in the average individual productivity as a result of the two types of group experience nor were there any clear differences in the amounts of individual learning which occurred during the discussions.[35]

Similar evidence was found in the study of 72 decision-making conferences by Fouriezos, Hutt, and Guetzkow.[36] Based on observer ratings of self-oriented need behavior, correlational evidence showed that such self-centered behavior was positively related to participant ratings of high group conflict and negatively related to participant satisfaction, group solidarity, and task productivity.

In general, the findings of these and other studies suggest that groups in which members share in goal attainment, rather than compete privately or otherwise seek personal needs, will be more satisfied and productive.[37]

---

[35] Hare, *Handbook of Small Group Research, op. cit.,* p. 263.
[36] Fouriezos, Hutt, and Guetzkow, *op. cit.*
[37] C. Stendler, D. Damrin and A. Haines, "Studies in Cooperation and Competition: I. The Effects of Working for Group and Individual Rewards on the Social Climate of Children's Groups," *Journal of Genetic Psychology,* 79 (1951), 173–197; Also A. Mintz, "Nonadaptive Group Behavior," *Journal of Abnormal and Social Psychology,* 46 (1951), 150–159; Also M. M. Grossack, "Some Effects of Cooperation and Competition Upon Small Group Behavior," *Journal of Abnormal and Social Psychology,* 49

Homogeneity or heterogeneity

The effects of member composition in the committee should also be considered from the standpoint of the homogeneity or heterogeneity of its membership. Homogeneous groups are those in which members are similar in personality, value orientation, attitudes to supervision, or predisposition to accept or reject fellow members. Heterogeneity is induced in the group by creating negative expectations regarding potential contributions by fellow members, by introducing differing personality types into the group, or by creating subgroups which differ in their basis of attraction to the group.

Here the evidence is much less clear. Some homogeneous groups become satisfied and quite unproductive, while others become satisfied and quite productive. Similarly, heterogeneity may be shown to lead to both productive and unproductive conditions. While the answer to this paradox may be related to the different definitions of homogeneity or heterogeneity in the studies, it appears to have greater relevance to the task and interpersonal requirements of the group task.

In some studies, homogeneity clearly leads to more effective group performance. The work of Schutz[38] is illustrative. In his earlier writing, Schutz distinguished between two types of interpersonal relationships: power orientation and personal orientation. The first emphasizes authority symbols. The power-oriented person follows rules and adjusts to external systems of authority. People with personal orientations emphasize interpersonal considerations. They assume that the way a person achieves his goal is by working within a framework of close personal relations, that is, by being a "good guy," by liking others, by getting people to like him. In his later work, Schutz[39] distinguished among three types of needs: *inclusion,* or the need to establish and maintain a satisfactory relation with people with respect to interaction and association; *control,* or the need to establish and maintain a satisfactory relation with people with respect to control and power; and *affection,* or the need to establish and maintain a satisfactory relation with others with respect to love and affection.

Using attitude scales, Schutz established four groups in which people were compatible with respect to high needs for personal relations with others, four whose members were compatible with respect to low personal orientation, and four which contained subgroups differing in these needs. Each of the twelve groups met twelve times over a period of six weeks and participated in a series of different tasks.

The results showed that groups which are compatible, either on a basis of personalness or counter-personalness, were significantly more productive than groups which had incompatible subgroups. There was no significant difference between the productivity of the two types of compatible

(1954), 341–348; Also E. Gottheil, "Changes in Social Perceptions Contingent Upon Competing or Cooperating," *Sociometry,* 18 (1955), 132–137; Also A. Zander and D. Wolfe, "Administrative Rewards and Coordination Among Committee Members," *Administrative Science Quarterly,* 9 (June 1964), 50–69.

38 W. C. Schutz, "What Makes Groups Productive?" *Human Relations,* 8 (1955), 429–465.

39 W. C. Schutz, *FIRO: A Three-Dimensional Theory of Interpersonal Behavior,* (New York: Holt, Rinehart and Winston, 1958).

groups. As might be expected, the difference in productivity between compatible and incompatible groups was greatest for tasks which required the most interaction and agreement under conditions of high time pressure.

A similar positive relationship between homogeneity and productivity is reported for groups in which compatibility is established on the basis of prejudice or degree of conservatism, managerial personality traits, congeniality induced by directions from the researcher, or status congruence.[40] In Adams' study, technical performance first increased, then decreased, as status congruence became greater. Group social performance increased continuously with greater homogeneity, however.

The relationship posited above does not always hold, however. In some studies, heterogeneous groups were more productive than homogeneous. For example, Hoffman[41] constructed heterogeneous and homogeneous groups, based on personality profiles, and had them work on two different types of problems. On the first, which required consideration of a wide range of alternatives of a rather specific nature, heterogeneous groups produced significantly superior solutions. On the second problem, which required primarily group consensus and had no objectively "good" solution, the difference between group types was not significant. Ziller[42] also found heterogeneity to be associated with the ability of Air Force crews to judge the number of dots on a card.

Collins and Guetzkow[43] explain these contradictory findings by suggesting that increasing heterogeneity has at least two effects on group interaction: it increases the difficulty of building interpersonal relations, and it increases the problem-solving potential of the group, since errors are eliminated, more alternatives are generated, and wider criticism is possible. Thus, heterogeneity would seem to be valuable where the needs for task facilitation are greater than the need for strong interpersonal relations.

Considering our original question, it appears that, from the standpoint of cooperation versus competition in committees, the cooperative committee is to be preferred. If we look at the effects of homogeneous or heterogeneous committee membership, the deciding factor seems to be the nature of the task and the degree of interpersonal conflict which the committee can tolerate.

[40] I. Altman and E. McGinnies, "Interpersonal Perception and Communication in Discussion Groups of Varied Attitudinal Composition," *Journal of Abnormal and Social Psychology,* 60 (May 1960), 390–393; Also W. A. Haythorn, E. H. Couch, D. Haefner, P. Langham and L. Carter, "The Behavior of Authoritarian and Equalitarian Personalities in Groups," *Human Relations,* 9 (1956), 57–74; Also E. E. Ghiselli and T. M. Lodahl, "Patterns of Managerial Traits and Group Effectiveness," *Journal of Abnormal and Social Psychology,* 57 (1958), 61–66; Also R. V. Exline, "Group Climate as a Factor in the Relevance and Accuracy of Social Perception," *Journal of Abnormal and Social Psychology,* 55 (1957), 382–388; Also S. Adams, "Status Congruency as a Variable in Small Group Performance, *Social Forces,* 32 (1953), 16–22.
[41] L. R. Hoffman, "Homogeneity of Member Personality and Its Effect on Group Problem-Solving, *Journal of Abnormal and Social Psychology* 58 (1959), 27–32.
[42] R. C. Ziller, "Scales of Judgment: A Determinant of Accuracy of Group Decisions," *Human Relations,* 8 (1955), 153–164.
[43] B. E. Collins and H. Guetzkow, *A Social Psychology of Group Process for Decision-Making,* (New York: John Wiley and Sons, 1965), p. 101.

Summary and conclusions

Research findings regarding committee size, leadership, and membership have been reviewed. Evidence has been cited showing that the ideal size is five, when the five members possess the necessary skills to solve the problems facing the committee. Viewed from the standpoint of the committee members' ability to attend to both the group and its members, or from the standpoint of balanced interpersonal needs, it seems safe to suggest that this number has normative value in planning committee operations. For technical problems additional members may be added to ensure the provision of necessary skills.

A second area of investigation concerned the functional separation of the leadership role and the influence of the role on other members. The research reviewed supports the notion that the committee chairman should be directive in his leadership, but a more specific definition of leadership roles makes questionable whether the chairman can or should perform as both the task and the social leader of the group. The evidence regarding the latter indicates that combined task and social leadership is an ideal which is seldom attained, but should be sought.

The final question concerned whether committee membership would be most effective when cooperative or competitive. When evaluated from the standpoint of research on cooperative versus competitive groups, it is clear that cooperative membership is more desirable. Committee operation can probably be enhanced by selecting members whose self-centered needs are of less intense variety and by directions to the group which strengthen motivations of a cooperative nature. When the proposition is evaluated from the standpoint of heterogeneity or homogeneity of group membership, the conclusion is less clear. Apparently, heterogeneity in a group can produce both ideas and a screening process for evaluating their quality, but the advantage of this process depends upon the negative effects of heterogeneous attitudes upon interpersonal cooperation.

III/F
Organizational design

17 Principles of organization
S. Avery Raube

Organization principles

Like the engineer who designs his bridge to meet special needs, the organization planner, in designing a company structure, applies principles. For through years of experience it has been learned that if certain principles are followed, regardless of the size of the enterprise, the result will be good organization. Some of these basic laws follow:

1 *There must be clear lines of authority running from the top to the bottom of the organization.*

Lt. Col. Lyndall Urwick[1] defines authority as "the formal right to require action of others." Mr. R. E. Gillmore[2] says it is "the right to direct, coordinate and decide."

Clarity is achieved through delegation by steps or levels from the leader to the working level, from the highest executive to the employee who has least responsibility in the organization and no authority over others. From the president, a line of authority may proceed to a vice president, to a general manager, to a foreman, to a leadman, and finally to a worker on an assembly line. It should be possible to trace such a line from the president, or whoever is top coordinating executive, to every employee in the company.

Following military parlance, this line is sometimes referred to as "the chain of command." The principle is known as the "scalar principle." It is the vertical division of authority.

Source: Reprinted with permission from *Company Organization Charts*. New York: National Industrial Conference Board (1954), pp. 7–13.
[1] Eminent British specialist in the field of organization.
[2] Vice-President, the Sperry Corporation, and author of many articles on organization subjects.

2 *No one in the organization should report to more than one line supervisor. Everyone in the organization should know to whom he reports, and who reports to him.*

This is known as the "unity of command" principle. Stated simply, everyone should have only one boss.

This principle is one of those most frequently violated and the cause of many internal difficulties. It may be a matter of several stenographers working for a group of executives, any one of whom can require directly the services of any of the individual girls. The best of the stenographers is overloaded with work; the least efficient has nothing to do.[3] It may be a matter of partners running a business, with each giving orders independently to the executive vice president.

The harassed individual who receives orders from several bosses is faced with problems such as whose orders to follow first, how to allocate his time so as to displease none and satisfy all, what to do if he receives conflicting orders from different sources. The lazy employee is afforded an excellent opportunity to avoid work by explaining to one boss that he cannot accept more tasks because he is busy carrying out (imaginary) assignments given by another.

3 *The responsibility and authority of each supervisor should be clearly defined in writing.*

Putting his responsibilities into writing enables the supervisor, himself, to know what is expected of him and the limits of his authority. It prevents overlapping of authority, with resultant confusion. It avoids gaps between responsibilities. And it enables quick determination of the proper point for decision.

Many executives say complacently, "We all know what we are supposed to do. There is no need to put our duties in writing." But in many companies management has been startled when top executives have been asked, independently, to list their duties. It is an eye-opener to discover that three and four individuals believe themselves responsible for an identical function, and that time and money are being wasted in duplicated effort. Therein, too, lie the seeds of jurisdictional dispute.

When an executive is lost suddenly, through death or lure of a competitor, it is not uncommon to find that no one knows exactly what the executive did, and therefore what to require of his successor. Even when a vacancy is expected, it is difficult to train a replacement without an accurate knowledge of the content of the position.

---

[3] In secretarial "pools," this situation is avoided and the principle adhered to by having all of the stenographers report to a single supervisor who receives all requests for stenographic assistance and assigns work to the individuals.

4 *Responsibility should always be coupled with corresponding authority.*

This principle suggests that if a plant manager in multi-unit organization is held responsible for all activities in his plant, he should not be subject to *orders* from company headquarters specifying the quantity of raw materials he should buy or from whom he should purchase them.[4] If a supervisor is responsible for the quality of work put out in his department, he should not have to accept as a member of his working force an employee who has been hired without consulting him.

There are many executives who delegate authority and then undermine it by making decisions that belong to the individual who is being held responsible. Over a luncheon table a company president makes a promise of delivery to a favored customer, which upsets the carefully planned schedules of the sales manager. A plant superintendent makes a casual statement to the press which strews rocks in the path of the director of public relations.

This principle can be stated conversely: "Authority should always be coupled with corresponding responsibility." Those given authority, unless they are held accountable, may easily become dictators.

5 *The responsibility of higher authority for the acts of its subordinates is absolute.*

Lt. Col. Urwick has expressed the principle in these words. Another way of saying it is that although a supervisor delegates authority, he still remains responsible for what is done by those to whom he has delegated it.

The head of maintenance is responsible for keeping the plant lighting systems in order. He does not screw a new electric light bulb in place when an old one burns out. That responsibility has been delegated to the plant electrician. But if the electrician fails to replace a bulb when one is needed, the head of maintenance is as accountable as the electrician. He is responsible for the electrician's inefficiency.

In accord with this principle, an executive cannot disassociate himself from the acts of his subordinates. He is as responsible as they, for what they do and neglect to do.

6 *Authority should be delegated as far down the line as possible.*

Permitting decisions to be made on as low a level as possible releases the energies of those on higher levels for matters which only they can attend to. The head of a pottery factory does not concern himself with whether the rose on the breakfast plate is to be red or yellow. The head of a large company does not personally sign every paycheck or personally approve the

---

[4] He may, however, welcome advice or suggestions from a purchasing specialist on the company's central staff.

salary increase of every typist. For those are duties that may easily and efficiently be delegated farther down the line.

Application of this principle can be observed in the current trend toward decentralization of large companies. Decision-making power is being placed nearer the scene of action. The plant or division manager is allowed to make all decisions in his unit, within the confines of a company-wide policy. This enables members of top corporate management to devote more time to over-all thinking and planning.

7 *The number of levels of authority should be kept at a minimum.*

The greater the number of levels, the longer is the chain of command, and the longer it takes for instructions to travel down and for information to travel up and down within the organization.

Too many levels encourage "run-arounds." To obtain a quicker decision, a worker fails to consult his immediate supervisor, but appeals to an executive higher up the line.

Mr. Gillmore has figured out mathematically that most organizations would never need more than six levels of supervision, including that of the top executive. With six such levels, he says, with a span of control of five at the top levels, and twenty workers reporting to each supervisor at the lowest level of supervision, there is room in an organization for 62,500 workers and 3,905 executives.[5]

8 *The work of every person in the organization should be confined as far as possible to the performance of a single leading function.*

This is the principle of specialization. It applies to departments and divisions as well as to individuals. It concerns delegation of authority *horizontally,* rather than vertically, as in the case of the scalar principle.

The total duties in the organization are divided according to functions, and a department or division is made responsible for each.[6]

There may be functional division according to the *kind* of work to be done—manufacturing, sales, finance, or engineering. Or, within a department, for example the financial department, a company may have subdivisions for billing, receiving, payroll, etc.

There may also be functional division according to the *way* in which the work is done. For example, divisions may be set up for typists, comptometer operators, etc.

This principle requires that if a person is held responsible for more

---

[5] "A Practical Manual of Organization," by R. E. Gillmore, Funk & Wagnalls Company, New York, 1948.

[6] There is no uniformity in the use of the terms "department" and "division." They mean whatever a company wants them to mean. Some companies have departments within divisions; some have divisions within departments. Some use "department" for their staff units and "division" for the operating units.

than one duty, and this is often the case in small companies, the duties should be similar. Public relations is grouped with industrial relations, rather than with engineering. The specialist specializes. In the interest of efficiency, he concentrates on the things he can do best.

In organizations which have been allowed to grow without design, individuals are frequently found who are performing two or more unrelated duties. Sometimes this comes about because a certain individual happens to have a little free time when an activity is added. Sometimes it is because a man happens to have some experience in his background which qualifies him to handle the new assignment, even though it has nothing to do with his major duties. Sometimes it is because he has a particular interest in the activity. Sometimes an individual seizes a floating activity simply because he is a power-grabber.

A combination of ill-related assignments often seems to work satisfactorily, so long as a particular person holds a post. But it is not considered good organization. Should he leave, the prospects of finding another person who has the identical abilities to handle the widely different duties are usually slim. The organization structure which has to be changed to fit persons cannot adhere to a design which it is believed will best achieve the company's objectives.

9 *Whenever possible, line functions should be separated from staff functions, and adequate emphasis should be placed on important staff activities.*

Line functions are those which accomplish the main objectives of the company. In many manufacturing companies, the manufacturing and distribution functions are considered line. The manufacturing and sales departments are considered the departments that are accomplishing the main objectives of the business.

In companies that are not attempting to reach the ultimate consumer with their products, for example those that sell their products to outside distributors or to the government, the sales function may not be considered a line function.

In some companies in which engineering is practically a part of production, it is considered a line function. In certain chemical companies, research is so closely integrated with production that it is thought of as a line activity. Procurement of raw materials may be considered line by a metal manufacturing company that does its own mining and quarrying.

Line departments are often called "operating" departments.

Staff functions are those which aid in, or are auxiliary to, the line functions. Some companies call their staff departments "auxiliary departments."

Members of staff departments provide service, advice, coordination and control for the line or operating departments. (They may perform one or more of these functions.) Purchasing and advertising departments, for instance, provide service. Legal and public relations departments provide advice. Production planning serves as an example of a coordinating agency. Industrial engineering and accounting departments are examples of departments that provide control. Many of these departments serve more than one of the purposes. The department which provides service may also provide advice; the department that coordinates may also help with control.

Committees are usually considered staff agencies. Their members advise, coordinate, and control.

There are also individuals, who are not members of a department or committee, who perform staff functions. These are called staff assistants. The specialist retained from an outside firm such as a legal consultant or public relations consultant, is an example. Or, within an organization, there may be an assistant to the president who has no supervisory duties but who investigates problems that are referred to him by the president, putting before the president data upon the basis of which the chief executive can make decisions. The staff assistant's duties are chiefly the detailed work of command, so that the energies of the line executive can be released for larger activities.

10 *There is a limit to the number of positions that can be coordinated by a single executive.*

This is known as the "span of control" principle.

The number of positions (groups of activities) which an executive is able to coordinate, depends on:

a. The similarity or dissimilarity of the subordinate positions and how interdependent they are. The more positions interlock, the greater is the work of coordination.

b. How far the people and activities are apart geographically. The manager who is coordinating activities within a single plant can coordinate more than if these activities are carried on a widely scattered locations.

c. The complexity of the duties of each of the positions to be coordinated.

d. The stability of the business.

e. The frequency with which new types of problems arise. If a company has been in business for many years, the problems which come up from day to day have probably been encountered before, and the work of coordination is therefore less than if the problems were brand new.

The span of control is seldom uniform throughout an organization. At the upper levels, where positions are interdependent and dissimilar, many organization specialists urge that the span of control embrace not more than five or six subordinates. In some decentralized companies, however, in which the operating units are practically autonomous, the top executive is successfully coordinating as many as twelve or fifteen positions.

At the lowest supervisory level—the level of the last executives who have any supervisory responsibilities—organization specialists say that a supervisor may supervise as many as twenty workers. This might be a foreman or leadman supervising men on an assembly line.

As attention has been given to the human relations aspects of the supervisor's responsibilities, there has been a tendency to shorten the span of control even at the lowest level. While a foreman might be able to supervise the work of twenty men, all of whom are performing an identical, simple operation, he might not have time to give them individual attention as persons. He might not have time to communicate information on company policies, listen to their suggestions or grievances, learn the causes of poor performance. For these reasons a large paper company announced that it had decided to limit the number of workers supervised by each of its foremen to ten. A manufacturer of metal products, because of such reasons, has adopted a maximum ratio of twelve workers to the lowest supervisor.

In separating packets of duties into manageable parts, so that no individual's span of control need be too great, three types of division are commonly employed: (1) functional, (2) product or service, and (3) regional or geographical. The functional type of division has been discussed in connection with the principle of specialization. A company that has a radio manufacturing department and a television manufacturing department is using product division. Examples of service divisions are provided by a public utility company which has a lighting department and a heating department, or a bank that has an insurance department and a mortgage department.

When operations are widely scattered, the most effective plan is sometimes to set up a unit in each geographical area. In public utilities such as railroads, this is a natural way of assigning duties. Life insurance companies, too, often have regional divisions.

Many companies use a combination of these methods. Within a sales department (a functional division) there may be a western and an eastern sales office (regional divisions). Or the refrigerator division of an electrical products company (product division) may use the functional basis for separating its activities into manageable parts—engineering, manufacturing, sales, etc.

Some point out that there is danger in oversupervision as well as in undersupervision, that is, in having the span of control too short. At the top levels, the executive coordinates dissimilar positions. He should not coordinate too many positions simply because they are dissimilar. Account must be taken of the frequency with which new problems arise and other factors which influence the span of control. If, however, the executive is not given enough positions to coordinate, he may have time on his hands. Such a person may have a tendency to inject himself into operational decisions, undermining authority which has been delegated.

11 *The organization should be flexible, so that it can be adjusted to changing conditions.*

The organization plan should stand up, in boom and in depression, in war and in peace, when new markets appear and when old ones disappear. The plan should permit expansion and contraction without disrupting the basic design. Good organization is not a straitjacket.

12 *The organization should be kept as simple as possible.*

Too many levels of authority, as has been noted, make communication difficult. Too many committees impede rather than achieve coordination.

All of these principles (there are more than the dozen listed, but these are ones that are frequently referred to in discussions of organization) are based on the idea of leadership and delegation of authority. Complete authority is delegated by the board of directors to an individual, who is able to carry out responsibilities by delegating authority to others.

Benefits of good organization

A few of the benefits of the application of these principles have been touched upon in describing the precepts. The following reiterate some of them, but include additional benefits that companies attribute to organization planning. Application of the principles

- Disposes of conflicts between individuals over jurisdiction.
- Prevents duplication of work.
- Decreases likelihood of "run-arounds."
- Makes communication easier through keeping the channels clear.
- Shows promotional possibilities, which is useful in executive development. Organization charts and position descriptions show where a man can expect to go, what qualifications are needed to fill a superior job, what additional training is needed to prepare a man in one position for a superior post.
- Provides a sound basis for appraisal and rating of individual performance and capabilities. If one knows what an individual is supposed to be doing, it is then possible to measure how well he is living up to the requirements of the job.
- Aids in wage and salary administration. The analysis of duties for the higher executives performs the same service as job descriptions for those in the lower echelons.
- Permits expansion with adequate control, and without killing off top executives. Activities are administered in manageable units, so that no one person has too heavy a load.
- Permits changes to be made in the right direction as opportunities present themselves. In the absence of a plan, changes are likely to be made on the basis of expediency, with the likelihood of perpetuating original mistakes.
- Increases cooperation and a feeling of freedom. Each person works best with others when he knows for what he is responsible, to whom he is responsible and the value of cooperation relationships with others. A feeling of freedom comes when responsibilities are definite and known and when delegation is actually practiced.

18 Organizational realities
Rocco Carzo, Jr.

Organizing is easy—at least, that is what one is led to believe from traditional writings on the subject. Traditional theory prescribes that organization be built around the work to be done. For maximum efficiency, this theory specifies that the work be divided into simple, routine, and repetitive tasks. These tasks or jobs should then be grouped according to similar work characteristics and arranged in an organization structure in which an executive has a limited number of subordinates reporting directly to him. Also, every member of the organization should be accountable to only one boss. Personnel assignments are to be made on the basis of the requirements of the job and each individual's ability to do the work.

These are not doctrinaire beliefs reserved for academic minds. In many quarters, they have gained enough stature to be called "principles" of management and/or organization, and they are also widely accepted in practice. Administrators and academicians will recognize the traditional organization pyramids that are based on these seemingly reasonable propositions. As an example, one administrator recommends the following for a "sound, flexible, and dynamic" organizational structure.[1]

1 Determine the objectives and the policies, programs, plans, and schedules that will best achieve those objectives for the company as a whole and, in turn, for each component of the business.
2 Determine the work to be done to achieve those objectives under such guiding policies.
3 Divide and classify or group related work into a simple, logical, understandable, and comprehensive organizational structure.
4 Assign essential work clearly and definitely to the various components and positions.
5 Determine the requirements and qualifications of personnel to occupy such positions.
6 Staff the organization with persons who meet these qualifications.
7 Establish methods and procedures that will help to achieve the objectives of the organization.

Now, however, there is enough research evidence to raise some significant doubts about the validity of prevailing organizational theories. Traditional theory is based on logical division of work. More recent social research is concerned with organizational arrangements that will facilitate the

Source: From *Business Horizons* (Spring 1961), pp. 95–104. Copyright © 1961 by the Foundation for the School of Business at Indiana University. Reprinted by permission.
[1] Ralph J. Cordiner, *New Frontiers for Professional Managers* (New York: McGraw-Hill Book Company, Inc., 1956), pp. 52–53.

joining of human efforts. Realistic organizational theory must be based on the real behavior of real people in real organizations, that is, the ways in which people join their efforts in any kind of cooperative system. The real test organizational theory is not abstract logic based on work but on arrangements that facilitate effective cooperative relationships. These relationships are the key to productivity. It is the purpose of this article to explain and illustrate the lack of concern for these realities in the traditional approach. In addition, some suggestions will be made for realistic organization.

Tradition vs. research

Specialization

The advantages of specialization are primarily economic. Both economists and formal organization theorists emphasize that greater efficiency and productivity are achieved through division of work. Adam Smith, in his *Wealth of Nations,* illustrated this thinking with his description of a pin factory. By dividing the work into specialized tasks, the factory could produce thousands of pins per man per day. But if the complete manufacturing process were left to individual workmen, each might produce only a few dozen per day. F. W. Taylor went a step further by proposing that management jobs be specialized so that "each man from the assistant superintendent down shall have as few functions as possible to perform. If practicable, the work of each man in the management should be confined to the performance of a single leading function."[2]

The approach that divides the work into simple, routine, and repetitive tasks utilizes *minimum* skills and abilities. James Worthy has attacked this approach as follows:

The gravest weakness (of specialization) was the failure to recognize and utilize properly management's most valuable resource: the complex and multiple capacities of people. On the contrary, the scientific managers deliberately sought to utilize as narrow a band of personality and as narrow a range of ability as ingenuity could devise. The process has been fantastically wasteful for the industry and society.[3]

Recently, the effects of specialization on employee attitudes have received more study. For example, Chris Argyris feels that congruency is lacking between the needs of healthy individuals and the demands of the formal organization. In his research of a seemingly healthy manufacturing operation

[2] Frederick W. Taylor, *Scientific Management* (New York: Harper & Brothers, 1941), p. 99.
[3] James C. Worthy, *Big Business and Free Man* (New York: Harper & Brothers, 1959), pp. 69–70.

that had very low indexes of employee turnover, absenteeism, and griev-ances, Argyris found the employees to be apathetic and indifferent toward management and the organization. He has said that the formal organization, with its emphasis on task specialization, utilizes a narrow range of skills and minimum abilities, and tends to create needs that are not characteristic of healthy, mature individuals.

The administrator and the social scientist might argue that these criti-cisms involve value judgments and are not really their concern. They may ask: Does it matter if human resources ar not fully utilized; and does it mat-ter that employees are apathetic and indifferent, as long as organization ob-jectives are accomplished efficiently or as long as profits are maximized in the case of a business enterprise? The administrator may argue further that he is forced to adopt specialization because it promises the greatest ef-ficiency and productivity. The social scientist may point out that, as a scien-tist, he cannot consider values; his concern must be limited to means and not ends.

Both administrators and social scientists would accept the position, however, that greater utilization of the physical and mental capabilities of the human resource may increase the scope of organizational accomplishment. They would also accept the argument that apathy and indifference may have long-run implications for the efficient attainment of goals. For example, Ar-gyris predicts that the dissatisfaction of employees manifested by apathy and indifference will result in demands for increased wages; these increases will be viewed "not as rewards for production but as management's moral obligation for placing the employees in the kind of working world where frustration, failure, and conflict are continuously being experienced." Accord-ing to this thesis, wage costs will tend to rise regardless of productivity changes. The employee in this situation views the increase as compensation for continued frustration.

Perhaps these realities imply even broader organizational objectives than those of maximum efficiency, productivity, and profits. The narrower view of organizations in terms of material achievements, such as profits as the prime goal (and some say the only goal) of business institutions, has permeated the classical as well as the popular and current versions of organized activity. The materialistic goals attributed to organizations are abstractions and serve only to facilitate simplified descriptions of organiza-tion and group behavior. These descriptions are usually devoid of human and moral values. Such values are important not only as ends in themselves but also for understanding human behavior. Oversimplification with regard to the multiple objectives of organizations and the complex motivations of individu-als will not lead to realistic organizational structure. Worthy has decried the prevailing theories of business organization and has called for a new theory that more adequately reflects and explains reality:

Such a theory will recognize that business is a social organ with functions far beyond the mere promotion of material prosperity, and with motivations

far broader than simple self-interest. It will give consideration to the perva-
sive influence of religious forces in American life, the profound conse-
quences of the rise of the large, publicly owned corporation, and certain
unique features of American historical development. It will, in other words,
shake off outmoded economic doctrine and take a fresh look at the truth
about today's business. [4]

This broader view of organizational goals implies that the administrator has responsibilities far beyond those dictated by material achievements. The fragmentation and routinization of work to the point where it loses significance has dire implications, not only for organizations that live by this action, but also for society in general. The organization may suffer because the rewards for submissive compliance produce apathy, indifference, noninvolvement, and alienation on the part of group members. They become highly dependent and incapable of solving problems and making decisions. The organization may become rigid and its members unwilling to accept and adapt to changes necessary for growth and changing socio-economic conditions. Furthermore, a democracy built on a foundation of free choice may carry over into everyday life.

Grouping

After the work has been divided into specialized tasks, the advocates of formal organization prescribe the grouping of these tasks according to similar work characteristics. This is called the principle of "functional homogeneity." According to one definition, the principle " . . . says that organizational effectiveness is increased and the cost of executive and operative labor is reduced when duties are grouped in accordance with functional similarities. The members of a group are able to *coordinate* and *cooperate* with one another directly when they are dealing with similar problems."[5]

The grouping of persons according to similarities in their work may be contrary to the natural development of human organization. Early researchers found that people tend naturally to organize on a basis other than the technical requirements of work. They organize in terms of sentiments, social customs, codes of behavior, status, friendships, and cliques. The significance of these findings lies in the researchers' conclusions that cooperation depends upon the natural relationships of informal organization and not necessarily on groupings based on work arrangements and/or economic incentives.

The simplicity and rationale of formal structuring is open to further criticism when one examines another prescription for organizing. The principle of "span of control" stipulates that the number of subordinates

---

[4] *Big Business and Free Man,* pp. 31–32.
[5] Ralph C. Davis, *Industrial Organization and Management* (New York: Harper & Brothers, 1957), p. 70. The emphasis is mine.

supervised directly by any one executive be limited. Some eminent students of administration have gone so far as to specify how many subordinates a superior can effectively manage. Urwick, for example, has said, "No superior can supervise directly the work of more than five or, at the most, six subordinates *whose work interlocks.*"[6] Two of the most outstanding criticisms (many have been made) of the span of control are those of Herbert A. Simon and Waino W. Suojanen. Simon points out that there is a basic contradiction between this principle and the principle that there should be as few levels as possible in an organization. By restricting or limiting the span of control, an organization—especially one that is growing—must increase the number of scalar levels and the administrative distance between individuals. This development inevitably produces excessive red tape and waste of time and effort. Obviously, adherence to the principle of span of control conflicts with the principle that requires a minimum number of organizational levels. Suojanen states:

If both principles are actually applicable to the large organization, then it must follow that many large government agencies and business corporations are less efficient than their smaller counterparts. However, large corporations not only continue to grow in size but also comparisons of various sizes of corporations are not convincing as to the superiority of smaller, as opposed to larger corporations.[7]

While Urwick's argument for the span-of-control concept is based on those situations where the work of subordinates interlocks, Suojanen offers this very reason as an explanation for the success of large organizations. Common purpose, willingness to cooperate, and coordinated action are characteristics of the executive unit. According to Suojanen, the ease of communication, the informality of relationships, and the personal satisfactions gained in association actually reduce rather than increase the number of relationships and the demands made on the superior.

If this is not enough to raise doubt about the span-of-control doctrine, one can consider the research done at the Institute for Social Research, University of Michigan. One of the researchers there has concluded that an organization will function best and will achieve the highest motivation when the people in the organization hold overlapping group memberships.[8] The very characteristic (interlocking relationships) that seems to make the span of control operative is in reality a necessity for cooperative and coordinated effort.

[6] Lydall F. Urwick, "The Manager's Span of Control," *Harvard Business Review,* XXXIV (May–June, 1956), 41.
[7] Waino W. Suojanen, "The Span of Control—Fact or Fable," *Advanced Management,* XX (November, 1955), 5.
[8] Rensis Likert, "A Motivational Approach to a Modified Theory of Organization and Management," in Mason Haire, ed., *Modern Organization Theory* (New York: John Wiley & Sons, Inc., 1959), pp. 184–217.

Effects of interaction

Evidence indicates that an organization initially framed according to work groupings will eventually function in a manner that parallels the natural social tendencies and personality characteristics of the persons in it.

In laboratory research undertaken by the author (the results have not yet been published), an attempt is being made to predict organizational success on the basis of the composition and interaction of group members. We have seen organizations, initially departmentalized according to similarities in work, actually operate under different systems. The new systems were based on the personalities and interaction of group members. In another study, where departments were established on the basis of work similarities and authority was delegated on the basis of work performance, researchers found that a system of relations had developed that was quite distinct from the formal organization. Furthermore, they suggest that difficulties of industrial cooperation could be avoided if organization would adapt the formal organization to the real relationships that develop over a period of time.[9]

Separation of line and staff

Another area where reality differs from theoretical prescriptions is the traditional separation of line (command) and staff (advisory) authority. According to traditional theory, staff departments are recommended for assisting line executives in work that requires technical knowledge and detailed attention. While the staff is supposed to remain advisory, it usually develops into a line capacity with both the higher and lower elements of the organizational hierarchy. Staff specialists become "experts" in their specialty and top management officials rely on them for "authoritative" advice. As lower management officials realize that staff recommendations are backed by top management, a line of command is established that covers a particular aspect of the work—in addition to general supervision of the line.

The development of this arrangement serves to obviate the neat separation of line and staff. Also, there is reason to question whether the unity-of-command doctrine (one boss) really operates in practice. The acceptance of staff recommendations and suggestions by lower management officials as authoritative and representative of the views of higher management creates a much more complicated organization than that portrayed by the simple line-and-staff (unity-of-command) type of structure.

The line-and-staff type of structure seems to suffer from some false assumptions: (1) staff specialists are able and willing to operate without formal authority, and (2) their advice, suggestions, and recommendations will

---

[9] Conrad M. Arensburg and Douglas McGregor, "Determination of Morale in an Industrial Company," *Applied Anthropology,* I (January–March, 1942), 12–34. In a more recent study, Melville Dalton, *Men Who Manage* (New York: John Wiley & Sons, Inc., 1959), Chapter 3, the author found that "real" or "actual" organization and authority differed from prescribed or formal organization and authority.

readily be accepted and applied by lower line officials. Under the true line-and-staff arrangement as it works out in practice, the staff officer finds he has little power. His advice may go unheeded and unheralded because he has no authority to implement his decisions in the organization. The lower line officers may resent and reject staff advice because it threatens the sacred position of the line. Melville Dalton, after a study of three industrial plants, concluded that line officers fear staff innovations for a number of reasons.

In view of their longer experience, presumably intimate knowledge of the work, and their greater remuneration, they fear being "shown up" before their line superiors for not having thought of the processual refinements themselves. They fear that changes in methods may bring personnel changes . . . and quite possibly reduce their area of authority. Finally, changes in techniques may expose forbidden practices and departmental inefficiency.[10]

These frustrations lead to a power struggle. The staff officer seeks more authority by reporting his frustrations and criticisms of line operations to higher line officials. Evidence indicates that staff officers, by virtue of their specialized knowledge, their continual contact with top management, and better education, are able to gain from top management the necessary functional authority over line operations. Some would bemoan this development because it violates the principle of unity of command and causes the lower line officials no end of confusion. However, as explained earlier, the overlapping and the various relationships are the basic ingredients for cooperation and coordination. Thus they should be encouraged, not circumscribed by the contrivances of those who draw organization charts.

Motivation

The doctrine of self-interest has long prevailed in traditional theory as well as in practice. The self-interest doctrine is illustrated in one of Adam Smith's basic assumptions: Every individual is continually exerting himself to discover the most advantageous employment for whatever capital he can command. It does not take much study to realize that this same doctrine still prevails. As an example, note the view of the president of one of the world's largest corporations: "Of all the motivations to which the human mechanism responds, none has proved so powerful as that of financial gain . . . self enrichment is a dream which must rank with the most compelling forces in shaping the destinies of the human race."[11]

---

[10] Melville Dalton, "Conflicts Between Staff and Line Management Officers," *American Sociological Review,* XV (June, 1950), 349. Also see *Men Who Manage,* Chapter 4.
[11] Crawford H. Greenewalt, *The Uncommon Man* (New York: McGraw-Hill Book Company, Inc., 1959), pp. 37–38.

While the concept of self-interest based on financial reward is important in explaining human behavior, it presents an incomplete and inadequate picture of human needs. It says nothing of the desire to feel important, to be respected, and to have prestige. Of even greater significance for the study of organizations is the basic human desire to associate, to belong, or to be accepted as a member of a group. This need far exceeds monetary enrichment as a factor in motivating human behavior. Elton Mayo has said, "The desire to stand well with one's fellows, the so-called human instinct of association, easily outweighs the merely individual interest and the logical reasoning upon which so many spurious principles of management are based."[12] He concluded that "If one observes either industrial workers or university students with sufficient care and continuity, one finds that the proportionate number actuated by motives of *self-interest logically elaborated* is exceedingly small. They have relapsed upon self-interest when social association has failed them."

The self-interest thesis falls down in another important respect. It was stated earlier that people organize naturally on a basis other than the technical requirements of work. This organization has been called the social structure or the informal organization. By satisfying men's basic needs for association, friendship, and belonging, it provides the setting that makes them willing to cooperate. Furthermore, individual behavior is influenced by the customs, traditions, and pressures of the group. Thus, individual interests and desires become subordinated to those of the social organization.

In this respect, one is reminded of the Coch and French experiments, which dealt with the problem of employee resistance to change at the Harwood Manufacturing Corporation.[13] The company had tried to solve this problem with monetary allowances for transfers. It would seem from the self-interest doctrine that economic incentives such as a transfer bonus should create acceptance toward job changes and attitudes favorable to relearning after transfer. On the contrary, the researchers found the general attitudes toward job changes markedly negative. Analysis of the relearning curves of several hundred experienced operators, rating standard or better prior to change, showed that 38 per cent of the operators recovered to the standard unit rating; the other 62 per cent either became chronically substandard operators or quit during the relearning period.

Four different groups were studied. One group was merely told of planned changes; a second group was allowed to participate through representation in designing changes; and the two remaining groups participated fully. The researchers found that the total participation groups not only returned to the previous production rate faster than the other groups, but showed sustained progress toward a higher rate. Coch and French

[12] Elton Mayo, *The Social Problems of an Industrial Civilization* (Boston: Division of Research, Graduate School of Business Administration, Harvard University, 1945). This and the following quotation are from p. 43.
[13] Lester Coch and John R. P. French, Jr., "Overcoming Resistance to Change," *Human Relations,* I (August, 1948), 512–32.

concluded that resistance to change in methods of work can be overcome by stimulating group participation in planning the changes.

This study dramatizes the significance of factors other than financial gain in motivating human behavior. First of all, the researchers observed that work standards, informally set by the groups, were important in determining output levels before and after the change. The nonparticipation group seemed to be governed by a standard set before the change, while the two total-participation groups were governed by a standard set when competition developed between them. However, it is important to note the authors' observation that a major determinant of the strength of these standards was probably the cohesiveness of the group. The power of the group over the members to increase or decrease productivity seemed to depend upon the amount of participation.

Secondly, changes in the social system that would be produced by technical or work changes may cause resistance to change. For example, the researchers indicated that employees would resist change because of the possibility of failure on the new job and a loss of status in the eyes of fellow employees. Furthermore, employees may resist because they are reluctant to leave friends or break social ties and are uncertain about being accepted in a new and different social system.

Thirdly, and most important for overcoming resistance and motivating human behavior, is the very nature of participation. Participation requires interaction, association, and involvement; as noted earlier, these are essential for cooperative effort.

Comparison and evaluation
The self-interest doctrine has prompted another organizational practice that is believed to stimulate greater productivity. This is the arrangement of individuals in a manner that permits their performance to be compared and evaluated. Rating and reward are based on how one individual compares to another doing similar work. Control is supposed to be easier because the organization has built-in standards for comparison and evaluation. Furthermore, it is believed that individuals will compete when they learn that they are being compared, and greater productivity will result.

Does competition increase production? Perhaps a more important first question is: Does competition stimulate cooperation? Competition is characterized by rivalry; one organization member strives against another for an objective of which he will be the principal beneficiary. Cooperation, on the other hand, is characterized by collaborative behavior; group members strive together for the attainment of a goal that is to be shared equally by each participating individual or unit. Cooperation, therefore, suppresses individual drives and goals so that common group objectives may be attained. An organization that promotes competition among its members will not have cooperation; it will have conflict. Group members have little reason to act jointly or collaborate with those against whom they are being measured or compared, or with whom they are competing.

Moreover, evidence indicates that a group will be more productive when its members are cooperative rather than competitive. Morton Deutsch, in an experiment designed to study the behavior of different groups (some cooperative, others competitive), found greater productivity among the cooperative groups.[14] Also, he found that the productivity was of a higher quality; these groups produced more fruitful ideas and showed more insight and understanding of problems. Measurement and reward of individual performance in the cooperative groups were made on the basis of group achievement. In this situation, each member received the same reward. Each member in the competitive groups was rated and rewarded on the basis of comparison with the efforts of the members in his group. In this situation, the reward each member received was different and was determined by his relative contribution to the solution of the problem with which the group was confronted. In contrast, the emphasis on group behavior in the cooperative groups produced the motivation, cooperation, and coordination that is necessary for the successful achievement of organization objectives.

Decentralization

Decentralization and "management by objectives" have often been offered by administrators and theorists as the best organizational arrangement for overcoming the suppressive aspects of a large organization while providing for the greatest motivation. Decentralization, as defined by its advocates, gives maximum authority and responsibility to the manager of each decentralized unit. Control by top management is exercised primarily by measuring end results and comparing performance with predetermined standards and the performance of other units. Once these measurements have been defined and applied, they are supposed to provide motivation. They are also used by top management as a basis for giving rewards such as promotions and bonuses. This practice may not only emphasize the wrong things in cooperative behavior, as explained earlier, but there is the possibility that measurements based on end results, such as earnings, production, costs, and sales, will encourage managers of decentralized units to adopt a pressure-oriented management. In other words, they may exercise pressure on the organization to meet the end results expected, while ignoring the quality of the human organization.

From a number of research studies, Rensis Likert has found that pressure-oriented supervision can achieve impressive short-run results. He reports that:

putting pressure on a well-established organization to produce can yield substantial and immediate increases in productivity. This increase is obtained, however, at a cost to the human assets of the organization. *In the company*

---

[14] Morton Deutsch, "A Theory of Co-operation and Competition," *Human Relations,* II (April, 1949), 129–52, and "An Experimental Study of the Effects of Co-operation Upon Group Process," *Human Relations,* II (July, 1949), 199–231.

we studied, for example, the cost was clear: hostilities increased, there was greater reliance upon authority, loyalties declined, and motivations to produce decreased while motivations to restrict production increased. In other words, the quality of the human organization deteriorated as a functioning social system.[15]

On the other hand, he has found that managers who are employee-centered and who support their subordinates will foster team spirit, greater productivity, and better employee satisfaction than pressure-oriented or production-centered managers.

Decentralization can, of course, provide the means for maximum utilization and development of the human resource as well as the basis for cooperative behavior. In contrast to organizations where there are many levels of supervision and elaborate systems of control, Worthy found that the flat type of structure with maximum decentralization develops self-reliance and initiative, and more fully utilizes individual capacities. At Sears, Roebuck and Co., for example, the typical store manager has forty-odd department managers reporting directly to him (thus violating the traditional limitations of the span-of-control doctrine), and has no alternative but to delegate decision-making authority to subordinates. When managers of departments were asked to manage, they learned to manage. Having to rely heavily on department managers, store managers at Sears took greater care in the selection, placement, and development of subordinates. Furthermore, Worthy says:

This pattern of administration not only gets today's job done better, but permits the individual to grow and develop in a way that is impossible in more centralized systems. Furthermore, it contributes strongly to morale because employees work in an atmosphere of relative freedom from oppressive supervision and have a sense of individual importance and personal responsibility which other types of arrangements often deny them.[16]

It is important to note also that Worthy attributes much of the success of the Sears organization to its ability to meet the personal and social demands of its employees and not to any "logical technology, division of labor, or hierarchy of control." The study showed that both low output and low morale prevailed where jobs were broken down minutely. The most sustained efforts were exerted by employees who performed the more complete sets of tasks; these likewise exhibited the highest levels of morale and *esprit de corps*. Further, the research revealed that size of the organization unit was unquestionably a most important factor in determining the

---

[15] Rensis Likert, "Measuring Organizational Performance," *Harvard Business Review*, XXXVI (March–April, 1958), 48.
[16] James C. Worthy, "Organizational Structure and Employee Morale," *American Sociological Review*, XV (April, 1950), 178. Worthy also observes that not all individuals can function effectively in this type of arrangement and that the system will tend to weed them out.

quality of employee relationships: the smaller the unit the higher the morale, and vice versa. It was clear that closer contact between executives and the rank and file in smaller organizations tends to result in friendlier, easier relationships.

In perspective

The research results that have been described are not conclusive, of course, but they do suggest that many of the so-called principles of management and organization are preconceived and have little value as descriptions of behavior or as prescriptions for success. Though specialization has its advantages, it may create employee attitudes and demands that are injurious to the organization. Similarly, efforts to departmentalize according to the requirements of work—while necessary for some degree of order, planning and control—may create arrangements that are contrary to the requirements for cooperative behavior. Also, while the importance of economic and material incentives cannot be denied, reliance on them as the prime or only means of motivation may produce behavior that is contrary to organization needs such as loyalty, honesty, and initiative.

The administrator's task is a difficult one. According to what has been suggested here, the administrator must provide a structure that is loose enough to gain the motivational benefits from the natural social inclinations of organization members, yet he must impose the technical or formal organization and controls so necessary for efficient goal achievement.

As an example of organizing on the basis of natural tendencies, consider the way people associate in small informal groups. They are not only influenced by customs, traditions, and structure, but also receive many satisfactions from and are motivated by membership in these simple social systems.

It seems appropriate, therefore, that the formal organization be structured to take advantage of the benefits provided by smallness. Small, loosely structured organizational units, coupled with maximum employee involvement in organization affairs, can provide the cooperation necessary for successful performance. Seemingly, as the number of organizational units increases, the task of coordination and control will become more difficult. However, the converse may be true, depending on the number of levels, the directness of communication, the amount of interaction and involvement that takes place in an organization. The flat or horizontal type of arrangement (wide spans of supervision and few levels), where the lines of communication are simple and direct, can more readily be coordinated than the organization with many levels where communication is relatively slow and subject to many interpretations. The coordination problem becomes simpler when components of the organization operate autonomously. Left to operate on their own, decentralized units need only to be coordinated on end results.

It is important to re-emphasize that overspecialization and over-functionalization in decentralized units can create not only the same problems as those experienced in the larger, more centralized organization but also more complex ones. The more a functional unit is defined as a separate entity, the greater the possibility that it will neglect its integrative purpose and be at odds with the over-all objectives of the decentralized unit as well as the whole organization. Furthermore, overfunctionalization may tend to make relationships at both the management and employee levels too formal. Cooperation may then be limited to that required by organization policy or the management hierarchy. Thus, the task of coordination becomes even more burdensome, increasing the necessity for elaborate systems and formal controls. This type of system, characterized by pressure-oriented management with undue regard for end results, can also be detrimental to the human organization. A loosely structured organization, where the emphasis is on teamwork and where there is a high degree of compatibility between goals of group members and the overall objectives of the organization, produces a human organization that is much more cooperative and productive.

Those who argue against organizing on the basis of human characteristics and tendencies emphasize the difficulties inherent in trying to diagnose human problems and in predicting human behavior. Diagnosis, of course, requires a much more learned and analytical administrator. He must be aware of and understand the research on organization behavior. He must be able to conduct and supervise research in his own organization concerning problems peculiar to his situation. With understanding and analysis, he should be better equipped to predict the outcome of anticipated courses of action and choose those that promise continued organizational success. Granted, this requires administration of a high order. It is, however, a necessity if organization in accord with reality is desired.

---

19 Frankly speaking
Phil Frank

I'd like to welcome Dean Hotchkiss, Campus Coffee Fund Coordinator, Member of the Committee to Study Committees, and President's Council on Hangnails , who will speak on the subject, Bureaucracy!

Source: Reprinted by permission from College Media Service.

---

20 Is there a best way to organize a business enterprise?
Y. K. Shetty

For many years an attempt to define an optimum organization structure has resulted in diverse approaches. In recent years, however, there has developed a new direction in the area of organization design. The research

Source: Reprinted by permission of the publisher from *S. A. M. Advanced Management Journal* (April 1973), pp. 47–52. © 1973 by Society for Advancement of Management.

evidence seems to suggest that there is no "one best" way to organize, as it was once postulated. The design is conditional. It must be tailor-made for the firm. An appropriate design to one technological-market condition may not be suitable to another. What type of design is more suitable in a particular setting depends on the internal and external environment of that particular organization.

The earliest attempt to explain the phenomena of organization was made by writers and practitioners who have come to be known as classicalists (1). The classical organization is characterized by a pyramid consisting of positions which are ordered into a hierarchical system of superior and subordinates. Each function has well-defined activities and responsibilities, demanding specialized conpetence and authority. The organization has complex mechanisms, rules, regulations and procedures. Human action within this framework is explained mechanistically by the obligations of position in a hierarchy. Ultimate control of the organization rests at the top of the hierarchy. Reliability of behavior is maintained by directives, by rules and regulations, and by standard operating procedures which prescribe the exact manner in which duties are to be performed. In short, the organization is a machine; the manager is the engineer who can draw on a body of principles to design the structure most suited to his ends—most rational instrument for implementing objectives and policies.

For quite some time the principles of classical organization largely based on bureaucracy have met with widespread acceptance among practitioners. However, in recent years the approach is coming under constant attack. The most insistent criticism leveled against classical organization theory comes from exponents of behavioral sciences. They claim that classical theory is too mechanistic and thus ignores major aspects of human nature. The rational model has been attacked as an abstraction that overlooks dynamic human behavior, in particular, the non-rational elements in human conduct and their implications for practicing managers. Some of the critics even go the extreme of claiming that the theory is incompatible with human nature. As an alternative to classical approach, behavioralists have suggested certain modifications in the structure.

The behavioral organization theorists (2) argue that organizational effectiveness is achieved by arranging matters so that people feel that they count, that they belong, and that work can be made more meaningful. They do not necessarily reject the classical principles, but they feel that there goes more into an organization design than rules and regulations and strict rationality.

For example, people, one of the major inputs in any organization, are all human beings, yet everyone is unique to some extent from the next one. Everything man does cannot necessarily be explained rationally. There is a certain amount of subjectivity to an individual's actions; that is, his actions are based on his personal value system. Behavioralists, particularly the earlier ones, do not necessarily prescribe any one form of organization structure but believe it can be improved by modifying it according to the informal structure by less narrow specialization, by less emphasis on hierarchy, by permitting more participation in decision-making on the part of the lower ranks, and by more democratic attitude on the part of the managers.

In recent years some writers have suggested a new type of organization structure known as the organic-structure—a structure in which there is a minimum of formal division of duties. In this structure, hierarchy will be deemphasized: people will be differentiated not vertically, according to rank and role, but flexibly and functionally according to skill and professional training. According to this view, organizations will be made up of temporary task forces in which membership will shift as needs and problems change. Warren Bennis (3) argues that bureaucracy—that is, the classical structure—is too rigid to be serviceable in the time of rapid technological change and that it will, therefore, eventually disappear, to be replaced by the task-force type of the organization of the future.

The design problem

If the organizer follows the classical principles, the resulting structure will necessarily be characterized by a hierarchy, a division of labor, and a series of rather precisely defined jobs and relationships. This is closer to the functional type of organization. On the other hand, the earlier behavioral scientists do not necessarily prescribe any one form of organization but believe the classical structure can be amended and improved by taking into account the human element. In recent years some theorists have suggested an "organic" type of structure, which deemphasizes specialization and authority and concentrates on problem solving. This comes closer to project organization.

Thus, organization models can be portrayed on a scale running between mechanistic at the one end and organic on the other. Organic organizations are characterized by less formalized definitions of jobs, by more stress on flexibility and adaptability and by communication networks involving more consultation than command. Mechanistic organizations are more rigidly specialized functionally and, in general, define the opposite pole from an organic continuum. In between this continuum there are various types of patterns which an organization can display. In other words, the range of patterns may fall anywhere on the scale's continuum. On the one extreme the organization is highly mechanical in structure and at the other extreme it is highly organic.

The relevant practical question is what factors or forces should a company consider in deciding how to design an organization? These are of particular importance:

Forces in the managers

The designing of an organization at any instance will be influenced greatly by the many forces operating within the managers' own personality. They will, of course, perceive their organization problems in a unique way on the basis of their background, knowledge and experience. Their initial decisions will be in terms of what industry the organization will enter, how it will compete, where it will be located, the kind of organization it will be, who will be the top managers and who will directly influence the organization structure. All these decisions have to be made in the context of the relationship between the environment and the managerial philosophy of the entrepreneurs involved.

Alfred Chandler (4) has clearly shown the relationship between the strategy a business adopts, consciously or otherwise, and the structure of its organization. He cites different kinds of organization structure [that] will be necessary for coping effectively with different strategies. The choice of corporate purpose and the design and administration of organizational process for accomplishing purposes are by no means impersonal procedures, unaffected by the characteristics of managers.

How strongly the manager feels that individuals should have freedom and autonomy in their own sphere of work will have an important influence in organizational design. Douglas McGregor (5) identified the bedrock assumptions about human nature which support markedly different approaches to organization and management—the theory "X" and "Y." The organization structure emerging from the managerial value system implied by the view that man is inherently lazy and pursues goals contrary to the interests of the company will not be the same as that which will emerge from the obverse image of the human nature. The implicitly held management value system manifests itself in contrasting organizational designs.

The manner in which work is organized, decision-making authority is distributed, span of control, shape of the organization, etc. all depend upon the underlying value system of managers. Theory "X" value system might predominantly lead to an organization closer to mechanistic structure, which will emphasize high specialization, close control, centralized decision-making etc. Theory "Y" value system might predominantly lead to less job specialization, wide span of control, flatter organization structure, and decentralized decision-making, etc.

Forces in the task

The task element in an organization situation is the central point of concern in any type of organization design and analysis. The nature of the task will have important influence on how the organization is designed. Significant empirical literature is emerging relating technology to various organizational variables. Joan Woodward, Charles Perrow (6), and several others consider technology to be a major determinant of organization structure. In her study, Joan Woodward reveals some interesting insights into the relationship between technology and organization structure. She found that successful organizations in industries with different methods were characterized by different organization structures. Successful firms in industries with a unit or job shop technology had wider spans of control and fewer hierarchical levels than did successful firms with continuous process technologies. According to her study, the companies at ends of the scale of technical complexity (unit production and continuous process production) were more likely to be characterized by organic systems than firms in the middle range of the scale.

One of the elements of technology which is also related to the organization pattern is the nature of workflow. The amount of discretion given to subordinates seems to vary according to the type of specialization—where the activities of one individual or department are closely dependent on other individuals or departments—is characterized by more lateral relationship in order to obtain effective coordination between specialized groups. At the same time, under this type of specialization the subordinates have a 'vested interest'' in their own typical point of view or approach to problems and are unable to see the impact of their actions on others. Only the personnel at the top would have the interest of the total organization and, thus, be able to see the overall picture and integrate the efforts of the different parts in order to achieve the overall organizational goals.

Under parallel specialization—where work-flow is organized so as to minimize the amount of coordination—employees see themselves as responsible for a total process, something with an observable output, and are able to see the total efforts rather than a part. Under this system natural teamwork develops as each man sees that his contribution is needed to complete the total work. For these reasons, under parallel specialization, a more organic type of organization may be appropriate, but the interdependent specialization may call for a less organic type of structure and less and less delegation of authority to the lower levels.

The size of an organization, especially in terms of the number of people employed and units produced, influences the kinds of coordination, direction and control, reporting systems and, hence the organization structure. Where an organization is small, interaction is confined to a relatively small group, communication is simpler, less information is required for decision-making and there is less need for formal organization aspects.

Forces in the environment

The environment in which an organization as a whole functions—its product and supply markets, the field of relevant technical knowledge, its political and socio-cultural environments—has a strong influence on the organization structure. Studies of Lawrence and Lorsch, Burns and Stalker, Emery and Trist, and Galbraith (7) suggest that the most effective pattern of organization is the one which enables an organization to adjust to the requirements of its environment. It is argued that the pattern of these environmental requirements over time, particularly with respect to their variability, may be such as to create different levels of uncertainty with which the organization has to cope through its structural arrangements. These different environments will tend to require different structural accommodation.

Lawrence and Lorsch (8) found that organizations operating effectively in different environments had different patterns of differentiation, and had developed different organizational mechanisms to achieve their differentiation and the integration required in their environment. They have found from their research of ten firms in three distinct industrial environments, that the environments of uncertainty and rapid rates of market and technological change, place different requirements on the organizational design than do stable conditions. According to their study organizations with less formal structure and widely shared influence are best able to cope with uncertain and heterogeneous environments. Conversely, organizations with rigid structure will be effective in more stable environments.

According to Burns and Stalker (9), in the science-based industries such as electronics where innovation is a constant demand, the organic type of organization is made appropriate. Lacking a frozen structure, an organic organization grows around the point of innovating success. Studies of communication reinforce the point that the optimal conditions for innovation are the lack of hierarchy; whereas an organization, not primarily concerned with technological innovation, but preoccupied with production problems, requires a mechanistic type of structure, where coordination is facilitated (10).

On the whole, considerable research has indicated that organizations with a low degree of formal structure could more profitably cope with changing environments than those which have a higher degree of formal structure.

Forces in the subordinates

Some research evidence seems to suggest that a major contribution to organizational effectiveness will derive from adapting the structure to accommodate more adequately the psychological needs of organizational members. Argyris, Herzberg (11) and others have drawn attention to the conflict which is likely to prevail between a traditional definition of formal organization structure and the needs of psychologically mature individuals. Herzberg has developed a two-factor theory of employee motivation which suggests specific structural adaptation to provide the "job enrichment" through which to enhance motivation and performance. Therefore, before designing organization structure, it is necessary to consider a number of forces affecting the subordinates' behavior and performance. The subordinates' desire for independence, skill and motivation for assuming responsibility, need for a sense of achievement, etc. will greatly influence the organization structure.

Research suggests that, compared to unskilled workers, skilled workers and professional personnel are more involved in their job and are more anxious for an opportunity to have a high degree of autonomy on the job and an opportunity to participate in making decisions relating to it (12). Studies consistently show that scientists as well as professional employees want autonomy and job freedom. They prefer not to be commanded in the same way as other employees in an organization.

There is also research evidence to suggest that some workers have positive attitudes toward work, who can be called "motivation seekers," while others, who seem relatively unaffected by the same conditions, can be called "maintenance seekers." Perhaps the significant difference is that maintenance reaches a state of relative fulfillment at the primary needs level, whereas motivation seekers continue to be motivated by the need for a higher level of social security (13). This implies that certain forces in the subordinates will have substantial influence in designing an organization structure.

The above is a brief analysis of selected elements which would indicate how they might influence a company's actions in designing an organization. This analysis scarcely exhausts all the elements in these forces. Looking at the selected few, however, one can begin to understand which types of design might lead to organizational effectiveness. The strength of each of them will, of course, vary from instance to instance, but the management which is sensitive to them can better assess the problems which face it and determine which mode of organization pattern is most appropriate for it.

Most organizations are formed through evolutionary processes [rather] than by conscious design. At certain stages design or redesign takes place, but this is merely a codification of modification of the results of the evolution. An adequate framework for developing organizational theory should make it possible to increase the role of a conscious design process in the development of an organization. Hopefully, the suggested model would provide such a framework.

References

1 The more important contributors to classical organization theory are: Henri Fayol, Frederick Taylor, Luther Gulick, James Mooney and Lyndall Urwick.
2 The contributions of behavioral scientists come from many sources. The more important among them are: Elton Mayo, F. J. Rothlisberger, Kurt Lewin, Mary Parker Follet, Chester Barnard, Chris Argyris, Rensis Likert, and Douglas McGregor.
3 Warren Bennis, "Organizational Developments and the Fate of Bureaucracy," *Industrial Management Review,* Spring 1966, p. 52.
4 Alfred D. Chandler, *Strategy and Structure,* (Cambridge, Mass.: M. I. T. Press, 1962).
5 Douglas McGregor, *The Human Side of Enterprise,* (New York: McGraw-Hill, 1960).
6 Joan Woodward, *Industrial Organization: Theory and Practice,* (Fair Lawn, N.J.: Oxford University Press, 1965): Charles Perrow, "A Framework for the Comparative Analysis of Organizations," *American Sociological Review,* April 1967, pp. 194–208.
7 Paul R. Lawrence and Jay W. Lorsch, *Organization and Environment,* (Boston: Harvard Business School, 1967): T. Burns and G. M. Stalker, *The Management of Innovation,* (London: Tavistock, 1961): F. E. Emery and E. L. Trist, "The Causal Texture of Organizational Environment," *Human Relations,*

February 1965, pp. 21–32: J. W. Lorsch and Paul R. Lawrence, *Studies in Organization Design,* (Homewood, Ill.: Richard D. Irwin, 1970), pp. 113–139.

8 Paul R. Lawrence and J. W. Lorsch, *op. cit.*

9 T. Burns and G. M. Stalker, *op. cit.*

10 J. W. Lorsch and Paul R. Lawrence, *Studies in Organization Design, op. cit.,* pp. 113–139.

11 Chris Argyris, *Integrating the Individual and the Organization,* (New York: Wiley, 1964): Frederick Herzberg, *Work and Nature of Man* (New York: The World Publishing Company, 1966).

12 Howard Vollmer, *Employment Rights and the Employment Relationship,* (Berkeley: University of California Press, 1960).

13 M. Scott Myers, "Who are Your Motivated Workers?" *Harvard Business Review,* (January-February, 1964), pp. 73–88.

21 People, productivity, and organizational structure
Joel E. Ross and Robert G. Murdick

Of all the current concerns of business and government, the most far-reaching is productivity, chiefly because it is so linked to foreign competition, and, related to that, because the declining rate of increase in productivity is a primary cause of monetary problems and inflation. If improved work output from both professional and production workers is the answer, threats certainly won't get it, and neither will exhortations. But organizational and management restructure might.

To quote chairman Gerstenberg of General Motors, "Better productivity results from better management." Another automotive executive, Chrysler's Eugene Cafiero, puts it more forcefully: "We've got to stop bossing and start managing." The 3M chief executive, Harry Heltzer, adds, "You can't press the button any harder and make the automated equipment run any faster. In a rising cost spiral you've just got to find ways of pressing it more intelligently." Among those more intelligent ways of pressing the button are innovative forms of organization and methods of managing.

By and large, managers have overlooked or underemphasized two major sources of increased productivity. The first is the salaried side of the company, that broad area known as white collar and middle management. One company that examined it was Hercules Incorporated, the chemical

Source: Reprinted by permission of the publisher from *Personnel* (September–October 1973), pp. 9–18. © 1973 by AMACOM, a division of American Management Associations.

giant. It reached the conclusion that those groups are overcompensated in relation to their attributable productivity gains to a greater extent than hourly workers. Other companies and studies have found that in general those groups are growing relative to direct labor; they exceed 60 percent in many cases. Moreover, few of them work to any standard of performance or under any productivity measurement system, and it is widely estimated that they seldom top 50 percent of their potential.

A possibility of immediate improvement here lies in stimulating and helping lower and middle managers to do a better job. They are often so bogged down in procedures, paperwork, red tape, and other trappings of organization structure that they have little time left for the more productive jobs of planning, organizing, and communicating. Their jobs are so narrowly defined and supervision is so close that motivation is killed.

The second source of increased productivity is the organization structure, the framework that facilitates organizational dynamics and guides company operations. Most managers are handling their physical and financial assets acceptably but are overlooking their human resources. A careful analysis of the costs of the human resources would very likely lead to better management and organization of these resources. In general, payrolls are running in the neighborhood of eight times earnings, so it is obvious that an increase of, say, 5 percent in productivity (through improved turnover, better organization, and so on) would have a really significant impact. Surely, such potential gains make trying new approaches to organization worthwhile. Let's see where our choices lie in this area.

The classical organization structure

The classical or bureaucratic, hierarchical organization continues to be the most common corporate structure. It is easily understood; it is traditional; and it works reasonably well. This traditional structure provides the foundation on which modern adaptations are constructed. The basic tenets of the classical structure are specialization of work (departments), span of management (nobody supervises over six subordinates), unity of command (nobody reports to more than one boss), and chain of command (authority delegation). The manager determines work activities to get the job done, writes job descriptions, and organizes people into groups and assigns them to superiors. He then establishes objectives and deadlines and determines standards of performance. Operations are controlled through a reporting system. The whole structure takes on the shape of a pyramid.

How do we arrive at a bureaucratic, pyramidal structure? The answer lies in an understanding of how a company grows and develops. In the beginning communication is simple and effective because activities and communications channels are few in number, but as operations grow in size and communications become more complex, proper coordination and direction demand written directives and procedures. Communication is between offices, not people. More growth means more complexity, and that calls for more policies, procedures, and further formalization. In time the proliferation of systems, procedures, and regulations demands greater departmentation and more staff people to coordinate operations. But a characteristic of the pyramidal structure is the rather tight hold the man at the top has on the reins of authority.

Criticizing the systems, formality, and controls of the bureaucracy is getting to be a profitable vocation—witness *Parkinson's Law, The Peter Principle,* and *Up the Organization.* Some of the charges leveled at the classical structure are these:

- It is too mechanistic and ignores major facets of human nature.
- It is too structured to adapt to change.
- Its formal directives and procedures hinder communication.
- It inhibits innovation.
- It pays the job and not the man.
- It relies on coercion to maintain control.
- Its job-defensive behavior encourages make-work.
- Its goals are incompatible with those of its members.
- It is simply out of date with the needs of the Seventies.

Many of those criticisms have a basis in truth, but except in small organizations, the classical structure appears to be the easiest way to cope effectively with complexity. Bureaucracy, with all of its "evils," is an organizational requirement when we go beyond the face-to-face stage of communication. The major arguments in favor of the classical approach are these:

- It has overwhelming acceptance by practicing businessmen.
- It works.
- It is easily understood and applied.
- It isn't set in concrete—it can accommodate modifications such as the behavioral organic ones when the need arises.

Recent business events point to the value of classical methods. In the late Sixties, LTV Corp., Litton Industries, Gulf & Western, and other conglomerates were having a field day with free-form management, which was characterized by loose controls and a high degree of decentralization of authority. For a while, it appeared that doing without some of the old standbys such as performance standards and controls was having some success, but now tight controls are back in favor. Two outstanding conglomerates, IT&T and TRW, never fell for the free-form management idea: both retained the fundamentals of planning and control, maintained strict reporting procedures that required substantial involvement on the part of division managers, and insisted on accurate projections, but they did establish an environment of reporting informality that made the best advice in the company accessible to everyone. In short, they used the old-time, proven methods with the necessary adaptation for human involvement to make them work.

Despite the criticisms frequently leveled at it, this structure will probably be around for a long time to come. Not long ago, a survey of the Fellows of the Academy of Management, a group of distinguished senior management professors, attempted to forecast the shape of the organization of the future. The result was a 75 percent probability prediction that the dominant organizational structure in 1985 will still be the classical pyramid.

The behavioral model of organization

The most persistent criticism of the classical organization structure comes from the behavioral scientists. Their basic quarrel with this structure is that it is too mechanistic and therefore tends to overlook human nature and the needs of people. Some maintain that organizational trappings such as structure, procedures, and controls actually violate human wants and inhibit productivity; others contend that the pyramidal structure, although perhaps suitable for a stable environment, is unable to accommodate the change that is characteristic of modern organizations.

In the behavioral model an attempt is made to overcome some of the mechanistic-structural objections to the classical organization. The model assumes the objective of economic productivity output as given, but it adds a new dimension—employee satisfaction. This satisfaction, which presumably leads to greater productivity, is a function not so much of structure as of individual perception and personal value systems. Harlan Cleveland, who has had a distinguished career in business, government, and higher education, expresses the view of the behaviorists fairly well when he decrees, "The pyramid structure of less than a generation ago must be replaced by 'horizontal systems' in which control is loose, power diffused, and centers of decision widespread."

Essentially, the idea is that the pyramid should be modified to provide:

- A more democratic attitude on the part of managers.
- More participation in major decisions at lower levels.
- Decentralization of decision making as far as possible.
- Less emphasis on hierarchy and authority delegation.
- Less narrow specialization of work tasks.

Most managers react to the behavioral model in one of four ways—with skepticism, with a pretense of acceptance but an actual intention to manipulate people and decisions, with general agreement but confusion about how to implement the model, or with an enthusiastic desire to adopt the model as a modern way to motivate people in the company. Among those who seem to be genuinely committed is Chrysler's Cafiero; he has said, "Let responsibility extend down to its lowest practical level and give authority to go along with it. The lowest level in a lot of cases is the guy right on the line."

At Chrysler, assembly workers in selected plants are authorized to reject substandard parts, work sitting instead of standing, and paint their machines any color they wish. Other companies that have acted to involve workers and let them participate in decisions about their work and to reduce the specialized and monotonous nature of the job include AT&T, where selected typists can now research, compose, and sign their own letters without supervision. Another is Motorola, where female hourly workers who formerly performed very specialized tasks (for example, wiring or soldering) on a walkie-talkie assembly line now assemble the entire product and approve its final checkout.

There is a lot of talk and speculation about the behavioral approach to improving organizational productivity, but its application is still limited and experimental. Companies that have tried to modify their organizational approach in that way are few and most have done so on a trial basis, but its acceptance should accelerate because it makes good economic sense and because it looks as if the work force, including lower and middle management, will demand it.

The organic model of organization

Also behavioral in nature, the organic approach to organizational design goes one step further in that it addresses itself to the fundamentals of structure and specialization of tasks. Warren Bennis, its foremost proponent, argues that the traditional structure is too rigid to adapt to the frequent changes brought about by modern technology, and to accommodate those changes, organizations should be made up of temporary task forces.

He summarizes his proposal this way:

First of all, the key word will be temporary. Organizations will become adaptive, rapidly changing temporary systems. Second, they will be organized around problems-to-be-solved. Third, these problems will be solved by groups of relative strangers who represent a diverse set of professional skills. Fourth, given the requirements of coordinating the various projects, articulating points or "linking pin" personnel will be necessary who can speak the diverse languages of research and who can relay and mediate between the various project groups. Fifth, the groups will be conducted on organic rather than on mechanical lines; they will emerge and adapt to the problems, and leadership and influence will fall to those who seem most able to solve the problems, rather than according to the programmed role expectations. People will be differentiated, not according to rank or roles, but according to skills and training. . . . Though no catchy phrase comes to mind, it might be called an organicadaptive structure.

Generally speaking, the organic approach to organization and productivity has had only moderate acceptance, although its use is spreading. In many ways it overcomes the familiar objections to bureaucracy by allowing more freedom of action and less narrow specialization.

Emerging concepts: The team approach

How can the essential characteristics of the organic model—described as temporary, flexible, and accommodating to change—be achieved within the traditional pyramidal structure? The answer is the team approach, which has several versions. The one called project management is widely used; matrix management and venture teams management are evolving.

The team, or plural, approach to problem solution and management is nothing new—committees and other coordinative devices have been with us for centuries. The modern team approach, however, was popularized by the Navy's Special Projects Office use of PERT in the Polaris program and is finding increased use in nondefense applications. Indeed, some form of team organization promises to be the major innovation in dealing with complexity and change during the coming decades.

Now let's turn to the various versions of the team approach.

Project management

Assume that you have a plan that requires the coordination of two or more functional departments, such as accounting, marketing, finance, or engineering. The plan may involve the development and design of a new product, deeper market penetration of an existing product, cost reduction, acquisition of or merger with an outside company, management development, new financing, construction and location of a new plant, or even overhaul of the entire company. How do you organize to accomplish the job?

The first inclination is to form a task force or committee, the device that comes to mind when one department has difficulty in handling a problem alone and where the organization structure is admittedly unable to deal with change. The drawback is that the committee is rarely given the power to make decisions and implement plans of action, and, in fact, that type of body, with its diffused power and lack of specific individual responsibility, is not appropriate for decision making.

Another solution might be to assign responsibilities for the various parts of the task to an operating manager of one of the functional departments, but here the problem is that serious top management involvement is necessary to resolve conflicts and to assure that all steps are coordinated and taken. Therefore, this tack is bound to be disruptive.

A third approach might be to establish a project manager with complete, undiluted authority for all aspects of the project. That is the organizational device being used more and more in aerospace as well as a variety of other industries, and we'll become better acquainted with it as we move away from process production systems into unit production and service output. The central idea is to assign one individual, the project manager, the responsibility for planning, work scheduling, budgeting, and controlling. His job is to ensure that the task or the project is completed within the established standards of time, cost and technical specifications.

Matrix management

Matrix organization gets its name from the fact that a number of project managers exercise planning, scheduling, and cost control over people who have been assigned to their projects, while the functional managers exert line control, in terms of technical direction, training, compensation, and the like, over the same workers. Thus, there is shared responsibility for the worker, and he must please two bosses.

Two excellent examples of this kind of management in operation can be found at Honeywell and Texas Instruments. When General Electric decided to quit the computer business, Honeywell acquired the pieces. It set up 20 managerial task forces, made up of about 200 people from both its own staff and GE's to integrate manufacturing, marketing, engineering, field services, personnel, software, and the inventory of actual product lines. Honeywell's chairman called it a textbook exercise in how to merge painlessly.

In the case of Texas Instruments, matrix management is a way of life, and has been carried to a high degree of sophistication. Broad company objectives are broken down into a series of strategies and methods for achieving them, and those strategies, in turn, are translated into several hundred tactical action programs (TAPS). Each TAP has a project management system.

By contrast, it should be mentioned, in the line project management organization each employee has only one home—the project to which he is assigned or an auxiliary service group. Usually, a number of projects are active at the same time but in different stages of their life cycles. As new projects build up, people are transferred from the projects that are approaching their ends. The project manager has complete responsibility for resources of money and men and contracts for auxiliary services, such as centralized testing in an R&D organization.

Venture teams

"The greatest challenge facing most corporations today is the development and marketing of new products or services that will produce a profit in the face of increased risks of failure," says a manager in a leading marketing research firm. The venture team is a recent organizational innovation designed to meet the demand for a breakthrough in product marketing.

The venture team is somewhat like the project matrix management team in that its personnel resources are obtained from the functional departments. Other similarities include organizational separation, the team of multidisciplinary personnel, and the goal-directed effort toward the achievement of a single result—here, product development and introduction. The venture team also may have a flexible life span, with a completion time loosely defined by broad time and financial goals. To be successful, members of venture teams have to be generally well accepted by others in the organization, because the interaction of the venture manager with those in other segments is considerable.

For companies that are committed to growth and for those whose success depends on the marketing of existing products and the development of new ones, the venture team approach offers a promising alternative to the operations traditionally found in marketing departments.

Emerging concepts: The contingency model

Thus far we have examined the classical, pyramidal form of organization structure, modifications of it, and a number of related approaches, behavioral and organic. Unfortunately, however, even taken together all of these concepts fail to come up with a workable systems approach to organization. The contingency model, which attempts to do so, represents the latest thinking and research in this area. (Howard M. Carlisle, of the University of Utah, explains it in detail in *Situational Management: A Contingency Approach to Leadership,* published by AMACOM, a division of American Management Associations.)

The contingency model seeks to answer the question of what factors, forces, or variables—contingencies—should be considered in deciding how to design an organization structure. The most important are these:

The manager

Corporate personality, strategy, policies, and plans reflect the personal, social, and ideological goals of the top-management group, frequently of the top man himself. It follows that top management is the most important variable in shaping the company's organization structure. Organizations per se don't have objectives; people have them, and through them, they set organizational goals. Their value systems and their philosophy of management combine to act as the shaping force in organizational design. For example, how do the managers view individual freedom to make decisions, as opposed to normal authority channels within the company? What is their attitude about leadership? How do they see the interaction between the company and its external environment?

The work

Since accomplishment of tasks to achieve organizational goals is the primary reason for organizing, a fundamental determinant of structure is the nature of the tasks. The work determines factors such as span of control, authority delegation, and the extent to which an organic, as opposed to a bureaucratic, structure is adopted. And a growing body of research evidence relates technology to organization design—different technologies seem to have different "management content." At this risk of oversimplification, we can

probably conclude that in low-technology, stable, continuous-process industries, there is less need for adaptive organizations.

The environment

The elements that set the climate of a company are social, political, economic, and technological, as well as those related to product and supply
markets. The environment is therefore complex, and the more a company
interacts with it, the greater its impact on the organization design.

   The greatest environmental interaction probably occurs in the context
of hard-headed market considerations, such as the availability of resources
and capital, the products or services the company sells, and the competition
anticipated. Other market considerations are the changing demand for the
company's output and the technological or other factors that may change
both demand and production methods. It isn't difficult to see why a stable
environment, such as that of the steel industry, would demand a different
pattern of design and behavior than would an environment of uncertainty
and flux, such as that of the computer industry.

The individual contributors

Because an organization structure is nothing without people to man it, the
human element is an essential factor. We now have a growing and perhaps
conclusive body of evidence that increased productivity and other desirable
results can be achieved by adapting the structure to accommodate the
needs of organizational members. That is not academic clap-trap, but practical business sense.

Building an adaptive organization

What does all this suggest and what practical use has it? It suggests that
the right structure is a function of the interaction of the variables, each of
which must be balanced against the effect of the others and against the desired output of the organization. In practice, no one style of organization design is universally appropriate; perhaps, however, there is a universal truth in
the observation of Joseph C. Wilson, of Xerox, that the greatest strength of
a company is the spirit of innovation and adaptation to change. To check the
presence of that spirit and the "adapability quotient," here are some questions:

- Do you blame most of your productivity problems on labor?
- Have you identified the output and costs of the nonhourly work force, including white collar and lower and middle management? If so, are those groups
  working to a standard and can you identify changes in their productivity?

- Do you know what a 5 percent increase in productivity of each category of worker would do for profits?
- Do you have a program for identifying the value of your human resources and the costs associated with them in much the same way as other assets?
- Do you have a true management of human resources program, not just a personnel department that maintains records?
- Do your people cling to old ways of working after they have been confronted with new situations?
- Are the older managers living in the past and passing their thinking along to the younger men?
- Is your reputation one of safety, security, and "a nice place to work"?
- Has management developed a low criticism tolerance?
- Does company esprit depend upon one or more outdated "rites"?
- Does your entire operation depend on tight controls?
- As you see it, is line-staff conflict nonexistent and are staff specialists doing their job properly?
- Have you reviewed the company situation to see whether some form of team organization would work?
- Are you willing to delegate and let subordinates make mistakes?
- Have you reviewed the relationship between these determinants of organizational design—managers, work, environment, individual contributors—to see whether you have a mix that fits your structure?

The focus of all this probing of the organizational structure is, obviously, human resource management. Here we come full circle, back to concern with productivity, because that is determined to a large extent by employees' reaction to the company's "socio-work" environment, and it, in turn, is determined to a large extent by company structure—the organization of work and people.

III/G
Organizing: Applications

22 A goal approach to organizational design
Patrick E. Connor and Stefan D. Bloomfield

Using organizational goals as a starting point in an organizational design study is suggested by the concept of organizational rationality. The predominant view in the literature on organizations—from the classicists (9, 21), to the open-systems advocates (11, 19), to the empiricists (1, 10, 17)—has been that "the organization is conceived as an 'instrument'—that is, as a rationally conceived means to the realization of . . . goals" (4, p. 404). Indeed, the essential purpose of formal organizations is "the pursuit of relatively specific objectives on a more or less continuous basis" (18, p. 488). Thus, as Gross (6, p. 277) observed, "The central concept in the study of organizations is that of the organizational goal . . . . It is the presence of a goal and a consequent organization of effort so as to maximize the probability of attaining the goal which characterizes modern organizations."

This viewpoint establishes a rationale for organizational structure: "The specific goals pursued will determine in important respects the characteristics of the structure" (18, p. 290). That is, within the framework of rationality, organizational structures are the tools for effectively pursuing organizational goals (4). The resurgence of contingency theories of organization reflects this idea; organizations are designed, continually redesigned, and managed to best accomplish their purposes under prevailing conditions. Borrowing from engineering terminology, goals are the specifications to which organizations are designed.

When goals serve as the basis for organizational design, the set of goal specifications must be comprehensive, yet analytically and operationally tractable. Unfortunately, the process of specifying goals is usually arduous and frustrating. Organizations have multiple goals (10, 16), of which many are difficult to define and often seemingly contradictory (22). Although goals

Source: From *Prescriptive Models of Organizations,* Paul C. Nystrom and William H. Starbuck (eds.), North-Holland/TIMS Studies in the Management Sciences, Vol. V, Amsterdam, The Netherlands, North-Holland Publishing Co., 1977.

such as production quotas, profit levels, and product parameters are relatively easily stated, goals relating to quality of service, internal morale, external image, and organizational flexibility are usually difficult to specify quantitatively. The familiar dependence on proxy variables in such cases may
yield precise results only at the expense of significant distortion in later
evaluation and analysis (3).

As a consequence, an attempt to elicit a comprehensive list of organizational goals usually produces a lengthy and awkward compilation of
statements—some relating directly to specific structural properties, and
others phrased in lofty generalities with heavy political overtones. Procedures must then be developed to reduce such sets of goal statements to a
form more amenable to analysis. In particular, the goals must be arrayed in a
way that facilitates assigning priorities among goals, and allows for their operational restatement.

Structuring organizational goals

The need to suitably structure sets of organizational goal statements is addressed by a developing body of evidence which finds that there exists only
a limited number of distinct goal types (10). Perrow (16), for example, observed that organizations are subject to many influences, and as a result
pursue five major goal categories. While differing in some respects from
Perrow's formulation, the findings of Edward Gross (6–8) support the
categorization of organizational goals into five goal types. The work of Bertram Gross (5) on organizational effectiveness led him to identify seven different goal types for organizations.

These typological approaches to defining organizational goals share
two important properties. First, each recognizes that organizations are
characterized by a variety of goals; as on-going social systems, organizations
maintain activities and resources directed to many purposes. But, significantly, these purposes can be conceptually grouped into a small number
of well-defined categories. Second, output goals constitute only one goal
type in each of the formulations, although these goals are usually distinguished by their importance to organizational survival and prosperity. In
comparison, other types may be most properly viewed as support goals
(6, 8).

A typological approach to organizational goals provides a helpful
mechanism for dealing with "complex sets of . . . attributes by identifying a
more parsimonious set of constructs" (13). Of course, organizations vary in
the relative emphases given to different categories of organizational goals,
particularly the support goals. Identifying the set of relative emphases, the
organization's *goal mix,* establishes a ranking of individual goals corresponding to the ranking of their goal category. For goals that suggest specific
structural properties (12, 14, 18), this ranking may be extended to the subsequent selection of design characteristics, providing a mechanism for
resolving conflicts among such characteristics. Finally, the structure imposed

on the goal identification process through use of a typology serves an auditing function by pointing out duplication within the list of goal statements, and by revealing areas in which important organizational goals may have been inadvertently omitted.

Specifying organizational correlates

A goal approach to organizational design requires specifying structural properties which will facilitate the accomplishment of these goals. That such a specification is possible follows from Etzioni's (3) concept of a real goal (or what Perrow [16] terms an operative goal): one that is actively being pursued by a substantial part of the organization. This pursuit is reflected in members' activities and resource utilization patterns. Directing resources toward goal accomplishment, however, requires a variety of organizational design characteristics—control mechanisms, departments, communication links, and so on. These characteristics comprise what may be termed the goals' organizational correlates. Conflicts between different organizational correlates may be resolved by reference to the priorities previously assigned to the goals themselves through use of the typology.

The specific methods used to categorize goals, assign priority rankings, identify organizational correlates, and specify a final organizational design probably will vary considerably among different types of organizations and between differently constituted organizational study teams. The following case study illustrates these methods.

An application

A unit of a large federal agency used a goal approach for their organizational redesign. The agency maintains its principal offices in Washington, D.C., with subordinate units at regional, local, and field office levels. A formal line and staff structure exists at the Washington offices, creating a clearly defined hierarchy for both staff specialists and line officers. Staff positions correspond to the agency's traditional missions, called functions. Staff personnel ostensibly act as technical specialists in their respective functional areas, reporting to and advising line officers. The line officers are delegated the sole authority to issue directions and orders within their specified areas of responsibility.

Two principal factors prompted the agency's decision to explore possible organizational redesign. The first was the gradual expansion of the agency's roster of functional specialists, paralleling the emergence of specialized technical disciplines within universities. The attempt to incorporate these disciplines into the prevailing organizational structure revealed basic incompatibilities between the traditional functional areas and the new technical specialties. These difficulties were compounded by the need to accommodate new interdisciplinary, and consequently interfunctional, specialties. Agency management believed that the resulting structural arrangements blurred the established functional roles, promoting interfunctional rivalry and reducing organizational effectiveness.

The second factor was a growing tendency for functional staff personnel to bypass designated authority and to issue orders directly. This was the most noticeable in the functional areas central to the agency's primary missions. The tendency of staff personnel to oversee directly operations within the central areas was extremely frustrating to the line officials whose managerial prerogatives were being usurped, especially since these line officers—in contrast to many other federal agencies—were career officials rather than political appointees.

These developments led agency management to believe that the formal organizational structure was no longer adequate to administer effectively the agency's missions. Therefore, selected regional and local offices were directed to develop new structures more appropriate to their individual needs. One such unit was a local office, of about 550 employees, that had played a flagship role in several aspects of the agency's missions.

Rather than unilaterally developing and imposing a new organizational design, local management appointed a study team of employees to propose a new organizational structure. The team was composed of six employees representing several different hierarchical levels and functional areas. These members were selected on the basis of their observed interest and commitment to the organization, without regard to their overall knowledge of the organization or their previous managerial experience. The resulting lack of managerial expertise within the team, coupled with a restrictive time constraint, precluded the use of many sophisticated procedures otherwise appropriate in such a redesign study. The authors participated in the study as technical resource personnel, charged with providing occasional guidance to the study process and monitoring its validity. In order that the final recommendations be credible as an in-house product, the authors were cautioned that all value judgments, decision criteria, and ultimate design specifications should be those of the study team members solely.

To augment its limited knowledge of the local office's missions, the design team initially compiled a comprehensive list of goal statements for the organization. This list was generated by soliciting inputs from employees at all levels of the local office, as well as obtaining official guidelines issued from the Washington and regional offices. This produced a set of forty-six goal statements, ranging from quite specific to extremely general. Several goals related directly to structural properties of the organization, and others had no apparent organizational correlates. The length and extreme diversity of this set of goal statements suggested the need for a goal typology to facilitate the analysis.

The goal typology

Selection of an appropriate goal typology was governed by three criteria: the typology must be scientifically supported, directly applicable to the organization, and meaningful to the design team. The authors suggested the classification scheme developed by Edward Gross (6–8) categorizing organizational goals into five principal classes as follows:

1 Output Goals. Those goals that are reflected in products or services intended to affect society.
2 Support Goals. a. Adaptation Goals—Those goals reflecting the need for the organization to cope effectively with its environment; these concern the need to attract clients and staff, to finance the enterprise, to secure needed resources, and so on.

   b. Management Goals—Those goals reflecting the need to administer the organization, to handle conflict, and to establish priorities for attending to output goals.

   c. Motivation Goals—Those goals directed toward developing a high level of satisfaction on the part of staff and clients.

   d. Positional Goals—Those goals aimed toward maintaining the organization's position and image in comparison to other organizations in the same industry, and in the face of attempts or trends to change its position.

   The authors considered the validity of this typology to compare most favorably with those of Perrow (16), Bertram Gross (5), and others (2, 15, 20). Edward Gross's categorization appeared to be the result of more systematic examination than the others, having been derived as part of an extensive empirical research program (7, 8).

   The design team agreed that Gross's typology was pertinent and would be useful. Team members endorsed the notion that output goals form a superordinate class of their own—the raison d'être of the organization. Other goals, by contrast, were seen as ends intended to better facilitate achievement of the output goals. The support-goal subcategories, moreover, seemed well-suited to the organization. Being employees of an agency subject to extensive and often sensitive dealings with the public, team members readily acknowledged the existence and importance of adaptation goals. Although lacking formal managerial training, team members appreciated the need for well-coordinated organizational maintenance activities, and thus endorsed the necessity of management goals. Finally, as representatives of different constituencies within the organization, team members expressed strong concern that the organization maintain as favorable a working climate as possible, and strive to retain the unique character distinguishing it from its sister agencies. This concern led the team to support identification of motivational and positional goals.

Establishing the goal mix

Realizing that the original list of goal statements might yield conflicting prescriptions for organizational structure, the study team thought it prudent to identify the agency's goal mix early in the redesign process. The team recognized, moreover, hat assigning priorities to the categories of the goal typology would serve not only to establish corresponding rankings for individual goals, but also would encourage team members to adopt a total-organization viewpoint emphasizing large-scale, overall goals.

The process used to assign goals to the five categories of the typology was tedious but straightforward. Each goal was thoroughly discussed and assigned—by consensus—to one or more categories. Many goals addressed several classes of organizational goals. For example, the goal statement, "Decision making . . . must de-emphasize intuitive reliance in favor of the increased capability and options offered by sophisticated analytical and computer systems," clearly pertained to the class of management goals, but was also thought to reflect adaptation and positional goals; it was therefore assigned to all three categories.

The subsequent process of assigning priorities to the typology was conditioned strongly by the context of the redesign study. Although many mechanisms exist for formally gathering and incorporating wide-scale organizational input into such a ranking task, the study team rejected such efforts as impractical within their time constraints. Instead, since the team was formed to represent several employee constituencies, team members decided to rely on their own perceptions of the agency's role, as reinforced or modified by the now-categorized goals. The goal typology, therefore, was extensively discussed within the group until a consensus was achieved for the assignment of priorities. Table 1 presents the goal typology as rewritten by the study team, and as ranked to display the agency's goal mix.

Developing organizational correlates

Developing structural properties corresponding to the set of goal statements was also a relatively straightforward, albeit judgmental, process. The design team examined each goal statement to identify one or more organizational correlates. For example, one goal statement was: "Increase public confidence in the organization's competence and credibility in long-range planning, especially by providing that decision making be open and visible to the public." The design team decided that pursuit of this goal would be facilitated by creating "a formal long-range planning unit whose charge includes acquiring input from the public." This organizational correlate was then designed into the emerging structure.

Through these activities, decision-making units were formed, linking pins were established, formal communication paths were identified, and job descriptions were modified. In short, a variety of organizational correlates were specified by the team and were then assigned priorities corresponding to those of the goal statements from which they derived.

It should be noted that the process of developing organizational correlates was actually less tidy than is suggested here. Each goal statement was exhaustively discussed and analyzed to isolate any content relevant to structural properties of the organization. Some goal statements had no implications for structure—for example, "Utilize available local unit personnel skills

Table 1 Goal typology adopted by the organization

Priority	Goal type	Organizational description
1	Output	The organization exists for the purpose of producing output. Normally output is tangible, although some may be intangible and feature lack of organizational activity such as pleasant experiences on the part of the public served.
2	Adaptability/ flexibility	This class of goals deals with the ability of the organization to respond to external stimuli whether they come from out-of-agency or from other and/or higher units in-agency. Examples: severe budget cut, increase in delegation to units, changing program needs, public concerns, emergencies.
3	Motivation	Synonym is morale. This class of goals involves maintenance and improvement of those forces which cause employees to want to perform tasks for the organization. A normal organization cannot function in the absence of employee motivation.
4	Positional	This class of goals speaks to the character of the organization as the public, customers, politicians, employees, and prospective employees see it. This is the general tenor of the organization; the impressions it gives to those that come into contact with it. This is what makes one organizational unit appear somewhat different from another. These goals are closely allied to motivational goals.
5	Management	Organizations have goals as to how they wish to administer organization resources in terms of such organizational properties as structure, communication processes, lines of authority, decision making processes, and control processes.

and training to meet program requirements." It was also discovered that many of the organizational correlates were implied by more than one goal statement; in such cases, the correlate was assigned a priority equal to that of the highest ranked statement. In all, the forty-six goal statements produced twenty-six distinct organizational correlates. Finally, many goal statements concerned factors not necessarily appearing on an organizational chart, but rather relating to tasks for managers or their departments. These tasks were described in a narrative forming an integral part of the redesign proposal.

Table 2 presents an illustrative sample of some goals and their organizational correlates.

Developing the organizational design

The final task facing the study team was to develop a new organizational design incorporating the organizational correlates. First, each team member

Table 2 Selected goal statements and their corresponding organizational correlates

Goal statement	Goal type	Organizational correlate
1. (a) Provide for an organization which can adjust to the imposition of additional work loads, changes in direction, and the addition of new skills. (b) Develop an organization which can respond to nonrecurring goals by adjusting current goals and subunit resource allocations as imposed goals are received. (c) Provide an organization having flexibility in program execution to respond quickly to emergency situations.	Adaptation	Provide as few distinct organizational units as possible consistent with smooth organizational functioning (Priority 2).
2. Decision making . . . must de-emphasize intuitive reliance in favor of the increased capability and options offered by sophisticated analytical and computer systems.	Adaptation Positional Management	Provide a unit charged with computer and systems development, capable of analytical work to furnish technical assistance to all levels of the organization (Priority 2).
3. Increase public confidence in the organization's competence and credibility in long-range planning, especially by providing that decision making be open and visible to the public.	Positional Management	Identify a formal long-range planning unit whose charge includes acquiring input from the public (Priority 4).
4. Provide for the minimum number of necessary reviews and review levels consistent with the costs, the risks of unsatisfactory performance, and the evaluation skills available.	Motivation Positional Management	Maintain absence of identifiable "review" units in the local office (Priority 3).
5. Provide for program execution based upon short-range planning and programming.	Management	Provide short organizational links between short-range planning and the program execution level (Priority 5).
6. A more precise control device needs to replace present accountability procedures as a means to effect accountability among agency subunits.	Management	Maintain in the local office an identifiable group with capability to audit or inspect against goals and standards (Priority 5).

independently developed a broadbrush design comprised solely of organizational elements implied by the correlates. This demonstrated the degree to which the correlates were perceived to specify an organizational structure. With these initial designs displayed before them, the team members developed their final recommendations after extensively discussing the strengths and weaknesses of their individual designs.

Specification of the final design was considerably simplified by the substantial overlap among the broadbrush designs, due in large measure to the high priority assigned to minimizing distinct organizational subunits. The extensive consolidation of tasks and functions implied by this organizational correlate was a clear distinguishing feature of each individual's design. Thus, the final design task was reduced primarily to rearranging five or six major organizational subunits to facilitate the communication needs addressed by other correlates. That being accomplished, equitable distribution of resources and power among the primary line officers was the criterion for final design selection.

The final design differed substantially from the existing organizational structure, shown in Figure 1. The existing structure had emphasized differentiation by function—that is, mission—with staff specialists ostensibly serving in an advisory capacity to line officials. As may be inferred from the organizational chart, this distinction between line and staff was often unclear, particularly to the line officials at the field office level. The new design, Figure 2, produced an organizational structure relatively free of functional emphasis. Instead, the design emphasized fundamental organizational processes, such as long-range planning and resource planning, through integration of the functional areas into these major processes.

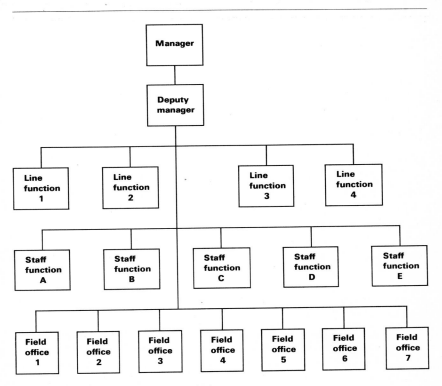

Figure 1 The original organizational design

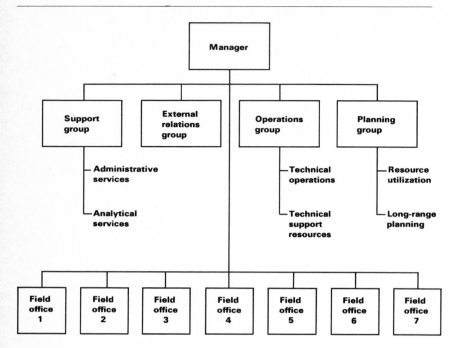

Figure 2 The new organizational design

Outcomes of the redesign

To integrate functional tasks into the organizational process units—support, operations, planning—the staff specialists' role was redefined explicitly as support to the decision makers. To emphasize this distinction, staff members were no longer invited to formal discussions among line officers except when specifically needed, and then were dismissed after their contribution had been made. The results of this change were threefold: line officers, especially at field office levels, became considerably more confident of their role as decision makers; staff officers went through a period of disorientation and anxiety with regard to their reduced role in the decision-making process; and lines of decision responsibility and accountability were significantly clarified, to the relief of top mamagement and their line officers.

Because local unit management could not be persuaded to conduct a formal evaluation, no systematic assessment of the new design's effectiveness can be presented. However, a series of interviews with top and middle managers revealed general agreement on two significant outcomes of the redesign. First, local-unit flexibility was improved. The new design allowed, even encouraged, an increased level of collaborative activity when unexpected events required a rapid organizational response. Officers directing the major organizational-process units report that they were able to quickly shift their personnel and resources to meet changing functional demands. Although increased flexibility within these large units was achieved at the expense of more formal communication needs between units, the trade-off was perceived to be greatly to the organization's advantage.

Second, the new design appeared after two years of operation to have been wholly accepted by the organizational membership. Local-unit management reported little tendency by organizational members to revert to previous modes of operation. The discomfort and disorientation initially experienced by many staff personnel appreciably eased, aided by the traditionally high personnel transfer rates within the agency and by personal counseling services made available during the reorganization. On balance, management concurred that the new design enabled a more effective pursuit of organizational goals.

References

1 Blau, Peter M., and Schoenherr, Richard A., *The Structure of Organizations,* Basic Books, New York, N.Y., 1971.

2 Etzioni, Amitai, *A Comparative Analysis of Complex Organizations,* Free Press, New York, N.Y., 1961.

3 Etzioni, Amitai, "Two Approaches to Organizational Analysis: A Critique and a Suggestion," *Administrative Science Quarterly,* Vol. 5 (September 1960), pp. 257–278.

4 Gouldner, Alvin W., "Organizational Analysis," in *Sociology Today,* Robert K. Merton, Leonard Broom, and Leonard S. Cottrell, Jr. (eds.), Harper and Row, New York, N.Y., 1959.

5 Gross, Bertram, "What Are Your Organization's Objectives? A General-Systems Approach to Planning," *Human Relations,* Vol. 18 (August 1965), pp. 195–216.

6 Gross, Edward, "The Definition of Organizational Goals," *British Journal of Sociology,* Vol. 20 (September 1969), pp. 277–294.

7 Gross, Edward, "Universities as Organizations: A Research Approach," *American Sociological Review,* Vol. 33 (August 1968), pp. 518–544.

8 Gross, Edward and Grambsch, Paul V., *Changes in University Organization, 1964–1971,* McGraw-Hill, New York, N.Y., 1974.

9 Gulick, L., and Urwick, L. (eds.), *Papers on the Science of Administration,* Institute of Public Administration, New York, N.Y., 1937.

10 Hall, Richard H., *Organizations: Structure and Process,* Prentice-Hall, Englewood Cliffs, N.J., 1972.

11 Katz, Daniel, and Kahn, Robert L., *The Social Psychology of Organizations,* Wiley, New York, N.Y., 1966.

12 Lawrence, Paul R., and Lorsch, Jay W., *Organization and Environment,* Irwin, Homewood, Ill., 1969.

13 McKelvey, Bill, "Guidelines for the Empirical Classification of Organizations," *Administrative Science Quarterly,* Vol. 20 (December 1975), pp. 509–525.

14 McKelvey, Bill and Kilmann, Ralph H., "Organization Design: A Participative Multivariate Approach," *Administrative Science Quarterly,* Vol. 20 (March 1975), pp. 24–36.

15 Parsons, Talcott, *Structure and Process in Modern Society,* Free Press, New York, N.Y., 1960.

16 Perrow, Charles, *Organizational Analysis: A Sociological Analysis,* Wadsworth, Belmont, Cal., 1970

17 Pugh, D. S., Hickson, D. J., and Hinings, C. R., "An Empirical Taxonomy of Structures of Work Organizations," *Administrative Science Quarterly,* Vol. 14 (March 1969), pp. 115–126.

18 Scott, W. Richard, "Theory of Organizations," in *Handbook of Modern Sociology,* Robert E. L. Faris (ed.), Rand McNally, Chicago, Ill., 1964.

19 Thompson, James D., *Organizations in Action,* McGraw-Hill, New York, N.Y., 1967.

20 Thompson, James D., and McEwen, William J., "Organizational Goals and Environment: Goal Setting as an Interaction Process," *American Sociological Review,* Vol. 23 (February 1958), pp. 23–31.

21 Weber, Max, From *Max Weber: Essays in Sociology,* H. H. Gerth and C. Wright Mills (eds.), Oxford University Press, London, England, 1958.

22 Wildavsky, Aaron, "The Self-Evaluating Organization," *Public Administration Review,* Vol. 32 (September–October 1972), pp. 509–520.

23 Organization and management techniques in the federal government
Forest W. Horton, Jr.

The population, knowledge and technology explosions which have taken place primarily since the end of World War II have had a profound effect on many of the fundamental assumptions and doctrines underlying traditional organization and management theory.

For example:

- Bureaucracy as we know it is becoming obsolete as a social system effective in organizing the efforts of human and other resources to achieve stated goals.
- Classic organization and management theories, such as span of control formulas prescribing "optimal" ratios of supervisors-to-workers, are proving to be either incorrect or no longer valid.

Source: Reprinted by permission of the publisher from *S.A.M. Advanced Management Journal,* 35, No. 1 (January 1970), pp. 66–67. © 1970 by Society for Advancement of Management.

● The emergence of a new discipline—Behavioral Science—is bringing with it a new concept of the relationship of man to his environment; a concept based on increased knowledge of his complex and changing needs which replaces the oversimplified, innocent push-button idea of man.

From a managerial standpoint, then, a key dimension to the problem of modern organizational structure is the *temporal dimension.* That is, the need for organizations to become more adaptive and reponsive to rapidly changing environments, problems, and objectives.

This article discusses one possible solution to this problem—the use of "task forces" and project managers as techniques in improving problem-solving and goal achievement as well as in motivating people to higher productivity and job satisfaction.

While some authors have argued that highly flexible and adaptive organic structures will eventually become the *only* viable form of organization, that thesis goes beyond the scope of this article. It will be my contention that task forces and project managers are useful management techniques even in the highly functionally-oriented, traditionally-structured organizations that characterize most of industry and government today.

Some conclusions

1 The Task Force and Project Manager concepts are very effective approaches to contemporary problem-solving and goal achievement in large and complex modern organizations.
2 The Task Force and Project Manager concepts are more rewarding and productive approaches to the ego-satisfaction and motivation needs of human behavior in modern organizational settings than are the more traditional approaches based on classic organizational theory.
3 As a first general rule, the larger and more complex an organization and the more specialized and diversified its product lines, services and objectives, the greater the utility of these approaches.
4 As a second general rule, the larger the number of individual skill categories needed to produce a product or service or accomplish an objective, the greater the utility of these approaches.
5 As a third general rule, the larger the number of organizational sub-elements (i.e., the greater the compartmentalization), the greater the utility of these approaches.
6 The Task Force and Project Manager concepts are most useful in organizational settings wherein top management is committed to that set of values embodied essentially by the late Douglas McGregor's Theory Y.[1]
7 The Task Force and Project Manager concepts are more useful in organizations with large numbers of professional personnel than in organizations with primarily semi-skilled or unskilled personnel.

[1] McGregor, Douglas, *The Human Side of Enterprise,* McGraw-Hill Book Company, 1960.

8 Even in organizations with primarily semi-skilled and unskilled personnel, these modern approaches will find increasing utility as the pressures of leisure time create increasing emotional needs for a higher order of job satisfaction.

Background

There is fairly widespread agreement of the concepts of the Task Forces and Project Management (use of Project Managers) developed as a new method of management during World War II in both the military establishment and in industry.

A number of different terms have been applied to what is essentially the same basic concept. They are:

- *"Project Management"* which is the term given to the concept as it originated primarily in the Defense Department. The aerospace industry–government relationship in World War II had developed a tendency toward greater use of *ad hoc* offices concerned exclusively with the managerial integration of a single major weapon. The head of the office responsible for the effort was generally called the Project Manager (or sometimes and more specifically, for example, the Weapons Systems Manager).
- *"Product Management"* was the more or less equivalent term introduced in industry. As new products began to appear with increasing frequency than ever before, and tended to be discounted after a shorter stay on the market, the idea of a Product Manager who could coordinate the traditional functions of engineering, manufacturing, purchasing, quality, sales and the other functions, came into being.
- *"Program Management"* was the term introduced in the non-defense side of the government establishment, as well as in other forms of organizations outside of the private industry, such as non-profit foundations. In these kinds of organizations, the "program" was the discrete task that cut across organizational boundaries and required coordination among the various functional departments.
- *"Task Force"* is a more general-purpose term used extensively even before World War II to describe the technique of bringing together a variety of specialists to perform a specific task. One connotation of this concept that has persisted over the years is the notion of the task itself having to be one of very high priority and having a relatively short or "tight" deadline for accomplishment.
- *"Matrix Management"* is perhaps the most recent title given to what is still essentially the same concept. It has won favor with the behavioral scientists particularly. Its focus is on the vertical, horizontal and diagonal relationships between and among staff and line managers. It emphasizes the critical importance of the coordination function and process as opposed to traditional chain of command, span of control, and similar notions.

The device of the "committee" also deserves attention in this context. While it, too, fits the basic criteria of a temporary organizational approach to problem-solving, through the years it has taken on some unfortunate negative connotations that probably account for its exclusion from the family of terms described above. For one thing, committees have often deliberately been used as a means of delaying or deferring problem-solving rather than promoting it. For another, committees have gained the reputation, perhaps underservedly, of "producing a camel from what is essentially a horse!" In government circles particularly, the comment is often heard that if one doesn't know what else to do with a problem, then one should turn it over to a committee! That, such cynics contend, will be sure to kill it!

Notwithstanding the cynics, the device of the committee does have its place and is perhaps used at least as widely as are task forces. There are some key differences, however.

First, committees are more formal than task forces and their very formality tends to run counter to some of the underlying purposes of task forces. Task forces thrive on informality, easy interpersonal relationships and the absence of rigid sets of rules that prescribe the modes and norms of "acceptable" behavior and procedure. The task force leader or project manager does not have to rely on a *Robert's Rules of Order* or other parliamentary conventions to achieve his goals and carry out his assigned tasks. Other aspects of the formality variable that differentiate these two approaches include the need for formal agendas, formal written periodic reports, "hearings," etc. Usually none of these are required of task forces and project managers.

Second, committees tend to be convened to deal with chronic and longstanding major policy and organizational problems that often have significant legal, legislative, or other "external" environmental aspects that may involve the interests, rights or obligations of diverse groups, whereas, task forces tend to be organized to deal with special, critical and sensitive high priority problems that have cropped up rather suddenly and which can be "solved" rather than just "studied."

I think a final word is necessary to distinguish the task force concept from the project management concept since I have chosen both as my subjects and have thus far referred to them in the text as if they were virtually synonymous in concept, purpose, and application.

They are in fact very closely related. The essential difference is that task forces are usually organized to deal with *problems* rather than monitor "from birth to death" a project or product. The project manager and his project office staff are dealing with a more tangible item—the project or product. But both are temporary, composed of specialists brought together because of their unique skills and abilities to contribute to the overall task, and are built upon the same fundamental assumptions about the nature of man and his needs espoused by McGregor and the modern behavioral scientists.

Therefore, for the balance of this article I will deal with them interchangeably—essentially as one concept, but recognizing that strictly and technically speaking they are in reality two very closely related species belonging to the same family.

Because the problems encountered in the defense industry have, in respect to the need to adjust to drastic and accelerated change, been perhaps more crucial than in other industries, it is not surprising that this industry has been in the forefront of the development of the task force concept.

Among those names most prominently mentioned in the literature as being on the leading edge in the use of this technique have been such groups as the RAND Corporation, Stanford Research Institute, Research Analysis Corporation (RAC), Systems Development Corporation (SDC), The Jet Propulsion Laboratory, Rocketdyne, Thomson-Ramo-Wolridge (TRW), Boeing Aircraft, Martin-Marietta Company, Lockheed Corporation and International Business Machines. Nearly all are members of the Aerospace and defense-related industries. Nearly all have reputations of "progressive" management philosophies; have felt keenly the competitive pressures of needing to act decisively in a very limited time frame in order to complete a proposal or respond to a bid; have felt the severe pressures of competing in very limited human resource markets for scarce skills such as electronic engineers, data processing systems analysts, physicists, mathematicians, etc.; and have been at the forefront in developing new technologies in the very exciting and challenging creative areas of satellites, missiles, high energy physics, nuclear reactors, atomic energy and others. In other words, these are the firms that have marched at the front of the modern technological revolution.

On the government side, as one might suspect, those government organizations and agencies which have been associated with the modern technological revolution also have experimented the most with this technique. Among these agencies, those most generally acknowledged to be the leaders have been such agencies as the Department of Defense, Atomic Energy Commission, National Aeronautics and Space Agency, Central Intelligence Agency and the Office of Economic Opportunity.

NASA

NASA's experience is perhaps the most instructive and in many ways the most typical of the agencies cited. Furthermore, its experiences have tended to meld the use of this technique as between government and industry. For these reasons, I think it would be useful to look at their experience a little more closely.

NASA's James E. Webb[2] recently said, "We are seeing increasing use of organizational concepts like product management and project management

---

[2] Webb, James E., "New Challenges for Organization," *Harvard Business School Bulletin,* March/April, 1967.

in which the responsibility for the development and marketing of a product or for the completion of an important project are put in the hands of one individual who has all of the required elements of command over all the resources he needs. What characterizes these new kinds of organizational structures is that they cut across the traditional proverbs used to express concepts of authority and responsibility. They utilize, rather than accept as limits, the differences of functional discipline or the division of work into bits and pieces. At NASA, for example, whenever possible, even while exercising very broad authority associated with his responsibility for performance, cost and schedule, an individual is left attached to the laboratory or technical group or department within his technical competence, where his skill was demonstrated and where the forward thrust of current research keeps him up to date. This also gives him easy access to colleagues who know how to wring out the facts needed for the difficult trade-off decisions."

Another idea advanced by Mr. Webb is that as organizations become more complex and their challenges more interdisciplinary in character, it is becoming increasingly apparent that there is nothing sacred about the notion of a single chief executive. Accordingly, he points out, there has been an increasing tendency to experiment with the idea of the "multiple executive," usually in the form of an "office of the president" concept.

Although Mr. Webb alluded to the context of the "multiple executives" in the context of NASA's *permanent* organizational structure, he was also drawing a parallel to the purpose and utility of such an arrangement within the context of the task force concept which embodies a *temporary* organizational structure. Underlying the multiple executive idea is the more fundamental notion beginning to take hold in both modern organizational and behavioral science theory that the leadership function can often be shared. Some research is even beginning to indicate that under certain conditions sharing the leadership function among the members of a group can be more effective than vesting the functions in a single individual.

This is not to say necessarily that the "chairmanship should rotate" among members or that sub-tasks should be divided up so that each man bosses his own piece of the pie; but rather that the atmosphere, structure, and values personified by the task force concept are more conducive to a participative approach to the leadership function than are traditional concepts.

Mr. Webb summarized his experiences using this technique saying that "in the complex challenge that we are talking about, it is rarely possible to attribute the solution or an achievement to one individual. In this kind of effort, the boundaries between disciplines are all but erased. The skills of individuals fuse with one another. It is virtually impossible to identify who has contributed some key elements to the final outcome."

Of course, what Mr. Webb leaves implicit is recognition that under such a system personal job satisfaction and reward come equally from feelings of being a member of an effective and competent *team* and from feelings of individual accomplishment, not solely from the latter.

Project managers

Cleland[3] points out that forerunners of the project manager are designated as "project expeditors;" they do not perform line functions but rather informally motivate those persons doing the work. The project expeditor is mainly concerned with schedules and relies upon his personal diplomacy and persuasive abilities to remove bottlenecks in the management process. He is perhaps the earliest kind of project manager; ranked slightly above him in terms of time and responsibility is the "project coordinator" who has a more formal role in the organization and who is concerned with the synchronization of organizational activities directed toward a specific objective in the overall functional activities. His limited independence is reflected in his freedom to make decisions within the framework of the overall project objectives; he does not actively enter into the management functions outside of his particular organization. The project coordinator has specific functional authority in certain areas such as budgeting, release of funds, and release of authority to act as in the dispatching function in the production control environment.

The difference, then, between the early beginnings of the project management concept and today's stage of evolution of the concepts is that today's project manager is *in every sense a manager.* He actively participates in the organic functions of planning, organizing, directing, and controlling the organization of the specific project. The project manager usually accomplishes the management process through other managers. Many of those feel the force of his leadership in the departments and organizations separate from the project manager's parent unit. Since these people are not subject to his operating supervision and owe their fidelity to a superior line manager, a unique set of conflicts of purpose and tenure (job seniority and rank) arise. The project manager has real and explicit authority but only over major considerations involved in the project plan. One of the project manager's biggest problems (which I shall examine in more detail later) is how to get full support when the functional people are responsible to someone else for pay raises, promotion, and the other expected line superior-subordinate relationships.

Discussion and analysis

First, I want to summarize some key assumptions which I think are crucial to any discussion and analysis of the concept of task forces and project management. They are:

- The need for organizations to react quickly and effectively to risks and opportunities before either the risk becomes seriously threatening or the opportunity is lost.

[3] Cleland, D. I., "Why Project Management," *Business Horizons,* Winter 1964, Vol. 7, No. 4.

- The need for organizations to utilize a wide variety of skills and expertise to solve problems, meet risks and take advantage of opportunities. Often many disciplines, experts in highly specialized fields and persons with broad experience backgrounds, must be brought together quickly. Rarely can all of the people "assigned" to any given standing functional unit solve a given problem.
- The need for organizations to create conditions in a working environment wherein people from different "cultures" and "subcultures" can come together with maximum interpersonal and intergroup effectiveness; where conflict is constructively channeled; and where there is a rapid and intense involvement with a minimum of cross-cultural "wasted motion."
- The recognition that problems and objectives are constantly in a state of flux; old ones are being resolved and new ones are being created. Rarely is the organization faced with long-standing, chronic and unresolved issues. (If it is, it will often go bankrupt or otherwise decay.)
- The hierarchical, traditional concept of authority is becoming increasingly less useful in solving modern organizational problems because more and more of these problems are cutting across jurisdictional lines within the organization. Therefore, all units that have an interest in the problem have virtually equal status and must work together without any particular one being considered the "boss" and thus having preemptive influence or authority over the others. Voluntary cooperation, therefore, becomes the only viable means of cohesiveness.
- The emphasis that bureaucracy places on structural maintenance leads to sanctification of procedure and to domineering attitudes of officials. Although apparently quite unlike, these two structural pathologies have one thing in common: the frequent failure of bureaucratic functionaries to separate means from ends. Procedures which are means become ends for the functionary who is imbued with the sanctity of impersonal application of abstract rules. This is not in the interest of problem-solving and goal achievement.

My contention in this article has been that task forces and project management offer a great deal of promise to organizations faced with the kinds of problems that stem from the foregoing assumptions.

The concept offers this promise by placing a premium on the conditions under which motivation, communication, goal-setting, decision-making, problem-solving, and performance evaluation can best take place. Rewards and punishments are geared to constructive group effort, not to the traditional measures of reward such as status, position, rank, pay, title, size of office, thickness of carpet on the floor and size of desk.

That is not to say that these considerations are entirely "missing" from the rewards and punishments system; but rather that they are given *secondary* rather than primary emphasis. Status, rank, pay, and similar considerations must always enter the motivation process. But if rewards and punishments are largely (if not entirely) based on *just* those kinds of considerations, then I would contend that in the long run productive, collaborative group effort will suffer and progressively deteriorate.

Now let us examine more closely some of the specific problems and issues which have given rise to these new theories.

First, recognition of the fact that people are basically different in makeup. Their values, attitudes, behavior, etc. vary widely. Janger[4] points out in studies he has made that project managers themselves feel that not all people fit into their project organization. There are some people who can't stand the informality. If two people have demands made on them, they feel that they have two bosses which to them is intolerable. There are people who want their work laid out for them precisely and who feel insecure without established procedures. Then there are people who misuse freedom of communication to go over their superior's head. Unless these people learn to work together as "responsible professionals" they don't stay on a team for long! Generally those groups which do not adapt as well to this permissive environment are in the less-skilled, lower-paid, and more security-conscious job categories such as those characterized by large numbers of blue collar, assembly-line workers in minimal competition industries and organizations.

Second, shifting people from project to project leaves them in a constant state of flux. Some people have more tolerance for such a state than others. Shifting people from project to project may disrupt the training of new employees and specialists, interfering with the growth and maturation of specialists within the fields of specialization. Furthermore, the long-term capability and effectiveness of an organization may be further impaired if project-team members fear they may not have their jobs when the project is over.

To offset this fear, some companies heavily involved with project work attempt to stablize employment in a number of ways: (1) by seeking enough new business to keep people working; (2) by avoiding, insofar as possible, projects that may go through periods of unpredictable delay or show likelihood of being cancelled; (3) by scheduling projects so that several do not begin or end at the same time; and (4) by scheduling the work in several projects so that, as specialists finish work on one project, they may be moved smoothly to another, cutting the likelihood of shortages or surpluses in particular specialities.

Third, since in the event of disagreements with the head of functional units project managers have only one "technically feasible," authoritative recourse, namely to go to their common superior to get what they want, how does the project manager really continue to get things done if he has "used up his currency" with the top common superior by going to him too often? The answer, of course, as has been implied above, is that the real key to the project management is to establish and maintain good, mutually helpful relationships with functional managers. The operative words here are consultation, involvement, participation, cooperation, collaboration and trying to develop and attain shared goals.

---

[4] Janger, A. R., "Anatomy of the Project Organization," *Business Management Record,* November 1963.

Fourth, in recognition of the immediately preceding point, does it necessarily follow that all managers make good project managers? Gaddis[5] thinks not. He says that a project manager is not a superman. He cannot be expected to double as a member of an executive committee and as a scientist or some other kind of expert or professional as well. Being a little of both, he is different from both. And it is, according to Gaddis, precisely this quality which makes him so valuable. In his own right he does what neither the front office executive nor the specialist can do: accomplish the aims of his corporate management, while serving as a perpetual buffer so that the engineers, scientists, and other technical and specialist personnel can meet the technological objectives that only they can define and only their output can meet.

Fifth, even if we wanted to, the pure functional approach cannot be applied when the task at hand involves the coordinated effort of hundreds of organizational elements and the coordinated efforts of hundreds of people. A combat aircraft, for example, is developed and produced through the coordinated efforts of literally dozens of industrial and governmental units. Certain advanced, functionally-oriented, management methods have been invented to help alleviate this problem of coordinating the efforts of so many elements and individuals—such as PERT. But even these, by themselves, cannot "automatically" coordinate the management of the totality of the efforts involved. The sheer magnitude is simply too great.

Handling the problems

Recognizing these problems, then, how does the project manager deal with them? Here, the perspectives and points of view of the three major groups or schools of management theorists—the "structuralists," the "functionalists" and the "behavioralists" all differ somewhat. Therefore, I think it would be useful to examine their various arguments.

First, the structuralists, such as Likert,[6] would argue that the project manager, as a unifying agent, integrates the parochial interests of autonomous organizational elements toward a common objective. Traditional lines of authority and responsibility are altered by the prerogatives of the project manager who possesses influence and power necessary to ensure unanimity of objective for all organizations involved in the project. More narrowly looked at from the commerical organization's point of view, the project organization offers an alternative to a functionally organized company or division that is big enough and complex enough to require some standard organization for product emphasis, but that cannot divisionalize along product lines.

[5] Gaddis, P. O., "The Project Manager," *Harvard Business Review,* Vol. 37, No. 3, May/June 1959.
[6] Likert, R., *The Human Organization: Its Management and Value,* McGraw-Hill, 1967.

Second, the functionalists such as Johnson *et al,* [7] would argue that project management is in reality simply the application of the systems concept to organization problems, given the recognition of the need for the breakdown of traditional functional specialization geared to optimizing performance of particular departments (which they allege is really sub-optimizing the overall organizational goals). The systems concept calls for integration, into a separate "organizational system," of activities related to particular projects or programs. The business organization, this school of thought contends, can no longer be thought of as a functional division of activities such as sales, finance, production, and personnel. Its breakdown into separate functional areas has been an artificial organizational device. Management science techniques, computer simulation approaches, and information-decision systems are just a few of the tools which will make it possible for management to visualize the firm as a total system.

Finally, the behavioralists such as Bennis[8] see the task force as organized around problems (not just products, programs, projects, or tasks, for example). They are, he says, often composed of groups of strangers who represent diverse sets of professional skills. They will, he contends, be arranged on an organic, rather than a mechanical model. The "executive" thus becomes a coordinator or "linking pin" between various task forces or projects. The task force leader or project manager must be a man, Bennis says, who can speak the diverse languages of research, with skills to relay information and to mediate between groups. People will be differentiated not vertically according to rank and status, but flexibly and functionally according to skill and professional training. This is the organizational form that will gradually replace bureaucracy as we know it. Bennis calls this form the "organic-adaptive" structure.

What is interesting, it seems to me, is that these three essentially disparate perspectives could come together on the utility of the task force as a useful device in group problem-solving situations. It is indeed rare (I know of only one or two other areas) where these schools of theorists agree! It would seem to be a strong argument, therefore, that the task force and project management concept should be given very serious attention as a useful approach to organizational problem-solving.

While companies and other organizations are reluctant as yet to go so far as to make explicit (in the form of stated policy, for example) their attitudes on this question, one cannot deny that pragmatic expediency, if nothing else, is causing more and more of them to experiment with the use of task forces and project management.

Let's look at some evidence.

First, Scott[9] points out that more and more companies are becoming

---

[7] Johnson *et al., Theory and Management of Systems,* McGraw-Hill, 1963, Part IV, "The Future."

[8] Bennis, Warren G., "Changing Organizations," *The Technology Review,* Vol. 68, No. 6, April 1966.

[9] Scott, W. G., *Organization Theory: A Behavioral Analysis for Management,* Richard D. Irwin, 1967.

international in character. There are, therefore, at least three major dimensions to the modern multinational company's problems—a geographic dimension, a product line dimension and a functional dimension. An increasing number of problems—in trying to find the location for a new plant, in trying to decide what new markets to enter, in deciding what new products to manufacture and which to discontinue—all of these kinds of problems cut across the organizational boundaries of compartmentalized elements.

Second, recognition of the hard and perhaps brutal fact that the official given the task of solving such problems doesn't last very long if he takes the position that he cannot tolerate the environmental and interpersonal ambiguity of reporting to more than one boss. Litterer[10] emphasizes that the official is finding that somehow he must acquire the interpersonal skills that will permit him to deal effectively with, for example, the engineering vice president, the head of the eastern division, and the chief of the advanced product line.

Third, Carzo[11] mentions that competition between companies and organizations is getting fiercer on a global scale every day. It has been predicted that the number of international firms doing business on a global scale will be reduced to 300 large multinational organizations by 1980. The organization which is not quick and effective in responding to problems of where to market, what to produce, how to finance, etc., will lose out to its competitors. This is not the prophet of doom—but the realization of the hard facts that are already staring many large corporations squarely in the face. Only through the use of the modern management technology, including modern organizational and structural approaches to problem-solving, can the organization survive.

In summary, I think the research evidence coming from management science in all three areas of endeavor—structure, technology, and behavioral science—clearly demonstrates that task forces and project management as organizational approaches are useful to problem-solving in organizational contexts.

Conclusions

1 The Task Force and Project Management concepts are very effective approaches to modern problem-solving and goal achievement problems in large and complex modern organizations. While not useful to all forms of organizations or all kinds of problems, they are becoming increasingly useful as organizations themselves become more complex in terms of products or services, markets, and specialization. They embody the fundamental assumption that compartmentalization, specialization and increasing technological sophistication are the "givens" of this last half of the twentieth century.

[10] Litterer, J. A., "Program Management: Organizing for Stability and Flexibility," *Personnel,* Vol. 40, No. 5, September/October, 1963.
[11] Carzo, R., and Yanouzas, J. N., *Formal Organization—A Systems Approach,* Richard D. Irwin, Inc., 1967.

2 The Task Force and Project Management concepts are more rewarding and productive approaches to the ego-satisfaction and motivation aspects of human behavior in modern organizational settings than are traditional approaches based on classic organizational theory. There is a harmony between the educated individual's need for meaningful, satisfactory and creative tasks and a flexible organizational structure. Greiner[12] points out that skills in human interaction will become more important, due to the growing needs for collaboration in complex tasks. There is a danger, however, that there may be reduced commitment to work groups, because these groups are transient and changing and not all people will be able to develop quick and intense relationships on the job and learn to bear the loss of more enduring work relationships.

3 As a first general rule, the larger and more complex an organization, the more specialized and diversified its product lines, services, and objectives, the greater the utility of these approaches. Organizations are, in fact, growing larger, more complex and more compartmentalized. No longer are small, "lean groups of a dozen or so old friends" able to come together to solve problems, except in very small organizations. In smaller organizations where personal relationships are closer simply by virtue of long-standing friendships, physical proximity of tasks performed and simplicity of functions to be performed, the task force approach will have minimal application.

4 As a second general rule, the larger the number of individual skill categories needed to produce a product or service or to accomplish an objective, the greater the utility of this approach. The greatest number of applications will continue to be in such industries as the aerospace and defense-related industries which will continue to be at the forefront of the technological revolution. For example, the production of a nuclear reactor or missile, which requires the close synchronization of the work of hundreds of different kinds of skills will make better use of this technique than will, for example, the production of relatively simple items of capital equipment such as a bus, motorboat, bulldozer or steam boiler.

5 As a third general rule, the larger the number of organizational sub-elements (i.e., the greater the compartmentalization), the greater the utility of this approach. For example, as Schultze[13] has indicated, in government there is a need for a single Federal manager to coordinate the various grant programs that may involve 25 or 30 different Federal Government agencies, all fifty states, perhaps several thousand counties, and tens of thousands of cities. Literally, such an overall manager must coordinate the work of hundreds or even thousands of managers vertically, horizontally, and diagonally.

6 The task force concept and approach are most useful in organizational settings wherein top management is committed to that set of values embodied by the late Douglas McGregor's Theory Y.

[12] Greiner, Larry E., "Successful Organization Change," *Harvard Business Review,* May–June 1967.
[13] Schultze, Charles L., Statement before the Subcommittee on Executive Reorganization on the Senate Committee on Government Operations on the Federal Role in Urban Affairs, June 28, 1967.

7 The task force approach and concept are more useful in organizations with large numbers of professional personnel than in organizations with primarily semi-skilled and unskilled personnel. For example, in general the approach is more useful in industrial settings than agricultural settings; in research and development organizations rather than production and assembly-line settings; in "white collar" settings rather than "blue collar" settings; and in specialty product/service organizations rather than in staple good industries with little competition—or publicly regulated industries such as public utility companies.

8 Even in organizations with primarily semi-skilled and unskilled personnel, the task force concept will find increasing utility as the pressures of leisure time create increasing emotional needs for greater job satisfaction and motivation. Bennis, for example, does not agree with those who emphasize a New Utopianism, in which leisure, not work, becomes the emotional-creative sphere of life. "Jobs," he contends, "should become more rather than less involving; man is a problem-solving animal and the tasks of the future guarantee a full agenda of problems."

---

24 Government simplification department
The Wall Street Journal

The two flow charts on p. 226 were found in a manila envelope appended to the back of "Issues '78, Perspectives on Fiscal Year 1978 Budget," a document which accompanied the budget proposals submitted to Congress by President Ford.

The top chart purports to describe how the Health, Education and Welfare Department's Office of Education presently works. The bottom chart illustrates how things would look if a number of reforms proposed in recent years to simplify the system were put into effect.

"I guess it shows we have a long way to go even if the reforms are adopted," says a spokesman for the Office of Management and Budget. "When President Ford saw it, he dubbed it a 'mess chart.'"

The top chart went through about eight separate revisions "before everybody in Congress, the Office of Education and elsewhere could even agree that it was accurate," reports the OMB spokesman. "The guy who drew it up was getting a little disturbed."

Source: From *The Wall Street Journal* (Jan. 25, 1977), p. 25. Reprinted with permission of *The Wall Street Journal*, © Dow Jones & Company, Inc., (1977). All Rights Reserved.

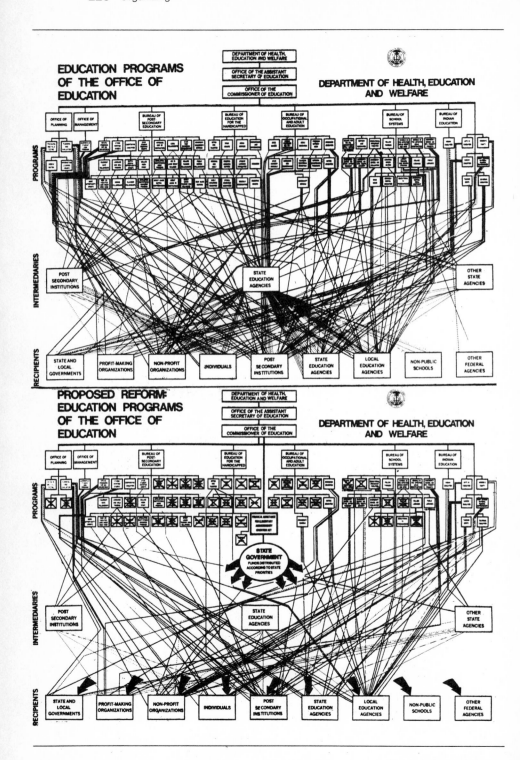

Part IV

Staffing

A good supervisor is a good teacher.
    Richard W. Wetherill

As we observed earlier, the manager must coordinate human and nonhuman resources to achieve organizational objectives. Staffing is often considered the responsibility of the personnel department, while the line manager is expected to cope with more immediate problems. As the reader will see, however, this is inaccurate; two of a manager's responsiblities are, first, to insure that qualified people are present to conduct the affairs of the enterprise, and second, to see that qualified people continue to be present.

   This section on staffing begins with discussion of two recent attempts to identify and place well-qualified personnel—assessment centers and affirmative-action programs. The next several selections deal, respectively, with developing managerial personnel, appraising managers' performance, and rewarding the manager.

IV/A
Identifying managerial competence

25 More concerns use "assessment centers" to gauge employees' managerial abilities
James C. Hyatt

The assignment was simple, the kind that managers face daily: Make a seven-minute speech to sell a new product.

But the first speaker was obviously nervous when he rose to address the group of about 20. He fumbled with his notes. Then his self-control vanished entirely. Tears streamed down his cheeks. "I'm sorry," he muttered as he walked out the door.

"That really upset me," recalls Tony DeLuca, who was watching from the audience. "I was the next speaker. And public speaking is the only subject where I got an F in college." (Mr. DeLuca did manage to get through his talk, however.)

Though the "new product" topic was imaginary, the task was dead-serious. Mr. DeLuca and his colleague were performing one of a series of problems that their employer, Gino's Inc., uses to measure managerial strengths and weaknesses.

Several times a year, a dozen middle managers for the fast-food chain gather at a Philadelphia conference center to undergo seven exercises. For four days, members of each group are observed for almost every trait from communications skill to what one executive calls "how their heads work," which means problem analysis and decision making.

Identifying talent

Although the experience is seldom so dramatic as the nervous speaker's collapse, this kind of testing is becoming common for many ambitious employers, whether they are supervisors or members of the management

Source: From The Wall Street Journal (Jan. 3, 1974), p. 15. Reprinted with permission of The Wall Street Journal. © Dow Jones & Company, Inc. (1974). All Rights Reserved.

suite. "Making hard decisions about people" remains one of management's toughest tasks, asserts Curt Russell, Gino's director of management and development. His firm and many others are convinced that the use of "assessment centers" makes the job of identifying and evaluating talent that much easier.

Recently the approach has been adopted by such well-known firms as Merrill Lynch, Pierce, Fenner & Smith, Knight Newspapers, Bendix Corp. and Prudential Insurance Co. Among the early recruits to the cause in the 1960s were IBM, General Electric and J. C. Penney Co.; they were following pioneering efforts by American Telephone & Telegraph Co. In all, it is estimated, over 800 companies have used this method of employee evaluation.

"Assessment centers are growing stronger in the U.S. and have taken off like a rocket in England," an official of the American Management Association says.

This year, more than 20,000 workers will be appraised in such centers, including 10,000 at AT&T, says William Byham, a psychologist whose consulting firm helped set up many such programs. The range of occupations involved is wide; included are stockbrokers and police officers, Social Security administrators and foremen on offshore oil rigs.

Predicting performance

Determining the effectiveness of assessment centers is difficult, but there are some data to indicate the method can help predict career performance.

At AT&T, a group of newly hired college graduates, all considered potential managers, was assessed years ago. The center staff decided that about half the group members would reach middle management early in their careers. However, that information wasn't given to the workers' supervisors. Eight years later, about 120 of the workers were still at AT&T; of those assessed favorably, 64% had reached middle management, while only 32% of those assessed unfavorably had achieved that level.

Moreover, the candidates assessed say they get better insight into handling themselves as managers. Mr. DeLuca, an area training manager for Gino's, found he did particularly well in an exercise testing his reactions to the administrative problems that might be dropped on an executive's desk. "Since then, I've spent less time on administration," he says. "I realized I was doing it totally out of enjoyment. Instead, I've spent more time with managers reporting to me."

On the other hand, his public-speaking results convinced him to enroll, at company expense, in a self-confidence course at night. "As managers, we're called on periodically to give a speech," he says.

Another assessment-center alumnus, James L. Hanchette, a marketing coordinator at Huyck Corp. of Wake Forest, N.C., recalls a follow-up session in which he watched himself on video-tape taking part in a group discussion. "I was more the kind of guy who is sort of a referee, working toward agreement," he says. "Now I'm trying to exert more leadership."

But the assessment procedure has its critics. They don't question that the method generates useful information. But they insist the results can't stand alone.

"The assessment center can become a kind of crutch," says Roy Walters, a management consultant. "I've seen organizations where nobody gets moved unless they've successfully passed a center. That can be a danger if it lets the line managers off the hook too easily." Managers still must learn to give workers the sort of real experiences they need for growth and development, he insists.

Others worry that, used too faddishly, the assessment center becomes "little more than a fraternity initiation," a symbol rather than a management tool to be taken seriously.

Rather than try to apply an objective method, of course, some employers have traditionally used arbitrary standards in making decisions on promotions—a prospect's race or sex, college background or golf manners. Or how he gets along with his supervisor. Or even the kind of marriage he has.

Present and future

In recent years, many firms have turned to elaborate tracking of on-the-job performance and intensive testing. But such methods also have obvious drawbacks. Present job performance, for instance, doesn't necessarily measure potential for a new job.

"All too often, we've taken the best craftsman we have and made him a foreman," says M. E. Haynes, an internal consultant for Shell Oil Co. "He may not have turned out to be a very good foreman."

So Shell is trying out a day-and-a-half assessment operation to give "an additional look at some areas we feel are necessary to successfully perform as a foreman." Shell's interests include leadership, managerial and administrative skill, problem analysis, mental alertness and tolerance of stress.

To bring those capabilities out, the company uses a variety of exercises. In one group exercise, prospective foremen are given a problem to analyze and discuss. In another, the group talks over a problem and reaches a solution. Each participant also takes a so-called in-basket test, handling a set of memos representing problems that might occur the first day on a new job.

None of the exercises is meant to test specific technical knowledge; rather, each is designed to bring out reactions to a situation. Two kinds of pressure are imposed on candidates, Mr. Haynes says: The stress of working under deadlines and the stress of "developing some solution, although the candidate may feel he isn't qualified to do that."

Such probing, psychologist Byham says, "is an answer to the Peter Principle," which holds that workers rise to their level of incompetence. "We try to evaluate how a person would perform at a higher level or at a new job before he or she is assigned to it."

26 Affirmative action program: Its realities and challenges
Gopal C. Pati and Patrick E. Fahey

Managers in many business organizations are increasingly feeling the impact of public policy in many functional areas of management.[1] This has created an unusual fermentation of mixed feelings of hope and frustration. It has been further compounded by the complexities and ineptness of the technological society which has demanded an unprecedented emphasis on human resource utilization and development.[2] As a matter of fact, in the last several years it has been the area of manpower planning and development in general, and equal employment opportunities in particular, where the role of government has been increasingly observed.[3] Many government-initiated and supported programs to ameliorate poverty, unemployment and wastage of human resources have generated numerous kinds of anxieties, debate and bewilderment among educators and practitioners. The affirmative action program is that part of the public policy which has induced many organizations to undertake a more vigorous approach to reach out for members of the minority groups, who have been traditionally left out as a consequence of socio-economic deprivation. More specifically the objective here has been to provide them with training, jobs and an opportunity to share the fruits of our economic system, thereby enabling them to assimilate themselves better in the greater participating democracy.

The experience of the last several years in the area of affirmative action program has been characterized by learning, relearning, and adjusting to things unheard of before, and clearly indicates the ineptness of many approaches to meet the great challenge. This has also required tremendous change in internal organization, values, climate and many organizational adjustments that were not thought of before. Consequently, the objective of this paper is not only to point out these changes and challenges, but also to point out the bumpy roads and detours that have been encountered by managers within the last several years. The issues to be examined will not only have implications for traditional personnel functions and practices but also for an unprecedented philosophical change that a corporation will have to undertake in order to keep up its commitment to the government and society.

Source: Reprinted, with permission of the publisher and the authors, from *Labor Law Journal,* 24, No. 6 (June 1973), pp. 351–361.
[1] Leon C. Megginson, *Personnel: A Behavioral Approach to Administration.* Homewood, Illinois, Richard D. Irwin, Inc., 1972, pp. 244–245.
[2] Elmer H. Burack and Gopal C. Pati, "Technology and Managerial Obsolescence," *MSU Business Topics,* Spring, 1970, Vol. 18, pp. 49–56.
[3] Robert A. Gordon, *Toward a Manpower Policy,* New York, John Wiley and Sons, Inc., 1967; also see Garth L. Mangum, *The Emergence of Manpower Policy,* New York, Holt, Rinehart and Winston, Inc., 1968, Elmer H. Burack, *Strategies for Manpower Planning and Programing,* New Jersey, General Learning Press, 1972.

Legal requirements in perspective

On July 2, 1965, Title VII of the Civil Rights Act of 1964 became effective. Title VII "Equal Employment Opportunity" covers companies, labor organizations, and employment agencies. It *prohibits* discrimination because of race, color, religion, sex or national origin. During the 1971 Fiscal Year, the Equal Employment Opportunity Commission (EEOC), established by Title VII as the primary federal enforcement agency for the Civil Rights Acts, received 22,920 new charges. This was a substantial increase over the 14,129 charges received during the previous fiscal year.[4]

Under the 1964 law, the EEOC was limited to "informal methods of conference, conciliation and persuasion" unless the Department of Justice concluded that a person or practice of resistance to Title VII was involved. If the employers refused to accept the conciliation conditions, it was the individual victim of discrimination who carried the burden of obtaining an enforceable court order.

Under the recently signed "Equal Employment Act of 1972," the EEOC, if unable to secure an acceptable agreement within thirty (30) days, may bring action in a U.S. District Court. In addition to the above, other provisions of the "Equal Employment Act of 1972" include: coverage of state and local government agencies, coverage of educational institutions, coverage of employers of fifteen (15) or more persons and labor unions with fifteen (15) or more members. The latter coverage is effective March 24, 1973.

The changes enacted by the "Equal Employment Act of 1972" will make increasingly stringent demands on employers in the future.

The other federal agency with jurisdiction in the field of employment discrimination is the Office of Federal Contract Compliance (OFCC). The authority of the OFCC is derived from Presidential Orders 11246 and 11375. These orders resulted from the government's decision to use its immense purchasing and regulatory powers to enforce equal employment opportunity.

A federal contractor, which term includes virtually every employer with a contractual, financial, or regulatory relationship with the federal government, is required to go beyond the prohibition to discriminate under the Civil Rights Act. The contractor must take "affirmative action," that is, results-oriented activities, not mere passive compliance.

The Office of Federal Contract Compliance has shifted the burden of proof from the government to the contractor and made eligibility for government contracts, services, financing, etc., dependent on compliance with OFCC guidelines.

Previously "Order #4" and currently "Order #14" set forth the components of an acceptable written affirmative action program, the basis for the compliance review.

An acceptable affirmative action program must include an analysis of

---

[4] Equal Employment Opportunity Commission, *6th Annual Report,* CCH, Chicago, June, 1972, p. 25.

minority and female participation in all levels of the organization to determine if minorities or women are being underutilized. Underutilization is defined as "having fewer minorities or women in a particular job category than would be reasonably expected by their availability."[5] Once the deficiencies are identified, the contractor must set goals and timetables to which good-faith efforts will be directed to increase the utilization of minorities and women at all levels where deficiencies exist.

Despite the confusion caused by President Nixon's declaration against quotas in his renomination speech on August 24, 1972, it is improbable that the current method of goal setting will be abandoned. Though the difference between goal and quota might be subtle, it is generally accepted that a goal is a reasonable objective based on the availability of qualified people and a quota would restrict employment opportunities to members of a specific group without regard to qualification.

Emerging trend

The above material provides a framework and perspective for understanding the role of government in the personnel decisions and suggests the kind of direction a manager will have to take in reexamining his own values and then reconciling these with those of corporate philosophy and posture in the area of manpower planning and development. Furthermore, it definitely indicates the emergence of more stringent rules and regulations as an answer to the partial failure of many organizations in achieving the result-oriented goals of the affirmative action program. The spirit and the realities of the regulations require that it is not just the personnel manager or department that has to carry the burden, but line and operating managers will also have to do their share to achieve the company objectives. In other words, it does affect the whole organization.

More specifically, this means that the operating manager will have to do things that he has never done before and yet his organization is demanding that he: (1) modify his recruitment, selection and testing policies; (2) vigorously and systematically reassess his training needs and criteria; (3) rechannel his training and developmental facilities and faculty; (4) become involved in better manpower inventory, manpower audit and control. He is further responsible for doing these things within the limitation of budget, without duplicating effort and coordinating better with the federal and state program without annihilating organizational climate. This requires not only broadening the knowledge base of individual managers, but also a serious effort in defrosting old ideas, relearning new developments and refreezing this newly learned knowledge to be useful in organizational growth. Thus, this challenge can only be met by more aggressive consolidation of managerial expertise supplemented by a strong corporate commitment.

[5] *Federal Register,* Section 60–2.11, Vol. 36, No. 234, October 4, 1971.

Recruitment

The immediate impact of AAP and the EEOC regulations has necessitated broadening the base of manpower supply. The basic objective of a traditional recruitment and selection policy has been to get the most qualified people at the least cost from those traditional sources which would be consistent with the organizational way of life in meeting the needs of the available job openings. The frequently used external sources have been (1) employee referrals, (2) private employment agencies, (3) walk-in recruiting, (4) newspaper ads, (5) major senior colleges and universities, (6) (to a lesser extent) vocational and correspondence schools. The traditional internal sources have been (1) transfer, (2) promotion, (3) job upgrading, without giving much attention to the potential of minority manpower within the organization.

Indeed, these sources once served their purpose in the past and still are doing so; however, in light of the developments in the area of reaching new elements of manpower these traditional sources may not be adequate. Consequently, the following sources are emerging as the kind of places that the employers are increasingly contacting to find people as required by the law:

1 Urban league offices,
2 Individual ministers and local religious organizations,
3 Minority-oriented media,
4 Senior and junior colleges with large minority populations,
5 Schools in the inner cities,
6 Local Spanish-American organizations,
7 Trade schools (more vigorously used now),
8 Women's organizations,*
9 Agencies dealing with correctional manpower.

As a consequence of this enlargement of the recruitment base, companies are definitely seeing more people to meet legal requirements as well as corporate ethic.

However, the rejection rate is usually high which can lead to many uneasy moments during a compliance review.

One company provided the following information which illustrates the difficulties that might arise as organizations appeal to minority-oriented agencies to fulfill their affirmative action commitments. During the effective period of an affirmative action program, the rejection rate for black female hourly applicants was 80 per cent while the rejection rate for white female hourly applicants was 68 per cent.

Though it certainly does not account for the entire disparity in rejection rates between black and white applicants, one statistic does give some insight into the depth of the problem employers are currently facing. In job categories for which a typing test meets the OFCC requirements for testing,

* For example, National Organization for Women, Professional Women's Caucus, Talent Bank from Business and Professional Women.

the average black female applicants ($N = 70$) typed 30 WPM—approximately 25 per cent below the average typing speed of the remainder of the applicant population.

Furthermore, many agencies do refer people without any skills who miserably fail to meet even the minimum requirements of the company. When qualified individuals are available, frequent lack of transportation to a suburban plant location may prevent them from even appearing for an interview. In addition, many agencies are often speculative about their knowledge of job availability and send applicants to plants without any job openings, creating frustration for many individuals. Needless to say, there is a steep competition among the companies themselves to attract the best qualified personnel available. Consequently, some companies in the area are facing difficulty even in gaining entrance to an organization or institution which might have qualified minority manpower.

Confrontation with the new types of manpower and the sources has also caused reconsideration of the qualification of company recruiters. Today, a recruiter has to be a person who understands the minority culture; if not, at least make[s] an attempt to understand and be sensitive to the needs of divergent groups. Several examples will clarify this point. In one instance a company representative went to a Spanish-American organization meeting to recruit. Ironically, no one spoke English and the entire meeting was conducted in Spanish. The recruiter could not communicate with the prospects and he returned to his office, of course, without recruiting anyone. The second example is of the case of a recruiter who went to a prominent black educational institution only to be asked "what the hell are you doing here?"* In another instance at a female dominated institution, a recruiter was asked about the real intention of the company for recruiting females. More specifically, a question such as, "Why, Honey, suddenly are you interested in us?" baffled the recruiter.

The implications of these examples are crucial. There exists a tremendous amount of mistrust about the real intent of the corporation in hiring minority groups. They are not sure about their future in these organizations where organizational posture of active recruitment is being considered as the ultimate consequence of severe government prodding and pressure rather than a genuine attempt by the organizations to hire them on an equal basis in any real sense. Accordingly, it is imperative that a recruiter know the sensitiveness of the issue, understand the dilemma, and is prepared to represent the corporation and carry on its objectives in spite of the realities of complex attitudinal crisis.

Employment testing

One employment procedure that has come under close scrutiny since the 1966 EEOC published guidelines is employment testing.

The field of industrial testing has grown substantially since World War

---

* Descriptive adjectives have been omitted in the interest of scholarship.

II. Far too often, testing programs have been incorporated in the selection process based only on the "professional judgment" of personnel executives with little or nor expertise, or on the recommendation of consultants motivated more by their fee than by the service they provide to industry.

Though the professionals in the field have for decades been recommending validation of personnel tests for their intended purpose, the widespread failure to establish criterion-related validity has resulted not only in the denial of employment to minorities but also in a waste of money. Contrary to generally accepted business practices, top corporate executives have been approving expenditures for testing programs that screen out people who would be productive employees and select people who will be marginal employees at best. Funds are allocated to production, advertising, research, etc., only if a reasonable return is anticipated but this requirement is lacking in the allocation of funds to personnel department testing programs in most cases.

In the U.S. Supreme Court decision *Griggs* v. *Duke Power Company,*[6] the Court adopted the interpretative guidelines of the EEOC that tests must fairly measure the knowledge or skills required in a job in order not to unfairly discriminate against minorities.

"Nothing in the Act precludes the use of testing or measuring procedures; obviously they are useful. What Congress has forbidden is giving these devices and mechanisms controlling force unless they are demonstrably a reasonable measure of job performance."[6a]

The Supreme Court decision in upholding the EEOC guidelines settled much of the confusion centered around test usage. A test can be used only if professionally developed and validated against job performance in accordance with the standards found in *Standards for Educational and Psychological Tests and Manuals*[7] and the burden of proof is placed on the employer in the area of business necessity.

Government contractors subject to the Rules and Regulations of Order #14 are required to provide an analysis of testing practices used in the past six months to determine if equal employment opportunity is being offered in all job categories. This will include the number of men and women acceptable on the test, the number of men and women not acceptable on the test, the same information for Negroes and Spanish-surnamed Americans, American Indians, Orientals and others when the group constitutes 2 per cent or more of the labor market or recruiting area for non-minority men and women. If there is a disparate rejection rate the test must be validated in accordance with the OFCC Testing Order (except for language arising from different legal authority, this order is the same as the EEOC guidelines).

Test validation will not bring about equal employment opportunity but will allow the employer to determine the relationship between the test and

---

[6] *Griggs* v. *Duke Power Company,"* Labor Law Reports, Commerce Clearing House, Inc., p. 15, 1971. (39 U.S.I., W., 4317.)
[6a] Ibid.
[7] *Standards for Education and Psychological Tests and Manuals,* Washington, D.C., American Psychological Association, 1966.

job performance and determine the significance of the test as a predictor of job performance for racial, sex or national origin groups. A test that has been validated against job performance, used with other selection or assessment tools, can significantly aid in the development and maintenance of an efficient work force. Such a test does not violate the civil rights law nor is it forbidden by the executive orders.

At this point it seems appropriate to discuss the validation study recently completed by one industrial organization.

A test battery was administered to 165 applicants over a four-month period. Though the battery included five short, professionally-developed tests, and the tests were chosen only after a thorough job analysis by an individual with a graduate degree and experience in both job analysis and testing, only one of the battery met the requirements for test usage.

The job is an inspection job that requires a background in electrical circuitry. The applicants selected for employment are enrolled in a company training school program for eleven days prior to actually starting on the job. During this period each employee is paid approximately $300.00. The selection tools used prior to the test validation study were considered unsatisfactory and the company considered it necessary to find additional tools to reduce the failures in the training school and the turnover on the job. (It should be noted that the training school evaluation was also validated against subsequent job performance by the Pearson product moment coefficient method with a coefficient of .4965.) The sample size was sixty-seven and the coefficient .4965 is significant at the 1 per cent level and satisfies the requirement of both the EEOC and OFCC.

The test was one of the Purdue Vocational Tests with two forms. In the study, Form B was used and Form A would be available for retesting purposes. Though the test carries a twenty-five minute time limit, this was disregarded and it was considered a work limit test.

The above clearly indicates that the classes projected by Title VII are adversely affected, that is, 48 per cent of Caucasians tested were subsequently enrolled in the training program but only 32 per cent of Negroes and 36 per cent of Spanish-Americans. As there is a disparate rejection rate, the test must be validated. The related criteria considered were (1) training school evaluation and (2) job performance criteria.

The training school evaluation consists of four paper and pencil tests on the subject matter taught during the eleven-day program. As noted previously the correlation coefficient between Training School Evaluation and job performance criteria is .4965.

I. Validity—test correlated to training school evaluation

N = 67
Mean = 39.7
Standard Deviation = 10.2
Correlation Coefficient = .4877

The Pearson product moment method results in a .4877 coefficient which is significant at the 1 per cent level and satisfies the testing requirements.

II. Validity—test correlated with job performance criteria

In this case the performance criteria consisted of a thirteen-week average percentage of a standard set by the Time-study Department.

N = 38
Mean = 41.2
Standard Deviation = 10.05
Correlation Coefficient = .3788 which is significant at the 5 per cent level and satisfies the requirements of the order and the guideline.

Number tested	Mean score	Race	Enrolled in training school
108	38.75	Caucasian	52
41	24.92	Negro	13
1	—	Oriental	1
1	—	American Indian	0
14	29.53	Spanish-American	5

Therefore, it is considered that the above meets the requirements set by the OFCC and EEOC. The authors are aware of the issues not considered above, that is, differential validity, etc. These were part of the study but not noted here.

III. Reliability

The method chosen was the split half estimate. The number in the sample was 158, none of which were retests. The scores of the odd number items were correlated against the even number items by the Pearson product moment correlation coefficient. The resultant correlation coefficient .857 was corrected by the Spearman-Brown formula to correct the reliability coefficient for the full length test to .9229, certainly in the acceptable area for continued test usage.

The test was validated in a period of economic downturn as clearly indicated by the number who successfully completed the training school (59) and the number included in the efficiency study (38). Nineteen employees were transferred out of the inspection group prior to the time meaningful proficiency data was available.

In view of the above, expectancy charts were constructed but a cut-off score was not determined until a later date and was based on "need" for inspectors as well as test score.

Though a complete explanation of the statistical data is not included here, it is obvious that the efforts generated to validate the test will not only reduce costs of failure and turnover, it will also be more objective evaluation of prospective employees which is expected to increase the chances of minority group members to be selected.

There was not a disparate rejection rate for female applicants and the test validity study did not report validity correlation coefficients by sex.

Promotion

Promotional opportunities for minorities and women has been thus far a neglected subject primarily because of the initial emphasis on economic opportunities and its delivery system rather than vertical mobility within the organizational structure. Since some progress has been made in the employment opportunity area, the promotional aspect becomes the next logical step. This is a recent phenomenon and has been effectively dramatized in those organizations with a large population of female employees. An example of this was the recent EEOC charge against the Bell system for lack of females in management level jobs.[8] As a result of this charge and consequent negotiation, Illinois Bell has agreed to promote 2,500 women employees by 1974. On the national level, the AT&T system has agreed to promote 50,000 women into higher paying jobs, including 10 per cent into management posts. Furthermore, 6,600 members of the minority groups will be promoted into higher paying jobs, 12 per cent of them into management. Before specifying the regulations for government contractors in this section, one must pause to consider the significance of the AT&T agreement. If it took eight long months for AT&T to conclude an agreement such as this, other organizations traditionally less committed to equal employment opportunity must now recognize that they cannot ignore this enormous responsibility they are charged with.

The emerging government regulations require government contractors to insure that minority and female employees are given equal opportunity for promotion. Suggestions for achieving this result include: (1) post or announce promotional opportunities, (2) take inventory of current minority and female employees to determine academic skill and experience level of individual employees, (3) initiate remedial training and work study programs, (4) develop and implement formal employee evaluation programs, when apparently qualified minority or female employees are passed over for upgrading and require supervisory personnel to submit written justification, (5) establish formal counseling programs and hold supervision responsible for having qualified and promotable minority or female employees in their organization.

The question of promotional opportunity is a twofold question.

One, minorities have been historically hired in the least desirable jobs,

---

[8] *Chicago Sun-Times,* Thursday, September 21, 1972.

if hired at all. It appears that recruiting minorities for supervisory, technical and clerical jobs is a step in the right direction. It will only be after qualified minorities are on the payroll that the question of promotion will occur. Promotions of minorities must be made on the basis of qualification and potential, not on how well they measure up to some undefined profile that has no proven relationship to job performance. The problem in this area is also related to the structural condition of the economy and the labor market in particular. During recent years there has been little turnover in managerial jobs and new jobs have not been created as anticipated. This has been further compounded by the lack of manpower planning and developmental efforts within organizations and the lack of consideration for people with potential within the organizational reservoir, particularly women and minorities.

Two, qualified women have always been hired but often not on jobs that truly utilize their abilities. To alleviate this problem organizations must open up their training program for females with management potential. Failure to open the facilities to women or minorities will invite stringent rules and regulations imposed by governmental authorities. This means that the burden of proof will not only affect personnel people but other line personnel who will be required to spend a great deal of time in manpower inventory and audit. This will be an additional burden to the line organizational personnel who will have to spend more time and energy in developing human resources, a task for which they are seldom trained.

Supervisory and corporate attitude

Perhaps it is the preoccupation with our own frustrations that emotionally isolates us from one another. This is particularly true for many supervisors and foremen who are frustrated because they feel that they are being "left-out" from some of the action of the great society. Affirmative action programs are a traumatic experience for them. To them government pressure signals the practice of dual standard; company commitment appears phony in view of his usual assumption of the role of responsibility without accompanied authority. His own values and his inability to understand the motivation of youth, women and black employees; his own changing neighborhood; his own employer's emphasis upon his reeducation for organizational mobility or survivial; increasing economic demand on him to make any significant headway in the inflationary economy—all these baffle him and place him in a very defensive mood. Thus, when the personnel department tries to select people *in,* the foreman seems to select them *out.* The supervisory groups just do not believe that "equal employment opportunity" is really happening and do not believe that the company is serious.

An unprecedented amount of attitudinal modification on the part of the top as well as supervisory groups is necessary if this program [is] to succeed. A strong support system within the organization is a necessity if any significant progress is intended to be made. And that support system can be developed if,

1 A vigorous organizational renewal program is pursued (at least partially),
2 an organizational development effort is seriously launched,
3 company reassurance of supervisory job security is strengthened,
4 100 per cent company commitment is demonstrated, and
5 reward is given to the supervisory and various support personnel for their
   cooperation in an effort to create a better organizational climate.

If the above-mentioned is not being done (and in most cases that we studied it is not), then we should not be surprised about the dubious impact of the action-oriented affirmative action program. First line supervisors in most instances do not know what it takes to make a good worker and performer out of an individual. Under this condition it is very unlikely that a person without training and previous work experience will survive in an organization once hired.

Implications

One, increasingly stringent goals and timetables as well as increased pressure from municipal Human Relations Commissions will emerge in the future. Only with specific goals derived from factual analysis will a company be able to carry the burden of proof against the OFCC and sell the program internally to non-persuaded upper management.

Two, the proposed regulations to require federal contractors to keep records of employees' religious and ethnic background will eventually be adopted in spite of protests from groups that consider such regulations an invasion of privacy.

Three, federal contractors will find it necessary to appoint a full-time Compliance Officer. An effective affirmative action program requires a strong results-oriented executive, not the average impotent personnel executive nor the unqualified token minority, too often administering programs at present.

Four, a considerable amount of money has been spent in recent years to fund neighborhood agencies to train and assist minority group members to secure employment. Many of these organizations have failed miserably. In the future, business organizations must take an interest, both financially and with their training expertise, to ensure that qualified applicants are available from the sources an affirmative action program requires companies to contact.

Five, this indeed is a very sensitive area and will continue to be a serious problem for those organizations who are passive. A strong corporate commitment supplemented by an internal support system will have to be undertaken to live up to the real spirit of the equal employment practices.

Six, in light of our experience in the Midwest it is very clear that recruiting a few warm bodies to meet the legal requirements is not enough. The real spirit of the law requires reevaluation of corporate philosophy, changes in traditional personnel practices, modification of attitude of the operating managers and a type of complete involvement which will help minorities to retain a job and grow within the organization. Otherwise, more interesting laws will be forthcoming.

And finally, with regard to continued progress by minorities in all job categories, comparative data for about 31 million employees covered by 1970 EEO-1 employment reports indicate that since 1966, Negro employment as a proportion of total employment is up 1.9 per cent in total employment, 1.0 per cent among officials and managers, 1.2 per cent in professional category, 2.1 per cent among technicians, 1.9 per cent among sales workers and 3.7 per cent in office and clerical category. Spanish-surnamed Americans and women also showed increases in each of these categories. While it can be assumed that the percentage gains would have been higher in a more dynamic economy, that is, minorities remain in a great many cases "last in," "first out," our conclusion is that minorities remain grossly underrepresented in the more desirable jobs in industry in spite of law and moral suasion. Furthermore, if we are to use our human resources to their potential, organizations must make total commitments to expend time, money, energy and expertise at least to the extent imparted to the other factors of production, for example, finance, plant acquisitions, technology, etc. If this is not done, the chances of living up to the real spirit of the burgeoning laws is very slim.

IV/B
Developing managerial skills

---

27 Management development as a process of influence
Edgar H. Schein

The continuing rash of articles on the subject of developing better managers suggests, on the one hand, a continuing concern that existing methods are not providing the talent which is needed at the higher levels of industry and, on the other hand, that we continue to lack clear-cut formulations about the process by which such development occurs. We need more and better managers and we need more and better theories of how to get them.

In the present paper I would like to cast management development as the problem of how an organization can influence the beliefs, attitudes, and values (hereafter simply called attitudes) of an individual for the purpose of "developing" him, i.e., changing him in a direction which the organization regards to be in his own and the organization's best interests. Most of the existing conceptions of the development of human resources are built upon assumptions of how people learn and grow, and some of the more strikingly contrasting theories of management development derive from disagreements about such assumptions. I will attempt to build on a different base: instead of starting with assumptions about learning and growth, I will start with some assumptions from the social psychology of influence and attitude change.

Building on this base can be justified quite readily if we consider that adequate managerial performance at the higher levels is at least as much a matter of attitudes as it is a matter of knowledge and specific skills, and that the acquisition of such knowledge and skills is itself in part a function of attitudes. Yet we have given far more attention to the psychology which underlies change in the area of knowledge and abilities than we have to the psychology which underlies change in attitudes. We have surprisingly few studies of how a person develops loyalty to a company, commitment to a job, or a professional attitude toward the managerial role; how he comes to

Source: From *Industrial Management Review* (May 1961), pp. 59–77. Reprinted with permission from *Sloan Management Review* (formerly *IMR*).

have the motives and attitudes which make possible the rendering of decisions concerning large quantities of money, materials, and human resources;
how he develops attitudes toward himself, his co-workers, his employees,
his customers, and society in general which give us confidence that he has
a sense of responsibility and a set of ethics consistent with his responsible
position, or at least which permit us to understand his behavior.

It is clear that management is becoming increasingly professionalized,
as evidenced by increasing emphasis on undergraduate and graduate education in the field of management. But professionalization is not only a matter
of teaching candidates increasing amounts about a set of relevant subjects
and disciplines; it is equally a problem of preparing the candidate for a role
which requires a certain set of attitudes. Studies of the medical profession
(Merton, Reader, and Kendall, 1957), for example, have turned their attention
increasingly to the unravelling of the difficult problem of how the medical
student acquires those attitudes and values which enable him to make responsible decisions involving the lives of other people. Similar studies in
other professions are sorely needed. When these are undertaken, it is likely
to be discovered that much of the training of such attitudes is carried out
implicitly and without a clearly formulated rationale. Law schools and medical schools provide various kinds of experiences which insure that the
graduate is prepared to fulfill his professional role. Similarly, existing approaches to the development of managers probably provide ample opportunities for the manager to learn the attitudes he will need to fulfill high level
jobs. But in this field, particularly, one gets the impression that such opportunities are more the result of intuition or chance than of clearly formulated
policies. This is partly because the essential or pivotal aspects of the managerial role have not as yet been clearly delineated, leaving ambiguous both
the area of knowledge to be mastered and the attitude to be acquired.

Existing practice in the field of management development involves activities such as: indoctrination and training programs conducted at various
points in the manager's career; systematic job rotation involving changes
both in the nature of the functions performed (e.g., moving from production
into sales), in physical location, and in the individual's superiors; performance appraisal programs including various amounts of testing, general personality assessment, and counseling both within the organization and
through the use of outside consultants; apprenticeships, systematic coaching, junior management boards, and special projects to facilitate practice by
the young manager in functions he will have to perform later in his career;
sponsorship and other comparable activities in which a select group of
young managers is groomed systematically for high level jobs (i.e., made
into "crown princes"); participation in special conferences and training programs, including professional association meetings, human relations workshops, advanced management programs conducted in business schools or
by professional associations like the American Management Association,
regular academic courses like the Sloan programs offered at Stanford and
MIT, or liberal arts courses, like those offered at the University of Pennsylvania, Dartmouth, Northwestern, etc. These and many other specific educa-

tional devices, along with elaborate schemes of selection, appraisal, and placement, form the basic paraphernalia of management development.

Most of the methods mentioned above stem from the basic conception that it is the responsibility of the business enterprise, as an institution, to define what kind of behavior and attitude change is to take place and to construct mechanisms by which such change is to occur. Decisions about the kind of activity which might be appropriate for a given manager are usually made by others above him or by specialists hired to make such decisions. Where he is to be rotated, how long he is to remain on a given assignment, or what kind of new training he should undertake, is master-minded by others whose concern is "career development." In a sense, the individual stands alone against the institution where his own career is concerned, because the basic assumption is that the institution knows better than the individual what kind of man it needs or wants in its higher levels of management. The kind of influence model which is relevant, then, is one which considers the whole range of resources available to an organization.

In the remainder of this paper I will attempt to spell out these general themes by first presenting a conceptual model for analyzing influence, then providing some illustrations from a variety of organizational influence situations, and then testing its applicability to the management development situation.

A model of influence and change

Most theories of influence or change accept the premise that change does not occur unless the individual is *motivated* and *ready* to change. This statement implies that the individual must perceive some need for change in himself, must be able to change, and must perceive the influencing agent as one who can facilitate such change in a direction acceptable to the individual. A model of the influence process, then, must account for the development of the motivation to change as well as the actual mechanisms by which the change occurs.

It is usually assumed that pointing out to a person some of his areas of deficiency, or some failure on his part in these areas, is sufficient to induce in him a readiness to change and to accept the influencing agent's guidance or recommendations. This assumption may be tenable if one is dealing with deficiencies in intellectual skills or technical knowledge. The young manager can see, with some help from his superiors, that he needs a greater knowledge of economics, or marketing, or production methods, and can accept the suggestion that spending a year in another department or six weeks at an advanced management course will give him the missing knowledge and/or skills.

However, when we are dealing with attitudes, the suggestion of deficiency or the need for change is much more likely to be perceived as a basic threat to the individual's sense of identity and to his status position vis-à-vis others in the organization. Attitudes are generally organized and

integrated around the person's image of himself, and they result in stabi-
lized, characteristic ways of dealing with others. The suggestion of the need
for change not only implies some criticism of the person's image of himself, but also threatens the stability of his working relationships because
change at this level implies that the expectations which others have about
him will be upset, thus requiring the development of new relationships. It is
not at all uncommon for training programs in human relations to arouse resistance or to produce, at best, temporary change because the expectations
of co-workers operate to keep the individual in his "normal" mold. Management development programs which ignore these psychological resistances to change are likely to be self-defeating, no matter how much attention is given to the actual presentation of the new desired attitudes.

Given these general assumptions about the integration of attitudes in
the person, it is appropriate to consider influence as a process which occurs
over time and which includes three phases:

1 *Unfreezing*[1] an alteration of the forces acting on the individual, such that
his table equilibrium is disturbed sufficiently to motivate him and to make
him ready to change; this can be accomplished either by increasing the
pressure to change or by reducing some of the threats or resistance to
change.
2 *Changing* the presentation of a direction of change and the actual process
of learning new attitudes. This process occurs basically by one of two
mechanisms: (a) *identification*[2]—the person learns new attitudes by identifying with and emulating some other person who holds those attitudes; or (b)
internalization—the person learns new attitudes by being placed in a situation where new attitudes are demanded of him as a way of solving problems which confront him and which he cannot avoid; he discovers the new
attitudes essentially for himself, though the situation may guide him or make
it probable that he will discover only those attitudes which the influencing
agent wishes him to discover.
3 *Refreezing* the integration of the changed attitudes into the rest of the personality and/or into ongoing significant emotional relationships.

In proposing this kind of model of influence we are leaving out two
important cases—the individual who changes because he is *forced* to
change by the agent's direct manipulation of rewards and punishments
(what Kelman calls "compliance") and the individual whose strong motivation to rise in the organizational hierarchy makes him eager to accept the attitudes and acquire the skills which he perceives to be necessary for advancement. I will ignore both of these cases for the same reason—they
usually do not involve genuine, stable change, but merely involve the adoption of overt behaviors which imply to others that attitudes have changed,
even if they have not. In the case of compliance, the individual drops the

---

[1] These phases of influence are a derivation of the change model developed by Lewin
(1947).
[2] These mechanisms of attitude change are taken from Kelman (1958).

overt behavior as soon as surveillance by the influence agent is removed. Among the upwardly mobile individuals, there are those who are willing to be unfrozen and to undergo genuine attitude change (whose case fits the model to be presented below) and those whose overt behavior change is dictated by their changing perception of what the environment will reward, but whose underlying attitudes are never really changed or refrozen.

I do not wish to imply that a general reward-punishment model is incorrect or inappropriate for the analysis of attitude change. My purpose, rather, is to provide a more refined model in terms of which it becomes possible to specify the differential effects of various kinds of rewards and punishments, some of which have far more significance and impact than others. For example, as I will try to show, the rewarding effect of approval from an admired person is very different in its ultimate consequences from the rewarding effect of developing a personal solution to a difficult situation.

The processes of unfreezing, changing, and refreezing can be identified in a variety of different institutions in which they are manifested in varying degrees of intensity. The content of what may be taught in the influence process may vary widely from the values of Communism to the religious doctrines of a nun, and the process of influence may vary drastically in its intensity. Nevertheless there is value in taking as our frame of reference a model like that proposed and testing its utility in a variety of different organizational contexts, ranging from Communist "thought reform" centers to business enterprises' management development programs. Because the value system of the business enterprise and its role conception of the manager are not as clear-cut as the values and role prescriptions in various other institutions, one may expect the processes of unfreezing, changing, and refreezing to occur with less intensity and to be less consciously rationalized in the business enterprise. But they are structurally the same as in other organizations. One of the main purposes of this paper, then, will be to try to make salient some features of the influence of the organization on the attitudes of the individual manager by attempting to compare institutions in which the influence process is more drastic and explicit with the more implicit and less drastic methods of the business enterprise.

Illustrations of organizational influence

Unfreezing

The concept of unfreezing and the variety of methods by which influence targets can be unfrozen can best be illustrated by considering examples drawn from a broad range of situations. The Chinese Communists in their attempt to inculcate Communist attitudes into their youth or into their prisoners serve as a good prototype of one extreme. First and most important was the removal of the target person from those situations and social relationships which tended to confirm and reinforce the validity of the old attitudes.

Thus the targets, be they political prisoners, prisoners of war, university professors, or young students, were isolated from their friends, families, and accustomed work groups and cut off from all media of communication to which they were accustomed. In addition, they were subjected to continuous exhortations (backed by threats of severe punishment) to confess their crimes and adopt new attitudes, and were constantly humiliated in order to discredit their old sense of identity.

The isolation of the target from his normal social and ideological supports reached its height in the case of Western civilians who were placed into group cells with a number of Chinese prisoners who had already confessed and were committed to reforming themselves and their lone Western cell mate. In the prisoner of war camps such extreme social isolation could not be produced, but its counterpart was created by the fomenting of mutual mistrust among the prisoners, by cutting off any supportive mail from home, and by systematically disorganizing the formal and informal social structure of the POW camp (by segregation of officers and noncommissioned officers from the remainder of the group, by the systematic removal of informal leaders or key personalities, and by the prohibition of any group activity not in line with the indoctrination program) (Schein, 1960, 1961).

The Chinese did not hesitate to use physical brutality and threats of death and/or permanent non-repatriation to enforce the view that only by collaboration and attitude change could the prisoner hope to survive physically and psychologically. In the case of the civilians in group cells, an additional and greater stress was represented by the social pressure of the cell mates who would harangue, insult, revile, humiliate, and plead with the resistant Westerner twenty-four hours a day for weeks or months on end, exhorting him to admit his guilt, confess his crimes, reform, and adopt Communist values. This combination of physical and social pressures is perhaps a prototype of the use of coercion in the service of unfreezing a target individual in attitude areas to which he is strongly committed.

A somewhat milder, though structurally similar, process can be observed in the training of a nun (Hulme, 1956). The novice enters the convent voluntarily and is presumably ready to change, but the kind of change which must be accomplished encounters strong psychological resistances because, again, it involves deeply held attitudes and habits. Thus the novice must learn to be completely unselfish and, in fact, selfless; she must adapt to a completely communal life; she must give up any source of authority except the absolute authority of God and of those senior to her in the convent; and she must learn to curb her sexual and aggressive impulses. How does the routine of the convent facilitate unfreezing? Again a key element is the removal of the novice from her accustomed routines, sources of confirmation, social supports, and old relationships. She is physically isolated from the outside world, surrounded by others who are undergoing the same training as she, subjected to a highly demanding and fatiguing physical regimen, constantly exhorted toward her new role and punished for any evidence of old behaviors and attitudes, and subjected to a whole range of social pressures ranging from mild disapproval to total humiliation for any failure.

Not only is the novice cut off from her old social identity, but her entry into the convent separates her from many aspects of her physical identity. She is deprived of all means of being beautiful or even feminine; her hair is cut off and she is given institutional garb which emphasizes formlessness and sameness; she loses her old name and chronological age in favor of a new name and age corresponding to the length of time in the convent; her living quarters and daily routine emphasize an absolute minimum of physical comfort and signify a total devaluation of anything related to the body. At the same time the threat associated with change is minimized by the tremendous support which the convent offers for change and by the fact that everyone else either already exhibits the appropriate attitudes or is in the process of learning them.

If we look at the process by which a pledge comes to be a full-fledged member of a fraternity, we find in this situation also a set of pressures to give up old associations and habits, a devaluation of the old self by humiliations ranging from menial, senseless jobs to paddling and hazing, a removal of threat through sharing of training, and support for good performance in the pledge role. The evangelist seeking to convert those who come to hear him attempts to unfreeze his audience by stimulating guilt and by devaluating their former selves as sinful and unworthy. The teacher wishing to induce motivation to learn sometimes points out the deficiencies in the student's knowledge and hopes at the same time to induce some guilt for having those deficiencies.

Some of the elements which all unfreezing situations have in common are the following: (1) the physical removal of the influence target from his accustomed routines, sources of information, and social relationships; (2) the undermining and destruction of all social supports; (3) demeaning and humiliating experience to help the target see his old self as unworthy and thus to become motivated to change; (4) the consistent linking of reward with willingness to change and of punishment with unwillingness to change.

Changing

Once the target has become motivated to change, the actual influence is most likely to occur by one of two processes. The target finds one or more models in his social environment and learns new attitudes by identifying with them and trying to become like them; or the target confronts new situations with an experimental attitude and develops for himself attitudes which are appropriate to the situation and which remove whatever problem he faces. These two processes—*identification* and *internalization*—probably tend to occur together in most concrete situations, but it is worthwhile, for analytical purposes, to keep them separate.[3]

[3] Both are facilitated greatly if the influence agent saturates the environment with the new message or attitude to be learned.

The student or prisoner of the Chinese Communists took his basic step toward acquiring Communist attitudes when he began to identify with his more advanced fellow student or prisoner. In the group cell it was the discovery by the Western prisoner that his Chinese cell mates were humans like himself, were rational, and yet completely believed in their own and his guilt, which forced him to re-examine his own premises and bases of judgment and led him the first step down the path of acquiring the Communist point of view. In other words, he began to identify with his cell mates and to acquire their point of view as the only solution to getting out of prison and reducing the pressure on him. The environment was, of course, saturated with the Communist point of view, but it is significant that such saturation by itself was not sufficient to induce genuine attitude change. The prisoner kept in isolation and bombarded with propaganda was less likely to acquire Communist attitudes than the one placed into a group cell with more re-formed prisoners. Having a personal model was apparently crucial.

In the convent the situation is essentially comparable except that the novice is initially much more disposed toward identifying with older nuns and has a model of appropriate behavior around her all the time in the actions of the others. It is interesting to note also that some nuns are singled out as particularly qualified models and given the appropriate name of "the living rule." It is also a common institution in initiation or indoctrination procedures to attach to the target individual someone who is labelled a "buddy" or "big brother," whose responsibility it is to teach the novice "the ropes" and to communicate the kinds of attitudes expected of him.

In most kinds of training and teaching situations, and even in the sales relationship, it is an acknowledged fact that the process is facilitated greatly if the target can identify with the influence agent. Such identification is facilitated if the social distance and rank difference between agent and target are not too great. The influence agent has to be close enough to the target to be seen as similar to the target, yet must be himself committed to the attitudes he is trying to inculcate. Thus, in the case of the Chinese Communist group cell, the cell mates could be perceived as sharing a common situation with the Western prisoner and this perception facilitated his identification with them. In most buddy systems, the buddy is someone who has himself gone through the training program in the recent past. If the target is likely to mistrust the influence attempts of the organization, as might be the case in a management-sponsored training program for labor or in a therapy program for delinquents in a reformatory, it is even more important that the influence agent be perceived as similar to the target. Otherwise he is dismissed as a "company man" or one who has already sold out, and hence is seen as someone whose message or example is not to be taken seriously.

Internalization, the discovery of attitudes which are the target's own solutions to his perceived dilemmas, can occur at the same time as identification. The individual can use the example of others to guide him in solving his own problems without necessarily identifying with them to the point of complete imitation. His choice of attitude remains ultimately his own in terms of what works for him, given the situation in which he finds himself. Internalization is only possible in an organizational context in which, from the organization's point of view, a number of different kinds of attitudes will be tolerated. If there is a "party line," a company philosophy, or a given way in which people have to feel about things in order to get along, it is hardly an efficient procedure to let trainees discover their own solutions. Manipulating the situation in such a way as to make the official solution the only one which is acceptable can, of course, be attempted, but the hazards of creating real resentment and alienation on the part of the individual when he discovers he really had no choice may outweigh the presumed advantages of letting him think he had a choice.

In the case of the Chinese Communists, the convent, the revival meeting, the fraternity, or the institutional training program, we are dealing with situations where the attitudes to be learned are clearly specified. In this kind of situation, internalization will not occur unless the attitudes to be learned happen to fit uniquely the kind of personal problem the individual has in the situation. For example, a few prisoners of the Communists reacted to the tremendous unfreezing pressures with genuine guilt when they discovered they held certain prejudices and attitudes (e.g., when they realized that they had looked down on lower class Chinese in spite of their manifest acceptance of them). These prisoners were then able to internalize certain portions of the total complex of Communist attitudes, particularly those dealing with unselfishness and working for the greater good of others. The attitudes which the institution demanded of them also solved a personal problem of long standing for them. In the case of the nun, one might hypothesize that internalization of the convent's attitudes will occur to the extent that asceticism offers a genuine solution to the incumbent's personal conflicts.

Internalization is a more common outcome in those influence settings where the direction of change is left more to the individual. The influence which occurs in programs like Alcoholics Anonymous, in psychotherapy or counseling for hospitalized or incarcerated populations, in religious retreats, in human relations training of the kind pursued by the National Training Laboratories (1953), and in certain kinds of progressive education programs is more likely to occur through internalization or, at least, to lead ultimately to more internalization.

Refreezing

Refreezing refers to the process by which the newly acquired attitude comes to be integrated into the target's personality and ongoing relationships. If the new attitude has been internalized while being learned, this has automatically facilitated refreezing because it has been fitted naturally into the individual's personality. If it has been learned through identification, it will persist only so long as the target's relationship with the original influence model persists unless new surrogate models are found or social support and reinforcement is obtained for expressions of the new attitude.[4]

In the case of the convent such support comes from a whole set of expectations which others have of how the nun should behave, from clearly specified role prescriptions, and from rituals. In the case of individuals influenced by the Chinese Communists, if they remained in Communist China they received constant support for their new attitudes from superiors and peers; if they returned to the West, the permanence of their attitude change depended on the degree of support they actually received from friends and relations back home, or from groups which they sought out in an attempt to get support. If their friends and relatives did not support Communist attitudes, the repatriates were influenced once again toward their original attitudes or toward some new integration of both sets.

The importance of social support for new attitudes was demonstrated dramatically in the recent Billy Graham crusade in New York City. An informal survey of individuals who came forward when Graham called for converts indicated that only those individuals who were subsequently integrated into local churches maintained their faith. Similar kinds of findings have been repeatedly noted with respect to human relations training in industry. Changes which may occur during the training program do not last unless there is some social support for the new attitudes in the "back home" situation.

The kind of model which has been discussed above might best be described by the term "coercive persuasion." The influence of an organization on an individual is coercive in the sense that he is usually forced into situations which are likely to unfreeze him, in which there are many overt and covert pressures to recognize in himself a need for change, and in which the supports for his old attitudes are in varying degrees coercively removed. It is coercive also to the degree that the new attitudes to be learned are relatively rigidly prescribed. The individual either learns them or leaves the organization (if he can). At the same time, the actual process by which new attitudes are learned can best be described as persuasion. In effect, the individual is forced into a situation in which he is likely to be influenced. The organization can be highly coercive in unfreezing its potential influence targets, yet be quite open about the direction of attitude change it will tolerate. In those cases where the direction of change is itself coerced (as contrasted with letting it occur through identification or internalization), it is highly unlikely that anything is accomplished other than surface behavioral change in the target. And such surface change will be abandoned the moment the coercive force of the change agent is lessened. If behavioral changes are coerced at the same time as other unfreezing operations are undertaken, actual influence can be facilitated if the individual finds himself having to learn attitudes to justify the kinds of behavior he has been forced to exhibit. The

---

[4] In either case the change may be essentially permanent, in that a relationship to a model or surrogate can last indefinitely. It is important to distinguish the two processes, however, because if one were to try to change the attitude, different strategies would be used depending upon how the attitude had been learned.

salesman may not have an attitude of cynicism toward his customers initially. If, however, he is forced by his boss to behave as if he felt cynical, he might develop real cynicism as a way of justifying his actual behavior.

Management development: Is it coercive persuasion?

Do the notions of coercive persuasion developed above fit the management development situation? Does the extent to which they do or do not fit such a model illuminate for us some of the implications of specific management development practices?

Unfreezing

It is reasonable to assume that the majority of managers who are being "developed" are not ready or able to change in the manner in which their organization might desire and therefore must be unfrozen before they can be influenced. They may be eager to change at a conscious motivation level, yet still be psychologically unprepared to give up certain attitudes and values in favor of untried, threatening new ones. I cannot support this assumption empirically, but the likelihood of its being valid is high because of a related fact which is empirically supportable. Most managers do not participate heavily in decisions which affect their careers, nor do they have a large voice in the kind of self-development in which they wish to participate. Rather, it is the man's superior or a staff specialist in career development who makes the key decisions concerning his career (Alfred, 1960). If the individual manager is not trained from the outset to take responsibility for his own career and given a heavy voice in diagnosing his own needs for a change, it is unlikely that he will readily be able to appreciate someone else's diagnosis. It may be unclear to him what basically is wanted of him or, worse, the ambiguity of the demands put upon him combined with his own inability to control his career development is likely to arouse anxiety and insecurity which would cause even greater resistance to genuine self-assessment and attitude change.[5] He becomes preoccupied with promotion in the abstract and attempts to acquire at a surface level the traits which he thinks are necessary for advancement.

If the decisions made by the organization do not seem valid to the manager, or if the unfreezing process turns out to be quite painful to him, to what extent can he leave the situation? His future career, his financial security, and his social status within the business community all stand to suffer if he resists the decisions made for him. Perhaps the most coercive feature is

[5] An even greater hazard, of course, is that the organization communicates to the manager that he is not expected to take responsibility for his own career at the same time that it is trying to teach him how to be able to take responsibility for important decisions!

simply the psychological pressure that what he is being asked to do is "for his own ultimate welfare." Elementary loyalty to his organization and to his managerial role demands that he accept with good grace whatever happens to him in the name of his own career development. In this sense, then, I believe that the business organization has coercive forces at its disposal which are used by it in a manner comparable to the uses made by other organizations.

Given the assumption that the manager who is to be developed needs to be unfrozen, and given that the organization has available coercive power to accomplish such unfreezing, what mechanisms does it actually use to unfreeze potential influence targets?

The essential elements to unfreezing are the removal of supports for the old attitudes, the saturation of the environment with the new attitudes to be acquired, a minimizing of threat, and a maximizing of support for any change in the right direction. In terms of this model it becomes immediately apparent that training programs or other activities which are conducted in the organization at the place of work for a certain number of hours per day or week are far less likely to unfreeze and subsequently influence the participant than those programs which remove him for varying lengths of time from his regular work situation and normal social relationships.

Are appraisal interviews, used periodically to communicate to the manager his strengths, weaknesses and areas for improvement, likely to unfreeze him? Probably not, because as long as the individual is caught up in his regular routine and is responding, probably quite unconsciously, to a whole set of expectations which others have about his behavior and attitudes, it is virtually impossible for him to hear, at a psychological level, what his deficiencies or areas needing change are. Even if he can appreciate what is being communicated to him at an intellectual level, it is unlikely that he can emotionally accept the need for change, and even if he can accept it emotionally, it is unlikely that he can produce change in himself in an environment which supports all of his old ways of functioning. This statement does not mean that the man's co-workers necessarily approve of the way he is operating or like the attitudes which he is exhibiting. They may want to see him change, but their very expectations concerning how he normally behaves operate as a constraint on him which makes attitude change difficult in that setting.

On the other hand, there are a variety of training activities which are used in management development which approximate more closely the conditions necessary for effective unfreezing. These would include programs offered at special training centers such as those maintained by IBM on Long Island and General Electric at Crotonville, N.Y.; university-sponsored courses in management, liberal arts, and/or the social sciences; and especially, workshops or laboratories in human relations such as those conducted at Arden House, N.Y., by the National Training Laboratories. Programs such as these remove the participant for some length of time from his normal routine, his regular job, and his social relationships (including his family in most cases), thus providing a kind of moratorium during which he can take stock of himself and determine where he is going and where he wants to go.

The almost total isolation from the pressures of daily life in the business world which a mountain chateau such as Arden House provides for a two-week period is supplemented by other unfreezing forces. The de-emphasis on the kind of job or title the participant holds in his company and the informal dress remove some of the symbolic or status supports upon which we all rely. Sharing a room and bath facilities with a roommate re-quires more than the accustomed exposure of private spheres of life to others. The total involvement of the participant in the laboratory program leaves little room for reflection about the back home situation. The climate of the laboratory communicates tremendous support for any efforts at self-examination and attempts as much as possible to reduce the threats inher-ent in change by emphasizing the value of experimentation, the low cost and risk of trying a new response in the protected environment of the lab, and the high gains to be derived from finding new behavior patterns and at-titudes which might improve back home performance. The content of the material presented in lectures and the kind of learning model which is used in the workshop facilitates self-examination, self-diagnosis based on usable feedback from other participants, and rational planning for change.[6]

The practice of rotating a manager from one kind of assignment to another over a period of years can have some of the same unfreezing ef-fects and thus facilitate attitude change. Certainly his physical move from one setting to another removes many of the supports to his old attitudes, and in his new job the manager will have an opportunity to try new be-haviors and become exposed to new attitudes. The practice of providing a moratorium in the form of a training program prior to assuming a new job would appear to maximize the gains from each approach, in that unfreezing would be maximally facilitated and change would most probably be lasting if the person did not go back to a situation in which his co-workers, superiors, and subordinates had stable expectations of how he should behave.

Another example of how unfreezing can be facilitated in the organiza-tional context is the practice of temporarily reducing the formal rank and re-sponsibilities of the manager by making him a trainee in a special program, or an apprentice on a special project, or an assistant to a high ranking member of the company. Such temporary lowering of formal rank can re-duce the anxiety associated with changing and at the same time serves of-ficially to destroy the old status and identity of the individual because he could not ordinarily return to his old position once he had accepted the path offered by the training program. He would have to move either up or out of the organization to maintain his sense of self-esteem. Of course, if such a training program is perceived by the trainee as an indication of his failing rather than a step toward a higher position, his anxiety about himself would

[6] Although, as I will point out later, such effective unfreezing may lead to change which is not supported or considered desirable by the "back home" organization.

be too high to facilitate effective change on his part. In all of the illustrations of organizational influence we have presented above, change was defined as being a means of gaining status—acceptance into Communist society, status as a nun or a fraternity brother, salvation, etc. If participants come to training programs believing they are being punished, they typically do not learn much.

The above discussion is intended to highlight the fact that some management development practices do facilitate the unfreezing of the influence target, but that such unfreezing is by no means automatic. Where programs fail, therefore, one of the first questions we must ask is whether they failed because they did not provide adequate conditions for unfreezing.

Changing

Turning now to the problem of the mechanisms by which changes actually occur, we must confront the question of whether the organization has relatively rigid prescribed goals concerning the direction of attitude change it expects of the young manager, or whether it is concerned with growth in the sense of providing increasing opportunities for the young manager to learn the attitudes appropriate to ever more challenging situations. It is undoubtedly true that most programs would claim growth as their goal, but the degree to which they accomplish it can only be assessed from an examination of their actual practice.

Basically the question is whether the organization influences attitudes primarily through the mechanism of identification or the mechanism of internalization. If the development programs stimulate psychological relationships between the influence target and a member of the organization who has the desired attitudes, they are thereby facilitating influence by identification but, at the same time, are limiting the alternatives available to the target and possibly the permanence of the change achieved. If they emphasize that the target must develop his own solutions to ever more demanding problems, they are risking that the attitudes learned will be incompatible with other parts of the organization's value system but are producing more permanent change because the solutions found are internalized. From the organization's point of view, therefore, it is crucial to know what kind of influence it is exerting and to assess the results of such influence in terms of the basic goals which the organization may have. If new approaches and new attitudes toward management problems are desired, for example, it is crucial that the conditions for internalization be created. If rapid learning of a given set of attitudes is desired, it is equally crucial that the conditions for identification with the right kind of models be created.

One obvious implication of this distinction is that programs conducted within the organization's orbit by its own influence agents are much more likely to facilitate identification and thereby the transmission of the "party line" or organization philosophy. On the other hand, programs like those conducted at universities or by the National Training Laboratories place much more emphasis on the finding of solutions by participants which fit their own particular needs and problems. The emphasis in the human relations courses is on "learning how to learn" from the participant's own interpersonal experiences and how to harness his emotional life and intellectual capacities to the accomplishment of his goals, rather than on specific principles of human relations. The nearest thing to an attitude which the laboratory staff, acting as influence agents, does care to communicate is an attitude of inquiry and experimentation, and to this end the learning of skills of observation, analysis, and diagnosis of interpersonal situations is given strong emphasis. The training group, which is the acknowledged core of the laboratory approach, provides its own unfreezing forces by being unstructured as to the content of discussion. But it is strongly committed to a method of learning by analysis of the member's own experiences in the group, which facilitates the discovery of the value of an attitude of inquiry and experimentation.

Mutual identification of the members of the group with each other and member identifications with the staff play some role in the acquisition of this attitude, but the basic power of the method is that the attitude of inquiry and experimentation *works* in the sense of providing for people valuable new insights about themselves, groups, and organizations. To the extent that it works and solves key problems for the participants, it is internalized and carried back into the home situation. To the extent that it is learned because participants wish to emulate a respected fellow member or staff member, it lasts only so long as the relationship with the model itself, or a surrogate of it, lasts (which may, of course, be a very long time).

The university program in management or liberal arts is more difficult to categorize in terms of an influence model, because within the program there are usually opportunities both for identification (e.g., with inspiring teachers) and internalization. It is a safe guess in either case, however, that the attitudes learned are likely to be in varying degrees out of phase with any given company's philosophy unless the company has learned from previous experience with a given course that the students are taught a point of view consistent with its own philosophy. Of course, universities, as much as laboratories, emphasize the value of a spirit of inquiry and, to the extent that they are successful in teaching this attitude, will be creating potential dissidents or innovators, depending on how the home company views the result.

Apprenticeships, special jobs in the role of "assistant to" somebody, job rotation, junior management boards, and so on stand in sharp contrast to the above methods in the degree to which they facilitate, indeed almost demand, that the young manager learn by watching those who are senior or more competent. It is probably not prescribed that in the process of acquiring knowledge and skills through the example of others he should also acquire their attitudes, but the probability that this will happen is very high if the trainee develops any degree of respect and liking for his teacher and/or supervisor. It makes little difference whether the teacher, coach, or supervisor intends to influence the attitudes of his trainee or not. If a good emotional relationship develops between them, it will facilitate the learning of knowledge and skills, and will, at the same time, result in some degree of attitude change. Consequently, such methods do not maximize the probability of new approaches being invented to management problems, nor do they really by themselves facilitate the growth of the manager in the sense of providing opportunities for him to develop solutions which fit his own needs best.

Job rotation, on the other hand, can facilitate growth and innovation provided it is managed in such a way as to insure the exposure of the trainee to a broad range of points of view as he moves from assignment to assignment. The practice of shifting the developing manager geographically as well as functionally both facilitates unfreezing and increases the likelihood of his being exposed to new attitudes. This same practice can, of course, be merely a convenient way of indoctrinating the individual by sending him on an assignment, for example, ''in order to acquire the sales point of view from Jim down in New York,'' where higher management knows perfectly well what sort of a view Jim will communicate to his subordinates.

Refreezing

Finally, a few words are in order about the problem of refreezing. Under what conditions will changed attitudes remain stable, and how do existing practices aid or hinder such stabilization? Our illustrations from the nonindustrial setting highlighted the importance of social support for any attitudes which were learned through identification. Even the kind of training emphasized in the National Training Laboratories programs, which tends to be more internalized, does not produce stable attitude change unless others in the organization, especially superiors, peers, and subordinates, have undergone similar changes and give each other stimulation and support, because lack of support acts as a new unfreezing force producing new influence (possibly in the direction of the original attitudes).

If the young manager has been influenced primarily in the direction of what is already the company philosophy, he will, of course, obtain strong support and will have little difficulty maintaining his new attitudes. If, on the other hand, management development is supposed to lead to personal growth and organizational innovation, the organization must recognize the reality that new attitudes cannot be carried by isolated individuals. The lament that we no longer have strong individualists who are willing to try something new is a fallacy based on an incorrect diagnosis. Strong individuals have always gained a certain amount of their strength from the support of others, hence the organizational problem is how to create conditions which make possible the nurturing of new ideas, attitudes, and approaches. If organizations seem to lack innovators, it may be that the climate of the organization and its methods of management development do not foster innovation, not that its human resources are inadequate.

An organizational climate in which new attitudes which differ from company philosophy can nevertheless be maintained cannot be achieved merely by an intellectual or even emotional commitment on the part of higher-ranking managers to tolerance of new ideas and attitudes. Genuine support can come only from others who have themselves been influenced, which argues strongly that at least several members of a given department must be given the same training before such training can be expected to have effect. If the superior of the people involved can participate in it as well, this strengthens the group that much more, but it would not follow from my line of reasoning that this is a necessary condition. Only some support is needed, and this support can come as well from peers and subordinates.

From this point of view, the practice of sending more than one manager to any given program at a university or human relations workshop is very sound. The National Training Laboratories have emphasized from the beginning the desirability of having organizations send teams. Some organizations like Esso Standard have created their own laboratories for the training of the entire management complement of a given refinery, and all indications are that such a practice maximizes the possibility not only of the personal growth of the managers, but of the creative growth of the organization as a whole.

Conclusion

In the above discussion I have deliberately focused on a model of influence which emphasizes procedure rather than content, interpersonal relations rather than mass media, and attitudes and values rather than knowledge and skills. By placing management development into a context of institutional influence procedures which also include Chinese Communist thought reform, the training of a nun, and other more drastic forms of coercive persuasion, I have tried to highlight aspects of management development which have remained implicit yet which need to be understood. I believe that some aspects of management development are a mild form of coercive persuasion, but I do not believe that coercive persuasion is either morally bad in any *a priori* sense nor inefficient. If we are to develop a sound theory of career development which is capable of including not only many of the formal procedures discussed in this paper, but the multitudes of informal practices, some of which are more and some of which are less coercive than those discussed, we need to suspend moral judgments for the time being and evaluate influence models solely in terms of their capacity to make sense of the data and to make meaningful predictions.

References

Alfred, T. M. Personal communication, 1960.

Hulme, K. *The nun's story.* Boston, Little, Brown, 1957.

Kelman, H. C. Compliance, identification, and internalization: three processes of attitude change. *Conflict Resolution,* 1958, *2,* 51–60.

Lewin, K. Frontiers in group dynamics: concept, method and reality in social science. *Hum. Relat.,* 1947, *I,* 5–42.

McGregor, D. *The human side of enterprise.* New York, McGraw-Hill, 1960.

Merton, R. K., Reader, G. G., and Kendall, Patricia L. *The student-physician.* Cambridge, Mass., Harvard University Press, 1957.

National Training Laboratory in Group Development: *Explorations in human relations training: an assessment of experience, 1947–1953.* Washington, D.C., National Education Association, 1953.

Schein, E. H. *Brainwashing.* Cambridge, Mass., Center for International Studies, M.I.T., 1961.

Schein, E. H. Interpersonal communication, group solidarity, and social influence. *Sociometry,* 1960, *23,* 148–161.

28 An additional thought on management development: A note from the editor
Patrick E. Connor

In the preceding article, Schein presented what is probably the classic statement on management development. His position is similar to that taken by most writers and practitioners in the field. Generally, this position states that the development of managers and executives involves changing them. Schein's concern emphasizes unfreezing and refreezing attitudes. Thus, management development typically is concerned with bringing about changes in the individual—in his attitudes and in his behavior.

You may ask whether the development of managers inherently requires that managers undergo some kind of change. The answer is, not necessarily. Remember that the basic objective of management development does not *directly* refer to the individual, but rather it has an organizational focus—namely, to insure that there are competent managers available to direct the activities of the organization on a continuous basis over time. The assumption that the best way to accomplish this objective is through changing individuals has been recently challenged. In particular, the extensive work being performed by Fiedler and his associates suggests a new approach. Dr. Fiedler has found that effective leadership depends on three basic factors:

1 *Leader-member relations* The degree to which the leader's subordinates trust and like him, and are willing to follow his guidance.
2 *Task structure* The degree to which the carrying out of the task (machining parts, designing equipment, performing an audit) is either specified step-by-step, or is nebulous and undefined.

3 *Position power*   The amount of power inherent to the position (as distinct from the personal power of a particular individual)—hiring and firing powers, security of the manager's own job, etc.

As you will see when you read Fiedler's article later in this volume (Selection 37, "How Do You Make Leaders More Effective? New Answers to an Old Puzzle"), these factors affect leadership effectiveness interdependently. For example, under a condition of high task structure and strong position power, "good" leader-member relations are not crucial—indeed, they may not be particularly relevant—for effective leadership.

Proceeding from these discoveries, we come to the same remarkable conclusion reached by Dr. Fiedler: it is easier—more straightforward, less costly, and less time-consuming—to alter characteristics of the job situation, especially task structure and position power, than to try to generate fundamental changes in the individuals. Additionally, as Fiedler notes, it is certainly easier to place people in a situation compatible with their natural leadership style than to force them to adapt to the demands of the job.

And so we have a different and intriguing view of management development. It is useful to consider that the objectives of management development are more fully served if, as Fiedler has put it, we engineer the job to fit the manager rather than try to engineer the manager to fit the job.

IV/C
Appraising managerial performance

29 Make performance appraisal relevant
Winston Oberg

These frequently voiced goals of performance appraisal programs underscore the importance of such programs to any ongoing business organization:

- Help or prod supervisors to observe their subordinates more closely and to do a better coaching job.
- Motivate employees by providing feedback on how they are doing.
- Provide back-up data for management decisions concerning merit increases, transfers, dismissals, and so on.
- Improve organization development by identifying people with promotion potential and pinpointing development needs.
- Establish a research and reference base for personnel decisions.

It has been estimated that over three fourths of U.S. companies now have performance appraisal programs.[1]

In actual practice, however, formal performance appraisal programs have often yielded unsatisfactory and disappointing results, as the growing body of critical literature attests.[2] Some critics even suggest that we abandon performance appraisal as a lost hope, and they point to scores of problems and pitfalls as evidence.

But considering the potential of appraisal programs, the issue should

Source: Reprinted with permission from *Harvard Business Review* (January–February 1972), pp. 61–67. © 1972 by the President and Fellows of Harvard College; all rights reserved.

[1] See W. R. Spriegel and Edwin W. Mumma, *Merit Rating of Supervisors and Executives* (Austin, Bureau of Business Research, University of Texas, 1961); and Richard V. Miller, "Merit Rating in Industry: A Survey of Current Practices and Problems," ILR Research, Fall 1959.
[2] See, for example, Douglas McGregor, "An Uneasy Look at Performance Appraisal," HBR May–June 1957, p. 89; Paul H. Thompson and Gene W. Dalton, "Performance Appraisals Managers Beware," HBR January–February 1970, p. 149; and Albert W. Schrader, "Let's Abolish the Annual Performance Review," *Management of Personnel Quarterly,* Fall 1969, p. 293.

not be whether to scrap them; rather, it should be how to make them better. I have found that one reason for failures is that companies often select indiscriminately from the wide battery of available performance appraisal techniques without really thinking about which particular technique is best suited to a particular appraisal objective.

For example, the most commonly used appraisal techniques include:

1 Essay appraisal.
2 Graphic rating scale.
3 Field review.
4 Forced-choice rating.
5 Critical incident appraisal.
6 Management-by-objectives approach.
7 Work-standards approach.
8 Ranking methods.
9 Assessment centers.

Each of these has its own combination of strengths and weaknesses, and none is able to achieve all of the purposes for which management institutes performance appraisal systems. Nor is any one technique able to evade all of the pitfalls. The best anyone can hope to do is to match an appropriate appraisal method to a particular performance appraisal goal.

In this article, I shall attempt to lay the groundwork for such a matching effort. First, I shall review some familiar pitfalls in appraisal programs; then, against this background, I shall assess the strengths and weaknesses of the nine commonly used appraisal techniques. In the last section, I shall match the organizational objectives listed at the outset of this article with the techniques best suited to achieving them.

Some common pitfalls

Obstacles to the success of formal performance appraisal programs should be familiar to most managers, either from painful personal experience or from the growing body of critical literature. Here are the most troublesome and frequently cited drawbacks:

- Performance appraisal programs demand too much from supervisors. Formal performance appraisals obviously require at least periodic supervisor observation of subordinates' performance. However, the typical first-line supervisor can hardly know, in a very adequate way, just what each of 20, 30, or more subordinates is doing.
- Standards and ratings tend to vary widely and, often, unfairly. Some raters are tough, others are lenient. Some departments have highly competent people; others have less competent people. Consequently, employees subject to less competition or lenient ratings can receive higher appraisals than equally competent or superior associates.

- Personal values and bias can replace organizational standards. An appraiser may not lack standards, but the standards he uses are sometimes the wrong ones. For example, unfairly low ratings may be given to valued subordinates so they will not be promoted out of the rater's department. More often, however, outright bias dictates favored treatment for some employees.
- Because of lack of communication, employees may not know how they are rated. The standards by which employees think they are being judged are sometimes different from those their superiors actually use. No performance appraisal system can be very effective for management decisions, organization development, or any other purpose until the people being appraised know what is expected of them and by what criteria they are being judged.
- Appraisal techniques tend to be used as performance panaceas. If a worker lacks the basic ability or has not been given the necessary training for his job, it is neither reasonable to try to stimulate adequate performance through performance appraisals, nor fair to base salary, dismissal, or other negative decisions on such an appraisal. No appraisal program can substitute for sound selection, placement, and training programs. Poor performance represents someone else's failure.
- In many cases, the validity of ratings is reduced by supervisory resistance to making the ratings. Rather than confront their less effective subordinates with negative ratings, negative feedback in appraisal interviews, and below-average salary increases, supervisors often take the more comfortable way out and give average or above-average ratings to inferior performers.
- Performance appraisal ratings can boomerang when communicated to employees. Negative feedback (i.e., criticism) not only fails to motivate the typical employee, but also can cause him to perform worse.[3] Only those employees who have a high degree of self-esteem appear to be stimulated by criticism to improve their performance.
- Performance appraisals interfere with the more constructive coaching relationship that should exist between a superior and his subordinates. Performance appraisal interviews tend to emphasize the superior position of the supervisor by placing him in the role of judge, thus countering his equally important role of teacher and coach. This is particularly damaging in organizations that are attempting to maintain a more participative organizational climate.

A look at methods

The foregoing list of major program pitfalls represents a formidable challenge, even considering the available battery of appraisal techniques. But attempting to avoid these pitfalls by doing away with appraisals themselves is

[3] See Herbert H. Meyer, Emanuel Kay, and John R. P. French, Jr., "Split Roles in Performance Appraisal," HBR January–February 1965, p. 123.

like trying to solve the problems of life by committing suicide. The more logical task is to identify those appraisal practices that are (a) most likely to achieve a particular objective and (b) least vulnerable to the obstacles already discussed.

Before relating the specific techniques to the goals of performance appraisal stated at the outset of the article, I shall briefly review each, taking them more or less in an order of increasing complexity. The best-known techniques will be treated most briefly.

1 Essay appraisal

In its simplest form, this technique asks the rater to write a paragraph or more covering an individual's strengths, weaknesses, potential, and so on. In most selection situations, particularly those involving professional, sales, or managerial positions, essay appraisals from former employers, teachers, or associates carry significant weight. The assumption seems to be that an honest and informed statement—either by word of mouth or in writing—from someone who knows a man well, is fully as valid as more formal and more complicated methods.

The biggest drawback to essay appraisals is their variability in length and content. Moreover, since different essays touch on different aspects of a man's performance or personal qualifications, essay ratings are difficult to combine or compare. For comparability, some type of more formal method, like the graphic rating scale, is desirable.

2 Graphic rating scale

This technique may not yield the depth of an essay appraisal, but it is more consistent and reliable. Typically, a graphic scale assesses a person on the quality and quantity of his work (is he outstanding, above average, average, or unsatisfactory?) and on a variety of other factors that vary with the job but usually include personal traits like reliability and cooperation. It may also include specific performance items like oral and written communication.

The graphic scale has come under frequent attack, but remains the most widely used rating method. In a classic comparison between the "old-fashioned" graphic scale and the much more sophisticated forced-choice technique, the former proved to be fully as valid as the best of the forced-choice forms, and better than most of them.[4] It is also cheaper to develop and more acceptable to raters than the forced-choice form. For many purposes there is no need to use anything more complicated than a graphic scale supplemented by a few essay questions.

[4] James Berkshire and Richard Highland, "Forced-Choice Performance Rating on a Methodological Study," *Personnel Psychology,* Autumn 1953, p. 355.

3 Field review

When there is reason to suspect rater bias, when some raters appear to be using higher standards than others, or when comparability of ratings is essential, essay or graphic ratings are often combined with a systematic review process. The field review is one of several techniques for doing this. A member of the personnel or central administrative staff meets with small groups of raters from each supervisory unit and goes over each employee's rating with them to (a) identify areas of inter-rater disagreement, (b) help the group arrive at a consensus, and (c) determine that each rater conceives the standards similarly.

This group-judgement technique tends to be more fair and more valid than individual ratings and permits the central staff to develop an awareness of the varying degrees of leniency or severity—as well as bias—exhibited by raters in different departments. On the negative side, the process is very time consuming.

4 Forced-choice rating

Like the field review, this technique was developed to reduce bias and establish objective standards of comparison between individuals, but it does not involve the intervention of a third party. Although there are many variations of this method, the most common one asks raters to choose from among groups of statements those which *best* fit the individual being rated and those which *least* fit him. The statements are then weighted or scored, very much the way a psychological test is scored. People with high scores are, by definition, the better employees; those with low scores are the poorer ones. Since the rater does not know what the scoring weights for each statement are, in theory at least, he cannot play favorites. He simply describes his people, and someone in the personnel department applies the scoring weights to determine who gets the best rating.

The rationale behind this technique is difficult to fault. It is the same rationale used in developing selection test batteries. In practice, however, the forced-choice method tends to irritate raters, who feel they are not being trusted. They want to say openly how they rate someone and not be second-guessed or tricked into making "honest" appraisals.

A few clever raters have even found ways to beat the system. When they want to give average employee Harry Smith a high rating, they simply describe the best employee they know. If the best employee is Elliott Jones, they describe Jones on Smith's forced-choice form. Thus, Smith gets a good rating and hopefully a raise.

An additional drawback is the difficulty and cost of developing forms. Consequently, the technique is usually limited to middle- and lower-management levels where the jobs are sufficiently similar to make standard or common forms feasible.

Finally, forced-choice forms tend to be of little value—and probably have a negative effect—when used in performance appraisal interviews.

5 Critical incident appraisal

The discussion of ratings with employees has, in many companies, proved to be a traumatic experience for supervisors. Some have learned from bitter experience what General Electric later documented; people who receive honest but negative feedback are typically not motivated to do better—and often do worse—after the appraisal interview.[5] Consequently, supervisors tend to avoid such interviews, or if forced to hold them, avoid giving negative ratings when the ratings have to be shown to the employee.

One stumbling block has no doubt been the unsatisfactory rating form used. Typically, these are graphic scales that often include rather vague traits like initiative, cooperativeness, reliability, and even personality. Discussing these with an employee can be difficult.

The critical incident technique looks like a natural to some people for performance review interviews, because it gives a supervisor actual, factual incidents to discuss with an employee. Supervisors are asked to keep a record, a "little black book," on each employee and to record actual incidents of positive or negative behavior.

For example: Bob Mitchell, who has been rated as somewhat unreliable, fails to meet several deadlines during the appraisal period. His supervisor makes a note of these incidents and is now prepared with hard, factual data: "Bob, I rated you down on reliability because, on three different occasions over the last two months, you told me you would do something and you didn't do it. You remember six weeks ago when I . . . ."

Instead of arguing over traits, the discussion now deals with actual behavior. Possibly, Bob has misunderstood the supervisor or has good reasons for his apparent "unreliability." If so, he now has an opportunity to respond. His performance, not his personality, is being criticized. He knows specifically how to perform differently if he wants to be rated higher the next time. Of course, Bob might feel the supervisor was using unfairly high standards in evaluating his performance. But at least he would know just what those standards are.

There are, however, several drawbacks to this approach. It requires that supervisors jot down incidents on a daily or, at the very least, a weekly basis. This can become a chore. Furthermore, the critical incident rating technique need not, but may, cause a supervisor to delay feedback to employees. And it is hardly desirable to wait six months or a year to confront an employee with a misdeed or mistake.

Finally, the supervisor sets the standards. If they seem unfair to a subordinate, might he not be more motivated if he at least has some say in setting, or at least agreeing to, the standards against which he is judged?

[5] Meyer, Kay, and French, op. cit.

6 Management by objectives

To avoid, or to deal with, the feeling that they are being judged by unfairly high standards, employees in some organizations are being asked to set—or help set—their own performance goals. Within the past five or six years, MBO has become something of a fad and is so familiar to most managers that I will not dwell on it here.

It should be noted, however, that when MBO is applied at lower organizational levels, employees do not always want to be involved in their own goal setting. As Arthur N. Turner and Paul R. Lawrence discovered, many do not want self-direction or autonomy.[6] As a result, more coercive variations of MBO are becoming increasingly common, and some critics see MBO drifting into a kind of manipulative form of management in which pseudo-participation substitutes for the real thing. Employees are consulted, but management ends up imposing its standards and its objectives.[7]

Some organizations, therefore, are introducing a work-standards approach to goal setting in which the goals are openly set by management. In fact, there appears to be something of a vogue in the setting of such work standards in white-collar and service areas.

7 Work-standards approach

Instead of asking employees to set their own performance goals, many organizations set measured daily work standards. In short, the work-standards technique establishes work and staffing targets aimed at improving productivity. When realistically used, it can make possible an objective and accurate appraisal of the work of employees and supervisors.

To be effective, the standards must be visible and fair. Hence a good deal of time is spent observing employees on the job, simplifying and improving the job where possible, and attempting to arrive at realistic output standards.

It is not clear, in every case, that work standards have been integrated with an organization's performance appraisal program. However, since the work-standards program provides each employee with a more or less complete set of his job duties, it would seem only natural that supervisors will eventually relate performance appraisal and interview comments to these duties. I would expect this to happen increasingly where work standards exist. The use of work standards should make performance interviews less threatening than the use of personal, more subjective standards alone.

The most serious drawback appears to be the problem of comparability. If people are evaluated on different standards, how can the ratings be

---

[6] *Industrial Jobs and the Worker* (Boston, Division of Research, Harvard Business School, 1965).
[7] See, for example, Harry Levinson, "Management by Whose Objectives?" HBR July–August 1970, p. 125.

brought together for comparison purposes when decisions have to be made on promotions or on salary increases? For these purposes some form of ranking is necessary.

8 Ranking methods

For comparative purposes, particularly when it is necessary to compare people who work for different supervisors, individual statements, ratings, or appraisal forms are not particularly useful. Instead, it is necessary to recognize that comparisons involve an overall subjective judgment to which a host of additional facts and impressions must somehow be added. There is no single form or way to do this.

Comparing people in different units for the purpose of, say, choosing a service supervisor or determining the relative size of salary increases for different supervisors, requires subjective judgment, not statistics. The best approach appears to be a ranking technique involving pooled judgment. The two most effective methods are alternation ranking and paired comparison ranking.

Alternation ranking
In this method, the names of employees are listed on the left-hand side of a sheet of paper—preferably in random order. If the rankings are for salary purposes, a supervisor is asked to choose the "most valuable" employee on the list, cross his name off, and put it at the top of the column on the right-hand side of the sheet. Next, he selects the "least valuable" employee on the list, crosses his name off, and puts it at the bottom of the right-hand column. The ranker then selects the "most valuable" person from the remaining list, crosses his name off and enters it below the top name on the right-hand list, and so on.

Paired-comparison ranking
This technique is probably just as accurate as alternation ranking and might be more so. But with large numbers of employees it becomes extremely time consuming and cumbersome.

To illustrate the method, let us say we have five employees: Mr. Abbott, Mr. Barnes, Mr. Cox, Mr. Drew, and Mr. Eliot. We list their names on the left-hand side of the sheet. We compare Abbott with Barnes on whatever criterion we have chosen, say, present value to the organization. If we feel Abbott is more valuable than Barnes, we put a tally beside Abbott's name. We then compare Abbott with Cox, with Drew, and with Eliot. The process is repeated for each individual. The man with the most tallies is the most valuable person, at least in the eyes of the rater; the man with no tallies at all is regarded as the least valuable person.

Both ranking techniques, particularly when combined with multiple rankings (i.e., when two or more people are asked to make independent rankings of the same work group and their lists are averaged), are among the best available for generating valid order-of-merit rankings for salary administration purposes.

9 Assessment centers

So far, we have been talking about assessing past performance. What about the assessment of future performance or potential? In any placement decision and even more so in promotion decisions, some prediction of future performance is necessary. How can this kind of prediction be made most validly and most fairly?

One widely used rule of thumb is that "what a man has done is the best predictor of what he will do in the future." But suppose you are picking a man to be a supervisor and this person has never held supervisory responsibility? Or suppose you are selecting a man for a job from among a group of candidates, none of whom has done the job or one like it? In these situations, many organizations use assessment centers to predict future performance more accurately.

Typically, individuals from different departments are brought together to spend two or three days working on individual and group assignments similar to the ones they will be handling if they are promoted. The pooled judgment of observers—sometimes derived by paired comparison or alternation ranking—leads to an order-of-merit ranking for each participant. Less structured, subjective judgments are also made.

There is a good deal of evidence that people chosen by assessment center methods work out better than those not chosen by these methods.[8] The center also makes it possible for people who are working for departments of low status or low visibility in an organization to become visible and, in the competitive situation of an assessment center, show how they stack up against people from more well-known departments. This has the effect of equalizing opportunity, improving morale, and enlarging the pool of possible promotion candidates.

Fitting practice to purpose

In the foregoing analysis, I have tried to show that each performance appraisal technique has its own combination of strengths and weaknesses. The success of any program that makes use of these techniques will largely depend on how they are used relative to the goals of that program.

For example, goal-setting and work-standards methods will be most effective for objective coaching, counseling, and motivational purposes, but some form of critical incident appraisal is better when a supervisor's personal judgment and criticism are necessary.

[8] See, for example, Robert C. Albrook, "Spot Executives Early," *Fortune,* July 1968, p. 106; and William C. Byham, "Assessment Centers for Spotting Future Managers," HBR July–August 1970, p. 150.

Comparisons of individuals, especially in win-lose situations when only one person can be promoted or only a limited number can be given large salary increases, necessitate a still different approach. Each person should be rated on the same form, which must be as simple as possible, probably involving essay and graphic responses. Then order-of-merit rankings and final averaging should follow. To be more explicit, here are the appraisal goals listed at the outset of this article and the techniques best suited to them.

Help or prod supervisors to observe their subordinates more closely and to do a better coaching job.

The critical incident appraisal appears to be ideal for this purpose, if supervisors can be convinced they should take the time to look for, and record, significant events. Time delays, however, are a major drawback to this technique and should be kept as short as possible. Still, over the longer term, a supervisor will gain a better knowledge of his own performance standards, including his possible biases, as he reviews the incidents he has recorded. He may even decide to change or reweight his own criteria.

Another technique that is useful for coaching purposes is, of course, MBO. Like the critical incident method, it focuses on actual behavior and actual results which can be discussed objectively and constructively, with little or no need for a supervisor to "play God."

Motivate employees by providing feedback on how they are doing.

The MBO approach, if it involves real participation, appears to be most likely to lead to an inner commitment to improved performance. However, the work-standards approach can also motivate, although in a more coercive way. If organizations staff to meet their work standards, the work force is reduced and people are compelled to work harder.

The former technique is more "democratic," while the latter technique is more "autocratic." Both can be effective; both make use of specific work goals or targets, and both provide for knowledge of results.

If performance appraisal information is to be communicated to subordinates, either in writing or in an interview, the two most effective techniques are the management-by-objectives approach and the critical incident method. The latter, by communicating not only factual data but also the flavor of a supervisor's own values and biases, can be effective in an area where objective work standards or quantitative goals are not available.

Provide back-up data for management decisions concerning merit increases, promotions, transfers, dismissals, and so on.

Most decisions involving employees require a comparison of people doing very different kinds of work. In this respect, the more specifically job-related techniques like management by objectives or work standards are not appropriate, or, if used, must be supplemented by less restricted methods.

For promotion to supervisory positions, the forced-choice rating form, if carefully developed and validated, could prove best. But the difficulty and cost of developing such a form and the resistance of raters to its use render it impractical except in large organizations.

Companies faced with the problem of selecting promotable men from a number of departments or divisions might consider using an assessment center. This minimizes the bias resulting from differences in departmental "visibility" and enlarges the pool of potential promotables.

The best appraisal method for most other management decisions will probably involve a very simple kind of graphic form or a combined graphic and essay form. If this is supplemented by the use of field reviews, it will be measurably strengthened. Following the individual appraisals, groups of supervisors should then be asked to rank the people they have rated, using a technique like alternation ranking or paired comparison. Pooled or averaged rankings will then tend to cancel out the most extreme forms of bias and should yield fair and valid order-of-merit lists.

Improve organization development by identifying people with promotion potential and pinpointing development needs.

Comparison of people for promotion purposes has already been discussed. However, identification of training and development needs will probably best—and most simply—come from the essay part of the combined graphic/essay rating form recommended for the previous goal.

Establish a reference and research base for personnel decisions.

For this goal, the simplest form is the best form. A graphic/essay combination is adequate for most reference purposes. But order-of-merit salary rankings should be used to develop criterion groups of good and poor performers.

Conclusion

Formal systems for appraising performance are neither worthless nor evil, as some critics have implied. Nor are they panaceas, as many managers might wish. A formal appraisal system is, at the very least, a commendable attempt to make visible, and hence improvable, a set of essential organization activities. Personal judgments about employee performance are inescapable, and subjective values and fallible human perception are always involved. Formal appraisal systems, to the degree that they bring these perceptions and values into the open, make it possible for at least some of the inherent bias and error to be recognized and remedied.

By improving the probability that good performance will be recognized and rewarded and poor performance corrected, a sound appraisal system can contribute both to organizational morale and organizational performance.

Moreover, the alternative to a bad appraisal program need not be no appraisal program at all, as some critics have suggested. It can and ought to be a better appraisal program. And the first step in that direction is a thoughtful matching of practice to purpose.

30 Measuring managers by results
Dale D. McConkey

The acid test of any manager is the results which he achieves. Expressed in terms of the physicist, nothing is accomplished unless efforts expended bring about results. The primary difficulty in applying the acid test to any manager is to agree upon the criteria by which the results can and will be measured—in other words, the formulation of standards of performance.

Undoubtedly the easiest and probably the most accurate standards are those established for factory workers based on methods analysis and work measurement, e.g., a machine operator must produce "X" number of units in "Y" time. This standard is rather easily related to performance simply by computing the actual number of units produced in the allowable time lapse. Unfortunately, the job characteristics which permit this minute type of performance measurement, i.e., the routine and repetitive nature of the job, do not lend themselves to similarly measuring the manager's performance.

Traditional measuring

Traditional measuring usually has taken the form of performance appraisal or merit rating reports—measuring which might be termed "personality" measuring in large part. These typically follow a civil service type of measurement, i.e., emphasis is on effort expended rather than output achieved (results). The writer has reviewed many of these forms and appraisal processes, including those in current use by many large corporations. Usually these forms are concerned with rating the individual according to a series of factors ostensibly designed to measure the incumbent's effectiveness. Factors frequently used include—Initiative—Grasp of Function—Cost Consciousness—Health—Judgment—Potential for Advancement—Ability to Deal with Others—etc. It is submitted that at best these factors are weak measuring devices in that they do not actually measure results achieved, and it is after all results which determine the success of an enterprise. For example, a particular executive could be bubbling with initiative, know his function well, be

Source: Reprinted with permission from *Personnel Journal* (December 1962), pp. 540–546. © December 1962 by *Personnel Journal.*

especially cost conscious, in the best of health, possess superb judgment, be a real comer, get along well with others—and still not produce any contribution whatsoever to company profit.

Again, to the writer's knowledge, one leading nationally known company has changed its appraisal form four times in as many years and is currently working on the fifth modification—all because actual results achieved by the executives are not jibing with the glowing words included on their appraisal forms. What better testimony is needed to the effect that merit rating forms, while probably good as guides for training and development purposes, are a poor means of results measurement.

In addition to the cardinal failure of not measuring what they are intended to measure, these so-called appraisal or merit rating forms perpetuate other ills. In many companies these rating reports form the basic premise on which: merit increases are granted—promotions are based—bonuses are awarded—efficiency awards are made—and a whole host of other rewards are "justified."

Critical analysis of the use of these forms will usually demonstrate that the primary reason why these forms and systems have failed is that they attempt to measure without first knowing what they are supposed to measure. To illustrate, let's take one of the more common factors appearing on managerial appraisal forms; namely, the factor of Cost Consciousness. This factor is usually spelled out in terms such as "Degree to which the Manager is Cost Conscious." In an attempt to guide the person doing the rating, the factor is usually further broken down into degrees such as, Manager is especially cost conscious—Manager is above average in cost consciousness—Manager is average in cost consciousness—Manager is below average in cost consciousness—Manager is poor in cost consciousness. Herein lies the joke! The degree in each factor is spelled out in indefinite, highly relative terms. This, coupled with the fact that many of these companies don't have any precise standard against which the manager is to be measured, makes the use of the words "appraisal," "rating" or "measurement" patently ridiculous on the surface. For example, take the case of a Plant Manager who spends $50,000 on plant maintenance during the year. Is he especially cost conscious, above average, average, below average, or poor? Naturally, without much more knowledge of the given situation no one in the possession of all of his faculties would attempt to answer the question. Yet, is this not the very "stabbing in the dark" which we are attempting when we endeavor to appraise or measure without first knowing precisely what we are measuring?

Measuring managers

The first step in the effective measurement of management must be a firm dedication on the part of people responsible for measuring that all managers must be measured—business cannot tolerate less; secondly, that management will be measured in precise, definite terms; and thirdly, that this precise measurement will be based solely on *Results Achieved*. Thus viewed, we find that measurement is reduced to two aspects—Results Achieved vs. Results Expected—and both can be solved by spelling out the results expected.

Because of the inability to apply precise standards such as those applied to factory workers to measuring the manager's job, resort is usually made to one or more of the following techniques in those companies which are dedicated to measuring their managers by results achieved:

A *Profit and loss centers* As private enterprises are in business to make a profit, the degree to which profits are achieved becomes one of our most effective measures. Usually profit and loss centers are established only for those managers having over-all responsibility for the management of a particular organizational unit, e.g., a company, a subsidiary or a division. The manager is responsible for combining production, sales and all other functions into a profitable enterprise and his performance is measured by the profit his efforts generate.

B *Cost centers* Comparable to profit and loss centers but differing primarily by scope. These are usually utilized when the basis on which the manager is to be measured is a particular function of an over-all unit rather than the over-all unit itself. An example is a production department which is part of an over-all profit and loss center. The production manager produces the articles and turns them over to the sales department for selling. The production manager does not determine how, where or at what price the articles will be sold and thus he cannot be held responsible for profits but he can be held responsible for the cost of producing the articles and thus he is measured on the basis of a cost center, e.g., producing a designated quantity of articles at a designated cost, and he is measured by the extent to which he achieves these cost standards.

C *Objectives* The performance of certain managers cannot be measured by either the profit and loss or cost center techniques; e.g., managers of staff departments. Because of the inherent nature of their jobs—which in most instances are concerned with intangibles or whose results are included with the over-all results of others—the primary measure of managers in industrial relations, law, research and accounting, must be by a method other than the two previously mentioned. In other instances, it may not be desired to establish profit and loss centers or cost centers.

Thus, we come to management and measuring by Objectives. A couple of examples will serve to illustrate this method of measurement. In the instance of an industrial relations manager, he might be measured by the standard of being required to formulate and implement a job evaluation plan for specified employees within a specified time period. A comptroller might be required to formulate and implement a particular cost accounting system in a specified time period. The research manager could be measured against the preset standard of developing a particular new product within a particular period of time. And so on, ad infinitum! Although less precise, these future objectives, if properly thought out and established, do provide an effective standard for measuring staff managers.

Because profit and loss and cost centers are generally more widely used and understood, the bulk of that which follows will be concerned with management and measurement by objectives.

Management and measurement by objective

One of the most critical aspects of measurement by objectives lies in the area of the manager's superior, in the form of evaluating the objectives against which the manager will perform and be measured. Again, it must be emphasized in this type of measurement that the objective must be set in advance for measuring at some particular future time. Thus, the superior must evaluate and pass on each objective in terms of:

1 Does the objective represent a sufficient task for the manager during the measuring period?
2 Is the objective a practical and attainable one?
3 Is the objective clearly stated in terms of:
   A. The task?
   B. The measuring period?
   C. The method of measuring to be used?
4 Is the objective compatible with the company's plans and over-all objectives for the period?

Only after the superior has answered the above is he in a position to pass upon the objective. If a "too easy" objective is approved—which is too easily attainable or is an insufficient task for the measuring period—the company will suffer in two ways. Number one, the company will not have received value due for the period and secondly, the development of the manager has been impeded as he has not been provided with a proper goal to spur his performance—his objective has contributed to sub-standard performance.

Returning again to the earlier point concerning the relative ease of setting work standards in rather routine, highly repetitive production operations, the superior has no such handy indices to use. Herein lies one of the greater parts of the problem. Once the superior has put his approval on the manager's objectives, the latter has every reason to accept that objective as being his mandate and operating procedure for the next two, three or five years—depending upon the measuring period. Thus, if at the end of the measuring period the manager has in fact satisfactorily completed his objective he has every right to believe he has done a good job. But! Take, for example, an objective to be completed in two years, but for which a period of 12 or 18 months was a realistic period for completion. Does this mean that a manager who took the full allowable two-year period was "goofing off"? I submit it does not altogether. In the first instance the manager knows he has two years to complete the objective and so he schedules each phase of the task for completion during a certain interval during the two-year period. If he completes one phase ahead of schedule he is very likely to use his time and that of his staff to work on other matters which he considers to be important—he does not necessarily pick up his golf clubs and head for the nearest green! However, by working on the "other matters" he may be making poor use of priority time which should be better spent working on his primary objective. But, on the other hand, he has been told by his boss that the main task is not required for the full two years.

How objectives are set

There is little doubt but that the better method for setting objectives is the one in which the objectives are drafted and recommended by the individual managers and then approved by their superiors. The first step should be a general briefing by the chief executive as to the goals and over-all objectives of the total company for a specified future period. From this general briefing the individual manager then translates these corporate goals into the impact they will have on his particular department, and in turn what objectives his department will have to achieve to play its part in the over-all goal.

The objectives of each manager are then routed to the chief executive for the review previously described and once approved they become the manager's:

1 Directive of required action, and
2 Standard against which he will be measured—and rewarded or removed.

To be effective, of course, measurement by objectives should not be limited to the top managers. Each of these top managers in turn should establish, and measure by, the same objective setting for each supervisor under the manager's jurisdiction. In this way we achieve multiple levels of responsibility with the result that the total enterprise is being held accountable for results. In addition to the measuring aspect, measuring in this fashion leads naturally into good forward planning—each manager is required to set future objectives and work toward them. In combining the future objectives of each manager, the chief executive establishes the forward planning for the total entity.

An effective system should also provide for interim measuring of performance within the total allowed time for the total objective, e.g., an objective approved for a two year period might be reviewed by the supervisor at interim periods of, say, every six months. This has two distinct advantages—one, it serves as a further check on the validity of the original objective setting; and two, it permits corrective action being taken before an improperly conceived objective or a poor manager has gone beyond the point of no return.

One last point about measurement by objectives. It is time-consuming and laborious. It requires much thinking in depth before, during and after objective-setting. No company should enter into such a program unless it is convinced that the effort and time is worth while, and it is willing to pay this cost.

Equally important, it must decide and dedicate itself to the principle that managers must be measured, that they must produce results and that unproductive ones must be removed. Results management is intolerant of mediocrity.

A comparison

A brief review and comparison of the "traditional" and the "results" appraisal will demonstrate the weaknesses and the strong points of the "results" type. This comparison of appraisal methods is equally applicable regardless of which of the previously discussed measuring indices is used, i.e., profit and loss centers, cost centers or objectives.

Exhibit 1 is a typical job description for a plant manager, and Exhibit 2 is an appraisal form currently used by a large corporation for measuring the plant manager. It will be noted that the job description in Exhibit 1 is the usual general type which gives little more than a vague idea of the incumbent's responsibilities. It is probably adequate for recruiting and development purposes, but of little value as a standard to measure against.

The appraisal form in Exhibit 2 is naturally general and vague; this is to be expected because the "standards" in the job description are similarly

---

Exhibit 1 Abbreviated example of common job description of plant manager

General responsibilities
Responsible for the manufacture of assigned products consistent with scheduled requirements, cost standards and quality specifications. Collaborates with functional departments in the development, installation and execution of specialized services to obtain production requirements. Formulates, develops and administers management activities in accordance with established policies and procedures.

Specific duties
1. Directs the manufacture of assigned products consistent with scheduled requirements, cost standards and quality specifications.
2. Directs the planning and construction of new plant and equipment.
3. Responsible for the formulation of employee relations policies designed to promote harmonious relations with employees.
4. Analyzes and reports on the development, installation, and progress of plans to improve manufacturing operations.

Supervises
1. Production manager
2. Plant engineer
3. Office manager
4. Personnel manager
5. Purchasing agent

Reports to
Vice President Operations

Exhibit 2 Example of typical appraisal form

Rater _____ _____1st _____2nd _____3rd Rater
              Name   Position

MANAGEMENT APPRAISAL FORM—PART II
(CONFIDENTIAL WHEN COMPLETED)

Name _____ Date _____

Job Title _____ Ranking _____ of _____

Department, Division, Plant or Office _____ How long in this position _____

Came with company _____ Age _____
              Date   Position   Present Age

How well is he doing the job? _____
            How does his performance compare with last year or previous periods;

with others doing similar work?

Strong points _____
              What is he doing unusually well?

Weak points _____
        What are his outstanding weaknesses? (Every one has some weaknesses, if this employee is to be

developed, helped to overcome his limitations, and properly placed, it is imperative that all of his weaknesses, shortcomings

and limitations be brought to light.)

11. Appearance, dress and manner _____
             Are they appropriate for the position?

2. Technical qualification _____
          Is it excessive?   If not qualified, where is he weak?

3. Industry _____
            Is he lazy?   Does he work too hard?

4. Energy, initiative and drive _____
          Is he a "self-starter?"   Does he find obstacles challenging?
          Is he a "doer?"

11. Self-reliance _____
        Is he a "leaner?"   How well does he stand on his own feet?   To what extent does he habitually

tell the boss what he wants to hear?

12. Willingness to accept responsibility for his and his subordinate's errors, etc. _____
              Does he "pass the buck" and alibi?

Will he admit that he is wrong?

weak. We cannot use something which is precise and definite to measure against something which is vague and general.

Exhibit 3 is a greatly abbreviated description of responsibilities for the same job under a "Results" type system. For purposes of brevity, only a few factors are spelled out in this illustration. No verbose, impressive

---

Exhibit 3 Simplified statement of results expected (accountability) [of] plant manager

Within the period specified the Plant Manager is accountable for achieving the following results. He may delegate to persons under his direction responsibility for certain of these activities but he may not delegate the accountability for the results expected.

1. Plant construction
Complete the construction and equipping of the approved addition to Plant Number 1 as follow:
A. Engineering completed by_____
B. Construction completed by_____
C. Equipment installed by_____
D. Plant producing by_____
E. Approved capital appropriation_____

2. Production costs
Produce product at Plant Number 1 in accordance with following unit costs:

Production level	Allowable unit cost
1000 units	$ .10
2000 units	.09
3000 units	.08
4000 units	.07
5000 units	.06

3. Equipment installation
Install and have operational the approved XYZ Packaging Line in Department A by_____

4. Operations analysis
Complete comprehensive operations analysis study of Departments A, B, and C and submit findings and recommendations by_____

5. Employee relations
Formulate service award program for recognizing employees with twenty-five or more years service and submit recommendation by_____

---

appraisal form is required to measure the manager's performance when accountability is spelled out as in Exhibit 3. Little more appraisal effort is needed than to review what the manager actually accomplished as compared to what he was responsible for accomplishing.

After comparing these two examples of pinpointing of responsibilities and results, the writer leaves it to the reader to determine which method is of most benefit to the success of the corporation.

Conclusion

The time is now at hand when industry must concentrate full time on improving the performance of the enterprise. We must determine and formalize the exact results for which an incumbent will be held responsible and the required results conveyed to him on a sink or swim, come hell or high water basis. Next we must define, delineate and grant to the incumbent every last ounce of authority which he requires to accomplish these results. And of major importance, we must clearly spell out the relationships which the incumbent must observe with his associates. We must discontinue spelling out responsibilities in broad, general terms which make measuring difficult if not impossible. We must not merely state that an industrial relations director, for instance, is "responsible for the successful formulation, installation and administration of an industrial relations program." We must, on the other hand, break down this broad responsibility into smaller, measurable segments. We must clearly define the objectives which the manager must fulfill in the area of wage and salary administration, of labor relations, of personnel administration, of training, of safety, et cetera, for each major component of the over-all field for which the manager is responsible. Failure to do this may permit excellence in one major area to overshadow lack of accomplishment in another, with the result that the manager is considered a satsifactory one when in reality his performance may have been only fair or poor in terms of over-all responsibility.

One or more, or a combination of all of the previously discussed measuring techniques—Profits—Costs—Objectives—can be tailored to each and every managerial job in the enterprise. It requires dedication and it takes time, but it more than pays its way in pay back. It puts money in the cash register, it develops a topflight management team, it pinpoints the glib faker, it highlights outstanding managers for promotion and, not to be neglected, it saves countless time and frustration of top management in completing the currently used, but virtually useless, merit rating forms. Candidly, it permits many a personnel director to clean out files which he currently regards as indispensable, but whose contents should have been moved long ago to the dead files.

IV/D
Rewarding the manager

31 Executive fringe benefit: Cold cash
Roger Ricklefs

Companies are latching on to an ingenious new executive fringe benefit: money.

Bonuses are becoming more popular, and executives who thought they would never see such a windfall now are collecting one. Many companies think the bonuses will make executives work harder. With changes in tax laws and recent poor results from long-term stock options, many executives say the are delighted with the cold, quick cash.

"Any time you can look for up to a 35% bonus, it really motivates you," says D. Dale Wood, a vice president of Crutcher Resources Corp., a Houston maker of pipeline equipment and other products, which started an executive-bonus plan two years ago. "I am very interested in the immediate recognition of performance, and this provides it," he adds.

In a McKinsey & Co. compensation survey of major companies, 71% had an annual executive-bonus plan last year, up from 63% two years earlier and only 50% in 1968. Even in industries where such plans were rare only a few years ago, they are prevalent today, the consulting firm found. In 23 of 31 industries surveyed last year, two-thirds of the companies had executive-bonus plans. Four years earlier, that was true in only six of 28 industries.

Middle management, too

Some companies say they have devised bonus plans for middle-management and other employes as well as for top executives. And companies that don't offer bonuses to executives in general increasingly grant special bonus arrangements to lure specific individuals from other companies, says Pearl Meyer, vice president of Handy Associates, a New York recruiting concern.

Even in banking and insurance, where bonuses were once as rare as mod suits, bonuses are arriving. "We're committed to a 15% growth rate in earnings per share, and we think that a bonus plan helps attract the kind of people to attain this," says Robert W. Feagles, senior vice president for personnel administration of First National City Corp. The holding company of First National City Bank of New York established an executive-incentive bonus plan this year.

Aetna Life & Casualty Co., Hartford, Conn., also established a bonus plan for 280 executives this year. In this fairly typical plan, directors first decide how much money will be made available for the bonuses. This sum depends on corporate performance but is limited to 1.5% of pretax operating earnings. Directors and management then allocate money to individuals based on their own performances.

Bonus plans are likely to grow even if the government gives final approval to executive pay restrictions the Cost of Living Council proposed last week, says George H. Foote, director and compensation expert at McKinsey. Among other things, the proposals would prohibit bonuses paid to top officers and employe-directors from rising more sharply than total company bonuses. And the new restrictions would renew the Phase 2 requirement that big companies obtain prior government approval before starting or revising bonus plans.

"The rationale for companies to start bonus plans still exists whether there are controls or not," Mr. Foote reasons. The approvals required are similar to those during Phase 2 of the government's anti-inflation program, and bonus plans grew then, Mr. Foote says.

Sensitive to performance

Some companies that already have bonus plans say they are revising them to make them more sensitive to performance. Leasco Corp. is one of these. Others are pushing bonuses outside the executive suite. Kennecott Copper Corp. is considering such a plan, and Aetna Life has established a system that will allow managers to grant bonuses to most workers whenever they exceed normal performance expectations.

"We feel it gives the manager more flexibility in relating total compensation to a person's performance that year," says Charles M. Cumming, Aetna's director of compensation. Of course, it also avoids saddling the company with a pay increase that will last indefinitely to reward a performance that may end tomorrow.

This is one reason companies like bonuses. But compensation experts say that some executives themselves are pressing for bonus plans, especially to supplement stock options. Such options give the recipient the right to purchase stock at a given price for a set period.

In many companies lately, stock prices have sunk below the option prices, meaning that executives made nothing on the options they once coveted. Some who borrowed money to exercise options lost large sums as stocks fell.

"The decline in the stock market has caused lots of guys to lose interest in pie in the sky," says Frederick A. Teague, vice president and compensation expert at Booz, Allen & Hamilton Inc., management consultants based in Chicago. Mrs. Meyer of Handy Associates contends: "What's happening is that a great many people have stopped wanting to bet. The attitude is 'bird in hand, master of my own destiny, give it to me now, and I'll take care of it myself.'"

Moreover, the federal tax-revision act of 1969 has gradually raised the maximum tax rate on capital gains (applicable to stock-option profits) to 35% from 25%. In addition, the act lowered the maximum tax rate on earned income, such as bonuses, to 50% from 70%.

Bonuses can create problems, however, especially if they are poorly administered, McKinsey's Mr. Foote says. "If the money doesn't get distributed in the right proportion to the people who actually generate the profits, the bonus is a poor incentive," he says.

And bonuses cost money. Aetna figures that its plan for general employes will cost $1.5 million a year—or a little under 1% of its payroll—and the executive bonuses can total as much as 50% of salary.

32 Executive rewards
Henry Martin

"This one's for keeping a neat and tidy cubicle at all times and this one's for not tying up lines with personal calls and this one's for not horsing around at the water cooler."

Source: Drawing by H. Martin; © 1975 The New Yorker Magazine, Inc.

33 What is an executive worth?
Arch Patton

A financial vice president who did not see eye to eye with the chief executive of a large manufacturer accepted the presidency of a much smaller company. The modest cut in salary he took was balanced by a substantial stock option. Within a few months after taking over, he identified his new employer's major problems and set about rectifying them. In three years' time, sales of the smaller company more than doubled, profits increased fourfold, return on invested capital jumped from 1.3% to 5.5%, and the total market value of the company's stock soared nearly $200 million.

Thus, the stockholders were vastly enriched, while the paper profits on the new president's stock option amounted to less than 0.5% of the total stock appreciation.

During the 1958 recession, the president of a leading raw material producing company proposed to enter into a contract with a major customer to supply a substantial volume of low-margin goods for a specified period in the future. Since his objective was to absorb overhead in a recession period, this apparently sensible proposal was favored by the sales and manufacturing vice presidents.

The controller, however, fought the decision on the ground that it tied up manufacturing equipment on low-margin goods for an extended period in the future—a period, moreover, that would be needed to produce the highest profit line the company manufactured as soon as customer inventories were moderately reduced. The debate was carried to the board of directors by the controller, over the bitter opposition of the president. The controller finally won his battle, saving the company an estimated $20 million in gross margin over a two-year period.

The research vice president of a major equipment manufacturing company turned down an invention offered to his company by an ex-employee. The gadget was purchased by a leading competitor, and it proved to have great consumer appeal. Heavy promotion of its convenience to the housewife plus a catchy and easily identifiable name, enabled it to boost the competitor's share of the market by approximately one-third. The company that originally turned it down lost a share of market which formerly accounted for 20% of its profits.

What is each of these executives worth? The answer, of course, is that the value of an upper echelon executive lies in the decisions he makes and influences. The question is not whether he reports to the president or a vice president, or what paper work he processes. Rather, it is what contribution he has made to the decisions that increase or decrease company profits.

Source: Reprinted with permission from *Harvard Business Review* (March–April 1961), pp. 65–73. Copyright © 1961 by the President and Fellows of Harvard College; all rights reserved.

As a staff man, the controller mentioned above may not make line decisions. But if he has "standing" with other executives, and the courage to back his judgment, he can influence line decisions and company profits. A lesser controller could have "gone along" with the president's proposal and quietly accommodated himself to the $20 million loss. He could have rationalized that it was not his responsibility, so why should he get in the president's hair? Unfortunately, this latter point of view is far more prevalent today than is generally recognized. Who would know, for instance, that the controller had the $20 million idea in the first place if he chose to keep silent in the face of presidential wishes?

The examples cited are more dramatic than the decisions executives are normally concerned with. But even run-of-the-mill decisions have results that eventually find their way into the profit and loss columns. For example, a sales manager turned down the job application of a young man some years ago. Today, as the sales vice president, he is conscious of being consistently undersold by a smaller competitor. But what he still does not know is that the young man whose job application he turned down more than a decade earlier is the guiding spirit behind the exuberant upstart that is undermining his company's profit margin.

Lack of standards

There is more than a little confusion in industry's answer to the question: *What is an executive worth?* To a great extent, this confusion arises from foggy notions as to what the "average" pay is for executives in various industries, from differing compensation philosophies, from some dim perceptions of what activities an executive should be paid for, and from prejudices which overpay one executive function at the expense of others. Let us take up each of these confusions.

What is average?

Careless use of executive compensation survey data accounts for a good share of the confusion. Actually, there is *no* "average" executive whose compensation is reported in industry surveys. The hypothetical average executive is made up not only of outstanding managers of well-run, rapidly growing companies who are probably paid substantially above the reported average, but also of weak executives in declining companies who may be paid well below the reported average. The mixture of the two extremes makes the true average—or modal—salary an unknown quantity.

This hodgepodge of variables frequently results in making the maximum and minimum salaries as much as 500% to 800% apart. For example, a well-known survey reports that the top sales executives in companies with sales of $50 million to $75 million received an "average" compensation of $48,000. However, a breakdown of the average showed that the highest paid executive in this group of companies was paid $96,600, while the lowest paid received only $18,750. In any given company, a particular executive is just as likely to be "worth" the maximum or minimum as he is the average, for his value depends on what he does, rather than on the title of his job. Yet the surveys necessarily focus attention *only* on the average.

What is fair play?

The second element in the confusion results from differences in top-management compensation philosophy. One president may buy executive talent the way he would buy coal—at the lowest possible price, offering little if any premium for quality. At the other extreme, the chief executive may regard quality of performance as a bargain at almost any price. One philosophy looks on compensation as a cost, the other looks on it as a motivational device. Some companies pay straight salary, others combine salery with bonus; some are generous, others are niggardly; some are committee-managed, others hold the individual accountable for specific responsibilities; some set high performance standards, others accept inadequate work without question. The possible combinations of basic company philosophy are so varied that sharp differences in compensation for similar jobs in the same industry are to be expected.

Paid for what?

The third ingredient in the confusion—and perhaps the most important—is the lack of uniform criteria as to what an executive should be paid *for.* For instance, the starting salary for a vice president in one large company was $25,000 over a period of many years. It made no difference that one vice president had the second most important job in the company, and that another was little more than an office boy for the retiring chairman. Both were vice presidents and, therefore, started even.

One of the most common prejudices in management circles is that by some mysterious alchemy a company officer—no matter what he does—is somehow worth more than other executives. The usual justification for this viewpoint is that, as officers they are liable before the law for corporate actions. This would be simply a harmless fiction (for it has little basis in reality) were it not for the fact that officers' remuneration is frequently published information. And when officers are paid more than other executives think they are worth, incentive-in-reverse throttles the very motivation that compensation seeks to foster. To the other executives, it seems just another case of, "It is, 'who you know,' not what you accomplish, that makes for progress in this company."

Overvaluing functions

Management prejudices in the compensation area are not confined to the value of an officer. Some companies whose basic economics emphasize a particular functional group (such as sales or engineering) frequently over-value this function and downgrade the others. Since the changing life cycle of products may shift the company's functional emphasis from research to manufacturing to selling to control—in that order—it also increases or de-creases the *relative* value of specific functions to the company. For example:

One important industry has been dominated by manufacturing executives almost from its inception. However, its principal product has for some years been in the maturity phase of the life cycle, which requires unusual sales and promotional skills in the executive group. Since the level of the com-pensation structure in this industry is related to soundly valued manufactur-ing positions, and these rather substantially outrank sales jobs, the latter are seriously downgraded. Unfortunately, the quality of executive talent attracted to the downgraded sales job is below the level necessary to make this a dynamic growth industry.

Parenthetically, as long as all companies in this particular industry con-tinue to undervalue the sales jobs, the only competitive loss occurs in the struggle for an increasing share of the consumer's dollar. And this, of course, is a difficult point to impress on a management that is making money today and has always considered "the competition" to be a relatively limited number of companies in its own industry. But the prospect of what would happen in this inudstry if one of the leading companies sensed the competitive advantage accruing from upgrading the quality of the sales func-tion has intrigued me for years.

Compensation factors

The question of what an executive is worth involves three basic considera-tions: the size of his company, the industry in which he works, and the im-portance of his contribution to the decision-making process. Obviously, the three are interrelated. However, it is useful to consider them separately as a means of maintaining perspective on the importance of each.

Company size

Compensation surveys, when properly used, provide reasonably factual yardsticks for assessing the effect of company size (and industry) on the value of an executive. On the basis of general agreement among the various compensation surveys, the larger a company is, the higher the compensation of the chief executive and his top-management group. This is entirely logical, for the stockholder has more at stake in the larger concern.

While numerous studies show that the compensation relationship between chief executives and their top staff is remarkably close, company size has its effect here, also. At each end of the size scale, in the very large and very small firms, second echelon executives are paid moderately closer to the chief executive than those in the middle of the size scale. The simplest explanation of this phenomenon is that the pay of a small company president is so low that a normal margin above his *chief* lieutenants cannot be maintained without damaging the full "spread" necessary over *all* the various echelons; and, at the other extreme, the responsibility of the big company chief executive is so broad that it is generally shared with several highly compensated executives.

Industry differences

While these conclusions regarding the effect of company size on executive compensation are generally accepted in management circles, the same can hardly be said of generalizations based on industry differences. Some time ago I wrote an article for a leading business magazine that pointed out the substantial compensation differentials between the chief executives of railroads and public utilities, on the one hand, and chemical and retail companies, on the other.[1] The conclusion drawn from an examination of the risk and importance of decisions made by the two executive groups was that a substantial compensation differential was warranted.

A few days after the article's appearance, however, the president of a company in one of the lower paid industries wrote me to the effect that the article "set our industry back five years," because it implied that its executives were worth less than those in other industries. The gist of his argument was that while one industry may face different types of problems than another, the jobs are equally difficult and therefore require the same management talents.

In all fairness, both positions are debatable. It is natural for executives in one industry to consider their jobs at least as difficult as "the other fellow's." No one likes to admit his job is even moderately less demanding than that of other executives. However, I feel confident that most professional men who have been exposed to problems in a reasonably wide cross section of industry would seriously question the letter writer's two main points: that jobs are equally difficult among *all* industries, or that identical management talents are needed.

The reasoning of such observers, I believe, would be that, on the one hand, the lower paid industries tend to lead a more sheltered competitive

---

[1] "What Management Should Know About Executive Compensation," *Dun's Review and Modern Industry,* February 1957, p. 43.

life. (Over the years, compensation surveys have identified banks, life insurance companies, air transport firms, meat packing concerns, railroads, and public utilities as falling in the relatively low-paid category.) Thus:

Many are monopolistic in character, and subject to governmental regulation of prices and profits. Products and services have tended to change slowly over the years.
Executives in a regulated industry feel uncomfortable asking for a rate increase when their salary level is unusually high.
Because promotion from within is generally a basic policy in such industries, there is little external job competition, and seniority carries great weight in promotional decisions. Job security is high, for job demands are such that few reasons for dismissal are found.
"Committee management" is common; equally so is the practice of using "assistants to" as a means of accommodating the management process to the incidental paper work of committee management.

On the other hand, these same independent observers would also agree, I think, that life tends to be more hectic among the higher paid industries on all counts. (Surveys list chemicals, department stores, automobiles, steel, textiles, and appliances among the top-paid industries.) To illustrate:

A high degree of creativity is usually found in these industries, in both product innovation and styling.
As a group, they will appear willing to reach "outside" the company for executive talent rather than promoting an inadequate man, and seniority usually carries less weight in promotional decisions.
The concept of individual accountability for decisions is more frequent in these industries. As a consequence, dismissal for failure is by no means uncommon; hence, job turnover is usually higher.

Decision differences

But the outstanding difference between the low-paid and high-paid industries is found in the nature of the decisions that influence profits, and in the decision-making process itself. Both, in my experience, have an important bearing on the value of executive jobs.

Generally speaking, the lower paid industries need huge sums of money; hence, the cost of this capital exerts a powerful leverage on profits. And when one industry, with $50 million in assets, can earn the same profits that it takes another industry $200 million in assets to produce, an important difference is involved. That difference usually lies in the talents required in its executives. In a sense, it might be said that the cost of the facility producing the profit reduces the value of the necessary executive talent. For example:

A power-generating station, or a fleet of aircraft, not only draws heavily on the skill of the electrical or aircraft manufacturer in the development phase, but the completed facilily has what amounts to a built-in earning power of its own. It is largely the location of the power plant, or the airline route franchise, that underwrites this earning power. One company's electricity is the same as another's, and some airlines with relatively poor customer relationships and service are among the most profitable because of their routes.

On the other hand, regardless of their locations, automobile, textile, chemical, or appliance plants only have earning power if their managements maintain style or innovational leadership over their competitors, and if the managements have developed a strong distribution organization and have been able to stimulate customer demand for their brands or products.

Moreover, in the lower paid industries the profit-influencing decisions are relatively few in number. Electric utilities, for example, infrequently buy new generating equipment, apply for a major rate increase, or raise new capital. The key profit-influencing decisions in the airlines industry are similarly few and infrequent. Banks are concerned primarily with securing deposits at the lowest cost and lending these funds at the highest rate consistent with banking laws and sound practice. Insurance companies sell insurance, accept risks, and earn money on their reserves.

It is true that the profit-influencing decisions in these industries, while relatively few, are "big" in terms of their individual impact on profits. However, they usually are circumscribed (or even ordained) by circumstances, and lend themselves to control on a "policy" basis so that a single decision on loans, type of aircraft, or investment policy may guide many subsequent decisions.

At the other extreme, the higher pay industries face a multitude of decisions that importantly influence profits. For instance:

In the chemical industry, the decision of a research chemist to probe in one direction rather than another has frequently made a small company big.
The decision of a salesman that a particular product might be useful in a new industry may make a dramatic difference in company volume a few years ahead.
The automobile designer who gives birth to a new look in fenders may start a trend that adds mightily to the profit record of his own company, and maybe the whole industry.

Such action-shaping decisions at lower levels do not reduce the responsibility of the chief executive in the high-pay industries. Indeed, these responsibilities are made more difficult by this dispersion of influence over decisions. He must depend on the thinking of specialists to a degree rarely found among the more centralized industries; and this calls for a high degree of administrative ability.

Team vs. individual

Even this brief review of the nature of the profit-influencing decisions in the low- and high-compensation industries clearly shows that in the former industries a few "big" decisions are made, while in the latter a relatively large number of important, profit-influencing decisions can be made at all executive levels. This difference in the decision-making process, it seems to me, is bound to cause considerable variations in executive compensation between the two groups of industries because of its effect on the way responsibility is placed.

The lower compensation industries, with a few major profit-influencing decisions, are able to concentrate decisions in the hands of a few top-level executives. To ensure that decisions are made at the very top, committees which tend to become decision-making bodies are widely used. This practice spreads the talents of a relatively few executives and protects company profits from the effects of "poor" decisions made by lower echelon executives. The "team" philosophy of the lower compensation industries is consistent with their other characteristics mentioned earlier: 100% promotion from within, emphasis on seniority, and job security.

On the other hand, the higher compensation industries, with many more activities that importantly influence profits, find it more difficult, but vitally necessary, to decentralize decisions, because there are so many potentially important decision-making areas. To help control the quality of lower echelon decisions, the high-compensation industries tend to hold individuals accountable for their actions to a greater degree than do the lower-compensation industries.

Protection and exposure

Both groups of industries require teamwork, of course, but the "togetherness" factor in the decision-making process of the lower compensation industries acts to protect the inadequate executive from his own insufficiency. He "participates" in the decision—by consultation, or as a member of a committee—but the risk is borne by the team rather than by the individual. Since he rarely has final authority (unless he is the chief executive), the individual cannot be held accountable.

The committee, like a wartime convoy which moves at the speed of the slowest ship, tends to be paced by its least effective member. By the same token, a relatively poor executive can survive in this environment without doing serious damage to the company, for his inadequacy is supported by the consultative decision-making process.

The executive in the higher compensation industries, by contrast, tends to be more exposed to his own weaknesses. Since he has the authority to make certain profit-influencing decisions, the effect of his individual actions are quickly translated into red or black ink on the P & L statement.

Since a weak executive can cost the company a lot of money, the decisions of the individual are under constant review. This assumes, of course, that adequate controls have been set up as part of the decentralization of the decision-making process.

Executives working in such an individual-centered environment are worth more than their opposites in a team-centered company, since their individual skill directly affects the profits. And, since they are accountable for their actions, their job security depends heavily on their individual effectiveness.

Mixed pattern

Having made what many executives will regard as invidious comparisons between the high- and low-compensation industries, I hasten to point out that some industries at each extreme have characteristics usually found at the opposite pole.

The food industry, for instance, is generally considered to be in the lower compensation group, yet is highly competitive and has decentralized the decision-making process more than most. At the other extreme, the steel industry is highly compensated; yet profit-influencing decisions are centralized, product innovation plays a minor role, and job security is relatively high.

The fact that exceptions exist is not surprising; nor does it vitiate the basic conclusion that some industries, for quite logical reasons, demand more of their executives than others do. Jobs in these industries are thus worth more than otherwise comparable positions. Further, a number of industries that were in the lower paid group a decade ago have risen to average or better during the interim. The reasons for this upsurge vary. Here is an interesting example:

One important industry had to recruit several major company presidents from the "outside" in a short span and paid well above its own industry rates to attract them. The new presidents in turn hired subordinates on the outside at levels that established entirely new compensation relationships for the individual company. Eventually, as a result of the influence of the industry's compensation level on the compensation surveys, companies in other industries increased their executive compensation levels.

Another factor in the upgrading process results when industry compensation falls well below the average. This hurts the pride of top management. The loss of an outstanding executive or two frequently serves as the rationale to convince directors that higher compensation is the solution to this "turnover problem."

Compensation values between industries can also be distorted by years of unusual prosperity. A number of raw material industries, for example, experienced 15 or more years when demand largely outstripped supply.

This created a situation in which even mediocre executives looked good, and higher compensation could readily be "afforded" by the companies. The natural result was to increase compensation to an unrealistic degree in terms of the contribution individual executives could be expected to make to company profitability under normal conditions.

Unreal job descriptions

The effect of industry characteristics and of company size on executive compensation has received more critical attention in recent years, from my observation, than has the more difficult assessment of the individual executive's value to the company.

Unfortunately, the evaluation of executive jobs for compensation purposes historically has followed the development of job evaluation for factory positions. And, as a result, the factory-oriented concept that evaluation is concerned with the job itself and not the performance of the jobholder has carried over into the evaluation process for executive positions. This concept is valid in the factory, where machine speeds and the pace of the assembly line limit the productivity of the individual. But when it governs the evaluation of executive jobs (particularly at upper levels), an unrealistic rigidity is built into the compensation structure. As an illustration:

Every time a top-level executive who has held his position for a long term retires or dies, problems result. If he was a good executive, he shaped his job over a period of years to fit his own talents. Then, too, during the years other senior executives may have come to rely on his "business" judgment in specific areas.

Suddenly he is replaced by a new man. While the "job descriptions" of the two men may read the same, the jobs are almost certain to be substantially different. The new man may not have the same talents as his predecessor. If he is strong where the other man was weak, it may well be that this particular talent will be wasted because some other executive long ago assumed this responsibility as the living organization accommodated itself to the individual. Even if he has all the strengths of his predecessor, and some to spare, his "chemistry" may be sufficiently different from that of the chief executive so that he never influences corporate policy to the extent that his predecessor did.

The typical factory-based approach to evaluating executive positions assumes that both executives hold the same job; therefore, the normal compensation range for the position will be adequate to pay both men. *Occasionally,* this philosophy holds true; the successor deserves the same pay as the executive he replaces, even though he has less seniority—simply because he is a better man than his boss was. But many promotions into upper level executive jobs actually involve a tangible downgrading of job value to the company that may last for some years. In such instances, the usual salary range for the position is inadequate to reflect the realities of the situation, yet few executive evaluation programs are sufficiently flexible to adjust for this situation.

Thus, the habits of almost a generation of usage—supported by much of the literature on job evaluation—have carried over the factory-job focus into the executive evaluation process. In my opinion, this basic weakness in executive position evaluation is an important element in the rapidly closing compensation gap between the various functional jobs. At best, it results in overpayment of some executives; at worst, it emasculates the motivational aspects of compensation by equating jobs having substantially different real worth to the company.

Impossible ideal

The job focus of the typical evaluation process finds support in the widely held concept that there is a "best" organization for a company. The proponents of this concept rightly point out that there are sound, logical groupings of responsibilities that result in nice, clean organization charts. All that needs to be done is to find executives whose talents match this "ideal" organization of responsibilities, they say, and decisions will be made faster and better at less cost.

The problem, of course, lies in finding the "right" men. Human experience from time immemorial indicates that great accomplishments result from the efforts of individuals, that strong organizations reflect the leadership of strong individuals. An organization soon sinks into bureaucracy when its inflexibility forces individuals to accommodate themselves to the structure, rather than the structure to the individual.

But the "ideal" organization concept, with its accent on structure, implies that an executive position *should* consist of a specific group of responsibilities whose importance remains constant. I believe this is unsound on two grounds:

1 The importance of the various responsibilities involved in running a company is in a constant state of flux. Some—for example, labor relations and the control function—are growing increasingly vital to success. Other responsibilities may be dwindling in importance as the life cycle of the company's products unfolds. When a product like automobile tires matures, the once dominant manufacturing function becomes less critical to success than marketing. As a result of such fluctuation, some responsibilities should be in the process of growing from part-time to full-time jobs for many people, while others should be shrinking (although Parkinson's Law results in strong resistance to such a course of action).[2]

2 A strong leader is so rare that the organization he leads, whether it is a

[2] See C. Northcote Parkinson, *Parkinson's Law* (Boston, Houghton Mifflin Company, 1957).

company, division, or function, soon learns to accommodate itself to his strengths and weaknesses. If he is weak in an area that is normally a part of the job, steps are taken to support this weakness in recognition of his great strengths in other directions.

Top of the pyramid

There is reasonable evidence that the typical job evaluation process has only moderate validity where the upper level executive is concerned. The closer to the top of the company pyramid an executive climbs, the more he makes his own job. Theoretically, a company's sales, or manufacturing, or research function has a value below which minimal performance requirements of the job are jeopardized. But, practically, corporate organization accommodates itself to a wide degree of individual skill and aggressiveness—or lack of it.

This being the case, it is pointless to talk about evaluating an executive job, when the real evaluation relates to what *an individual has made of his job, compared with what others have made of their jobs.* In effect, such an evaluation is little more than an assessment of the situation that exists at any given point of time. These values, as we have seen, are in a state of constant change. They reflect the skill and aggressiveness of the individual in the ever-changing "mix" of other individuals' skill and aggressiveness, as well as the fluctuating profit contribution of the several functions to the corporate picture that stems from shifting internal or external economic tides.

Evaluating contributions

In my view, the critical element to evaluate in an upper level executive position is its contribution to the decision-making process. It is simply a question of the relative worth to the company P & L statement of the decisions made or influenced by the individual. Needless to say, such an assessment should be in terms of what the individual actually does, not what a job description or organization chart says he should do—the difference is frequently profound. Many an executive abdicates his responsibilities to subordinates, or passes them along to his peers by failure to act himself.

Probably the most difficult aspect of the upper level executive job to judge is the contribution the incumbent makes to company policies that go beyond his functional responsibilities. The chief executive frequently (and often unconsciously) selects some senior executive whose strengths supplement his own and uses him as a sounding board in reaching decisions on broad policies. Such a man may have great influence over top-level decisions because of his proven judgment, or his personal "chemistry" with the president. In fact, this sounding board responsibility is frequently worth more to the company than the traditional functional responsibilities of the executive. Yet many formal job evaluation programs entirely overlook this intangible and informal policy support in arriving at position-oriented job values.

Assessment of risk

Evaluating executive positions in terms of decisions made and influenced is certainly no science.[3] Decisions cannot be put on a scale that will weigh the importance and difficulty of each, and crank out a number reflecting their value. However, the spectrum of decisions required by the economics of the individual company can be studied, and as assessment made of the relative risk to profits that may reasonably be expected from each under varying conditions. In other words, the decision-making process can be examined in detail, and an evaluation made of each executive's contribution to the total process.

Obviously, decisions that are *made* are more valuable than decisions that are merely *influenced*. The sales manager who can only *recommend* a price change has no effect on the profit and loss statement until someone *decides* to make the change. Needless to say, influencing big decisions may well be more important than making small ones.

It is relatively easy to judge who makes what decisions, and not overly difficult to distinguish the important ones from the less important. But the problem of judging who influences which decisions, and to what degree, has proved to be a major stumbling block. The formal organizational structure, for example, may call for the sales manager to provide the critical judgment of market reaction to a price change, but the treasurer actually may have far greater influence with the executive who makes the real decision. In other words, the "informal" organization frequently has a louder voice in the decision-influencing process than is recognized.

Two scales of value

Any assessment of executive jobs needs to recognize and integrate two scales of value in the evaluation process.

The first basic measure of value involves those elements that we have been discussing: specifically, the size of the company, the industry of which it is a part, and the relative responsibility each executive assumes in the decision-making and decision-influencing process. In this phase, the value of the chief executive's job becomes a relatively solid bench mark—at the apex of the compensation pyramid—against which to judge the contributions of other executives whose decisions have an effect on company-wide activities.

But at a lower point on the executive pyramid, company size is displaced as a yardstick of position value by some other measure. A regional sales manager's value will be reflected by the size and importance of his territory; a plant manager will be paid on a basis that relates to the size of his plant, regardless of whether over-all company sales are $20 million or $200 million. Professional men in industry—lawyers, accountants, doctors—will be

[3] See my article, "How to Appraise Executive Performance," HBR January–February 1960.

compensated in terms of still another gauge of value; i.e., what they can expect to earn on the outside in the practice of their profession.

This dual scale of executive job valuation is another frequently ignored aspect of the evaluation process. As a result, many compensation structures are either higher or lower than they need be for the company to remain competitive. In one case, costs are substantially increased, for relatively large numbers of employees are usually involved. In the other, the effect is to attract poorer quality personnel, the most expensive of all costs.

It is this second group of executive jobs whose values are related to some other factor than company size that makes the normal job evaluation process practical at the executive level. Most middle and lower echelon positions fall in this group. And while these jobs are also "made" by the incumbent to some degree, this individually developed element is far less important than is the case among upper level jobs. The reason, of course, is that policies originating at the top level normally restrict the freedom of the lower echelon executive to influence profits directly.

Hence, this latter group of jobs lends itself to an evaluation process that seeks to measure such job factors as (1) scope of responsibility, (2) skills required, and (3) decisions made or influenced (largely the latter). For the most part, these positions are stable enough not to require changes in basic values with every promotion or every retirement.

Conclusion

What, finally, constitutes a practical theory of executive compensation? Essentially a compensation structure is expected to attract men who are competent to attain company objectives, and to motivate them to seek ever-greater responsibility in the company. However, this relatively simple statement of principle involves some complicating elements.

In the first place, just as side show barkers and clergymen are likely to have vastly differing temperaments and viewpoints, a company needs to attract and motivate men having characteristics essential to success in their own industry. For example:

A bank recruited 20 top graduates from several business schools a few years ago. These men were outstanding academically, and psychological tests indicated they were go-getters as well. Within 18 months, all but 2 had left the bank. A checkup indicated that these men did not leave because they were dissatisfied with their salaries, but rather because they found the lack of individual responsibility devastating. The bank had committed the cardinal recruiting sin of attracting men whose competitive characteristics did not happen to be compatible with the industry environment.

Motivating executives to seek increased responsibility also involves problems. Thus, if a company has long had a philosophy of promotion from within, rarely fires anyone, and tries to shore up an inadequate executive by "organizing around him," a relatively narrow compensation spread between boss and subordinate is sufficient to encourage the latter to accept a higher level job. However, if the company seeks out the best man available for a job—in or out of the company—and expects him to produce on the new job or be fired, a substantially wider spread will be required between boss and subordinate to accomplish the same purpose.

The reason for the difference in "spreads," of course, lies in the demands on the individual. In one case, he can accept promotion in a relaxed frame of mind, confident that if he does not measure up, the job will be adjusted to his shortcomings. No real risk is involved for this executive. In the other case, however, the acceptance of promotion carries the threat of a severe penalty for failure—dismissal. This difference warrants a substantial compensation spread between levels to maintain the attractiveness of promotion.

In the final analysis, an executive is "worth" what his superiors believe he is worth. The market for his skills has a bearing on this valuation, as does his "trading position." Needless to say, the latter assumes major importance when the man's contributions are critical to the success of the enterprise. But it is primarily the skill, aggressiveness, and leadership qualities of the individual that make the difference.

Part V

Influencing

The biggest trouble with industry is that it is full of human beings.
    John L. McCaffrey

The selections in Part V deal with the other major human aspect of the manager's task: influencing. Although the management process occurs within the framework of the formal organization, it is performed by, for, and with people. People perceive and interpret; they have diverse attitudes, values, and beliefs; they bring different backgrounds, aspirations, feelings, needs, and drives to their positions; and they form and dissolve alliances not prescribed by the official structure of the organization. The effective manager recognizes these facts.

 The first two sets of articles deal with topics critical to the effective manager: leadership and motivation. Next come three "so-what?" articles. Thus we conclude our treatment of the human element in managing by focusing on the organizational setting. Nonformal relations, satisfaction-performance relationships, and organizational change are all central to the manager's task. Finally, Professor Lawler points out some managerial practices that can provide high payoffs to both the worker and the organization.

V/A
Influence and leadership

34 The bases of social power
John R. P. French, Jr., and Bertram Raven

The processes of power are pervasive, complex, and often disguised in our society. Accordingly one finds in political science, in sociology, and in social psychology a variety of distinctions among different types of social power or among qualitatively different processes of social influence (1, 7, 14, 18, 19, 21, 22, 26, 28). Our main purpose is to identify the major types of power and to define them systematically so that we may compare them according to the changes which they produce and the other effects which accompany the use of power. The phenomena of power and influence involve two points of view: (a) What determines the behavior of the agent who exerts power? (b) What determines the reactions of the recipient of this behavior? We take this second point of view and formulate our theory in terms of P, the person upon whom the power is exerted.

The bases of power

By the basis of power we mean the relationship between O and P which is the source of that power.[1] It is rare that we can say with certainty that a given empirical case of power is limited to one source. Normally, the relation between O and P will be characterized by several qualitatively different variables which are bases of power (22). Although there are undoubtedly many possible bases of power which may be distinguished, we shall here define five which seem especially common and important. These five bases of O's power are: (a) reward power, based on P's perception that O has the ability to mediate rewards for him; (b) coercive power, based on P's perception that O has the ability to mediate punishments for him; (c) legitimate power,

Source: Abridged from *Studies in Social Power,* D. Cartwright, ed. Ann Arbor: University of Michigan Press, 1959, pp. 118–149.
[1] Editor's Note: O refers to the agent who exercises influence on a person P.

based on the perception by P that O has a legitimate right to prescribe behavior for him; (d) referent power, based on P's identification with O; (e) expert power, based on the perception that O has some special knowledge or expertness.

Our first concern is to define the bases which give rise to a given type of power. Next, we describe each type of power according to its strength, range, and the degree of dependence of the new state of the system which is most likely to occur with each type of power. We shall also examine the other effects which the exercise of a given type of power may have upon P and his relationship to O. Finally, we shall point out the interrelationships between different types of power, and the effects of use of one type of power by O upon other bases of power which he might have over P.

Reward power

Reward power is defined as power whose basis is the ability to reward. The strength of the reward power of O/P increases with the magnitude of the rewards which P perceives that O can mediate for him. Reward power depends on O's ability to administer positive valences and to remove or decrease negative valences. The strength of reward power also depends upon the probability that O can mediate the reward, as perceived by P. A common example of reward power is the addition of a piece-work rate in the factory as an incentive to increase production.

The new state of the system induced by a promise of reward (for example, the factory worker's increased level of production) will be highly dependent on O. Since O mediates the reward, he controls the probability that P will receive it. Thus P's new rate of production will be dependent on his subjective probability that O will reward him for conformity minus his subjective probability that O will reward him even if he returns to his old level. Both probabilities will be greatly affected by the level of observability of P's behavior. Incidentally, a piece rate often seems to have more effect on production than a merit rating system because it yields a higher probability of reward for conformity and a much lower probability of reward for nonconformity.

The utilization of actual rewards (instead of promises) by O will tend over time to increase the attraction of P toward O and therefore the referent power of O over P. As we shall note later, such referent power will permit O to induce changes which are relatively independent. Neither rewards nor promises will arouse resistance in P, provided P considers it legitimate for O to offer rewards.

The range of reward power is specific to those regions within which O can reward P for conforming. The use of rewards to change systems within the range of reward power tends to increase reward power by increasing the probability attached to future promises. However, unsuccessful attempts to exert reward power outside the range of power would tend to decrease the power; for example, if O offers to reward P for performing an impossible act, this will reduce for P the probability of receiving future rewards promised by O.

Coercive power

Coercive power is similar to reward power in that it also involves O's ability to manipulate the attainment of valences. Coercive power of O/P stems from the expectation on the part of P that he will be punished by O if he fails to conform to the influence attempt. Thus negative valences will exist in given regions of P's life space, corresponding to the threatened punishment by O. The strength of coercive power depends on the magnitude of the negative valence of the threatened punishment multiplied by the perceived probability that P can avoid the punishment by conformity, i.e., the probability of punishment for nonconformity minus the probability of punishment for conformity (11). Just as an offer of a piece-rate bonus in a factory can serve as a basis for reward power, so the ability to fire a worker if he falls below a given level of production will result in coercive power.

Coercive power leads to dependent change also, and the degree of dependence varies with the level of observability of P's conformity. An excellent illustration of coercive power leading to dependent change is provided by a clothes presser in a factory observed by Coch and French (3). As her efficiency rating climbed above average for the group the other workers began to "scapegoat" her. That the resulting plateau in her production was not independent of the group was evident once she was removed from the presence of the other workers. Her production immediately climbed to new heights.[2]

At times, there is some difficulty in distinguishing between reward power and coercive power. Is the withholding of a reward really equivalent to a punishment? Is the withdrawal of punishment equivalent to a reward? The answer must be a psychological one—it depends upon the situation as it exists for P. But ordinarily we would answer these questions in the affirmative; for P, receiving a reward is a positive valence as is the relief of suffering. There is some evidence (5) that conformity to group norms in order to gain acceptance (reward power) should be distinguished from conformity as a means of forestalling rejection (coercive power).

The distinction between these two types of power is important because the dynamics are different. The concept of "sanctions" sometimes lumps the two together despite their opposite effects. While reward power may eventually result in an independent system, the effects of coercive power will continue to be dependent. Reward power will tend to increase the attraction of P toward O; coercive power will decrease this attraction (11, 12).

---

[2] Though the primary influence of coercive power is dependent, it often produces secondary changes which are independent. Brainwashing, for example, utilizes coercive power to produce many primary changes in the life space of the prisoner, but these dependent changes can lead to identification with the aggressor and hence to secondary changes in ideology which are independent.

Legitimate power

Legitimate power is probably the most complex of those treated here, embodying notions from the structural sociologist, the group-norm and role oriented social psychologist, and the clinical psychologist.

There has been considerable investigation and speculation about socially prescribed behavior, particularly that which is specific to a given role or position. Linton (21) distinguishes group norms according to whether they are universals for everyone in the culture, alternatives (the individual having a choice as to whether or not to accept them), or specialties (specific to given positions). Whether we speak of internalized norms, role prescriptions and expectations (24), or internalized pressures (15), the fact remains that each individual sees certain regions toward which he should locomote, some regions toward which he should not locomote, and some regions toward which he may locomote if they are generally attractive for him. This applies to specific behaviors in which he may, should, or should not engage; it applies to certain attitudes or beliefs which he may, should, or should not hold. The feeling of "oughtness" may be an internalization from his parents, from his teachers, from his religion, or may have been logically developed from some idiosyncratic system of ethics. He will speak of such behaviors with expressions like "should," "ought to," or "has a right to." In many cases, the original source of the requirement is not recalled.

Legitimate power of O/P is here defined as that power which stems from internalized values in P which dictate that O has a legitimate right to influence P and that P has an obligation to accept this influence. We note that legitimate power is very similar to the notion of legitimacy of authority which has long been explored by sociologists, particularly by Weber (29), and more recently by Goldhammer and Shils (14). However, legitimate power is not always a role relation: P may accept an induction from O simply because he had previously promised to help O and he values his word too much to break the promise. In all cases, the notion of legitimacy involves some sort of code or standard, accepted by the individual, by virtue of which the external agent can assert his power. We shall attempt to describe a few of these values here.

Bases for legitimate power

Cultural values constitute one common basis for the legitimate power of one individual over another. O has characteristics which are specified by the culture as giving him the right to prescribe behavior for P, who may not have these characteristics. These bases, which Weber (29) has called the authority of the "eternal yesterday," include such things as age, intelligence, caste, and physical characteristics. In some cultures, the aged are granted the right to prescribe behavior for others in practically all behavior areas. In most cultures, there are certain areas of behavior in which a person of one sex is granted the right to prescribe behavior for the other sex.

Acceptance of the social structure is another basis for legitimate power. If P accepts as right the social structure of his group, organization, or society, especially the social structure involving a hierarchy of authority, P will accept the legitimate authority of O, who occupies a superior office in the hierarchy. Thus legitimate power in a formal organization is largely a relationship between offices rather than between persons. And the acceptance of an office as *right* is a basis for legitimate power—a judge has a right to levy fines, a foreman should assign work, a priest is justified in prescribing religious beliefs, and it is the management's prerogative to make certain decisions (10). However, legitimate power also involves the perceived right of the person to hold the office.

Designation by a legitimizing agent is a third basis for legitimate power. An influencer O may be seen as legitimate in prescribing behavior for P because he has been granted such power by a legitimizing agent whom P accepts. Thus a department head may accept the authority of his vice-president in a certain area because that authority has been specifically delegated by the president. An election is perhaps the most common example of a group's serving to legitimize the authority of one individual or office for other individuals in the group. The success of such legitimizing depends upon the acceptance of the legitimizing agent and procedure. In this case it depends ultimately on certain democratic values concerning election procedures. The election process is one of legitimizing a person's right to an office which already has a legitimate range of power associated with it.

Range of legitimate power of O/P

The areas in which legitimate power may be exercised are generally specified along with the designation of that power. A job description, for example, usually specifies supervisory activities and also designates the person to whom the job-holder is responsible for the duties described. Some bases for legitimate authority carry with them a very broad range. Culturally derived bases for legitimate power are often especially broad. It is not uncommon to find cultures in which a member of a given caste can legitimately prescribe behavior for all members of lower castes in practically all regions. More common, however, are instances of legitimate power where the range is specifically and narrowly prescribed. A sergeant in the army is given a specific set of regions within which he can legitimately prescribe behavior for his men.

The attempted use of legitimate power which is outside of the range of legitimate power will decrease the legitimate power of the authority figure. Such use of power which is not legitimate will also decrease the attractiveness of O (11, 12, 25).

Legitimate power and influence

The new state of the system which results from legitimate power usually has high dependence on O though it may become independent. Here, however, the degree of dependence is not related to the level of observability. Since legitimate power is based on P's values, the source of the forces induced by O include both these internal values and O. O's induction serves to activate the values and to relate them to the system which is influenced, but thereafter the new state of the system may become directly dependent on the values with no mediation by O. Accordingly this new state will be relatively stable and consistent across varying environmental situations since P's values are more stable than his psychological environment.

We have used the term legitimate not only as a basis for the power of an agent, but also to describe the general behaviors of a person. Thus, the individual P may also consider the legitimacy of the attempts to use other types of power by O. In certain cases, P will consider that O has a legitimate right to threaten punishment for nonconformity; in other cases, such use of coercion would not be seen as legitimate. P might change in response to coercive power of O, but it will make a considerable difference in his attitude and conformity if O is not seen as having a legitimate right to use such coercion. In such cases, the attraction of P for O will be particularly diminished, and the influence attempt will arouse more resistance (11). Similarly the utilization of reward power may vary in legitimacy; the word "bribe," for example, denotes an illegitimate reward.

Referent power

The referent power of O/P has its basis in the identification of P with O. By identification, we mean a feeling of oneness of P with O, or a desire for such an identity. If O is a person toward whom P is highly attracted, P will have a desire to become closely associated with O. If O is an attractive group, P will have a feeling of membership or a desire to join. If P is already closely associated with O he will want to maintain this relationship (28). P's identification with O can be established or maintained if P behaves, believes, and perceives as O does. Accordingly O has the ability to influence P, even though P may be unaware of this referent power. A verbalization of such power by P might be, "I am like O, and therefore I shall behave or believe as O does," or "I want to be like O, and I will be more like O if I behave or believe as O does." The stronger the identification of P with O the greater the referent power of O/P.

We must try to distinguish between referent power and other types of power which might be operative at the same time. If a member is attracted to a group and he conforms to its norms only because he fears ridicule or expulsion from the group for nonconformity, we would call this coercive power. On the other hand if he conforms in order to obtain praise for conformity, it is a case of reward power. The basic criterion for distinguishing referent power from both coercive and reward power is the mediation of the punishment and the reward by O: to the extent that O mediates the sanctions (i.e., has means [of] control over P) we are dealing with coercive and reward power; but to the extent that P avoids discomfort or gains satisfaction by conformity based on identification, regardless of O's responses, we are dealing with referent power. Conformity with majority opinion is sometimes based on a respect for the collective wisdom of the group, in which case it is expert power. It is important to distinguish these phenomena, all grouped together elsewhere as "pressures toward uniformity," since the type of change which occurs will be different for different bases of power.

The concepts of "reference group" (27) and "prestige suggestion" may be treated as instances of referent power. In this case, O, the prestige-ful person or group, is valued by P; because P desires to be associated or identified with O, he will assume attitudes or beliefs held by O. Similarly a negative reference group which O dislikes and evaluates negatively may exert negative influence on P as a result of negative referent power.

It has been demonstrated that the power which we designate as refe-rent power is especially great when P is attracted to O (2, 6, 8, 9, 13, 19, 22). In our terms, this would mean that the greater the attraction, the greater the identification, and consequently the greater the referent power. In some cases, attraction or prestige may have a specific basis, and the range of referent power will be limited accordingly: a group of campers may have great referent power over a member regarding campcraft, but consid-erably less effect on other regions (22). However, we hypothesize that the greater the attraction of P toward O, the broader the range of referent power of O/P.

The new state of a system produced by referent power may be de-pendent on or independent of O; but the degree of dependence is not af-fected by the level of observability to O (7, 19). In fact, P is often not con-sciously aware of the referent power which O exerts over him. There is probably a tendency for some of these dependent changes to become inde-pendent of O quite rapidly.

Expert power

The strength of the expert power of O/P varies with the extent of the knowledge or perception which P attributes to O within a given area. Proba-bly P evaluates O's expertness in relation to his own knowledge as well as against an absolute standard. In any case expert power results in primary social influence on P's cognitive structure and probably not on other types of systems. Of course changes in the cognitive structure can change the direc-tion of forces and hence of locomotion, but such a change of behavior is secondary social influence. Expert power has been demonstrated experi-mentally (9, 23). Accepting an attorney's advice in legal matters is a com-mon example of expert influence; but there are many instances based on much less knowledge, such as the acceptance by a stranger of directions given by a native villager.

Expert power, where O need not be a member of P's group, is called "informational power" by Deutsch and Gerard (4). This type of expert power must be distinguished from influence based on the content of communica-tion as described by Hovland et al. (16, 17, 19, 20). The influence of the content of a communication upon an opinion is presumably a secondary influ-ence produced after the *primary* influence (i.e., the acceptance of the infor-mation). Since power is here defined in terms of the primary changes, the influence of the content on a related opinion is not a case of expert power as we have defined it, but the initial acceptance of the validity of the content does seem to be based on expert power or referent power. In other cases, however, so-called facts may be accepted as self-evident because they fit into P's cognitive structure; if this impersonal acceptance of the truth of the fact is independent of the more-or-less enduring relationship between O and P, then P's acceptance of the fact is not an actualization of expert power. Thus we distinguish between expert power based on the credibility of O and informational influence which is based on characteristics of the stimulus such as the logic of the argument or the "self-evident facts."

Wherever expert influence occurs it seems to be necessary both for P to think that O knows and for P to trust that O is telling the truth (rather than trying to deceive him).

Expert power will produce a new cognitive structure which is initially relatively dependent on O, but informational influence will produce a more independent structure. The former is likely to become more independent with the passage of time. In both cases the degree of dependence on O is not affected by the level of observability.

The range of expert power, we assume, is more delimited than that of referent power. Not only is it restricted to cognitive systems but the expert is seen as having superior knowledge or ability in very specific areas, and his power will be limited to these areas, though some "halo effect" might occur. Recently, some of our renowned physical scientists have found quite painfully that their expert power in physical sciences does not extend to regions involving international politics. Indeed, there is some evidence that the attempted exertion of expert power outside of the range of expert power will reduce that expert power. An undermining of confidence seems to take place.

Summary

We have distinguished five types of power: referent power, expert power, reward power, coercive power, and legitimate power. These distinctions led to the following hypotheses.

1 For all five types, the stronger the basis of power the greater the power.
2 For any type of power the size of the range may vary greatly, but in general referent power will have the broadest range.
3 Any attempt to utilize power outside the range of power will tend to reduce the power.
4 A new state of a system produced by reward power or coercive power will be highly dependent on O, and the more observable P's conformity the more dependent the state. For the other three types of power, the new state is usually dependent, at least in the beginning, but in any case the level of observability has no effect on the degree of dependence.
5 Coercion results in decreased attraction of P toward O and high resistance; reward power results in increased attraction and low resistance.
6 The more legitimate the coercion the less it will produce resistance and decreased attraction.

References

1 Asch, S. E. *Social psychology.* New York: Prentice-Hall, 1952.
2 Back, K. Influence through social communication. *Journal of Abnormal and Social Psychology,* 1951, 46, 9–23.
3 Coch, L., & French, J. R. P., Jr. Overcoming resistance to change. *Human Relations,* 1948, 1, 512–532.
4 Deutsch, M., & Gerard, H. A study of normative and informational influences upon individual judgment. *Journal of Abnormal and Social Psychology,* 1955, 51, 629–636.
5 Dittes, J., & Kelley, H. Effects of different conditions of acceptance upon conformity to group norms. *Journal of Abnormal and Social Psychology,* 1956, 53, 629–636.
6 Festinger, L. Informal social communication. *Psychological Review,* 1950, 57, 271–282.
7 Festinger, L. An analysis of compliant behavior. In M. Sherif & M. O. Wilson (Eds.), *Group relations at the crossroads.* New York: Harper, 1953. Pp. 232–256.
8 Festinger, L., Schachter, S., & Back, K. *Social pressures in informal groups.* New York: Harper, 1950, Chap. 5.
9 Festinger, L., *et al.* The influence process in the presence of extreme deviates. *Human Relations,* 1952, 5, 327–346.
10 French, J. R. P., Jr., Israel, J., & Ås, D. *Arbeidernes medvirkning i industribedriften: En eksperimentell undersøkelse.* Oslo, Norway: Institute for Social Research, 1957.
11 French, J. R. P., Jr., Morrison, H. W., & Levinger, G. Coercive power and forces affecting conformity. *Journal of Abnormal and Social Psychology,* 1960, 61, 93–101.
12 French, J. R. P., Jr., & Raven, B., Legitimate power, coercive power, and observability in social influence. *Sociometry,* 1958, 21, 83–97.
13 Gerard, H. The anchorage of opinions in face-to-face groups. *Human Relations,* 1954, 7, 313–325.
14 Goldhammer, H., & Shils, E. Types of power and status. *American Journal of Sociology,* 1939, 45, 171–178.
15 Herbst, P. Analysis and measurement of a situation. *Human Relations,* 1953, 2, 113–140.
16 Hovland, C., Lumsdaine, A., & Sheffield, F. *Experiments on mass communication.* Princeton, N.J.: Princeton Univ. Press, 1949.
17 Hovland, C., & Weiss, W. The influence of source credibility on communication effectiveness. *Public Opinion Quarterly,* 1951, 15, 635–650.
18 Jahoda, M. Psychological issues in civil liberties. *The American Psychologist,* 1956, 11, 234–240.
19 Kelman, H. Three processes of acceptance of social influence: Compliance, identification, and internalization. Paper read at the meetings of the American Psychological Association, August, 1956.
20 Kelman, H., & Hovland, C. Reinstatement of the communicator in delayed

measurement of opinion change. *Journal of Abnormal and Social Psychology,* 1953, 48, 327–335.

21 Linton, R. *The cultural background of personality.* New York: Appleton-Century-Crofts, 1945.

22 Lippitt, R., *et al.* The dynamics of power. *Human Relations,* 1952, 5, 37–64.

23 Moore, H. The comparative influence of majority and expert opinion. *American Journal of Psychology,* 1921, 32, 16–20.

24 Newcomb, T. *Social psychology.* New York: Dryden, 1950.

25 Raven, B., & French, J. Group support, legitimate power, and social influence. *Journal of Personality,* 1958, 26, 400–409.

26 Russell, B. *Power: A new social analysis.* New York: Norton, 1938.

27 Swanson, G., Newcomb, T., & Hartley, E. *Readings in social psychology.* New York: Holt, 1952.

28 Torrance, E., & Mason, R. Instructor effort to influence: An experimental evaluation of six approaches. Paper presented at USAF-NRC Symposium on Personnel, Training, and Human Engineering. Washington, D.C., 1956.

29 Weber, M. *The theory of social and economic organization.* Oxford: Oxford Univ. Press, 1947.

---

35 How to choose a leadership pattern
Robert Tannenbaum and Warren H. Schmidt

- "I put most problems into my group's hands and leave it to them to carry the ball from there. I serve merely as a catalyst, mirroring back the people's thoughts and feelings so that they can better understand them."
- "It's foolish to make decisions oneself on matters that affect people. I always talk things over with my subordinates, but I make it clear to them that I'm the one who has to have the final say."
- "Once I have decided on a course of action, I do my best to sell my ideas to my employees."
- "I'm being paid to lead. If I let a lot of other people make the decisions I should be making, then I'm not worth my salt."
- "I believe in getting things done. I can't waste time calling meetings. Someone has to call the shots around here, and I think it should be me."

Each of these statements represents a point of view about "good leadership." Considerable experience, factual data, and theoretical principles could

Source: Reprinted with permission from *Harvard Business Review* (March–April 1958), pp. 95–101. © 1958 by the President and Fellows of Harvard College. All rights reserved.

be cited to support each statement, even though they seem to be inconsistent when placed together. Such contradictions point up the dilemma in which the modern manager frequently finds himself.

New problem

The problem of how the modern manager can be "democratic" in his relations with subordinates and at the same time maintain the necessary authority and control in the organization for which he is responsible has come into focus increasingly in recent years.

Earlier in the century this problem was not so acutely felt. The successful executive was generally pictured as possessing intelligence, imagination, initiative, the capacity to make rapid (and generally wise) decisions, and the ability to inspire subordinates. People tended to think of the world as being divided into "leaders" and "followers."

New focus

Gradually, however, from the social sciences emerged the concept of "group dynamics" with its focus on *members* of the group rather than solely on the leader. Research efforts of social scientists underscored the importance of employee involvement and participation in decision making. Evidence began to challenge the efficiency of highly directive leadership, and increasing attention was paid to problems of motivation and human relations.

Through training laboratories in group development that sprang up across the country, many of the newer notions of leadership began to exert an impact. These training laboratories were carefully designed to give people a first-hand experience in full participation and decision making. The designated "leaders" deliberately attempted to reduce their own power and to make group members as responsible as possible for setting their own goals and methods within the laboratory experience.

It was perhaps inevitable that some of the people who attended the training laboratories regarded this kind of leadership as being truly "democratic" and went home with the determination to build fully participative decision making into their own organizations. Whenever their bosses made a decision without convening a staff meeting, they tended to perceive this as authoritarian behavior. The true symbol of democratic leadership to some was the meeting—and the less directed from the top, the more democratic it was.

Some of the more enthusiastic alumni of these training laboratories began to get the habit of categorizing leader behavior as "democratic" *or* "authoritarian." The boss who made too many decisions himself was thought of as an authoritarian, and his directive behavior was often attributed solely to his personality.

New need

The net result of the research findings and of the human relations training based upon them has been to call into question the stereotype of an effective leader. Consequently, the modern manager often finds himself in an uncomfortable state of mind.

Often he is not quite sure how to behave; there are times when he is torn between exerting "strong" leadership and "permissive" leadership. Sometimes new knowledge pushes him in one direction ("I should really get the group to help make this decision"), but at the same time his experience pushes him in another direction ("I really understand the problem better than the group and therefore I should make the decision"). He is not sure when a group decision is really appropriate or when holding a staff meeting serves merely as a device for avoiding his own decision-making responsibility.

The purpose of our article is to suggest a framework which managers may find useful in grappling with this dilemma. First, we shall look at the different patterns of leadership behavior that the manager can choose from in relating himself to his subordinates. Then, we shall turn to some of the questions suggested by this range of patterns. For instance, how important is it for a manager's subordinates to know what type of leadership he is using in a situation? What factors should he consider in deciding on a leadership pattern? What difference do his long-run objectives make as compared to his immediate objectives?

Range of behavior

Exhibit I presents the continuum or range of possible leadership behavior available to a manager. Each type of action is related to the degree of authority used by the boss and to the amount of freedom available to his subordinates in reaching decisions. The actions seem on the extreme left characterize the manager who maintains a high degree of control while those seen on the extreme right characterize the manager who releases a high degree of control. Neither extreme is absolute; authority and freedom are never without their limitations.

Now let us look more closely at each of the behavior points occurring along this continuum.

The manager makes the decision and announces it.

In this case the boss identifies a problem, considers alternative solutions, chooses one of them, and then reports this decision to his subordinates for implementation. He may or may not give consideration to what he believes his subordinates will think or feel about his decision; in any case, he provides no opportunity for them to participate directly in the decision-making process. Coercion may or may not be used or implied.

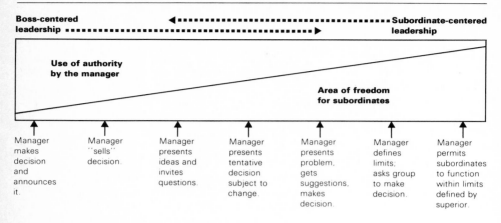

Boss-centered leadership ◀ ■■ ■ **Subordinate-centered leadership**

Use of authority by the manager

Area of freedom for subordinates

| Manager makes decision and announces it. | Manager "sells" decision. | Manager presents ideas and invites questions. | Manager presents tentative decision subject to change. | Manager presents problem, gets suggestions, makes decision. | Manager defines limits; asks group to make decision. | Manager permits subordinates to function within limits defined by superior. |

Exhibit I Continuum of leadership behavior

The manager "sells" his decision.

Here the manager, as before, takes responsibility for identifying the problem and arriving at a decision. However, rather than simply announcing it, he takes the additional step of persuading his subordinates to accept it. In doing so, he recognizes the possibility of some resistance among those who will be faced with the decision, and seeks to reduce this resistance by indicating, for example, what the employees have to gain from his decision.

The manager presents his ideas, invites questions.

Here the boss who has arrived at a decision and who seeks acceptance of his ideas provides an opportunity for his subordinates to get a fuller explanation of his thinking and his intentions. After presenting the ideas, he invites questions so that his associates can better understand what he is trying to accomplish. This "give and take" also enables the manager and the subordinates to explore more fully the implications of the decision.

The manager presents a tentative decision subject to change.

This kind of behavior permits the subordinates to exert some influence on the decision. The initiative for identifying and diagnosing the problem remains with the boss. Before meeting with his staff, he has thought the problem through and arrived at a decision—but only a tentative one. Before finalizing it, he presents his proposed solution for the reaction of those who will be affected by it. He says in effect, "I'd like to hear what you have to say about this plan that I have developed. I'll appreciate your frank reactions, but will reserve for myself the final decision."

The manager presents the problem, gets suggestions, and then makes his decision.

Up to this point the boss has come before the group with a solution of his own. Not so in this case. The subordinates now get the first chance to suggest solutions. The manager's initial role involves identifying the problem. He might, for example, say something of this sort: "We are faced with a number of complaints from newspapers and the general public on our service policy. What is wrong here? What ideas do you have for coming to grips with this problem?"

The function of the group becomes one of increasing the manager's repertory of possible solutions to the problem. The purpose is to capitalize on the knowledge and experience of those who are on the "firing line." From the expanded list of alternatives developed by the manager and his subordinates, the manager then selects the solution that he regards as most promising.[1]

The manager defines the limits and requests the group to make a decision.

At this point the manager passes to the group (possibly including himself as a member) the right to make decisions. Before doing so, however, he defines the problem to be solved and the boundaries within which the decision must be made.

An example might be the handling of a parking problem at a plant. The boss decides that this is something that should be worked on by the people involved, so he calls them together and points up the existence of the problem. Then he tells them:

"There is the open field just north of the main plant which has been designated for additional employee parking. We can build underground or surface multilevel facilities as long as the cost does not exceed $100,000. Within these limits we are free to work out whatever solution makes sense to us. After we decide on a specific plan, the company will spend the available money in whatever way we indicate."

The manager permits the group to make decisions within prescribed limits.

This represents an extreme degree of group freedom only occasionally encountered in formal organizations, as, for instance, in many research groups. Here the team of managers or engineers undertakes the identification and diagnosis of the problem, develops alternative procedures for solving it, and decides on one or more of these alternative solutions. The only limits directly imposed on the group by the organization are those specified by the superior of the team's boss. If the boss participates in the decision-making process, he attempts to do so with no more authority than any other

[1] For a fuller explanation of this approach, see Leo Moore, "Too Much Management, Too Little Change," HBR January–February 1956, p. 41.

member of the group. He commits himself in advance to assist in implementing whatever decision the group makes.

Key questions

As the continuum in Exhibit I demonstrates, there are a number of alternative ways in which a manager can relate himself to the group or individuals he is supervising. At the extreme left of the range, the emphasis is on the manager—on what *he* is interested in, how *he* sees things, how *he* feels about them. As we move toward the subordinate-centered end of the continuum, however, the focus is increasingly on the subordinates—on what *they* are interested in, how *they* look at things, how *they* feel about them.

When business leadership is regarded in this way, a number of questions arise. Let us take four of especial importance:

Can a boss ever relinquish his responsibility by delegating it to someone else?

Our view is that the manager must expect to be held responsible by his superior for the quality of the decisions made, even though operationally these decisions may have been made on a group basis. He should, therefore, be ready to accept whatever risk is involved whenever he delegates decision-making power to his subordinates. Delegation is not a way of "passing the buck." Also, it should be emphasized that the amount of freedom the boss gives to his subordinates cannot be greater than the freedom which he himself has been given by his own superior.

Should the manager participate with his subordinates once he has delegated responsibility to them?

The manager should carefully think over this question and decide on his role prior to involving the subordinate group. He should ask if his presence will inhibit or facilitate the problem-solving process. There may be some instances when he should leave the group to let it solve the problem for itself. Typically, however, the boss has useful ideas to contribute, and should function as an additional member of the group. In the latter instance, it is important that he indicate clearly to the group that he sees himself in a *member* role rather than in an authority role.

How important is it for the group to recognize what kind of leadership behavior the boss is using?

It makes a great deal of difference. Many relationship problems between boss and subordinate occur because the boss fails to make clear how he plans to use his authority. If, for example, he actually intends to make a certain decision himself, but the subordinate group gets the impression that he has delegated this authority, considerable confusion and resentment are likely to follow. Problems may also occur when the boss uses a "democratic" facade to conceal the fact that he has already made a decision which he hopes the group will accept as its own. The attempt to "make them think it was their idea in the first place" is a risky one. We believe that it is highly important for the manager to be honest and clear in describing what authority he is keeping and what role he is asking his subordinates to assume in solving a particular problem.

Can you tell how "democratic" a manager is by the number of decisions his subordinates make?

The sheer *number* of decisions is not an accurate index of the amount of freedom that a subordinate group enjoys. More important is the *significance* of the decisions which the boss entrusts to his subordinates. Obviously a decision on how to arrange desks is of an entirely different order from a decision involving the introduction of new electronic data-processing equipment. Even though the widest possible limits are given in dealing with the first issue, the group will sense no particular degree of responsibility. For a boss to permit the group to decide equipment policy, even within rather narrow limits, would reflect a greater degree of confidence in them on his part.

Deciding how to lead

Now let us turn from the types of leadership which are possible in a company situation to the question of what types are *practical* and *desirable*. What factors or forces should a manager consider in deciding how to manage? Three are of particular importance:

- Forces in the manager.
- Forces in the subordinates.
- Forces in the situation.

We should like briefly to describe these elements and indicate how they might influence a manager's action in a decision-making situation.[2] The strength of each of them will, of course, vary from instance to instance, but the manager who is sensitive to them can better assess the problems which face him and determine which mode of leadership behavior is most appropriate for him.

[2] See also Robert Tannenbaum and Fred Massarik, "Participation by Subordinates in the Managerial Decision-Making Process," *Canadian Journal of Economics and Political Science,* August 1950, p. 413.

Forces in the manager

The manager's behavior in any given instance will be influenced greatly by the many forces operating within his own personality. He will, of course, perceive his leadership problems in a unique way on the basis of his background, knowledge, and experience. Among the important internal forces affecting him will be the following:

1 *His value system* How strongly does he feel that individuals should have a share in making the decisions which affect them? Or, how convinced is he that the official who is paid to assume responsibility should personally carry the burden of decision making? The strength of his convictions on questions like these will tend to move the manager to one end or the other of the continuum shown in Exhibit I. His behavior will also be influenced by the relative importance that he attaches to organizational efficiency, personal growth of subordinates, and company profits.[3]

2 *His confidence in his subordinates* Managers differ greatly in the amount of trust they have in other people generally, and this carries over to the particular employees they supervise at a given time. In viewing his particular group of subordinates, the manager is likely to consider their knowledge and competence with respect to the problem. A central question he might ask himself is: "Who is best qualified to deal with this problem?" Often he may, justifiably or not, have more confidence in his own capabilities than in those of his subordinates.

3 *His own leadership inclinations* There are some managers who seem to function more comfortably and naturally as highly directive leaders. Resolving problems and issuing orders come easily to them. Other managers seem to operate more comfortably in a team role, where they are continually sharing many of their functions with their subordinates.

4 *His feelings of security in an uncertain situation* The manager who releases control over the decision-making process thereby reduces the predictability of the outcome. Some managers have a greater need than others for predictability and stability in their environment. This "tolerance for ambiguity" is being viewed increasingly by psychologists as a key variable in a person's manner of dealing with problems.

The manager brings these and other highly personal variables to each situation he faces. If he can see them as forces which, consciously or unconsciously, influence his behavior, he can better understand what makes him prefer to act in a given way. And understanding this, he can often make himself more effective.

[3] See Chris Argyris, "Top Management Dilemma: Company Needs vs. Individual Development," *Personnel,* September 1955, pp. 123–134.

Forces in the subordinate

Before deciding how to lead a certain group, the manager will also want to consider a number of forces affecting his subordinates' behavior. He will want to remember that each employee, like himself, is influenced by many personality variables. In addition, each subordinate has a set of expectations about how the boss should act in relation to him (the phrase "expected behavior" is one we hear more and more often these days at discussions of leadership and teaching). The better the manager understands these factors, the more accurately he can determine what kind of behavior on his part will enable his subordinates to act most effectively.

Generally speaking, the manager can permit his subordinates greater freedom if the following essential conditions exist:

- If the subordinates have relatively high needs for independence. (As we all know, people differ greatly in the amount of direction that they desire.)
- If the subordinates have a readiness to assume responsibility for decision making. (Some see additional responsibility as a tribute to their ability; others see it as "passing the buck.")
- If they have a relatively high tolerance for ambiguity. (Some employees prefer to have clear-cut directives given to them; others prefer a wider area of freedom.)
- If they are interested in the problem and feel that it is important.
- If they understand and identify with the goals of the organization.
- If they have the necessary knowledge and experience to deal with the problem.
- If they have learned to expect to share in decision making. (Persons who have come to expect strong leadership and are then suddenly confronted with the request to share more fully in decision making are often upset by this new experience. On the other hand, persons who have enjoyed a considerable amount of freedom resent the boss who begins to make all the decisions himself.)

The manager will probably tend to make fuller use of his own authority if the above conditions do *not* exist; at times there may be no realistic alternative to running a "one-man show."

The restrictive effect of many of the forces will, of course, be greatly modified by the general feeling of confidence which subordinates have in the boss. Where they have learned to respect and trust him, he is free to vary his behavior. He will feel certain that he will not be perceived as an authoritarian boss on those occasions when he makes decisions by himself. Similarly, he will not be seen as using staff meetings to avoid his decision-making responsibility. In a climate of mutual confidence and respect, people tend to feel less threatened by deviations from normal practice, which in turn makes possible a higher degree of flexibility in the whole relationship.

Forces in the situation

In addition to the forces which exist in the manager himself and in his subordinates, certain characteristics of the general situation will also affect the manager's behavior. Among the more critical environmental pressures that surround him are those which stem from the organization, the work group, the nature of the problem, and the pressures of time. Let us look briefly at each of these:

Type of organization

Like individuals, organizations have values and traditions which inevitably influence the behavior of the people who work in them. The manager who is a newcomer to a company quickly discovers that certain kinds of behavior are approved while others are not. He also discovers that to deviate radically from what is generally accepted is likely to create problems for him.

These values and traditions are communicated in numerous ways—through job descriptions, policy pronouncements, and public statements by top executives. Some organizations, for example, hold to the notion that the desirable executive is one who is dynamic, imaginative, decisive, and persuasive. Other organizations put more emphasis upon the importance of the executive's ability to work effectively with people—his human relations skills. The fact that his superiors have a defined concept of what the good executive should be will very likely push the manager toward one end or the other of the behavioral range.

In addition to the above, the amount of employee participation is influenced by such variables as the size of the working units, their geographical distribution, and the degree of inter- and intra-organizational security required to attain company goals. For example, the wide geographical dispersion of an organization may preclude a practical system of participative decision making, even though this would otherwise be desirable. Similarly, the size of the working units or the need for keeping plans confidential may make it necessary for the boss to exercise more control than would otherwise be the case. Factors like these may limit considerably the manager's ability to function flexibly on the continuum.

Group effectiveness

Before turning decision-making responsibility over to a subordinate group, the boss should consider how effectively its members work together as a unit.

One of the relevant factors here is the experience the group has had in working together. It can generally be expected that a group which has functioned for some time will have developed habits of cooperation and thus be able to tackle a problem more effectively than a new group. It can also be expected that a group of people with similar backgrounds and interests will work more quickly and easily than people with dissimilar backgrounds, because the communication problems are likely to be less complex.

The degree of confidence that the members have in their ability to solve problems as a group is also a key consideration. Finally, such group variables as cohesiveness, permissiveness, mutual acceptance, and commonality of purpose will exert subtle but powerful influence on the group's functioning.

The problem itself

The nature of the problem may determine what degree of authority should be delegated by the manager to his subordinates. Obviously he will ask himself whether they have the kind of knowledge which is needed. It is possible to do them a real disservice by assigning a problem that their experience does not equip them to handle.

Since the problems faced in large or growing industries increasingly require knowledge of specialists from many different fields, it might be inferred that the more complex a problem, the more anxious a manager will be to get some assistance in solving it. However, this is not always the case. There will be times when the very complexity of the problem calls for one person to work it out. For example, if the manager has most of the background and factual data relevant to a given issue, it may be easier for him to think it through himself than to take the time to fill in his staff on all the pertinent background information.

The key question to ask, of course, is: "Have I heard the ideas of everyone who has the necessary knowledge to make a significant contribution to the solution of this problem?"

The pressure of time

This is perhaps the most clearly felt pressure on the manager (in spite of the fact that it may sometimes be imagined). The more that he feels the need for an immediate decision, the more difficult it is to involve other people. In organizations which are in a constant state of "crisis" and "crash programming" one is likely to find managers personally using a high degree of authority with relatively little delegation to subordinates. When the time pressure is less intense, however, it becomes much more possible to bring subordinates in on the decision-making process.

These, then, are the principal forces that impinge on the manager in any given instance and that tend to determine his tactical behavior in relation to his subordinates. In each case his behavior ideally will be that which makes possible the most effective attainment of his immediate goal within the limits facing him.

Long-run strategy

As the manager works with his organization on the problems that come up day by day, his choice of a leadership pattern is usually limited. He must take account of the forces just described and, within the restrictions they impose on him, do the best that he can. But as he looks ahead months or even years, he can shift his thinking from tactics to large-scale strategy. No longer need he be fettered by all of the forces mentioned, for he can view many of them as variables over which he has some control. He can, for example, gain new insights or skills for himself, supply training for individual subordinates, and provide participative experiences for his employee group.

In trying to bring about a change in these variables, however, he is faced with a challenging question: At which point along the continuum *should* he act?

Attaining objectives

The answer depends largely on what he wants to accomplish. Let us suppose that he is interested in the same objectives that most modern managers seek to attain when they can shift their attention from the pressure of immediate assignments:

1 To raise the level of employee motivation.
2 To increase the readiness of subordinates to accept change.
3 To improve the quality of all managerial decisions.
4 To develop teamwork and morale.
5 To further the individual development of employees.

In recent years the manager has been deluged with a flow of advice on how best to achieve these longer-run objectives. It is little wonder that he is often both bewildered and annoyed. However, there are some guidelines which he can usefully follow in making a decision.

Most research and much of the experience of recent years give a strong factual basis to the theory that a fairly high degree of subordinate-centered behavior is associated with the accomplishment of the five purposes mentioned.[4] This does not mean that a manager should always leave all decisions to his assistants. To provide the individual or the group with greater freedom than they are ready for at any given time may very well tend to generate anxieties and therefore inhibit rather than facilitate the attainment of desired objectives. But this should not keep the manager from making a continuing effort to confront his subordinates with the challenge of freedom.

Conclusion

In summary, there are two implications in the basic thesis that we have been developing. The first is that the successful leader is one who is keenly

[4] For example, see Warren H. Schmidt and Paul C. Buchanan, *Techniques that Produce Teamwork* (New London, Arthur C. Croft Publications, 1954); and Morris S. Viteles, *Motivation and Morale in Industry* (New York, W. W. Norton & Company, Inc., 1953).

aware of those forces which are most relevant to his behavior at any given time. He accurately understands himself, the individuals and group he is dealing with, and the company and broader social environment in which he operates. And certainly he is able to assess the present readiness for growth of his subordinates.

But this sensitivity or understanding is not enough, which brings us to the second implication. The successful leader is one who is able to behave appropriately in the light of these perceptions. If direction is in order, he is able to direct; if considerable participative freedom is called for, he is able to provide such freedom.

Thus, the successful manager of men can be primarily characterized neither as a strong leader nor as a permissive one. Rather, he is one who maintains a high batting average in accurately assessing the forces that determine what his most appropriate behavior at any given time should be and in actually being able to behave accordingly. Being both insightful and flexible, he is less likely to see the problems of leadership as a dilemma.

36 Retrospective commentary
Robert Tannenbaum and Warren H. Schmidt

Since this HBR Classic was first published in 1958, there have been many changes in organizations and in the world that have affected leadership patterns. While the article's continued popularity attests to its essential validity, we believe it can be reconsidered and updated to reflect subsequent societal changes and new management concepts.

The reasons for the article's continued relevance can be summarized briefly:

- The article contains insights and perspectives which mesh well with, and help clarify, the experiences of managers, other leaders, and students of leadership. Thus it is useful to individuals in a wide variety of organizations— industrial, governmental, educational, religious, and community.
- The concept of leadership the article defines is reflected in a continuum of leadership behavior (see Exhibit I in original article). Rather than offering a choice between two styles of leadership, democratic or authoritarian, it sanctions a range of behavior.
- The concept does not dictate to managers but helps them to analyze their

Source: Reprinted with permission from *Harvard Business Review* (May–June 1973), pp. 166–168. © 1973 by the President and Fellows of Harvard College. All rights reserved.

own behavior. The continuum permits them to review their behavior within a context of other alternatives, without any style being labeled right or wrong.

(We have sometimes wondered if we have, perhaps, made it too easy for anyone to justify his or her style of leadership. It may be a small step between being nonjudgmental and giving the impression that all behavior is equally valid and useful. The latter was not our intention. Indeed, the thrust of our endorsement was for the manager who is insightful in assessing relevant forces within himself, others, and the situation, and who can be flexible in responding to these forces.)

In recognizing that our article can be updated, we are acknowledging that organizations do not exist in a vacuum but are affected by changes that occur in society. Consider, for example, the implications for organizations of these recent social developments:

- The youth revolution that expresses distrust and even contempt for organizations identified with the establishment.
- The civil rights movement that demands all minority groups be given a greater opportunity for participation and influence in the organizational processes.
- The ecology and consumer movements that challenge the right of managers to make decisions without considering the interest of people outside the organization.
- The increasing national concern with the quality of working life and its relationship to worker productivity, participation, and satisfaction.

These and other societal changes make effective leadership in this decade a more challenging task, requiring even greater sensitivity and flexibility than was needed in the 1950's. Today's manager is more likely to deal with employees who resent being treated as subordinates, who may be highly critical of any organizational system, who expect to be consulted and to exert influence, and who often stand on the edge of alienation from the institution that needs their loyalty and commitment. In addition, he is frequently confronted by a highly turbulent, unpredictable environment.

In response to these social pressures, new concepts of management have emerged in organizations. Open-system theory, with its emphasis on subsystems' interdependency *and* on the interaction of an organization with its environment, has made a powerful impact on managers' approach to problems. Organization development has emerged as a new behavioral science approach to the improvement of individual, group, organizational, and interorganizational performance. New research has added to our understanding of motivation in the work situation. More and more executives have become concerned with social responsibility and have explored the feasibility of social audits. And a growing number of organizations, in Europe and in the United States, have conducted experiments in industrial democracy.

In light of these developments, we submit the following thoughts on how we would rewrite certain points in our original article.

The article described forces in the manager, subordinates, and the situation as givens, with the leadership pattern a resultant of these forces. We would now give more attention to the *interdependency* of these forces. For example, such interdependency occurs in: (a) the interplay between the manager's confidence in his subordinates, their readiness to assume responsibility, and the level of group effectiveness; and (b) the impact of the behavior of the manager on that of his subordinates, and vice versa.

In discussing the forces in the situation, we primarily identified organizational phenomena. We would now include forces lying outside the organization, and would explore the relevant interdependencies between the organization and its environment.

In the original article, we presented the size of the rectangle in Exhibit I as a given, with its boundaries already determined by external forces—in effect, a closed system. We would now recognize the possibility of the manager and /or his subordinates taking the initiative to change those boundaries through interaction with relevant external forces—both within their own organization and in the larger society.

The article portrayed the manager as the principal and almost unilateral actor. He initiated and determined group functions, assumed responsibility, and exercised control. Subordinates made inputs and assumed power only at the will of the manager. Although the manager might have taken into account forces outside himself, it was *he* who decided where to operate on the continuum—that is, whether to announce a decision instead of trying to sell his idea to his subordinates, whether to invite questions, to let subordinates decide an issue, and so on. While the manager has retained this clear prerogative in many organizations, it has been challenged in others. Even in situations where he has retained it, however, the balance in the relationship between manager and subordinates at any given time is arrived at by interaction—direct or indirect—between the two parties.

Although power and its use by the manager played a role in our article, we now realize that our concern with cooperation and collaboration, common goals, commitment, trust, and mutual caring limited our vision with respect to the realities of power. We did not attempt to deal with unions, other forms of joint worker action, or with individual workers' expressions of resistance. Today, we would recognize much more clearly the power available to *all* parties, and the factors that underlie the interrelated decisions on whether to use it.

In the original article, we used the terms "manager" and "subordinate." We are now uncomfortable with "subordinate" because of its demeaning, dependency-laden connotations and prefer "nonmanager." The titles "manager" and "nonmanager" make the terminological difference functional rather than hierarchical.

We assumed fairly traditional organizational structures in our original article. Now we would alter our formulation to reflect newer organizational

modes which are slowly emerging, such as industrial democracy, intentional communities, and "phenomenarchy."* These new modes are based
on observations such as the following:

- Both manager and nonmanagers may be governing forces in their group's
  environment, contributing to the definition of the total area of freedom.
- A group can function without a manager, with managerial functions being
  shared by group members.
- A group, as a unit, can be delegated authority and can assume responsibility
  within a larger organizational context.

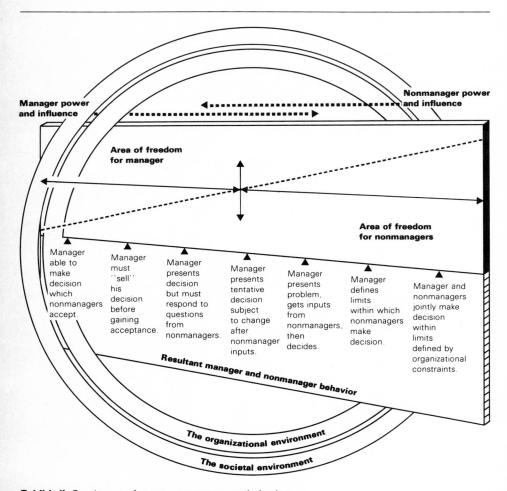

Exhibit II Continuum of manager-nonmanager behavior

---

* For a description of phenomenarchy, see Will McWhinney, "Phenomenarchy: A
  Suggestion for Social Redesign," *Journal of Applied Behavioral Science,* May 1973.

Our thoughts on the question of leadership have prompted us to design a new behavior continuum (see Exhibit II) in which the total area of freedom shared by manager and nonmanagers is constantly redefined by interactions between them and the forces in the environment.

The arrows in the exhibit indicate the continual flow of interdependent influence among systems and people. The points on the continuum designate the types of manager and nonmanager behavior that become possible with any given amount of freedom available to each. The new continuum is both more complex and more dynamic than the 1958 version, reflecting the organizational and societal realities of 1973.

---

37 How do you make leaders more effective? New answers to an old puzzle
Fred. E. Fiedler

Let's begin with a basic proposition: The organization that employs the leader is as responsible for his success or failure as the leader himself. Not that this is a new insight—far from it. Terman wrote in 1904 that leadership performance depends on the situation, as well as on the leader. Although this statement would not be questioned by anyone currently working in this area, it also has been widely ignored. Practically all formal training programs attempt to change the individual; many of them assume explicitly or implicitly that there is one style of leadership or one way of acting that will work best under all conditions. Most military academies, for example, attempt to mold the individual into a supposedly ideal leader personality. Others assume that the training should enable the individual to become more flexible or more sensitive to his environment so that he can adapt himself to it.

Before going further let's define a few terms. I will confine my discussion to *task groups* rather than the organization of which the group is a part. Furthermore, we will assume that anyone who is placed in a leadership position will have the requisite technical qualifications for the job. Just as the leader of a surgical team obviously has to have medical training, so a manager must know the essential administrative requirements of his job. We will here talk primarily about training *as a leader* rather than training as a specialist. The effectiveness of the leader will be defined in terms of how well his group or organization performs the primary tasks for which the group exists. We measure the effectiveness of a football coach by how many games his team wins and not by the character he builds, and the excellence of an orchestra conductor by how well his orchestra plays, not by

Source: Reprinted by permission of the publishers from *Organizational Dynamics* (Autumn 1972), pp. 3–18. © 1972 by American Management Association, Inc.

the happiness of his musicians' or his ability as a musicologist. Whether the musicians' job satisfaction or the conductor's musicological expertness do, in fact, contribute to the orchestra's excellence is an interesting question in its own right, but it is not what people pay to hear. Likewise, the performance of a manager is here measured in terms of his department's or group's effectiveness in doing its assigned job. Whether the accomplishment of this job is to be measured after a week or after five years depends, of course, upon the assignment the organization gives the group, and the accomplishments the organization considers important.

When we think of improving leadership, we almost automatically think of training the individual. This training frequently involves giving the man a new perspective on his supervisory responsibilities by means of role playing, discussions, detailed instructions on how to behave toward subordinates, as well as instruction in the technical and administrative skills he will need in his job. A training program might last a few days, a few months, or as in the case of college programs and military academies, as long as four years. What is the hard evidence that this type of training actually increases organizational performance?

Empirical studies to evaluate the effectiveness of various leadership training programs, executive development, and supervisory workshops have been generally disappointing. Certainly, the two field experiments and two studies of ongoing organizations conducted by my associates and me failed to show that training increases organizational performance.

The first experiment in 1966 was conducted at a Belgian naval training center. We chose 244 Belgian recruits and 48 petty officers from a pool of 546 men. These men were assembled into 96 three-men groups: 48 groups had petty officers and 48 groups had recruits as leaders. The recruits ranged in age from 17 to 24, and none had been in the service longer than six weeks. The petty officers ranged in age from 19 to 45 years, and had an average of ten years' experience. All petty officers had received a two-year technical and leadership training course at petty officer candidate school. Since most successful graduates enlist for a 20-year term, Belgian petty officers are not only well-trained but they are also truly motivated and committed career men.

The petty officers were matched with the recruit leaders on intelligence and other relevant scores. Each group worked on four cooperative tasks which were considered fair samples of the type of work petty officers might perform. One task consisted of writing a recruiting letter urging young men to join the Belgian navy as a career; the second and third tasks required the groups to find the shortest route for a convoy first through ten and then through twelve ports; the fourth task required the leader to train his men without using verbal instructions in the disassembling and reassembling of a .45-caliber automatic pistol.

Despite the fact that the recruits had had no leadership experience or training, their groups performed as well as those led by petty officers.

To test whether these results were not simply due to the chance or to a fault in our experimental design, we conducted a second experiment at a leadership training workshop for officers of Canadian military colleges. This study compared the performance of groups led by captains and majors with groups led by enlisted men who had just finished their eight weeks of basic training. All of the officers were, themselves, graduates of a Canadian military college. In addition, the officers had from 5 to 17 years of leadership experience and training after graduation. The 32 enlisted men were basic trainees between 19 and 22 years of age, and their intelligence scores were substantially below those of the officers'. To reduce the possibility that they might feel anxious or inhibited by working with officers, the officers wore casual clothes and the enlisted men were told that they would work with civilian instructors.

The officers and men worked as three-men groups on three different tasks. They were asked to (a) write a fable, (b) find the shortest route for a truck convoy, and (c) draw bar graphs from score distributions that first had to be converted from one scale to another. As in the Belgian study, the tasks were designed so that all three group members had to participate in the work. As in the Belgian study, the groups led by the trained and experienced officers performed no better than the groups led by untrained and inexperienced enlisted men.

It is, of course, possible that experimental tasks do not give realistic results. For this reason we further checked in real-life situations whether the amount of training influenced performance by a study of 171 managers and supervisors in U.S. post offices. The performance of each of these supervisors was rated by two to five of his superiors. Amount of training ranged from zero hours of training to three years, with a median of 45 hours. The number of hours of supervisory training received by these managers was totally unrelated to their rated performance. We also investigated whether the post offices with highly trained supervisors were more effective on such objective post office performance measures as target achievement in number of first-class pieces handled, indirect costs, mail processing, etc. However, 12 of the 15 correlations were slightly *negative*; none was significant. Thus, training apparently did not improve organizational performance.

Another study related the amount of training received by police sergeants with the performance ratings made by their supervisors and other sergeants. Here again, training was unrelated to performance. Thus, neither the two controlled experiments nor the two field studies provide any basis for assuming that leadership training of the type given in these institutions, or in the training programs taken by postal managers or police sergeants, contributed to organizational performance.

I repeat that these findings are by no means unusual. Empirical studies to determine whether or not leadership training improves organizational performance have generally come up with negative findings. Newport, after surveying 121 large companies, concluded that not one of the companies had obtained any scientifically acceptable evidence that the leadership training for their middle management had actually improved performance.

T-group and sensitivity training, which has become fashionable in business and industry, has yielded similarly unsatisfactory results. Reviews of the literature by Campbell and Dunnette and by House found no convincing evidence that this type of training increased organizational effectiveness, and a well-known study at the International Harvester Company by Fleishman, Harris, and Burtt on the effects of supervisory training concluded that the effects of supervisory training in modifying behavior were very short-lived and did not improve performance.

Effect of experience on leadership

Let us now ask whether supervisory experience improves performance. Actually, since leadership experience almost always involves on-the-job training, we are dealing with a closely related phenomenon.

Interestingly enough, the literature actually contains few, if any, studies which attempt to link leadership experience to organizational effectiveness. Yet, there seems to be a firmly held expectation that leadership experience makes a leader more effective. We simply have more trust in experienced leaders. We can infer this, for example, from the many regulations that require time in grade before promotion to the next higher level, as well as the many specifications of prior job in hiring executives for responsible positions.

We have already seen that the experienced petty officers and military academy officers did not perform more effectively than did the inexperienced enlisted men, nor did the more experienced officers or petty officers perform better than the less experienced.

In addition, we also anlyzed data from various other groups and organizations. These included directors of research and development teams at a large physical research laboratory, foremen of craftshops, general foremen in a heavy machinery manufacturing company, managers of meat, and of grocery markets in a large supermarket chain as well as post office supervisors and managers, and police sergeants. For all these managers we could obtain reliable performance ratings or objective group effectiveness criteria. None of the correlations was significant in the expected direction. The median correlation relating leadership experience to leadership performance for all groups and organizations was −.12—certainly not significant in the positive direction!

To summarize the findings, neither orthodox leadership training nor leadership experience nor sensitivity training appear[s] to contribute across the board to group or organizational effectiveness. It is, therefore, imperative first that we ask why this might be so, and second that we consider alternative methods for improving leadership performance.

The contingency model

The "Contingency Model," a recent theory of leadership, holds that the effectiveness of group performance is contingent upon (a) the leader's motivational pattern, and (b) the degree to which the situation gives the leader power and influence. We have worked with a leadership motivation measure called the "Esteem for the Least Preferred Coworker," or LPC for short. The subject is first asked to think of all the people with whom he has ever worked, and then given a simple scale on which he describes the one person in his life with whom he has been able to work *least well*. This "least preferred coworker" may be someone he knows at the time, or it may be someone he has known in the past. It does not have to be a member of his present work group.

In grossly oversimplified terms, the person who descibes his least preferred coworker in relatively favorable terms is basically motivated to have close interpersonal relations with others. By contrast, the person who rejects someone with whom he cannot work is basically motivated to accomplish or achieve on the task, and he derives satisfaction from being recognized as having performed well on the task. The task-motivated person thus uses the task to obtain a favorable position and good interpersonal relations.

Classifying leadership situations

The statement that some leaders perform better in one kind of situation while some leaders perform better in different situations is begging a question. "What kinds of situations are best suited for which type of leader?" In other words, how can we best classify groups if we wish to predict leadership performance?

We can approach this problem by assuming that leadership is essentially a work relationship involving power and influence. It is easier to be a leader when you have complete control than when your control is weak and dependent on the good will of others. It is easier to be the captain of a ship than the chairman of a volunteer group organized to settle a school bussing dispute. The *job* may be more complex for the navy captain but *being in the leadership role* is easier for him than for the committee chairman. It is, therefore, not unreasonable to classify situations in terms of how much power and influence the situation gives the leader. We call this "situational favorableness." One simple categorization of groups on their situational favorableness classifies leadership situations on the basis of three major dimensions:

1 *Leader-member relations* Leaders presumably have more power and influence if they have a good relationship with their members than if they have a poor relationship with them, if they are liked, respected, trusted, than if they are not. Research has shown that this is by far the most important single dimension.
2 *Task structure* Tasks or assignments that are highly structured, spelled out, or programmed give the leader more influence than tasks that are vague, nebulous and unstructured. It is easier, for example, to be a leader whose

task it is to set up a sales display according to clearly delineated steps than it is to be a chairman of a committee preparing a new sales campaign.

3 *Position power* Leaders will have more power and influence if their position is vested with such prerogatives as being able to hire and fire, being able to discipline, to reprimand, and so on. Position power, as it is here used, is determined by how much power the leader has over his subordinates. If the janitor foreman can hire and fire, he has more position power in his own group than the chairman of a board of directors who, frequently, cannot hire or fire—or even reprimand his board members.

Using this classification method we can now roughly order groups as being high or low on each of these three dimensions. This gives us an eight-celled classification (Figure 1). This scheme postulates that it is easier to be a leader in groups that fall into Cell 1 since you are liked, have position power, and have a structured task. It is somewhat more difficult in Cell 2 since you are liked, have a structured task, but little position power, and so on to groups in Cell 8 where the leader is not liked, has a vague, unstructured task, and little position power. A good example of Cell 8 would be the disliked chairman of the volunteer committee we mentioned before.

Figure 1 Cells or "octants"

	Very favorable			Intermediate in favorableness			Unfavorable	
	1	**2**	**3**	**4**	**5**	**6**	**7**	**8**
Leader-member relations	Good	Good	Good	Good	Poor	Poor	Poor	Poor
Task structure	High	High	Low	Low	High	High	Low	Low
Position power	Strong	Weak	Strong	Weak	Strong	Weak	Strong	Weak

The critical question is, "What kind of leadership does each of these different group situations call for?" Figure 2 summarizes the results of 63 analyses based on a total of 454 separate groups. These included bomber and tank crews, antiaircraft artillery units, managements of consumer cooperative companies, boards of directors, open-hearth shops, basketball and surveying teams, and various groups involved in creative and problem-solving tasks.

The horizontal axis of the group indicates the "situational favorableness," namely, the leader's control and influence as defined by the eightfold classification shown in Figure 1. The vertical axis indicates the relationship between the leader's motivational pattern, as measured by the LPC score, and his group's performance. A median correlation above the midline shows that the relationship-motivated leaders tended to perform better than the task-motivated leaders. A correlation below the midline indicates that the task-motivated leaders performed better than the relationship-motivated leaders. Figure 3 shows the predictions that the model would make in each of the eight cells.

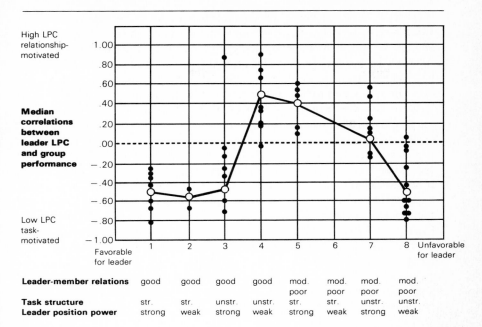

Figure 2

	1	**2**	**3**	**4**	**5**	**6**	**7**	**8**
Leader-member relations	good	good	good	good	mod. poor	mod. poor	mod. poor	mod. poor
Task structure	str.	str.	unstr.	unstr.	str.	str.	unstr.	unstr.
Leader position power	strong	weak	strong	weak	strong	weak	strong	weak

Figure 3 Prediction of the performance of relationship- and task-motivated leaders

	1	**2**	**3**	**4**	**5**	**6**	**7**	**8**
High LPC (relationship-motivated)				Good	Good	Some-what better	Some-what better	
Low LPC (task-motivated)	Good	Good	Good					Good

These findings have two important implications for our understanding of what makes leaders effective. First, Figure 2 tells us that the task-motivated leaders tend to perform better than relationship-motivated leaders in situations that are very favorable and in those that are unfavorable. Relationship-motivated leaders tend to perform better than task-motivated leaders in situations that are intermediate in favorableness. Hence, both the relationship- and the task-motivated leaders perform well under some conditions and not under others. It is, therefore, not correct to speak of any person as generally a good leader or generally a poor leader. Rather, a leader may perform well in one situation but not in another. This is also borne out by the repeated findings that we cannot predict a leader's performance on the basis of his personality traits, or even by knowing how well he performed on a previous task unless that task was similar in situational favorableness.

Second, the graph on Figure 2 shows that the performance of a leader depends as much on the situational favorableness as it does on the individual in the leadership position. Hence, the organization can change leadership performance either by trying to change the individual's personality and motivational pattern or by changing the favorableness of the leader's situation. As we shall see, this is really what training is all about.

Before we go further, we must ask how valid the Contingency Model is. How well does it predict in new situations? There have been at least 25 studies to date that have tested the theory. These validation studies included research on grocery and meat markets, a physical science laboratory, a machinery plant, a hospital, an electronics company, and teams of volunteer public health workers in Central America, as well as various experimentally assembled groups in the laboratory. Of particular importance is a large experiment that used cadets at West Point to test the entire eight cells of the model. This study almost completely reproduced the curve shown on Figure 2. In all studies that were recently reviewed, 35 of the 44 obtained correlations were in the predicted direction—a finding that could have occurred by chance less than one time in 100. An exception is Cell 2, in which laboratory experiments—but nor field studies—have yielded correlations showing the relationship-motivated leaders perform better than task-motivated leaders.

Effect of leadership training?

The main question of this paper is, of course, how we can better ultilize leadership training and experience to improve leadership performance. While appropriate leadership training and experience apparently do not increase organizational performance, there is considerable evidence that they do affect the manager's attitudes, behavior, and of course, his technical skills and administrative knowhow. These programs teach the leader better methods of getting along with his subordinates, more effective handling of administrative routines, as well as technical background required for the job. In other words, the leader who is trained or experienced will have considerably greater control and influence over his job and his subordinates than one who is untrained and inexperienced.

In contrast, the inexperienced and untrained leader confronts numerous problems that are new to him, and for which he does not have a ready answer. As a result, he cannot give clear and concise instructions to his subordinates. Moreover, since so many situations are novel, he will be more anxious and less sure of himself, which will tend to make him more dependent upon his group and others in the organization. Not even the most detailed manual of operating instructions will enable a new manager to step into his job and behave as if he had been there for years. Thus, situations will be correspondingly less favorable for the untrained and inexperienced leader than for the trained and experienced leader.

What we are really saying here is that leadership training and experience primarily improve the favorableness of the leadership situation. But, if the Contingency Model is right, a more favorable situation requires a different type of leadership than a less favorable situation. Hence, leadership training and experience that will improve the performance of one type of leader *will decrease the performance of the other.* On the average, it will have little or no measurable effect on organizational performance. This is schematically shown by Figure 4. The arrows indicate that effect of training and experience in improving the favorableness of the leadership situation.

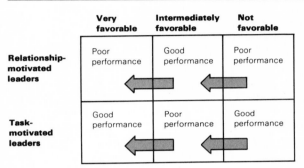

Arrows indicate the predicted effect of experience and training

Figure 4 Favorableness of the situation for the trained or experienced leader

The headings on Figure 4 indicate the situational favorableness for the already trained or experienced leader. The untrained or inexperienced leader obviously would face a correspondingly less favorable situation. Thus, while the situation at the left of the table is very favorable for the trained leader, it is likely to be intermediate for the leader who lacks training and experience. The training or experience, as indicated by the arrow, would then change the untrained leader's situation from one which is intermediate to one which is very favorable. Likewise, if the trained leader's situation is intermediate in favorableness, the untrained leader's situation would be unfavorable. Training would, then, improve the untrained leader's situation from an unfavorable one to a situation which is intermediate in favorableness.

But why should an inexperienced and untrained leader perform better than someone with training and experience? Under certain conditions this is not too difficult to see. An individual who is new on the job is likely to seek good interpersonal relations with his coworkers so that he can enlist their full cooperation. He is not likely to throw his weight around and he will, therefore, be less likely to antagonize his group members. In other words, the proposition is far from absurd, and it is quite compatible with the behavior of the manager who learns to rely on his staff of experts in making various decisions.

The proof of this theoretical pudding lies in various studies that bear out our suppositions.

Study of school principals

One study was conducted by McNamara on principals of rural elementary schools and of urban secondary schools in Canada. The performance of elementary principals was evaluated by means of ratings obtained from school superintendents and their staffs. The performance of secondary school principals was measured on the basis of province-wide achievement tests given to all students in the 11th grade. The average test score was used as the measure of the principal's effectiveness.

McNamara divided his group into task- and relationship-motivated principals, and again into inexperienced principals who had been on their job less than two years and those with three or more years of experience.

Let us now consider the favorableness of the leadership situation of elementary school principals. Their position power is reasonably high, and their task is fairly structured. The schools in McNamara's sample were quite small, the curricula of these schools are determined by the authorities of the province and by the school superintendent's office, and the elementary school principal typically is not called upon to make many policy decisions or innovations. His task is, therefore, structured. Hence, the experienced principal will have a very favorable leadership situation, and we would expect the task-motivated principals to perform better than the relationship-motivated principals.

The inexperienced principal faces a considerably less favorable situation. While his position power is high, he does not know his teachers well, and many of the administrative problems that arise will have to be handled in a manner that is new to him. We would predict that his task is unstructured and that the situation is intermediate. Without much experience the relationship-motivated principals will, therefore, perform better than their task-motivated colleagues. That this is the case is shown on Figure 5.

The secondary principal also has high position power. However, his organization is considerably more complex. In McNamara's sample, the schools had from 25 to 40 teachers who, in turn, were supervised by department heads. Thus, the principal's control over the teachers is less direct. In addition, of course, the curriculum of a high school varies from school to school and the high school principal generally has to make a considerable number of policy decisions about the teaching program, his staff, as well as the activities and disciplinary problems of his students. For this reason, the experienced principals of secondary schools were judged to have a situation of intermediate favorableness. Relationship-motivated principals should perform best. The inexperienced high school principal will have to set new precedents and he will have to think through many of the problems for the first time as they arise. Hence, the situation will be relatively unfavorable. We would predict, therefore, that the task-motivated principals with less than two years' experience will perform best in these situations. Here, again, the data follow the prediction. (See Figure 5.)

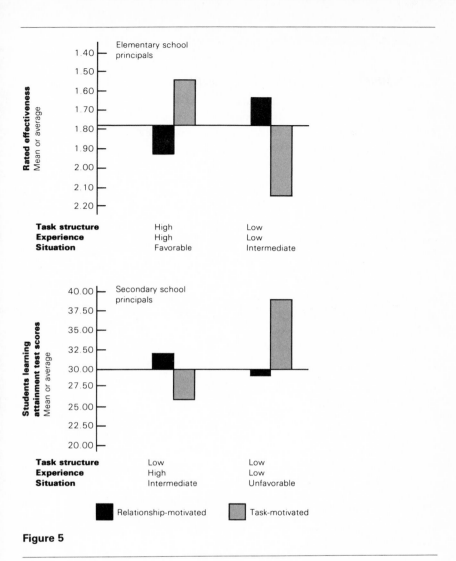

Figure 5

It is particularly important to note that the relationship-motivated elementary school principal with longer experience actually performed *less well* than the relationship-motivated elementary school principal with less experience. Likewise, the task-motivated secondary school principal with more experience had significantly *poorer* performance than the task-motivated principal with considerably less experience. Thus, for these particular administrators, the more extensive experience not only failed to improve their performance but actually decreased their effectiveness.

Study of consumer cooperatives

Another study that illustrates the effect of training and experience was conducted some years ago on 32 member companies of a large federation of consumer cooperatives. The federation used two indices for measuring company effectiveness and managerial performance. These were (a) the operating efficiency of the company, that is, roughly the proportion of overhead to total sales, and (b) the proportion of net income to total sales. We used the three-year average of these measures for our study.

In a reanalysis of these data, the managers were divided into those with task- and relationship-motivated leadership patterns, and of these, the ten with the most and the ten with the least years of experience in the organization. Since the federation of the companies maintained a strong management development program, managers with long experience also tended to have the most extensive training.

The leadership situation for the experienced managers was judged to be relatively favorable. They had considerable position power, and their job was relatively structured. As in the case of school administrators, the inexperienced and less well trained managers would, of course, face a larger number of problems that they had not encountered before, and the task would, therefore, be correspondingly less structured. Hence, for the inexperienced managers the situation would be intermediate in favorableness.

The Contingency Model would then predict that the experienced managers with task-oriented leadership patterns would perform better, as would the inexperienced managers with relationship-motivated leadership patterns. That this was the case is shown on Figure 6 for operating efficiency. Somewhat weaker results were obtained for the net income criterion. It is again apparent that the experienced and trained relationship-motivated managers performed less well than did the relatively inexperienced and untrained managers who are relationship-motivated.

We have also studied the effect of training and experience on the performance of the post office managers and supervisors, police sergeants, and formal and informal leaders of company boards. These studies have yielded essentially similar results.

New studies of military leadership

Two studies were recently conducted specifically for the purpose of testing the hypothesis on completely new data. These were of field artillery sections and navy aircraft maintenance shops. Training and experience data were available for the noncommissioned officers in charge of these groups. In these studies, groups were assigned to cells 1, 3, 5, and 8 of the model. (See Figure 7.) Just as predicted, the task-motivated leaders performed best in cells 1, 3, and 8, while the relationship-motivated leaders performed best in cell 5. All findings were statistically significant.

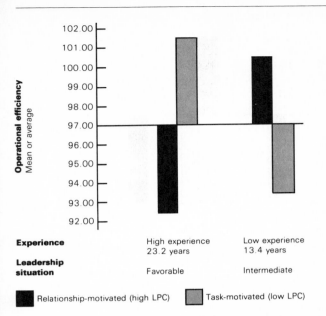

Figure 6 Performance of relationship- and task-motivated managers with relatively high and relatively low levels of experience

To train or not to train

What does all this mean for improving managerial performance, and how can we apply the findings that we have described?

In sum, if we want to improve leadership performance, we can either change the leader by training, or we can change his leadership situation. Common sense suggests that it is much easier to change various aspects of a man's job than to change the man. When we talk about leadership behavior, we are talking about fairly deeply ingrained personality factors and habits of interacting with others. These cannot be changed easily, either in a few hours or in a few days. In fact, as we have seen, not even four years of military academy and 5 to 17 years of subsequent experience enable a leader to perform significantly better on different tasks than someone that has had neither training nor experience.

We have seen that a leader's performance depends not only on his personality, but also on the organizational factors that determine the leader's control and influence, that is, the "situational favorableness." As we have shown, appropriate training and experience improve situational favorableness. Whether or not they improve performance depends upon the match between the leader's motivational pattern and the favorableness of the situation. This means that a training program that improves the leader's control

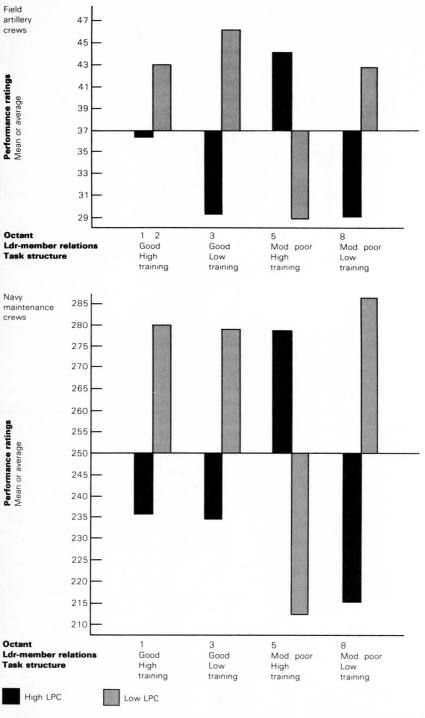

Figure 7

and influence may benefit the relationship-motivated managers, but it will be detrimental to the task-motivated managers, or vice versa, depending upon the situation.

The idea that we can improve a leader's performance by increasing the favorableness of his situation is, of course, far from new. A poorly performing manager may be given more authority, more explicit instructions, more congenial coworkers in the hope that it will help him do a better job. Moreover, decreasing the favorableness of the situation in order to improve a manager's performance is also not quite as unusual as it might appear at first blush. If a man becomes bored, stale, or disinterested in his job, a frequent remedy is to transfer him to a more challenging job. As it turns out, "challenging" is just another way of saying that the job is less structured, has less position power, or requires working with difficult people. It is certainly well known that some men perform best under pressure and that they get into difficulty when life is too calm. These are the trouble shooters who are dispatched to branch offices or departments that need to be bailed out.

What, then, can an organization do to increase managerial performance? As a first step, it is necessary to determine which of the managers are task- and which are relationship-motivated. This can be accomplished by means of a short scale. Second, the organization needs to categorize carefully the situational favorableness of its managerial jobs. (Scales are available in Fiedler, F. E., *A Theory of Leadership Effectiveness,* McGraw-Hill, 1967.) Third, the organization can decide on a number of options in its management of executive personnel.

The least expensive and probably most efficient method is to develop a careful program of managerial rotation that moves some individuals from one job to another at a faster rate than it moves others. For example, it will be recalled that the relationship-motivated elementary school principals on the average became less effective after two years on the job. Moving these men to new jobs probably would have made them more effective than leaving them at the same school for many years. Likewise, moving the task-motivated secondary school principals after two years probably would have increased their performance. In the case of the consumer cooperatives, it took 15 to 20 years in the organization (as employee and assistant manager, as well as manager) before the relationship-motivated managers began to go stale. How long a man should stay on a particular job must, of course, be determined empirically in each organization.

A second major option is management training. The problem here is whether to train only some people or all those who are eligible: training a task-motivated manager who is accepted by his group and has a structured task is likely to improve his performance; training a relationship-motivated manager for the same job is likely to make him less effective. The organization would, therefore, be better off if it simply did not train relationship-motivated managers for these particular jobs. On the other hand, the relationship-motivated but not the task-motivated managers should be trained for jobs in which the situational favorableness is intermediate.

Leadership training should devote more effort to teaching leaders how to modify their environment and their own job so that they fit their style of leadership. We must get rid of the implicit assumption that the environment and the organization, or a particular leadership position, are constant and unchanging. In addition to changes which occur as the leaders gain experience, they also continuously modify their leadership positions. They often speak of showing their men who is boss, presumably to assert their position power or of "being one of the boys" to de-emphasize it; they speak of getting to know their men, presumably to establish better relations with them; they speak of different approaches to their work; they look for certain types of assistants who complement their abilities; they demand more authority, or they play down the authority they already have; they ask for certain types of assignments and try to avoid others. The theory that has here been described merely provides a basis for a more rational modification of the leadership job.

How can we train leaders to determine the conditions under which they are most likely to succeed or fail, and how can they learn to modify their own leadership situation? The frequently negative relationship between leadership experience and leader performance undoubtedly stems in part from the difficulties in obtaining feedback about one's own leadership effectiveness. As research has shown, unless the group fails utterly in its task, most leaders are unable to say with any degree of accuracy how well their group performed in comparison with other groups.

Leadership training away from the organization should provide the prospective leader with a wide range of leadership situations in which he can get immediate feedback on how well he has performed. On the basis of these experiences, he must learn to recognize which situations fit his particular style of leadership and how he can best modify situations so that they will enable him to perform effectively. This may involve the development of six to eight short leadership tasks and situations, or adequately measured organizational tasks, in which each trainee is required to lead. He must then be given an objective appraisal of how well his group's performance compared with the performance of others under the same conditions.

The closest approximation to the all-around good leader is likely to be the individual who intuitively or through training knows how to manage his environment so that the leadership situation best matches his leadership style.

It may be desirable for various reasons to train all managers of a certain level, especially since being sent to executive training programs has in many organizations become a symbol of success. Men are sent to these training programs not because they need to learn, but because they need to be rewarded. If this is the case, the organization might do well to place the manager who completes the training program into a position that matches his leadership motivation pattern. For example, in the consumer cooperative companies, the relationship-motivated managers might have been given staff jobs, or jobs with troubled companies at the conclusion of an extensive training program.

Conclusion

As a consequence of our research, we have both discredited some old myths and learned some new lessons.

The old myths:

- That there is one best leadership style, or that there are leaders who excel under all circumstances.
- That some men are born leaders, and that neither training, experience, or conditions can materially affect leadership skills.

The lessons, while more pedestrian and less dogmatic, are more useful. We know that people differ in how they respond to management situations. Furthermore, we know that almost every manager in an organization can perform effectively, providing that we place him in a situation that matches his personality, providing we know how to match his training and experience to the available jobs—and providing that we take the trouble.

38 The golden rule
Brent Parker and Johnny Hart

Source: THE WIZARD OF ID by permission of Johnny Hart and Field Enterprises, Inc.

V/B
Motivation

39 That urge to achieve
David C. McClelland

Most people in this world, psychologically, can be divided into two broad groups. There is that minority which is challenged by opportunity and willing to work hard to achieve something, and the majority which really does not care all that much.

For nearly twenty years now, psychologists have tried to penetrate the mystery of this curious dichotomy. Is the need to achieve (or the absence of it) an accident, is it hereditary, or is it the result of environment? Is it a single, isolatable human motive, or a combination of motives—the desire to accumulate wealth, power, fame? Most important of all, is there some technique that could give this will to achieve to people, even whole societies, who do not now have it?

While we do not yet have complete answers for any of these questions, years of work have given us partial answers to most of them and insights into all of them. There is a distinct human motive, distinguishable from others. It can be found, in fact tested for, in any group.

Let me give you one example. Several years ago, a careful study was made of 450 workers who had been thrown out of work by a plant shutdown in Erie, Pennsylvania. Most of the unemployed workers stayed home for a while and then checked back with the United States Employment Service to see if their old jobs or similar ones were available. But a small minority among them behaved differently: the day they were laid off, they started job-hunting.

They checked both the United States and the Pennsylvania Employment Office; they studied the "Help Wanted" sections of the papers; they checked through their union, their church, and various fraternal organizations; they looked into training courses to learn a new skill; they even left town to look for work, while the majority when questioned said they would

Source: Reprinted by permission from *Think* magazine, published by IBM, copyright 1966 by International Business Machines Corporation. Pages 19–23.

not under any circumstances move away from Erie to obtain a job. Obviously the members of that active minority were differently motivated. All the men were more or less in the same situation objectively: they needed work, money, food, shelter, job security. Yet only a minority showed initiative and enterprise in finding what they needed. Why? Psychologists, after years of research, now believe they can answer that question. They have demonstrated that these men possessed in greater degree a specific type of human motivation. For the moment let us refer to this personality characteristic as "Motive A" and review some of the other characteristics of the men who have more of the motive than other men.

Suppose they are confronted by a work situation in which they can set their own goals as to how difficult a task they will undertake. In the psychological laboratory, such a situation is very simply created by asking them to throw rings over a peg from any distance they may choose. Most men throw more or less randomly, standing now close, now far away, but those with Motive A seem to calculate carefully where they are most likely to get a sense of mastery. They stand nearly always at moderate distances, not so close as to make the task ridiculously easy, nor so far away as to make it impossible. They set moderately difficult, but potentially achievable goals for themselves, where they objectively have only about a 1-in-3 chance of succeeding. In other words, they are always setting challenges for themselves, tasks to make them stretch themselves a little.

But they behave like this only if *they* can influence the outcome by performing the work themselves. They prefer not to gamble at all. Say they are given a choice between rolling dice with one in three chances of winning and working on a problem with a one-in-three chance of solving in the time allotted, they choose to work on the problem even though rolling the dice is obviously less work and the odds of winning are the same. They prefer to work at a problem rather than leave the outcome to chance or to others.

Obviously they are concerned with personal achievement rather than with the rewards of success *per se,* since they stand just as much chance of getting those rewards by throwing the dice. This leads to another characteristic the Motive A men show—namely, a strong preference for work situations in which they get concrete feedback on how well they are doing, as one does, say in playing golf, or in being a salesman, but as one does not in teaching, or in personnel counseling. A golfer always knows his score and can compare how well he is doing with par or with his own performance yesterday or last week. A teacher has no such concrete feedback on how well he is doing in "getting across" to his students.

The *n* Ach men

But why do certain men behave like this? At one level the reply is simple: because they habitually spend their time thinking about doing things better. In fact, psychologists typically measure the strength of Motive A by taking samples of a man's spontaneous thoughts (such as making up a story about a picture they have been shown) and counting the frequency with which he mentions doing things better. The count is objective and can even be made these days with the help of a computer program for content analysis. It yields what is referred to technically as an individual's *n* Ach score (for "need for Achievement"). It is not difficult to understand why people who think constantly about "doing better" are more apt to do better at job-hunting, to set moderate, achievable goals for themselves, to dislike gambling (because they get no achievement satisfaction from success), and to prefer work situations where they can tell easily whether they are improving or not. But why some people and not others come to think this way is another question. The evidence suggests it is not because they are born that way, but because of special training they get in the home from parents who set moderately high achievement goals but who are warm, encouraging and nonauthoritarian in helping their children reach these goals.

Such detailed knowledge about one motive helps correct a lot of common sense ideas about human motivation. For example, much public policy (and much business policy) is based on the simpleminded notion that people will work harder "if they have to." As a first approximation, the idea isn't totally wrong, but it is only a half-truth. The majority of unemployed workers in Erie "had to" find work as much as those with higher *n* Ach, but they certainly didn't work as hard at it. Or again, it is frequently assumed that *any* strong motive will lead to doing things better. Wouldn't it be fair to say that most of the Erie workers were just "unmotivated"? But our detailed knowledge of various human motives shows that each one leads a person to behave in *different* ways. The contrast is not between being "motivated" or "unmotivated" but between being motivated toward A or toward B or C, etc.

A simple experiment makes the point nicely: subjects were told that they could choose as a working partner either a close friend or a stranger who was known to be an expert on the problem to be solved. Those with higher *n* Ach (more "need to achieve") chose the experts over their friends, whereas those with more *n* Aff (the "need to affiliate with others") chose friends over experts. The latter were not "unmotivated"; their desire to be with someone they liked was simply a stronger motive than their desire to excel at the task. Other such needs have been studied by psychologists. For instance, the need for Power is often confused with the need for Achievement because both may lead to "outstanding" activities. There is a distinct difference. People with a strong need for Power want to command attention, get recognition, and control others. They are more active in political life and tend to busy themselves primarily with controlling the channels of communication both up to the top and down to the people so that they are more "in charge." Those with high *n* Power are not as concerned with improving their work performance daily as those with high *n* Ach.

It follows, from what we have been able to learn, that not all "great achievers" score high in *n* Ach. Many generals, outstanding politicians, great research scientists do not, for instance, because their work requires other personality characteristics, other motives. A general or a politician must be more concerned with power relationships, a research scientist must be able to go for long periods without the immediate feedback the person with high *n* Ach requires, etc. On the other hand, business executives, particularly if they are in positions of real responsibility or if they are salesmen, tend to score high in *n* Ach. This is true even in a Communist country like Poland: apparently there, as well as in a private enterprise economy, a manager succeeds if he is concerned about improving all the time, setting moderate goals, keeping track of his or the company's performance, etc.

Motivation and half-truths

Since careful study has shown that common sense notions about motivation are at best half-truths, it also follows that you cannot trust what people tell you about their motives. After all, they often get their ideas about their own motives from common sense. Thus a general may say he is interested in achievement (because he has obviously achieved), or a businessman that he is interested only in making money (because he has made money), or one of the majority of unemployed in Erie that he desperately wants a job (because he knows he needs one); but a careful check of what each one thinks about and how he spends his time may show that each is concerned about quite different things. It requires special measurement techniques to identify the presence of *n* Ach and other such motives. Thus what people say and believe is not very closely related to these "hidden" motives which seem to affect a person's "style of life" more than his political, religious or social attitudes. Thus *n* Ach produces enterprising men among labor leaders or managers, Republicans or Democrats, Catholics or Protestants, capitalists or Communists.

Whenever people begin to think often in *n* Ach terms, things begin to move. Men with higher *n* Ach get more raises and are promoted more rapidly, because they keep actively seeking ways to do a better job. Companies with many such men grow faster. In one comparison of two firms in Mexico, it was discovered that all but one of the top executives of a fast growing firm had higher *n* Ach scores than the highest scoring executive in an equally large but slow-growing firm. Countries with many such rapidly growing firms tend to show above-average rates of economic growth. This appears to be the reason why correlations have regularly been found between the *n* Ach content in popular literature (such as popular songs or stories in children's textbooks) and subsequent rates of national economic growth. A nation which is thinking about doing better all the time (as shown in its popular literature) actually does do better economically speaking. Careful quantitative studies have shown this to be true in Ancient Greece, in Spain in the Middle Ages, in England from 1400–1800, as well as among contemporary nations, whether capitalist or Communist, developed or underdeveloped.

Contrast these two stories for example. Which one contains more *n* Ach? Which one reflects a state of mind which ought to lead to harder striving to improve the way things are?

Excerpt from story A (4th grade reader) "Don't Ever Owe A Man— The world is an illusion. Wife, children, horses and cows are all just ties of fate. They are ephemeral. Each after fulfilling his part in life disappears. So we should not clamour after riches which are not permanent. As long as we live it is wise not to have any attachments and just think of God. We have to spend our lives without trouble, for is it not time that there is an end to grievances? So it is better to live knowing the real state of affairs. Don't get entangled in the meshes of family life."

Excerpt from story B (4th grade reader) "How I Do Like to Learn—I was sent to an accelerated technical high school. I was so happy I cried. Learning is not very easy. In the beginning I couldn't understand what the teacher taught us. I always got a red cross mark on my papers. The boy sitting next to me was very enthusiastic and also an outstanding student. When he found I couldn't do the problems he offered to show me how he had done them. I could not copy his work. I must learn through my own reasoning. I gave his paper back and explained I had to do it myself. Sometimes I worked on a problem until midnight. If I couldn't finish, I started early in the morning. The red cross marks on my work were getting less common. I conquered my difficulties. My marks rose. I graduated and went on to college."

Most readers would agree, without any special knowledge of the *n* Ach coding system, that the second story shows more concern with improvement than the first, which comes from a contemporary reader used in Indian public schools. In fact the latter has a certain Horatio Alger quality that is reminiscent of our own McGuffey readers of several generations ago. It appears today in the textbooks of Communist China. It should not, therefore, come as a surprise if a nation like Communist China, obsessed as it is with improvement, tended in the long run to outproduce a nation like India, which appears to be more fatalistic.

The *n* Ach level is obviously important for statesmen to watch and in many instances to try to do something about, particularly if a nation's economy is lagging. Take Britain, for example. A generation ago (around 1925) it ranked fifth among 25 countries where children's readers were scored for *n* Ach—and its economy was doing well. By 1950 the *n* Ach level had dropped to 27th out of 39 countries—well below the world average— and today, its leaders are feeling the severe economic effects of this loss in the spirit of enterprise.

Economics and *n* Ach

If psychologists can detect *n* Ach levels in individuals or nations, particularly before their effects are widespread, can't the knowledge somehow be put to use to foster economic development? Obviously detection or diagnosis is not enough. What good is it to tell Britain (or India for that matter) that it needs more *n* Ach, a greater spirit of enterprise? In most such cases, informed observers of the local scene know very well that such a need exists, though they may be slower to discover it than the psychologist hovering over n Ach scores. What is needed is some method of developing n Ach in individuals or nations.

Since about 1960, psychologists in my research group at Harvard have been experimenting with techniques designed to accomplish this goal, chiefly among business executives whose work requires the action characteristics of people with high n Ach. Initially, we had real doubts as to whether we could succeed, partly because like most American psychologists we had been strongly influenced by the psychoanalytic view that basic motives are laid down in childhood and cannot really be changed later, and partly because many studies of intensive psychotherapy and counseling have shown minor if any long-term personality effects. On the other hand we were encouraged by the nonprofessionals: those enthusiasts like Dale Carnegie, the Communist ideologue or the Church missionary, who felt they could change adults and in fact seemed to be doing so. At any rate we ran some brief (7 to 10 days) "total push" training courses for businessmen, designed to increase their n Ach.

Four main goals

In broad outline the courses had four main goals: (1) They were designed to teach the participants how to think, talk and act like a person with high n Ach, based on our knowledge of such people gained through 17 years of research. For instance, men learned how to make up stories that would code high in n Ach (i.e., how to think in n Ach terms), how to set moderate goals for themselves in the ring toss game (and in life). (2) The courses stimulated the participants to set higher but carefully planned and realistic work goals for themselves over the next two years. Then we checked back with them every six months to see how well they were doing in terms of their own objectives. (3) The courses also utilized techniques for giving the participants knowledge about themselves. For instance, in playing the ring toss game, they could observe that they behaved differently from others—perhaps in refusing to adjust a goal downward after failure. This would then become a matter for group discussion and the man would have to explain what he had in mind in setting such unrealistic goals. Discussion could then lead on to what a man's ultimate goals in life were, how much he cared about actually improving performance v. making a good impression or having many friends. In this way the participants would be freer to realize their achievement goals without being blocked by old habits and attitudes. (4) The courses also usually created a group *esprit de corps* from learning about each other's hopes and fears, successes and failures, and from going through an emotional experience together, away from everyday life, in a retreat setting. This membership in a new group helps a man achieve his goals, partly because he knows he has their sympathy and support and partly because he knows they will be watching to see how well he does. The same effect has been noted in other therapy groups like Alcoholics Anonymous. We are not sure which of these course "inputs" is really absolutely essential—that remains a research question—but we were taking no chances at the outset in view of the general pessimism about such efforts, and we wanted to include any and all techniques that were thought to change people.

The courses have been given: to executives in a large American firm, and in several Mexican firms; to underachieving high school boys; and to businessmen in India from Bombay and from a small city—Kakinada in the state of Andhra Pradesh. In every instance save one (the Mexican case), it was possible to demonstrate statistically, some two years later, that the men who took the course had done better (made more money, got promoted faster, expanded their businesses faster) than comparable men who did not take the course or who took some other management course.

Consider the Kakinada results, for example. In the two years preceding the course 9 men, 18 percent of the 52 participants, had shown "unusual" enterprise in their businesses. In the 18 months following the course 25 of the men, in other words nearly 50 percent, were unusually active. And this was not due to a general upturn of business in India. Data from a control city, some forty-five miles away, show the same base rate of "unusually active" men as in Kakinada before the course—namely, about 20 percent. Something clearly happened in Kakinada: the owner of a small radio shop started a chemical plant; a banker was so successful in making commercial loans in an enterprising way that he was promoted to a much larger branch of his bank in Calcutta; the local political leader accomplished his goal (it was set in the course) to get the federal government to deepen the harbor and make it into an all-weather port; plans are far along for establishing a steel rolling mill, etc. All this took place without any substantial capital input from the outside. In fact, the only costs were for four 10-day courses plus some brief follow-up visits every six months. The men are raising their own capital and using their own resources for getting business and industry moving in a city that had been considered stagnant and unenterprising.

The promise of such a method of developing achievement motivation seems very great. It has obvious applications in helping underdeveloped countries, or "pockets of poverty" in the United States, to move faster economically. It has great potential for businesses that need to "turn around" and take a more enterprising approach toward their growth and development. It may even be helpful in developing more *n* Ach among low-income groups. For instance, data show that lower-class Negro Americans have a very low level of *n* Ach. This is not surprising. Society has systematically discouraged and blocked their achievement striving. But as the barriers to upward mobility are broken down, it will be necessary to help stimulate the motivation that will lead them to take advantage of new opportunities opening up.

Extreme reactions

But a word of caution: Whenever I speak of this research and its great potential, audience reaction tends to go to opposite extremes. Either people remain skeptical and argue that motives can't really be changed, that all we are doing is dressing Dale Carnegie up in fancy "psychologese," or they become converts and want instant course descriptions by return mail to solve their local motivational problems. Either response is unjustified. What I have described here in a few pages has taken 20 years of patient research effort, and hundreds of thousands of dollars in basic research costs. What remains to be done will involve even larger sums and more time for development to turn a promising idea into something of wide practical utility.

Encouragement needed

To take only one example, we have not yet learned how to develop n Ach really well among low-income groups. In our first effort—a summer course for bright underachieving 14-year-olds—we found that boys from the middle class improved steadily in grades in school over a two-year period, but boys from the lower class showed an improvement after the first year followed by a drop back to their beginning low grade average. (See the graph below.) Why? We speculated that it was because they moved back into an environment in which neither parents nor friends encouraged achievement or

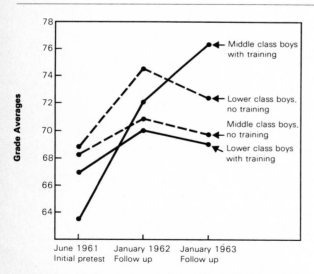

In a Harvard study, a group of underachieving 14-year-olds was given a six-week course designed to help them do better in school. Some of the boys were also given training in achievement motivation, or n Ach (solid lines). As graph reveals, the only boys who continued to improve after a two-year period were the middle-class boys with the special n Ach training. Psychologists suspect the lower-class boys dropped back, even with n Ach training, because they returned to an environment in which neither parents nor friends encouraged achievement.

upward mobility. In other words, it isn't enough to change a man's motivation if the environment in which he lives doesn't support at least to some degree his new efforts. Negroes striving to rise out of the ghetto frequently confront this problem: they are often faced by skepticism at home and suspicion on the job, so that even if their *n* Ach is raised, it can be lowered again by the heavy odds against their success. We must learn not only to raise *n* Ach but also to find methods of instructing people in how to manage it, to create a favorable environment in which it can flourish.

Many of these training techniques are now only in the pilot testing stage. It will take time and money to perfect them, but society should be willing to invest heavily in them in view of their tremendous potential for contributing to human betterment.

40 The motivation-hygiene concept and problems of manpower
Frederick Herzberg

I wish to preface my remarks in this article with a disclaimer of competence in the field of manpower. My research and contemplative efforts are more directly related to an equally large and protean problem, that of industrial mental health. From my investigations in the latter area, I have formulated a general theory of mental health, and a specific application to job attitudes that may have bearing on certain aspects of "manpower" questions.

I apologize to the reader who already has familiarity with the Motivation-Hygiene theory of job attitudes for occupying the next few pages with a repetition of data and comments which have appeared a number of times elsewhere. I must lay the groundwork for my thoughts on "manpower" by first presenting my theory of job attitudes, without which I have very little excuse for accepting the invitation to contribute to this issue.

The Motivation-Hygiene theory of job attitudes began with a depth interview study of over 200 engineers and accountants representing Pittsburgh industry. (10) These interviews probed sequences of events in the work lives of the respondents to determine the factors that were involved in their feeling exceptionally happy and conversely exceptionally unhappy with their jobs. From a review and an analysis of previous publications in the general area of job attitudes, a two-factor hypothesis was formulated to guide the original investigation. This hypothesis suggested that the factors involved in producing job satisfaction were separate and distinct from the

Source: From *Personnel Administration* (January–February 1964), pp. 3–7. Reprinted by permission of the International Personnel Management Association, 1313 East 60th Street, Chicago, Illinois 60637.

factors that led to job dissatisfaction. Since separate factors needed to be considered depending on whether job satisfaction or job dissatisfaction was involved, it followed that these two feelings were not the obverse of each other. The opposite of job satisfaction would not be job dissatisfaction, but rather *no* job satisfaction; and similarly the opposite of job dissatisfaction is *no* job dissatisfaction—not job satisfaction. The statement of the concept is awkward and may appear at first to be a semantic ruse, but there is more than a play with words when it comes to understanding the behavior of people on jobs. The fact that job satisfaction is made up of two unipolar traits is not a unique occurrence. The difficulty of establishing a zero point in psychology with the procedural necessity of using instead a bench mark (mean of a population) from which to start our measurement, has led to the conception that psychological traits are bipolar. Empirical investigations, however, have cast some shadows on the assumptions of bipolarity; one timely example is a study of conformity and nonconformity, where they were shown not to be opposites, but rather two separate unipolar traits. (3)

Methodology

Before proceeding to the major results of the original study, three comments on methodology are in order. The investigation of attitudes is plagued with many problems, least of which is the measurement phase; although, it is measurement to which psychologists have hitched their scientific integrity. First of all, if I am to assess a person's feeling about something, how do I know he has a feeling? Too often we rely on his say so, even though opinion polling is replete with instances in which respondents gladly respond with all shades of feeling when in reality they have never thought of the issue and are devoid of any practical affect. They respond to respond and we become deceived into believing that they are revealing feelings or attitudes. Secondly, assuming the respondent does have genuine feelings regarding the subject under investigation, are his answers indicative of his feelings; or are they rationalizations, displacements from other factors which are for many reasons less easy to express, coin of the realm expressions for his particular job classification, etc.? Those who have had experience with job morale surveys recognize these ghosts and unfortunately some have contributed to the haunting of companies. Thirdly, how do you equate feelings? If two persons state that they are happy with their jobs, how do you know they are equally happy? We can develop scales, but in truth we are only satisfying our penchant for rules which do not get inside the experience and measure the phenomenological reality, but rather have significance wholly within our devices.

To meet these objections, the methodology of the original study was formulated. It included a study of changes in job attitudes in the hope that if attitudes change there is more likelihood that an attitude exists. Further, it focused on experiences in the lives of the respondents which contained substantive data that could be analyzed apart from the interpretations of the respondents. Finally, rather than attempt to measure degree of feeling, it focused on peak experiences and contrasted negative peaks with positive peaks; without being concerned with the quality of the peaks. Briefly, we asked our respondents to describe periods in their lives when they were exceedingly happy and unhappy with their jobs. Each respondent gave as many "sequences of events" as he could which met certain criteria including a marked change in feeling, a beginning and an end, and contained some substantive description other than feelings and interpretations.

A rational analysis of the "sequences of events" led to the results shown in the accompanying chart. For a more complete description of the methodology as well as the results, see *The Motivation to Work.* (10)

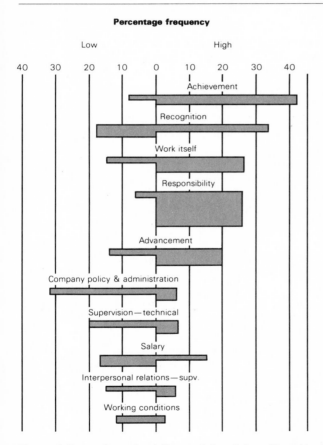

Figure 1 Comparison of satisfiers and dissatisfiers. The wider the box the longer the duration of the attitude.

The proposed hypothesis appears verified. The factors on the right that led to satisfaction (achievement, recognition for achievement, intrinsic interest in the work, responsibility, and advancement) are mostly unipolar; that is, they contribute very little to job dissatisfaction. Conversely, the dissatisfiers (company policy and administrative practices, supervision, interpersonal relationships, working conditions, and salary) contribute very little to job satisfaction.

Satisfiers and dissatisfiers

What is the explanation for such results? Do the two sets of factors have two separate themes? It appears so, for the factors on the right all seem to describe man's relationship to what he does, to his job content, achievement on the task, recognition for task achievement, the nature of the task, responsibility for a task, and professional advancement or growth in task capability.

What is the central theme for the dissatisfiers? Restating the factors as the kind of administration and supervision received in doing the job, the nature of interpersonal relationships and working conditions that surround the job, and the amount of salary that accrues to the individual for doing his job, suggest the distinction with the nature of the task, responsibility for a task, and professional what he does, the "dissatisfier" factors describe his relationship to the context or environment in which he does his job. One cluster of factors relates to what the person does and the other to the situation in which he does it.

As usual with any new theory, a new jargon is invented, perhaps to add some fictitious uniqueness to the theory, although I prefer to think that these new terms better convey the meaning of the theory. Because the factors on the left serve primarily as preventatives, that is to prevent job dissatisfaction, and because they also deal with the environment, I have named these factors "the hygiene" factors in a poor analogy with the way the term is used in preventive medicine. The factors on the right I call the "motivators" because other results indicate they are necessary for improvement in performance beyond that pseudo-improvement which in substance amounts to coming up to a "fair day's work."

In these terms we can recapitulate the major findings of the original study by stating that it is the hygiene factors that affect job dissatisfaction and the motivator factors that affect job satisfaction; with the further understanding that there are two parallel continua of satisfactions. I have only reported on the first study because of the required brevity of this paper. Corroboration can be found in the studies with the following references: (1), (2), (4), (13), (14), (15), (16).

Significance of hygiene factors

Why? We next explore the reasons given by our respondents for the differential effects that the two sets of factors have on job attitudes. In brief, the hygiene factors meet man's needs to avoid unpleasantness. "I don't like to be treated this way; I don't want to suffer the deprivation of low salary; bad interpersonal relationships make me uncomfortable." In other words they want their lives to be hygienically clean. The motivator factors on the other hand make people happy with their jobs because they serve man's basic and human need for psychological growth; a need to become more competent. A fuller commentary on these two separate needs of man are contained in the following publications: (5), (6), (7), (8), (10), (11), (12).

This theory opens wide the door for reinterpretations of industrial relations phenomena. To begin with, job attitudes must be viewed twice; what does the employee seek—what makes him happy; and then a separate question not deducible from the first, what does he wish to avoid—what makes him unhappy? Industrial relations that stress sanitation as their modus operandi can only serve to prevent dissatisfactions and the resultant personnel problems. Of course such attention to hygienic needs is important, for without it any organization, as we well know, will reap the consequences of unhappy personnel. The error of course lies in assuming that prevention will unleash positive health and the returns of increased productivity, lowered absenteeism, turnover, and all the other indices of manpower efficiency. One additional deduction from the theory which is supported by empirical findings should be added. The effect of improved hygiene lasts for only a short time. In fact man's avoidance needs are recurrent and of an infinite variety, and as such we will find that demands for improved salary, working conditions, interpersonal relations and so on will continue to occupy the personnel administrator without any hope of escaping the "what have you done for me lately."

There is nothing wrong with providing the maximum of hygienic benefits to the employee, as much as the society can afford (which appears to be more than the historic cries of anguish which have always accompanied the amelioration of work hygiene would indicate). What is wrong is the summation of human needs in totally hygienic terms. The consequences of this one-sided view of man's nature has led to untoward consequences of much greater import than the direct monetary costs of these programs to our organizations. The more pertinent effect has been on the psychological premises of industrial relations and its effect in turn on the self concepts of the employees.

Since hygiene is the apparent key to industrial success, the motivators are given but lip service, and attention to the challenge and meaningfulness of jobs is satisfied via the pious espousal of cultural noises. We are today familiar with the industrial engineering principle of leveling jobs down to the lowest common talent as it applies to the rank and file assembly operation. The same denigration of human talent at the managerial and professional level, the sacrificing of human performance and potentiality to insure that no one will fail or make for unpleasantness, is obscured by referring to the rank and file when acknowledging the lack of meaning in work. At these higher levels, the effects of the assembly line are accomplished by the overuse of rules and regulations, rational organizational principles and the insidious use of interpersonal *skills*. We find that more and more training and education is required to do less and less; more and more effort on surround and less and less substance on accomplishment. Pride in work, in successful accomplishment, in maximizing one's talent is becoming socially gauche or more tragically a victim of progress. We cry for nurturance of human talent and find that we have no place for most of it; human talent on the job has become as much of a surplus commodity as our wheat. And where are our personnel managers? Their problem is hygiene, not the creative function of maximizing human resources.

Significance of motivators

The Protestant Ethic is being replaced by an Avoidance Ethic in our world of work, and those in charge of personnel utilization have almost totally directed their efforts to maintenance procedures. This is seen from the very beginning of employment in the practice of college recruitment on the campus, where each company sets up its own enticing tent, and selection is transformed into public relations, luring of candidates, and in fact the incredible situation of the candidate interviewing the interviewer.

Job attitude data suggest that after the glow of the initial year on the job, job satisfaction plummets to its lowest level in the work life of individuals. (9) From a lifetime of diverse learning, successive accomplishment through the various academic stages, and periodic reinforcement of efforts, the entrant to our modern companies finds, that rather than work providing an expanding psychological existence, the opposite occurs; and successive amputations of his self-conceptions, aspirations, learning, and talent are the consequence of earning a living. Of course as the needs and values of our industrial enterprises have become the template for all aspects of our lives, the university is preparing many young people by performing the amputations early, and they enter already primed for work as only a means of hygienic improvement; or for those still capable of enjoying the exercise of their human talents, as means of affording off the job satisfactions. If the number of management development programs is a valid sign, the educational system has done its job too well.

A reaction to retirement policies is beginning to set in as the personal consequences of organizational definitions of human obsolescence are being told. Prior to retirement, however, are 30 to 40 years of partial retirement and partial commitment to work for the too many who have not "succeeded" in terms of organizational advancement. From the first orientation to the farewell party, the history of work careers is a history of human waste. What a paradox we face. There is a shortage of talent in the country at a time when our problems are defined in planetary dimensions and to meet these circumstances we have evolved a system and a philosophy to use and motivate our talent that serves to decrease further this precious resource.

What alternatives are there? A spate of new research and literature is becoming available that is reacting to personnel and managerial psychology that has too long tried to emulate the vast and short term goals of the military. The new literature, while encompassing diverse problems, exhortations, solutions and conceptions, seems to have the common theme of emphasizing the motivator needs of man and the necessity for the personnel function of industry to pause in its search for the Holy Grail of instruments, to become creative in finding ways to meet the motivator needs. Man is distinguished from all other animals in that he alone is a determiner. How strange that when it comes to the satisfactions of his special psychological growth needs he finds himself a victim of outside determinisms and helpless in affecting the way he is utilized in work. The short term economic "necessities" cannot justify the larger economic loss and the denial of human satisfaction that the restriction of human talent inevitably costs. I might add that many of the barriers to fuller utilization of manpower that are "justified" by economic reasons are, in reality, devices of fearful and inadequate managers who are not prepared to meet the challenge of managing adults. The philosophy of management which prizes such men is changeable. We need a goal of industry which includes the expansion of manpower utilization in addition to the expansion of productivity and profit. The acceptance of such a goal as basic will lead to the means for its implementation. Personnel cannot remain the one management function that only establishes objectives for which techniques and procedures are available.

References

1 Frantz, R. *Motivation Factors in Rehabilitation.* Unpublished doctoral dissertation, Western Reserve University Library, Cleveland, 1961.
2 Gibson, J. *Sources of Job Satisfaction and Job Dissatisfaction.* Unpublished doctoral dissertation, Western Reserve University Library, Cleveland, 1961.
3 Guilford, J. P., Christensen, P. R., Bond, N. and Sutton, M. "A Factor Analysis Study of Human Interests." *Res. Bull.,* 53–11, Human Resources Research Center, San Antonio, 1953.
4 Hamlin, R. and Nemo, R. "Self-actualization in Choice Scores of Improved Schizophrenics." *J. Clin. Psychol.,* 18, 1962.
5 Herzberg, F. "New Approaches in Management Organization and Job Design." *Industrial Med. and Surgery,* November 1962.
6 Herzberg, F. "Basic Needs and Satisfactions of Individuals." *Industrial Relations Monograph,* No. 21, Industrial Relations Counselors, Inc., New York, 1962.
7 Herzberg, F. "Comment on the Meaning of Work. Proceedings of Symposium of the Worker in the New Industrial Environment." *Industrial Med. and Surgery,* June 1963.
8 Herzberg, F. "The Meaning of Work to the Individual." In *Basic Psychology and Physiology of Work,* edited by H. Hellerstein, C. C. Thomas Press, Ft. Lauderdale.

9 Herzberg, F. et al. *Job Attitudes: Research and Opinion.* Psychological Service of Pittsburgh, 1957.

10 Herzberg, F., Mausner, B., and Snyderman, B. *The Motivation to Work.* New York: John Wiley and Sons, 1959.

11 Herzberg, F., and Hamlin, R. "A Motivation-Hygiene Concept of Mental Health." *Mental Hygiene,* July 1961.

12 Herzberg, F., and Hamlin, R. "Motivation-Hygiene Concept and Psychotherapy." *Mental Hygiene,* July 1961.

13 Lodahl, T. *Patterns of Job Attitudes in Two Assembly Technologies.* Graduate School of Business and Public Administration, Cornell University, Ithaca, New York, 1963.

14 Saleh, S. *Attitude Change and Its Effect on the Pre-Retirement Period.* Unpublished doctoral dissertation, Western Reserve University Library, Cleveland, 1962.

15 Schwarz, P. *Attitudes of Middle Management Personnel.* Pittsburgh: American Institute for Research, 1961.

16 Schwartz, M., Jenusaitis, E. and Stark, H. "Motivation Factors Among Supervisors in the Utility Industry. *Personnel Psychology,* 16, 1963.

41 Facts and fictions about working women explored; several stereotypes prove false in national study
Institute for Social Research

The American working woman does not fit many of the stereotypes that have been created for her, a study derived from the ISR Survey of Working Conditions has shown.

Several popular notions about women that were proved untrue in the study are that women work only for "pin money," that they are more often satisfied than men with intellectually undemanding jobs, or that they are less concerned that a job help them realize their full potential.

These and other findings from the ISR investigation of the job-related attitudes and beliefs of a nationwide sample of 539 working women and 993 working men are presented in a paper authored by Joan E. Crowley, Teresa E. Levitin and Robert P. Quinn titled "Facts and Fictions About the American Working Woman."

Source: Reprinted with permission from *ISR Newsletter* (Autumn 1972), pp. 4–5. © 1972 Institute for Social Research, University of Michigan, Ann Arbor.

Noticeable differences

The study is based on information gathered in late 1969 from a representative group of American workers who were 16 years old or older and working at least 20 hours a week.

While many stereotypes proved false, men and women did show several noticeable differences in their attitudes toward their jobs. For example, the study found that women were much less inclined than men to say that they would continue to work if they could be freed from the economic necessity to do so. Women also showed more concern for their physical work surroundings, with the hours of work, and with travel to and from work than did men, and they were less likely to say that taking the initiative on a job was important to them.

Much of the difference in attitudes and beliefs, the authors conclude, can be attributed to early childhood socialization which prepares males and females to fulfill different work and family roles as adults. But additional social forces which act on men and women workers later in life—such as educational and professional training or the demands of the job itself—have some influence on job-related attitudes, they say.

Straw women

The researchers tested their study results against eight "straw women" which embodied many common stereotypes:

1 *American women work just for pin money*   "According to this stereotype of working women, women are always supported economically by men, usually their husbands or fathers," the authors say. "The data indicated that about two out of every five working women could *not* be regarded as economically dependent on a male wage earner, be he either a husband or a father. A third of the women in the sample were the sole wage earners in their households. An additional 8 percent were not the sole wage earners but nevertheless reported that they were the *major* wage earners, providing the bulk of their families' incomes."

2 *Women should not work if they did not absolutely have to for economic reasons*   "While 74 percent of the men indicated that they would continue to work under such circumstances, only 57 percent of the women indicated that they would do so," the researchers report. Most of this observed sex difference was, however, produced by the small number of married women who would continue to work were work not an economic necessity for them.

3 *Women are more satisfied than men with intellectually undemanding jobs*   The report notes that "this idea is at times invoked in order to account for the high proportion of women in routine, repetitive, and otherwise uninspiring work." Women do hold down a high proportion of the intellectually

undemanding jobs; the study found that 55 percent of the men said they had intellectually demanding jobs, compared to 37 percent of the women. But when men and women in demanding jobs were compared, both sexes reported the same amount of satisfaction, as they did when those in similarly undemanding jobs were compared.

4 *Women are less concerned than men with getting ahead on their jobs* The study found "no difference between men and women in terms of the importance they attached to having a job where the chances for promotion are good." But when asked of their present job, "Approximately when would you *like* to take on a job at a higher level?" significantly more women than men said that they never wanted to be promoted.

The study discovered, however, that women's attitudes toward promotion were strongly tied to their *expectation* of being promoted. "That women in general were less interested than men with promotions on their present job was mainly a result of their resignation to their expectations that they were *not* going to be promoted," the researchers conclude.

5 *Women prefer not to take initiative on the job* "There was a significant sex difference between men and women in their desires to be given freedom to decide how they did their jobs, with men attaching greater importance to such freedom," the researchers conclude. "Somewhat smaller was the sex difference in terms of workers' desires to have their responsibilities clearly defined, with men being less concerned with such clear role definitions."

These sex differences are explained by the researchers as being, in part, the result of childhood socialization practices which "discourage the training of girls to work on their own" and, in part, the smaller proportion of women with positions that require them to exercise independent behavior or that make other people dependent on them. To support the latter explanation they note that "the present study indicated that while 59 percent of the men said that their present jobs gave them a lot of freedom to decide how they did their work, significantly fewer women, 44 percent, reported having such freedom."

6 *Women are more concerned than men with the hygienic aspects of their jobs* "The present study provided some support for this assertion when the desire for a "hygienic" job was measured by workers' importance ratings of three job facets: good hours, pleasant physical surroundings, and convenient travel to and from work. Women attached significantly more importance to each of these facets than did men."

7 *Women are more concerned than men with the socio-emotional aspects of their jobs* Four questions concerning workers' emotional ties with co-workers and supervisors revealed only one basic sex difference—more women than men said that it was very important to them that their co-workers be friendly and helpful. The researchers suggested, however, that the source of this sex difference may really have been the fact that women were over-represented in jobs demanding interpersonal relations. "Without friendly and helpful co-workers, their job performance might be impaired," they explain.

8 *Women are less concerned than men with obtaining self-actualizing work*
"This assertion, like some of the other straw women, suggests that
women are less involved with their work than are men, viewing their work
as 'just a job' without any meaningful, self-relevant implications," the authors say. After analyzing workers' ratings of three aspects of their jobs: (1)
having an opportunity to develop one's special abilities through work, (2)
doing interesting work, and (3) having a chance to do the things that one
does best, they concluded that women are just as concerned as men with
self-actualization on the job.

42 Beyond Theory Y
John J. Morse and Jay W. Lorsch

During the past 30 years, managers have been bombarded with two competing approaches to the problems of human administration and organization.
The first, usually called the classical school of organization, emphasizes the
need for well-established lines of authority, clearly defined jobs, and authority equal to responsibility. The second, often called the participative approach, focuses on the desirability of involving organization members in decision making so that they will be more highly motivated.

Douglas McGregor, through his well-known "Theory X and Theory Y,"
drew a distinction between the assumptions about human motivation which
underlie these two approaches, to this effect:

- Theory X assumes that people dislike work and must be coerced, controlled,
  and directed toward organizational goals. Furthermore, most people prefer to
  be treated this way, so they can avoid responsibility.
- Theory Y—the integration of goals—emphasizes the average person's intrinsic interest in his work, his desire to be self-directing and to seek responsibility, and his capacity to be creative in solving business problems.

It is McGregor's conclusion, of course, that the latter approach to organization is the more desirable one for managers to follow.[1]

McGregor's position causes confusion for the managers who try to
choose between these two conflicting approaches. The classical organizational approach that McGregor associated with Theory X does work well in

Source: Reprinted with permission from *Harvard Business Review* (May–June 1970,
pp. 61–68. © 1970 by the President and Fellows of Harvard College; all rights reserved.
[1] Douglas McGregor, *The Human Side of Enterprise* (New York: McGraw-Hill Book
Company, Inc., 1960), pp. 34–35 and pp. 47–48.

some situations, although, as McGregor himself pointed out, there are also some situations where it does not work effectively. At the same time, the approach based on Theory Y, while it has produced good results in some situations, does not always do so. That is, each approach is effective in some cases but not in others. Why is this? How can managers resolve the confusion?

A new approach

Recent work by a number of students of management and organization may help to answer such questions.[2] These studies indicate that there is not one best organizational approach; rather, the best approach depends on the nature of the work to be done. Enterprises with highly predictable tasks perform better with organizations characterized by the highly formalized procedures and management hierarchies of the classical approach. With highly uncertain tasks that require more extensive problem solving, on the other hand, organizations that are less formalized and emphasize self-control and member participation in decision making are more effective. In essence, according to these newer studies, managers must design and develop organizations so that the organizational characteristics *fit* the nature of the task to be done.

While the conclusions of this newer approach will make sense to most experienced managers and can alleviate much of the confusion about which approach to choose, there are still two important questions unanswered:

1 How does the more formalized and controlling organization affect the motivation of organization members? (McGregor's most telling criticism of the classical approach was that it did not unleash the potential in an enterprise's human resources.)
2 Equally important, does a less formalized organization always provide a high level of motivation for its members? (This is the implication many managers have drawn from McGregor's work.)

We have recently been involved in a study that provides surprising answers to these questions and, when taken together with other recent work, suggests a new set of basic assumptions which move beyond Theory Y into what we call "Contingency Theory: the fit between task, organization, and people." These theoretical assumptions emphasize that the appropriate pattern of organization is *contingent* on the nature of the work to be done and on the particular needs of the people involved. We should emphasize that we have labeled these assumptions as a step beyond Theory Y because of

[2] See for example Paul R. Lawrence and Jay W. Lorsch, *Organization and Environment* (Boston, Harvard Business School, Division of Research, 1967); Joan Woodward, *Industrial Organization: Theory and Practice* (New York, Oxford University Press, Inc., 1965); Tom Burns and G. M. Stalker, *The Management of Innovation* (London, Tavistock Publications, 1961); Harold J. Leavitt, "Unhuman Organizations," HBR July–August 1962, p. 90.

McGregor's own recognition that the Theory Y assumptions would probably be supplanted by new knowledge within a short time.[3]

The study design

Our study was conducted in four organizational units. Two of these performed the relatively certain task of manufacturing standardized containers on high-speed, automated production lines. The other two performed the relatively uncertain work of research and development in communications technology. Each pair of units performing the same kind of task were in the same large company, and each pair had previously been evaluated by that company's management as containing one highly effective unit and a less effective one. The study design is summarized in Exhibit I.

Exhibit I Study design in "fit" of organizational characteristics

Characteristics	Company I (predictable manufacturing task)	Company II (unpredictable R&D task)
Effective performer	Akron containers plant	Stockton research lab
Less effective performer	Hartford containers plant	Carmel research lab

The objective was to explore more fully how the fit between organization and task was related to successful performance. That is, does a good fit between organizational characteristics and task requirements increase the motivation of individuals and hence produce more effective individual and organizational performance?

An especially useful approach to answering this question is to recognize that an individual has a strong need to master the world around him, including the task that he faces as a member of a work organization.[4] The accumulated feelings of satisfaction that come from successfully mastering one's environment can be called a "sense of competence." We saw this sense of competence in performing a particular task as helpful in understanding how a fit between task and organizational characteristics could motivate people toward successful performance.

Organizational dimensions

Because the four study sites had already been evaluated by the respective corporate managers as high and low performers of tasks, we expected that such differences in performance would be a preliminary clue to differences in the "fit" of the organizational characteristics to the job to be done. But,

[3] McGregor, op cit., p. 245.
[4] See Robert W. White, "Ego and Reality in Psychoanalytic Theory," *Psychological Issues,* Vol. III, No. 3 (New York, International Universities Press, 1963).

first, we had to define what kinds of organizational characteristics would determine how appropriate the organization was to the particular task.

We grouped these organizational characteristics into two sets of factors:

1 Formal characteristics, which could be used to judge the fit between the kind of task being worked on and the formal practices of the organization.
2 Climate characteristics, or the subjective perceptions and orientations that had developed among the individuals about their organizational setting. (These too must fit the task to be performed if the organization is to be effective.)

We measured these attributes through questionnaires and interviews with about 40 managers in each unit to determine the appropriateness of the organization to the kind of task being performed. We also measured the feelings of competence of the people in the organizations so that we could link the appropriateness of the organizational attributes with a sense of competence.

Major findings

The principal findings of the survey are best highlighted by contrasting the highly successful Akron plant and the high-performing Stockton laboratory. Because each performed very different tasks (the former a relatively certain manufacturing task and the latter a relatively uncertain research task), we expected, as brought out earlier, that there would have to be major differences between them in organizational characteristics if they were to perform effectively. And this is what we did find. But we also found that each of these effective units had a better fit with its particular task than did its less effective counterpart.

While our major purpose in this article is to explore how the fit between task and organizational characteristics is related to motivation, we first want to explore more fully the organizational characteristics of these units, so the reader will better understand what we mean by a fit between task and organization and how it can lead to more effective behavior. To do this, we shall place the major emphasis on the contrast between the high-performing units (the Akron plant and Stockton laboratory), but we shall also compare each of these with its less effective mate (the Hartford plant and Carmel laboratory respectively).

Formal characteristiscs

Beginning with differences in formal characteristics, we found that both the Akron and Stockton organizations fit their respective tasks much better than did their less successful counterparts. In the predictable manufacturing task environment, Akron had a pattern of formal relationships and duties that was highly structured and precisely defined. Stockton, with its unpredictable research task, had a low degree of structure and much less precision of definition (see Exhibit II).

Exhibit II Differences in formal characteristics in high-performing organizations

Characteristics	Akron	Stockton
1. Pattern of formal relationships and duties as signified by organization charts and job manuals	Highly structured, precisely defined	Low degree of structure, less well defined
2. Pattern of formal rules, procedures, control, and measurement systems	Pervasive, specific, uniform, comprehensive	Minimal, loose, flexible
3. Time dimensions incorporated in formal practices	Short-term	Long-term
4. Goal dimensions incorporated in formal practices	Manufacturing	Scientific

Akron's pattern of formal rules, procedures, and control systems was so specific and comprehensive that it prompted one manager to remark: "We've got rules here for everything from how much powder to use in cleaning the toilet bowls to how to cart a dead body out of the plant." In contrast, Stockton's formal rules were so minimal, loose, and flexible that one scientist, when asked whether he felt the rules ought to be tightened, said: "If a man puts a nut on a screw all day long, you may need more rules and a job definition for him. But we're not novices here. We're professionals and not the kind who need close supervision. People around here *do* produce, and produce under relaxed conditions. Why tamper with success?"

These differences in formal organizational characteristics were well suited to the differences in tasks of the two organizations. Thus:

• Akron's highly structured formal practices fit its predictable task because behavior had to be rigidly defined and controlled around the automated, high-speed production line. There was really only one way to accomplish the plant's very routine and programmable job; managers defined it precisely and insisted (through the plant's formal practices) that each man do what was expected of him.

On the other hand, Stockton's highly unstructured formal practices made just as much sense because the required activities in the laboratory simply could not be rigidly defined in advance. With such an unpredictable, fast-changing task as communications technology research, there were numerous approaches to getting the job done well. As a consequence, Stockton managers used a less structured pattern of formal practices that left the scientists in the lab free to respond to the changing task situation.

• Akron's formal practices were very much geared to *short-term* and *manufacturing* concerns as its task demanded. For example, formal production reports and operating review sessions were daily occurrences, consistent with the fact that the through-put time for their products was typically only a few hours.

By contrast, Stockton's formal practices were geared to *long-term* and *scientific* concerns, as its task demanded. Formal reports and reviews were made only quarterly, reflecting the fact that research often does not come to fruition for three to five years.

At the two less effective sites (i.e., the Hartford plant and the Carmel laboratory), the formal organizational characteristics did not fit their respective tasks nearly as well. For example, Hartford's formal practices were much less structured and controlling than were Akron's, while Carmel's were more restraining and restricting than were Stockton's. A scientist in Carmel commented: "There's something here that keeps you from being scientific. It's hard to put your finger on, but I guess I'd call it 'Mickey Mouse.' There are rules and things here that get in your way regarding doing your job as a researcher."

Climate characteristics

As with formal practices, the climate in both high-performing Akron and Stockton suited the respective tasks much better than did the climates at the less successful Hartford and Carmel sites.

Perception of structure

The people in the Akron plant perceived a great deal of structure, with their behavior tightly controlled and defined. One manager in the plant said: "We can't let the lines run unattended. We lose money whenever they do. So we make sure each man knows his job, knows when he can take a break, knows how to handle a change in shifts, etc. It's all spelled out clearly for him the day he comes to work here." In contrast, the scientists in the Stockton laboratory perceived very little structure, with their behavior only minimally controlled. Such perceptions encouraged the individualistic and creative behavior that the uncertain, rapidly changing research task needed. Scientists in the less successful Carmel laboratory perceived much more structure in their organization and voiced the feeling that this was "getting in their way" and making it difficult to do effective research.

Distribution of influence

The Akron plant and the Stockton laboratory also differed substantially in how influence was distributed and on the character of superior-subordinate and colleague relations. Akron personnel felt that they had much less influence over decisions in their plant than Stockton's scientists did in their laboratory. The task at Akron had already been clearly defined and that definition had, in a sense, been incorporated into the automated production flow itself. Therefore, there was less need for individuals to have a say in decisions concerning the work process.

Moreover, in Akron, influence was perceived to be concentrated in the upper levels of the formal structure (a hierarchical or "top-heavy" distribution), while in Stockton influence was perceived to be more evenly spread out among more levels of the formal structure (an egalitarian distribution).

Akron's members perceived themselves to have a low degree of freedom vis-à-vis superiors both in choosing the jobs they work on and in handling these jobs on their own. They also described the type of supervision in the plant as being relatively directive. Stockton's scientists, on the other hand, felt that they had a great deal of freedom vis-à-vis their superiors both in choosing the tasks and projects, and in handling them in the way that they wanted to. They described supervision in the laboratory as being very participatory.

It is interesting to note that the less successful Carmel laboratory had more of its decisions made at the top. Because of this, there was a definite feeling by the scientists that their particular expertise was not being effectively used in choosing projects.

Relations with others

The people at Akron perceived a great deal of similarity among themselves in background, prior work experiences, and approaches for tackling job-related problems. They also perceived the degree of coordination of effort among colleagues to be very high. Because Akron's task was so precisely defined and the behavior of its members so rigidly controlled around the automated lines, it is easy to see that this pattern also made sense.

By contrast, Stockton's scientists perceived not only a great many differences among themselves, especially in education and background, but also that the coordination of effort among colleagues was relatively low. This was appropriate for a laboratory in which a great variety of disciplines and skills were present and individual projects were important to solve technological problems.

Time orientation

As we would expect, Akron's individuals were highly oriented toward a relatively short time span and manufacturing goals. They responded to quick feedback concerning the quality and service that the plant was providing. This was essential, given the nature of their task.

Stockton's researchers were highly oriented toward a longer time span and scientific goals. These orientations meant that they were willing to wait for long-term feedback from a research project that might take years to complete. A scientist in Stockton said: "We're not the kind of people here who need a pat on the back every day. We can wait for months if necessary before we get feedback from colleagues and the profession. I've been working on one project now for three months and I'm still not sure where it's going to take me. I can live with that, though." This is precisely the kind of behavior and attitude that spells success on this kind of task.

Managerial style

Finally, the individuals in both Akron and Stockton perceived their chief executive to have a "managerial style" that expressed more of a concern for the task than for people or relationships, but this seemed to fit both tasks.

In Akron, the technology of the task was so dominant that top managerial behavior which was not focused primarily on the task might have reduced the effectiveness of performance. On the other hand, although Stockton's research task called for more individualistic problem-solving behavior, that sort of behavior could have become segmented and uncoordinated, unless the top executive in the lab focused the group's attention on the overall research task. Given the individualistic bent of the scientists, this was an important force in achieving unity of effort. All these differences in climate characteristics in the two high performers are summarized in Exhibit III.

Exhibit III Differences in "climate" characteristics in high-performing organizations

Characteristics	Akron	Stockton
1. Structural orientation	Perceptions of tightly controlled behavior and a high degree of structure	Perceptions of a low degree of structure
2. Distribution of influence	Perceptions of low total influence, concentrated at upper levels in the organization	Perceptions of high total influence, more evenly spread out among all levels
3. Character of superior-subordinate relations	Low freedom vis-à-vis superiors to choose and handle jobs, directive type of supervision	High freedom vis-à-vis superiors to choose and handle projects, participatory type of supervision
4. Character of colleague relations	Perceptions of many similarities among colleagues, high degree of coordination of colleague effort	Perceptions of many differences among colleagues, relatively low degree of coordination of colleague effort
5. Time orientation	Short-term	Long-term
6. Goal orientation	Manufacturing	Scientific
7. Top executive's "managerial style"	More concerned with task than people	More concerned with task than people

As with formal attributes, the less effective Hartford and Carmel sites had organization climates that showed a perceptibly lower degree of fit with their respective tasks. For example, the Hartford plant had an egalitarian distribution of influence, perceptions of a low degree of structure, and a more participatory type of supervision. The Carmel laboratory had a somewhat top-heavy distribution of influence, perceptions of high structure, and a more directive type of supervision.

Competence motivation

Because of the difference in organizational characteristics at Akron and Stockton, the two sites were strikingly different places in which to work. But these organizations had two very important things in common. First, each organization fit very well the requirements of its task. Second, although the behavior in the two organizations was different, the result in both cases was effective task performance.

Since, as we indicated earlier, our primary concern in this study was to link the fit between organization and task with individual motivation to perform effectively, we devised a two-part test to measure the sense of competence motivation of the individuals at both sites: Thus:

The *first* part asked a participant to write creative and imaginative stories in response to six ambiguous pictures.

The *second* asked him to write a creative and imaginative story about what he would be doing, thinking, and feeling "tomorrow" on his job. This is called a "projective" test because it is assumed that the respondent projects into his stories his own attitudes, thoughts, feelings, needs, and wants, all of which can be measured from the stories.[5]

The results indicated that the individuals in Akron and Stockton showed significantly more feelings of competence than did their counterparts in the lower-fit Hartford and Carmel organizations.[6] We found that the organization-task fit is simultaneously linked to and interdependent with both individual motivation and effective unit performance. (This interdependency is illustrated in Exhibit IV.)

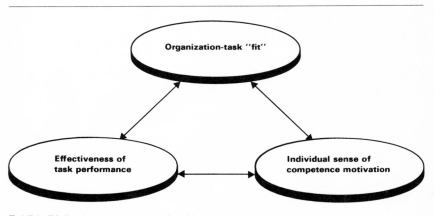

Exhibit IV Basic contingent relationships

[5] For a more detailed description of this survey, see John J. Morse, *Internal Organizational Patterning and Sense of Competence Motivation* (Boston, Harvard Business School, unpublished doctoral dissertation, 1969).
[6] Differences between the two container plants are significant at .001 and between the research laboratories at .01 (one-tailed probability).

Putting the conclusions in this form raises the question of cause and effect. Does effective unit performance result from the task-organization fit or from higher motivation, or perhaps from both? Does higher sense of competence motivation result from effective unit performance or from fit?

Our answer to these questions is that we do not think there are any single cause-and-effect relationships, but that these factors are mutually interrelated. This has important implications for management theory and practice.

Contingency theory

Returning to McGregor's Theory X and Theory Y assumptions, we can now question the validity of some of his conclusions. While Theory Y might help to explain the findings in the two laboratories, we clearly need something other than Theory X or Y assumptions to explain the findings in the plants.

For example, the managers at Akron worked in a formalized organization setting with relatively little participation in decision making, and yet they were highly motivated. According to Theory X, people would work hard in such a setting only because they were coerced to do so. According to Theory Y, they should have been involved in decision making and been self-directed to feel so motivated. Nothing in our data indicates that either set of assumptions was valid at Akron.

Conversely, the managers at Hartford, the low-performing plant, were in a less formalized organization with more participation in decision making, and yet they were not as highly motivated like the Akron managers. The Theory Y assumptions would suggest that they should have been more motivated.

A way out of such paradoxes is to state a new set of assumptions, the Contingency Theory, that seems to explain the findings at all four sites:

1 Human beings bring varying patterns of needs and motives into the work organization, but one central need is to achieve a sense of competence.
2 The sense of competence motive, while it exists in all human beings, may be fulfilled in different ways by different people depending on how this need interacts with the strengths of the individuals' other needs—such as those for power, independence, structure, achievement, and affiliation.
3 Competence motivation is most likely to be fulfilled when there is a fit between task and organization.
4 Sense of competence continues to motivate even when a competence goal is achieved; once one goal is reached, a new, higher one is set.

While the central thrust of these points is clear from the preceding discussion of the study, some elaboration can be made. First, the idea that different people have different needs is well understood by psychologists. However, all too often, managers assume that all people have similar needs. Lest we be accused of the same error, we are saying only that all people have a need to feel competent; in this *one* way they are similar. But in many other dimensions of personality, individuals differ, and these differences will determine how a particular person achieves a sense of competence.

Thus, for example, the people in the Akron plant seemed to be very different from those in the Stockton laboratory in their underlying attitudes toward uncertainty, authority, and relationships with their peers. And because they had different need patterns along these dimensions, both groups were highly motivated by achieving competence from quite different activities and settings.

While there is a need to further investigate how people who work in different settings differ in their psychological makeup, one important implication of the Contingency Theory is that we must not only seek a fit between organization and task, but also between task and people and between people and organization.

A further point which requires elaboration is that one's sense of competence never really comes to rest. Rather, the real satisfaction of this need is in the successful performance itself, with no diminishing of the motivation as one goal is reached. Since feelings of competence are thus reinforced by successful performance, they can be a more consistent and reliable motivator than salary and benefits.

Implications for managers

The major managerial implication of the Contingency Theory seems to rest in the task-organization-people fit. Although this interrelationship is complex, the best possibility for managerial action probably is in tailoring the organization to fit the task and the people. If such a fit is achieved, both effective unit performance and a higher sense of competence motivation seem to result.

Managers can start this process by considering how certain the task is, how frequently feedback about task performance is available, and what goals are implicit in the task. The answers to these questions will guide their decisions about the design of the management hierarchy, the specificity of job assignments, and the utilization of rewards and control procedures. Selective use of training programs and a general emphasis on appropriate management styles will move them toward a task-organization fit.

The problem of achieving a fit among task, organization, and people is something we know less about. As we have already suggested, we need further investigation of what personality characteristics fit various tasks and organizations. Even with our limited knowledge, however, there are indications that people will gradually gravitate into organizations that fit their particular personalities. Managers can help this process by becoming more aware of what psychological needs seem to best fit the tasks available and the organizational setting, and by trying to shape personnel selection criteria to take account of these needs.

In arguing for an approach which emphasizes the fit among task, organization, and people, we are putting to rest the question of which organizational approach—the classical or the participative—is best. In its place we are raising a new question: What organizational approach is most appropriate given the task and the people involved?

For many enterprises, given the new needs of younger employees for more autonomy, and the rapid rates of social and technological change, it may well be that the more participative approach is the most appropriate. But there will still be many situations in which the more controlled and formalized organization is desirable. Such an organization need not be coercive or punitive. If it makes sense to the individuals involved, given their needs and their jobs, they will find it rewarding and motivating.

Concluding note

The reader will recognize that the complexity we have described is not of our own making. The basic deficiency with earlier approaches is that they did not recognize the variability in tasks and people which produces this complexity. The strength of the contingency approach we have outlined is that it begins to provide a way of thinking about this complexity, rather than ignoring it. While our knowledge in this area is still growing, we are certain that any adequate theory of motivation and organization will have to take account of the contingent relationship between task, organization, and people.

43 The jackpot
Anonymous

Until well after the turn of the century it was the custom for many of the New York banks and insurance companies to distribute shiny new twenty dollar gold pieces—double eagles—at their board meetings to each of the directors present. Some companies, such as the New York Life Insurance Company, attempted to encourage attendance by placing all the gold pieces in a cut-glass bowl in the center of the table and then dividing them among the directors present. It was a rare occasion when as many as half of the full board showed up, and the directors would match for the odd coins. In the case of New York Life, whose directors were among the wealthiest members of the financial community, the value of the fee meant nothing, but there was always a good deal of gleeful chaffing of absent members when the distribution amounted to as much as three or even four twenty dollar gold pieces for each of those present.

Source: Reprinted with permission from the November 1966 issue of the *Michigan Business Review,* published by the Graduate School of Business Administration, The University of Michigan.

On only one occasion in the history of the company, according to a former director, the late Charles Dewey Hilles (1867–1949), was there ever a full attendance at a board meeting, and that was on March 13, 1888. The occasion—the worst blizzard that the City of New York has ever experienced, and every single member of the board braved the hazards of slippery streets, icy winds, and high voltage wires from fallen electric light poles to walk a mile or more to the company's offices at 346 Broadway, each sure in the belief that he alone would win the jackpot of double eagles.

44 Motivation on Fiji
Reuters News Service

SUVA, Fiji—Gold miners here are seeking a 30-minute midday sex break.

The miners believe this is the best time for sex, their union secretary, Navita Raqona, said Friday.

The demand is one of a number of issues the 1,600 strong union is discussing with a mining company at Vatukoula.

Raqona said a man has a sexual obligation to his wife and if he goes home exhausted at 5 p.m., he cannot fulfill it.

The union wants the sex break added to the normal lunch break.

After lunch and a short rest, a man is in prime mental and physical condition to meet his sexual obligations, Raqona said.

The union proposes to limit the sex break to married men. What he termed "alternative arrangements" would have to be made to compensate bachelors.

"We don't want to overdo this," Raqona said.

Source: Reuters News Service, January 23, 1975.

V/C
Influencing:
Organizational implications

45 Non-formal aspects of the organization
John M. Pfiffner and Frank P. Sherwood

I. Modifying processes as overlays on formal structures

The formal structure of an organization represents as closely as possible the deliberate intention of its framers for the processes of interaction that will take place among its members. In the typical work organization this takes the form of a definition of task specialties, and their arrangement in levels of authority with clearly defined lines of communication from one level to the next. (See Chart 1.)

It must be recognized, however, that the actual processes of interaction among the individuals represented in the formal plan cannot adequately be described solely in terms of its planned lines of interaction. Coexisting with the formal structure are myriad other ways of interacting for persons in the organization; these can be analyzed according to various theories of group behavior, but it must not be forgotten that in reality they never function so distinctively, and all are intermixed together in an organization which also follows to a large extent its formal structure.

These modifying processes must be studied one at a time; a good way to do so without forgetting their "togetherness" is to consider each as a transparent "overlay" pattern superimposed on the basic formal organizational pattern. The totality of these overlays might be so complex as to be nearly opaque, but it will still be a closer approach to reality than the bare organization chart so typically used to diagram a large group structure.

Five such overlay patterns will be considered here; many more or less might be chosen from the kinds of studies that have been made, but these five might well be considered basic:

Source: John M. Pfiffner and Frank P. Sherwood, *Administrative Organization,* © 1960, pp. 18–27. Reprinted by permission of Prentice-Hall, Inc. Englewood Cliffs, New Jersey.

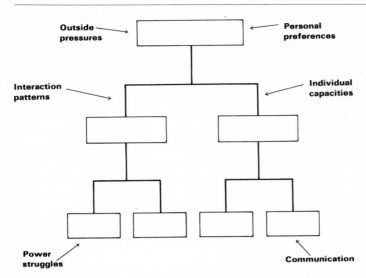

Chart 1 The typical job pyramid of authority and some of its interacting processes

- The sociometric network
- The system of functional contacts
- The grid of decision-making centers
- The pattern of power
- Channels of communication[1]

The idea that these processes are overlays upon the conventional job-task pyramid does not require that the latter take a subordinate position, although much of the research in organization might give this impression. The overlay approach aims to be realistic in recognizing that organization also consists of a wide variety of contacts that involve communication, sociometry, goal centered functionalism, decision-making, and personal power. Let us consider this complex of processes one at a time.

The job-task pyramid

The job-task pyramid constitutes the basis from which all departures are measured. It is the official version of the organization as the people in the organization believe that it is and should be. It would be correct to say that

---

[1] For much of the conceptual underpinnings of this chapter we are indebted to John T. Dorsey, Jr., "A Communication Model for Administration," *Administrative Science Quarterly* 2:307–324, December 1957. While Dorsey would seem to view communication as the central component of administration, we would put it on a level with others dealt with here.

in most production organizations today, whether private or public, this official version of the organization-as-it-should-be reflects the view of those in the top echelons of the job-task pyramid. The actual operating organizations may differ in some respects from the formal organization; this difference can be expressed by showing the manner in which the other networks vary from the job-task hierarchy.

Job-task hierarchy as foundation. Variations of the other networks from the job-task hierarchy should not be taken as an indication that the latter is being undermined or has no acceptance in the organization. It is well recognized in practice that there is an operating organization that varies from the chart with the full knowledge of those in authority. Day-to-day and hour-to-hour adjustments must be made, and there is no need to revise the chart for each of these. Nevertheless, the job-task hierarchy as depicted by the organization manual does set forth the grid of official authority as viewed by those in the organization. Without it the other networks would simply not exist.[2]

The sociometric overlay (see Chart 2A)

In any organization there is a set of relationships among people which is purely social in nature; it exists because of a net feeling of attraction or rejection. This pattern of person-to-person contacts is called sociometric because it is revealed in the kind of group testing that was given that name by its originator, J. L. Moreno. Some investigators have felt that individual attitudes lending themselves to sociometric measurement include as many as the following:

1 The *prescribed* relations, which are identical with the official or formal organization.
2 The *perceived* relations, which consist of people's interpretations of the meaning of the official network.
3 The *actual* relations are those interactions which in fact take place among persons.

4 The *desired* relations are people's preferences regarding interactions they want with other persons.

5 The *rejected* relations are the relationships with other people which are not wanted.[3]

It is, however, the last two categories that are primarily sociological in nature, and it is these that will be considered sociometric here. Desired and rejected relationships are fairly easy to ascertain with statistical reliability, and

---

[2] William Brownrigg deals with the job-task hierarchy most provocatively in *The Human Enterprise Process and Its Administration* (University, Ala.: University of Alabama Press, 1954).

[3] Fred Massarik, Robert Tannenbaum, Murray Kahane, and Irving Wescheler, "Sociometric Choice and Organizational Effectiveness: a Multi-Relational Approach." *Sociometry* 16:211–238, August 1953.

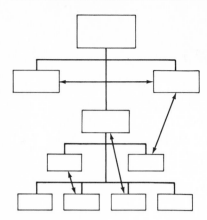

Chart 2A Social overlay: The special friendships in the organization ("I'll talk to my friend George in purchasing. He'll know what to do.")

are found to be very responsive to the other dynamics of the group. Ohio State studies of naval leadership have effectively utilized sociometric charts (sociograms—graphic representations of social relations) superimposed on the traditional job-task charts.[4]

The functional overlay (see Chart 2B)

There is in the organization a network of functional contacts that is important to and yet different from the formal authority structure. Functional contacts occur most typically where specialized information is needed; through them the staff or other specialist, the intellectual "leader," exerts his influence upon operations without direct responsibility for the work itself. This relationship, something like that between a professional man and his client, is a phenomenon of the twentieth century, and more markedly of the mid-century period.

Frederick Taylor was so perceptive as to understand the importance of the network of functional contacts in a management institution. Taylor called these functional contacts "functional supervision"; this term upset many theorists who worshipped the concept of clear cut supervisor-subordinate authority relationships.[5]

While Taylor's orginal concept of multiple supervision was rejected as a theoretical instrument at the time, it is still true that most organizations exhibit a system of functional supervision. Many charts of formal authority

[4] Ralph M. Stogdill, *Leadership and Structure of Personal Interaction* (Columbus: Ohio State University, Bureau of Business Research, Monograph No. 84, 1957), p. 10.
[5] A collection of excerpts from the literature of the early scientific management movement relating to staff specialization and functionalism is contained in Albert Lepawsky, *Administration* (New York: Alfred A. Knopf, Inc., 1949), pp. 299–306.

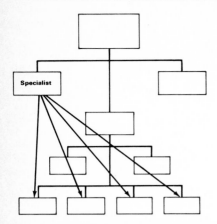

Chart 2B Functional overlay: The direct relationships between the specialist assistant and the operating departments ("You have to see Personnel for approval to take that training course.")

structures, such as those of the military, also show functional contacts through such devices as broken connecting lines.

The decision overlay (see Chart 2C)

Simon maintains that the best way to analyze an organization is to find out where the decisions are made and by whom.[6] It can perhaps be assumed that normally in an organization the decision pattern follows the structure of the formal hierarchy, that is, the job-task pyramid. However, the power and authority network, together with the functional network, may cut across hierarchical channels. It is in this sense that they take on the configuration of a grid or network. Thus the network pattern of approach is helpful, not in undermining the concept of hierarchy but in conveying the picture of actual practice. It modifies the harsh overtones of hierarchy by pointing out that actual organizations permit a great many cross-contacts.

Network of influence

It might be more correct to say that there is a network of influence, not a network of decision. This, of course, depends upon one's definition of decision-making and if one insists upon there being a clear cut choice between alternatives by a person in authority, then decision-making usually follows clear hierarchical paths and channels. However, if we think in terms of a decision *process* rather than a decision *point,* the sense of interaction and influence is more appropriately conveyed. In this connection it is helpful to

[6] Herbert A. Simon, *Administrative Behavior,* 2nd edition (New York: The Macmillan Company, 1947), p. xix. Simon's decision model is discussed in detail in Chapter 21.

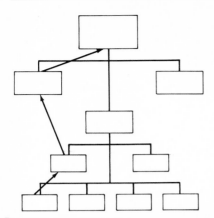

Chart 2C Decision overlay: Flow of significant decisions in the organization ("Don't worry about Joe. He doesn't concern himself about this. Our next step is to go top-side.")

refer to Mary Parker Follett's concept of order giving in which she says "an order, command, is a step in a process, a moment in the movement of interweaving experience. We should guard against thinking this step a larger part of the whole process than it really is."[7]

The power overlay (see Chart 2D)

Any discussion of power as a factor in organizational dynamics rather quickly encounters difficulties of definition and terminology. Since this is a subject upon which there will be considerable discussion at a later point in this book, let it be noted here that many of these problems arise from a confusion of the terms *power* and *authority*. They are not necessarily synonymous; yet there has been a tendency to look at the organization chart, note the various status levels, and to assume that power increases as one rises in the pyramid. Much of this attitude is based on old concepts of authority as they are found in jurisprudence. Within this framework there is an assumption that a rule laid down by a political superior who is ultimately sovereign can be enforced by the imposition of sanctions. Translated into the terminology of management institutions, this means that authority, and hence power, rests with those at the top echelons of the job-task pyramid.

Power no longer viewed as synonymous with authority
However there has been a considerable rebellion against this narrow view of the power factor in organization environment. Almost everyone who has had

---

[7] Henry C. Metcalf and L. Urwick, editors, *Dynamic Administration: The Collected Papers of Mary Parker Follett* (New York: Harper and Brothers, 1940), p. 49.

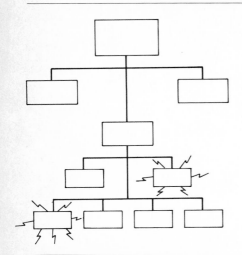

Chart 2D Power overlay: Centers of power in the organization ("Before you go further, you had better clear that with Jack in Production Planning.")

any experience in a management institution has encountered a situation where the boss's secretary, or his assistant, or the executive officer, is the "person to see." For a great variety of reasons, these people may be effective decision-makers in the situation. Thus power is really personal; it is political; and it may or may not be legitimate in that it has been authorized by formal law or has achieved hierarchical legitimization. Involving a person-to-person relationship, power exists when one has the ability to influence someone to behave in a particular way or to make decisions. As a result the mapping of power centers would seldom follow the pattern of a typical hierarchy.

Management institutions are political

It seems desirable to emphasize that management institutions are political in nature and that the basis of politics is power. While the use of the adjective "political" may be jarring to students of business administration who regard politics and government as being synonymous, the fact remains that business organizations are also political to an important degree. The maneuvering for proxies to gain control of an industrial corporation is certainly a political act and the same is true of struggles on the part of individuals to "build empires," or the use of artifice to gain the ear of the president.

The important consideration from the standpoint of organization theory is that there is a network or a grid of personal power centers, though sometimes latent and not expressed.[8] They may or may not coincide with the

[8] Robert Dubin, *Human Relations in Administration: The Sociology of Organization* (Englewood Cliffs, N.J.: Prentice-Hall, Inc., 1951), p. 173. See also Dubin, *The World of Work* (Englewood Cliffs, N.J.: Prentice-Hall, Inc., 1958), pp. 47–54.

official structure of authority. Power is not institutionalized in the sense that one can look in the organization manual and find out where it resides. As a matter of fact one might find it in unsuspected places. The person of comparatively low status may be a power center because he has been around so long that only he knows the intricate rules and the regulations well enough to make immediate decisions.

The communication overlay (see Chart 2E)

Perhaps nowhere is the inter-relationship of the various overlays more clearly to be seen than in communication. As will be observed at countless points in this book, the information process is central to organizational system. It affects control and decision-making, influence and power, interpersonal relationships, and leadership, to name only a few facets. Dorsey, in making a case for the significance of communications, says that "power consists of the extent to which a given communication influences the generation and flow of later communications. Points in the patterned flow where this occurs . . . are positions of power. . . ."[9] Furthermore, the communication net "consists physically of a complex of *decision centers* and *channels* which seek, receive, transmit, subdivide, classify, store, select, recall, recombine and retransmit *information*."[10] This net consists not only of

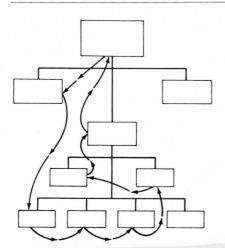

Chart 2E Communications overlay: The route of telephone calls on a particular matter ("If we had to go through channels, we never would get anything done around here!")

---

[9] Dorsey, "A Communication Model for Administration," *Administrative Science Quarterly*, p. 310.
[10] *Ibid.*, p. 317.

the technical information apparatus, but also of the human nervous systems of the people who make up the organization.

It is important to recognize that communication is itself a clearly identifiable facet of behavior. Redfield tells, for example, of the consultant who "starts his studies in the mail room, for, by plotting the lines of actual communication, he can sometimes build a more accurate organization chart than the one that hangs on the wall in the president's office."[11] Such a chart is, of course, one of communications. And it may tell a great deal more about how life is really lived in an organization than the formal authority picture. Thus an important and useful means of taking a look at an organization is to ask the question, "Who talks to whom about what?"

Answers to the question will often reveal that patterns of communication are at variance with official prescriptions. That is something the consultant mentioned in the previous paragraph frequently found. Furthermore there have been enough experiments with small groups to give great strength to the proposition that "the mere existence of a hierarchy sets up restraints against communication between levels."[12] Gardner has pointed out that factory production reports on productivity are sometimes rigged in order to give higher echelons the type of information which will make them happy. Such blockages and distortions are certainly frequent enough to force us to recognize that the communications overlay represents an important dimension of organization analysis.

[11] Charles Redfield, *Communication in Management* (Chicago: University of Chicago Press, 1953), p. 7.
[12] Burleigh B. Gardner and David G. Moore, *Human Relations in Industry,* 3rd edition (Homewood, Ill.: Richard D. Irwin, Inc., 1955), pp. 213 ff.

46 The satisfaction-performance controversy: New developments and their implications
Charles N. Greene

As Ben walked by smiling on the way to his office, Ben's boss remarked to a friend: "Ben really enjoys his job and that's why he's the best damn worker I ever had. And that's reason enough for me to keep Ben happy." The friend replied: "No, you're wrong! Ben likes his job because he does it so well. If you want to make Ben happy, you ought to do whatever you can to help him further improve his performance."

Source: From *Business Horizons* (October 1972), pp. 31–41. Copyright © 1972 by the Foundation for the School of Business at Indiana University. Reprinted by permission.

Four decades after the initial published investigation on the satisfaction-performance relationship, these two opposing views are still the subject of controversy on the part of both practitioners and researchers. Several researchers have concluded, in fact, that "there is no present technique for determining the cause-and-effect of satisfaction and performance." Current speculations, reviewed by Schwab and Cummings, however, still imply at least in theory that satisfaction and performance are causally related although, in some cases, the assumed cause has become the effect, and, in others, the relationship between these two variables is considered to be a function of a third or even additional variables.[1]

Theory and evidence

"Satisfaction causes performance"

At least three fundamental theoretical propositions underlie the research and writing in this area. The first and most pervasive stems from the human relations movement with its emphasis on the well-being of the individual at work. In the years following the investigations at Western Electric, a number of studies were conducted to identify correlates of high and low job satisfaction. The interest in satisfaction, however, came about not so much as a result of concern for the individual as concern with the presumed linkage of satisfaction with performance.

According to this proposition (simply stated and still frequently accepted), the degree of job satisfaction felt by an employee determines his performance, that is, satisfaction causes performance. This proposition has theoretical roots, but it also reflects the popular belief that "a happy worker is a productive worker" and the notion that "all good things go together." It is far more pleasant to increase an employee's happiness than to deal directly with his performance whenever a performance problem exists. Therefore, acceptance of the satisfaction-causes-performance proposition as a solution makes good sense, particularly for the manager because it represents the path of least resistance. Furthermore, high job satisfaction and high performance are both good, and, therefore, they ought to be related to one another.

At the theoretical level, Vroom's valence-force model is a prime example of theory-based support of the satisfaction-causes-performance case.[2] In

---

[1] Initial investigation by A. A. Kornhauser and A. W. Sharp, "Employee Attitudes: Suggestions from a Study in a Factory," *Personnel Journal,* X (May, 1932), pp. 393–401.

First quotation from Robert A. Sutermeister, "Employee Performance and Employee Need Satisfaction—Which Comes First?" *California Management Review.* XIII (Summer, 1971), p. 43.

Second quotation from Donald P. Schwab and Larry L. Cummings, "Theories of Performance and Satisfaction: a Review," *Industrial Relations,* IX (October, 1970), pp. 408–30.

[2] Victor H. Vroom, *Work and Motivation* (New York: John Wiley & Sons, Inc., 1964).

Vroom's model, job satisfaction reflects the valence (attractiveness) of the job. It follows from his theory that the force exerted on an employee to remain on the job is an increasing function of the valence of the job. Thus, satisfaction should be negatively related to absenteeism and turnover, and, at the empirical level, it is.

Whether or not this valence also leads to higher performance, however, is open to considerable doubt. Vroom's review of twenty-three field studies, which investigated the relationship between satisfaction and performance, revealed an insignificant median static correlation of 0.14, that is, satisfaction explained less than 2 percent of the variance in performance. Thus, the insignificant results and absence of tests of the causality question fail to provide support for this proposition.

"Performance causes satisfaction"

More recently a second theoretical proposition has been advanced. According to this view, best represented by the work of Porter and Lawler, satisfaction is considered not as a cause but as an effect of performance, that is, performance causes satisfaction.[3] Differential performance determines rewards which, in turn, produce variance in satisfaction. In other words, rewards constitute a necessary intervening variable and, thus, satisfaction is considered to be a function of performance-related rewards.

At the empirical level, two recent studies, each utilizing time-lag correlations, lend considerable support to elements of this proposition. Bowen and Siegel, and Greene reported finding relatively strong correlations between performance and satisfaction expressed later (the performance-causes-satisfaction condition), which were significantly higher than the low correlations between satisfaction and performance which occurred during the subsequent period (the "satisfaction-causes-performance" condition).[4]

In the Greene study, significant correlations were obtained between performance and rewards granted subsequently and between rewards and subsequent satisfaction. Thus, Porter and Lawler's predictions that differential performance determines rewards and that rewards produce variance in satisfaction were upheld.

"Rewards" as a causal factor

Closely related to Porter and Lawler's predictions is a still more recent theoretical position, which considers both satisfaction and performance to be

---

[3] Lyman W. Porter and Edward E. Lawler, III, *Managerial Attitudes and Performance* (Homewood, Ill.: Richard D. Irwin, Inc., 1968).
[4] Donald Bowen and Jacob P. Siegel, "The Relationship Between Satisfaction and Performance: the Question of Causality," paper presented at the annual meeting of the American Psychological Association, Miami Beach, September, 1970.

functions of rewards. In this view, rewards cause satisfaction, and rewards that are based on current performance affect subsequent performance.

According to this proposition, formulated by Cherrington, Reitz, and Scott from the contributions of reinforcement theorists, there is no inherent relationship between satisfaction and performance.[5] The results of their experimental investigation strongly support their predictions. The rewarded subjects reported significantly greater satisfaction than did the unrewarded subjects. Furthermore, when rewards (monetary bonuses, in this case) were granted on the basis of performance, the subjects' performance was significantly higher than that of subjects whose rewards were unrelated to their performance. For example, they found that when a low performer was not rewarded, he expressed dissatisfaction but that his later performance improved. On the other hand, when a low performer was in fact rewarded for his low performance, he expressed high satisfaction but continued to perform at a low level.

The same pattern of findings was revealed in the case of the high performing subjects with one exception; the high performer who was not rewarded expressed dissatisfaction, as expected, and his performance on the next trial declined significantly. The correlation between satisfaction and subsequent performance, excluding the effects of rewards, was 0.00, that is, satisfaction does *not* cause improved performance.

A recent field study, which investigated the source and direction of causal influence in satisfaction-performance relationships, supports the Cherrington-Reitz-Scott findings.[6] Merit pay was identified as a cause of satisfaction and, contrary to some current beliefs, was found to be a significantly more frequent source of satisfaction than dissatisfaction. The results of this study further revealed equally significant relationships between (1) merit pay and subsequent performance and (2) current performance and subsequent merit pay. Given the Cherrington-Reitz-Scott findings that rewards based on current performance cause improved subsequent performance, these results do suggest the possibility of reciprocal causation.

In other words, merit pay based on current performance probably caused variations in subsequent performance, and the company in this field study evidently was relatively successful in implementing its policy of granting salary increases to an employee on the basis of his performance (as evidenced by the significant relationship found between current performance and subsequent merit pay). The company's use of a fixed (annual) merit

---

Charles N. Greene, "A Causal Interpretation of Relationship Among Pay, Performance, and Satisfaction," paper presented at the annual meeting of the Midwest Psychological Association, Cleveland, Ohio, May, 1972.

[5] David J. Cherrington, H. Joseph Reitz, and William E. Scott, Jr., "Effects of Contingent and Non-contingent Reward on the Relationship Between Satisfaction and Task Performance," *Journal of Applied Psychology*, LV (December, 1971) pp. 531–36.

[6] Charles N. Greene, "Source and Direction of Causal Influence in Satisfaction-Performance Relationships," paper presented at the annual meetings of the Eastern Academy of Management, Boston, May, 1972. Also reported in Greene, "Causal Connections Among Managers' Merit Pay, Satisfaction, and Performance," *Journal of Applied Psychology*, 1972.

increase schedule probably obscured some of the stronger reinforcing effects of merit pay on performance.

Unlike the Cherrington-Reitz-Scott controlled experiment, the fixed merit increase schedule precluded (as it does in most organizations) giving an employee a monetary reward immediately after he successfully performed a major task. This constraint undoubtedly reduced the magnitude of the relationship between merit pay and subsequent performance.

Implications for management

These findings have several apparent but nonetheless important implications. For the manager who desired to enhance the satisfaction of his subordinates (perhaps for the purpose of reducing turnover), the implication of the finding that "rewards cause satisfaction" is self-evident. If, on the other hand, the manager's interest in his subordinates' satisfaction arises from his desire to increase their performance, the consistent rejection of the satisfaction-causes-performance proposition has an equally clear implication: increasing subordinates' satisfaction will have no effect on their performance.

The finding that rewards based on current performance affect subsequent performance does, however, offer a strategy for increasing subordinates' performance. Unfortunately, it is not the path of least resistance for the manager. Granting differential rewards on the basis of differences in his subordinates' performance will cause his subordinates to express varying degrees of satisfaction or dissatisfaction. The manager, as a result, will soon find himself in the uncomfortable position of having to successfully defend his basis for evaluation or having to put up with dissatisfied subordinates until their performance improves or they leave the organization.

The benefits of this strategy, however, far outweigh its liabilities. In addition to its positive effects on performance, this strategy provides equity since the most satisfied employees are the rewarded high performers and, for the same reason, it also facilitates the organization's efforts to retain its most productive employees.

If these implications are to be considered as prescriptions for managerial behavior, one is tempted at this point to conclude that all a manager need do in order to increase his subordinates' performance is to accurately appraise their work and then reward them accordingly. However, given limited resources for rewards and knowledge of appraisal techniques, it is all too apparent that the manager's task here is not easy.

Moreover, the relationship between rewards and performance is often not as simple or direct as one would think, for at least two reasons. First, there are other causes of performance that may have a more direct bearing on a particular problem. Second is the question of the appropriateness of the reward itself, that is, what is rewarding for one person may not be for another. In short, a manager also needs to consider other potential causes of performance and a range of rewards in coping with any given performance problem.

Nonmotivational factors

The element of performance that relates most directly to the discussion thus far is effort, that element which links rewards to performance. The employee who works hard usually does so because of the rewards or avoidance of punishment that he associates with good work. He believes that the magnitude of the reward he will receive is contingent on his performance and, further, that his performance is a function of how hard he works. Thus, effort reflects the motivational aspect of performance. There are, however, other nonmotivational considerations that can best be considered prior to examining ways by which a manager can deal with the motivational problem.

Direction

Suppose, for example, that an employee works hard at his job, yet his performance is inadequate. What can his manager do to alleviate the problem? The manager's first action should be to identify the cause. One likely possibility is what can be referred to as a "direction problem."

Several years ago, the Minnesota Vikings' defensive end, Jim Marshall, very alertly gathered up the opponent's fumble and then, with obvious effort and delight, proceeded to carry the ball some fifty yards into the wrong end zone. This is a direction problem in its purest sense. For the employee working under more usual circumstances, a direction problem generally stems from his lack of understanding of what is expected of him or what a job well done looks like. The action indicated to alleviate this problem is to clarify or define in detail for the employee the requirements of his job. The manager's own leadership style may also be a factor. In dealing with an employee with a direction problem, the manager needs to exercise closer supervision and to initiate structure or focus on the task, as opposed to emphasizing consideration or his relations with the employee.[7]

In cases where this style of behavior is repugnant or inconsistent with the manager's own leadership inclinations, an alternative approach is to engage in mutual goal setting or management-by-objectives techniques with the employee. Here, the necessary structure can be established, but at the subordinate's own initiative, thus creating a more participative atmosphere. This approach, however, is not free of potential problems. The employee is more likely to make additional undetected errors before his performance improves, and the approach is more time consuming than the more direct route.

Ability

What can the manager do if the actions he has taken to resolve the direction problem fail to result in significant improvements in performance? His

[7] For example, a recent study reported finding that relationships between the leader's initiating structure and both subordinate satisfaction and performance were moderated by such variables as role ambiguity, job scope, and task autonomy perceived by the subordinate. See Robert J. House, "A Path Goal Theory of Leader Effectiveness," *Administrative Science Quarterly,* XVI (September, 1971), pp. 321–39.

subordinate still exerts a high level of effort and understands what is expected of him—yet he continues to perform poorly. At this point, the manager may begin, justifiably so, to doubt his subordinate's ability to perform the job. When this doubt does arise, there are three useful questions, suggested by Mager and Pipe, to which the manager should find answers before he treats the problem as an ability deficiency: Could the subordinate do it if he really had to? Could he do it if his life depended on it? Are his present abilities adequate for the desired performance?[8]

If the answers to the first two questions are negative, then the answer to the last question also will be negative, and the obvious conclusion is that an ability deficiency does, in fact, exist. Most managers, upon reaching this conclusion, begin to develop some type of formal training experience for the subordinate. This is unfortunate and frequently wasteful. There is probably a simpler, less expensive solution. Formal training is usually required only when the individual has never done the particular job in question or when there is no way in which the ability requirement in question can be eliminated from his job.

If the individual formerly used the skill but now uses it only rarely, systematic practice will usually overcome the deficiency without formal training. Alternatively, the job can be changed or simplified so that the impaired ability is no longer crucial to successful performance. If, on the other hand, the individual once had the skill and still rather frequently is able to practice it, the manager should consider providing him greater feedback concerning the outcome of his efforts. The subordinate may not be aware of the deficiency and its effect on his performance, or he may no longer know how to perform the job. For example, elements of his job or the relationship between his job and other jobs may have changed, and he simply is not aware of the change.

Where formal training efforts are indicated, systematic analysis of the job is useful for identifying the specific behaviors and skills that are closely related with successful task performance and that, therefore, need to be learned. Alternatively, if the time and expense associated with job analysis are considered excessive, the critical incidents approach can be employed toward the same end.[9] Once training needs have been identified and the appropriate training technique employed, the manager can profit by asking himself one last question: "Why did the ability deficiency develop in the first place?"

Ultimately, the answer rests with the selection and placement process. Had a congruent man-job match been attained at the outset, the ability deficiency would have never presented itself as a performance problem.[10]

---

[8] Robert F. Mager and Peter Pipe, *Analyzing Performance Problems* (Belmont, Calif.: Lear Siegler, Inc., 1970), p. 21.

[9] See, for example, J. D. Folley, Jr., "Determining Training Needs of Department Store Personnel," *Training Development Journal,* XXIII (January, 1969), pp. 24–27, for a discussion of how the critical incidents approach can be employed to identify job skills to be learned in a formal training situation.

[10] For a useful discussion of how ability levels can be upgraded by means of training and selection procedures, the reader can refer to Larry L. Cummings and Donald P. Schwab, *Performance in Organizations: Determinants and Appraisal* (Glenview, Ill.: Scott, Foresman & Co., 1973).

Performance obstacles
When inadequate performance is not the result of a lack of effort, direction, or ability, there is still another potential cause that needs attention. There may be obstacles beyond the subordinate's control that interfere with his performance. "I can't do it" is not always an alibi; it may be a real description of the problem. Performance obstacles can take many forms to the extent that their number, independent of a given situation, is almost unlimited.

However, the manager might look initially for some of the more common potential obstacles, such as a lack of time or conflicting demands on the subordinate's time, inadequate work facilities, restrictive policies or "right ways of doing it" that inhibit performance, lack of authority, insufficient information about other activities that affect the job, and lack of cooperation from others with whom he must work.

An additional obstacle, often not apparent to the manager from his face-to-face interaction with a subordinate, is the operation of group goals and norms that run counter to organizational objectives. Where the work group adheres to norms of restricting productivity, for example, the subordinate will similarly restrict his own performance to the extent that he identifies more closely with the group than with management.

Most performance obstacles can be overcome either by removing the obstacle or by changing the subordinate's job so that the obstacle no longer impinges on his performance. When the obstacle stems from group norms, however, a very different set of actions is required. Here, the actions that should be taken are the same as those that will be considered shortly in coping with lack of effort on the part of the individual. In other words, the potential causes of the group's lack of effort are identical to those that apply to the individual.

The motivational problem

Thus far, performance problems have been considered in which effort was not the source of the performance discrepancy. While reward practices constitute the most frequent and direct cause of effort, there are, however, other less direct causes. Direction, ability, and performance obstacles may indirectly affect effort through their direct effects on performance. For example, an individual may perform poorly because of an ability deficiency and, as a result, exert little effort on the job. Here, the ability deficiency produced low performance, and the lack of effort on the individual's part resulted from his expectations of failure. Thus, actions taken to alleviate the ability deficiency should result in improved performance and, subsequently, in higher effort.

Effort is that element of performance which links rewards to performance. The relationship between rewards and effort is, unfortunately, not a simple one. As indicated in the figure, effort is considered not only as a function of the (1) value and (2) magnitude of reward, but also as a function of the (3) individual's perceptions of the extent to which greater effort on his part will lead to higher performance, and (4) that his high performance, in turn, will lead to rewards. Therefore, a manager who is confronted with a subordinate who exerts little effort must consider these four attributes of reward practices in addition to the more indirect, potential causes of the lack of effort. The key issues in coping with a subordinate's lack of effort—the motivation problem—or in preventing such a problem from arising involve all four of the attributes of rewards just identified.[11]

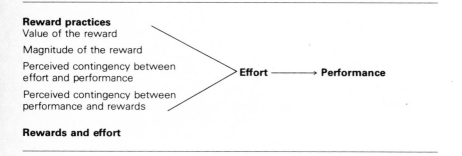

Reward practices
Value of the reward

Magnitude of the reward

Perceived contingency between effort and performance

Perceived contingency between performance and rewards

Effort ⟶ **Performance**

Rewards and effort

Appropriateness of the reward

Regardless of the extent to which the individual believes that hard work determines his performance and subsequent rewards, he will obviously put forth little effort unless he *values* those rewards—that is, the rewards must have value in terms of his own need state. An accountant, for example, may value recognition from his boss, an opportunity to increase the scope of his job, or a salary increase; however, it is unlikely that he will place the same value on a ten-year supply of budget forms.

In other words, there must be consistency between the reward and what the individual needs or wants and recognition that there are often significant differences among individuals in what they consider rewarding. Similarly, individuals differ in terms of the *magnitude* of that valued reward they consider to be positively reinforcing. A 7 or 8 percent salary increase may motivate one person but have little or no positive effect on another person at the same salary level. Furthermore, a sizable reward in one situation might be considered small by the same individual in a different set of circumstances.

These individual differences, particularly those concerning what rewards are valued, raise considerable question about the adequacy of current organization reward systems, virtually none of which make any formal recognition of individual differences. Lawler, for example, has suggested that organizations could profit greatly by introducing "cafeteria-style" wage

---

[11] The discussion in this section is based in part on Cummings and Schwab, *Performance in Organizations,* and Lyman W. Porter and Edward E. Lawler, III, "What Job Attitudes Tell About Motivation," *Harvard Business Review,* LXVI (January–February, 1968), pp. 118–26.

plans.[12] These plans allow an employee to select any combination of cash and fringe benefits he desires. An employee would be assigned "X" amount in compensation, which he may then divide up among a number of fringe benefits and cash. This practice would ensure that employees receive only those fringe benefits they value; from the organization's point of view, it would reduce the waste in funds allocated by the organization to fringe benefits not valued by its members. As a personal strategy, however, the manager could profit even more by extending Lawler's plan to include the entire range of nonmonetary rewards.

Rewards can be classified into two broad categories, extrinsic and intrinsic. Extrinsic rewards are those external to the job or in the context of the job, such as job security, improved working facilities, praise from one's boss, status symbols, and, of course, pay, including fringe benefits. Intrinsic rewards, on the other hand, are rewards that can be associated directly with the "doing of the job," such as a sense of accomplishment after successful performance, opportunities for advancement, increased responsibility, and work itself.

Thus, intrinsic rewards flow immediately and directly from the individual's performance of the job and, as such, may be considered as a form of self-reward. For example, one essentially must decide for himself whether his level of performance is worthy of a feeling of personal achievement. Extrinsic rewards, to the contrary, are administered by the organization; the organization first must identify good performance and then provide the appropriate reward.

Generally speaking, extrinsic rewards have their greatest value when the individual is most strongly motivated to satisfy what Maslow has referred to as lower level needs, basic physiological needs and needs for safety or security, and those higher level ego needs that can be linked directly to status. Pay, for example, may be valued by an individual because he believes it is a determinant of his social position within the community or because it constitutes a means for acquiring status symbols.

Intrinsic rewards are likely to be valued more by the individual after his lower level needs have been largely satisfied. In other words, there must be an adequate level of satisfaction with the extrinsic rewards before intrinsic rewards can be utilized effectively. In order to make the subordinate's job more intrinsically rewarding, the manager may want to consider several actions.

Perhaps most important, the manager needs to provide meaningful work assignments, that is, work with which the subordinate can identify and become personally involved. He should establish challenging yet attainable goals or, in some cases, it may be more advantageous for him to create conditions that greatly enhance the likelihood that his subordinate will succeed, thus increasing the potential for attaining feelings of achievement, advancement, and recognition. The manager may also consider such means as

[12] Edward E. Lawler, III, *Pay and Organizational Effectiveness: a Psychological View* (New York: McGraw-Hill Book Company, 1971).

increased delegation and job enlargement for extending the scope and depth of the subordinate's job and thereby increasing the subordinate's sense of responsibility and providing greater opportunity to make the job into something more compatible with his own interests.

In short, the manager should as best he can match the rewards at his disposal, both extrinsic and intrinsic rewards, with what the subordinate indicates he needs or wants. Second, he should, by varying the magnitude and timing of the rewards granted, establish clearly in the subordinate's mind the desired effort-performance-reward contingencies.

Establishing the contingencies

The contingency between effort and performance (that is, the extent to which the individual believes that by working harder, he will improve his performance) is largely a function of his confidence in his own abilities and his perceptions of the difficulty of the task and absence of obstacles standing in the way of successful task performance. When the effort-performance contingency is not clear for these reasons, the manager should consider several actions. He can reassign work or modify the task to be more consistent with the individual's perceptions of his own abilities; treat the problem as a "real" ability deficiency; remove the apparent performance obstacles; or simply reassure the individual.

The second contingency, the individual's belief that the rewards he receives reflect his accomplishments, is usually more difficult to establish. Here, two rather vexing predicaments are frequently encountered, both of which stem primarily from administration of extrinsic rewards. First, the instrument (usually a merit evaluation or performance appraisal device) may inaccurately measure the individual's contribution and thus his performance is rewarded in error. Reward schedules constitute the source of the second problem. Given fixed reward schedules (that is, the ubiquitous annual salary increase) adopted by the great majority of organizations, there is more frequently than not a considerable delay between task accomplishment and bestowal of the reward. As a result, the individual may not only fail to perceive the intended contingency but may incorrectly associate the reward with his behavior just prior to being rewarded. In other words, he may perceive a nonexistent contingency, and his subsequent behavior will reflect that contingency and, this time, go unrewarded.

Reward schedules

The manner in which a given reward, or reinforcer, is scheduled is as strong a determinant of the effectiveness of that reward as is the value of the reward itself, or, for that matter, any other attribute of the reward. In organizations, the only plausible forms of reward schedules are intermittent as opposed to the continuous reward schedule in which the reward or punishment is administered after every behavioral sequence to be conditioned. In the case of the intermittent schedules, the behavior to be conditioned is reinforced only occasionally. There are four schedules of interest to the manager, each with varying effects on performance as a number of investigations in the field of experimental psychology have revealed.

1 *Fixed-interval schedule*   Rewards are bestowed after a fixed period, usually since the last reward was granted. This schedule is equivalent to the annual salary increase schedule in organizations, and its effects on performance are well-known. Typically, the individual "saves up," that is, he exerts a high level of effort just prior to the time of the reinforcement, usually his annual performance review. His performance more than likely will then taper off until the time just prior to his next annual review.

2 *Variable-interval schedule*   Rewards are administered at designated time periods, but the intervals between the periods vary. For example, a reward may be given one day after the last rewarded behavior sequence, then three days later, then one week later, and so on, but only if the behavior to be conditioned actually occurs. This schedule results in fairly consistent rates of performance over long periods of time. Praise or other forms of social reinforcement from one's peers and superior, as an example, usually occur according to a variable-interval schedule, not by intention but simply because they are too involved with their own affairs to provide systematic reinforcement.

3 *Fixed-ratio schedule*   Reinforcement is provided after a fixed number of responses or performances by the individual. Incentive wage plans so frequently utilized in organizations constitute the prime example of this type of schedule. It is characterized by higher rates of effort than the interval schedules unless the ratio is large. When significant delays do occur between rewards, performance, much like in the fixed schedule, declines immediately after the reward is bestowed and improves again as the time for the next reward approaches.

4 *Variable-ratio schedule*   The reward is administered after a series of responses or performances, the number of which varies from the granting of one reward to the next.

For example, an individual on a 15:1 variable-interval schedule might be reinforced after ten responses, then fifteen responses, then twenty responses, then ten responses, and so on, an average of one reinforcement for every fifteen responses. This schedule tends to result in performance that is higher than that of a comparable fixed ratio schedule, and the variation in performance both before and after the occurrence of the reward or reinforcement is considerably less.

Virtually all managers must function within the constraints imposed by a fixed-interval schedule (annual salary schedule) or fixed-ratio schedule (wage incentives). However, this fact should not preclude consideration of the variable schedules, even within the framework of fixed schedules. Given their more positive effects on performance, such consideration is indeed highly desirable. It is conceivable, at least in a sales organization, for example, that monetary rewards (bonuses in this case) could be administered according to a variable-ratio schedule. From a more practical point of view, the entire range of nonmonetary rewards could be more profitably scheduled on a variable-interval basis, assuming that such scheduling was done in a systematic fashion.

Conclusions

This article has reviewed recent research concerning the relationship between satisfaction and performance and discussed the implications of the results of this research for the practicing manager. As noted at the outset, current speculation on the part of most practitioners and researchers continues to imply that satisfaction and performance are causally related, although confusion exists concerning the exact nature of the relationship. While the performance-cause-satisfaction proposition is a more recent development, the contention that satisfaction causes performance, nonetheless, remains the more widely held of the two beliefs, particularly among practitioners.

The recent research findings, however, offer only moderate support of the former view and conclusively reject the latter. Instead, the evidence provides rather strong indications that the relationship is more complex: (1) rewards constitute a more direct cause of satisfaction than does performance and (2) rewards based on current performance (and not satisfaction) cause subsequent performance.

For the manager who is concerned about the well-being of his subordinates, the implication of the finding that rewards cause satisfaction is self-evident. In order to achieve this end, the manager must provide rewards that have value or utility in terms of the subordinate's own need state and provide them in sufficient magnitude to be perceived as positively reinforcing. The manager whose goal is to increase a subordinate's performance, on the other hand, is faced with a more difficult task for two reasons. First, the relationship between rewards and performance is not a simple one. Second, there are other causes of performance—direction, the subordinate's ability, and existence of performance obstacles standing in the way of successful task performance—which the manager must also deal with.

The relationship between rewards and performance is complex because in reality there is at least one intervening variable and more than one contingency that needs to be established. An employee exerts high level effort usually because of the valued rewards he associates with high performance. Effort, the intervening variable, may be considered a function of the value and magnitude of the reward and the extent to which the individual believes that high effort on his part will lead to high performance and that his high performance, in turn, will lead to rewards.

Therefore, the manager in addition to providing appropriate rewards, must establish contingencies between effort and performance and between performance and rewards. The first contingency, the extent to which the individual believes that "how hard he works" determines his performance, is perhaps the more readily established. This contingency is a function, at least in part, of the individual's confidence in his own abilities, his perceptions of the difficulty of the task, and the presence of performance obstacles. When a problem does arise here, the manager can take those actions indicated earlier in this article to overcome an apparent ability deficiency or performance obstacle. The performance-reward contingency requires the manager, by means of accurate performance appraisals and appropriate reward practices, to clearly establish in the subordinate's mind the belief that his own performance determines the magnitude of the rewards he will receive.

The establishment of this particular contingency, unfortunately, is becoming increasingly difficult as organizations continue to rely more heavily on fixed salary schedules and nonperformance-related factors (for example, seniority) as determinants of salary progression. However, the manager can, as a supplement to organizationally determined rewards, place more emphasis on nonmonetary rewards and both the cafeteria-style reward plans and variable-interval schedules for their administration.

It is apparent that the manager whose objective is to significantly improve his subordinates' performance has assumed a difficult but by no means impossible task. The path of least resistance—that is, increasing subordinates' satisfaction—simply will not work.

However, the actions suggested concerning reward practices and, particularly, establishment of appropriate performance-reward contingencies will result in improved performance, assuming that such improvement is not restricted by ability or direction problems or by performance obstacles. The use of differential rewards may require courage on the part of the manager, but failure to use them will have far more negative consequences. A subordinate will repeat that behavior which was rewarded, regardless of whether it resulted in high or low performance. A rewarded low performer, for example, will continue to perform poorly. With knowledge of this inequity, the high performer, in turn, will eventually reduce his own level of performance or seek employment elsewhere.

---

47 A situational change typology
Robin Stuart-Kotzé

The trainer or internal change agent in a firm undergoing an organizational development program may be instrumental in designing the implementation of a change strategy. The situational change typology proposed below may be of use as a training instrument to:

Source: Reproduced by special permission from the January 1972 *Training and Development Journal.* Copyright © 1972 by the American Society for Training and Development, Inc.

1 present a number of different change strategies,
2 examine the situational demands surrounding the change,
3 focus attention on the match of situation to strategy,
4 escape from the concept of the "ideal" organizational change strategy and
5 focus on existing and required management skills.

Two independent determinants of organizational change strategy—managers' interpersonal competence and technical competence—are used to build the situational change typology. This typology is then linked with a recent management style model to demonstrate a tactical approach to implementation.[1]

As Warren Bennis notes, "All change is not 'planned change'."[2] The success with which management is able to implement change depends on a number of factors; and depending on the factor "mix," what is intended as planned change may well turn out to be something quite different.

Findings in a number of studies suggest that the subjects of change must be approached in a consultative manner and be invited to participate in the change decision as equal (no power differential) partners, for change to be implemented most effectively.[3] This underlying idea is supported by research into social or cultural change.[4] It seems that the subjects of change must be sure that their basic value system is not being threatened by the proposed change and that they are afforded a sense of security by being allowed to participate in the change decision, determination of the plan, and introduction or implementation.

Bennis's "Paradigm for Change Processes" (see Figure 1) reflects the general emphasis of the literature on the importance of the informal or social group as the subject of change. He considers (1) the power ratio between the originator and the subject of the change, (2) whether there is mutual or unilateral goal-setting and (3) the deliberateness of goal-setting, as the three independent variables which determine types of change.

Figure 1 Bennis's paradigm for change processes

Power ratio	Mutual goal setting		Nonmutual goal setting (or goals set by one side)	
	Deliberate on the part of one or both sides of the relationship	Nondeliberate on the part of both sides	Deliberate on the part of one side of the relationship	Nondeliberate on the part of both sides
.5/.5	Planned change	Interactional change	Technocratic change	"Natural" change
1/0	Indoctrinational change	Socialization change	Coercive change	Emulative change

Taken from Warren G. Bennis, "A Typology of Change Processes," *The Planning of Change*, ed. W. G. Bennis, K. D. Benne and R. Chin, Holt, Rinehart and Winston, 1964, p. 154.

While the weight of the evidence seems against him, the average manager might not agree that the participative approach is the best one. As he sees it, there are other variables than those used by Bennis which affect the method of change he should use. These include such situational demands of his position as the underlying technology, the time horizon, availability and effect of rewards and punishments, competence of organizational members, etc. Therefore, while Bennis is proposing a normative model in which the optimal change strategy is participative in nature, a situational approach to change, which includes the type of factors mentioned above, would offer a more descriptive model.

Level of competence

A powerful variable determining types of organizational change is the level of competence of the organization's members, that is, the degree and type of skill, or competence, possessed by the managers of the organization. Argyris states that, "The administrative competence of an organization is composed of two interrelated but analytically separable components. They are intellective, rational, technical competence and interpersonal competence. The former deals with things and ideas, the latter with people."[5] Thus we could operationally define *technical competence* as referring to the ability of the organization's members to plan, control, design, schedule, produce, etc., and *interpersonal competence* as a function of the degree to which organizational members are aware of their impact upon others, and they upon them.

If these two aspects of competence are independent, that is, a manager can possess varying degrees of technical competence whether he possesses a high degree or a low degree of interpersonal competence, or vice-versa, then the relationship may be represented by Figure 2.

The type of change which will be most effective will depend on the degree of technical and interpersonal competence of the organization's members; i.e., their competence mix in a given situation. A typology of change processes based on the organization members' competence mixes could be represented by Figure 3.

Types of change

Natural change would be most effective where the organization's members have low technical competence and low interpersonal competence. Where management lacks the ability to plan, control, direct and schedule in other than the short run, and at the same time communication skills are minimal, there is a lack of mutual trust, and problem-solving is not attempted in other than a superficial manner, any attempt at implementing a specific organizational change strategy will be ineffective.

	Low←Technical competence→High	
Low←Interpersonal competence→High	High interpersonal competence Low technical competence	High interpersonal competence High technical competence
	Low interpersonal competence Low technical competence	Low interpersonal competence High technical competence

Low←Technical competence→High

Figure 2 Four types of competence mix; cutting the two scales into two produces four types

Interpersonal competence		
Cooperative change	Planned change
Natural change	Directed change

Technical competence

Figure 3 A situational change typology; four change strategies correspond to the four types of competence mix

Directed change would be most effective where the organization's members have high technical competence, but low interpersonal competence. Where management is highly skilled in the techniques of planning, scheduling and controlling, but trust levels are low and communication tends to be one-way, from the top down, decisions concerning organizational change will tend to be based on technical factors, and implementation will rely on "rational" explanation of the benefits of the change. Rewards and punishments will be closely tied-in to the proposed change for reinforcement, and implementation will be rapid and "all at once." Types of change, other than directed change, will tend to be less effective in this situation because they will either require more time to implement and/or a different set of skills than those possessed by management.

Cooperative change would be most effective where the organization's members have low technical competence, but high interpersonal competence. Management is not highly skilled "technically," but they have developed a high trust level within the organization, and communication flows freely up and down. Management's jobs may entail creativity, or counseling and training. Because of a desire for freedom from direction, they may not indulge in tight, long-term planning and scheduling, or be concerned with formal structural relationships and rapid feedback of end-product measures. Other types of change will be incongruent with the established patterns of communication and the atmosphere of mutual trust within the organization, and hence will tend to be less effective.

Planned change would be most effective where the organization's members have both high technical and interpersonal competence. Stimulated by an image of potential, management will consider a wide range of alternatives for organizational development, requiring a high degree of competence in long range planning, scheduling, organizing, directing and controlling, and a high degree of interpersonal competence to allow for the provision of clear feedback and ideas concerning change. Management is willing to spend a considerable amount of time examining and working through the various alternatives available and ensuring commitment to objectives throughout the organization. Given the mix of both high technical and interpersonal competence, planned change is more effective than any of the other types simply because it employs all the organization's resources to the fullest.

Change and management style

This situational change typology is primarily concerned with effective change strategies as determined by the mix of technical and interpersonal competence of the organization's members. But it can also be tied in with a *situational management style typology,* indicating which management styles are optimally employed in the implementation of each type of change. The link with managerial styles is suggested by a finding drawn from Berelson and Steiner that, "Leaders of small groups tend to direct the group's activities along lines at which they themselves are proficient and away from those areas where they are less competent."[6] In other words, managers who possess a high degree of technical competence will tend to use a managerial style which emphasizes this technical competence, while managers who possess a high degree of interpersonal competence will tend to use a managerial style which emphasizes or makes use of this particular skill.

W. J. Reddin's situational management style typology has been chosen here for integration with the situational change typology.[7] As with other situationists, Reddin sees managerial effectiveness as a match of style to situation; to match style and situation, a manager needs situational sensitivity (to size up a situation) and style flexibility (to adapt to it) or situational management (to change it) if necessary.

Tactics and strategy

When Reddin's management style typology, as shown in Figure 4, is combined with the situational change typology in Figure 3, both the strategy and tactics of organizational change are shown as being dictated by the situational demand elements of interpersonal and technical competence.

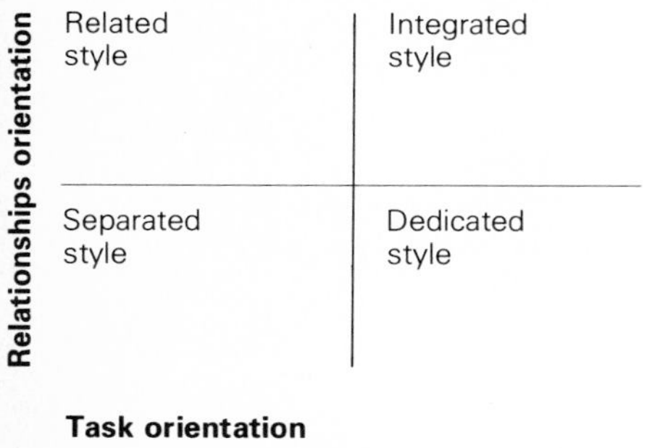

Related style	Integrated style
Separated style	Dedicated style

(Vertical axis label: Relationships orientation)

Task orientation

Figure 4 Reddin's four basic styles; these are four basic styles of managerial behavior

Brief descriptions of Reddin's four basic managerial styles, as shown in Figure 4, may aid in demonstrating the close relationship between management tactics and organizational change strategy.

The *separated* manager is oriented towards procedures, methods and systems, and emphasizes accuracy, conservatism, prudence and noninvolvement. He is low in both relationships orientation (extent to which he is likely to have personal job relations characterized by mutual trust, respect for subordinates' ideas, and consideration of their feelings) and task orientation (extent to which he is likely to direct his subordinates' efforts to goal attainment; characterized by planning, organizing and controlling), and therefore, rather than becoming involved with his subordinates in an interpersonal manner, or becoming committed to his job, he takes refuge in rules and procedures, and operates "by the book."

The *related* manager is oriented to other people and produces an atmosphere of security and trust. He stimulates "noise-free" communication and feedback, but is less concerned for the accomplishment of the task at hand than for the well-being of the individuals involved.

The *dedicated* manager directs the work of others and shows little concern for the well-being of his subordinates. He is concerned with conserving time and increasing production, lowering costs, etc., and relies on his own judgment in making decisions. Communication is directed downward toward his subordinates, and feedback is in terms of information which he specifically requests.

The *integrated* manager has both high-task orientation and high-relationships orientation, and tends to indulge in long range planning and motivational techniques. While he is deeply concerned with production in both the short- and long-run, he is interested in developing a highly cooperative approach to achieving organizational objectives. He is interested in stimulating commitment, on the part of his subordinates, to the organization's goals, and wants to integrate the needs of the individual to the needs of the organization.[8]

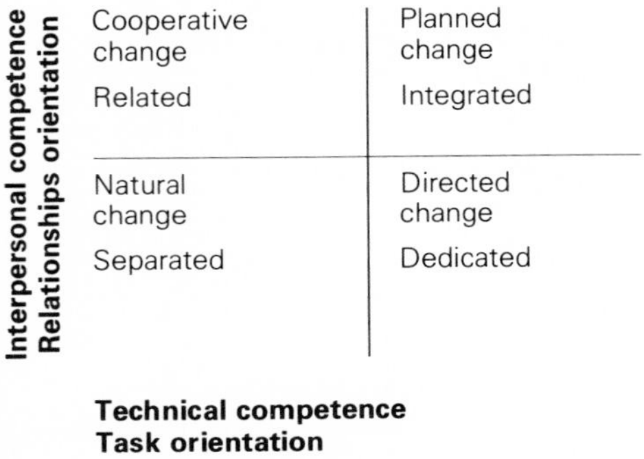

Interpersonal competence / Relationships orientation		
Cooperative change	Planned change
Related	Integrated
Natural change	Directed change
Separated	Dedicated

Technical competence
Task orientation

Figure 5 A combination of the situational change typology and Reddin's management style typology; both the appropriate strategy and tactics for implementing organizational change are determined by the competence mix

Useful approach

This situational approach to organizational change is useful for several reasons. First, it implies that training programs can be designed to increase awareness of the organization's existing competence mix so that commitment to an appropriate change strategy may be obtained. Or it can be used to alter the competence mix of various members of the organization to optimize the effectiveness of a chosen change strategy. Or, finally, it can be used to decide on one organizational change strategy rather than another by fitting the strategy to the organization's competence mix. This is a very different approach to training from the one usually adopted, where a set of values is agreed upon as a normative goal, and training is instituted to implement these values. While there is no doubt that a participative approach to change (e.g., cooperative change) can be effective, this is a far cry from being able to say that it is always optimally effective.

This typology also points out the importance of the congruency of managerial style and organizational change strategy. Neither one determines the other, but rather both managerial style and organizational change strategy are tied to situational requirements. It is interesting to note that a certain management style may be used more effectively in implementing a certain organizational change strategy, but this effectiveness is caused by the independent matching of the managerial style and the change strategy to the *situation,* and not to one another. Given a certain strategy for change then, the question is not "What managerial style would be most effective?" but, "Is this organizational change *strategy* likely to be effective here, and if so, what is the most effective managerial style to adopt in implementing it?"

In addition, the typology has significance for the individual manager since it aids situational sensitivity by serving to point out the variance between his managerial style and that required by the rest of the organization. The alternatives open to the individual manager include developing his style flexibility by adapting his style to that required by the situation, or developing his skill at situational management and changing the situation to adapt to his style.

Finally, the most important and basic contribution of the situational change typology is the idea that there is no best stategy. All arguments for one approach to organizational change versus another are hollow unless they take into account the requirements of the situation. While the typology presented here defines the situation in terms of two variables only, it remains useful as a training tool to focus attention on different approaches to change and the underlying factors determining the effectiveness of the change.

References

1 Reddin, W. J., *Managerial Effectiveness,* McGraw-Hill, 1970.
2 Bennis, Warren G., "A Typology of Change Processes," *The Planning of Change,* ed. W. G. Bennis, K. D. Benne and R. Chin, Holt, Rinehart and Winston, 1964, p. 154.
3 This suggestion has been made by F. J. Roethlisberger and W. J. Dickson, *Management and the Worker,* Wiley, 1964; L. Coch and J. R. P. French, "Overcoming Resistance to Change," *Human Relations,* 1, 1948, pp. 512–532; and in a more recent study by J. J. O'Connell, *Managing Organizational Innovation,* Irwin-Dorsey, 1968.
4 Erasmus, C. J., *Man Takes Control,* Bobbs-Merrill, 1961, and W. H. Goodenough, *Cooperation in Change,* Wiley, 1963.
5 Argyris, Chris, *Interpersonal Competence and Organizational Effectiveness.* Irwin-Dorsey, 1962, p. 16.
6 Berelson, Bernard and Steiner, Gary A., *Human Behavior,* Harcourt, Brace and World, 1964, p. 343.
7 Reddin, *op. cit.*
8 Reddin, *op. cit.*

48 Workers can set their own wages—responsibly
Edward E. Lawler

Decisions about pay are usually made behind closed doors by someone at a higher level in the company. And pay, not surprisingly, is a frequent subject of employee complaint. Managers and employees somehow assume that pay decisions must always be made at the top, and that pay will always be a source of dissatisfaction. But recent research in organizational behavior has demonstrated the possibility of practical alternatives to the standard pay systems, alternatives that are more attractive and equitable for employees, and more effective for their employers. These alternatives embrace the radical proposition that employees can take a strong part in setting their own remuneration.

Management usually assumes that lower-level employees don't have the necessary information to make such decisions, and can't be trusted to keep the company's interest in mind if they did. To find out if these assumptions are valid, I have conducted a number of studies of existing employee-participation pay systems, and have helped introduce such plans in several companies. The results suggest that managements should reexamine their standard pay practices.

The pay-and-benefits package

For most employees, the pay package consists of a mixture of salary and fringe benefits. The value of the benefits ranges from 10 to 40 percent of salary. Employees generally have no choice as to what benefits they receive; management simply makes the decision for them. Corporate executives usually defend this policy on two grounds: to make sure employees have the "proper" kind of benefit coverage; and to gain the cost advantages of buying the same benefits for all employees.

Stanley Nealey and I have found that this approach results in many employees receiving costly benefits they neither want nor, in some cases, even need. Employees with different family situations often want very different benefits. For example, young married men generally prefer less vacation and more insurance coverage; young unmarried males want more vacation time and less insurance coverage. Our recommended solution to this problem was simple; the employees should choose the benefits they want.

Two years ago one large West Coast electronics company followed our recommendation, and let about 12,000 employees decide—within cost

Source: From *Psychology Today* 10 (February 1977), pp. 109–110, 112. Copyright © 1977 Ziff-Davis Publishing Company. Reprinted by permission of *Psychology Today Magazine.*

limits—what mixture of salary and fringe benefits they wanted. More than 80 percent of them changed their benefits. They behaved responsibly, picking benefits that fit their family situation. In many cases this meant taking lower salaries in order to increase the benefit coverage. As a result of this experiment, the employees generally became more satisfied with their pay package because they now received the benefits they really wanted.

In most organizations, employees have no say about when they receive pay raises. Although many companies speak in terms of annual salary increases, all but a few actually give raises by adjusting the regular pay checks of their employees, thereby effectively spreading the increase out over the ensuing year.

This approach allows the employees no flexibility with respect to when they receive their raises. To get the full amount of their annual increase they have to wait an entire year. Once the raise is divided up among the regular pay checks, and the tax deductions are taken out, the increase in take-home pay is often minimal. Perceptually, this has the effect of burying a raise so that it is hardly visible to the recipient.

Lump-sum pay increases

Recognizing these problems, two companies—one engaged in food processing, the other in insurance—have started programs aimed at giving their managerial employees more choice about when they receive salary increases. Under this program, each individual gets the opportunity to decide when and how the annual increase will be distributed. Available options include spreading the increase out over the year, in the standard manner; getting it all in one lump sum at the beginning of the year; or receiving the increase in quarterly or semiannual installments. Increases advanced to employees in the form of lump-sum payments at the beginning of the year are treated as loans; if an employee quits before the end of a full year, he or she has to pay back the unearned part of the raise.

It is too early to evaluate the effectiveness of these salary-increase plans totally, but so far employees seem to like them, particularly because of the opportunity to get large sums of cash in advance for major purchases. While these two companies have offered their increase options only to managerial employees, the B.F. Goodrich Company recently extended such a plan to all its employees.

The evidence we have thus far suggests that when employees make decisions about their pay package, it benefits both the individuals involved as well as their company. But changing the components of the pay package is the easiest area for agreement, since the interests of the employees and the company are not in direct conflict. Changing the design and the amount of the pay package presents more potential for argument.

Pay plans are usually complicated systems designed by specialists in wage and salary administration. But becuase the employees are rarely consulted, the plans often ignore their needs and desires. Because of this lack of communication the employees often do not understand the pay plans, and feel no commitment to ensuring their success.

Employee-designed pay plans

I decided to find out if these problems might be overcome by having employees design their own pay system. In one study of 300 janitorial workers at an East Coast cleaning-service company, J. Richard Hackman and I asked several work groups to design a bonus system that would reward them for good attendance. The plan they developed was also put into effect for several other groups.

The results of this experiment came as quite a surprise to the company's management. The plan the workers created was carefully thought out, conservative in the amount of money it asked for, and quite effective in improving attendance. It worked particularly well for the groups that designed it because they were committed to making it work. Significantly, when management discontinued the bonus plan in two work groups, their attendance dropped back to previous levels.

In another experiment, Douglas Jenkins and I worked with a small, Midwest manufacturing firm with 100 employees, that was having trouble with its pay system. We arranged for a representative group of eight employees to develop a new pay plan. They first took courses in wage and salary administration, and did a survey of pay practices and rates in other local firms.

The plan they developed included a new approach to determining base-pay rates, and a bonus system that depended on the overall performance of the company. The base-pay system rated employees according to their skill levels, and paid them accordingly. The bonus system was based upon corporate return on investment, and covered all employees. The plan turned out to be simple, conservative in the amount it paid employees, and, most important, it worked.

A before-and-after survey showed that employee satisfaction with pay increased from seven to 38 percent. Employee commitment to the company also increased; the number of workers willing to consider another job dropped from 60 percent to 44 percent. Interviews with employees showed they were committed to seeing the plan work because they had designed it.

Individual pay decisions

All these studies and experiments, although heartening, don't tell us whether employees are capable of deciding intelligently how much they and their peers should actually be paid. These decisions are difficult because they most directly pit the employee's self-interest against that of the organization that employs them.

A few companies in the U.S. and Europe have been experimenting with employee participation in deciding individual pay rates. I have studied a number of these organizations. A good example of how peer-group decisions can be built into a pay plan is provided by the plan now in use at a fairly new General Foods dog-food-processing plant in Topeka, Kansas. The plan there is based upon a starting rate given to workers when they first join the plant's 120-man work force. After they have mastered five different jobs, employees move up to the next higher pay rate. After they have mastered all 10 jobs in the plant, they move to the top rate. The members of the person's work team decide when the person has mastered a job, and thus when he or she gets a pay increase.

Douglas Jenkins and I recently studied this General Foods plant. It is a fairly automated factory requiring relatively untechnical skills from its work force. We found that the new pay plan seems to be contributing to organizational effectiveness and an improved quality of work life. Because the pay plan encourages training for new jobs, the plant now has a very knowledgeable and flexible work force, with very low absenteeism and turnover rates. The new pay rates have not gotten out of control through overly lenient evaluations. Although the members of the work teams help each other to learn new jobs, it still takes a minimum of two years for an employee to be certified for all 10 jobs.

When we compared the attitudes toward pay of the Topeka employees with those of employees in similar plants without a peer-based pay plan, the results were dramatic. The Topeka plant had much higher levels of pay satisfaction and trust in the company. Much of the trust and commitment was due to the fact that the employees were making their own pay decisions.

Perhaps the most interesting case of workers setting their own pay has occurred at the Friedman-Jacobs Company, a small Oakland, California, appliance sales firm with 15 employees. Friedman decided to allow his employees to set their own wages, set their own hours, and take their vacations whenever they wanted to. This radical approach has apparently worked well.

Instead of the all-out raid on the company coffers that some people might expect, the 15 employees displayed astonishing restraint. They demanded wages just slightly higher than the scale of the union to which they belong. Some did not even take a raise. When one appliance serviceman who was receiving considerably less than his coworkers was asked why he did not insist on equal pay, he replied, "I don't want to work that hard." In this case, employees behaved quite realistically when given the responsibility for setting their own pay rates.

Not for everyone

The participative approach to pay plans may not work in all situations for all companies. And the success of new pay plans depends a great deal on how those involved, employees and management, perceive them. A good deal of past research has demonstrated that for pay plans to be successful at motivating effective performance, there must be a relationship between their pay and their performance. For pay plans to be successful in attracting and retaining employees they must create feelings of pay satisfaction.

The best source of information about how different pay systems and rates affect employees is the employees themselves, a source rarely consulted by management. Their participation in the design and administration of company pay systems should lead to more effective and more equitable policies for both employees and employers.

Of course, not all managers are ready or willing to give up their traditional power of the purse over employees. Most managers I have talked with reject the kind of employee participation described in this article. Those I have worked with are unusual in their commitment to democratic management. Without such commitment on the part of a company's senior executives, no such revisions in the pay system are possible.

I am not surprised that participation in pay decisions has led to greater trust and responsible behavior among employees. They are more likely to trust a system of their own design because they have more control over it. They become committed to it because they have contributed to its development. If this surprises some observers, it shouldn't. There is a great deal of evidence from other research indicating that when individuals are trusted and given responsibility, they respond accordingly. Why should they behave differently when dealing with their own pay?

Part VI

Controlling

Fortune is arbiter of half our actions, but she still leaves the control of the other half to us.
       Machiavelli

In this part we encounter the last of the traditional management functions: controlling. Ample evidence of the importance of planning, organizing, staffing, and influencing has been given. In a complex system, however, where the components and processes are interdependent, there must be some control of the activities to ensure successful accomplishment of ultimate goals. The managerial control function allows activities in progress to be evaluated in relation to expectations. Thus, according to Kast and Rosenzweig, the control function is defined as:

that phase of the managerial process which maintains organization activity within allowable limits as measured from expectations. These expectations may be implicit or explicitly stated in terms of objectives, plans, procedures, or rules and regulations.[1]

Note that the control function relates to much more than output at a given point in time. According to the definition, the control process serves a feedback function, often resulting in the identification of a need for new or adjusted plans. In brief, control forms one stage in the managerial cycle: planning—implementing—controlling.

The first selection, by Sayles, is a fairly recent examination of the many aspects of formal control systems. Sayles provides a comprehensive treatment of a multifaceted subject.

In the next three selections, the authors present several ideas concerning managerial control. In the first, Brummet, Pyle, and Flamholtz discuss a budgeting control device that is becoming increasingly important to

[1] Fremont E. Kast and James E. Rosenzweig, *Organization and Management: A Systems Approach* (New York: McGraw-Hill, 1970), p. 468. The first part of these comments has relied on Kast and Rosenzweig's discussion, Chapter 16.

industry: human resource accounting. Strong and Smith briefly describe break-even charts, and Daugherty and Harvey conclude the section by suggesting an additional facet that is critical to the control process—people. The authors demonstrate that controls in general and budgets in particular carry important implications for human behavior.

49 The many dimensions of control
Leonard Sayles

The subject of management controls is one of the oldest in the field of administration. No matter which theory or system of management one favors or practices, controls inevitably turn up as a central element—and properly so. After all, controls are the techniques by which the manager decides how to expand his most valuable asset, his time. Be they formal or informal, it is through controls that he knows where things are going badly that require his intervention—and where and when he can relax because things are going well. All managers from presidents to foremen make use of controls, some more effectively than others.

We have recently finished a review of the management of the National Aeronautics and Space Agency, extending from first-line technical managers and project managers up to the top of the agency. Although NASA has many special complications that wouldn't be found in most companies, its experience in the use of controls has direct relevance to any organization, public or private. Therefore, what follows is a general discussion of the use of management controls, with examples drawn from the space program.

Perhaps more problems are created by the manager's failure to recognize differences among types of control than by anything else. As we begin to look more closely at the functioning of any large organization, we observe four quite distinct types of control that perform very different functions for the manager.

1 *Reassurance to sponsors*   Higher management and sources of funds and support need reassurance that the major objectives are likely to be met efficiently and on time.
2 *"Closing the loop"*   The manager seeks to prove that technical and legal requirements have been met, and therefore that neither he nor the program is vulnerable to obvious omissions.
3 *Guidance to subordinates from managers*   The subjects their superiors pay

Source: Reprinted by permission of the publisher from *Organizational Dynamics* (Summer 1972). © 1972 by the American Management Association, Inc.

attention to, as demonstrated by both written documents and informal observations, give guidance to subordinates as to what is important and what they should concentrate on.

4 *Guidance to lower-level managers by higher management*   Perhaps the most important function of controls is to direct the attention and energies of managers to subjects and locations where accomplishment is lagging and management action is required.

We shall term number 1 high-level controls, number 2 low-level controls, and numbers 3 and 4 middle-level controls, the last being both the most important and the most easily neglected.

High-level controls

In a large organization, top management needs to be convinced that any individual program is reasonably efficient in moving toward its major goals. At the simplest level, this might mean showing the percentage of the total program completed in a given fiscal year. If possible, it is always useful to show that either the rate of completion or the rate of accomplishment per dollar of expenditure is improving.

The distinctive feature of these high-level measures is that they are intended to reassure those who are not sufficiently close to the scene to be able to see any of the detailed activities or to evaluate them. If properly done, they may ward off investigatory activities and provide sponsors and top management with ammunition to counter skeptics and the opposition. These measures, therefore, have a public relations quality about them, and it is unfortunate that a good deal of internal effort may have to be expended to accumulate statistical information to support pre-established contentions. Nevertheless, in any large organization, public or private, the higher echelons are sufficiently far removed so that they require this type of reassurance.

The business enterprise has the advantage of a slightly less arbitrary system called profit accounting, but is limitations in measuring managerial performance are also well known. Changes in inventory evaluation, decisions as to which costs will be capitalized and which will be expensed, formulas for "distributing" overhead, and similar accounting decisions can influence profitability by a modest factor of 100 percent or more. Even the general public is beginning to realize that profits are rather arbitrary numbers that can be manipulated within a wide range.

High-level controls are not controls in the usual management sense of the term. However, in complex endeavors necessitating substantial expenditures to complete high-risk programs that require many years to show results, it is necessary to provide some regularized feedback to those whose dollars or reputations are involved. The measures that are used demonstrate but do not prove efficiency, nor do they provide adequate bases for continuing supervision.

By this we mean simply that these reports demonstrate that managers are trying to improve performance, but they are not adequate measures of real performance. We are reminded, by analogy, of consulting firms installing new incentive plans that cut labor costs by 25 percent or even 40 percent. The reports made to top management appear to more than justify the investment in heavy installation costs. What the reports don't disclose is the increasing number of grievances over standards and the time and money involved in their settlement, the growing foreman-worker antipathy over the incentive program, and the costs of the continuing industrial engineering needed to update standards as jobs and technology change, as well as the growing resistance to technological change caused by the constant need to negotiate new standards. Added together, as they rarely are, these may show quite a different "profit" on the new incentive plan!

Low-level controls

Low-level controls are checking procedures established to insure that neither financial nor technical decisions are taken without adequate review, and that no necessary step has been omitted. Such procedures as these are typical examples:

- All expenditures over $500 have to be approved by the controller's office.
- When "off-standard" temperature prevails for more than five minutes, written authorization from the chief engineer is required to continue processing procedures.
- Storage of flammables within 50 feet of Building 209 requires the permission of the safety officer.
- Any substitution of materials must be approved by the subsystem engineer, the functional manager, and a representative of the project office.

These are old hat in classical scientific management, but they present recurring problems. Perhaps the most obvious problem is the predecision as distinct from a postdecision position of these controls. Nervous managers want to know before, of course, but every advance check is a potential delay; when there are many such checks, gaining the required authorizations, permissions, and what have you can hold up work on a specific problem for weeks or even months.

Important decisions are often subject to before-the-fact review by a number of people. Thus, in a technical program a design decision by an engineer may be reviewed by his functional manager, a technical specialist in the project office, the project manager, and then the program office. In addition, parallel system managers may also be involved. Such "sign offs" are time-consuming both for the project and for those who must review the technical details. When there are a great number of these to be made, there is a temptation for each echelon to give just a cursory glance.

Many after-the-fact checks are done on a sampling basis to assure functional managers that adequate technical expertise is being utilized and existing organizational policies are being upheld.

One of the most serious defects of these low-level controls is that they divert energy from critical problems to those where someone is checking up. It is the "numbers game" with which every experienced manager is familiar. Efforts are diverted to making oneself and one's department look good at the expense of larger goals and often at the expense of other managers.

The manager of the "frame and mechanics" unit, for example, was approached by the manager responsible for final assembly, who asked whether he would put some re-engineering efforts into reducing frame weight. It was clear that weight was an increasing problem and the total system would not get through final acceptance tests at the rate that the weight was increasing. The frame manager nodded agreement, but he knew he would do nothing. In the history of these projects, he knew that weight was always a problem, and furthermore one to which many managers contributed. The problem wouldn't get critical until the final tests, at which point it would be a problem for everyone, meaning no one—he wouldn't be blamed. On the other hand, if he diverted engineering effort now, a subsystem test next week might be in trouble, and those test results were watched closely by his boss. This manager minimized his potential losses by ensuring that a problem that involved him personally wouldn't occur next week and risking minor trouble a few months from now when the overweight problem would come up.

Many observers have noted what game theorists have called the "minimax" solution to individual efforts to cope with win-lose situations. The manager consistently chooses a decision by which he is guaranteed to minimize his losses, rather than seeking a large payoff at the risk of a big loss.

One all-too-common expression of the playing-it-safe syndrome is making sure that all rules, procedures and orders are followed and that easily measured quantitative benchmarks are met. Then, if a problem emerges, it can be argued that it is the "other guy's fault" because everything specified was done, as proved by the check results. Naturally, this hinders responsiveness to larger system interests, to facilitating the work of groups who may need your collaboration or modifications in your procedures, and who are dependent on your being flexible. The controls introduce rigidities that can become a serious problem whenever the work is not routine, the technology has intrinsic uncertainties, and the employee is not simply doing the same thing over and over again repeatedly.

Evidence of management concern in most organizations over these control-induced rigidities shows itself in the extent to which middle and upper management seek to see what is really happening, as distinct from what the controls tell them. Even relatively high-level managers, particularly when dealing with advanced technologies, seek to gain a feel for the raw technical data. They are not content to look at staff summary or exception reports. Nor is their concern misplaced. Evidence suggests that this immersion in technical detail is necessary to keep abreast and knowledgeable. Some even insist on sampling all the original correspondence concerning project progress and problems. Of course, this raises the obvious question of whether technically unsophisticated managers can properly serve in these posts.

Typical of this point of view is the following remark made by a project office engineer:

There is just no substitute for having the technical sophistication and willingness to go into the other guy's shop and look around. In R&D you've got to find out what he is not willing to tell you. The estimates, the test reports, and the progress reports tend to be too optimistic, and you'll go under every time if you take them at face value. The designers are always optimistic about future performance, and the project people naturally cover up their problems, so you've got to be their technical equal and get into the real data to know where you stand.

Of course, this effort also represents what we have called middle-level controls—that is, assessing the organizational effectiveness of various contributors to the system and seeking to predict where breakdowns are likely to occur.

Middle-level controls

Middle-level controls are signals to guide managers to act in ways that contribute to overall systems effectiveness, not to paper "wins" or immediate payoffs. They concentrate on what is necessary to keep the organization functioning. As techniques for keeping in touch with the progress of the dispersed parts of the program, assessing information received, and responding to a variety of information inputs, they are vital to any project manager. The project manager here is no different from any manager; handling middle-level controls is the heart of his job, because it determines where and when he must go into action.

Much of traditional management literature dealing with delegation and controls stresses the autonomy that must be given to subordinates for motivational reasons. The superior waits to intervene until the subordinate has manifestly failed; otherwise he stays out of the process.

This is a luxury that the manager and the organization can't afford. In the NASA launch control procedure, there are numerous engineers whose job it is to call a halt to the countdown if the pressure or temperature they are watching goes beyond some precisely defined limits. However, they can't afford to wait until the limit is exceeded; they must seek to predict if it is likely to go out, particularly during the later stages of the countdown. Of course, this takes more judgment and has greater elements of risk, responsibility, and personal stress than simply waiting for a clear signal of trouble.

Obviously, in highly costly programs, even the subordinates can't afford to wait for a technical process to go "out of limits." Failures must be prevented at all costs. NASA managers appear to suffer no ill effect from

having their actions reviewed with substantial regularity, even when there is
no evidence of failure. They speak with some pride about having developed
"over-the-shoulders management" in which the superior endeavors to
guarantee success, not to wait for failure. When everyone knows the costs
of failure and everyone is committed to the same goal—and not to individual
goals, such as the numerical scores so characteristic of low-level controls—
there is acceptance of the need for constant review in the most critical
areas. Engineers are not distressed because their superiors are watching
their actions, ready to step in should the system show signs of breaking
down—they appreciate the need, and even welcome the possibility of intervention.

Sizing up the other organization

Whether the work is being done by a contractor, within another functional
group, by one's own employees, or in another part of the organization not
immediately accessible to the project manager, there is the constant problem of predicting the likelihood of successful completion. In complex projects, managers learn to expect the unexpected; they realize that what looks
good today may be in deep trouble tomorrow, and that highly effective im-
provisation may be necessary to overcome very serious problems. Thus it
becomes important to assess the capability of the organizations that are
dealing with the various subsystems, their leadership, diligence, and competence; to ask what those people are like and how they are really performing.

To find out, the project manager and the coordinators reporting to him
seek to build a network of contacts within the various organizations whose
work will be vital to the completion of his responsibilities. He seeks contacts at sufficiently low levels to provide him with firsthand information instead of information that is highly filtered and refined, and thus deservedly
suspect. Many of these contacts will be "worked" daily during critical
periods or when the relationships are being established.

Information assessed

The project manager obviously needs information on schedules and budgets,
but he must also collect information on the organization itself. These are the
principal questions posed: How energetic and qualified are the managers
and their key technical people? How much priority do they assign to this
project, compared with other work that may be in process or in prospect?
How effectively do they work together, and what kind of support do they
usually receive from upper management and service groups?

The frequency of checking can have a strong effect on the amount of
information collected. When a manager is concerned about how the work of
a subordinate or a contractor is progressing, or when the participants are

strangers to each other, he will tend to increase the frequency of checking. From the point of view of the man or group being checked upon, a high frequency of checking communicates lack of trust, and it may also be a material handicap because of the time consumed responding to initiations and filling out reports. Moreover, when an individual detects that information will be used against him he tends to be circumspect about what is revealed. It is easy to get into a position in which the person being controlled restrains the flow of information and the controller is required to keep increasing the pressure required to extract valid progress reports. A dangerous spiral of administrative costs and conflicts can ensue.

This process shows itself most acutely when cutbacks are required, and it is necessary to calculate alternative costs and the impact of various budget amounts on existing programs. Lower echelons have a variety of ways of protecting certain programs by "proving" that any cutback will strike at the heart of their favorites.

With trust on both sides, the respondent is more candid, and less time and effort are required to obtain information.

Sensitivity to signals

Anyone experienced in R&D work learns not to jump at the first sign of trouble; troubles are endemic to these nonroutinized, one-of-a-kind activities. The question the manager must always ask is, what is *significant* trouble? He is concerned primarily with the kinds of difficulties that the other organization seems incapable of handling with its normal problem-handling apparatus. Put another way, the project manager is endeavoring to assess their reaction to stress situations.

Most managers make the mistake of using "absolutes" as signals of trouble—or its absence. A quality problem emerges—that means trouble; a test is passed—we have no problems. Outside of routine organizations, there are always going to be such signals of trouble or success, but they are not very meaningful. Many times everything looks good, but the roof is about to cave in because something no one thought about—and for which there is no rule, procedure, or test—has been neglected. The specifics of such problems cannot be predicted, but they are often signaled in advance by changes in the organizational system: Managers spend less time on the project; minor problems proliferate; friction in the relationships between adjacent work groups of departments increases; verbal progress reports become overly glib—or overly reticent; changes occur in the *rate* at which certain events happen, not in whether or not they happen. And *they* are monitored by random probes into the organization—seeing how things are going.

In addition, of course, the manager assesses the normal statistical reports on manpower, performance, cost, etc., checks PERT charts, and notes any significant deviations.

Further evaluation of signals: When to proceed

The project manager has to decide what signals that suggest potential trouble spots are worth following up by further probes. As we have already suggested, a probe is costly in terms of both the time and energy expended on the probe itself and the lost opportunity of pursuing an alternative probe. All leads can't be followed up.

The information he has is usually combined with other information to determine this decision: previous experience with this particular organization, its reputation, rumors in the field, and other data that may be available—labor problems, materials shortages, pending or recently completed negotiations, and the like. Another element in the manager's decision to act or not are the potential losses in future rapport and the driving up of reliable information once privileged information is revealed.

Preliminary steps

If it seems clear that a real problem is emerging, the manager who has made the evaluation may do one or more of the following:

1 Alert higher levels within his own management. Frequently the man who makes the observation is a technical coordinator who must decide when the project office is to be alerted.
2 Alert higher levels within management of the group in trouble. Many coordinators have told us that they observe things that local management hasn't learned, and it often takes a good deal of effort to persuade the organization that they have a problem.
3 Undertake further explorations and probings.
4 Alert other subsystems or stages that may be affected if the problem continues. Timing here is important. Doing this too soon can provide a signal to relax to the other units, and may reduce everyone's effort, particularly when it appears as though the schedule will be changed because of someone else's problems.

Next steps

So far the manager has contented himself with alerting the various parties affected by the problem—higher levels of his own management, higher levels in the management of the group in trouble and in interrelated subsystems. If the group in trouble seems unable to resolve the problem, the manager has several options: He may increase the pressure on local management; he may urge local management to take specific measures that he believes will resolve the problem; finally, he may attempt to work around the problem by changing the master plan and allowing stage three to begin, even though stage two has not been completed successfully, or he may authorize another and different method for doing stage two in the hopes that one or the other method will work. Both methods involve increased risks and sharply higher costs, but they may save the schedule.

If these efforts fail and the situation still is not "turning around," then the next step is to consider structural changes. Administrative action is apparently not sufficiently drastic to solve the problem.

Structural changes include evaluating other sources of supply, changing managers, renegotiating certain parts of the contract to reflect changes in requirements or capability, modifications of the specifications, and so forth. More modest examples include providing direct assistance to the troubled unit by sending in specialists from the headquarters organization, requiring more or less subcontracting, and the like.

Structural changes should never be contemplated lightly. Most of these actions involve significant changes in cost; they endanger personal relationships, have wide and sometimes unpredictable impacts, and require substantial effort to implement. A prime test of the effective manager is his ability to anticipate most of the potential ramifications involved in any such drastic action.

Assessing organizational effectiveness

Another way of viewing these middle-level controls is that they seek to assess how the organizational system is functioning as a system. They assume that organizational malfunctioning precedes technical malfunctioning; failures in the former are a good predictor of failures in the latter. Let us look at some examples of both the kinds of organizational relationships that can be monitored and their predictive value.

Workflow responsiveness

Organizationally, this means that managers responsible for adjacent workflow stages be willing to engage in some give and take and be responsive to each other's needs so that there can be swift resolution of difficulties that span two or more jurisdictions.

Unfortunately, it is quite easy for any group to refuse to consider alternatives, unless "bribed" excessively by mustering a number of reasonable technical arguments. Evidence that a given manager consistently responds to the project office or other adjacent groups with flat refusals is a sign that upper management should give the manager its concentrated attention and intervene directly whenever it becomes necessary.

The generalization is true for any large-scale organization: Waiting to look at results guarantees a kind of "crisis management" characterized by turmoil and high costs in both material and human resources. Every organization increasingly needs good middle-level controls, which by continuously measuring the degree to which the organization is holding together as an organization can pinpoint potential trouble spots before they become serious.

Finally, these middle-level controls, because they concentrate on the total system, concern themselves with integration and coordination. This means that they assess the ability of subordinates, managers, and work groups to coordinate their activities, make mutually satisfying trade-offs, and get the total job done. By doing so, they contribute to breaking down departmental boundaries and help to unify the organization.

Polarization of issues

Human groups obtain major satisfactions and facilitate their own cohesiveness by sharing in a common dislike or even hatred. In highly integrated systems, work-related groups cannot afford the luxury of these polarizations.

This happens in any organization. For example, marketing and production are at each other's throats over their relative balance of power. No matter what problem comes up—even if it is only a trivial request by marketing for an advance copy of production's next month's schedule—becomes part of the struggle: "Do they want that schedule early to use it with top management to hang us? In some way or other are they trying to show us that they have the power to get us to change our reporting system, to show that we have to defer to them?" Polarization means that everything is evaluated in terms of a power struggle and that divisiveness dominates all decisions.

Monitoring headquarters-field relationships

Typically, the program and project manager have a somewhat blurred division of labor. It is easy for the program manager to be either too assertive in project affairs or too distant.

In the division of labor between field and headquarters, it is important for the program manager to act as a buffer between the field-level technical staff and external demands. He should be the one who responds to the questions, criticisms, and pressures of other headquarters' functional and program people, as well as to external political, technical, and economic pressures.

There are several reasons for this: A reasonable amount of risk-taking is essential if innovative solutions to both the predicted and unanticipated technical barriers are to be found. An excessively "safe" approach can lead to high costs, delayed schedules, cumbersome redundancy, and uninspired design. This is not to say that field personnel should make imprudent changes, but that long-run success is probably a function of a somewhat protected development environment in which every step does not have to be justified immediately.

This also represents a functional division of labor. Headquarters personnel should have more time; more experience; supplementary resources, such as readily available advisory services; and greater skill in coping with external initiations. Field personnel need all the time they can get for technical coordination, monitoring, and developmental efforts.

Finally, we have a good deal of evidence that a durable field headquarters relationship, as is true of most leadership situations, requires the higher-status "partner" to prove to those dependent upon him that he has the willingness, the power, and the skill to represent them and protect them from external threats. Lacking this, the headquarters manager will find it increasingly difficult to communicate to field personnel and get the response he is seeking.

Conclusion

There is an old theme in economics about bad money driving out good, and social scientists have noted an analogous tendency for easily quantified measures to drive out more subjective ones. The problem in the control area of management is that it is easier to give numerical scores to what we have called high-level and low-level performance. The result is that the manager is induced—or seduced—into doing things that make him and his unit look good, often at the expense of larger organizational goals and the larger system.

This is not to deny the usefulness of high- and low-level controls that try to measure accomplishments by comparing cost, schedule, and performance to date with what was predicted or budgeted. Equally important, however, is what these controls fail to do and fail to show. They are misleading as a measure of performance because they assume rigid plans and unified responsibilities, a misconception that is particularly dangerous in an organization in which the nature of the projects insures that unanticipated obstacles will become expected problems on an almost daily basis.

50 Human resource accounting in industry
R. Lee Brummet, William C. Pyle, and Eric G. Flamholtz

Investments in the business enterprise

Investments are expenditures made for the purpose of providing future benefits beyond the current accounting period. If a firm purchases a new plant

Source: From Personnel Administration, 32: 4 (1969), pp. 34–46. Reprinted by permission of the International Personnel Management Association, 1313 East 60th Street, Chicago, Illinois 60637.

with an expected useful life of fifty years, it is treated as an investment on the corporate balance sheet, and is depreciated over its useful life. If the structure should be destroyed or become obsolete, it would lose its service potential and be written off the books as a loss which would be reflected as an offset against earnings on the company's statement of income.

Firms also make investment in *human* assets. Costs are incurred in recruiting, hiring, training, and developing people as individual employees and as members of viable interacting organizational groups. Furthermore, investments are made in building favorable relationships with *external* human resources such as customers, suppliers, and creditors. Although such expenditures are made to develop future service potential, conventional accounting practice assigns such costs to the "expense" classification, which, by definition, assumes that they have no value to the firm beyond the current accounting year.

For this reason human assets neither appear on a corporate balance sheet, nor are changes in these assets reflected on the statement of corporate income. Thus, conventional accounting statements may conceal significant changes in the condition of the firm's unrecognized human assets. In fact, conventional accounting statements may spuriously reflect *favorable* performance when human resources are actually being liquidated (1). If people are treated abusively in an effort to generate more production, short term profits may be derived through liquidation of the firm's organizational assets. If product quality is reduced, immediate gains may be made at the expense of customer loyalty assets.

A need exists, therefore, to develop an organizational accounting or information system which will reflect the current condition of and changes in the firm's human assets. Some accountants have recognized such a need, but measurement difficulties pose problems for them. As early as 1922, William A. Paton observed:

In the business enterprise, a well-organized and loyal personnel may be a more important "asset" than a stock of merchandise. . . . At present there seems to be no way of measuring such factors in terms of the dollar; hence, they cannot be recognized as specific economic assets. But let us, accordingly, admit the serious limitations of the conventional balance sheet as a statement of financial condition (2).

Importance of human resources

Why have industry and the accounting profession steadfastly neglected accounting for human resources? Aside from the measurement difficulties, the answer may be found, partly, in the perpetuation of accounting practices which trace their origins to an early period in our industrial history when human resource investments were relatively low. In more recent years, however, those occupational classifications exhibiting the highest rates of growth, such as managerial and technical groupings, are those which require the greatest investment in human resources (3). In addition, rising organizational complexity has created new demand for developing more sophisticated interaction capabilities and skills within industry (4). These and other factors, coupled with persistent shortages in highly skilled occupational groupings increase the need for information relevant to the management of human resources.

Resource management needs

Although oversimplified, management may be viewed as a process of *acquisition and development, maintenance,* and *utilization* of a "resource mix" to achieve organizational objectives, as suggested in Figure 1. Accounting and information systems contribute to this process by identifying, measuring, and communicating economic information to permit informed judgments and decisions in the management of the resource mix. Management needs information regarding: (1) resource acquisition and development, (2) resource maintenance or condition, and (3) resource utilization.

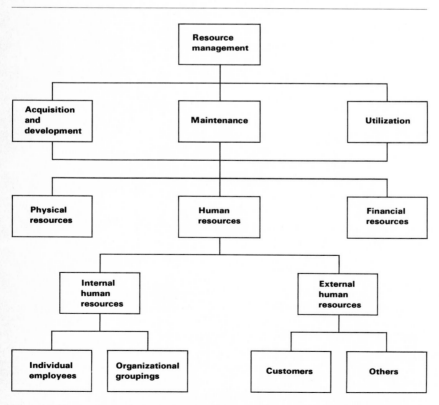

Figure 1 The process of resource management

Resource acquisition and development information needs

Organizations acquire a wide variety of resources to achieve their purposes. Investments are undertaken in those resources which offer the greatest potential returns to the enterprise given an acceptable degree of risk. Calculation of resource acquisition and development costs is necessary, therefore, not only for investment planning, but also as a base for determining differential returns which accrue to those investments. The *resource acquisition and development information needs* reflect themselves along two dimensions; (1) the need for measurement of *outlay costs* when assets are actually acquired, and (2) the need for estimating the *replacement cost* of these investments in the event they should expire.

Resource maintenance or condition information

Investments are undertaken in resources with the objective of creating new capabilities, levels of competency, types of behavior, forms of organization, and other conditions which will facilitate achieving organizational objectives. An information need exists, therefore, to ascertain the degree to which investments in resources actually produce and sustain the desired new capabilities, levels of competency, types of behavior, and forms of organization.

Resource utilization information

Once new capabilities, levels of competency, and other "system states" are achieved, *resource utilization information* needs become more salient. Management should know the degree to which changes in resource conditions or "system states" are translated into organizational performance. The answer to this question is reflected in the rate of return on the investments which created the new "system state" or resource condition.

Conventional accounting and information needs

Conventional accounting or information systems answer these three basic information needs for *non-human resources.* Measurement of investment in plant and equipment fulfills the "acquisition information need." Over time, these assets are depreciated, and new investments are recorded. The current "book values" of such investments reflect, at least in theory, the "resource condition" of the organization's physical assets. Finally, "utilization information needs" are supplied in the form of return on investment calculations.

Unfortunately, conventional accounting systems do not answer these three basic information needs for human assets. The objective of our research effort, therefore, is to develop a body of human resource accounting theory and techniques which will, at least in part, alleviate these information deficiences.

Human resource accounting model

The development of human resource accounting in the business enterprise derives from the pioneering work of Rensis Likert and his colleagues at the University of Michigan's Institute for Social Research. For more than two decades, their research studies have revealed that relationships exist between certain variable constructs and organizational performance. *"Causal variables,"* such as organizational structure and patterns of management behavior have been shown to affect *"intervening variables"* such as employee loyalties, attitudes, perceptions, and motivations, which in turn have been shown to affect *"end-result variables"* such as productivity, costs, and earnings (5). Furthermore, research by Likert and Seashore indicates that time lags of two years or more often exist between changes in the "causal variables" and resultant changes in the "end-result variables" (6).

As seen in Figure 2, Likert's three variable models have been adopted into a human resource accounting model with the addition of two variable constructs—*"Investment variables"* and *"return on investment variables."* Why have these new variable classifications been added? All business firms wish to improve organizational performance. In doing so, however, a more crucial question is, *how much* will performance be improved and *what will it cost?* When a firm invests in new capital equipment, the costs of various alternatives are estimated for each along with projected rates of return. For example, one piece of equipment may cost $75,000 and have an estimated rate of return of 20 percent, while another may cost $100,000 with a return estimate of 15 percent.

An important objective of our research is to extend capital budgeting concepts to the firm's human resources. If the company invests $50,000 in a new training program, what is the anticipated return? If the firm invests $75,000 in an organizational development program, what return will accrue to that investment?

Human resource variables and information needs

Investment variables

Investments in both human and non-human assets are recorded in dollar units and are measured to fulfill the *"resource acquisition and development information"* needs of management through identification of investment *outlay costs* and *replacement costs.* Conventional accounting practice now identifies *non-human* resource investments, at least on an outlay cost basis. In January 1968, a human resource accounting system was operationalized at the R. G. Barry Corporation to measure "individual employee" investments. Development work is now in progress to provide a system for identifying "organizational investments."

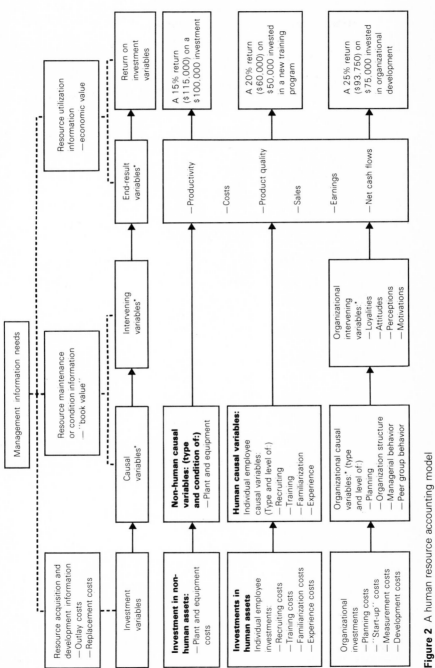

Figure 2 A human resource accounting model
*A more complete listing of variables is found in Rensis Likert, *The Human Organization: Its Management and Value*, Appendix III.

"Causal variables"

These are independent variables which management may alter to affect the course of developments within the organization. These variables include the type and condition of plant and equipment, and the type and level of employee competency, managerial behavior, organizational structure, and related factors. As suggested by the arrows in Figure 2, the state of the "individual employee causal variables" is more likely to *directly* affect the "end-result variables" (e.g., productivity, costs, and product quality) than the "organizational causal variables," whose effects tend to pass through a series of "intervening variables," which will be discussed shortly.

"Causal variables" are measured to supply the "resource maintenance or condition information" needs of management. Both dollar and socio-psychological based measurements may be employed to reflect the condition of the "causal variables." Conventional accounting practice now provides "non-human causal variable" data in the form of asset book values which, at least in theory, reflect the current state of those assets. A similar system for measuring "individual employee causal variables" has been implemented at the R. G. Barry Corporation. Questionnaire survey techniques developed by the Institute for Social Research are being employed to measure "organizational causal variables."

Intervening variables

As stated above, the effect of "organizational causal variables" may not be directly reflected in the "end-result variables." Time lags of two years or more have been observed between changes in these "causal variables" and resultant changes in the "end-result variables." The effects of changes in "organizational causal variables" have been traced through a series of *intervening variables,*" which include employee loyalties, attitudes, perceptions, and motivations.

"Intervening variables" are not measured in dollar units, but in terms of a scaling of perceptions derived from a socio-psychological questionnaire. Measurements of the "intervening variables" are directed toward the "resource maintenance or condition information" needs of the organization.

End-result variables

These are dependent variables which reflect the achievements of the organization. The particular "end-result variables" for a given enterprise are a function of performance objectives which have been defined by that organization. These may include the level of productivity, costs, product quality, sales, earnings, net cash flows, employee health and satisfaction, and related factors.

"End-result variables" are normally measured in monetary terms, but they may also be reflected in socio-psychological units, as in the case of employee satisfaction. Changes in "end-result variables" may be associated with variations in "investment," "causal," and "intervening" variables through multiple correlation analyses of data collected in each of the variable classifications over an extended period of time. In this fashion, "end-result variables" may be expressed in the form of *"return on investment variables"* where a particular change in the "end-result variables" can be significantly associated with a particular "investment variable" change. For example, if $75,000 were invested in an organizational development program, and a $93,750 change in predetermined "end-result variables" was observed, a return of 25 percent would be realized on the investment. Such analyses may be employed to improve the allocation of organizational resources by indicating which investment patterns should be increased, reduced, or maintained at their current level.

Ultimately, it may be possible to place a current valuation on the firm's human resources through a process of discounting estimates of future "end-result variables," using time lags and relationships which have been observed among the variable classifications. The results of this valuation can be cross-checked against the unexpired costs which are recorded in the human asset accounts.

Human resource accounting objectives

The ultimate objective of the research is to develop an integrated accounting function which fulfills basic information needs with respect to physical, financial, and human resources both internal and external to the organization. As an intermediate objective, we are concentrating on the development of an *internal human resource* accounting capability. This research effort divides itself into three functions: (1) *the development of a human resource accounting system oriented to basic managerial information needs,* (2) *the development and refinement of managerial applications of human resource accounting, and* (3) *the analysis of the behavioral impact of human resource accounting on people.* These objectives are being pursued in a five-year inter-company research program which has been initiated by the University of Michigan's Institute for Social Research and Graduate School of Business Administration in cooperation with several corporations.

Research at the R. G. Barry Corporation (7)

Since October 1966, the University of Michigan has been engaged, along with the management of the R. G. Barry Corporation, in development of what is believed to be the first human resource accounting system. The Barry Corporation's 1,300 employees manufacture a variety of personal comfort items including foam-cushioned slippers, chair pads, robes, and other leisure wear, which are marketed in department stores and other retail out-lets under brand names such as Angel Treds, Dearfoams, Kush-ons, and Gustave. The corporate headquarters and four production facilities are in Columbus, Ohio. Several other plants, warehouses, and sales offices are lo-cated across the country. The firm has expanded from a sales volume of about $5½ million in 1962 to approximately $20 million in 1968.

Implementation of a human resource accounting system

The first phase of a human resource accounting system became operational at the R. G. Barry Corporation during January 1968. This system measures investments which are undertaken in the firm's some 96 members of man-agement, on both *outlay cost* and *replacement cost* bases. An account structure applicable to organizational investments is now being developed. The Barry Corporation is now in the process of extending human resources accounting to other occupational classifications in the firm. In the future, a system will be developed for its customer resources. A model of an outlay cost measurement system for employees is presented in Figure 3.

Historical and replacement investments measured

An outlay cost measurement system

Investments in human resources may be measured in terms of outlay costs. *Outlay costs* are sacrifices incurred by the firm in the form of out-of-pocket expenditures associated with a particular human resource investment. These are measured in terms of *non-salary* and *salary* costs. Examples of the former include travel costs in support of recruiting or training, and tuition charges for management development programs. The latter would include employee salary allocations during an investment period. For example, if an executive attends a two-week management seminar, his salary for this time period should be viewed as part of the investment, in addition to the tuition and travel costs. Similarly, if during the first year of tenure with a firm, 30 percent of a new manager's time is devoted to familiarization with company policy, precedents, organization structure, interaction patterns, and the like, 30 percent of his salary should be recorded as an outlay cost associated with the familiarization investment.

At the R. G. Barry Corporation, instruments have been designed to measure investments undertaken in *individual managers* for each of the functional accounts indicated in Figure 3. To qualify as assets, specific expenditures must meet the test of offering service potential beyond the current accounting period in relation to long term written corporate objec-tives. Charges to the functional accounts are also entered in "individualized accounts" for each manager. With a few modifications the individual man-ager account structure will also be applied to other occupational groupings

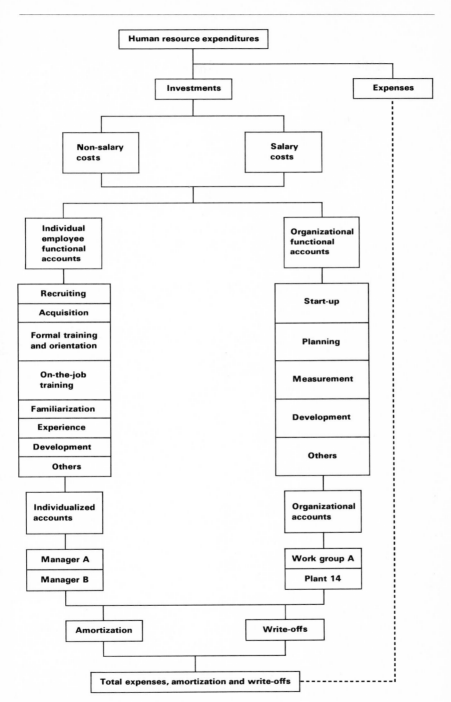

Figure 3 Model of an outlay cost measurement system

within the firm. However, it is not contemplated that "individualized accounts" will be developed for factory and clerical personnel.

Procedures have also been designed to record investment expirations. Asset accounts are amortized on two bases: (1) *maximum life* and (2) *expected life.* Functional investments are separately identified in each manager's account and are amortized according to the *maximum life* of each investment type. For example, recruiting and acquisition costs provide benefits to the firm so long as an employee remains with the organization. The *maximum life* of this investment would be the mandatory retirement age less the employee's age when hired. If *maximum life* were relied on exclusively for amortization, asset accounts would be overstated since employees frequently leave the firm prior to the mandatory retirement age. To assure a more realistic statement of assets, maximum life amortization periods are adjusted to expected life by application of weighted probabilities which reflect a particular individual's likelihood of remaining until mandatory retirement based upon his age, tenure, organizational level, marital status, job satisfaction, and related factors. *Expected life* periods are employed in the amortization of the functional accounts.

The choice between these two bases is essentially a choice between relevance and verifiability. "Maximum life" provides a highly verifiable base, but it is less relevant than "expected life." "Expected life" may, to some degree, be influenced by job satisfaction as well as many other factors. For this reason, a firm may wish to obtain a range of estimates. To be more conservative, "expected life" is employed to calculate the investments shown on the firm's balance sheet and an adjustment to net income based upon changes occurring in those investments. Other estimates may be more useful for planning purposes.

Specific measurement instruments have been designed to record human asset losses resulting from turnover, obsolescence, and health deteriorations. Turnover is immediately identifiable; however, obsolescence is much more elusive. For this reason individual employee asset accounts are reviewed quarterly for obsolescence by each supervisor. Review also occurs when an employee is transferred to a new position. Accounts are also adjusted for known health deteriorations in proportion to the seriousness of the impairment as reflected in actuarial data.

As suggested in Figure 3, an outlay cost measurement system designed to record *organizational investments* is now being developed at the R. G. Barry Corporation. Investments are undertaken in human resources *over and above* those made in *individual employees as individuals.* Organizational "start-up" costs are reflected in heavy individual employee investments and in production below standard during the initial period when the organization is building and developing group interaction patterns for the first time. Additional investments are also made in the form of organizational planning. Furthermore, periodic measurement of organizational causal and intervening variables are in themselves investments in the organization when they lead to development activities which improve the functioning of the enterprise as an interacting system. Finally, investments are undertaken in the organization which cannot be readily traced to individual employees. A portion of the operating costs of the personnel department, company library, health service, safety department, and similar departments may be traced to activities which offer long term benefits to the organization.

Charges made to the "organizational functional accounts" will also be allocated to appropriate entities such as work groups, plants, divisions, or the enterprise as a whole. In addition, a capability is being developed to reflect expirations which occur in these accounts. Many "organizational investments" differ *in kind* from "individual employee investments" which lose their usefulness to the firm when a particular individual leaves the firm. For example, benefits could be derived indefinitely from costs incurred in molding the organization into a system of effective interacting groups despite a moderate level of individual employee turnover within the system. This suggests the possibility that some organizational investments may be non-depreciable.

This would not, however, preclude the possibility of expirations. If for example, an enterprise invests $50,000 in an organizational development program which succeeds in improving employee attitudes and motivations by a measurable amount, subsequent deterioration in those attitudes and motivations could justify a write-off of the original investment.

A replacement cost measurement system

The outlay cost system described above is designed to record human resource investments, obsolescence, and losses as they are actually incurred. These data, however, only partially fulfill the "resource information" needs of the organization. For planning purposes, the *positional replacement cost of* human resources becomes more salient. Positional replacement costs are the outlay costs (recruiting, training, etc.) which would be incurred if an incumbent should leave his position. The human resource accounting system which has been installed at the R. G. Barry Corporation has the capability of supplying average positional replacement cost data for each manager. These positional replacement cost data reflect annual adjustments for price level changes. The system also records "compositional" investment changes since some investments undertaken in the past will not be repeated and, conversely, others not made in the past will be undertaken in the future. For these and other reasons, positional replacement cost may be less than, equal to, or greater than historical outlay cost.

Appropriate measurement units

As noted above, "investment variables" are measured exclusively in dollar or socio-psychologically based units. However, "causal variables"(8) may be measured in either dollars or socio-psychological terms. For example, the current condition of the firm's plant and equipment (a "causal variable") should be reflected at its current book value, although other indicators can also be employed. Similarly, the *current condition* of the company's "individual employee investments" (a "causal variable") should be reflected at the book values recorded in the functional asset accounts discussed above. However, other indicators are being developed as cross-checks. Socio-psychological survey questions are now being used to measure employee perceptions of the current condition of "individual employee causal variables" such as the quality of recruiting and training. Trends in these data are being compared with trends in the individual employee asset account balances. These socio-psychological data may suggest more realistic amortization procedures for individual employee investments." The current condition of "organizational causal variables" may also be reflected in the current book value of "organizational investments," recorded in dollar units. However, socio-psychological survey instruments may prove more valid since managerial behavior (a "causal variable") may be altered independently of cost outlays.

"Intervening variable" measurements have been undertaken at the R. G. Barry Corporation and additional surveys are planned. However, an accumulation of several years' data will be required before meaningful "return on investment variables" may be calculated.

Human resource accounting applied

Human resource accounting system applications are oriented toward fulfilling the three basic organizational information needs: (1) resource acquisition and development information, (2) resource maintenance or condition information and (3) resource utilization information. Inasmuch as the human resource accounting system at the R. G. Barry Corporation is in an early stage of development, its potential applications can only be stated in tentative terms at this time.

It is contemplated that the system will generate two types of data: (1) information which is integrated with conventional accounting statements and (2) information which is presented independently of these statements.

Human resource data integrated and conventional financial reports

One of the first reports generated by the system is a *balance sheet* indicating the firm's investment in human resources. The corporate *income statement* is also affected to the degree that there is a net change in the firm's investment in human resources during the reporting period. This situation is illustrated in Figure 4. The two balance sheets indicate that a hypothetical company experienced a *net increase* in its investment in *individual employees* during the period. This change taken by itself, would result in a positive adjustment to the firm's net income (9) of $100,000. However, this firm also experienced a *net decline* in its organizational investments during the period. (This could result, for example, from a plant being closed in one location with operations being moved to another state.) This change, taken by itself, would result in a negative net income adjustment of $200,000. When the two changes are taken together, a negative adjustment of $100,000 is reflected in the firm's net income.

Figure 4

Balance sheet

Assets	Dec. 31, 1967	Dec. 31, 1968
Current assets (cash, etc.)	$1,000,000	$1,500,000
Plant and equipment	8,000,000	8,000,000
Investment in individual employees (recruiting, training, development, etc.)	750,000	850,000
Organizational investments (start-up, planning, development, etc.)	900,000	700,000
Total assets	$10,650,000	$11,050,000
Equities		
Liabilities	$2,000,000	$2,000,000
Owner's equity: Stock	6,000,000	6,000,000
Retained earnings (including investment in human resources)	2,650,000	3,050,000
Total equities	$10,650,000	$11,050,000

Income statement
Year ending December 31, 1968

Sales		$2,000,000
Expenses		1,500,000
Net income		$ 500,000
Adjustment for change in investment in human resources		
—Individual employee adjustment	+$100,000	
—Organizational adjustment	−$200,000	−100,000
Adjusted net income		$ 400,000

Data generated by the human resource accounting system at the R. G. Barry Corporation indicate that the replacement investment of their some 96 managers is approximately $1,000,000, while the current "book value" is about $600,000. The firm invests around $3,000 in a first line supervisor and upwards of $30,000 in a member of top management.

Other human resource accounting reports

A variety of additional reports are now being generated by a human resource accounting system. Periodic comparative data for different work groups, plants, and divisions contrast human resource investment changes during reporting periods. Turnover losses are also being quantified and analyzed according to such factors as employee job satisfaction, age, occupation, tenure and the like. Special purpose reports are also being prepared to evaluate various organizational alternatives which require investments in human resources. To increase production capacity, for example, should a firm expand its existing plant or construct a new facility? For each alternative these reports indicate projected new investments, write-offs, and the effect on net cash flows. Once a particular alternative is chosen, actual investment, write-offs and cash flows may then be contrasted against projections. As patterns of return on investments in human resources become apparent, the firm will learn which investment types should be increased, reduced, or maintained at their current level.

The ultimate success of any accounting system is determined by its impact on the behavior of people. Where the goals of employees and the organization are reasonably consistent, data may be employed as a problem solving tool to achieve organizational objectives. However, the social science literature is replete with evidence of the distortions which may be introduced into an information system when individual and organizational goals are not congruent (10). For this reason, an integral part of human resource accounting research will focus on determining the behavioral impact of an operational human resource accounting system on employees. Socio-psychological survey instruments supplemented by personal interviews will be employed to assess the impact. These data will, in turn, be used to design organization development activities which will facilitate installation and sustained operation of the human resource accounting system

Conclusions

Human resource accounting is now in an early stage, and a host of problems remain to be resolved before a fully-developed system can become operational. However, the initial results are encouraging as many beneficial results are being derived prior to full scale operation. Investments in human resources may be determined at a relatively early stage. The techniques developed to measure these assets may also be employed in extended organizational and manpower planning which underlie and sustain corporate growth. Even before return on investment data become available, measurement of trends and rates of change in "causal" and "intervening" variable data may suggest new behaviors and investment routes which will improve organizational effectiveness.

Notes

1 Rensis Likert, *The Human Organization: Its Management and Value,* New York: McGraw-Hill, 1967, pp. 101–115.
2 W. A. Paton, *Accounting Theory,* New York: The Ronald Press, 1922, pp. 486–87.

3 U. S. Bureau of the Census, Historical Statistics of the United States, Colo-
nial Times to 1957, Washington, D.C. 1960, pp. 74–75; pp. 202–14.
4 Likert, *op. cit.*, pp. 156–160.
5 *Ibid.*
6 Likert, R. and Seashore, S., "Making Cost Control Work," *Harvard Business
Review,* November–December 1963, pp. 96–108.
7 This research was described in greater depth in a monograph prepared
by the authors and published in 1969.
8 Where relationships between the level of job satisfaction and expected tenure can be identified, turnover losses may be calculated in dollar terms and
predicted for varying levels of job satisfaction, as a function of measured
changes in causal and intervening variables.
9 The net income that would be indicated without a human resource accounting system
10 Argyris, C., "Human Problems with Budgets," *Harvard Business Review,*
January–February 1953, pp. 97–110; Whyte, W. F., *Money and Motivation,*
New York: Harper & Row, 1955.

---

51 Break-even charts
Earl P. Strong and Robert D. Smith

The break-even chart, Figure 1, gives an executive a financial picture of his
operation. By drawing a vertical line at any point in the graph, a quick, visual
profit and loss statement can be determined simply by measuring the vertical lengths of the line segments. For instance, line A develops the following
data:

Sales		$420,000
Fixed costs	$320,000	
Variable costs	120,000	440,000
Loss		$ 20,000

Line B develops the following data:

Sales		$720,000
Fixed costs	$320,000	
Variable costs	220,000	540,000

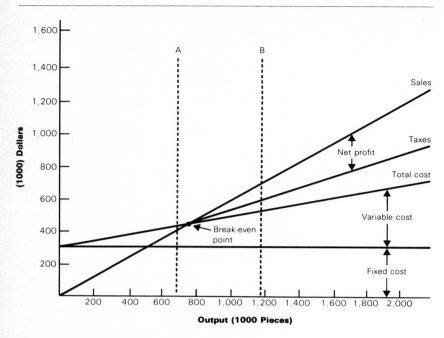

Figure 1 Break-even chart for a manufacturing concern

Gross profit	180,000
Taxes	30,000
Net profit	$150,000

If more detail is desired, fixed and variable costs could each be broken down further and plotted. The components of fixed costs might be depreciation on property, depreciation on equipment, salaries of key personnel, interest on borrowed money, floor space expense, and real estate expenses. The components of variable costs might be direct labor, direct material, transportation, and variable overhead.

The executive can use the break-even chart to predict the effect of changes of various kinds in the overall profit picture of his business. An increase in material cost or direct labor, a decrease in sales price in an effort to increase volume, or the purchase of an expensive piece of equipment can be pictured quickly on the break-even chart.

Figure 2 shows the effect of such changes in the break-even point for no gain, no loss. Such break-even charts assume linear relationships among all variables and the reader should remember that, in the event nonlinear functions are involved, this type of analysis may lead to erroneous conclusions.

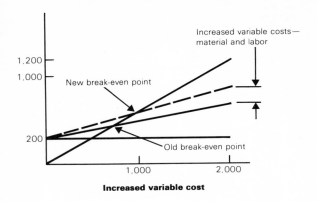

Increased variable cost

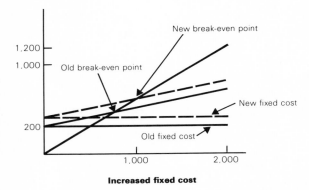

Increased fixed cost

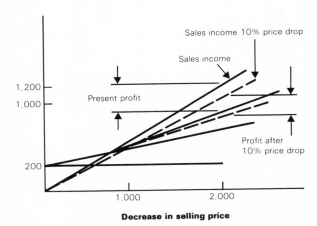

Decrease in selling price

Figure 2 Changes in break-even point due to various changes in operating expenses

52 Some behavioral implications of budgeting systems
William Daugherty and Donald Harvey

The motivational impact of budgeting has often been neglected or ignored, as Robert Townsend has suggested:

Budgets must not be prepared on high and cast as pearls before swine. They must be prepared by the operating divisions. Since a division must believe in the budget as its own plan for operations, management cannot juggle figures just because it likes to. Any changes must be sold to the division or the whole process is a sham.[1]

There has been a tendency to emphasize the negative or punishment aspects of budgets, which has tended to reinforce the use of budgetary systems as pressure devices. A recent survey by the authors suggests that budget systems may actually operate as a negative motivational force in many organizations.

The results of the survey suggest that the budgeting process may involve unintended consequences that stifle change and innovation, restrict managerial initiative, induce inappropriate pressures, and tend to reinforce management leadership by the rule book. All of these behavioral consequences tend to have dysfunctional results in terms of overall organizational objectives.

Clearly, these findings lead to an increasing realization of the pervasiveness and significance of the human component and the importance of recognizing the behavioral implications that are inherent in planning and control systems. Therefore, it is the purpose of this article to examine briefly the multiplicity of objectives and models within the budgeting process, to identify some behavioral consequences of planning and control systems, and to suggest some directions for developing more effective systems.

The multiplicty of budget objectives and models

Budgets are now used extensively as an essential element in organizational planning and control systems by almost all major organizations. Budgeting is the process of taking management's plans and expressing these plans in dollars and cents, allocating or factoring total system resources into a set of subsystem plans, and providing a common language for communicating a description of planned operations and activities for a given period of time.

Source: From *Arizona Business* (April 1973), pp. 3–7. Reprinted by permission of the publisher, College of Business Administration, Arizona State University.
[1] R. Townsend, *Up the Organization* (New York: Knopf, 1970).

Generally, with regard to initiation of budget objectives, budget systems fall into one of two general categories or some combination thereof: "top down" where the targets and goals are determined by top management and sent down to lower departmental levels, or "bottom up" where departmental goals and objectives are defined at subordinate levels and integrated with other departmental plans at higher levels. Many organizations combine the two approaches. This involves the determination of guidelines at the higher level of management and actual budget preparation by lower level units.

The survey conducted by the authors revealed a multiplicity of budget functions and budget models used in major organizations. Among the different functions of the budget systems were the following:

1 *Promotion of efficiency* In this aspect, the budget is seen as a tool to make operations more efficient; an important measure of managerial performance is the ability of a manager to conform to the budget. An entire operating division's efficiency is usually measured in terms of its performance in relation to planned performance as set out in the division budget.
2 *Control* The budget is often mentioned as a measurement tool, which management uses in the control of cost by comparing actual costs to budgeted targets and by investigating significant variances.
3 *Planning, information, and feedback* The budgeting system is used to provide information and feedback to management at many organizational levels as an aid to the decision-making process. In this sense, the budget is used to determine where and why the organization is spending time, resources, and dollars.
4 *Pressure-exertion* Budgets are often used as an instrument for putting pressure on operating supervisors to increase productivity and efficiency. In this sense, the budget is often used as a threat or coercive force.
5 *Motivation* Budgets are used to present a goal or a challenge for operating units; that is, something to shoot for or a goal to achieve.

From previous studies, in line with this multiplicity of functions, at least three different models of the budgeting process may be derived:

A *Pressure-oriented budget model* Evidence from a number of studies[2] indicates that most individuals and groups perform more effectively under certain degrees and types of pressure, but on the other hand, that inordinate or unrealistic pressures tend to result in performance deterioration. DeCoster and Fertakis[3] reported research on the relationship between budgetary pressures and leader behavior. They found a positive relationship between budget-induced pressure and supervisory behavior in both directive and considerate leadership styles.

---

[2] See, for example, R. Kahn and D. Wolfe, *et al., Organizational Stress* (New York: Wiley, 1964).
[3] D. DeCoster and T. Fertakis, "Budget-Induced Pressure and Its Relationship to Supervisory Behavior," *Journal of Accounting Research,* Autumn, 1968.

B *Aspiration level model* The aspiration level is that level of future performance in a familiar task that an individual, knowing his level of performance in
that task, explicitly undertakes to reach. Andrew Stedry[4] conducted research
into the motivational aspects of budgeting and reported that performance is
affected by the type of budget chosen, the conditions of administration, and
the way in which aspiration levels of a task are determined. Since the aspiration level represents the manager's internal goal, then a budget goal that
significantly varies from this level will tend to have adverse consequences
upon managerial behavior.

C *Participative model* A frequently suggested solution to motivational problems is that of active participation in budget preparation. Participation has
been defined as "the process of joint decision making by two or more parties in which the decisions have future effects on those making them."[5] The
use of participation involves sophistication on the part of the supervisor and
an increased inner security in his ability to delegate portions of his own
decision-making powers. Participation also usually requires increased time
commitments. Consequently, many firms have substituted "pseudo-
participation"; that is, the appearance of participation but without giving up
decision-making powers to subordinate members or units.

Chris Argyris[6] conducted a study examining the human relation problems of budgets, and found that finance people often tended to view their
function as primarily *controlling* and *criticizing* the performance of operating
managers. His finding emphasized the need for participation of all key organizational members in establishing budgetary parameters. Becker and
Green[7] arrived at similar conclusions; that is, a successful participative
budget induces proper motivation and acceptance of specific goals and provides information that makes it possible to associate reward and punishment
with performance.

In comparing these models, it may be noted that the evidence suggests that budgets do have a significant influence on behavior and motivational levels. Although the models differ in their basic assumptions about
the motivational consequences, the participative systems appear to be
more successful in reinforcing positive motivation. Consequently, this multiplicity of functions and objectives in models of budgeting systems often leads
to dysfunctional behavioral consequences as a result of the approach that is
emphasized.

Some dysfunctional behavioral consequences

The preceding sections have pointed out some of the behavioral consequences of administering budgeting systems. Often for every pressure

[4] A. Stedry, *Budget Control and Cost Behavior* (Englewood Cliffs: Prentice-Hall, 1960).
[5] S. Becker and D. Green, "Budgeting and Employee Behavior," *Journal of Business,*
Oct., 1962.
[6] C. Argyris, *The Impact of Budgets Upon People* (New York: Controllership Foundation,
1952).
[7] Becker and Green, *loc. cit.*

applied from above, subordinate levels devise countermeasures to offset the pressure. Consequently, budgets tend to lose their control, information, and motivational functions, and become one of the games managers play. These consequences include the following:

Padding the budget or "building in fat"

This tactic is often used where organizational management (or any other decision group) reacts to budget requests by "trimming the fat" out. Over a period of budget reviews, the operating groups learn to anticipate the amount of trimming necessary to satisfy the reviewing body. This will probably be a percentage, and is usually expressed in some ingroup slogan such as "Every budget has X percent of fat in it."

Therefore, in order to perform well against the budget goals, the manager builds X percent into his budget so that in effect he is building into his estimates an amount that he anticipates will be cut out. Consequently, his expenditure level can be reduced and he will come out with what he really wanted in the first place. Another consequence is that the manager who submits a realistic budget (but who also suffers the percentage reduction) is forced to work under a handicap. The system then, tends to reward defensive budgets and to penalize realistic estimates.

Refill the empty tank or "oil the squeaking wheel"

Another tactic managers often utilize is the forecast based upon past use plus a growth factor. In this situation, future allocations are based upon past consumption, therefore, a wise manager strives for a deficit. For example, the allocation of fuel to military units is based upon the previous year's expense. If the unit is underrunning the allocation, usage levels are raised to use up the budget. It is not unusual to find a high increase in flight time in May and June at the end of the fiscal year. No budget negotiator wants to go in with an unused allocation for any item—advertising, manpower, supplies, travel costs, because the budgeted targets tend to decrease. This in effect is a Parkinsonian Law: *Expenditure rises to fill the amount allocated to it.*

Put off till tomorrow what could be charged to today

It is not unusual for budget managers to learn to manipulate the budget variables, and in a sense, defer the bad news. This is done by either manipulating the recording of sales between periods, or deferring cost items from period to period. The result, of course, is to distort the budget in a favorable direction. If done adroitly, this may be continued for years, and a real gamesman can gain a promotion on the basis of his fine performance, and then hand the whole mess to a new man. It will probably take the new manager six months to a year to find out why he is in such big trouble. Further, when he understands what has happened, he is motivated to continue the game to avoid an adverse effect on *his* performance.

Underground operations or "midnight research supply"

This game is usually concerned with R & D Management. Here the game involves subsidizing one activity by hiding it or burying it in another, usually larger, more ambiguous budget section. This usually occurs when scientists feel they have a better knowledge of where R & D efforts should be expended than does top management. Therefore, they operate a subterranean research project on some other budget. For example, they might "sell" some engineering budget for a product that actually has already been designed, then apply it to their *pet* project. If it succeeds, it is approved, if it doesn't, no one outside is aware of the losses.

Counterbudget systems or "do unto others before they do unto you"

Another consequence of the budget game, as we have already suggested, is the use of evasive tactics requiring increased information gathering and control systems. This in turn tends to create the development of counter-budget groups. These are staff people who gather information for the operating level manager to support his budget demands. Consequently, he is able to go into budget negotiations armed with supporting data. Trend analyses, ratios, and percentages are generally assembled on flip charts to back up and "sell" his budget demands. Obviously such systems themselves introduce a significant cost factor into the budget and into the overhead costs.

Our preliminary survey suggests that these counter strategies often introduce added costs and cause dysfunctional reactions because budgets become too arbitrary, too rigid, and unrelated to the real world at the operating level. When this happens, participation by managers in the budgeting process may become a perfunctory ritual, devoid of operational significance.

Implications

There is evidence that the human component plays a significant and important part in the effectiveness of planning and control systems. Unwise use of budget systems or ignoring of behavioral implications can have dysfunctional consequences upon organizational effectiveness. It appears that these problems are often the unintended consequences of using the budget as a pressure device. Although the budgeting system appears to be an effective and efficient tool of management, when the underlying attitudes of managers and the effectiveness of budget systems are critically analyzed, it is often found that dysfunctional reactions result from the budgeting process because the human component has been ignored or neglected.

The proposed solution to this problem includes:

Active participation in the preparation of the budget

Considerable evidence indicates that participation tends to provide better plans, increased understanding of goals, and especially, increased acceptance of and commitment to these goals throughout the organization.

An improved reporting structure

An initial step in determining behavioral consequences involves an examination of the reporting structure to identify its weaknesses and shortcomings in providing for the needs of operating managers. This should include isolation of critical factors for both short-term results and for long-term growth and competitive strength. These critical factors may then be utilized in implementing management by objectives or participative budget programs. Each executive or manager must receive the feedback he needs to control his own performance parameters.

Increased responsibility and accountability for realistic objectives

Once an effective system of reporting and setting budget objectives is attained, management information systems should feed back information about actual performance results in relation to these objectives. The key words here are *realistic budget objectives.* Our survey data indicates that too often unrealistic budget targets are set. After a few months, this type of budget is no longer an effective motivator to individual aspiration levels or performance measures.

The use of positive motivations that appeal to higher level needs of organization members

Behavioral science research indicates that the most important factor in motivating managers today is a sense of accomplishment in the achievement of challenging goals, and recognition for these achievements. Consequently, it seems reasonable to assume that the human factors in budgeting systems must be given as much consideration as is currently given to the financial and technical aspects.

Given the multiplicity of budget system functions and models, it appears that more research needs to be aimed at determining the relationship between these dimensions and the impact of budgets upon the behavior of organizational members. For example, more needs to be known about the relationship between planning groups and operating groups, the effects on future performance of success and failure to meet budget goals, and the consequences of pressure-oriented systems.

Modern managers cannot be expected to be experts in the psychology of human behavior. It is not unreasonable, however, to expect them to have an awareness of the behavioral implications of the budgeting process and to use the budget wisely in administering their organizations. Clearly, the behavioral consequences can result in increased success for managers who are aware of the human factor in budget systems.

Part VII

Linking processes

Ever since Adam and Eve made the wrong one, decisions have been be-deviling people.
      Robert L. Heilbroner

Communication is a process of mutual information.
      Douglas McGregor

The major managerial functions already discussed—planning, organizing, staffing, influencing, and controlling—are not performed independently of each other, but are interconnected. In this section we consider the two major processes that perform this connecting or linking function.

    The first set of articles deals with the linking process of decision making. When all is said and done, the principal distinction between managers and nonmanagers is that the former are responsible for the rational allocation of organizational resources. We call such a task "decision making." The articles by Rowe and Simon discuss some principles to guide effective decision making, while Browne's piece presents some specific techniques to apply.

    Of equal importance to managers is the communication process, for it is through communicating that information relevant to the major functions can be interrelated. In the first selection on communicating, Rogers and Roethlisberger point out various obstacles—and paths—to effective communications. Planty and Machaver present ways to stimulate and conduct the communication process in the next article. Finally, in one of the most succinct and effective selections in *Dimensions in Modern Management,* the American Management Association describes ten important "commandments" of good communication.

VII/A
Decision making

---

53 Making effective decisions
Alan J. Rowe

To know whether a decision is effective, a manager must first have a basis for determining what is a good decision. In one study involving chief executives, the consensus was that a good decision is one that "feels" good. On the other hand, when looking at the question from the point of view of "management by objectives," the soundness of a decision is determined by the results achieved.

Of course, after the fact, one can ascertain whether the decision met the objectives desired, but how can we tell ahead of time whether a proposed course of action will achieve desired results? As might be expected, there are no simple answers to this question. Rather, what is required is a recognition that any approach proposed will have to be based on a "current appraisal of a future occurrence."

Decision factors

Undoubtedly, any basis for determining the soundness of a decision will have to be multidimensional, because there are a number of considerations that must be met. The following list attempts to identify factors, which, if considered ahead of time, offer the highest likelihood of the decision being successful:

- *Perception* Has the right problem been defined and the objectives clearly stated?
- *Priority* Does the decision deal with priorities in an appropriate order?
- *Acceptability* Will the results be accepted by the persons who have to implement the decision?
- *Risk* Is there an understanding of the risk involved, and the strategy to follow when dealing with uncertainty?

Source: Reprinted by special permission from *Chemical Engineering* (September 16, 1974), pp. 126–132. Copyright © 1974 by McGraw-Hill, Inc., New York, N.Y. 10020.

- *Resources*   Is there an analysis of the resources required and a forecast of return on investment?
- *Goals*   Does the decision fit within the stated goals and objectives of the organization?
- *Values*   Does the decision reflect the values of the decision-maker and of the organization?
- *Demands*   Does time pressure or lack of information present unreasonable demands on the individuals involved?
- *Style*   Has the decision involved participation on the part of persons in the organization and achieved support from power blocks?
- *Judgment*   Does the decision meet the test of intuition or experience, and is there a validation of the expected results by experts?

One could easily say that most decisions do not warrant the extensive "looking into" that is implied by the list. The intention here is not to say that all decisions must satisfy the foregoing factors, but rather to suggest that a measure such as "results" is not useful in determining, before action was taken, whether the decision would be a good one.

We are concerned here mainly with determining the soundness of a decision before it is carried out. Thus, "results" would only be what is expected rather than what actually happens. The effective decision-maker is able to determine which factors apply in a given situation and then is able to carry through on the proposed course of action.

Understanding the decision-maker

To understand the decision process, we might start by examining how individuals make decisions. A powerful, yet very simple, approach is based on a model of decision-making that considers the decision-maker as responding to a series of forces, as shown:

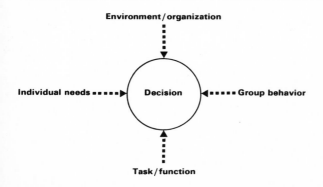

All decision-makers operate in an environment in which they are expected to perform some meaningful function. Performance depends not only
on the capability of the manager, but also on the environment in which he
operates. For example, every manager responds to the pressure of small
and large groups with whom he must interact and, at the same time, he has
personal needs. These personal needs include such things as his aspirations,
goals and values. The environment consists of both social and managerial
influences. His responses to managerial pressures will depend on the management style being used.

The model can be extended to show the behavior of groups or entire
organizations. For example, McGregor describes the behavior of a group as
consisting of a number of interacting variables, including:

- *Members* Attitudes, knowledge, skills and capabilities.
- *Task* The nature of the job and variables related to the primary task.
- *Structure* The internal controls of the organizational subsystem.
- *Leader* Skills, capabilities and other personal characteristics.
- *Environment* Variables in the larger organizational system and society.

These variables are included in the preceding model as forces imping-
ing on the decision-maker.

If we next put the decision-maker into a problem-solving situation, the
model in Figure 1 could be used to describe his behavior and response.

Although the model in Figure 1 is at best a simplified description of
how decisions are carried out, it nevertheless illustrates the fact that

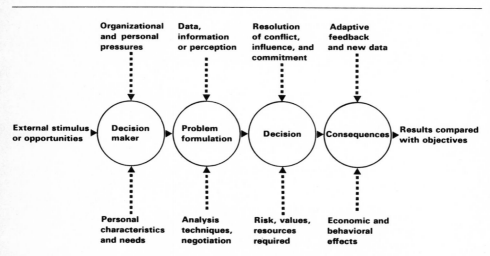

Figure 1 Decision-making is only the first step in achieving results; carrying out a
decision is often more complex.

decision-making consists of a number of phases, and involves more than merely choosing from among a number of alternatives. It shows that both the behavioral and analytic factors must be included in order to have a correct description of decision-making.

Although the decision model attempts to incorporate behavioral and rational aspects of decision-making, such a model often does not explain what happens in actual decision-making. For example, it assumes that a rational choice can be made between conflicting values and that problem-solving is an orderly process. It also suggests that the decision-maker can rank all the sets of consequences. Of course, no human being can solve problems in a completely rational manner.

There is a growing body of evidence that behavioral factors are perhaps more important than analytical ones in "making decisions work." It is thus incumbent on the manager to properly balance these considerations and not be trapped into thinking that merely having the right information or the right analysis will lead to good decisions.

Making decisions work

Let us now examine how to effectively carry out decisions. As can be seen in Figure 1, decision-making is really only a part—even only the beginning—of the process of achieving effective results. Carrying out the decision is often more complex and trying on the manager than the analysis performed to arrive at an appropriate course of action.

It is because of the increasing complexity of decisions in organizations and the rising desire for involvement and commitment on the part of subordinates that managers have been turning more and more to the practice of participative management.

As with any approach, participative management has benefits and shortcomings. The theory rests on assumptions that employees at all levels of an organization are capable of contributing usefully to the decision process, and that, in general, this willingness and capability have not been used.

Collins and Guetzkow have examined the questions of power and influence in an organization, and concluded that when subordinates are more involved in decision-making, superiors have more influence in how decisions are carried out.

Perhaps we can best examine participative management if we define participation as the sharing of power and influence in decision situations. Heller's monumental study of participative management showed that senior managers use prior consultation 37% of the time, whereas they make decisions on their own only 36% of the time, and that delegation is the least frequently used decision style. (On the other hand, his research indicated that power is shared between senior managers and their immediate subordinates in nearly 50% of all important decisions.)

What accounts for the fact that participation is not more widely used?

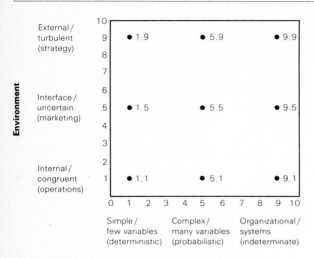

Figure 2 Style depends on environment and decision type.

Perhaps it is that the sharing of power is not really practical when managers are solely accountable for results. Further, it may be unreasonable to expect a subordinate who has less information and often less experience to have the same perspective as the manager.

Most important is the willingness of the subordinate to assume responsibility. There is evidence that the workers councils that have existed in Europe for some time are rather apathetic toward decision-making that does not directly involve their work or expertise. For example, Mulder in his study of "power equalization through participation" found that participation by those who are less powerful in decision-making processes actually increases power differences between those who are more powerful and those who are less powerful.

He supports this with empirical research, and states: "In research on the functioning of Dutch work councils, half the voluntary members of work councils were not strongly motivated to participate in decision-making; the other half complained about insufficient expertise, even though the work councils had been functioning for as long as eight years. This combination of low levels of motivation and expertness has appeared in all the investigations made in Dutch-speaking areas."

If we consider participation as being contingent upon environmental conditions and the kinds of decisions being made, we observe a variety of decision styles. For example, if we examine participative decision style as shown in the matrix (Figure 2), we find that the style changes at each of the points shown.

The categories shown in the matrix can be described by nine typical decisions shown in Figure 3.

External	Forecasts	Strategies	Adaptive strategies
Interface	Budgets	Market plans	Managerial control
Internal	Procedures, rules	Plans, policies	Motivation, commitment

Figure 3 Decision types fit categories of Figure 2 matrix

The decision styles actually used could include:

M_a = Manager makes decision alone.

M_i = Manager makes decisions and informs subordinates.

M_c = Manager consults subordinate before making decisions.

M_m = Manager consults other managers before decisions.

M_s = Manager depends on staff for input to decision.

M_d = Manager delegates decision.

M_j = Manager makes decision jointly with subordinates.

For example, M_a and M_i are often used for internal simple decisions; whereas, M_c, M_m and M_s generally are used for external/complex decisions. When the decisions directly involve the organization, M_d and M_j are most often used. Results obtained in using the foregoing decision-style categories with a number of management groups confirmed the point made by Heller that there is "no one best way" of making decisions. This, of course, differs with the approach that assumes there is a best style of decision-making.

As shown, situational leadership or structural variables are the key to the decision process; that is, a decision cannot be taken out of its environmental context.

Subordinates' expectations of managers

What do subordinates expect in the men they work for? It is obvious they expect specific decision characteristics and do not like the compulsive individual. Sadler and Hofstede found in an international survey resulting in almost 20,000 responses from marketing and service organizations the following:

Decision style	Preferred style	Actually perceived style	Employees perceived preferred style in their manager
Tells	3%	17%	29%
Sells	25	31	43
Consults	56	30	34
Joins	16	7	21
None of these		14	
No reply	5	8	

Thus, although the preferred style was "consults," this was not the managerial behavior perceived either in general or in the employees' own managers. Interestingly, "sells" seems to dominate the actually perceived styles.

Bond, Leabo and Swinyard found that the major contributors to successful performance of the chief executive officer were:

Attributes	Percent of respondents
Special skills	
Mental skills, analytic ability	56
Ability to work with and lead people	45
Ability to appraise staff	39
Ability to organize and delegate	29
Communication ability	23
Personal characteristics	
Attitude toward work	44
General leadership qualities	29
Mental capacity, inquiring mind	27
Attitude toward decision-making	23
Ethical values	21
Attitude toward people	21
Acquired knowledge	
Knowledge of industry and firm	18
Business-economic understanding	9
General management techniques	8
General experience	8

The results would seem to indicate that special skills are most important, although attitude toward work appears more important (in the personal-characteristics category) than mental capacity (which was at the top of the special skills).

Heller used twelve skill factors to define a manager's requirements. He compared the perception of two senior levels of management regarding their own job and that of the other level:

Skill	Agree	Disagree
Knowledge of technical matters	X	
Close contact with people		X
Knowledge of human nature		X
Imagination		X
Self-confidence		X
Sense of responsibility		X
Decisiveness		X
Tact		X
Adaptability		X
Forcefulness		X
Intelligence	X	
Initiative		X

In addition, he found that the skills that most affect a senior manager's decision styles are: technical ability, decisiveness, and intelligence. Not only did he consider the question of how the manager and his subordinate viewed their respective capabilities, he also found that subordinates consistently overestimated the power they held. An important finding was that senior managers and subordinates do not agree on the amount of skill needed for their respective levels of work, except as regards technical specialists. Thus, we can see the need for a clearer relationship between subordinate and superior.

Conclusion

Our purpose in trying to better understand the decision process has been not only to show how to make better decisions, but also to be able to predict the outcome of decisions. Although this might imply a rigid approach to decision-making, it instead has been meant to demonstrate that some of the accepted methods in use are, perhaps, incomplete and could benefit from a more comprehensive or systems view of the problem. For example, when considering decision style, we should look at the characteristics of the decision-maker, the problems he is most likely to encounter, and the environment in which the decision must be carried out.

Although much has been written about the importance of communication, we still find goal conflicts arising because there often is a lack of mutual understanding. Further, because change is inherent in any organization and the future always involves risk, goal-adaptation and risk-taking must be related to the dynamics of the environment confronting every organization. Our ability to predict or forecast the consequences of decisions is a critical requirement for effective operations.

We have only attempted to deal with a limited number of factors in decision-making, the most significant of which is undoubtedly the behavioral aspect. It has remained important despite the advent of computers and quantitative analysis. Still, we do not mean to deny the value of the rational approach to decision-making. Rather, we have attempted to reconcile the two approaches in the expectation that the better understanding of the decision process will contribute to the making of more effective decisions.

References

1 McGregor, D., "The Professional Manager," McGraw-Hill, 1967.
2 Heller, F. A., "Managerial Decision-Making," Tavistock, London, 1971.
3 Collins, B. E. and Guetzkow, H., "A Social Psychology of Group Processes for Decision-Making," Wiley, 1964.
4 Blankenship, L. V., Miles, R. E., "Organizational Structure and Managerial Decision Behavior," *Administrative Sci. Quart.,* June 1968.
5 Mulder, M., "Power Equalization Through Participation," *Administrative Sci. Quart.,* March 1971.
6 Sadler, P. J. and Hofstede, G. H., "Leadership Styles," *Mens en Ondernem- ing* 26, 1972, 43–63.
7 Bond, F. A., Leabo, D. A. and Swinyard, A. W., "Preparation for Business Leadership," *Business Research,* 1964.
8 Diesing, P., "Socioeconomic Decisions," *Ethics,* 69, October 1958.
9 Mockler, R. J., "Management Decision Making and Action in Behavioral Situations," Austin Press, 1973.
10 Drucker, P. F., "The Effective Decision," *Harvard Bus. Rev.,* Jan.–Feb. 1967.
11 Zaleznick, A., "Power and Politics in Organizational Life," *Harvard Bus. Rev.,* May–June 1970.
12 Mott, P. E., "The Characteristics of Effective Organizations," Harper and Row, 1972.
13 Tosi, H. L. and Hamner, W. C., "Organizational Behavior and Management—A Contingency Approach," St. Clair Press, 1974.
14 Lawless, D. J., "Effective Management—Social Psychological Approach," Prentice-Hall, 1972.

54 Administrative decision making
Herbert A. Simon

Behavioral alternatives[1]

At each moment the behaving subject, or the organization composed of numbers of such individuals, is confronted with a large number of alternative

Source: Reprinted with permission of Macmillan Publishing Company, Inc., from *Administrative Behavior* by Herbert A. Simon, pp. 67, 75–77, 80–84, xxv–xxvii. Copyright © 1947, 1957 by Herbert A. Simon.
[1] The theory presented here was worked out by the author in 1941. Its present refor-

behaviors, some of which are present in consciousness and some of which are not. Decision, or choice, as the term is used here, is the process by which one of these alternatives for each moment's behavior is selected to be carried out. The series of such decisions which determines behavior over some stretch of time may be called a *strategy*.

If any one of the possible strategies is chosen and followed out, certain consequences will result. The task of rational decision is to select that one of the strategies which is followed by the preferred set of consequences. It should be emphasized that *all* the consequences that follow from the chosen strategy are relevant to the evaluation of its correctness, not simply those consequences that were anticipated.

The task of decision involves three steps: [1] the listing of all the alternative strategies; [2] the determination of all the consequences that follow upon each of these strategies; [3] the comparative evaluation of these sets of consequences. The word "all" is used advisedly. It is obviously impossible for the individual to know *all* his alternatives or *all* their consequences, and this impossibility is a very important departure of actual behavior from the model of objective rationality.

Roughly speaking, rationality is concerned with the selection of preferred behavior alternatives in terms of some system of values whereby the consequences of behavior can be evaluated. Does this mean that the process of adaptation must be conscious, or are unconscious processes included as well? It has been shown that many of the steps in mathematical invention—than which there can presumably be nothing more rational—are subconscious; and this is certainly true of the simpler processes of equation-solving.[2] Moreover, if consciousness is not stipulated as an element of rationality, are only deliberate processes of adaptation admitted, or non-deliberate ones as well? The typist trains herself to strike a particular key in response to the stimulus of a particular letter. Once learned, the act is unconscious, but deliberate. On the other hand, any person instinctively withdraws a finger that has been burned. This is "rational" in the sense that it serves a useful purpose, but is certainly neither a conscious nor a deliberate adaptation.

Shall we, moreover, call a behavior "rational" when it is in error, but only because the information on which it is based is faulty? When a subjective test is applied, it is rational for an individual to take medicine for a disease if he believes the medicine will cure the disease. When an objective test is applied, the behavior is rational only if the medicine is in fact efficacious.

Finally, in terms of what objectives, whose values, shall rationality be judged? Is behavior of an individual in an organization rational when it serves

---

mulation has been greatly influenced by the remarkable work of John von Neumann and Oskar Morgenstern, *The Theory of Games and Economic Behavior* (Princeton: Princeton University Press, 1944), chap. 2. It is fair to point out that von Neumann first published that portion of his theory which is germane to the present discussion in 1928, "Zur Theorie der Gesellschaftsspiele," *Math. Annalen* 100:295–320 (1928).
[2] See Jacques Hadamard, *Essay on the Psychology of Invention in the Mathematical Field* (Princeton: Princeton University Press, 1945).

his personal objectives, or when it serves the organizational objectives? Two soldiers sit in a trench opposite a machine-gun nest. One of them stays undercover. The other, at the cost of his life, destroys the machine-gun nest with a grenade. Which is rational?

Perhaps the only way to avoid, or clarify, these complexities is to use the term "rational" in conjunction with appropriate adverbs. Then a decision may be called "objectively" rational if *in fact* it is the correct behavior for maximizing given values in a given situation. It is "subjectively" rational if it maximizes attainment relative to the actual knowledge of the subject. It is "consciously" rational to the degree that the adjustment of means to ends is a conscious process. It is "deliberately" rational to the degree that the adjustment of means to ends has been deliberately brought about (by the individual or by the organization). A decision is "organizationally" rational if it is oriented to the organization's goals; it is "personally" rational if it is oriented to the individual's goals.

The limits of rationality

Objective rationality, as that term was defined in the previous chapter, would imply that the behaving subject molds all his behavior into an integrated pattern by (a) viewing the behavior alternatives prior to decision in panoramic fashion, (b) considering the whole complex of consequences that would follow on each choice, and (c) with the systems of values as criteria singling out one from the whole set of alternatives.

Real behavior, even that which is ordinarily thought of as "rational" possesses many elements of disconnectedness not present in this idealized picture. If behavior is viewed over a stretch of time, it exhibits a mosaic character. Each piece of the pattern is integrated with others by their orientation to a common purpose; but these purposes shift from time to time with shifts in knowledge and attention, and are held together in only slight measure by any conception of an over-all criterion of choice. It might be said that behavior reveals "segments" of rationality—that behavior shows rational organization within each segment, but the segments themselves have no very strong interconnections.

Actual behavior falls short, in at least three ways, of objective rationality as defined in the last chapter:

1 Rationality requires a complete knowledge and anticipation of the consequences that will follow on each choice. In fact, knowledge of consequences is always fragmentary.
2 Since these consequences lie in the future, imagination must supply the lack of experienced feeling in attaching value to them. But values can be only imperfectly anticipated.
3 Rationality requires a choice among all possible alternative behaviors. In actual behavior, only a very few of all these possible alternatives ever come to mind.

Incompleteness of knowledge

Rationality implies a complete, and unattainable, knowledge of the exact consequences of each choice. In actuality, the human being never has more than a fragmentary knowledge of the conditions surrounding his action, nor more than a slight insight into the regularities and laws that would permit him to induce future consequences from a knowledge of present circumstances.

For instance, to achieve a completely successful application of resources to a city's fire protection problem, the members of the fire department would need to know in comprehensive detail the probabilities of fire in each portion of the city—in fact, in each structure—and the exact effect upon fire losses of any change in administrative procedure or any redistribution of the fire-fighting forces.

Even to state the problem in this form is to recognize the extent to which complete rationality is limited by lack of knowledge. If each fire were reported to the department at the moment ignition occurred, fire losses would miraculously decline. Lacking such omniscience, the fire department must devote considerable effort to securing as promptly as possible, through special alarm systems and otherwise, information regarding situations where its action is needed.[3]

This point has been developed in some detail in order to emphasize that it poses an extremely practical problem of administration—to secure an organization of the decision-making process such that relevant knowledge will be brought to bear at the point where the decision is made. The same point might have been illustrated with respect to a business organization—the dependence of its decisions, for example, on the correct prediction of market prices.

The human being striving for rationality and restricted within the limits of his knowledge has developed some working procedures that partially overcome this difficulty. These procedures consist in assuming that he can isolate from the rest of the world a closed system containing only a limited number of variables and a limited range of consequences.

There is a story to the effect that a statistician once found a very high correlation between the number of old maids and the size of the clover crop in different English counties. After puzzling over this relation for some time, he was able to trace what appeared to him to be the causal chain. Old maids, it appeared, kept cats; and cats ate mice. Field mice, however, were natural enemies of bumble-bees, and these latter were, in turn, the chief agents in fertilizing the flowers of the clover plants. The implication, of course, is that the British Parliament should never legislate on the subject of marriage bonuses without first evaluating the effect upon the clover crop of reducing the spinster population.

[3] With respect to similar considerations involved in military tactics, see *United States Army Field Service Regulations, 1923* (Washington: Government Printing Office, 1924), p. 4.

In practical decision-making, devious consequences of this sort must of necessity be ignored.[4] Only those factors that are most closely connected with the decision in cause and time can be taken into consideration. The problem of discovering what factors are, and what are not, important in any given situation is quite as essential to correct choice as a knowledge of the empirical laws governing those factors that are finally selected as relevant.

Rational choice will be feasible to the extent that the limited set of factors upon which decision is based corresponds, in nature, to a closed system of variables—that is, to the extent that significant indirect effects are absent. Only in the cases of extremely important decisions is it possible to bring to bear sufficient resources to unravel a very involved chain of effects. For instance, a very large amount spent for research to determine the indirect effects of a governmental fiscal policy upon employment in the economy would, if it achieved its aim, be well spent. On the other hand, a physician treating a patient does not take time to determine what difference the life or death of his patient will make to the community.

Difficulties of anticipation

It is a commonplace of experience that an anticipated pleasure may be a very different sort of thing from a realized pleasure. The actual experience may be considerably more or less desirable than anticipated.

This does not result merely from failure to anticipate consequences. Even when the consequences of a choice have been rather completely described, the anticipation of them can hardly act with the same force upon the emotions as the experiencing of them. One reason for this is that the mind cannot at a single moment grasp the consequences in their entirety. Instead, attention shifts from one value to another with consequent shifts in preference.

Valuation, therefore, is limited in its accuracy and consistency by the power of the individual to trace the varied value elements in the imagined consequence and to give them the same weight in anticipation as they will have for him in experience.

This is probably an important influence in "risky" behavior. The more vividly the consequences of losing in a risky venture are visualized—either through past experience of such consequences or for other reasons—the less desirable does the risk assumption appear. It is not so much that the experience of loss leads to attaching a higher probability to the occurrence of loss as that the desire to avoid the consequences of loss has been strengthened.

[4] Cf. Dewey, *The Public and Its Problems* (New York: Henry Holt & Co., 1927), pp. 106–107.

The scope of behavior possibilities

Imagination falls down also in conceiving all the possible patterns of behavior that the individual might undertake. The number of things that a man, restricted only by physical and biological limitations, could do in even so short an interval as a minute is inconceivable. He has two legs, two arms, a head, two eyes, a neck, a trunk, ten fingers, ten toes, and many sets of voluntary muscles governing each. Each of these members is capable of complex movements individually or in coordination.

Of all these possible movements, only a very few come to mind at any moment as possible behavior alternatives. Since each alternative has distinct consequences, it follows that many sets of possible consequences never reach the stage of valuation, since it is not recognized that they are possible consequents of available behavior alternatives.

Relatively speaking, of course, human beings come much closer to exploiting in purposive action their physiological capacities of movement than other animals. The relatively simple "tool behaviors" of which the great apes are capable[5] are very elementary, judged by human standards.

In some fields, considerable ingenuity has been shown in devising methods for exploiting possibilities of behavior. Elaborate devices have been constructed in phonetics for observing and correcting lip and tongue movements. Time-and-motion studies are made to observe, in great detail, hand movements in industrial processes, to improve these movements, and to facilitate them through revision of the process. In the same category could be placed the whole field of tool-invention and skill-training. Both involve a close observation of behavior processes, and a consequent enlargement of the alternatives available for choice.

Rationality and decision-making

It must be concluded from the above that the perfectly rational decision maker—economic man—does not exist in everyday organizational life. Rather, the decision maker operates under a condition of limited rationality—i.e., administrative man:

1 While economic man maximizes—selects the best alternative from among all those available to him; his cousin, whom we shall call administrative man, satisfices—looks for a course of action that is satisfactory or "good enough." Examples of satisficing criteria that are familiar enough to businessmen, if unfamiliar to most economists, are "share of market," "adequate profit," "fair price."[6]

[5] See Tolman, *op. cit.,* pp. 219–226, and the literature there cited.
[6] See, for example, R. M. Cyert and James G. March, "Organizational Factors in the Theory of Oligopoly," *Quarterly Journal of Economics* 70:44–64 (February, 1956).

2 Economic man deals with the "real world" in all its complexity. Administrative man recognizes that the world he perceives is a drastically simplified model of the buzzing, blooming confusion that constitutes the real world. He is content with this gross simplification because he believes that the real world is mostly empty—that most of the facts of the real world have no great relevance to any particular situation he is facing, and that most significant chains of causes and consequences are short and simple. Hence, he is content to leave out of account those aspects of reality—and that means *most* aspects—that are substantially irrelevant at a given time. He makes his choices using a simple picture of the situation that takes into account just a few of the factors that he regards as most relevant and crucial.

What is the significance of these two characteristics of administrative man? First, because he satisfices, rather than maximizes, administrative man can make his choices without first examining all possible behavior alternatives and without ascertaining that these *are* in fact all the alternatives. Second, because he treats the world as rather "empty," and ignores the "interrelatedness of all things" (so stupefying to thought and action), administrative man is able to make his decisions with relatively simple rules of thumb that do not make impossible demands upon his capacity for thought.

This description of administrative man is essentially a development and formalization of the description in pages 81—84 of *Administrative Behavior*. But how do we know that it is a *correct* description—more accurate, for example, than the model of economic man? The first test, and perhaps not the least important, is the test of common sense. It is not difficult to imagine the decision-making mechanisms that administrative man would use. Our picture of him fits pretty well our introspective knowledge of our own judgemental processes as well as the more formal descriptions that have been made of those processes by the few psychologists who have studied them.[7]

Formalization of the theory over the past several years—as exemplified by the papers cited in footnote 6 and by subsequent work—has made a sharper test possible. For within the past six months, Allen Newell and I have succeeded in describing in detail a decision-making mechanism capable of exhibiting certain complex human problem-solving behavior—specifically, the discovery of proofs for theorems in logic.[8] In fact, we are now able to simulate such complex human behavior, using this decision-making program, with the aid of an ordinary electronic computer. A more complete description of our results will have to be left to other publications. They are mentioned here simply to emphasize that I do not regard the description of human rationality as hypothetical, but as now having been verified in its main features.

[7] See, for example, Max Wertheimer, *Productive Thinking* (New York: Harper & Bros., 1945), and A. D. de Groot, *Het Denken van den Schaker* (Amsterdam: Noord-Hollondsche Uitgevers Maatschappij, 1946).

[8] For an account of the general approach represented by this work, see Allen Newell and Herbert A. Simon, "The Logic Theory Machine," *Transactions on Information Theory,* Institute of Radio Engineers, Vol. IT–2, No. 3 (September, 1956), pp. 61–79.

55 Techniques of operations research
William G. Browne

Operations research is a scientific approach to management problems that was introduced during and used since World War II. "Its purpose is to provide a basis for directing and controlling operations." (1) Operations research does not point to any one particular tool for the scientific approach. "Operations research differs from almost anything else industry has done in the past, chiefly in method and approach to a problem. The techniques of operations research require an exacting statement of the problem with all the variables and factors included with their proper relationships." (2)

The management of businesses, institutions, and governments have a number of operations research techniques available for investigation and analysis of their particular problems. The technique that is ultimately used may depend on the type of problem, the complexity of the problem, the types of input available or the type of output desired, the ability and experience of the users of the technique and the amount that is budgeted for the project. Operations research techniques may be used anywhere in the spectrum of day-to-day decisions and problems to once-in-a-lifetime decisions and problems. The number of people involved varies widely.

The model, in most cases, provides a systematic analysis of the problem or problems confronting the user. For example, one authority finds that, "Simulation models of operating systems have been growing rapidly and promise to become a dominant technique for assisting management, in the decision-making process for day-to-day problems, as well as for comparing basic alternatives of operating policies." (3) The model gives the user material and time to explore the environment, solution alternatives, and objectives of the problem in greater depth. Generally, a model will fall into one of the five following areas in regard to its applications:

1 It may be used to study a system for possible improvement or to look at the present system to compare it with a renovated or suggested system.
2 The model can be utilized to design systems or outputs of systems for optimal returns. It is a tool for the analysis of different possible alternatives so that the one bringing the optimal or near optimal results can be initiated.
3 A model may help in the clarification of the objectives or goals and the tentative plans of the organizers, planners, and decision makers.
4 Models may be used for training personnel to give them experience that may be used to their advantage when placed on the job.
5 Techniques may be used to set up a model for forecasting or showing possible outputs of the system when there are changes in exogenous or endogenous variables.

Source: Reprinted with permission from the *Journal of Systems Management* (September 1972), pp. 3–13. © 1972 by the *Journal of Systems Management.*

Modeling process

Fred Hansman (4) of the University of Munich and formerly of the Caste Institute Operations Research Group relates an ultimate model to the real
world in a very fundamental diagram shown in Figure 1. The flowchart, itself
a model, is a good framework for studying the process by which the operations research techniques are applied.

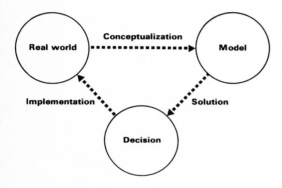

Figure 1

The terms in the diagram need some explanation to give the reader
further depth on how it can be used. The *Real World* is the environment in
which we find ourselves confronted with the problems that may require the
application of an operations research technique to efficiently find an optimal
or improved solution. Once the problem is established the operations researcher tries to *conceptualize* the problem's complete environment. He
looks for the critical variables or limiting constraints that should be incorporated into the model.

At this point it is necessary for him to decide if one of the techniques
is applicable. Once this analysis is completed and it is decided to use an operations research technique, a *Model* is developed that can best relate the
significant variables, operating constraints and the stated objectives. To do
this one or more of the techniques are used. The model should be tested or
verified to see if it has captured all of the characteristics that were to be included.

Relevant data is gathered and prepared for the model's format to obtain a *solution* from the model. The solution will be transformed from
abstract terms into terms that will be applicable to the users of the system
being modeled. The solution(s) may then be evaluated to ascertain its

usefulness. If all or parts of the solution are found to be beneficial a *Decision* has to be made by management concerning the *implementation* of the acceptable solution to the problem. If it is decided to implement the solution, plans and controls will have to be established to put the solution into action with a minimum disruption to the system and to gain assurance that the intended results will be obtained.

Emphasis on the different components of the cycle would vary in each type of application. Most of the time the model should not be considered a routine decision maker, but as a tool to explore the different alternatives. In some very routine applications, however, users may justify using the model to select the alternatives to be used.

While Figure 1 is appropriate in relating the modeling process to the real world, Figure 2 presents the more formal steps that take place in the modeling process. These steps are self explanatory. The situation being modeled will determine, to a large extent, the attention and resources

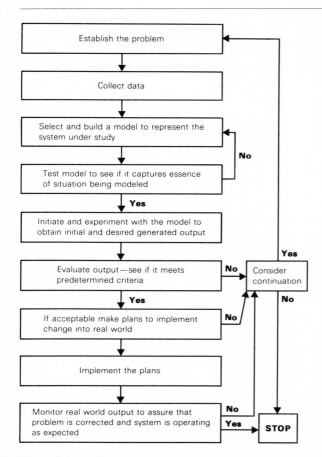

Figure 2 Modeling process

placed on any one of these steps. Most individuals or operations research groups usually focus and give adequate consideration to the first six steps in the process, but many of those employed in model construction tend to treat the last three steps of the process too lightly. This results in confusion and distrust of the models being used. Managers should insure that sufficient attention is provided by the model builders in the last three steps.

Most modeling techniques discussed here may be useful in situations unrelated to their original purpose. The theoretical foundations of any one of them may make it feasible to employ it in noncorporate applications or in different situations from its original intent. The format presented in Figure 2 is generally applicable to all model types listed here with changing emphasis on each of the steps. The word "model" is open to many interpretations. The range covered by this term when it is used without regard to any specific application may include (5; Also see Figure 3):

1 Physical models
2 Pictorial models
3 Mathematical programming
      a) Gaming models
      b) Input-output models
      c) Linear programming models
4 Queuing or waiting line models
5 Critical path models (CPM), and
      a) PEP
      b) IMPACT
      c) PERT
6 Simulation models
      a) Special purpose
      b) General

Although specific types of models can be used in several ways, each type of model has a set of applications for which it is best suited. The classification system presented should give the manager insight into a hierarchical organization and general foundations leading to each of the modeling methods. The practitioner's responsibility is to ascertain and use the modeling method best suited for the particular situation being analyzed and/or researched.

Physical models

The physical model portrays some aspect of the general problem by physically imitating the problem's pertinent environment. Many companies use physical layout models to study the feasibility of the alternatives available to them for handling different components of their production function and its related activities so that their goods or services can be produced with improved efficiency. Physical models may be used in direct experimentation to

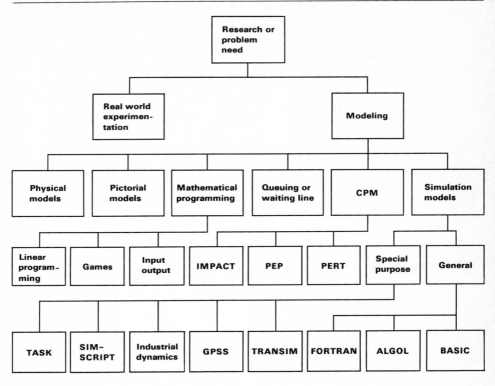

Figure 3 Structure of general types of models

see if there are any possible improvements, such as saving floor space or more direct product movement, that could be made to further economize the process of proceedings within an activity.

Thus, predominantly, management use of the physical model is to find more efficient alternatives of equipment arrangement or for pretesting to ascertain the suitability of the various alternatives. This approach may add safety to the final layout or it may save time and cost in the ultimate production line. Physical models consider only physical size and arrangement and not the operating characteristics of the equipment being studied, information flows or decision processes. Because of their limited nature and inflexibility, they are of little use in more complex problems.

Pictorial models

Pictorial models show a simple relationship between a system's different components or the dimensional characteristics of one component. For example, they can be used to find the best arrangement of the present components or to fit a new component into the company's production function. Flowcharts or diagrams would be another type of pictorial model representing the various elements of a system.

Since pictorial models are usually the easiest and cheapest to construct and understand, they are widely used. Many times they are used to give managers or researchers background material for construction of more sophisticated models. One advantage of this type is the ease in manipulation once the decision is made to look at something new. This model can be scaled to virtually any size so that components can be easily visualized or handled. The economies of small size have to be played against completeness or coverage of the model. Pictorial models suffer from many of the physical model's disabilities. They may, however, be used as an integral part of other more complex methods. For instance, the flowchart, a part of many of the computer methods, is really a pictorial model of the computer program.

Mathematical programming

"Mathematics in operations research is the means by which the findings of modern investigations can be expressed, analyzed and computed with the aim of reaching an objective result." (6) The objective result of mathematical programming which has been defined as a symbolic model, is usually a maximization or minimization of some function. Mathematical programming refers to problem analysis in which some function of one or more variables with non-negative values is to be maximized or minimized when these variables are subject to a number of constraints or conditions, at least one of which is expressed as an inequality.

There are a number of branches of mathematical programming which can be categorized into major headings. Three of the more familiar subdivisions of mathematical programming are input-output analysis, linear programming, and game theory. The common characteristic that permits these three methods to be grouped together is that all require linear restrictions and objective functions. The linear requirement is to keep the problem and analysis in the simplest of all mathematical functions (first degree) so that many functions can be handled with ease. Applications of the mathematical technique are quite general. "Some of the most fertile applications of programming have involved welfare economics and advice to businessmen, both of which aim to tell the relevant persons how they can most efficiently go about working toward their objectives." (7)

Many mathematical programs are either specialized for particular uses or they are of a static nature rendering them useless for broad applications or for dynamic situations. The following quote expresses this problem, "Until recently there has been widespread dependence on the use of 'mathematical models'; these are mathematical relationships describing the operations of the real-life system. However, in a large number of instances, mathematical tools have been inadequate to represent complex system interrelationships and variables with sufficient accuracy." (8)

The linear programming and input-output models are static in nature. Some research is currently underway that has, as a goal, modifications that could make these two methods dynamic. The dynamic developments have not reached a state of maturity that makes it useful for most managers. Generally, mathematical programming models do not have provisions for handling all of the types of input, different kinds of relationships between the phenomenon being analyzed, or the different forms of output required. Mathematical models that do contain sophistication that would be useful in many situations are usually specialized to a point that make them useless. In the future as the state of the art develops, there will probably be deterministic models available to handle many more problem types.

Queuing or waiting line models

The queuing or waiting line model is used in situations in which customers, servers, objects, or products arrive at a service point at irregular intervals. If there is a possibility of a queue being formed, because of faster arrival than departure, a manager may find queuing models useful for identifying more efficient methods of operation. "Waiting-line theory or queuing theory usually provides models which are capable of providing 'solutions' for 'random or nonrandom demands,' in order to predict the behavior of the system." (9) With this model one is able to ascertain if he has enough capacity to serve his customers or products and the general characteristics of the system as it operates under different conditions.

The investigator also may discover some other characteristics about the facility, such as the average length of the waiting line and the average amount of time spent in that line. Costs are estimated to the waiting line periods in terms of lost customers and are derived for providing each of the server configurations under study. These two costs will be compared with one another to discover the optimal point for operating the facility with maximum returns. Except in forced situations (e.g., emergency hospital rooms, landing strips at an airport, or war maneuvers), this optimal point is where marginal costs equal marginal revenues. A study of this information may indicate to the investigator and/or manager that a priority system may be beneficial for optimization or that more alternatives should be available at certain times.

A critical path model is used normally to study an integrated series of activities required for completion of a project. The activities are first placed in a sequential relationship, then the time to complete each activity is estimated. The data are used to construct a network. With this network the required sequencing, interdependencies, and the intradependencies of the different intermediate required steps of a project can be visualized and analyzed. The data in the network are used by a computer program to assign schedules to the different implements and resources being used in the construction of the project. Status information of the various activities is constantly fed into the program so that schedules can be updated. The analysis should help insure that the project is finished in an efficient manner.

The critical path programs most widely used for the network analysis and scheduling are Critical Path Method (CPM), Program Evaluation Procedure (PEP), Program Evaluation and Review Technique (PERT), and Integrated Management Planning and Control Technique (IMPACT). All have the same basic objective—to schedule efficiently all the project's activities in order to complete the project by a particular date or at a minimal cost. The CPM approach is finding wide usage in the construction industry and in many governmental projects. Many requests for proposals now require that a contractor include provisions for monitoring their work through use of CPM.

Simulation model

"A simulation model is a model of some situation in which the elements of the situation are represented by arithmetic or logical processes that can be executed on a computer to predict the dynamic properties of the situation." (10) Most simulation techniques provide a medium for interconnecting the activities being considered so that cause and effect patterns can be studied in relation to time. The goals of simulation models are spread over a wide spectrum. They may assist an individual or group in formalizing plans, making forecasts, decision making, experimentation, or searching out new problems.

For a more specific area of assistance, dynamic output simulation models may be useful in showing some of the effects of time lags in information systems of a company (11). They may also provide insight into the complete operation of an enterprise. Useful information, in many forms, can be obtained for advancing a company towards its objectives or subobjectives. The methods of simulation are few and largely untried. Ones given considerable attention in recent literature are TASK, SIMSCRIPT, GPSS, Industrial Dynamics and GASP.

Even though simulation is a non-deterministic type of model in relation to optimal solutions, it does provide a means of studying many different types of phenomena simultaneously. For instance, normal mathematical techniques have been developed to determine the optimal order quantity, best reorder point and most economic inventory level for one point in a system, but mathematical programming techniques have not been developed to handle simultaneously a system with a growing number of inventory points and a growing activity at each point.

Along with the accommodation of the above phenomenon, a simulation model, for example, could also simultaneously accommodate: a changing failure rate of a system's component parts, changing utilization rate, changing schedule for resource inputs, and/or arbitrary assignments repair capabilities. Simulation provides a means of studying a system, but it does not provide a means of directing one to an optimal solution. In many cases the path to the problem's satisfactory solution is completed through sequential experimentation.

The history of simulation models is not extensive since the field is relatively new in relation to the other modeling techniques. To construct a dynamic model and encompass a wide spectrum of considerations, one needs a systematic and fast medium for handling and processing the necessary material and data. The combination of simulation and the computer partially fills this need. The simulation is needed to organize the input information, and the computer is needed because of its capability to systematically and accurately handle all of the mathematical iterations required by a dynamic simulation model. The computer can quickly process the data, sometimes in minutes, once the model is finished.

Summary

Some of the techniques that have fallen under a heading of their own are used as an agent by other techniques (e.g., linear programming may be, but normally is not, used by a critical path model), so the structures presented here cannot be considered ironclad.

Each potential user of operations research will have to make his framework for evaluating and using the techniques.

Figure 4 shows a structure that imposes the different operations research techniques on the decision making process of the three levels of management. It shows where each technique *might* be used in an organization. It by no means limits the use of the technique to the specified area, but gives an indication where it may be used most frequently. Since some techniques (e.g., Linear Programming, Graphs) are used by all levels, they are not firmly placed at one point.

References

1 Haskins and Sells, *Operations Research* (Haskin and Sells, 1958), p. 8.
2 Robert W. Metzger, *Elementary Mathematical Programming* (John Wiley and Sons, Inc., New York, N. Y., 1958), p. 2.
3 Elwood S. Buffa, *Models for Production and Operations Management* (New York: John Wiley and Sons, Inc., 1964), p. 505.
4 Fred Hansman, *Operations Research in Production and Inventory Control* (New York: John Wiley and Sons, Inc., 1962), p. 8.
5 James R. Emshoff and Roger L. Sisson in *Design and Use of Computer Simulation Models* (New York: The Macmillan Company, 1970), pages 5–7, classify the modeling field into four major categories: Descriptive, Physical, Symbolic and Procedural. While this breakdown is helpful and covers the same material here, the category titles do not give the reader insights to the possible methodology.
6 Giuseppe M. Ferrero di Roccaferrera, *Operations Research for Business and Industry* (Cincinnati: Southwestern Publishing Company, 1964), p. 295.

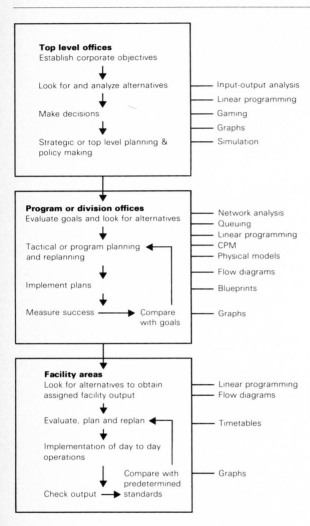

Figure 4

7 William J. Baumol, *Economic Theory and Operations Analysis,* Second Edition (Englewood Cliffs, N. J.: Prentice-Hall, Inc., 1965), p. 71.

8 *TRANSIM—General Purpose Transportation System Simulator—User's Manual,* No. 66-6 (Springfield, Va.: U.S. Department of Commerce, May, 1966), p. 31

9 Giuseppe M. Ferrero di Roccaferrera, *Operations Research for Business and Industry* (Cincinnati: Southwestern Publishing Company, 1964), p. 802.

10 James R. Emshoff and Roger L. Sisson, *Design and Use of Computer Simulation Models* (N. Y.: The Macmillan Company, 1970), p. 8.

11 Adolph F. Moravec, "Using Simulation to Design a Management Information System," *Management Services,* May–June, 1966, pp. 50–58.

VII/B
Communicating

56 Barriers and gateways
to communication
Carl R. Rogers and F. J. Roethlisberger

Part I

It may seem curious that a person like myself, whose whole professional effort is devoted to psychotherapy, should be interested in problems of communication. What relationship is there between obstacles to communication and providing therapeutic help to individuals with emotional maladjustments?

Actually the relationship is very close indeed. The whole task of psychotherapy is the task of dealing with a failure in communication. The emotionally maladjusted person, the "neurotic," is in difficulty, first, because communication within himself has broken down and, secondly, because as a result of this his communication with others has been damaged. To put it another way, in the "neurotic" individual parts of himself which have been termed unconscious, or repressed, or denied to awareness, become blocked off so that they no longer communicate themselves to the conscious or managing part of himself; as long as this is true, there are distortions in the way he communicates himself to others, and so he suffers both within himself and in his interpersonal relations.

The task of psychotherapy is to help the person achieve, through a special relationship with a therapist, good communication within himself. Once this is achieved, he can communicate more freely and more effectively with others. We may say then that psychotherapy is good communication,

Source: Reprinted by permission of The Belknap Press of Harvard University Press from *Man-In-Organization: Essays of F. J. Roethlisberger,* 1968. Originally published in *Harvard Business Review,* July–August 1952, pp. 46–52. © 1952 by the President and Fellows of Harvard College.
Author's note: For the concepts I use to present my material I am greatly indebted to some very interesting conversations I have had with my friend, Irving Lee.—F. J. R.
Editors' note: Professors Rogers' and Roethlisberger's observations are based on their contributions to a panel discussion at the Centennial Conference on Communications, Northwestern University, October 1951.

within and between men. We may also turn that statement around and it will still be true. Good communication, free communication, within or between men, is always therapeutic.

It is, then, from a background of experience with communication in counseling and psychotherapy that I want to present two ideas: (1) I wish to state what I believe is one of the major factors in blocking or impeding communication, and then (2) I wish to present what in our experience has proved to be a very important way of improving or facilitating communication.

Barrier: The tendency to evaluate

I should like to propose, as a hypothesis for consideration, that the major barrier to mutual interpersonal communication is our very natural tendency to judge, to evaluate, to approve (or disapprove) the statement of the other person or the other group. Let me illustrate my meaning with some very simple examples. Suppose someone, commenting on this discussion, makes the statement, "I didn't like what that man said." What will you respond? Almost invariably your reply will be either approval or disapproval of the attitude expressed. Either you respond, "I didn't either; I thought it was terrible," or else you tend to reply, "Oh, I thought it was really good." In other words, your primary reaction is to evaluate it from *your* point of view, your own frame of reference.

Or take another example. Suppose I say with some feeling, "I think the Republicans are behaving in ways that show a lot of good sound sense these days." What is the response that arises in your mind? The overwhelming likelihood is that it will be evaluative. In other words, you will find yourself agreeing, or disagreeing, or making some judgment about me such as "He must be a conservative," or "He seems solid in his thinking." Or let us take an illustration from the international scene. Russia says vehemently, "The treaty with Japan is a war plot on the part of the United States." We rise as one person to say, "That's a lie!"

This last illustration brings in another element connected with my hypothesis. Although the tendency to make evaluations is common in almost all interchange of language, it is very much heightened in those situations where feelings and emotions are deeply involved. So the stronger our feelings, the more likely it is that there will be no mutual element in the communication. There will be just two ideas, two feelings, two judgments, missing each other in psychological space.

I am sure you recognize this from your own experience. When you have not been emotionally involved yourself and have listened to a heated discussion, you often go away thinking, "Well, they actually weren't talking about the same thing." And they were not. Each was making a judgment, an evaluation, from his own frame of reference. There was really nothing which could be called communication in any genuine sense. This tendency to react to any emotionally meaningful statement by forming an evaluation of it from our own point of view is, I repeat, the major barrier to interpersonal communication.

Gateway: Listening with understanding

Is there any way of solving this problem, of avoiding this barrier? I feel that we are making exciting progress toward this goal, and I should like to present it as simply as I can. Real communication occurs, and this evaluative tendency is avoided, when we listen with understanding. What does that mean? It means to see the expressed idea and attitude from the other person's point of view, to sense how it feels to him, to achieve his frame of reference in regard to the thing he is talking about.

Stated so briefly, this may sound absurdly simple, but it is not. It is an approach which we have found extremely potent in the field of psychotherapy. It is the most effective agent we know for altering the basic personality structure of an individual and for improving his relationships and his communications with others. If I can listen to what he can tell me, if I can understand how it seems to him, if I can see its personal meaning for him, if I can sense the emotional flavor which it has for him, then I will be releasing potent forces of change in him.

Again, if I can really understand how he hates his father, or hates the company, or hates Communists—if I can catch the flavor of his fear of insanity, or his fear of atom bombs, or of Russia—it will be of the greatest help to him in altering those hatreds and fears and in establishing realistic and harmonious relationships with the very people and situations toward which he has felt hatred and fear. We know from our research that such empathic understanding—understanding *with* a person, not *about* him—is such an effective approach that it can bring about major changes in personality.

Some of you may be feeling that you listen well to people and yet you have never seen such results. The chances are great indeed that your listening has not been of the type I have described. Fortunately, I can suggest a little laboratory experiment which you can try to test the quality of your understanding. The next time you get into an argument with your wife, or your friend, or with a small group of friends, just stop the discussion for a moment and, for an experiment, institute this rule: "Each person can speak up for himself only *after* he has first restated the ideas and feelings of the previous speaker accurately and to that speaker's satisfaction."

You see what this would mean. It would simply mean that before presenting your own point of view, it would be necessary for you to achieve the other speaker's frame of reference—to understand his thoughts and feelings so well that you could summarize them for him. Sounds simple, doesn't it? But if you try it, you will discover that it is one of the most difficult things you have ever tried to do. However, once you have been able to see the other's point of view, your own comments will have to be drastically revised. You will also find the emotion going out of the discussion, the differences being reduced, and those differences which remain being of a rational and understandable sort.

Can you imagine what this kind of an approach would mean if it were projected into larger areas? What would happen to a labor-management dispute if it were conducted in such a way that labor, without necessarily agreeing, could accurately state management's point of view in a way that management could accept; and management, without approving labor's stand, could state labor's case in a way that labor agreed was accurate? It would mean that real communication was established, and one could practically guarantee that some reasonable solution would be reached.

If, then, this way of approach is an effective avenue to good communication and good relationships, as I am quite sure you will agree if you try the experiment I have mentioned, why is it not more widely tried and used? I will try to list the difficulties which keep it from being utilized.

Need for courage

In the first place it takes courage, a quality which is not too widespread. I am indebted to Dr. S. I. Hayakawa, the semanticist, for pointing out that to carry on psychotherapy in this fashion is to take a very real risk, and that courage is required. If you really understand another person in this way, if you are willing to enter his private world and see the way life appears to him, without any attempt to make evaluative judgments, you run the risk of being changed yourself. You might see it his way; you might find yourself influenced in your attitudes or your personality.

This risk of being changed is one of the most frightening prospects many of us can face. If I enter, as fully as I am able, into the private world of a neurotic or psychotic individual, isn't there a risk that I might become lost in that world? Most of us are afraid to take that risk. Or if we were listening to a Russian Communist, or Senator Joe McCarthy, how many of us would dare to try to see the world from each of their points of view? The great majority of us could not *listen*; we would find ourselves compelled to *evaluate*, because listening would seem too dangerous. So the first requirement is courage, and we do not always have it.

Heightened emotions

But there is a second obstacle. It is just when emotions are strongest that it is most difficult to achieve the frame of reference of the other person or group. Yet it is then that the attitude is most needed if communication is to be established. We have not found this to be an insuperable obstacle in our experience in psychotherapy. A third party, who is able to lay aside his own feelings and evaluations, can assist greatly by listening with understanding to each person or group and clarifying the views and attitudes each holds.

We have found this effective in small groups in which contradictory or antagonistic attitudes exist. When the parties to a dispute realize that they are being understood, that someone sees how the situation seems to them, the statements grow less exaggerated and less defensive, and it is no longer necessary to maintain the attitude, "I am 100% right and you are 100% wrong." The influence of such an understanding catalyst in the group permits the members to come closer and closer to the objective truth involved in the relationship. In this way mutual communication is established, and some type of agreement becomes much more possible.

So we may say that though heightened emotions make it much more difficult to understand *with* an opponent, our experience makes it clear that a neutral, understanding, catalyst type of leader or therapist can overcome this obstacle in a small group.

Size of group

That last phrase, however, suggests another obstacle to utilizing the approach I have described. Thus far all our experience has been with small face-to-face groups—groups exhibiting industrial tensions, religious tensions, racial tensions, and therapy groups in which many personal tensions are present. In these small groups our experience, confirmed by a limited amount of research, shows that this basic approach leads to improved communication, to greater acceptance of others and by others, and to attitudes which are more positive and more problem-solving in nature. There is a decrease in defensiveness, in exaggerated statements, in evaluative and critical behavior.

But these findings are from small groups. What about trying to achieve understanding between larger groups that are geographically remote, or between face-to-face groups that are not speaking for themselves but simply as representatives of others, like the delegates at Kaesong? Frankly we do not know the answers to these questions. I believe the situation might be put this way: As social scientists we have a tentative test-tube solution of the problem of breakdown in communication. But to confirm the validity of this test-tube solution and to adapt it to the enormous problems of communication breakdown between classes, groups, and nations would involve additional funds, much more research, and creative thinking of a high order.

Yet with our present limited knowledge we can see some steps which might be taken even in large groups to increase the amount of listening *with* and decrease the amount of evaluation *about*. To be imaginative for a moment, let us suppose that a therapeutically oriented international group went to the Russian leaders and said, "We want to achieve a genuine understanding of your views and, even more important, of your attitudes and feelings toward the United States. We will summarize and resummarize these views and feelings if necessary, until you agree that our description represents the situation as it seems to you."

Then suppose they did the same thing with the leaders in our own country. If they then gave the widest possible distribution to these two views, with the feelings clearly described but not expressed in name-calling, might not the effect be very great? It would not guarantee the type of understanding I have been describing, but it would make it much more possible. We can understand the feelings of a person who hates us much more readily when his attitudes are accurately described to us by a neutral third party than we can when he is shaking his fist at us.

Faith in social sciences

But even to describe such a first step is to suggest another obstacle to this approach of understanding. Our civilization does not yet have enough faith in the social sciences to utilize their findings. The opposite is true of the physical sciences. During the war when a test-tube solution was found to the problem of synthetic rubber, millions of dollars and an army of talent were turned loose on the problem of using that finding. If synthetic rubber could be made in milligrams, it could and would be made in the thousands of tons. And it was. But in the social science realm, if a way is found of facilitating communication and mutual understanding in small groups, there is no guarantee that the finding will be utilized. It may be a generation or more before the money and the brains will be turned loose to exploit that finding.

Summary

In closing, I should like to summarize this small-scale solution to the problem of barriers in communication, and to point out certain of its characteristics.

I have said that our research and experience to date would make it appear that breakdowns in communication, and the evaluative tendency which is the major barrier to communication, can be avoided. The solution is provided by creating a situation in which each of the different parties comes to understand the other from the *other's* point of view. This has been achieved, in practice, even when feelings run high, by the influence of a person who is willing to understand each point of view empathically, and who thus acts as a catalyst to precipitate further understanding.

This procedure has important characteristics. It can be initiated by one party, without waiting for the other to be ready. It can even be initiated by a neutral third person, provided he can gain a minimum of cooperation from one of the parties.

This procedure can deal with the insincerities, the defensive exaggerations, the lies, the "false fronts" which characterize almost every failure in communication. These defensive distortions drop away with astonishing speed as people find that the only intent is to understand, not to judge.

This approach leads steadily and rapidly toward the discovery of the truth, toward a realistic appraisal of the objective barriers to communication. The dropping of some defensiveness by one party leads to further dropping of defensiveness by the other party, and truth is thus approached.

This procedure gradually achieves mutual communication. Mutual communication tends to be pointed toward solving a problem rather than toward attacking a person or group. It leads to a situation in which I see how the problem appears to you as well as to me, and you see how it appears to me as well as to you. Thus accurately and realistically defined, the problem is almost certain to yield to intelligent attack; or if it is in part insoluble, it will be comfortably accepted as such.

This then appears to be a test-tube solution to the breakdown of communication as it occurs in small groups. Can we take this small-scale answer, investigate it further, refine it, develop it, and apply it to the tragic and well-nigh fatal failures of communication which threaten the very existence of our modern world? It seems to me that this is a possibility and a challenge which we should explore.

Part II

In thinking about the many barriers to personal communication, particularly those that are due to differences of background, experience, and motivation, it seems to me extraordinary that any two persons can ever understand each other. Such reflections provoke the question of how communication is possible when people do not see and assume the same things and share the same values.

On this question there are two schools of thought. One school assumes that communication between A and B, for example, has failed when B does not accept what A has to say as being fact, true, or valid; and that the goal of communication is to get B to agree with A's opinions, ideas, facts, or information.

The position of the other school of thought is quite different. It assumes that communication has failed when B does not feel free to express his feelings to A because B fears they will not be accepted by A. Communication is facilitated when on the part of A or B or both there is a willingness to express and accept differences.

As these are quite divergent conceptions, let us explore them further with an example. Bill, an employee, is talking with his boss in the boss's office. The boss says, "I think, Bill, that this is the best way to do your job." Bill says, "Oh yeah!" According to the first school of thought, this reply would be a sign of poor communication. Bill does not understand the best way of doing his work. To improve communication, therefore, it is up to the boss to explain to Bill why his way is the best.

From the point of view of the second school of thought, Bill's reply is a sign neither of good nor of bad communication. Bill's response is indeterminate. But the boss has an opportunity to find out what Bill means if he so desires. Let us assume that this is what he chooses to do, i.e., find out what Bill means. So this boss tries to get Bill to talk more about his job while he (the boss) listens.

For purposes of simplification, I shall call the boss representing the first school of thought "*Smith*" and the boss representing the second school of thought "*Jones*." In the presence of the so-called same stimulus each behaves differently. Smith chooses to *explain*; Jones chooses to *listen*. In my experience Jones's response works better than Smith's. It works better because Jones is making a more proper evaluation of what is taking place between him and Bill than Smith is. Let us test this hypothesis by continuing with our example.

What Smith assumes, sees, and feels

Smith assumes that he understands what Bill means when Bill says, "Oh yeah!" so there is no need to find out. Smith is sure that Bill does not understand why this is the best way to do his job, so Smith has to tell him.

In this process let us assume Smith is logical, lucid, and clear. He presents his facts and evidence well. But, alas, Bill remains unconvinced. What does Smith do? Operating under the assumption that what is taking place between him and Bill is something essentially logical, Smith can draw only one of two conclusions: either (1) he has not been clear enough, or (2) Bill is too damned stupid to understand. So he either has to "spell out" his case in words of fewer and fewer syllables or give up. Smith is reluctant to do the latter, so he continues to explain. What happens?

If Bill still does not accept Smith's explanation of why this is the best way for him to do his job, a pattern of interacting feelings is produced of which Smith is often unaware. The more Smith cannot get Bill to understand him, the more frustrated Smith becomes and the more Bill becomes a threat to his logical capacity. Since Smith sees himself as a fairly reasonable and logical chap, this is a difficult feeling to accept. It is much easier for him to perceive Bill as uncooperative or stupid. This perception, however, will affect what Smith says and does. Under these pressures Bill comes to be evaluated more and more in terms of Smith's values. By this process Smith tends to treat Bill's values as unimportant. He tends to deny Bill's uniqueness and difference. He treats Bill as if he had little capacity for self-direction.

Let us be clear. Smith does not see that he is doing these things. When he is feverishly scratching hieroglyphics on the back of an envelope, trying to explain to Bill why this is the best way to do his job, Smith is trying to be helpful. He is a man of good will, and he wants to set Bill straight. This is the way Smith sees himself and his behavior. But it is for this very reason that Bill's "Oh yeah!" is getting under Smith's skin.

"How dumb can a guy be?" is Smith's attitude, and unfortunately Bill will hear that more than Smith's good intentions. Bill will feel misunderstood. He will not see Smith as a man of good will trying to be helpful. Rather he will perceive him as a threat to his self-esteem and personal integrity. Against this threat Bill will feel the need to defend himself at all cost. Not being so logically articulate as Smith, Bill expresses this need, again, by saying, "Oh yeah!"

What Jones assumes, sees, and feels

Let us leave this sad scene between Smith and Bill, which I fear is going to terminate by Bill's either leaving in a huff or being kicked out of Smith's office. Let us turn for a moment to Jones and see what he is assuming, seeing, hearing, feeling, doing, and saying when he interacts with Bill.

Jones, it will be remembered, does not assume that he knows what Bill means when he says, "Oh yeah!" so he has to find out. Moreover, he assumes that when Bill said this, he had not exhausted his vocabulary or his feelings. Bill may not necessarily mean one thing; he may mean several different things. So Jones decides to listen.

In this process Jones is not under any illusion that what will take place will be eventually logical. Rather he is assuming that what will take place will be primarily an interaction of feelings. Therefore, he cannot ignore the feelings of Bill, the effect of Bill's feelings on him, or the effect of his feelings on Bill. In other words, he cannot ignore his relationship to Bill; he cannot assume that it will make no difference to what Bill will hear or accept.

Therefore, Jones will be paying strict attention to all of the things Smith has ignored. He will be addressing himself to Bill's feelings, his own, and the interactions between them.

Jones will therefore realize that he has ruffled Bill's feelings with his comment, "I think, Bill, this is the best way to do your job." So instead of trying to get Bill to understand him, he decides to try to understand Bill. He does this by encouraging Bill to speak. Instead of telling Bill how he should feel or think, he asks Bill such questions as, "Is this what you feel?" "Is this what you see?" "Is this what you assume?" Instead of ignoring Bill's evaluations as irrelevant, not valid, inconsequential, or false, he tries to understand Bill's reality as he feels it, perceives it, and assumes it to be. As Bill begins to open up, Jones's curiosity is piqued by this process.

"Bill isn't so dumb; he's quite an interesting guy" becomes Jones's attitude. And that is what Bill hears. Therefore Bill feels understood and accepted as a person. He becomes less defensive. He is in a better frame of mind to explore and re-examine his own perceptions, feelings, and assumptions. In this process he perceives Jones as a source of help. Bill feels free to express his differences. He feels that Jones has some respect for his capacity for self-direction. These positive feelings toward Jones make Bill more inclined to say, "Well, Jones, I don't quite agree with you that this is the best way to do my job, but I'll tell you what I'll do. I'll try to do it that way for a few days, and then I'll tell you what I think."

Conclusion

I grant that my two orientations do not work themselves out in practice in quite so simple or neat a fashion as I have been able to work them out on paper. There are many other ways in which Bill could have responded to Smith in the first place. He might even have said, "O.K., boss, I agree that your way of doing my job is better." But Smith still would not have known how Bill felt when he made this statement or whether Bill was actually going to do his job differently. Likewise, Bill could have responded to Jones in a way different from my example. In spite of Jones's attitude, Bill might still be reluctant to express himself freely to his boss.

The purpose of my examples has not been to demonstrate the right or wrong way of communicating. My purpose has been simply to provide something concrete to point to when I make the following generalizations:

1 Smith represents to me a very common pattern of misunderstanding. The misunderstanding does not arise because Smith is not clear enough in expressing himself. It arises because of Smith's misevaluation of what is taking place when two people are talking together.

2 Smith's misevaluation of the process of personal communication consists of certain very common assumptions, e.g., (a) that what is taking place is something essentially logical; (b) that words in themselves apart from the people involved mean something; and (c) that the purpose of the interaction is to get Bill to see things from Smith's point of view.

3 Because of these assumptions, a chain reaction of perceptions and negative feelings is engendered which blocks communication. By ignoring Bill's feelings and by rationalizing his own, Smith ignores his relationship to Bill as one of the most important determinants of the communication. As a result, Bill hears Smith's attitude more clearly than the logical content of Smith's words. Bill feels that his individual uniqueness is being denied. His personal integrity being at stake, he becomes defensive and belligerent. As a result, Smith feels frustrated. He perceives Bill as stupid. So he says and does things which only provoke more defensiveness on the part of Bill.

4 In the case of Jones, I have tried to show what might possibly happen if we made a different evaluation of what is taking place when two people are talking together. Jones makes a different set of assumptions. He assumes (a) that what is taking place between him and Bill is an interaction of sentiments; (b) that Bill—not his words in themselves—means something; (c) that the object of the interaction is to give Bill an opportunity to express freely his differences.

5 Because of these assumptions, a psychological chain reaction of reinforcing feelings and perceptions is set up which facilitates communication between Bill and him. When Jones addresses himself to Bill's feelings and perceptions from Bill's point of view, Bill feels understood and accepted as a person; he feels free to express his differences. Bill sees Jones as a source of help; Jones sees Bill as an interesting person. Bill in turn becomes more cooperative.

6 If I have identified correctly these very common patterns of personal communication, then some interesting hypotheses can be stated:

(a) Jones's method works better than Smith's, not because of any magic, but because Jones has a better map than Smith of the process of personal communication.

(b) The practice of Jones's method, however, is not merely an intellectual exercise. It depends on Jones's capacity and willingness to see and accept points of view different from his own, and to practice this orientation in a face-to-face relationship. This practice involves an emotional as well as an intellectual achievement. It depends in part on Jones's awareness of himself, in part on the practice of a skill.

(c) Although our colleges and universities try to get students to appreciate intellectually points of view different from their own, very little is done to help them to implement this general intellectual appreciation in a simple face-to-face relationship—at the level of a skill. Most educational institutions train their students to be logical, lucid, and clear. Very little is done to help them to listen more skillfully. As a result, our educated world contains too many Smiths and too few Joneses.

(d) The biggest block to personal communication is man's inability to listen intelligently, understandingly, and skillfully to another person. This deficiency in the modern world is widespread and appalling. In our universities as well as elsewhere, too little is being done about it.

7 In conclusion, let me apologize for acting toward you the way Smith did. But who am I to violate a long-standing academic tradition!

57 Stimulating upward communication
Earl G. Planty and William Machaver

Managers, by and large, have been relatively quick to perceive the problems of downward communication. The growth and complexity of modern industry have placed pressure upon management at all levels to develop effective means of transmitting to lower echelons information that is vital to the continuing, efficient operation of the business.

Executives and supervisors recognize, too, that misinformation and the resulting misunderstanding lessen working efficiency. Sharing information with subordinates at all levels of the organization tends to diminish the fears and suspicions that we all sometimes have in our work and toward our employer; it affords the security and feeling of belonging so necessary for efficiency and morale. In general, it may be said that *downward* communication is an integral part of the traditional industrial organization and is readily accepted and made use of—more or less effectively—by management.

The neglected other half

Unfortunately, however, some managers tend to consider communication a one-way street. They fail to see the values obtained from encouraging employees to discuss fully the policies and plans of the company. They do not provide a clear channel for funneling information, opinions, and attitudes up through the organization.

There are many values, however, that accrue to those managers who listen willingly, who urge their subordinates to talk freely and honestly. Upward communication reveals to them the degree to which ideas passed down are accepted. In addition, it stimulates employees to participate in the operation of their department or unit and, therefore, encourages them to defend the decisions and support the policies cooperatively developed with management. The opportunity for upward communication also encourages

Source: Reprinted by permission of the publisher from *Effective Communication on the Job,* pp. 123–130. © 1956 by the American Management Association, Inc.

employees to contribute valuable ideas for improving departmental or company efficiency. Finally, it is through upward communication that executives and supervisors learn to avert the many explosive situations which arise daily in industry.

If these advantages are to be achieved, we must realize that communication is dynamic. It must flow constantly up as well as down if it is to stimulate mutual understanding at all levels of the organization.

Faced as all industry is with the need for education in this complex and emotion-laden problem of upward communication, Johnson & Johnson and affiliated companies established a committee of operating executives to make a thorough investigation of the problems of upward communication. The personnel directors, a sales director, and two vice presidents in charge of manufacturing constituted the committee. They met, read, studied, interviewed specialists, argued the question among themselves, and then prepared the material which constitutes the body of the following report. Operating in panel style, they presented the report to the board of directors of the parent company, to the boards of affiliated companies, and to major operating executives, inviting their suggestions and criticisms.[1] Other committees similarly prepared themselves, presented reports, and invited discussions with middle and lower levels of management. Thus the report which follows represents practical recommendations dealing with the fundamentals and techniques of upward communication—a program developed by the joint effort of operating executives.

I. The value of effective upward communication[2]

A. Values to superiors

1 Many of management's best ideas are sown on cold and sour soil, not tilled and prepared in advance for the information. Where attitudes and feelings are transmitted freely upward, however, management is forewarned of possible failure and can better prepare the seed bed before its own ideas are broadcast. Upward communications tell us not only when our people are ready to hear our story, but also how well they accept our story when we do tell it. We have no better means than upward communication of knowing whether our downward communications have been believed.

---

[1] The writers wish to acknowledge the assistance of the following members of the committee who presented the report: E. A. Carlson, Controller at Johnson & Johnson; J. T. Freeston, Assistant Personnel Director at Johnson & Johnson; J. F. Kiley, Vice President, General Line Field Sales Force at Johnson & Johnson; W. S. McCord, Director of Industrial Relations at Personal Products; C. V. Swank, Vice President in Charge of Manufacturing at Johnson & Johnson; and H. A. Wallace, Vice President in Charge of Manufacturing at Ethicon Suture Laboratories, Inc.

[2] The points outlined in this section were developed by the panel in reply to the moderator's question, "What values may we expect in business and industry from improved upward communications?"

2 If we are to gain understanding and full acceptance of our decisions, subordinates must be given the opportunity to participate in their making or at
least to discuss the merits and defects of proposed actions. Social scientists
tell us that employee understanding and loyalty do not come solely from
hearing facts, even true facts. Appreciation and loyalty result from self-
expression in a situation in which the subordinate feels there is personal
sympathy toward him and his views. Therefore the superior should encourage subordinates at any level to ask questions and contribute their own
ideas. Above all, he should listen, sincerely and sympathetically, with intention to use workable ideas that are proposed.

3 From upward communication we discover whether subordinates get the
meaning from downward communication that is intended by the superior. It
is highly unlikely that a subordinate left completely to his own interpretation
will understand a directive or an action just as the originator intended it. In
the first place, management may phrase its messages vaguely or ambigu-
ously. Second, recipients interpret even the clearest communication in the
light of their own biases and experience. Even though it may seem to us
most logical that they should draw only one conclusion, we can never be
sure what subordinates think unless we get them to relay back to us their
interpretations and reactions to what we do and say.

4 Finally, effective upward communication encourages subordinates to offer
ideas of value to themselves and the business. The need here is to devise
and use every form of upward communication that will draw these ideas
from all who are qualified to make them.

B. Values to subordinates

1 Upward communication helps satisfy basic human needs. All subordinates
look upon themselves as having inherent worth at least as great as the personal worth of their superiors. This is true even if they feel their own inferiority in managerial ability or in some other skill. They still think, just as
you and I do, that because they are individual human beings they have certain values and rights. This sense of personal worth is always injured when
people do not get a chance to express their ideas—when they are merely
told, without opportunity to comment or reply. This principle applies even if
the telling is very well done. We respect our employees' dignity only when
we allow, or better still invite, them to express their reactions to what is
told—preferably before action is taken.

2 Employees who are encouraged to talk directly and frankly with their
superiors get a release of emotional tensions and pressures which otherwise may find outlet in criticism to other members of the company and the
community, or in loss of interest or efficiency. Some superiors feel that by
listening to fanatics, crackpots, and neurotics they encourage their complaints. If complaints seem to arise from physical or mental ailments, treatment by a physician or psychiatrist may be necessary. But to the degree

that the maladjustment lies in the man's work relations, listening to him may identify failures and sore spots in the organization that cause his problems. Moreover, it is well established that the right kind of listening enables many individuals to understand and solve their own problems. For the *normal* individuals in industry, it is likely that the more you listen willingly to what employees are inclined to tell you, the less time you will in the future be called upon to give.

3 Unlike the organizational structure of the church, the school, the local and even the national government, industry in its organization is essentially authoritarian. This makes it even more necessary in industry than in, say, education or government that every opportunity be given subordinates to express their views freely and to make their influence felt. Many think that business cannot continue to exist as we know it today unless more and more ways are found to bring the essentials of democracy into the workplace. Fortunately, the principles of democracy do not require that such business functions as financing, expansion or curtailment of production, and hiring be decided upon by vote of the majority. However, the fact that by nature we must be authoritarian in some matters makes it imperative that we be more democratic in those business matters where employee participation is appropriate. Nothing is more fundamental to democracy than upward communication in which the ideas of subordinates are given prompt and sympathetic hearing followed by such action as is desirable.

II. Barriers to upward communication

Even though management may appreciate the need for effective upward communication, it may not translate this need into action. It becomes apparent at once that to swim up the stream of communication is a much harder task than to float downstream. The currents of resistance, inherent in the temperament and habits of supervisors and employees and in the complexity and structure of modern industry, are persistent and strong. Let us examine some of these deterrents to upward communication.[3]

A. Barriers involving business organization

1 The physical distance between superior and subordinate impedes upward communications in several ways. Communication becomes difficult and infrequent when superiors are isolated so as to be seldom seen or spoken to.

[3] Panel discussions with various groups revealed that until the obstacles to effective communications were clearly identified and accepted it was difficult to discuss techniques and methods profitably. A clear understanding of what impedes upward communications must precede removal of obstructions. In many cases an open channel is all we need for ideas and attitudes to flow upward. It was the thought of the syndicate that more could be gained by first emphasizing the removal of barriers than by first putting out enticements and formal devices for stimulating communication upward. Group meetings, written reports, and individual contacts become mere window dressing and will fail in their purpose if superiors have not first dispelled completely any feeling of disinterest or impatience with what their subordinates are telling them.

In large organizations executives are located in headquarters or divisional centers, at points not easily reached by their subordinates. In smaller organizations their offices are sometimes remotely placed, or they hold themselves needlessly inaccessible.

2 Complexity also delays communication up. Suppose there is at the employee's level a significant problem that eventually must be settled at the top. The employee tells his supervisor. They talk it over and try to settle it. This takes a day or two. Then it goes to the department head. He requires some time to hear the case, thinks about it a day or two, and then tells the divisional manager, who holds the case a week while he investigates, unwilling to bother the vice president with it. Since there may appear to be an admission of failure in passing the problem up, each level of supervision is reluctant to do so, thus causing more delay. By the time the problem reaches the top echelon, months may have elapsed since it first arose.

3 Movement of information through many levels dilutes or distorts it. Since each supervisor consciously or unconsciously selects and edits the information he passes up, the more levels of supervision, or filter stations, it passes through before it reaches the top, the less accurate it becomes. Also, in a large company with a hierarchy of management, contacts become fewer and more hurried as one ascends in the organization. A group leader contacts his workers more often than a president contacts his vice presidents.

B. Barriers involving superiors

1 The superior's attitude and behavior in listening will play a vital role in either encouraging or discouraging communication up. If the boss seems anxious to get the interview over with or appears to be impatient with his subordinate, or annoyed or distressed by the subject being discussed, this attitude will place an insurmountable communications barrier between them in the future.

2 A boss may fall into the familiar error of thinking that "no news is good news," whereas lack of complaint or criticism is often a symptom that upward communication is working in very low gear; or he may assume, often wrongly, that he knows what subordinates think or feel; or he may have such an exaggerated sense of duty that he feels it disloyal to listen to complaints, especially if made intemperately. This attitude tends to discourage employees with justifiable complaints from approaching their superiors.

3 We all have a natural defensiveness about ourselves and our actions. As managers, we are prone to resent and resist communications which indicate that some of our actions have been less than perfect. Where this attitude is evident, loyal workers who could be most helpful to us sometimes withhold information. In such cases communicating is of necessity done by the less loyal workers and the maladjusted. In other words, unless we are willing to hear criticism freely, much we learn about our organization comes from those who are the least loyal to it.

4 Superiors often resist becoming involved with the personal problems of their subordinates. This resistance to listening may affect the subordinates'

willingness to communicate up on other matters more directly related to the job. Moreover, job problems and personal problems are often closely linked, and it is difficult to discuss the one without the other.

5 One of the strongest deterrents to communication up is the failure of management to act on undesirable conditions previously brought to its attention. The result is that the workers lose faith both in the sincerity of management and in the value of communication.

6 Listening is time-consuming. Many executives feel that they are too involved with daily problems and responsibilities to provide adequate time for listening fully to their subordinates' ideas, reports, and criticisms. Nevertheless, many time-consuming problems could be minimized or eliminated if superiors were free to listen to their employees, for in listening they can discover solutions to present problems or anticipate causes for future ones. The subordinate who has free access to his boss can get the answers to many budding problems and thus eliminate heavier demands made when the problems have gotten complex, emotion-laden, and possibly out of control.

A man's philosophy of management determines the value he places upon communications and the time he gives to it. A manager who has freed himself of much of his routine responsibilities and is engaged in building individual subordinates and developing teamwork in his group will rank communications high in priority and will allow time for it, since it is the nerve center of such a leader's management. In contrast, the boss who acts alone, solves most of his department's problems himself and lets the growth of subordinates take its own course may well be too busy to communicate.

C. Barriers involving subordinates

1 Communications down may run more freely than communications up because the superior is free to call in the subordinate and talk to him at will. The subordinate does not have the same freedom to intrude upon the superior's time. A man is discouraged from going freely over his boss's head or from asking appeal from his decisions by the line of authority that prevails in industry.

2 Neither the facilities available nor the rewards offered to the subordinate for upward communication equal those for messages downward. Management can speed the flow of information down by the use of company publications, in-plant broadcasts, meetings, bulletin boards, form letters, etc. By praise, promotions, and other signs of recognition management can reward subordinates who act upon communications down, as it can penalize those who fail to act. Few such facilities or incentives for encouraging communications upward are available to the employee.

3 Communications from subordinate to superior cannot be prepared with as much care as those that move down. A sales manager, for example, may address a message to a dozen men—a message resulting from the combined thinking of his staff, strengthened by research, careful writing, editing,

and visual aids. He and his staff are free to give that message far more time and thought than a salesman in the field can expend on a message back to the sales manager.

4 Because tradition, authority, and prestige are behind communications down, they flow more easily in that direction than do communications up. In communicating up, the subordinate must explain himself and get acceptance from one who has greater status and authority. The subordinate's difficulties are greater also because he is likely to be less fluent and persuasive than the man who communicates down to him.

   The semantics barrier is likewise greater for the subordinate. His superior, probably having worked at one time on the subordinate's job, knows the attitudes, the language, and the problems of that level. On the other hand, the man who is communicating up faces the difficulty of talking to a person with whose work and responsibilities he is not familiar.

5 Like all of us, employees are emotional and prejudiced. Their feelings mix freely with their facts, creating further barriers to objective upward communications. Their observations and reports to management are prejudiced by their own personal habits and sentiments. The establishment of rapport through judicious listening will help the superior to understand and interpret what employees are trying to tell him. The superior, of course, must recognize and minimize his own prejudices and idiosyncrasies before he can do this.

6 Unless superiors are particularly receptive, subordinates generally prefer to withhold or temper bad news, unfavorable opinions, and reports of mistakes or failures. Because some managers are defensive about listening to bad news, those who like and respect them withhold information or minimize omissions and errors out of friendly motives; others keep back information from fear, dislike, or indifference.

---

58 Ten commandments of good communication
American Management Association

As a manager, your prime responsibility is to get things done through people. However sound your ideas or well-reasoned your decisions, they become effective only as they are transmitted to others and achieve the desired action—or reaction. Communication, therefore, is your most vital management tool. On the job you communicate not only with words but through

Source: Reprinted by permission of the publisher from *Ten Commandments of Good Communication.* © 1955 by American Management Association, Inc.

your apparent attitudes and your actions. For communication encompasses all human behavior that results in an exchange of meaning. How well you manage depends upon how well you communicate in this broad sense. These ten commandments are designed to help you improve your skills as a manager by improving your skills of communication—with superiors, subordinates, and associates.

1 *Seek to clarify your ideas before communicating* The more systematically we analyze the problem or idea to be communicated, the clearer it becomes. This is the first step toward effective communication. Many communications fail because of inadequate planning. Good planning must consider the goals and attitudes of those who will receive the communication and those who will be affected by it.

2 *Examine the true purpose of each communication* Before you communicate, ask yourself what you *really* want to accomplish with your message—obtain information, initiate action, change another person's attitude? Identify your most important goal and then adapt your language, tone, and total approach to serve that specific objective. Don't try to accomplish too much with each communication. The sharper the focus of your message the greater its chances of success.

3 *Consider the total physical and human setting whenever you communicate* Meaning and intent are conveyed by more than words alone. Many other factors influence the over-all impact of a communication, and the manager must be sensitive to the total setting in which he communicates. Consider, for example, your sense of timing—i.e., the circumstances under which you make an announcement or render a decision; the *physical setting*—whether you communicate in private, for example, or otherwise; the *social climate* that pervades work relationships within the company or a department and sets the tone of its communications; *custom and past practice*—the degree to which your communication conforms to, or departs from, the expectations of your audience. Be constantly aware of the total setting in which you communicate. Like all living things, communication must be capable of adapting to its environment.

4 *Consult with others, where appropriate, in planning communications* Frequently it is desirable or necessary to seek the participation of others in planning a communication or developing the facts on which to base it. Such consultation often helps to lend additional insight and objectivity to your message. Moreover, those who have helped you plan your communication will give it their active support.

5 *Be mindful, while you communicate, of the overtones as well as the basic content of your message* Your tone of voice, your expression, your apparent receptiveness to the responses of others—all have tremendous impact on those you wish to reach. Frequently overlooked, these subtleties of communication often affect a listener's reaction to a message even more than its basic content. Similarly, your choice of language—particularly your awareness of the fine shades of meaning and emotion in the words you use—predetermines in large part the reactions of your listeners.

6 *Take the opportunity, when it arises, to convey something of help or value to the receiver*   Consideration of the other person's interests and needs— the habit of trying to look at things from his point of view—will frequently point up opportunities to convey something of immediate benefit or long-range value to him. People on the job are most responsive to the manager whose messages take their own interests into account.

7 *Follow up your communication*   Our best efforts at communication may be wasted, and we may never know whether we have succeeded in expressing our true meaning and intent, if we do not follow up to see how well we have put our message across. This you can do by asking questions, by encouraging the receiver to express his reactions, by follow-up contacts, by subsequent review of performance. Make certain that every important communication has a "feed-back" so that complete understanding and appropriate action result.

8 *Communicate for tomorrow as well as today*   While communications may be aimed primarily at meeting the demands of an immediate situation, they must be planned with the past in mind if they are to maintain consistency in the receiver's view; but, most important of all, they must be consistent with long-range interests and goals. For example, it is not easy to communicate frankly on such matters as poor performance or the shortcomings of a loyal subordinate—but postponing disagreeable communications makes them more difficult in the long run and is actually unfair to your subordinates and your company.

9 *Be sure your actions support your communications*   In the final analysis, the most persuasive kind of communication is not what you say but what you *do*. When a man's actions or attitudes contradict his words, we tend to discount what he has said. For every manager this means that good supervisory practices—such as clear assignment of responsibility and authority, fair rewards for effort, and sound policy enforcement—serve to communicate more than all the gifts of oratory.

10 *Last, but by no means least: Seek not only to be understood but to understand—be a good listener*   When we start talking we often cease to listen—in that larger sense of being attuned to the other person's unspoken reactions and attitudes. Even more serious is the fact that we are *all* guilty, at times, of inattentiveness when others are attempting to communicate to us. Listening is one of the most important, most difficult—and most neglected—skills in communication. It demands that we concentrate not only on the explicit meanings another person is expressing, but on the implicit meanings, unspoken words, and undertones that may be far more significant. Thus we must learn to listen with the inner ear if we are to know the inner man.

Conclusion

Since 'tis Nature's law to change,
Constancy alone is strange.
    John Wilmot, Earl of Rochester

There is only one thing that's a cinch, and that's the strap that holds the
saddle on.
    Barnaby Jones

This volume has covered the evolution of management from its beginnings to its present state. This section concludes the discussion by considering where management is going.

We begin by examining a difficult issue for today's—and tomorrow's— managers: "social responsibility." Davis and Burck provide us with somewhat opposing treatments of this issue. Following these discussions are two short items that focus sharply on the problem.

The punch line for managers—the essential managerial purpose, as it were—is organizational effectiveness. Buchele delivers a detailed examination of what this purpose means operationally.

The third set of articles deals with three major dimensions of our managerial future. Bennis offers an intriguing view of the organization of the future, predicting that the bureaucratic organization will simply be unable to cope. Etzioni, for his part, expands the analysis, and describes a new type of organization that is becoming increasingly important to our society. Professor Mee then describes what he calls the "manager of the future."

This volume concludes with two items that have been included for one basic reason: the editor considers them amusing reminders that we should not become too ingrained in, and smug about, our various perspectives.

Conclusion/A
Managing social
responsibility

59 Can business afford to ignore social responsibilities?
Keith Davis

Few persons would deny that there are significant changes taking place in social, political, economic, and other aspects of modern culture. Some of these changes businessmen may want and others they may dislike, but in either instance the changes do exist and must be faced. As our culture changes, it is appropriate—even mandatory—that businessmen re-examine their role and the functions of business in society. One area undergoing extensive re-examination is the responsibility businessmen have to society in making business decisions. These are the questions that are being asked:

- Why do businessmen have social responsibilities, if in fact they do?
- How does a businessman know in what directions his social responsibilities lie?
- If businessmen fail to accept social responsibilities incumbent upon them, what consequences may be expected?

It is my purpose in this article to discuss these questions in a very fundamental way. Without looking at specific company practices and without insisting upon a particular program of action, I wish to discuss three basic ideas which must underlie all of our thinking about social responsibility, regardless of what choices we eventually make. The first two ideas are constant and enduring, no matter what social changes occur. The third is more directly related to social changes today, but I believe it is just as fundamental as the others.

Social responsibility is a nebulous idea and, hence, is defined in various ways. It is used here within a management context to refer to *businessmen's decisions and actions taken for reasons at least partially beyond the firm's direct economic or technical interest.*[1] Thus, social responsibility has two rather different faces. On the one hand, businessmen recognize that since they are managing an economic unit in society, they have a broad obligation to the community with regard to economic developments affecting the public welfare (such as full employment, inflation, and maintenance of competition). A quite different type of social responsibility is, on the other hand, a businessman's obligation to nurture and develop human values (such as morale, cooperation, motivation, and self-realization in work). These human values cannot be measured on an economic value scale. Accordingly, the term "social responsibility" refers to both socio-economic and socio-human obligations to others. Popular usage often omits or underplays the socio-human side, but I shall suggest later in this article that it deserves more emphasis.

Note that the importance of social responsibility in this context derives from the fact that it affects a businessman's decisions and consequently his actions toward others. Social responsibility has applied in any situation if it *influences* a businessman's decision even partially. It is not necessary that a decision be based wholly on one's attitude of social responsibility in order to qualify. For example, when a businessman decides to raise or lower prices, he is normally making an economic decision; but if the management of a leading automobile firm decided not to raise prices because of possible effects on inflation, social responsibility would be involved. As a matter of fact, *rarely* would social responsibility be the exclusive reason for a decision.

While it is true that only businessmen (rather than businesses *per se*) make socially responsible decisions, they decide in terms of the objectives and policies of their business institution, which over a period of time acquires social power in its own right. Thus each business institution and the entire business system eventually come to stand for certain socially responsible beliefs and actions. But in the last analysis it is always the businessman who makes the decision. The business institution can only give him a cultural framework, policy guidance, and a special interest.

Responsibility goes with power

Most persons agree that businessmen today have considerable social power. Their counsel is sought by government and community. What they say and do influences their community. This type of influence is *social power*. It comes to businessmen because they are leaders, are intelligent men of affairs, and speak for the important institution we call business. They

---

[1] Some socially responsible business decisions by a long, complicated process of reasoning can be "justified" as having a good chance of bringing long-run economic gain to the firm and thus paying it back for its socially responsible outlook. This long-run economic gain is often merely rationalization of decisions made for non-economic reasons, and in any case the connection is so problematical that some social responsibility is bound to be present also. An example is a decision to retain a very old employee even though his productivity is low.

speak for free enterprise, for or against right-to-work policies, for or against their local school bond election, and so on, *in their roles as businessmen.* When they speak and act as citizens only, and those involved recognize this fact, then whatever social power businessmen possess is that of a citizen and is beyond the bounds of this discussion. In practice, however, it is often difficult to distinguish between these two roles, thereby further complicating the situation.

To the extent that businessmen or any other group have social power, the lessons of history suggest that their social responsibility should be equated with it. Stated in the form of a general relationship, it can be said that *social responsibilities of businessmen need to be commensurate with their social power.* Though this idea is deceptively simple on its face, it is in reality rather complicated and is often overlooked by discussants of social responsibility. On the one hand, it is argued that business is business and anything which smacks of social responsibility is out of bounds (i.e., keep the power but accept no responsibility). On the other, some would have business assume responsibilities as sort of a social godfather, looking after widows, orphans, water conservation, or any other social need, simply because business has large economic resources. Both positions are equally false.

The idea that responsibility and power go hand in hand appears to be as old as civilization itself. Wherever one looks in ancient and medieval history—Palestine, Britain—men were concerned with balancing power and responsibility. Men, being somewhat less than perfect, have often failed to achieve this balance, but they generally sought it as a necessary antecedent to justice. This idea appears to have its origins in logic. It is essentially a matter of balancing one side of an equation with the other.

The idea of co-equal power and responsibility is no stranger to business either. For example, one of the tenets of scientific management is that authority and responsibility should be balanced in such a way that each employee and manager is made responsible to the extent of his authority, and vice-versa.[2] Although this tenet refers to relationships *within* the firm, it seems that it would apply as well to the larger society outside the firm. As a matter of fact, businessmen have been one of the strongest proponents of co-equal social power and responsibility, particularly in their references to labor unions.

Based upon the evidence, it appears that both business leaders and the public accept the ideas of co-equal power and responsibility. Although businessmen accept the logic of this idea, their problem is learning to respect and apply it when making decisions. Granted that there are no pat answers, they still need some guides, else each shall take off in a different direction. At this point, the idea already stated continues to offer help. If "social responsibilities of businessmen need to be commensurate with their social power," then, in a general way, *in the specific operating areas* where there is power, responsibility should also reside. Let us take an example:

[2] Harold Koontz and Cyril O'Donnell, *Principles of Management,* Second Edition, McGraw-Hill Book Company, New York, 1959, p. 95.

Company "A" is the only major employer in a small town. It is considering moving its entire plant out of the area. Company "B" is considering moving its plant of the same size out of a large city where it is one of many employers. It would seem that, other things being equal, Company "A" should give more weight to social responsibilities to the community when considering its move.

Even accepting the greater responsibility of Company "A," and some would not go this far, we still do not know how much greater nor in what way Company "A" should let its decision be amended, if at all. Thus the principle of co-equal power and responsibility can at best serve only as a rough guide, but a real one. For example:

- Do businessmen by their industrial engineering decisions have the power to affect workers' feelings of accomplishment and self-fulfillment on the job? If so, there is roughly a co-equal responsibility.
- Do businessmen have power as businessmen to influence unemployment? To the extent that is so, is there not also social responsibility?
- Do businessmen have power to determine the honesty of advertising? To the degree that they do, is there also social responsibility?

One matter of significance is that the conditions causing power are both internal and external to the firm. In the example of advertising honesty, power is derived primarily internally from the authority structure of the firm and management's knowledge of product characteristics. In the case of Company "A" described earlier, much of its social power is derived from the external fact that it is the only employer in a small town. Each case is situational, requiring reappraisal of power-responsibility relationships each time a major decision is made.

There are, of course, other viewpoints concerning the extent of business social responsibility, and most of them offer a much easier path for businessmen than the one I have been describing. Levitt, in a powerful attack on social responsibility of businessmen, points out that if business assumes a large measure of social responsibility for employee welfare it will lead to a sort of neo-feudalism with all its paternalistic and autocratic ills. The result would be socially less desirable than in the days before businessmen were concerned with social responsibility.[3] Selekman, in an important new analysis, suggests that attention to social responsibility will undermine the main objective of all business, which is to provide economic goods and services to society.[4] A collapse of business' basic economic objectives would indeed be a catastrophe. Certainly the primary economic objectives of

[3] Theodore Levitt. "The Danger of Social Responsibility," *Harvard Business Review,* September–October, 1958, pp. 41–50.
[4] Benjamin M. Selekman, *A Moral Philosophy for Business,* McGraw-Hill Book Company, New York, 1959, especially chapter 27.

business must come first, else business will lose its reason for existence. Selekman's solution is a form of constitutionalism in which the responsibility of the business, other than its economic goals, is to administer its affairs with justice according to a constitutional framework mutually established by all groups involved. These criticisms and others raise questions about putting much social responsibility into business' kit of tools, a fact which leads directly to the second fundamental point of this discussion.

Less responsibility leads to less power

Certainly, if social responsibilities could be avoided or kept to insignificant size in the total scheme of business, a weighty, difficult burden would be raised from businessmen's shoulders. Business progress would be a primrose path compared to the path of thorns which responsibilities entail. But what are the consequences of responsiblibility avoidance? If power and responsibility are to be relatively equal, *then the avoidance of social responsibility leads to gradual erosion of social power*. To the extent that businessmen do not accept social-responsibility opportunities as they arise, other groups will step in to assume these responsibilities. Historically, government and labor have been most active in the role of diluting business power, and probably they will continue to be the principal challenging groups.[5] I am not proposing that this *should* happen, but on basis of the evidence it appears that this will tend to happen to the extent that businessmen do not keep their social responsibilities approximately equal with their social power. In this same vein Howard R. Bowen, in his study of business social responsibilities, concluded, "And it is becoming increasingly obvious that a freedom of choice and delegation of power such as businessmen exercise, would hardly be permitted to continue without some assumption of social responsibility."[6]

Admiral Ben Moreell, Chairman of the Board, Jones and Laughlin Steel Corporation, put this idea more dramatically:

I am convinced that unless we do [accept social responsibilities], the vacuum created by our willingness will be filled by those who would take us down the road to complete statism and inevitable moral and social collapse.[7]

---

[5] For government's role, see George A. Steiner, *Government's Role in Economic Life,* McGraw-Hill Book Company, New York, 1953 and Wayne L. McNaughton and Joseph Lazar, *Industrial Relations and The Government,* McGraw-Hill Book Company, New York, 1954. For labor's role, see Neil W. Chamberlain, *Collective Bargaining,* McGraw-Hill Book Company, New York, 1951 and John A. Fitch, *Social Responsibilities of Organized Labor,* Harper and Brothers, New York, 1957.

[6] Howard R. Bowen, *Social Responsibilities of the Businessman,* Harper and Brothers, New York, 1953, p. 4.

[7] Admiral Ben Moreell, "The Role of American Business in Social Progress," Indiana State Chamber of Commerce, Indianapolis, 1956, p. 20.

History supports these viewpoints. Under the protection of common law, employers during the nineteenth century gave minor attention to worker safety. Early in the twentieth century, in the face of pressure from safety and workmen's compensation laws, employers genuinely accepted responsibility for safety. Since then there have been very few restrictions on business power in this area, because business in general has been acting responsibly. At the opposite extreme, business in the first quarter of this century remained callous about technological and market layoff. As a result, business lost some of its power to government, which administers unemployment compensation, and to unions, which restrict it by means of tight seniority clauses, supplemental unemployment benefits (SUB), and other means. *Now business finds itself in the position of paying unemployment costs it originally denied responsibility for, but having less control than when it did not pay!*

A current problem of social responsibility is gainful employment for older workers. The plight of workers in the over-45 age bracket is well known. In spite of public pronouncements of interest in them and in spite of their general employability, many of them find job opportunities quite limited or even nonexistent. I have said elsewhere that "unless management . . . makes reasonable provision for employing older persons out of work, laws will be passed prohibiting employment discrimination against older workers."[8] Just as a glacier grinds slowly along, the responsibility-power equation gradually, but surely, finds its balance.

In line with the foregoing analysis, Levitt's proposal of "business for business' sake" loses some of its glamor, because it means substantial loss of business power. Historian Arnold J. Toynbee predicts this result when he speaks of business managers being part "of a new world civil service," not necessarily working for government, but working under such stability and elaborate rules both from within and without that they form a relatively powerless bureaucracy similar to the civil service.[9]

It is unlikely that businessmen will concede their social power so easily, and I for one do not want them to do so. Businessmen are our most capable core of organization builders and innovators. We need them. In spite of pessimistic views, businessmen during the next fifty years probably will have substantial freedom of choice regarding what social responsibilities they will take and how far they will go. As current holders of social power, they can act responsibly to hold this power if they wish to do so. If their philosophy is positive (i.e., *for* something, rather than against almost any change) they can take the initiative as instruments of social change related to business. They will then be managers in the true sense of shaping the future, rather than plaintive victims of a more restrictive environment. The choice *is* theirs.

[8] Keith Davis, *Human Relations in Business,* McGraw-Hill Book Company, New York, 1957, p. 415.
[9] Arnold J. Toynbee, "Thinking Ahead," *Harvard Business Review,* September–October, 1958, p. 168.

Non-economic values in business

Early in this discussion I distinguished two types of social responsibilities. One was socio-economic responsibility for general economic welfare. The other was socio-human and referred to responsibility for preserving and developing human values. Let us now further discuss this dintinction as it relates to a third idea underlying the entire problem of social responsibility.

There is general consensus that the "economic man" is dead if, indeed, he ever did exist. Men at work, as customers, and as citizens of a plant community do expect more than straight economic considerations in dealing with business. Since man is more than an economic automaton computing market values, what will be the role of business in serving his other needs? My third basic idea is that *continued vitality of business depends upon its vigorous acceptance of socio-human responsibilities along with socio-economic responsibilities.* A number of people accept the general idea of social responsibility, but they argue that business is wholly an economic institution and, therefore, its responsibilities are limited only to economic aspects of general public welfare. Following this line of reasoning, businessmen might be concerned with economic costs of unemployment, but not with the loss of human dignity and the social disorganization that accompany it. They would be concerned with making work productive in order to better serve society's economic needs but not with making it meaningful in a way that provided worker fulfillment.

The idea of confining social responsibility within economic limits fails on several counts. In first place, it is hardly possible to separate economic aspects of life from its other values. Business deals with a *whole* man in a *whole* social structure, and all aspects of this situation are interrelated. It is agreed that the economic functions of business are primary and the non-economic are secondary, but the non-economic do exist. Second, even if economic aspects of life could be wholly separated out, the general public does not seem to want business confined only to economics. They also have human expectations of business. Third, businessmen currently have socio-human power; hence, if they ignore responsibility in this area, they will be inviting further loss of power. On three counts, then, it appears unwise to equate social responsibility with economic public welfare.

As a matter of fact, it is not a question of "Will these non-economic values be admitted to the decision matrix?" but "To what extent will they be admitted?" Regardless of professions to the contrary, businessmen today are influenced by other than technical-economic values when making decisions. Businessmen are human like all the rest of us. They do have emotions and social value judgments. It is foolish to contend that they, like a machine and unlike other human beings, respond only to economic and technical data.

Businessmen in making decisions typically apply three separate value systems, along with overriding ethical-moral considerations. These are:

- *Technical*   Based upon physical facts and scientific logic.

- *Economic*   Based upon market values determined by consumers.

- *Human*   Based upon social-psychological needs other than economic consumption needs. This value system often goes by the term "human relations."

In many business decisions all three of these value systems exert some weight upon the final decision. Because man is human this aspect of his life cannot be ignored by any institution that deals with him.

But there are dangers in generalizations which are too sweeping, such as, "Business is responsible for human values in general." What is needed is a concept which marks business as an instrument *for specific human goals* (along with technical-economic ones) in the life of man and his society—something which gives direction and hope to the climb of mankind from the depths of the Stone Age to the great potential which his Creator has given him. This kind of concept does not come easily but it must come eventually. By giving people motivation, social goals and work fulfillment, business might over the long pull be termed a "movement" in the same way that history refers to the labor movement.

Certainly some major efforts at being explicit have been made recently. Theodore V. Houser, writing from the point of view of big business, stated five specific areas of social responsibility, ranging from employees to government.[10] Selekman's idea of constitutional justice was discussed earlier.[11] Crawford Greenewalt emphasized the importance of individual creativity and stated, "The important thing is that we bring into play the full potential of all men whatever their station."[12] And there are many others. For my own use I have summed these ideas into a single manageable phrase, as follows: *To fulfill the human dignity, creativity, and potential of free men.*[13] This can be businessmen's long-run guide to socially responsible action in each situation they face. The term "fulfill" is used because business cannot award goals such as human dignity. It can only develop the proper climate for their growth. The term "man" is used because unless *man* is free, men cannot be free. Other institutions and groups will also be interested in this goal. Businessmen are not wholly responsible here, but only partially so, approximately to the extent of their social power.

[10] Theodore V. Houser, *Big Business and Human Values,* McGraw-Hill Book Company, New York, 1957.
[11] Selekman (see note 4), p. 7.
[12] Crawford H. Greenewalt, *The Uncommon Man: The Individual in the Organization,* McGraw-Hill Book Company, New York, 1959.
[13] One analyst has put this point even more strongly: "The making of goods is incidental and subordinate to the making of men." Raphael Demos, "Business and the Good Society," in Edward C. Bursk, Ed., *Business and Religion,* Harper and Brothers, New York, 1959, p. 190.

An important choice ahead

The subject of social responsibility places business at an important cross-roads in its history. Which way it will go is not known, but in any event social responsibility will tend to equate with social power, which means that avoidance of responsibilities as they develop will lead to loss of business power. Some hard thinking is needed so that the right course can be charted. This is not the time for pat slogans, clichés, and wheezes. Clearly, economic functions of business are primary, but this does not negate the existence of non-economic functions and responsibilities. The price of social freedom is its responsible exercise.

Because society is changing, evidence suggests that the continued vigor of business depends upon its forthright acceptance of further socio-human responsibilities. In spite of protestations of impending corporate feudalism and dilution of economic objectives, the trend in this direction is already apparent. Some of the more fruitful avenues of interest are: making work meaningful, developing persons to their fullest potential, preservation of creativity and freedom, and fulfillment of human dignity.

In summary, the *first* social responsibility of businessmen is to find workable solutions regarding the nature and extent of their own social responsibilities.

We can be confident that modern business leadership does have the capacity to deal with questions of social responsibility. Although the next fifty years will bring major social change, business should perform effectively in this instability because it is geared for change. Typically, during the last century it has had an unstable economic environment; yet it has learned to live and prosper therein. It can do the same during a period of social reevaluation by developing flexible responses to the needs of society. But if it does not do so, it will use up its capital in human and spiritual values, which is a sure way to go socially bankrupt.

60 The hazards of corporate responsibility
Gilbert Burck

Every Friday evening, Walter Fackler, professor of economics at the University of Chicago's Graduate School of Business, has been addressing a class of seventy-five high-ranking executives on the problems of public policy and corporate social responsibility. A more appropriate and exigent activity

Source: Reprinted from the June 1973 issue of *Fortune Magazine,* pp. 114–117, by special permission; © 1973 Time Inc.

these days is hard to imagine. Fackler says he has never seen businessmen so confused and defensive. The doctrine that business has responsibilities "beyond business," which began to gather momentum a dozen or so years ago, is still picking up steam. Never before has the U.S. business establishment been confronted with such a bewildering variety of animadversion, such a Vanity Fair of conflicting demands and prescriptions. A detailed inventory of the "social" demands being made on business would fill several volumes; reconciling the numerous and conflicting prescriptions would baffle a synod of Solomons.

Perhaps because businessmen are so defensive, they themselves have not done much talking back to those who are making all the demands. When businessmen essay to discuss their role in society these days, they all too often sound like young ladies fifty years ago talking about sex. They cough and clear their throats and come up with moralistic platitudes. The back talk has come principally from economists—notably from some, like Milton Friedman and Henry Manne, who have generally been identified with the classical school. These "strict constructionists" argue that business serves society best when it minds its business well, and that it should take part in social activities only to the extent that these are necessary to its own well-being.

Fackler himself manages to sound like a strict constructionist much of the time. The great, the dominant, the indispensable *social* role of business, he tells his executive students, is a familiar one. In this most uncertain world, their prime job is to evaluate risks wisely, to allocate the nation's resources prudently, and to use them with optimum efficiency. Business fulfills its real social role by striving endlessly to take in more money than it pays out, or, as some of its critics would put the case, by lusting incessantly after the Almighty Dollar.

Arrayed on the other side of the argument are the social-responsibility advocates—those who want an enlarged social role for industry. For all the immense variety of their prescriptions, these advocates agree on one general proposition: business ought to accept social responsibilities *that go beyond the requirements of the law.* In addition to mere compliance with the law, say the advocates, business should actively initiate measures to abate pollution, to expand minority rights, and in general to be an exemplary citizen, and should cheerfully accept all the costs associated with this good citizenship.

Suppressing the controversy

Many of the most vocal social-responsibility advocates, including those affiliated with one or another band of Nader's raiders, tend to extreme forms of self-righteousness. Their proposals are often couched in rather general terms; they imply that the justice of their ideas is self-evident and that only a moral delinquent, or a businessman consumed by greed, could resist them. The notion that some schemes for implementing the proposals might actually be controversial, or that there might be serious questions of equity involved in asking corporate executives to tackle social problems with money belonging to other people (i.e., their stockholders)—these thoughts often seem to be suppressed in the advocates' minds.

But there is also a more sophisticated version of the social-responsibility proposition. According to this version, corporate executives who are strict constructionists at heart, and who harbor powerful lusts for Almighty Dollars, might nevertheless conclude that an activist social posture was good for their companies. They might decide, in other words, that social activism was good public relations. They might agree with Paul Samuelson, the Nobel laureate, who takes a simple view of the new demands on corporations. "A large corporation these days," he says, "not only may engage in social responsibility; it had damn well better try to do so."

A similarly pragmatic view of the matter has been propounded by Professor Neil Jacoby of the Graduate School of Management at the University of California, Los Angeles. Jacoby has been a dean of the school, a member of the Council of Economic Advisers under Eisenhower, a fellow of the Center for the Study of Democratic Institutions, and a member of the Pay Board. His forthcoming book, *Corporate Power and Social Responsibility,* describes corporate social involvement as a fact of life. "I don't really ask companies to do a single thing that isn't profitable," Jacoby remarked recently. "But political forces are just as real as market forces, and business must respond to them, which means it often must be content with optimizing and not maximizing immediate profits."

Corporations do it better

Professor Henry Wallich of Yale has also advanced a rather sophisticated case for corporate social responsibility. Writing in *Fortune* last year ("Books & Ideas," March, 1972), Wallich made the point that corporations can perform some social activities better than can government; and in undertaking to do more than the law requires, they are shifting activities from the public to the private sector. When one corporation undertakes social obligations not borne by its competitors, it would, of course, be at a disadvantage. Therefore, Wallich proposes, companies in an industry should be allowed to work together toward social goals without fear of antitrust action.

Some serious economists regard the social-responsibility movement as a harbinger of major changes in the business environment. Professor George Steiner of the U.C.L.A. Graduate School of Management, for instance, believes the movement implies "a new area of voluntarism" that will change large corporations' basic operating style. Generally speaking, Steiner says, the old authoritarian way of running a company will give way to permissive and statesmanlike methods; the single-minded entrepreneur will be succeeded by the broad-gauge "renaissance" manager. Centralized decision making will be accompanied, if not largely superseded, by decision making in small groups. Financial accounting will be augumented by human-resources accounting, and the "social" costs of production will be increasingly internalized. Inevitably, government and business planning will complement each other. "We are," says Steiner prophetically, "in the process of redefining capitalism"

How Supreme Life got the business

A few companies are beginning to act as if they believe Steiner. One is Standard Oil Co. (Indiana), which is spending about $40 million a year on pollution control—far more than it legally has to. It also boasts a long list of other social achievements, including efforts on behalf of Chicago's schools and a determined program to hire and promote minority employees and to help minority suppliers and businessmen. Recently, for example, Standard arranged with Chicago's Supreme Life Insurance Co. of America, a company owned by blacks, to insure two plants of is Amoco chemical subsidiary in California. Standard's policy is to use not only qualified but "qualifiable" minority suppliers—i.e., it helps some to qualify.

The company's director of public affairs these days is Phillip Drotning, author of three books on the black movement in the U.S., and an advocate of a high level of corporate involvement. If Drotning has his way—and so far he has been backed by top management—the promotion of executives will depend not only on their cost and profit records but on their approach to social objectives. Managers will be supplied with the information they need to evaluate the social consequences of their decisions, and they will plan strategies that benefit both the company and society. "The heads of the company," says Drotning, "will exercise leadership among their peers in the broad business community and the public at large, to generate support for the far-reaching, long-range changes in social policy that must occur."

The goals of Chicago's CNA Financial Corp., an insurance-centered company with revenues of $1.6 billion, are pretty ambitious too. Last year the company spent close to $660,000 on dozens of selected social projects, compelled its insurance subsidiaries to demand that their clients take "corrective action" on a variety of pollution problems, and insisted on a 30 percent minority representation among the workers erecting its new headquarters building.

CNA's vice president in charge of social policy is a former social-agency administrator named David Christensen, who argues that companies typically go through several phases in the perception of their social responsibilities. First there is the "do-good" phase, in which the company builds libraries with its name on them—but goes right on dumping waste in the lake. Later comes a more systematic effort to coordinate public relations and corporate involvement in, say, urban affairs. Finally the company gets to the phase of genuine corporate responsibility, in which it is concerned less with public relations than with developing responsible ways to improve society. Conscience money is no longer needed, because the company doesn't have a bad conscience.

Nobody talks about cost

Christensen says that CNA is just now entering the third phase. To guide it in this period he has helped the company develop an elaborate manual on corporate responsibility—a document that details just how CNA proposes to involve all its executives in social goals, and how they in turn should involve their charges. The whole opus has a somewhat evangelical tone, suggesting the marching orders for an all-out war on the devil. What it all will cost and who will finally pay for it are matters nobody seems to talk about. Presumably, however, CNA can afford it. That is to say, CNA, unlike many less opulent and more price-competitive companies, can absorb the costs—i.e., reduce the profits of its shareholders.

Given the natural inclination of managers to demand records and evaluations, it is not surprising that many businessmen who are interested in being socially responsible are also interested in what is known as the "social audit." Just as a conventional audit sums up a company's financial performance, a social audit would describe its social performance. Hundreds of articles, pamphlets, and books have already been written about the social audit, scores of workshops and seminars have been held to discuss it, and some sizable companies are experimenting with ways to implement the idea.

So far, it is fair to say, little has come of the effort. The problem, says Professor S. Prakash Sethi of the University of California at Berkeley, is that nobody has yet drawn up an objective definition of socially responsible behavior; hence nobody has succeeded in measuring it consistently. And who, in any case, would certify that the accounting was accurate? Professor Raymond Bauer of the Harvard Graduate School of Business Administration says, "We still need to learn how to get on the learning curve."

The social-audit concept has been scoffed at even by some of the most ardent advocates of corporate social responsibility. Milton Moskowitz, a financial columnist who edits a crusading biweekly sheet called *Business & Society,* derides the social-audit concepts as "nonsense, redemption through mathematics, and useful to companies only as a laundry list." F. Thomas Juster, until recently a senior economist at the National Bureau of Economic Research, has been exploring social and economic measurement. "Given the state of the art," says Juster, "we're all kidding ourselves if we think we can measure [social] output. One reason is that real outputs are very long range. . . . We can't measure that, not now . . . probably can't measure it in ten years."

One of the most insistent of all recent efforts to develop a social audit was presented in the Winter 1972–73 issue of the quarterly *Business and Society Review,* in an article by David Linowes, a partner in the accounting firm of Laventhol Krekstein Horwath & Horwath. Linowes, who likes to be alluded to as the father of socioeconomic accounting, presents a model of a social audit. The model differentiates, logically, between mandatory and voluntary corporate outlays, and proposes to put dollar figures on the employee time, the facilities, the training, etc., that a company voluntarily invests in social areas. Linowes anticipates that *Fortune's* 500 list will someday include a corporate responsibility rating. In the same issue of the review, however, six friendly critics who were asked to comment on Linowes' suggestions raise a host of substantive and technical objections. As one puts it, Linowes tries "to shoehorn . . . into the framework of the orthodox income statement model" what are essentially nonfiscal data containing highly subjective determinations.

Meanwhile, the social-audit enthusiasts seem determined to find a way of making the thing work. A host of consultants who specialize in advising companies on the art and mystery of carrying out their responsibilities to society have got behind the idea of the social audit. "Anytime there is money to be made in some area requiring newly developed expertise," says Ralph Lewis, editor of the *Harvard Business Review,* "a new breed of consultants seems to arise." Several serious enterprises are also showing interest in the social-responsibility audit. Abt Associates Inc., a contract research organization, publishes an annual report accompanied by its version of a social audit. Meanwhile, imaginative newspapermen are setting themselves up as experts, and social audits seem to be giving the public-relations profession a new lease on life.

The great social increment

All this may sound highly laudable at best and harmless enough at worst. But in some circumstances it might be very harmful indeed. It could very well threaten the phenomenon known as rising productivity.

Perhaps because most people are so used to the phrase, they often forget what a stupendous phenomenon it describes. Last year American business produced more than $900 billion worth of goods and services, more than two-thirds of which were accounted for by corporations. Owing in large part to the corporations' striving to make money, national productivity rose by 4 percent. (Corporations earned some $88 billion before taxes, $41 billion of which was taxed away for government and other social needs.)

That 4 percent figure means that business turned out roughly $36 billion *more* of goods and services than it would have if it had maintained only the productivity level of the year before. This great social increment, fluctuating from year to year but expanding at an average of about 3 percent a year, is the very foundation of the nation's way of life; these gains afford the only basis on which a better society can be built. Rising productivity alone made possible the first eight-hour day more than eighty years ago, just as rising productivity has more recently brought higher real pay, shorter hours, and larger fringe benefits. And rising productivity alone will enable the U.S. to achieve without inordinate sacrifice the benefits that the advocates of social responsibility are now demanding.

This is so important a matter that it deserves to be viewed from another perspective. Suppose productivity ceased to rise, or that it even fell a little. Unless more people worked longer, the average living standard would then remain constant or decline. The costs associated with cleaner air, training for minorities, and other socially desirable programs would increase the total price of other things by precisely the amount of those costs. Every benefit would be offset by a sacrifice. If productivity did not rise, one man's gain would be another man's loss.

It's the consumer who pays

Productivity, however, rises only when a business manages to innovate successfully and when it manages to cut costs, either by using fewer resources to make a product or by turning out a better product with the same resources. As the man in charge of costs, the businessman is the agent of what might be called the "consumer at large." When the businessman wastes resources on a bad risk, it is this consumer who principally pays (although the stockholders are presumably losers too). When he reduces his costs or innovates successfully, it is the consumer who benefits.

And so, precisely because the businessman's drive for profitability is identical with his drive for lower costs, his profit is a pretty good measure of social welfare. Suppose two companies make similar products and sell them at about the same price. Company A nets $10 million, but Company B nets twice as much because it is run by a tough crew of hardheaded, no-nonsense, endlessly striving managers motivated by abundant bonuses—the kind of men corporate critics often like to describe as s.o.b.'s. To an individual consumer, the two companies might seem to offer little choice. But so far as society at large is concerned, Company B has done a much better job, because it has used $10 million less of our resources, i.e., raw material and manpower, in doing the same job. So, obviously, the s.o.b.'s have been better for society than easygoing and irresolute managers would have been. As the Lord remarked of Faust, "He who strives endlessly, him we can redeem."

It is just possible, then, that the U.S. could use more endless strivers, redeemed or not. The advocates of corporate social responsibility, indeed, seem to have overlooked what may be the real case against U.S. business: it may be using too many resources for what it turns out. Suppose, at all events, that U.S. corporations had managed to turn out that 1972 volume for 2 percent less than they actually spent. The incremental profit would have amounted to $11 billion, enough to eliminate, over the year, practically all pollution. "If the responsibility buffs really want to promote national welfare," one strict constructionist observed recently, "they should be complaining that companies aren't making *enough* money."

And so it seems reasonable to ask what effect the businessman's increasing preoccupation with those other social "responsibilities" will have on
his endless striving to elevate productivity. Thirty-one years ago the late
Joseph Schumpeter predicted that, as corporations grew bigger, businessmen would cease to behave like aggressive entrepreneurs, and would
degenerate into mere bureaucrats. Schumpeter's prediction hasn't come
true, but some now worry that it may. They fear that the new emphasis on
Good Works will sicken the businessman o'er with the pale cast of thought,
vitiate his drive to innovate and cut costs, and gradually convert him and his
fellows into the kind of bureaucrats that infest so many marble halls of government.

Our socially responsible monopolists

These are the kinds of considerations that bother Milton Friedman when he
contemplates the contentions in favor of social responsibility. Friedman likes
to dramatize his position by making the superficially shocking statement that
the businessman's *only* social responsibility is to increase profits. He is
against the acceptance of social responsibilities, because it implicitly expresses the socialist view that political, and not market, considerations
should govern the allocation of resources, and over the long run this means
reduced efficiency. What's more, Friedman says, "no businessman has
money to spend on social responsibility unless he has monopoly power. Any
businessman engaged in social responsibility ought to be immediately
slapped with an antitrust suit."

In the same vein, Professor Harold Demsetz of U.C.L.A. insists that
the word "responsibility" is being misused: "The only responsibility of businessmen or anyone else is to obey the laws of the land, no more, no less."
If our society wants business to set up day-care centers for employees'
children, for example, then it should pass a law to that effect, so that the
burden will be shared by all business enterprises.

The problem of sharing that burden is one that most social-
responsibility advocates seem not to have thought through. One trouble with
leaving good deeds up to individual executives is that not all of their companies are equally prosperous. Now that the Kaiser empire is in trouble, for
example, Edgar Kaiser is taking a hard line on demands for "responsibility"
in his companies. "Not to husband resources," Kaiser says with considerable feeling, "would be social irresponsibility of the highest order." Hard-
pressed companies obviously cannot undertake the social programs supported by companies with strong market power, such as utilities (whose
regulated rates are based on costs). And healthily profitable companies like
Standard of Indiana and CNA obviously have a great advantage over companies that are constantly battling to stay in the black.

Even companies that have the resources to undertake socially responsible projects do not necessarily possess the skills to solve most complex
social problems. "The job of the public and government," says F. Thomas

Juster, "is to tell business what the appropriate social objectives are; they shouldn't want business messing around with its own set of social objectives." Professor Paul Heyne of Southern Methodist University, a strict constructionist, argues that the economic system is not a playground in which businessmen should be exercising their own preferences. "Any economic system," he explains, "ought to be a social mechanism for picking up the preferences of everyone, matching these against available resources, and obtaining from what we have a maximum of what we want. The market is a mechanism of almost incredible effectiveness in the accomplishment of this task. The market works effectively because those who have command over resources continually reallocate them in response to the signals provided by relative prices. The businessman who wants to behave in a socially responsible way must depend heavily, overwhelmingly, on this information."

Just like embezzlement

Probably no economist has given more thought to corporate social responsibility than Henry Manne, professor of law at the University of Rochester, who began writing about the subject a dozen years ago. He observed that most companies maintained enough reserves to meet unforseen contingencies and to offset unintended mistakes, and so could *temporarily* spend some money on social activities that raise costs without raising revenues or income. So far as consumers and employees are concerned, Manne has observed, somewhat caustically, this spending is indistinguishable in its effects from simple inefficiency or outright embezzlement.

Manne believes that the whole concept of corporate responsibility suits government officials and intellectuals —particuarly intellectuals who deride and even hate the idea of a free market. It also goes down just fine with bloviating businessmen who don't mind casting themselves as members of the divine elect. Of course, businessmen often interpret "socially responsible" policies as long-term profit maximization, i.e., "in the long run we make more money by spending to be good citizens now." Manne doesn't object to this line of reasoning so long as the spending really does maximize profits in the long run—and helps the firms survive in a free market. He says, however, that voluntary corporate altruism has never made a significant dent in any but insignificant problems. Manne has developed his own economic model of corporate responsibility—the first of its kind—and reports that it can accommodate a little, but not much, corporate giving; he finds it impossible to justify a model of substantial corporate social action.

Above all, Manne avers, any such action will result in more government controls. It implies that business and government should work together to promote social progress. "Corporate social responsibility, a doctrine offered by many as a scheme to popularize and protect free enterprise," Manne concludes, "can succeed only if the free market is abandoned in favor of government controls. The game isn't worth the candle."

There seem to have been some cases in which "socially responsible" behavior has actually hampered business operations. California's Bank of America, upset and moved by radicals' demonstrations against it, went in some time ago for being socially responsible in a big way. It appointed an executive vice president, G. Robert Truex, Jr., as custodian of social policy, and he is now dabbling with a social audit. The bank also set aside no less than $200 million for low-interest loans that would help to provide housing for minority-group members and other under-privileged persons.

But the bank has found itself in a dilemma. The 2,500 loan officers in its thousand California branches pride themselves on knowing the credit-worthiness of people in their areas. Now many of these officers have been asked to lend money to people who had no conventional credit standing at all—indeed, they were being asked to *persuade* people to borrow. How, in these circumstances, do you preserve the loan officers' morale and esprit? The Bank of America is wrestling with that problem.

Some proponents of increased corporate responsibility have given high marks to Levi Strauss & Co. of San Francisco, maker of the famous Levi's and other informal apparel. As its many admirers note, the company contributes 3 percent of its net after taxes to carefully chosen social programs, does a lot of hiring from among disadvantaged minority groups, helps finance minority suppliers, and has established day-care centers for employees' children. At the same time, the company has done well. It has expanded sales from $8 million in 1946 to more than $504 million last year, and net income from $700,000 to $25 million.

Getting their money's worth

But Levi Strauss is obviously getting a lot for that 3 percent. It does business in an intensely liberal city and has a market in which tastes are heavily influenced by young people. And so, whatever its top executives believe in their heart of hearts, their social-responsibility outlays would appear to be rather effective public relations. So far as an outsider can determine, these outlays cost no more than would conventional high-pressure public relations in a different kind of company.

Many of the costs associated with social responsibility, such as minority training and aid, are often marginal, out of proportion to all the time and talent that have gone into arguing about them. Behaving responsibly often means no more or less than acting humanely, treating employees and customers with consideration, avoiding ineptitudes and blunders, cultivating a sharp eye for the important little things, and knowing how to spend where the returns are high. In this sense, responsibility can accomplish a lot with relatively small cost.

But many other expenses of behaving in a socially acceptable way, such as the cost of meeting the escalating demands of the consumer advocates, will not come cheap, and might easily get out of hand. Heavy social involvements can also cost a company dear in terms of managerial talent. And so the impact of the corporate-responsibility movement on companies that must husband their resources, on the endlessly striving cost cutters, indeed on competition itself, is not yet clear. Americans can only hope that businessmen will retain enough of the old Adam Smith in them to keep productivity rising.

61 The small society
Morrie Brickman

Source: June 5, 1969.

62 Feeding 3rd-world babies
Phillip West

NEW YORK—While affluent American mothers with Doctor Spock's blessing now bare their breasts to feed their babies, mothers in poor Third World countries are turning to the bottle, encouraged by the manufacturers of synthetic baby formulas. The results can be disastrous.

Bristol-Meyers' Enfamil and Abbot Laboratories' Similac, sold here in cans, are marketed throughout Asia and Latin America in powdered form.

Source: Reprinted with permission from Pacific News Service (April 2, 1974).

Similac is also widely sold in the Middle East and Africa, where it competes with similar products from European companies like Nestle's and Unigate.

The change to bottle-feeding in developing countries is a "noticeable trend," according to World Health Organization (WHO) information officer Peter Ozorio.

To persuade poor women to give up breast-feeding, which is convenient and free, for bottles which must be washed and formulas which must be paid for requires some hard selling. Unhappily for millions of babies, manufacturers have risen to the challenge.

British companies in Africa dress their sales girls in nurses' uniforms to give their pitch the appearance of nutritional counselling. Companies stock rural health clinics with free paper supplies, all bearing pictures of their products. The illiterate mother sees the picture of the bottle but misses the clinic's printed message, "Breast feed your baby as long as you can."

"We've heard that breast-feeding is best, and of course we try to promote that," says a spokesman for Similac. But nutritionists complain that formula advertising everywhere promotes the notion that educated, up-to-date mothers feed their babies from bottles.

Throughout Africa, manufacturers' posters brighten the bare walls of baby clinics. One Nestle's series pictures pre-natal care, bathing and dressing the baby, preparing solid foods—among them Cerelac, a Nestle's product—and feeding, with a Nestle's bottle.

A survey taken in Nigeria, where only 14 per cent of the population reads newspapers, showed that 38 per cent of 400 mothers recalled at least one formula advertisement.

The modern kitchens, sparkling white baby clothes, and new cribs shown in ads are beyond the reach of most families, but the bottle is often supplied free by the clinic—a gift from the formula company, along with free samples.

A mother need not stay "sold" on store milk for long to become a dependable customer: when breast-feeding is delayed or interrupted, she soon has no milk.

In most Third World countries, Ozorio points out, the woman who starts her baby on formula takes on a heavy financial burden. In the U.S., a week's supply of Similac costs about $1.40. The equivalent price in many developing countries is half or more of the average weekly wage.

According to WHO nutritionists, the high price of formula drives many mothers to "stretch" it by adding too much water, depriving the baby of protein and calories. Thus, while parents scrimp to buy the "best" food, their babies cry constantly from hunger.

A survey made in Chile before the recent coup showed that the death rate for babies bottle-fed during the first three months was three times that for breast-fed babies. One reason for the difference is hygiene: breast milk can rarely be contaminated, but traditional living conditions make it difficult to keep bottles clean and formulas sterile.

Another reason is that bottle-fed babies are deprived of the immunities provided by mother's milk. Numerous U.S. studies show that breast-fed babies suffer half as many illnesses as bottle-fed ones. Where modern medical care is unavailable, this natural protection is indispensable. Intestinal infections, which thrive in unsanitary conditions, kill ten times as many bottle-fed infants as breast-fed ones.

Bottle-feeding may also raise the birth rate in developing countries. Since 80 to 90 per cent of women remain infertile as long as they are nursing, breast-feeding, which often continues until a child is two or three, has traditionaly served as a child-spacer.

Alarmed by the statistics, WHO is emphasizing breast-feeding in its 1974 campaign for "Better Food for a Healthier World," as are several African governments in public information drives.

Questioned as to the effect of these campaigns on Similac sales, Abbott marketing executive Gene Curry replied, "As far as I know, we haven't felt any pressure yet."

Conclusion/B
Organizational
effectiveness

63 How to evaluate a firm
Robert B. Buchele

The sharp drops in earnings and even losses recently suffered by many so-
called "growth" companies, whose stocks had been bid so high, have cast
doubts upon the adequacy of the established methods which are used by
investment specialists to evaluate companies.

Equally dramatic but less evident have been the serious declines of
numerous companies shortly after having been rated as "excellently managed" by the best known of the evaluation systems using a list of factors
covering numerous aspects of corporate management.

What has happened to render these evaluation systems so inadequate? What lessons can be learned by persons whose work requires
them to do over-all evaluations of companies—investors, acquisition
specialists, consultants, long-range planners, and chief executives? Finally,
what are the requirements for a system for evaluating firms that will function reliably under today's conditions?

After all, the decline of even blue chip companies is not a new phenomenon. To quote from an unpublished paper recently presented by Ora C.
Roehl before a management conference at UCLA:

"The Brookings Institution some time ago made a study of the 100
top businesses in the USA in the early 1900's, and they found that after 40
years only 36 were still among the leaders.

"We all look at the Dow-Jones Industrial Average practically every day
and we know the companies that are a part of the Average today—from Allied Chemical, Aluminum Company of America, and American Can to U.S.
Steel, Westinghouse, and Woolworth. But, as we go back in time a bit, we
find names that once were important enough to be a part of the Average
and which we have heard of, such as Hudson Motors, Famous Players-
Lasky, and Baldwin Locomotive. It is not long, however, before we run into

Source: © 1962 by the Regents of the University of California. Reprinted by permission from *California Management Review,* volume VI, number 1 (Fall 1962), pp. 5–16,
by permission of the Regents.

one-time business leaders whose names are strange to us, such as Central Leather, U.S. Cordage Company, Pacific Mail, American Cotton Oil Company, and one with a nostalgic sort of name, The Distilling and Cattle Feeding Company."[1]

What is new, however, is the current pace of such events. Stemming in part from the rise of industrial research expenditures from less than $200 million in 1930 to an estimated $12.4 billion in 1960,[2] the pace of industrial change has been accelerating for many years. It is now so rapid that firms can rise or fall more quickly than ever before.

Sophisticated technologies are spreading to many industries; in addition, as we shall see in this article, various management techniques contribute to the quickening pace of change. In consequence, the rapid rate of change now affects a great many American firms rather than just that minority known as "growth" companies.

Present evaluation methods

Financial Analysis

This method typically consists of studying a "spread" of profit and loss figures, operating statements and balance sheet ratios for the past five or ten years. The underlying assumption is that the future performance of a company can be reliably projected from trends in these data. The reasoning is that these data represent the "proof of the pudding." If they're sound, the company as a whole, particularly its top management, must be sound, for a competent top management will keep a firm healthy.

Through the years this method has worked well because the basic assumption has been reasonably valid. Despite the fact that some blue chip companies have failed, it is still reasonably valid for the large firms who are thoroughly entrenched in their markets and who make substantial investments in executive development, in market development, and in any technology that promises to threaten one of their market positions.

However, the assumption is becoming less safe, especially in connection with medium-sized and small firms, as the pace of industrial change steadily accelerates. Thus, a firm whose financial record is unimpressive may be on the verge of a technological breakthrough that will send its profits rocketing ahead; conversely, a company that looks good in financial analyses may be doomed because it is being bypassed technologically or marketing-wise or because rigor mortis has taken over the executive offices.

In practice the financial analysis method is often supplemented by

---

[1] "Evaluating Your Company's Future," an unpublished paper presented at the Fourth Annual Management Conference, UCLA Executive Program Association, Los Angeles, October 20, 1960, p. 2.

[2] Data from the National Science Foundation, cited in: *Research Management,* Autumn, 1960, Volume III, No. 3, p. 129.

market research in the form of interviews with leading customers, by interviews with the firm's top executives, and by consultation with scientists capable of evaluating technological capabilities and trends. While these supplementary activities help, financial analysis still is neither adequately comprehensive nor adequately oriented to the future.

Thus, this type of market research can yield some insights into the effectiveness of past and present performance but is too superficial to tell much about the future. The interviews with top executives can be more misleading than informative simply because they are conducted by financial people inexperienced in management, marketing, or technology.[3] The use of scientists is a commendable step forward. However, it provides help in only one and possibly two of the many areas essential to a thorough evaluation.

Outline for evaluation of a firm

I. Product lines and basic competitive position

A. Past
What strengths and weaknesses in products (or services) have been dominant in this firm's history—design features, quality-reliability, prices, patents, proprietary position?

B. Present
What share of its market(s) does the firm now hold, and how firmly? Is this share diversified or concentrated as to number of customers? In what phases of their life-cycles are the present chief products and what is happening to prices and margins? How do customers and potential customers regard this firm's products? Are the various product lines compatible marketing-wise, engineering-wise, manufacturing-wise? If not, is each product line substantial enough to stand on its own feet?

C. Future
Is the market(s) as a whole expanding or contracting and at what rate? What is the trend in this firm's share of the market(s)? What competitive trends are developing in numbers of competitors, technology, marketing, pricing? What is its vulnerability to business cycle (or defense spending) changes? Is management capable of effectively integrating market research, R & D, and market development into a development program for a new product or products?

---

[3] Lee Dake explains in detail a case in which a financial analyst and a management consultant arrived at opposite conclusions about a firm's prospects in "Are Analysts' Techniques Adequate for Growth Stocks?" *The Financial Analysts Journal,* Volume 16, No. 6, Nov.–Dec., 1960, pp. 45–49. Dake's thesis can be confirmed many times over in the present author's experience. Particularly distressing was the case where a persuasive but incompetent chief executive persuaded three investment firms to recommend his stock less than six months before declaration of losses exceeding the firm's tangible net worth!

II. R & D and operating departments

A. R & D and engineering

What is the nature and the depth of its R & D capability? Of engineering capability? What are engineering's main strengths and weaknesses re creativity, quality-reliability, simplicity? Is the R & D effort based on needs defined by market research, and is it an integral part of an effective new product development program? Are R & D efforts well planned, directed, and controlled? What return have R & D dollars paid in profitable new products? Have enough new products been produced? Have schedules been met?

B. Marketing

Nature of the Marketing Capability—What channels of distribution are used? How much of the total marketing job (research, sales, service, advertising and promotion is covered? Is this capability correctly tailored to match the nature and diversity of the firm's product lines? Is there a capability for exploiting new products and developing new markets? Quality of the marketing capability—Is market research capable of providing the factual basis that will keep the firm, especially its new product development and R & D programs, truly customer-oriented? Is there a capability for doing broad economic studies and studies of particular industries that will help management set sound growth and/or diversification strategies?

C. Manufacturing

What is the nature of the manufacturing processes, the facilities and the skills—are they appropriate to today's competition? How flexible are they—will they be, or can they be made, appropriate to tomorrow's competition? What is the quality of the manufacturing management in terms of planning and controlling work schedule-wise, cost-wise, and quality-wise? Is there evidence of an industrial engineering capability that steadily improves products and methods? Does manufacturing management effectively perform its part of the process of achieving new products?

D. Summary on R & D and operating departments

Is this a complete, integrated, balanced operation; or have certain strong personalities emphasized some functions and neglected others? What is the quality of performance of key R & D and operating executives; do they understand the fundamental processes of management, namely planning, controlling, organizing, staffing and directing? Are plans and controls in each department inadequate, adequate or overdeveloped into a "paperwork mill?" Is there throughout the departments a habit of steady progress in reducing overhead, lowering break-even points and improving quality? Are all departments future-minded? Do they cooperate effectively in developing worthy new products geared to meet the customer's future needs?

III. Financial and analysis and financial management

A. Financial Analysis

What main strengths and weaknesses of the firm emerge from analysis of the trends in the traditional financial data: earnings ratios (to sales, to tangible net worth, to working capital) and earnings-per-share: debt ratios (current and acid tests, to tangible net worth, to working capital, to inventory); inventory turnover; cash flow; and the capitalization structure? What do the trends in the basic financial facts indicate as to the firm's prospects for growth in sales volume and rate of earnings? Does "quality of earnings" warrant compounding of the earnings rate?

B. Financial management

What is the quality of financial management? Is there a sound program for steadily increasing return on investment? Do the long-range financial plans indicate that management understands the cost of capital and how to make money work hard? Have balance sheets and operating statements been realistically projected for a number of years into the future? Is there careful cash planning and strong controls that help the operating departments lower break-even points? Are capital expenditures inadequate or excessive with respect to insuring future operating efficiently? Are capital investment decisions based on thorough calculations? Does management have the respect of the financial community? Is the firm knowledgeable and aggressive in tax admininstration?

IV. Top management

A. Identification of top management and its record

What person or group constitutes top management? Has present top management been responsible for profit-and-loss results of the past few years?

B. Top management and the future

What are top management's chief characteristics? How adequate or inadequate is this type of management for coping with the challenges of the future? Will the present type and quality of top management continue? Will it deteriorate, will it improve, or will it change its basic character?

C. Board of Directors

What influence and/or control does the Board of Directors exercise? What are the capabilities of its members? What are their motivations?

V. Summary and evaluation strategy

What other factors can assume major importance in this particular situation? (Use a check list.) Of all the factors studied, which if any, is overriding in this particular situation? Which factors are of major importance by virtue of the fact that they govern other factors? What are the basic facts-of-life about the economics and competition of this industry now and over the next decade? In view of the firm's particular strengths and weaknesses, what are the odds that it will succeed, and at what level of success, in this industry? What are the prospects of its succeeding by diversifying out of its industry?

Key factor ratings

Systems more comprehensive than the financial analysis method have been developed, mainly by consultants seeking to understand firms' overall strengths and weaknesses in order to be able to prescribe for them. Such systems typically involve ratings based on a series of key factors underlying the financial factors themselves. Little has been published about these systems because the consulting firms regard them as proprietary secrets. One system that has been published and, therefore, is well known is that developed by the American Institute of Management.[4] That this system is not adequately future-oriented is clearly proved by the fact that numerous companies have encountered deep trouble shortly after being rated "excellently managed" by the AIM.[5]

Professor Erwin Schell a decade ago set forth a comprehensive system with some future-oriented elements; however, he recently stated that his system should be revised to give greater emphasis to the future via more attention to the R & D function.[6]

As indicated in the Outline for evaluation which accompanies this article, the evaluation of a firm, as it is at present and as it will be in the future,

[4] The factors are: (a) Economic Function; (b) Corporate Structure; (c) Health of Earnings; (d) Services to Stockholders; (e) Research and Development; (f) Directorate Analysis; (g) Fiscal Policies; (h) Production Efficiency; (i) Sales Vigor; (j) Executive Evaluation. The factors and their use are explained in detail in a series of ten reports: *The Management Audit Series* (New York: The American Institute of Management, starting in 1953).

[5] Most dramatic was the case of the Douglas Aircraft Company whose "excellently managed" rating for 1957–8–9 was followed by staggering losses in late '59 and '60. Among numerous other examples that can be cited are the 1957 ratings of Olin Mathieson Chemical Co. and Allis-Chalmers Manufacturing Company, both of whom, soon after receiving "excellently managed" ratings, suffered serious declines that have been openly discussed in business magazines. For the ratings, see: *Manual of Excellent Managements* (New York: The American Institute of Management, 1957). For accounts of the travails of these firms see *Business Week,* April 15, 1961, pp. 147–149 and April 9, 1960, p. 79.

[6] "Industrial Administration Through the Eyes of an Investment Company," *Appraising Managerial Assets—Policies, Practices and Organization,"* General Management Series #151 (New York: American Management Association, 1950). The new emphasis is suggested in a postscript to a reprint published in 1960 by the Keystone Custodian Funds, Inc. (Boston, Mass.: 1960, p. 13). Professor Schell suggested increased emphasis on tax administration, too. The original factors were: (a) Breadth and variety of viewpoint in administration; (b) Vigor and versatility in operating management; (c) Clarity and definiteness of long-term objectives; (d) Vigilance in matters of organization; (e) Dependence upon far-reaching plans; (f) Maintenance of integrated controls; (g) Upkeep in harmony with an advancing art; (h) Improvement as a normal expectancy; (i) Creativeness through high morale; (j) Effectiveness of managerial attitudes; (k) Resources for consistently distinguished leadership in a specific industry.

can be organized around a series of penetrating questions. Thorough study of the areas covered by these questions will yield a picture, oriented to the future, of the strengths and weaknesses of the firm under consideration and a reliable indication of its chances for success in the future.

There are, as the outline shows, four vital areas in a firm about which you should ask questions. They are: its product lines and basic competitive position; its R & D and operating departments; its financial position as revealed by analysis of the traditional financial data plus an estimate of the quality of its financial management; its top management with emphasis not only upon its past record, but also on its adequacy to cope with the future.

When these data have been assembled and summarized, you are in a position to evaluate both the present situation and potential of the firm under study as an investment possibility or as a management problem.

The rest of this article will be devoted to a discussion of these factors one by one. First we shall pose the questions contained in the outline; then we shall discuss the techniques professional analysts use for obtaining such data and determining what it means.

Product lines and competition

The first things to investigate are a firm's product lines and its basic competitive position. This involves a study of its past, present, and future. Here are the lines your inquiry should take:

- *Past* What strengths and weaknesses in products (or services) have been dominant in this firm's history—design features, quality-reliability, prices, patents, proprietary position?
- *Present* What share of its market(s) does the firm now hold, and how firmly? Is this share diversified or concentrated as to number of customers? In what phases of their life cycles are the present chief products and what is happening to prices and margins? How do customers and potential customers regard this firm's products? Are the various product lines compatible marketing-wise, engineering-wise, manufacturing-wise? If not, is each product line substantial enough to stand on its own feet?
- *Future* Is the market(s) as a whole expanding or contracting, and at what rate? What is the trend in this firm's share of the market(s)? What competitive trends are developing in numbers of competitors, technology, marketing, pricing?

What is the vulnerability to business cycle (or defense spending) changes?

Is there the capability effectively to integrate market research, R & D and market development into a new products development program?

The past-present-future structure furnishes the material needed to determine whether the firm has presently or in-the-pipeline the type of products needed for success in the future.

A key technique here is to determine how much quantitative information the company executives have and, then, to spot-check the quality of that information by the evaluator's own research. The firm that has sound, pertinent market data usually has achieved the first step to success—a clear definition of the job to be done. Conversely, the firm that has only sparse, out-of-date, out-of-focus data and relies heavily on executives' opinions is usually a poor bet for the future. Unsupported opinions, no matter how strongly held or ably stated, can be misleading. Although top management often must rely on such opinions, failure to secure the data that are available is a serious weakness.

Life cycle curves for products made

Another device for focusing on the basic facts of life about a product line is the building of S, or life cycle curves. These curves plot sales and/or margins for a product against time. For a given firm such plots picture clearly the life expectancy of products. Composite plots can show the trends in life expectancies. Also, they can indicate developing gaps. When past data are joined to carefully projected estimates of the future, dangerous situations can be revealed. Thus, the firm that is currently highly profitable but has not provided for the future will show virtually all of its products at or near the period of peak profitability.[7]

The question of compatibility of product lines may seem too elementary for mention; however, major mistakes are made in this area, especially by firms headed by scientists. Seeing their own skill as the key one in business, scientists tend to underestimate the importance and difficulty of other management activities. In consequence, they often develop or acquire products that present marketing problems far beyond the financial or managerial capability of the firm.

One science-based and scientist-led company, after an acquistion binge, was attempting to market ten distinct product lines through one centralized market organization, all with a total of less than $18 million annual volume. None of the products could individually support a top-flight marketing organization; yet no two of them could be effectively marketed through the same people. The result was disaster.

Integration of market research, R & D, and market development into an effective new product development program is one of the newer and more difficult arts of management. Such integration, which is the heart of profit planning, apparently accounted for much of the success of the Bell and Howell Company during the decade of the '50's.[8]

---

[7] For an illustration and discussion of use of life cycle curves, see C. Wilson Randle, "Selecting the Research Program. A Top Management Function," *California Management Review,* Volume II, No. 2 (Winter, 1960), pp. 10–11.

[8] The Bell and Howell methods are described in two articles: "How to Coordinate Executives," *Business Week,* September 12, 1953, p. 130 ff., and "How to Plan Profits Five Years Ahead," *Nation's Business,* October 1955, p. 38.

In vivid contrast to the coordinated profit planning of Bell and Howell, is the case of the small glamor firm that "went public" in early 1961 for $1,000,000 and has since seen the price of its stock triple. The scientist-president and his associates have developed a dazzling array of technically ingenious new products; however, they have little data on the market for the products and have not yet started to build an organization for distributing and selling them.

R & D and operating departments

Having probed a firm's product lines and competitive position, the second vital area for investigation is its R & D, marketing, and operating divisions. Good questions to guide your analysis are:

R & D and Engineering   What is the nature and the depth of the R & D capability? Of the engineering capability? What are the main strengths and weaknesses re creativity, quality-reliability, simplicity?

Is the R & D effort based on needs defined by market research, and is it an integral part of an effective new product development program? Are R & D efforts well planned, directed and controlled? What return have R & D dollars paid in profitable new products? Have enough new products been produced, and have schedules been met?

A truly basic change in American industry since the start of World War II has been that thousands of companies have R & D programs whereas earlier only a handful of firms did so. The figures cited earlier concerning the growth of R & D expenditures indicate that sophisticated technologies and rapidly changing products and markets characterize not only electronics and defense industries but also such diverse fields as food processing, photography, communications, pharmaceuticals, metallurgy, plastics, and equipments used in industrial automation processes. The consequence is that most firms beyond the "small business" category must have R & D programs; increasingly a firm must take on the characteristics of a "growth" firm in order to survive.

How to evaluate a firm's R & D

One of the newest of management activities, R & D management, is one of the hardest to evaluate. For lack of better technique, the vogue has been to assume that the volume of dollars spent on R & D is commensurate with results achieved. However, we now know that there has been great waste; also, there has been deception by firms "padding" their reported R & D expenditures to give the impression of being more R & D oriented than they really are.

A growing literature reports useful techniques for conceiving, planning, controlling and directing R & D programs and for evaluating R & D output.[9] The truth is being established that R & D management is a capability different from and much rarer than the capability of performing straight engineering or scientific work.

The first task of the evaluator is to determine whether the selection of R & D programs is integrated with a sound overall long-range plan and is based on market research findings. The next task is to compare the nature and depth of the R & D capability with the job to be done. Can it cope with the firm's future needs in regard to maintaining and improving market position by an integrated new products program? The third job is to compare cost and output. Techniques for evaluating output include assessing the quantity and quality of patents produced, measurement of the contribution of R & D to increased (or maintained) sales volume and profit margins, and measurement of the contribution to lowered break-even points via improved materials and methods.

Are its innovations well-timed?

An evaluator needs to understand the time cycle required for research, development and introduction to application; also, he must be able to relate this understanding to the basic facts about the market being served. Such an evaluator can tell when a firm is proceeding in the vanguard of the competition or when it is jumping on a bandwagon too late—as so many electronics firms did with respect to the transistor bandwagon.

Marketing

Closely allied with R & D and product innovation are the marketing skills of the firm under analysis. Strengths and weaknesses in this area can be uncovered by digging into the following topics.

Nature of the marketing capability   What channels of distribution are used? How much of the total marketing job (research, sales, service, advertising, and promotion) is covered? Is this capability correctly tailored to match the nature and diversity of the firm's product lines?

---

[9] An invaluable review of this literature up to early 1957 is given in: Albert H. Rubenstein, "Looking Around: Guide to R & D," *Harvard Business Review,* Volume 35, No. 3, May–June, 1957, p. 133 ff. Among the most pertinent articles since Rubenstein's review are: Ora C. Roehl, "The Investment Analyst's Evaluation of Industrial Research Capabilities," *Research Management,* Volume III, No. 3, Autumn, 1960, 127 ff.; Maurice Nelles, "Changing the World Changers," a paper presented at the Ninth Annual Management Conference, The Graduate School of Business Administration, University of Chicago, March 1, 1961; C. Wilson Randle," "Problems of R & D Management, *Harvard Business Review,* Volume 37, No. 1, January–February 1959, p. 128 ff.; James B. Quinn, "How to Evaluate Research Output," *Harvard Business Review,* Volume 38, No. 2, March–April 1960, pp. 69 ff,; and "Long-Range Planning of Industrial Research, *Harvard Business Review,* Volume 39, No. 4, July–August 1961, pp. 88 ff.

Is there a capability for exploiting new products and for developing new markets?

Quality of the marketing capability   Is market research capable of providing the factual basis that will keep the firm, especially its new product development and R & D programs, truly customer-oriented? Is there a capability for doing broad economic studies and studies of particular industries that will help management set sound growth and/or diversification strategies?

The evaluator will already have learned much about market research capability in answering the product line questions posed earlier in this article. There it was indicated that the firm that knows the facts about trends in its market and technologies is well on the way to success in the future. This clearly places great responsibility on market research, a field still neglected or abused by many science-based firms, especially those in defense work.

To cope adequately with challenges of the future requires more than market research in the old narrow concept; rather, it requires an ability at economic analysis of entire industries. Survival and growth in a rapidly changing economy sometimes demands more than a stream of new products; often it requires diversification into substantially different fields that offer greater growth and better profits for a given time period.

Diversification strategy is another subject that is currently being developed.[10] The aircraft industry today presents a case study in which certain firms are prospering because ten years ago they started to diversify while other firms are suffering badly because they failed to do so.

The accelerating rate of change in industry is a process that feeds on itself. Thus, sophisticated methods of market research and planning not only help a firm cope with rapid change but also foster more rapid change.

The evaluator must know enough about quantitative methods of research to be able to distinguish between valid use and abuse of market research. If not so equipped, he is at the mercy of the super-salesman with a smattering of scientific lore who can spin great tales about how a given firm has made a technological breakthrough that soon will have tremendous impact upon the market.

The evaluator must also be able to distinguish between creative market research and pedestrian fact-gathering that plods along a year too late to help management conquer the future. Only when market research secures fresh quantitative data on future markets can management integrate market development with product development.

Manufacturing

Next area to be studied is production. Questions to be asked include:

Manufacturing   What is the nature of the manufacturing processes, the facilities and the skills—are they appropriate to today's competition? How

[10] H. Igor Ansoff, "Strategies for Diversification," *Harvard Business Review,* September–October, 1957.

flexible are they—will they be or can they be made appropriate to tomorrow's competition?

What is the quality of the manufacturing management in terms of planning and controlling work schedule-wise, cost-wise, and quality-wise? Is there evidence of an industrial engineering capability that steadily improves products and methods? Does manufacturing management effectively perform its part of the process of achieving new products?

The answers to these questions call mainly for conventional type analysis which need not be commented upon here. This is not to say that there are not now, as always, new and better techniques being developed in the manufacturing field. Certainly an alert manufacturing management will use such progressive techniques as "value engineering" to simplify product designs and, thus, reduce costs; and it will use electronic data processing and other modern industrial engineering methods of controlling the work pace and other cost elements.

But, basically, manufacturing management still is, and long has been, evaluated on the basis of performance schedule-wise, cost- and quality-wise, and techniques for such evaluations are among the oldest and best-developed tools of management consultants and others concerned with industrial engineering.

The quickening pace of technological change does, however, require special attention to the ability of the engineering and manufacturing departments to cooperate effectively in bringing new products into production and in utilizing new processes. Also, it requires special caution with respect to firms with heavy investments in inflexible capital equipment because such investments might be susceptible to almost sudden obsolesence.

Summary on R & D and operations

To make the most of information acquired about a firm's operating departments and R & D, it is well at this point to pull all this sometimes diffuse information together into a sight summary that pulls the whole picture of operations into focus. Questions running along lines such as these help clarify it.

The overall picture   Is this a complete, integrated, balanced operation; or have certain strong personalities emphasized some functions and neglected others?

What is the quality of performance of key R & D and operating executives; do they understand the fundamental processes of management, namely planning, controlling, organizing, staffing, and directing? Are plans and controls in each department inadequate, adequate, or over-developed into a "paperwork mill"?

Is there throughout the departments a habit of steady progress in reducing overhead, lowering break-even points and improving quality?

Are all departments future-minded; do they cooperate effectively in developing worthy new products geared to meet the customer's future needs?

Finance is the third area of a corporation which should be analyzed carefully in appraising its present and future development. In this connection, both the men handling a company's finances and the figures on the balance sheet should be studied. Beginning inquiries could be:

Financial analysis What main strength and weaknesses of the firm emerge from analysis of the trends in the traditional financial data: earnings ratios (to sales, to tangible net worth, to working capital) and earnings-per-share; debt ratios (current and acid tests, to tangible net worth, to working capital, to inventory); inventory turnover; cash flow; and the capitalization structure?

What do the trends in the basic financial facts indicate as to the firm's prospects for growth in sales volume and rate of earnings? Does "quality of earnings" warrant compounding of the earnings rate?

Although this article has already pointed out limitations of financial analysis standing alone as a method of evaluating firms, its importance as one of the key elements of an evaluation should never be overlooked. Because financial analysis has been so important for so long, its techniques have been well developed. Therefore, it is not necessary to discuss them here.

One concept concerning "growth" companies, however, does require comment. The technique of evaluating a growth firm on the basis of an assumption that it will "plow back" its earnings and thereby achieve a compounded rate of increase in earnings per share is of questionable validity. By compounding earnings on a straight-line (or uninterrupted) basis, financial analysts arrive at estimates of future earnings that justify stock prices from 40 to 100 times present earnings per share.

No firm progresses evenly

The concept of straight-line progress just doesn't square with the facts of life as observed by students of management. Especially in small and medium-sized companies, progress typically occurs in a sawtooth, rather than a straight-line pattern. This phenomenon is based partly on the existence of business cycles and partly on the fact that firms are affected by the strengths and limitations of humans in key positions. There are stages in which the typical growing firm requires managerial talents greater than—or, possibly, only different from—those talents essential to its start.

At these critical periods the earnings per share may slow down or even turn into losses. Such events devastate the compounding process; if one compounds a more realistic 5–10 percent rate of growth per year, the result is far less sensational than is secured by compounding a 20–25 percent rate. It is exceedingly rare that a firm achieves the higher percentages for any sustained period; Litton Industries and IBM appear to be the exception that prove the rule. The reference to quality of earnings is meant to shed light on the sustainability of the rate of improvements in earnings. Here the evaluator must distinguish between continuous, sustainable improvement and isolated events (such as a single acquisition or securing an especially favorable contract) or cyclical events (a period of high profitability certain to be followed by a corresponding low).

The money men

Figures alone don't tell the complete financial story of a firm. Its money management must be rated and this involves an evaluation of both policies and men, not only those in the financial division but also the men in charge of planning and top management. You need to know their attitudes about . . .

Financial management Is there a sound program for steadily increasing return on investment? Do the long-range financial plans indicate that management understands the costs of capital and how to make money work hard? Have balance sheets and operating statements been realistically projected for a number of years into the future?

Is there careful cash planning and strong controls that help the operating departments lower break-even points? Are capital expenditures inadequate, adequate, or excessive with respect to insuring future operating efficiency? Are capital investment decisions based on thorough calculations?

Does management have the respect of the financial community?

Is the firm knowledgeable and aggressive in tax administration?

While many financial departments function only as record-keepers and rules-enforcers, some play a truly creative role. Financial management can today contribute as much or more to improvement in earnings per share as can any other part of management.[11] In fact, in recent years bold use of the newer forms of financing have in many cases contributed as much to the rapid rise of companies as have technological innovations. And, alas, bold but unwise financing has ruined many a promising young company.

The questions here are designed to help the evaluator discover whether or not the financial people are vigorously contributing in a number of ways to the steady improvement of earnings currently and in the long run.

Rating top management

All study of management invariably and understandably leads to a searching examination of the top management men. Here there are pitfalls for the un-

[11] For an exposition of this thought as applied to large firms, see: "The New Power of the Financial Executive," *Fortune,* Volume LXV, No. 1, January 1962, p. 81 ff. See also the new text by J. Fred Weston, *Managerial Finance* (New York: Holt, Rinehart & Winston, 1962).

wary. The analyst must first identify the true top management before he can examine their performance record. Things, in terms of who actually runs the show, are not always what they seem on the organization chart. So key topics are:

Top management and its record   What person or group constitutes top management? Has present top management been responsible for profit-and-loss results of the past few years?

The problem is to determine the individual or group of individuals who contribute directly and regularly to those decisions that shape the basic nature of this business and significantly affect profit-and-loss results. This usually cannot be determined reliably by direct questions to persons in key positions; few men are objective about themselves on these matters.

Watch them work

Rare is the top executive who will admit that he is a one-man rule type; rare is the vice-president or department head who will admit that he is a highly-paid errand boy. Accordingly, direct observation of management at work is needed. Some additional information can also be gained through examination of minutes of meetings and files of memos.

After top management has been identified, the evaluator must ask whether this management has had time to prove itself one way or the other. The criterion is whether or not major decisions and programs put forth by this top management have come to fruition. It is not simply a matter of looking at profit and loss figures for a few years. We all know that in certain situations factors other than top management capability (for example, an inherited product line that is unusually strong) can produce good profits for a number of years.

Next comes consideration of:

Top management and the future   What are top management's chief characteristics? How adequate or inadequate is this type of management for coping with the challenges of the future?

Will the present type and quality of top management continue, or will it deteriorate, will it improve, or will it change its basic character?

We must ask how and why top management has achieved the results that it has achieved so that we can judge how adequate it will be for meeting tomorrow's challenges. Exploring the how and why gets the evaluator into the subject of types of management and their effects on profitability—the thorniest area of contemporary management theory. Over the past twenty years a tremendous literature has accumulated on such subjects as participative leadership, autocratic vs. bureaucratic vs. democratic types of management, and related subjects.

Some writers have claimed or implied great virtues for participative-democratic methods; others have attacked such methods as wasteful and ineffective, wholly inappropriate in industrial life and have advocated "benevolent autocracy." The confusion recently reached a zenith with the almost simultaneous publication of conflicting views by eminent professors from the same university.[12]

Industrial psychologists and sociologists have provided valuable insights into management practices and their effects upon profitability. While a skilled social scientist could contribute importantly to the evaluation of a firm's top management, there is a more direct way of evaluating top management's capability for coping with future challenges.

The direct method is to determine how top management has in the past coped with the future. This technique is based on the idea that management is essentially the process of planning to achieve certain goals and, then, controlling activities so that the goals are actually attained. It is in the processes of planning and controlling that top management does its major decision-making. Since planning and controlling are the heart of the managerial process, it is in these activities that top management most fully reveals its vital characteristics.

The evaluator can probe deeply into the content of the firm's past and current long-range and short-range plans, into the methods by which the plans are formulated, and into the controls used to bring those plans to fruition. This technique gets away, to a considerable extent, from subjective judgments; it deals with such facts as what was planned, how it was planned and what actually happened.

Fortunately these activities can be studied without great difficulty and by persons who do not have formal training in the behavioral sciences. A simple yet highly informative procedure is to compare succeeding sets of old long-range plans with one another, with present plans and with actual events.

Do their plans work?

First, a firm that is effectively tomorrow-minded will have long-range plans. These may not be neatly bound in a cover labeled "long-range plans"; however, they will exist either in minutes of meetings, in memos, in reports to stockholders or in other places. Second, the old plans will contain evidence as to whether top management truly has studied the future to determine and anticipate the nature of the opportunities and threats that will inevitably arise.

Third, the old plans will contain evidence of the nature and quality of

[12] Rensis Likert, reporting on a decade of social science research into patterns of management makes a case for participative management in *New Patterns of Management* (New York: McGraw-Hill Publishing Company, 1961). George Odiorne, reporting on studies of successful managements, warns strongly against the views of social scientists and makes a case for the more traditional, somewhat autocratic, business leader in *How Managers Make Things Happen* (New York: Prentice-Hall, Inc., 1961). Both authors are professors at the University of Michigan.

the solutions developed for meeting the challenges of the future—how creative, aggresive and realistic management has been in initiative matters such
as selecting R & D programs, establishing diversification strategy and program, developing new markets, planning the organizational changes needed
to keep fit for new tasks, and effectively utilizing advanced techniques (e.g.,
operations research, automation, etc.) when feasible.

Special attention to initiative matters will indicate whether or not top
management is creative and aggressive enough to keep up with an accelerating rate of change.

Fourth, comparison of succeeding sets of plans will indicate whether
consistent progress has been made or top management is recklessly aggressive in that it undertakes unrealistic, ill-conceived, unachievable plans.

The same technique can be applied to short-range plans such as annual budgets, sales forecasts and special developmental programs of many
types. This study will indicate whether or not forecasts are typically accurate, whether or not plans typically are successfully completed, whether or
not new products are developed on schedule, and whether or not they are
supported by marketing, finance, and management programs ready to go at
the right time. Again, as in the case of long-range plans, the inquiry will reveal whether decision-making is mature or immature. Has management
made profitability a habit, or just a subject of wishful thinking?

A management that knows how to bring plans to fruition builds into
every plan a set of controls designed to give early warning of problems and
an indication that corrective action is needed. Examination of the controls
and the ways in which they are used will indicate whether or not top management is on top of its problems or vice versa.

Who makes the plans?

Investigation of the methods by which plans are formulated and control is
exercised will reveal a great deal about whether top management is autocratic, bureaucratic or democratic. This inquiry holds more than academic interest; the extent to which lower levels of management contribute to the formulation of plans and the extent to which they are held accountable for
results will tell much about the firm's down-the-line strength.

Executive turnover

Also, these factors are particularly important indicators of whether top management will retain its vigor, will improve or will deteriorate. Thus, they indicate whether or not top management is making sincere efforts to recruit and
develop middle management that will become a new and better generation
of top management. Other insights into whether management is bringing in
too little or too much new blood can be gained by examining age patterns

and statistics on turnover in executive ranks, by reviewing formal executive development efforts and by interviews with some of the men.

Yardstick to gauge growth factors

In summary, the technique of probing deeply into the firm's actual plans and controls and methods of planning and control can yield abundant evidence to indicate whether or not top management has the characteristics of a growth firm. These characteristics have been set forth in a major study by Stanford Research Institute of the factors that usually distinguish growth from non-growth firms. They are:

- Affinity for growth fields.
- Organized programs to seek and promote new opportunities.
- Proven competitive abilities in present lines of business.
- Courageous and energetic managements, willing to make carefully calculated risks.
- Luck.

Incidentally, this study found that high growth companies had twice the earning power of low growth companies, while maintaining four times the growth rate.[13]

The Board of Directors

Rounding out the top management of every corporation is an enigmatic, unpublicized group of men about whom a competent analyst should be most curious. They are the Board of Directors. Questions such as these should be asked about them: What influence and/or control does the Board of Directors exercise? What are the capabilities of its members? What are their motivations?

In the author's experience one of the most frequent and serious errors of small-and medium-sized firms is failure to have and use effectively a strong Board of Directors. Too often the entrepreneurial types who start firms disdain help until they are in deep trouble.

Especially in firms headed by a scientist or a super-salesman, a strong

[13] The title is *Environmental Change and Corporate Strategy* (Menlo Park, California: Stanford Research Institute, 1960), p. 8. A more recent report on this continuing research project is given by Robert B. Young, "Keys to Corporate Growth," *Harvard Business Review,* Vol. 39, No. 6, November–December 1961, pp. 51–62. Young concludes: "In short, the odds for corporate growth are highest when the top executives of a firm treat their future planning as a practical decision-making challenge requiring personal participation and direct their planning efforts toward the origins of opportunity itself. Such an approach can make the difference between having constantly to adapt to day-to-day crises and enjoying profitable future growth."

and active Board can be invaluable in helping make up for the top executives' lack of rounded managerial training and experience. Except in a few
unusual situations, a Board must be an "outside," or nonemployee, Board to
be strong.

Dummies or policy makers

To be active and helpful, an "outside" Board must have some motivation,
either financial or the psychic motivation involved in being confronted with
real problems and being able to contribute to their solution. Examination of
files and minutes of Board meetings will reveal whether or not there is a
good flow of information to the outside directors and a contribution by them
to the solution of significant problems.

Adding up the facts

With all the data in about the four vital areas of a firm, products and competition, operations and R & D, finance, and top management, the analyst ends
his task by posing one more set of questions which might be called Summary and Evaluation Strategy. They should run something like this:

What other factors (use a checklist)[14] can assume major importance in
this particular situation?

Of all the factors studied, which, if any, is overriding in this particular
situation? Which factors are of major importance by virtue of the fact that
they govern other factors?

What are the basic facts of life about the economics and competition
of this industry now and over the next decade? In view of this firm's particular strengths and weaknesses, what are the odds that it will succeed and at
what level of success, in this industry? What are the prospects of its succeeding by diversifying out of its industry?

Determing other vital factors

There is a purpose behind every evaluation study. That purpose or the particular nature of the firm and its industry might place importance upon any
of an almost infinite number of factors. Accordingly, the evaluator must
thoughtfully run through a checklist containing such considerations as: personnel management practices (e.g., labor relations, profit-sharing, compensation levels), valuation questions (e.g., valuation of fixed or real assets or inventory or unique assets), geographical location as related to labor markets,
taxes, cost of distribution, seasonality factors, in-process or impending

---

[14] For one such check list, see: Robert G. Sproul, Jr. "Sizing Up New Acquisitions,"
Management Review, XLIX, No. 1, February 1960, pp. 80–82.

litigation, or any matter footnoted in the financial reports so that the auditing firm is, in effect, warning of an unusual circumstance.

The purpose of a particular evaluation study often will determine which factor, if any, is overriding. Logically, the quality of top management should usually be the overriding factor. By definition a highly competent top management group can solve the other problems such as securing competent scientists and other personnel, developing new products, getting financing, etc. However, there may be an investment or acquisition situation in which the product line, for example, is the overriding factor because it is so obsolete that even the finest management could not effect a recovery within existing time and financial parameters.

Matching buyer and acquisition

If the evaluation is being done to help decide the advisability of an acquisition, many additional considerations come into play. The problem is one of matching the acquiring and acquired firms; many firms have acquired grief rather than growth because they have neglected this point. At one extreme, acquistion of one healthy company by another may be unwise because the two are so different that the acquirer may mismanage the acquired company. At the other extreme, it may be wise for one unhealthy company to acquire another unhealthy one if the strengths of one remedy the weaknesses of the other, and vice versa.

The character of the company

The acquirer must precisely define his objectives in acquiring. Also, he must carefully consider the "character," or "climate," of the other firm in relation to his own. The subject of "company character" has not been well developed in management practice or literature.[15] Nevertheless, a consideration of the "character" of the two companies is highly relevant, and the outline presented in this article will help the evaluator consider some of the more obvious elements of "company character" such as the nature of its engineering and manufacturing skills, the type of distribution channels and marketing skills required, the type of managerial leadership practiced and top management's aggressiveness and the quality of its decisions in initiative matters.

In sum, the evaluation of a firm requires a clinical judgment of the highest order. The purposes of the evaluation study set the criteria for the judgment. Except in a few instances in which conditions are highly stable, the day is rapidly passing when simple financial analyses, or even financial analyses supplemented by a few interviews and judgments of scientists will suffice for evaluation of a firm.

[15] A new textbook brings together for the first time the few and scattered writings on the subject of "company character." See William B. Wolf's *The Management of Personnel* (San Francisco: Wadsworth Publishing Co., Inc., 1961), pp. 8–43.

Conclusion/C
Managing in the future

---

64 The coming death of bureaucracy
Warren G. Bennis

Not far from the new Government Center in downtown Boston, a foreign visitor walked up to a sailor and asked why American ships were built to last only a short time. According to the tourist, "The sailor answered without hesitation that the art of navigation is making such rapid progress that the finest ship would become obsolete if it lasted beyond a few years. In these words which fell accidentally from an uneducated man, I began to recognize the general and systematic idea upon which your great people direct all their concerns."

The foreign visitor was that shrewd observer of American morals and manners, Alexis de Tocqueville, and the year was 1835. He would not recognize Scollay Square today. But he had caught the central theme of our country: its preoccupation, its *obsession* with change. One thing is, however, new since de Tocqueville's time: the *acceleration* of newness, the changing scale and scope of change itself. As Dr. Robert Oppenheimer said, " . . . the world alters as we walk in it, so that the years of man's life measure not some small growth or rearrangement or moderation of what was learned in childhood, but a great upheaval."

How will these accelerating changes in our society influence human organizations?

A short while ago, I predicted that we would, in the next 25 to 50 years, participate in the end of bureaucracy as we know it and in the rise of new social systems better suited to the 20th-century demands of industrialization. This forecast was based on the evolutionary principle that every age develops an organizational form appropriate to its genius, and that the prevailing form, known by sociologists as bureaucracy and by most businessmen as "damn bureaucracy," was out of joint with contemporary realities. I realize now that my distant prophecy is already a distinct reality so that prediction is already foreshadowed by practice.

I should like to make clear that by bureaucracy I mean a chain of

Source: Reprinted by permission from *Think* magazine, pages 30–35, published by IBM, copyright 1966 by International Business Machines Corporation.

command structured on the lines of a pyramid—the typical structure which coordinates the business of almost every human organization we know of: industrial, governmental, of universities and research and development laboratories, military, religious, voluntary. I do *not* have in mind those fantasies so often dreamed up to describe complex organizations. These fantasies can be summarized in two grotesque stereotypes. The first I call "Organization as Inkblot"—an actor steals around an uncharted wasteland, growing more restive and paranoid by the hour, while he awaits orders that never come. The other specter is "Organization as Big Daddy"—the actors are square people plugged into square holes by some omniscient and omnipotent genius who can cradle in his arms the entire destiny of man by way of computer and TV. Whatever the first image owes to Kafka, the second owes to George Orwell's *Nineteen Eighty-four.*

Bureaucracy, as I refer to it here, is a useful social invention that was perfected during the industrial revolution to organize and direct the activities of a business firm. Most students of organizations would say that its anatomy consists of the following components:

- A well-defined chain of command.
- A system of procedures and rules for dealing with all contingencies relating to work activities.
- A division of labor based on specialization.
- Promotion and selection based on technical competence.
- Impersonality in human relations.

It is the pyramid arrangement we see on most organizational charts.

The bureaucratic "machine model" was developed as a reaction against the personal subjugation, nepotism and cruelty, and the capricious and subjective judgments which passed for managerial practices during the early days of the industrial revolution. Bureaucracy emerged out of the organizations' need for order and precision and the workers' demands for impartial treatment. It was an organization ideally suited to the values and demands of the Victorian era. And just as bureaucracy emerged as a creative response to a radically new age, so today new organizational shapes are surfacing before our eyes.

First I shall try to show why the conditions of our modern industrialized world will bring about the death of bureaucracy. In the second part of this article I will suggest a rough model of the organization of the future.

Four threats

There are at least four relevant threats to bureaucracy:

1 Rapid and unexpected change.
2 Growth in size where the volume of an organization's traditional activities is

not enough to sustain growth. (A number of factors are included here, among them: bureaucratic overhead; tighter controls and impersonality due to bureaucratic sprawls; outmoded rules and organizational structures.)
3 Complexity of modern technology where integration between activities and persons of very diverse, highly specialized competence is required.
4 A basically psychological threat springing from a change in managerial behavior.

It might be useful to examine the extent to which these conditions exist right now:

1 *Rapid and unexpected change*   Bureaucracy's strength is its capacity to efficiently manage the routine and predictable in human affairs. It is almost enough to cite the knowledge and population explosion to raise doubts about its contemporary viability. More revealing, however, are the statistics which demonstrate these overworked phrases:

- Our productivity output per man hour may now be doubling almost every 20 years rather than every 40 years, as it did before World War II.
- The Federal Government alone spent $16 billion in research and development activities in 1965; it will spend $35 billion by 1980.
- The time lag between a technical discovery and recognition of its commercial uses was: 30 years before World War I, 16 years between the Wars, and only 9 years since World War II.
- In 1946, only 42 cities in the world had populations of more than one million. Today there are 90. In 1930, there were 40 people for each square mile of the earth's land surface. Today there are 63. By 2000, it is expected, the figure will have soared to 142.

Bureaucracy, with its nicely defined chain of command, its rules and its rigidities, is ill-adapted to the rapid change the environment now demands.

2 *Growth in size*   While, in theory, there may be no natural limit to the height of a bureaucratic pyramid, in practice the element of complexity is almost invariably introduced with great size. International operation, to cite one significant new element, is the rule rather than exception for most of our biggest corporations. Firms like Standard Oil Company (New Jersey) with over 100 foreign affiliates, Modil Oil Corporation, The National Cash Register Company, Singer Company, Burroughs Corporation and Colgate-Palmolive Company derive more than half their income or earnings from foreign sales. Many others—such as Eastman Kodak Company, Chas. Pfizer & Company, Inc., Caterpillar Tractor Company, International Harvester Company, Corn Products Company and Minnesota Mining & Manufacturing Company—make from 30 to 50 percent of their sales abroad. General Motors Corporation sales are not only nine times those of Volkswagen, they are also bigger than the Gross National Product of the Netherlands and well over the GNP of a

hundred other countries. If we have seen the sun set on the British Empire, we may never see it set on the empires of General Motors, ITT, Shell and Unilever.

Labor boom

3 *Increasing diversity*   Today's activities require persons of very diverse, highly specialized competence.

Numerous dramatic examples can be drawn from studies of labor markets and job mobility. At some point during the past decade, the U.S. became the first nation in the world ever to employ more people in the service occupations than in the production of tangible goods. Examples of this trend:

- In the field of education, the *increase* in employment between 1950 and 1960 was greater than the total number employed in the steel, copper and aluminum industries.
- In the field of health, the *increase* in employment between 1950 and 1960 was greater than the total number employed in automobile manufacturing in either year.
- In financial firms, the *increase* in employment between 1950 and 1960 was greater than total employment in mining in 1960.

These changes, plus many more that are harder to demonstrate statistically, break down the old, industrial trend toward more and more people doing either simple or undifferentiated chores.

Hurried growth, rapid change and increase in specialization—pit these three factors against the five components of the pyramid structure described on page 536, and we should expect the pyramid of bureaucracy to begin crumbling.

4 *Change in managerial behavior*   There is, I believe, a subtle but perceptible change in the philosophy underlying management behavior. Its magnitude, nature and antecedents, however, are shadowy because of the difficulty of assigning numbers. (Whatever else statistics do for us, they most certainly provide a welcome illusion of certainty.) Nevertheless, real change seems under way because of:

a. A new concept of *man,* based on increased knowledge of his complex and shifting needs, which replaces an oversimplified, innocent, push-button idea of man.

b. A new concept of *power,* based on collaboration and reason, which replaces a model of power based on coercion and threat.

c. A new concept of *organizational values,* based on humanistic-democratic ideals, which replaces the depersonalized mechanistic value system of bureaucracy.

The primary cause of this shift in management philosophy stems not from the bookshelf but from the manager himself. Many of the behavioral scientists, like Douglas McGregor or Rensis Likert, have clarified and articulated—even legitimized—what managers have only half registered to themselves. I am convinced, for example, that the popularity of McGregor's book, *The Human Side of Enterprise,* was based on his rare empathy for a vast audience of managers who are wistful for an alternative to the mechanistic concept of authority, i.e., that he outlined a vivid utopia of more authentic human relationships than most organizational practices today allow. Furthermore, I suspect that the desire for relationships in business has little to do with a profit motive per se, though it is often rationalized as doing so. The real push for these changes stems from the need, not only to humanize the organization, but to use it as a crucible of personal growth and the development of self-realization.*

The core problems confronting any organization fall, I believe, into five major categories. First, let us consider the problems, then let us see how our 20th-century conditions of constant change have made the bureaucratic approach to these problems obsolete.

1 *Integration* The problem is how to integrate individual needs and management goals. In other words, it is the inescapable conflict between individual needs (like "spending time with the family") and organizational demands (like meeting deadlines).

Under 20th-century conditions of constant change there has been an emergence of human sciences and a deeper understanding of man's complexity. Today, integration encompasses the entire range of issues concerned with incentives, rewards and motivations of the individual, and how the organization succeeds or fails in adjusting to these issues. In our society, where personal attachments play an important role, the individual is appreciated, and there is genuine concern for his well-being, not just in a veterinary-hygiene sense, but as a moral, integrated personality.

Paradoxical twins

The problem of integration, like most human problems, has a venerable past. The modern version goes back at least 160 years and was precipitated by an historical paradox: the twin births of modern individualism and modern industrialism. The former brought about a deep concern for a passionate interest in the individual and his personal rights. The latter brought about increased mechanization of organized activity. Competition between the two

* Let me propose an hypothesis to explain this tendency. It rests on the assumption that man has a basic need for transcendental experiences, somewhat like the psychological rewards which William James claimed religion provided—"an assurance of safety and a temper of peace, and, in relation to others, a preponderance of loving affections." Can it be that as religion has become secularized, less transcendental, men search for substitutes such as close interpersonal relationships, psychoanalysis—even the release provided by drugs such as LSD?

has intensified as each decade promises more freedom and hope for man and more stunning achievements for technology. I believe that our society has opted for more humanistic and democratic values, however unfulfilled they may be in practice. It will "buy" these values even at loss in efficiency because it feels it can now afford the loss.

2 *Social influence*   This problem is essentially one of power and how power is distributed. It is a complex issue and alive with controversy, partly because of an ethical component and partly because studies of leadership and power distribution can be interpreted in many ways, and almost always in ways which coincide with one's biases (including a cultural leaning toward democracy).

The problem of power has to be seriously reconsidered because of dramatic situational changes which make the possibility of one-man rule not necessarily "bad" but impractical. I refer to changes in top management's role.

Peter Drucker, over twelve years ago, listed 41 major responsibilities of the chief executive and declared that "90 percent of the trouble we are having with the chief executive's job is rooted in our superstition of the one-man chief." Many factors make one-man control obsolete, among them: the broadening product base of industry; impact of new technology; the scope of international operation; the separation of management from ownership; the rise of trade unions and general education. The real power of the "chief" has been eroding in most organizations even though both he and the organization cling to the older concept.

3 *Collaboration*   This is the problem of managing and resolving conflicts. Bureaucratically, it grows out of the very same social process of conflict and stereotyping that has divided nations and communities. As organizations become more complex, they fragment and divide, building tribal patterns and symbolic codes which often work to exclude others (secrets and jargon, for example) and on occasion to exploit differences for inward (and always fragile) harmony.

Recent research is shedding new light on the problem of conflict. Psychologist Robert R. Blake in his stunning experiments has shown how simple it is to induce conflict, how difficult to arrest it. Take two groups of people who have never before been together, and give them a task which will be judged by an impartial jury. In less than an hour, each group devolves into a tightly-knit band will all the symptoms of an "in group." They regard their product as a "masterwork" and the other group's as "commonplace" at best. "Other" becomes "enemy." "We are good, they are bad; we are right, they are wrong."

Rabbie's reds and greens

Jaap Rabbie, conducting experiments on intergroup conflict at the University of Utrecht, has been amazed by the ease with which conflict and stereotype develop. He brings into an experimental room two groups and distributes green name tags and pens to one group, red pens and tags to the other. The two groups do not compete; they do not even interact. They are only in sight of each other while they silently complete a questionnaire. Only 10 minutes are needed to activate defensiveness and fear, reflected in the hostile and irrational perceptions of both "reds" and "greens."

4 *Adaptation*   This problem is caused by our turbulent environment. The pyramid structure of bureaucracy, where power is concentrated at the top, seems the perfect way to "run a railroad." And for the routine tasks of the 19th and early 20th centuries, bureaucracy was (in some respects it still is) a suitable social arrangement. However, rather than a placid and predictable environment, what predominates today is a dynamic and uncertain one where there is a deepening interdependence among economic, scientific, educational, social and political factors in the society.

5 *Revitalization*   This is the problem of growth and decay. As Alfred North Whitehead has said: "The art of free society consists first in the maintenance of the symbolic code, and secondly, in the fearlessness of revision. . . . Those societies which cannot combine reverence to their symbols with freedom of revision must ultimately decay. . . ."

Growth and decay emerge as the penultimate conditions of contemporary society. Organizations, as well as societies, must be concerned with those social structures that engender buoyancy, resilience and a "fearlessness of revision."

I introduce the term "revitalization" to embrace all the social mechanisms that stagnate and regenerate, as well as the process of this cycle. The elements of revitalization are:

1. An ability to learn from experience and to codify, store and retrieve the relevant knowledge.

2. An ability to "learn how to learn" that is, to develop methods for improving the learning process.

3. An ability to acquire and use feedback mechanisms on performance, in short, to be self-analytical.

4. An ability to direct one's own destiny.

These qualities have a good deal in common with what John Gardner calls "self-renewal." For the organization, it means conscious attention to its own evolution. Without a planned methodology and explicit direction, the enterprise will not realize its potential.

Integration, distribution of power, collaboration, adaptation and *revitalization*—these are the major human problems of the next 25 years. How organizations cope with and manage these tasks will undoubtedly determine the viability of the enterprise.

Against this background I should like to set forth some of the conditions that will dictate organizational life in the next two or three decades.

1 *The environment*   Rapid technological change and diversification will lead to more and more partnerships between government and business. It will be a

truly mixed economy. Because of the immensity and expense of the projects, there will be fewer identical units competing in the same markets and organizations will become more interdependent.

The four main features of this environment are:

- Interdependence rather than competition.
- Turbulence and uncertainty rather than readiness and certainty.
- Large-scale rather than small-scale enterprises.
- Complex and multinational rather than simple national enterprises.

"Nice"—and necessary

2 *Population characteristics*   The most distinctive characteristic of our society is education. It will become even more so. Within 15 years, two thirds of our population living in metropolitan areas will have attended college. Adult education is growing even faster, probably because of the rate of professional obsolescence. The Killian report showed that the average engineer required further education only 10 years after getting his degree. It will be almost routine for the experienced physician, engineer and executive to go back to school for advanced training every two or three years. All of this education is not just "nice." It is necessary.

One other characteristic of the population which will aid our understanding of organizations of the future is increasing job mobility. The ease of transportation, coupled with the needs of a dynamic environment, change drastically the idea of "owning" a job—or "having roots." Already 20 percent of our population change their mailing address at least once a year.

3 *Work values*   The increased level of education and mobility will change the values we place on work. People will be more intellectually committed to their jobs and will probably require more involvement, participation and autonomy.

Also, people will be more "other-oriented," taking cues for their norms and values from their immediate environment rather than tradition.

4 *Tasks and goals*   The tasks of the organization will be more technical, complicated and unprogrammed. They will rely on intellect instead of muscle. And they will be too complicated for one person to comprehend, to say nothing of control. Essentially, they will call for the collaboration of specialists in a project or a team-form of organization.

There will be a complication of goals. Business will increasingly concern itself with its adaptive or innovative-creative capacity. In addition, supra-goals will have to be articulated, goals which shape and provide the foundation for the goal structure. For example, one might be a system for detecting new and changing goals; another could be a system for deciding priorities among goals.

Finally, there will be more conflict and contradiction among diverse standards for organizational effectiveness. This is because professionals tend to identify more with the goals of their profession than with those of their immediate employer. University professors can be used as a case in point. Their inside work may be a conflict between teaching and research, while more of their income is derived from outside sources, such as foundations and consultant work. They tend not to be good "company men" because they divide their loyalty between their professional values and organizational goals.

Key word: "Temporary"

5 *Organization*   The social structure of organizations of the future will have some unique characteristics. The key word will be "temporary." There will be adaptive, rapidly changing *temporary* systems. These will be task forces organized around problems-to-be-solved by groups of relative strangers with diverse professional skills. The group will be arranged on an organic rather than mechanical model; they will evolve in response to a problem rather than to programmed role expectations. The executive thus becomes a coordinator or "linking pin" between various task forces. He must be a man who can speak the polyglot jargon of research, with skills to relay information and to mediate between groups. People will be evaluated not vertically according to rank and status, but flexibly and functionally according to skill and professional training. Organizational charts will consist of project groups rather than stratified functional groups. (This trend is already visible in the aerospace and construction industries, as well as many professional and consulting firms.)

Adaptive, problem-solving, temporary systems of diverse specialists, linked together by coordinating and task-evaluating executive specialists in an organic flux—this is the organization form that will gradually replace bureaucracy as we know it. As no catchy phrase comes to mind, I call this an organic-adaptive structure. Organizational arrangements of this sort may not only reduce the intergroup conflicts mentioned earlier; it may also induce honest-to-goodness creative collaboration.

6 *Motivation*   The organic-adaptive structure should increase motivation and thereby effectiveness, because it enhances satisfactions intrinsic to the task. There is harmony between the educated individual's need for tasks that are meaningful, satisfactory and creative and a flexible organizational structure.

There will also be, however, reduced commitment to work groups, for these groups will be, as I have already mentioned, transient structures. I would predict that in the organic-adaptive system, people will learn to develop quick and intense relationships on the job, and learn to bear the loss of more enduring work relationships. Because of the added ambiguity of roles, time will have to be spent on continual rediscovery of the appropriate organizational mix.

I think that the futuure I describe is not necessarily a "happy" one.

Coping with rapid change, living in temporary work systems, developing meaningful relations and then breaking them—all augur social strains and psychological tensions. Teaching how to live with ambiguity, to identify with the adaptive process, to make a virtue out of contingency, and to be self-directing—these will be the tasks of education, the goals of maturity, and the achievement of the successful individual.

No delightful marriages

In these new organizations of the future, participants will be called upon to use their minds more than at any other time in history. Fantasy, imagination and creativity will be legitimate in ways that today seem strange. Social structures will no longer be instruments of psychic repression but will increasingly promote play and freedom on behalf of curiosity and thought.

One final word: While I forecast the structure and value coordinates for organizations of the future and contend that they are inevitable, this should not bar any of us from giving the inevitable a little push. The French moralist may be right in saying that there are no delightful marriages, just good ones; it is possible that if managers and scientists continue to get their heads together in organizational revitalization, they *might* develop delightful organizations—just possibly.

I started with a quote from de Tocqueville and I think it would be fitting to end with one: "I am tempted to believe that what we call necessary institutions are often no more than institutions to which we have grown accustomed. In matters of social constitution, the field of possibilities is much more extensive than men living in their various societies are ready to imagine."

65 The third sector and domestic missions*
Amitai Etzioni

What tools are best suited to serve our economic and social needs? This question has been debated for more than a century, usually in the name of the virtue of capitalism, which lauds the market system, and socialism, which favors, in effect, state administration. Each ideological system has

Source: Reprinted with permission from *Public Administration Review,* 33, No. 4 (July–August 1973), pp. 314–323.
* The author is indebted to Nancy Castleman who served as a research assistant in preparing this report which is part of a larger work in progress under the auspices of the Center for Policy Research.

sought purity in its guiding principles, despite the fact that they are not mutually exclusive.

Thus, private enterprise plays a significant role in the production and distribution of goods and services in socialist republics, but this activity is considered an exception, a residue, a transitory element, or a concession to the old-fashioned, something to be eliminated later. Similarly, in the United States, the existence of large-scale government business—for example, the Atomic Energy Commission and the Postal Service—is viewed as exceptional, and either undesirable or to be condoned for special purposes, such as security or lack of profitability in a vitally needed service.

Actually, over the years, the private sector has grown in the Soviet Union and government business has expanded in the United States.[1] Nevertheless, this fact is either disregarded or bemoaned by each side as a sure sign of increasing "softness"—if not outright deterioration—in the respective system. Like many other ideological debates, this one has concealed more truth than it has highlighted and it is particularly unhelpful in providing insight into the dynamics of the societies involved. As several keen analysts already have indicated, the capitalist and socialist systems, contrary to their avowed intentions, are actually moving toward each other[2]—or, as I see it, they are moving toward a third system, one in which both profit making and administrative principles of organization, production, and distribution are widely used.[3] This is *not* to suggest that the differences will disappear; the state enterprise will surely continue to play a major role in the Soviet Union in the foreseeable future, just as the profit motive will continue to dominate in the United States, but the two systems are becoming ever less "pure," more "mixed," and hence closer to a third type.

Moreover, even this picture—i.e., the notion of a private economy with a public ingredient, and a public economy with a private factor—does not get close enough to the societal reality to allow careful analysis of the main options for economic, social, and domestic efforts, nor does it reveal the proportion or direction that the mixes will change. To achieve this we must move closer to the situation, which we attempt to do by focusing here one country at one state in time—the U.S.A.—at the end of the '60s, early '70s.

Where we are

In the U.S.A. ever since the Republicans returned to the White House in 1969, frequent tribute has been paid to the capitalist, market, profit-making ideology. The expansion of government in any form is seen as evil by the modern conservative ideologists, who suggest that tasks and funds should

---

[1] For example, see Eli Ginsberg, Dale L. Hiestand, and Beatrice G. Reubens, *The Pluralistic Economy* (New York:McGraw-Hill Book Company, 1965).

[2] For example, see Zbigniew Brzezinski and Samuel P. Huntington, *Political Power: USA/USSR* (New York: The Viking Press, 1964).

[3] For more on the author's views, see Amitai Etzioni, *The Active Society* (New York: The Free Press, 1968), chapters 16–18.

be shifted from the government to the private sector. One spokesman for this approach, Peter Drucker, professor at the New York University Business School, has called the change "reprivatization"; he has written that the government should act like a conductor in a concert—initiating, guiding, coordinating, but not actually carrying out the missions. That job would be returned to the private sector.[4]

However, in the formative years of the Nixon Administration, the chief advisor to the President in domestic affairs was a New Deal liberal, Pat Moynihan, not Drucker. And practically all the major programs initiated or advocated by the Nixon Administration have been those that entail increased governmental efforts. Thus, the major anti-poverty, welfare plan of the Nixon Administration has been based not on black capitalism, JOBS (a businessmen-based drive for work to the unemployed), or any other private enterprise approach, but on the federally funded, federally administered, notion of guaranteed annual income, known as the Family Assistance Plan. Nixon,s "full-employment" budget attempts to give an added boost to the economy through such measures as expanding the money in circulation, increasing the national debt, and reducing some taxes—all made on the federal level. And Nixon's "revolutionary," "bold," and "most significant" domestic proposal—revenue sharing—only involves the transference of some monies from Washington to states, cities, and other local governments. But of more consequence than all this, of course, is the setting up of price and wage controls.They will subject to government review and control most aspects of the private sector previously untouched by the state. At least theoretically, all businesses (and especially larger ones) now have a status similar to that heretofore reserved for utilities, which cannot adjust rates, approve raises, or basically change their services without government approval or without adhering to government guidelines.

The major exception to this general trend of increased federal involvement is Nixon's proposed health plan, which calls for a "partnership" between the business community, its employees, and the federal government. (This plan is discussed in greater detail below.) Private insurance companies would administer a plan whereby the business community would have to provide health insurance for employees, who themselves would contribute about one third of the necessary funds for their health care. The federal government would supply the funds for the poor and the unemployed. The proposed national health insurance plan points the way that many new domestic plans might follow.

The third sector

While debate over how to serve our needs has focused on the public versus the private alternative, a third alternative, indeed sector, has grown between the state and market sector. Actually this third sector may well be the most

---

[4] Peter Drucker, *The Age of Discontinuity* (New York: Harper & Row, 1969).

important alternative for the next few decades, *not* by replacing the other two, but by matching and balancing their important roles.

The situation is analogous to the early days of the capitalist era. Rapid industrial growth "took off" only after a new legal and organizational concept paved its way, namely the limited liability corporation. This allowed for the accumulation of the large amount of capital necessary for industrialization and large-scale marketing—amounts which most families or partnerships could not amass.

In the present era, when society increasingly turns to provide public goods such as education, health, and welfare, *the search is on for appropriate legal and organizational tools.* Of course some public goods are, and will continue to be, provided by the private sector, e.g., production of textbooks for schools. And there certainly is no question that the government does and will provide many services, like social security. But increasingly we find missions—such as pollution control—where the profit motive is not great enough and/or costs involved in making the mission profitable seem too high. At the same time, we are ever more tired of the reliance on multiplying, expanding government bureaucracies. A method must be developed to combine "the best of both worlds"—efficiency and expertise from the business world with public interest, accountability, and broader planning from government.

An answer is coming not from theory but from a large variety of experimentations with new forms which are developing to carry out our domestic missions. All of these may be seen as attempts to find the appropriate vehicle through which to conduct the social as well as the economic "business" of mature capitalism. These developing forms are mainly in the *third sector,* which is neither governmental nor private. Some are created out of a mix of private business and governmental elements. Others take the form of voluntary associations (e.g., the Red Cross or the League of Women Voters) and the non-profit corporations (e.g., the Ford Foundation). Not all are successful, not by a long shot; but many seem to do significantly superior work than either the federal or local governments, and they are able to carry out missions which are not profitable enough to attract the private sector. *In fact, the most promising solutions to our domestic problems are among the third sector approaches now evolving.*

It should be noted that there is a semantic difficulty indicative of the ideological confusion and novelty of the development we seek to highlight, which often clouds the debate about different approaches to domestic problems. Usually reference is made to the private vs. the public sector. This, though, hides the fact that the term "public" refers to both governmental and voluntary (or not-for-profit) beings. Moreover, while often the "nonprofit" beings are lumped with the government ones, on other occasions they are treated as part of the private sector, e.g., Columbia University is referred to as a "private" university. As the third sector beings differ significantly from both dominant sectors, we suggest reference shall be made to *private* (profit), *governmental* (state), and *public* sectors (not-for-profit, voluntary).

That there is a need for such a concept can be seen by the semantic contortions writers have engaged in to point to the divergent type they recognized but had no category for. Thus, writing about the condition in which the United Kingdom government has a majority or minority holding of the shares of an "undertaking" which remains juristically a "private" company (quotation marks in original), one author uses the term "mixed enterprise," in quotes, to indicate its novelty.[5] No wonder; the author uses the term public corporation to refer to fully nationalized, i.e., state, ones.

Professor Hokan Stromberg, discussing the situation in Sweden, tries to play the distinction at hand by referring to two kinds of public corporations: state-controlled company" and "public institutions."[6]

And, when discussing the Children's Television Workshop, the producer of the world-renowned *Sesame Street,* Linda Francke, writes: "Legally, CTV is a 'public' rather than a 'private', non-profit foundation, the essential difference being that it is not only supported by government, but also gets additional income for the sales of shows. . . ."[7]

Third sector bodies

We turn to review the large variety of third sector beings.

Health insurance

One major type is the government-private sector partnership. It is illustrated by an idea which so far has not been enacted, the health insurance plan that has already been mentioned.

The national health insurance plan that the Nixon Administration proposed places part of the financial burden on employers, part on the workers. Employees:

would pay 35 percent of the cost on insurance premiums at the start of the program and 25 percent after 1976. . . . [In addition, there is a suggested government contribution of] provisions costing about $1.4 billion for covering the poor with a family health insurance program, increasing the supply of doctors and other health professionals and streamlining the manner in which medicine has been practiced in the United States.[8]

Nixon's plan requires, in fact depends on, the participation of private health insurance firms in this "governmental" effort. These companies

---

[5] J. F. Garner, "Introduction" to W. G. Friedman and J. F. Garner (ed.), *Government Enterprise* (New York: Columbia University Press, 1970), p. 5.

[6] *Ibid.,* p. 168.

[7] Linda Francke, "The Games People Play on Sesame Street," *New York Magazine,* April 5, 1971, pp. 26–29.

[8] Richard D. Lyons, "Nixon's Health Care Plan Proposes Employers Pay $2.5 Billion More a Year," *New York Times,* February 19, 1971.

would underwrite the increased employer costs as well as the family health insurance plan (for the poor, unemployed, and self-employed). Nixon recognized the "mix" nature of the plan. He stated in his message to Congress:

Good health care should be readily available to all of our citizens. . . . I believe the public will always be better served by a pluralistic system than by a monolithic one, by a system which creates many effective centers of responsibility—both in public and private—rather than one that concentrates authority in a single governmental source.[9]

He did not suggest that, in effect, a third being, pieced together from private and governmental elements into one system, be generated.

Student loans

Another program, similar in basic conception, is already at work in the student loan program. In this plan, the loan is taken by a student. The interest accumulated during the school years is paid by the government. The student repays the loan and the remaining interest after graduation at a rate of 7 per cent. The program is administered differently in different states, with some states guaranteeing a part of the loan against default and other states playing no role whatsoever. However, there are a number of features which are common to all of the loan programs regardless of the specific mechanisms of administration: (1) the federal government guarantees the loans against default, death, or disability of the borrower; (2) the family income of the student must be below $15,000 after adjustment for number of dependents and number of dependents in school; (3) the student may use the loan for tuition or for living expenses; (4) the total amount of loans may not exceed $7,500; and (5) the school plays no part in the loan procedures other than to certify the student's good standing

The growth of the guaranteed loan program has been large and the ambitions held for it yet larger.[10] In 1969 approximately 75,000 students received $670 million, with government financing totalling $71,200,000. In 1970, 923,500 students received loans adding up to $794,241,000, with $114 million of government financing.

It must be pointed out that in comparison to federal fellowships, with their monumental paperwork (announcements, application forms, recommendation letters, transcripts of grades, evaluation, forms, accounting) and high cost to the taxpayer, the student loan program involves little red tape, and the costs to the taxpayer are minor. It should also be noted that the administrative costs of the program are remarkably low. For instance, the appropriation for 1969–70 included $62.4 million for interest subsidies, $10.8

9 "Excerpts from the President's Message Urging a New National Health Strategy," *New York Times,* February 19, 1971.
10 The figures and estimates have been reported in the *Chronicle of Higher Education* based on Office of Education figures.

million for default insurance, and only $1.5 million for computer services.

The program is far from perfect; the rates are still too high, and many fear that the funds will soon run out. It is also criticized for not being responsive to the needs of poor and minority group students. The "Survey of Guaranteed Student Loan Accessibility," done by an independent firm *(Chronicle of Higher Education,* 3/16/70), found this to be true. While 42 per cent of the applicants were female, females accounted for 51 per cent of the refusals. Although 11.7 per cent of the sample was non-white, non-whites accounted for 36.4 per cent of the refusals. The report concluded that "the proportion of females and non-whites not receiving loans was significantly higher than could be explained by chance occurrence." But these shortcomings are being overcome by an increase in the federal contribution and the development of closer cooperation between banks and financial aid officers of universities. By and large, the student loan program provides a fine model for management of federal aid, in which the effects of dollars spent are multiplied many times through the economy.

NASA

Perhaps the most famous of the government-private sector mixes was developed under NASA for project Apollo. The successful completion of the program was made possible by the combination of government facilities and funds, third sector beings, and private corporations. Thus, aeronautical engineers at universities and research foundations worked on government contracts with the businessmen from the aerospace industry to build spacecrafts that were tested and launched on government land. In reporting on their four years of intensive study of NASA, Sayles and Chandler point out that:

NASA, at its peak in the mid-1960s, sought contributions from 20,000 different organizations! . . . A scientist may be part of a university, responsible for the design and testing of an experiment to be flown by a NASA spacecraft, serving as a consultant to an industrial contractor that builds equipment for the agency, and a member of an advisory board that helps shape future science policy for NASA and other government agencies. [11]

Sayles and Chandler go on to say:

thousands of engineers, scientists, technicians, and administrative personnel are employed in laboratory and field-development work, in basic research, in launching and tracking spacecraft, and in a whole host of support activities. While outsiders employed by contractors may comprise 90 percent of the work force, a critical amount of designing, testing, planning, and operating is

[11] Leonard R. Sayles and Margaret K. Chandler, *Managing Large Systems* (New York: Harper & Row, 1971), p. 6.

*conducted "in-house" by NASA personnel. Further, NASA believes, with
substantial justification, that outsiders cannot be successfully stimulated,
managed, or coordinated without a technologically sophisticated internal organization.* [12]

Given the successes of NASA, it seems clear that it was able to overcome many difficulties and coordinate the efforts of all these individuals who
worked for NASA at different points in time, with different perspectives and
training, etc.

*The key to making the NASA structure work rests upon creating an effective
network of formal and informal communications. . . . To be on the safe side,
NASA may err in over-communicating upward, laterally, and downward. It
engulfs anyone who can conceivably influence or implement the decision. It
establishes various "management councils" composed of co-equal associates to share progress and problems on a frequent basis. In an unending
effort to exchange information in real-time, it uses telephone, hot lines,
executive aircraft, datafax, long distance conference hook-ups by voice and
data display and computer data transmission.* [13]

Most of these networks cut across the sectors and thus help integrate
them. The details of this necessarily well-coordinated operation are not important for our discussion. However, it should be remembered that no such
approach has been attempted on our domestic problems. Imagine what effective an attack could be made on heroin addiction if government funds,
hospital staffs, community groups, and local businesses got together to
tackle the program under a well-coordinated and well-financed system! The
same holds for pollution control, crime reduction, and consumer protection.

Postal Service

Sometimes third sector beings are created by governmental fiat. The U.S.
Postal Service is an example of such a public corporation. While the pre-
1970 Post Office Department was dependent on Congress for rate increases, the new one must become entirely self-supporting. In fact, the last
attempt of the old Post Office Department to increase its rate was vetoed
by Congress. A year later, the Postal Service increased its rates. According
to the Postal Reform Act, increased charges can be levied once the Postal
Commission, not Congress, approves them. The enacting legislation requires
the Postal Service to do what is necessary to maintain itself as a financially
independent corporation.

In order to provide better service, this semi-independent corporation

[12] *Ibid.,* p. 161.
[13] Albert Siepert, "NASA's Management of the Civilian Space Program," speech prepared for presentation to the Institute for Management Science meeting, March 28,
1969, mimeo.

has altered its traditional way of operating. Thus, local postmasters used to have to turn to Washington (or at least regional offices) for every decision; now, the local branches seem to be remarkably free from centralization. For example,

Until a year ago the Baltimore office couldn't pay its own utility bills. . . . The bills had to be certified and forwarded to a center in Atlanta for payment. Baltimore and other major post offices have also recently received authority to open small branch offiices without higher approval and to make repairs and improvements costing up to $2,000. . . . Next fall the Baltimore office will move into a spacious new building filled with modern mail-processing equipment. The budgeting basis will be different, too. For the fiscal year beginning July 1, Postmaster Bloomberg is asking for a budget of about $60 million. Previously, postmasters in big cities had no budget; everything was decided by regional bosses.[14]

Before the Postal Service was formed, postmasters were often outsiders, appointed because of political connections. Now, on the other hand, men and women selected for these jobs are experienced and qualified. Their skills, rather than who they know, get them their jobs; thus, it is much more conceivable that one will go up through the ranks of the new postal system. This must lead to higher morale, if not to greater efficiency on the part of Postal Service employees. Although the average letter writer may not notice any difference, except in the color of the mailboxes, it is inconceivable to me that the new system, which cuts through many of the bureaucratic hassles created by an overly centralized operation, could be doing as poor a job as the old Department did. In fact, according to one source, improvements have been made. The *San Francisco Examiner* repeated a survey it did before the Postal Service was formed. Mailings were sent to over 675 individuals in the U.S., Great Britain, Mexico, and the Orient. People who had complained to the *Examiner* in the past about the postal system were reinterviewed as were postal officials and employees. Post offices were also revisited. The findings of this survey when compared to the past survey were:

- The public attitude towards mail service has vastly improved.
- More mail (especially packages) is damaged in transit.
- There is less personnel dissatisfaction with pay (workers have had a 39.4 increase all-around) and with working conditions.
- There is less political manipulation.
- There is less overt racism and greater minority participation.
- There is more dissatisfaction in respect to service to and from APO and FPO addresses (service men).
- Special delivery service is almost an utter waste of time and money.
- San Francisco originating complaints (once many and varied) are largely limited to plaintive wishes from the public that "the mailman would show up

---

[14] Kenneth H. Bacon, "New Postal Corporation Seeks to Become a Business Rather Than a Bureaucracy," *Wall Street Journal,* February 18, 1971.

earlier than he does." (No complaints about hairy or barefoot postmen any longer.)
- Infinitely worse service between Bay Area cities; some of it incredibly bad.
- Infinitely better service (than in 1963) to and from business and banking firms in the area.[15]

Amtrak

Amtrak, the new federally chartered corporation that now runs the intercity passenger trains in this country, is another example of a third sector being created by governmental fiat. The long-range task of the National Railroad Passenger Corporation (Amtrak is its nickname) is "turning a collection of rickety, money-losing passenger trains into a swift, modern transportation system that will attract more riders and make a profit—before it goes broke."[16] Amtrak started operations on May 1, 1971. It received $40 million from Congress and an additional $300 million in loans and guarantees.

Amtrak has since taken a number of steps to remodel passenger railroad transportation, not all of which have been well received. Amtrak reduced the number of trains from 300 to 186. And passenger trains are now given the priority—formerly granted to freight trains—to make inter-city trips shorter; trains no longer stop in many of the very small towns where trains used to stop. In addition, new train service has been added to heavily travelled routes. Connections have been improved because schedules have been revised.

Amtrak continues to have a number of problems that may have more to do with the recentness of the change than with the third sector approach. Many trains are not filled to capacity or even full enough to allow Amtrak to meet its costs.

Initially, Amtrak was set up as a for-profit corporation. However, it suffered unanticipated financial problems less than six months after it took over the largely unprofitable passenger trains and could not achieve the aim of financial independence from Congress. There are many who see Amtrak as the first step in nationalizing the railroads in this country. Companies like the Penn Central can no longer foot the bills created by their large work crews, the loss of business to trucking firms, and the disappearance of certain markets. "As the government moves toward subsidizing long-haul passenger operations through Amtrak, it's an easy jump to rationalize federal support for short-haul freight operation," an Interstate Commerce Commission official says.[17] Many railroad officials, Congressmen, and other public spokesmen are opposed to efforts toward nationalization of the railroads, while union members, creditors, and some Congressmen favor this solution. "And though the industry is generally horrified at the thought of government

---

[15] Robert Patterson, "Postal Service Found Better in New Study," *San Francisco Examiner,* December 6, 1971.
[16] Albert R. Karr, "Government Train Service Is Set to Begin, but Few Improvements Are Likely at First," *Wall Street Journal,* April 27, 1971.
[17] Albert R. Karr, "The Takeover Route," *Wall Street Journal,* January 6, 1972.

takeover, some railroad executives do see public demand for maintaining maximum rail service as tending to force public ownership."[18]

It is far too early to judge where all this will end. If large deficits will continue to plague the railroads, Amtrak might become little more than a "Department of Railroads," a way to nationalize passenger trains, thus becoming a new *government* arm. If miraculously the trains would be profitable enough to be entirely self-supporting, Amtrak may move toward the *private* sector. Most likely it will continue to be partially subsidized and otherwise mix or bridge the two sectors.

Other organizations

There are other branches of our federal government, aside from the postal system, which might be profitably cut off from the bureaucratic maze and made into what the press refers to as semi-private agencies. It has been suggested that since the U.S. Office of Economic Opportunity is becoming mainly a research unit, it would be more effective if it were isolated from political pressures. One way to remove it from direct bureaucratic control would be to set up a public corporation and semi-private agency that would be partially funded by Washington. In an earlier publication, this author suggested a reorganization of the Food and Drug Administration which would be similar to the one our postal system recently underwent.[19]

The Food and Drug Testing Corporation, as the liberated FDA might be called, would be a public corporation endowed by Congress. Its trustees would be appointed from the scientific community, the National Science Foundation, the consumer protection movement, labor unions, etc. The newly formed non-profit corporation would charge a nominal fee to industries desiring the certification of their products. In this way, some of the costs of testing and research could be covered.

The new organization would be removed from the political pressures which hamper the effective operation of the FDA. Its long-term endowment could insure its semi-independent status and its financial security. Our purpose here is not to review all the recent criticisms of the FDA and to show how our own idea would save the day, but as has already been said, it is inconceivable that the new public corporation could do as bad a job as the old one.

The possibilities of the creation by government of public corporations are tremendous. For example, there is evidence that the public would be willing to try a radically different approach to our welfare problems. According to a poll conducted by the Center for Policy Research in 1969, 48 per cent of Americans would pay an average of $6 a month (or $72 a year) to insure themselves against poverty.[20] Given that about a million Americans

---

[18] *Ibid.*

[19] Amitai Etzioni, "Freeing the Food and Drug Administration," *The Conference Board Record,* Vol. 7 (October 1970), pp. 37–39.

[20] Reprints of this unpublished report may be obtained from the Center for Policy Research, Inc., 475 Riverside Drive, New York, New York 10027.

fall into poverty each year, the income generated by the premiums would provide all Americans a minimal income of $1,600 a year. Higher income could be provided if the premiums are raised. Welfare could be handled at least in part through the development of a public corporation that would be in charge of anti-poverty insurance.

Another way to modify anti-poverty programs has been suggested by a bipartisan group of 98 senators and representatives. They introduced "legislation to create an independent National Legal Services Corporation, which would be funded by Congress and operated by an autonomous board of public and private members."[21]

The suggested National Legal Services Corporation would be much more insulated from the political pressures that have surrounded government-run attempts at providing legal aid for the poor. Like my proposed Food and Drug Testing Corporation, the National Legal Services Corporation would be cut off from the bureaucratic maze of governmental agencies because of its autonomous status as a public corporation.

These governmentally created public corporations *do not* have to be on the national level. In New York City, the massive hospital system has been turned into the New York City Health and Hospitals Corporation. The quality of hospital care was rapidly deteriorating in New York City. If the budget for the Corporation is not cut too drastically, we will be able to see what a difference the third sector approach can make in this area. It is hard to imagine that the newly formed corporation will do nearly as poor a job as the worn out agency did.

There have been other corporations that have been public, third sector *from inception.* The Public Broadcasting Corporation which, though far from an unmitigated success, is widely regarded as more effective than governmental agencies in the same business (e.g., New York City's own TV program on channel 31), or commercial TV, as far as broadcasting public education and information is concerned.

Third sector beings can operate in another fashion. Public nongovernmental authorities can be formed to carry out domestic services. One of the problems we frequently run into in this area is caused by the semantics I discussed earlier. The difference between "public" and "private" often hides the possibilities and the achievements of nongovernmental enterprises. For example, we have public universities, like the New York State Universities, and private ones, like Harvard. The same holds for hospitals— the Veterans Administration Hospitals are viewed as public while hospitals like the Columbia Presbyterian are private.

Universities

The *really* "private" sector schools are created for profit. Famous Artists and Career Academy would be examples. And the truly private hospitals are

---

[21] "Bipartisan Group in Congress Urges a Legal Services Corporation for Poor," *New York Times,* March 18, 1971.

proprietary. Nonprofit hospitals, research organizations, universities and colleges, legal aid societies, abortion referral agencies, etc., differ markedly in organization, accountability, and cost-effectiveness from either governmental *or* private sector beings which produce the same kind of public goods.

Given our present situation, where the private sector has not been sufficiently mobilized to produce public goods on a large scale, the best services and facilities can often be found in the third sector. In the educational system, for instance, the universities most highly thought of are not governmental nor are they commercial (Harvard, MIT, Yale, Princeton, Columbia, etc.). And the state-run universities that are highly respected are treated as if they were in the third sector. Berkeley and the University of Wisconsin would be good examples of these. Interestingly, those whose autonomy from state control is being violated are the ones which are on the decline.

There have been some recent attempts to allow the private sector to be more directly involved in the teaching of children. Thus, private concerns were to be paid only to the degree that they improve the performance of students. "Performance contracting," as it is called, was tried out in at least 16 states at a cost of $6.5 million to the federal government. "On the average, each private contractor must improve students' performance in reading and mathematics by 1.6 grades in order to break even."[22]

Indications so far are that contract teaching does not work. A study carried out for HEW by the Rand Corporation found that the programs run by private contractors produced no overall gains in the performance of the children[;] in most cases, the children progressed at the same rate as those not involved in performance contracting.[23]

Hospitals

"Voluntary" hospitals are considered to be the best in our country. Ten experts on hospital care were asked the following question: "If you or your family required major hospital services—diagnosis or treatment—which 25 hospitals in the United States would you select as representative of the best?"[24] The following hospitals were the most popular: (1) Massachusetts General, Boston; (2) Johns Hopkins, Baltimore; (3) University of Chicago, Chicago; (4) Columbia Presbyterian, New York; (5) New York Hospital, New York; (6) (tied) Barnes, St. Louis, and Henry Ford, Detroit; (7) Mount Sinai, New York; (8) St. Mary's, Rochester, Minn.; (9) (tied) Palo Alto-Stanford, Palo-Alto, California, and Yale-New Haven, New Haven, Conn.; (10) (tied) University Hospital, Ann Arbor, Mich., and University of Minnesota Hospital,

[22] Jack Rosenthal, "U.S. Plans Test of the Teaching of Pupils by Private Contractors," *New York Times,* July 15, 1970.
[23] See *Science News,* Vol. 100, No. 25 (1972).
[24] Roul Tunley, "America's 10 Best Hospitals," *Ladies Home Journal,* Vol. 85 (February 1967), pp. 34, 134.

Minneapolis, Minn. All of these hospitals are also non-profit teaching institutions. They are all in the third sector—none are proprietary and none are governmental.

Proprietary medical schools were forced to close down as long ago as 1910 when the American Medical Association began to set new standards for accreditation.[25] Proprietary hospitals in general seem to be of lower quality than third sector ones. Government hospitals do not usually measure up to the third sector ones either. A good example of this would be a comparison of mental hospitals. The state institutions are basically inferior to third sector facilities.

Since July 1, 1970, abortions have been legal in the state of New York. Two different kinds of abortion referral agencies developed. The first kind is offered as a free service by groups like Planned Parenthood, the Family Planning Information Service, the Clergy Consultation Services on Abortion, and other non-profit groups. The other group consists of profit-making firms. These "have found in the hard-won reform the basis for 'one of the most lucrative businesses of the year.' . . . [according to] Stephen E. Mindell, an assistant attorney general in the office of the State Attorney General Louis J. Lefkowitz. . . ."[26]

The State Attorney General's Office now has an operating injunction against these commercial firms. They found that the profit-making abortion referral agencies were splitting fees with doctors and advertising medicine in a way that was contrary to the common law of the state. The case against Abortion Information Agency, Incorporated, a profit-making firm, is now in the Court of Appeals. (The state won its case in the New York State Supreme Court and the decision was affirmed in the Appellate Division.)

In addition, the New York State Legislature passed a statute which prohibited the operation of for-profit abortion agencies. This statute has been upheld by a panel of three federal judges convened to hear the case.

The non-profit abortion referral agencies, which neither split fees nor advertise specific doctors, may continue to operate. In this case, the merits of the public sector over the private one, for this kind of service, are particularly evident.

These brief comments on relative quality of services may seem gratuitous, especially to those familiar with the complexities of making full-fledged evaluative studies. However, only few such studies have been undertaken, and hence statements which compare the merits of doing things one way or another are necessarily tentative, until more studies are conducted.

Of course, not all third sector beings are superior on all counts, as is illustrated by the New York Triboro Bridge and Tunnel Authority. The Authority is reported to use its monopoly power to generate excessive income and

[25] See editorial entitled "Higher Education and the Nation's Health" by John H. Knowles, general director, Massachusetts General Hospital, in *Science,* Vol. 171 (January 1971).
[26] Linda Charlton, "Abortion Brokers Are Under Study," *New York Times,* February 10, 1971.

keep its facilities in unnecessarily good condition. The New York Port Authority is certainly not known for its efficiency. Maybe the reason is that most of these ineffective bodies, *within* the third sector, are on the less "privatized," more "governmental" side.

Two success stories

Those third sector beings which have been relatively more "privatized" seem to be, on balance, much more successful. Two major cases in point are COMSAT and Fannie Mae.

Fannie Mae

Fannie Mae (or FNMA), which stands for the Federal National Mortgage Association, is reported in the press daily as a high volume stock on the New York Stock Exchange. But it is far from just another stock of a typical corporation. (Even technically it has had a special status which reflects its government support: until April 1971 the "margin" required for it was much lower than for other common stocks; it was closer to that required for government bonds.) Originally a government agency, which issued some *non-voting* stocks to the public, with the balance being funded by the treasury, it was "privatized" in 1968. All the stocks were sold to the public and made into voting stocks which elect up to 10 of the 15 board members (the rest being appointed by the Secretary of HUD).

However, about one-third of Fannie Mae's volatile stock is owned by companies involved in housing-related industries; they are, for the most part, the mortgage bankers with whom Fannie Mae does a major part of its business.

Fannie Mae now ranks as the eighth largest corporation in the United States. Its aim has been to meet the public's need for housing by providing a secondary market for government-insured mortgages.

Investment-wise, Fannie Mae is a unique animal. One reason is the complex nature of its earnings. Despite the fact that there has probably never been a company on which more information was available, the variables are so great that a line-by-line prediction is extremely difficult to make. Management stresses that when one component such as fees goes one way, another element, perhaps the sale of mortgages, will move in the opposite direction.

Skeptics insist that Fannie Mae is a near monopoly, government-sponsored and controlled, which will never be allowed to earn more than a public utility or other regulated companies. If Congress thinks Fannie Mae is making too much money, they say, it could intervene and change the charter of the company. Further, the Secretary of HUD, George Romney, holds the power to narrow or broaden the ratio of debt to equity.[27]

While there are clearly a number of problems like these that potential investors in Fannie Mae must take into account, it is also clear that Fannie Mae has made money available to potential home buyers in a time of tight credit and high interest rates. For example, Fannie Mae's "net new business in 1970 totaled 25 per cent of U.S. residential mortgage credit. Moreover, in 1969 and 1970, Fannie Mae helped boost FHA and VA financed housing starts 140 per cent, while conventional starts declined 7 per cent."[28]

In the last few years, Fannie Mae has been trying to balance its responsibility to the public with its responsibility to achieve stable returns for its stockholders. In the process Fannie Mae has been reorganized in a more efficient manner by *cutting* its staff substantially as the volume of work *rose*.

Comsat

The Communications Satellite Corporation, known as Comsat, was created by the government through a congressional act in 1962. Federal money appropriated for defense and space financed the development of its chief technology—the world-hugging satellites. Civilian use was made possible through a corporation financed half by the public and half by the commercial communications companies. Comsat's board of directors includes representatives of the industries involved, presidential-appointed directors, and public officials. The *Economist* referred to orbiting a world-wide system within seven years, as "magnificent."[29]

Conclusion

Surely other third types, either to be composed of government and business elements or third sector beings from inception, can be identified, and others could be evolved if there were greater experimentation. There is no doubt that we need more information and evaluation on the production of public goods in the various sectors and mixes of sectors. But it seems that enough is known for us to be able to state now that greater reliance on the third sector, both as a way of reducing government on all levels and as a way of involving the private sector in the service of domestic missions, would be significantly more effective than either expanding the federal or other levels of government or dropping them on the private sector.

[27] Robert Lenzner, "What Makes Fannie Run?" *Barrons,* July 12, 1971.
[28] *Ibid.*
[29] *The Economist,* August 9, 1969.

66 The manager of the future
John F. Mee

Coming events cast their shadows before—if we study those shadows, we can observe the forces and factors that are shaping the manager of the future.

There will be managers in the future. The pathologists can predict with certainty that bleeding will always stop; managers can predict with certainty that the future will eventually involve them. Their concern is whether or not they are prepared for the changing social, economic, technological, and political environments that emerge as the future unfolds.

Managers of the past

Managers of the past can be described and classified in relation to the environments in which they operated. The antecedents of the managers in our English-influenced culture can be recognized in sixteenth-century Tudor England. They were the office-holders in the royal household, in the major departments of state, and in the army and the navy. They were men to whom administration and management was a professional life commitment, and their function was to administer the affairs of the state and the economy within the rules of the social order.

After the separation of the United States from England, our constitution provided that individuals might own private property. Our government founded on the concept of government by law rather than government by men, established an environment of opportunity for the owner-manager in a private enterprise economy. For over a century, the owner-managers of small enterprises flourished, managing by right of ownership rather than by birthright in a predominantly agricultural society.

Some of those owner-managers thrived with the changing environment at the turn of the century, and, using their authority of ownership, developed our basic industries and promoted our industrial society. Facing death from the impact of the Sherman Act they resorted to corporate forms of business organizations to perpetuate their firms. The growth of large and complex organizations with the capability of generating a trillion dollar gross national product originated with these "captains of industry."

They were followed by a new breed of managers who are now classified as corporate speculators and exploiters. These managers, who had financial or legal backgrounds, gained control of the business organizations that they managed for corporate share owners. The era of the speculators and exploiters was rather short. They met with an ignominious end in the decade of the 1930s because they were unable to manage business organi-

Source: From *Business Horizons* (June 1973), pp. 5–14. Copyright © 1973 by the Foundation for the School of Business at Indiana University. Reprinted by permission.

zations for the benefit of society through the intelligent use of human and capital resources.

During that decade the federal government set about helping managers with legislative guidelines and regulations. The health of the economy was deemed too important to trust to capricious managers with improper human values and undesirable social ethics. The flow of legislation regulating business activities and the pressures for social responsibilities and objectives of business were initiated by the failures of these managers.

Following the debacle of the thirties, a class of managers known as professional managers appeared; most operating managers of business enterprise today are in this category. The term professional managers is used because these men manage for pay and do not own any significant share of the enterprises they manage. They profess to have the knowledge, the skills and the value systems suitable for setting objectives and then attaining them through the utilization of other people's money, talents, and physical facilities. Some of them acquire professional manager citations from their professional associations to reinforce their image.

Evaluated by their records of economic progress and the creation of material wealth, our American managers have the best performance records in the history of the world. U.S. resources include 6 percent of the world's population and 7 percent of the land area of the world; with these, our managers have generated over half of the wealth of the world and about 35 percent of the world's annual income. They have achieved the world's first trillion dollar gross national product. The combined efforts of Russia, Japan, West Germany, and the United Kingdom—with double the population of the United States—would be required to equal that figure.

That is a formidable record of managerial achievement; why, then, are managers experiencing so much dissatisfaction with their performance? Why are today's professional managers, working on the objectives established for the decade of the sizzling sixties, absorbing attacks for matters that previously have not been considered germane to operating businesses? Despite the most outstanding performance of managers in all history, they are criticized and attacked by:

- Consumer groups and regulatory agencies
- Aroused antipollutionists who often press for hasty, costly, or sometimes unavailable solutions
- Ecologists who are more concerned with preserving the wilderness than creating employment opportunities
- Civil rights activists who demand more jobs for minority groups from top to bottom ranks
- Naive and well-meaning activists who clamor for democracy on boards of directors
- Employees who want relief from boring and monotonous work assignments

Recognizing merit in some of the criticism, perhaps too many well-meaning people are finding themselves influenced by the extremists and activists who can proclaim without responsibility. James Roche of General Motors Corporation has tried to bring the extremist view into perspective:"Profits are the incentives, the driving force behind economic expansion and rising employment. It takes about $25,000 investment to create one new job opportunity. Just to keep pace with the rising labor force each year requires an opening of about 1.75 million new jobs."

Obviously, the managers of the future must be mindful of several worthwhile corporate objectives, but they had better not lose sight of the primary objective of a business, that of staying in business. No profits, no business. Survival is the first priority of managing.

Managers in the future will be expected to create wealth, generate profits, and provide employment for the fulfillment of the public policy outlined in the Employment Act of 1946. Furthermore, they will be expected to utilize the human resources of the nation in accordance with the spirit of equal economic opportunity, civil rights, equal employment opportunity, and, at the same time, adhere to the clean air and clean water guidelines of the Environmental Protection Agency within the Occupational Health and Safety Act standards. Managers will be challenged to create almost 2 million new employment opportunities a year with people working fewer hours per week. The four-day work week is on the horizon with "gliding work time" a probability. A 28-hour work week has been predicted for the turn of the century, compared with 37.3 hours in 1970, 49 hours in 1930, 57 hours in 1900, 70 hours in 1850, and 84 hours in 1800.

Future managers will be expected to create more goods and services with more profits and more employment, and to deal with employees' demands for more leisure, more services, and more conveniences in a technological economy in a scientific society. The role of future managers will be complicated further by energy and power shortages and pressure to guard the environment from damage.

Some of the most obvious and pressing factors and forces in the changing economic, social, and political situation have been cited to illustrate that managers of the future will be operating in an environment different from that in which managers of the past operated. The question of managerial concern is now posed. What knowledge, skills, and values will be required for the future manager's survival and success?

Managers of the future

According to the time schedule, a new type of manager should now be emerging to cope with the complexity of factors and forces in a society that is struggling to adapt to changing human values and rapid technological advances. It is probable that the manager of the future will be classified as a "public manager" or a "public oriented executive." Harlan Cleveland, in his recent book *The Future Executive,* predicts the role of the future public executive and gives reasons for his or her emergence.

Today's professional manager will modify his style and begin the transition toward the era of the public manager; the potential managers among the some 8 million students in the universities today will complete the transition during the last portion of the century. The manager will develop from a hired man for private corporation shareholders into a business institutional leader who will manage enterprise for the best balanced interests of the state and the nation to preserve and maintain our private enterprise system. This development could be changed, of course, in the event of war, epidemic, depression, or some other unforeseen catastrophe.

The environmental factors and forces at work, such as changing human values along with the growing size and complexity of organizational patterns, are blurring the traditional lines between what is private and what is public. The future managers of private enterprise—profit or nonprofit—will gravitate toward the concept that they are responsible for people in general and reluctantly accept the government as a monitor of business affairs. Concurrently, the government will contract to the private sector of the economy a growing proportion of the public business because public managers will be better qualified to achieve the results desired by the body politic.

The National Aeronautics and Space Administration is a prime example of this method of operation. No large business organization, whatever its formal ownership, will be able to escape social and public responsibility. Public managers will be faced with the major responsibility for merging human values with the potential from technological advances to conserve human energy in the creation and distribution of goods and services for improved life styles.

For the managers of the future, policies for the conduct of their firms will be formulated mostly by their sense of direction as modified by negotiation with their colleagues and peers. Private enterprise will prevail, but managers will be sensitive to the need to satisfy multiple claimants for the benefits flowing from national and multinational corporations.

Actually, it is the success of past managers that has developed this trend toward the concept of the public manager. The managers of our corporate enterprises have succeeded in creating most of the wealth of the nation; they also have attracted most of the nation's competent personnel into the work force of the corporations. Corporations, therefore, have the greatest capability of achieving state and national goals for economic and social progress. If the managers of private enterprise do not adopt the public manager concept, the alternative would not be acceptable to the advocates of the private enterprise system that has been the foundation of the American dream.

Future managerial situation

The first priority for managers of the future will be the survival of the companies that they manage and their own survival as managers. If present professional managers could send a scout into the future, receive reports, and ensure their survival by being prepared, such reports probably would include subject areas that already are discernible. The public manager in the future will perform functions with resources that may have names the same as or similar to present ones, but they will change in concept and nature in response to changing human values and environmental conditions.

The manager of the future will deal with highly complex organizations. The organizational vehicle will not be the hierarchical pyramid in which decisions are centralized and most of the planning and control are done at the top. The future manager's organizational mechanism will be in the nature of systems that will have interlaced webs of tension with loose control; power will be diffused among plural centers of decision. Decision making will become an increasingly intricate process of multilateral brokerage both inside and outside the organization.

As organizations become more horizontal and less vertical in structure, the style by which they will be governed will be more consensual, collegial, and consultive. The more challenging the objective and the more formidable the problems to be resolved, the more authority and power will be diffused so that a larger number of capable people can work toward achievement and problem solving. Collective leadership is not for the expression of democratic feelings; it is an imperative of size and complexity. The manager of the future must manage more complexity for survival.

Evidence of the increasing complexity of organizations is easily observable in the growth and influence of multinational firms, bank holding companies, and conglomerate corporations. Multinational firms already dominate much of the production of the world, and they are growing at a rate double the purely domestic companies. Some of them exert great influence on the world's financial affairs and have grown in economic size beyond all but the wealthiest nations. They are creating an economic and social movement that rivals the impact of the industrial revolution. Bank holding companies, as of mid-1972, held nearly 40 percent of all commercial banks in the nation with 58 percent of all deposits and 60 percent of all U.S. assets. The responsibilities of the managers of these complex organizations are greater than those faced by previous managers; the consequences of error and mismanagement could have serious negative impacts on the world economy.

Managers of these organizations have the opportunity to influence the peace of the world and the living standards and life styles of the peoples of less developed nations because the influence of their operations can transcend national boundaries more readily than that of governments or religious orders. However, they can only achieve their potential by managing with the concept and style of a public oriented manager. J. J. Servan-Schreiber, in his book *The American Challenge* paid tribute to the genius and viability of American managers: "American industry spills out across the world primarily because of the energy released by the American system—by the opportunity for individual initiative, by the innovative knack of teams, by the flexibility of business structure and by the decentralization of business decision."

The manager of the future will encounter an accelerating growth in the size and complexity of organizational systems that seem destined to move away from formal, authoritarian, and hierarchical managing. The trend is toward more informal, fluid ways of bargaining, brokerage, advice, and consent. Management will be practiced less as a system of authority and more as a resource in an organizational system to achieve desired results.

The view of William Blackie, the past chairman of Caterpillar Tractor Company, reflects the changing concept: "Insofar as authority has meant the power to order or command, its definition will be modified by the addition of some such qualification as 'but expect or deserve to be obeyed or followed only if you can satisfy those being ordered or led'." According to Blackie, the boss-man relationship will prevail and embrace both a superior and a subordinate. The gap will be narrowed, however, because of the rapidity with which the well-educated subordinate is acquiring skill and experience. The essential requirement is that both parties understand and appreciate the basic nature of their respective responsibilities.

The manager of the future will realize that employees will be more inclined to take authority from agreed-upon objectives and the nature of the work than from the dictation of an authoritarian boss. More than one mode of thinking can be utilized. The future manager will be a multiplier of the work of others; in the more complex organizations of the future, he will find it necessary to utilize the knowledge and skills that others possess. He will be responsible for results and for "getting it all together," rather than for preoccupying himself with individual processes.

Authority as used by the future manager will be modified by the changing values and motivations of university students as they populate the organizations of business. By 1985, college graduates will outnumber those without a high school education in the U.S. work force, and managers will have as a resource the most highly educated personnel in the history of the world. Employees will regard themselves as partners in management and expect to have their talents utilized for self-esteem and self-realization. The better educated young people today, especially those in the so-called new culture or counter culture, tend to demand their rights, resist authority and regimentation that try to put them into an organizational harness too tight for comfort, and search for their own identity instead of allowing themselves to be "house-broken" by endless procedures and processes.

Before anyone makes a quick decision that universities are subversive places and our young people have revolutionary ideas, it might be enlightening to read *The Unanimous Declaration of the Thirteen United States of America*. In this document, popularly known as the Declaration of Independence, one will find written:

We hold these truths to be self-evident, that all men are created equal, that they are endowed by their Creator with certain unalienable Rights, that among these are Life, Liberty, and the pursuit of Happiness—That to secure these rights, governments are instituted among Men, deriving their just powers from the consent of the governed—That whenever any form of government becomes destructive of these ends, it is the Right of the People to alter or to abolish it, and to institute new government, laying its foundation on such principles, and organizing its powers in such form, as to them shall seem most likely to effect their Safety and Happiness.

If a substitution of the words "management" for "government" and "employees" for "people" is made in the reading of that document, one can better understand why there is a trend in the concept of management by the consent of those managed. Of course, there is no reference to women. The proposed 27th amendment to the constitution might remedy this original writing. Some thirty states have ratified the amendment with thirty-eight required to provide equal rights for women by the enactment of an Equal Rights Act. Depending upon one's point of view, an equal rights act may be necessary to enlarge opportunities for women. With few exceptions, most professions and trades employed about the same percentage of women in 1970 as in 1950, twenty years previously.

Henry B. Schacht, commenting on the changing trend in organizational design and the use of human resources, has stated that managers must learn to handle both the underprivileged and the bright young people, especially those who are calling for a change [*Business Horizons,* August, 1970, pp. 29–34]. He adds:

What this means is shorter, flatter organizations; it means responsive management; it means a true willingness to allow people to participate in setting their own destiny; it means that the militaristically-oriented hierarchy that has characterized societies and most business enterprises is a thing of the past, and the quicker we recognize it the better . . . all organizations will have to think of their key assets in terms of people and knowledge. People can be the most flexible of all assets; knowledge is the one thing that will give us insight into change and the consequences of change. Many companies say that people are its most important resource, but few believe it. Many people say that they live or die with their people but then spend all of their time analyzing balance sheets and income statements.

Current professional managers who make the transition to public oriented managers will master the methods required to achieve objectives in organizations with more complex and decentralized ralationships; they will develop the skills to use as a modified concept of authority that will enable personnel to exercise self-commitment and self-control for the achievement of agreed upon results instead of emphasizing processes.

For the realization of high motivation and performance of personnel in more complex organizational relationships, authority must be applied with the consent and cooperation of those managed. Future managers will cope with the challenge of generating purposeful action while more and more employees demand the satisfaction of getting into the act.

Future external forces on managers

All organizations exist and operate in an environment of some kind. External forces and factors in the environment will complicate the work of future managers. Before the end of the present decade, for example, managers of all organizations in the United States will be faced with the problem of adapting their operations to the metric system of weights and measurements. (The meter unit of measurement was determined by measuring the distance from the North Pole to the equator and then dividing by 10 million. The meter is 3.3 feet or 1.1 yards in the English system.) At present, the United States and Burma are the only major nations still using the English system. Because of the world trend, Congress asked in 1968 for a sweeping investigation of the question. This investigation involved public hearings and surveys on almost every activity in our society—from education, manufacturing, and the consumer to international trade and national security. The recommendation of the Secretary of Commerce was that the United States should adopt the metric through a nationally coordinated program.

This conversion will affect all managers of business enterprise, especially the manufacturers. Temperature will be measured by Celsius instead of Fahrenheit; length will be computed by centimeters and kilometers rather than by inches and miles; mass weight will change from ounces and pounds to grams and kilograms; area will be determined by square meters and square kilometers instead of by square feet and square miles; hectares will replace acres; and volume will be measured by milliliters and liters.

Present managers are planning for the costs of conversion, which will be relatively greater in the manufacturing industry. The greatest burden of costs will be in production and industrial educational programs, particularly the machine tool and automotive industries. The conversion will entail considerable costs for manufacturers during a time when costs will be increasing for pollution and environmental damage control.

The material wealth of the nation, measured by either the metric system or the passing English system, stems from the managerial use of the basic factors of production, land, labor, and capital. The manager of the future will be more restricted in his use of land than his predecessors. Managers of the past have enjoyed freedom of decision in the use of private land, regardless of whether or not it was devoted to its highest and best use. The market system prevailed. The future manager, however, will be confined to operating within federal and state land-use policy. A bill now in Congress (S. 268) will give grants to states for the development of plans for private land use.

J. Irwin Miller, a prominent Indiana industrialist, in a recent issue of *U.S. News and World Report,* expressed his views concerning corporate survival by serving effectively and well some real current need of society. He wrote:

We have a fixed amount of land in the continental United States. Contained in that fixed amount of land is a fixed amount of natural resources. On the fixed amount of land, then, with a finite quantity of resources, there exists a growing population of human beings. By the end of the century there will be somewhere between 50 and 100 million more people in this country. . . . Growing demand for a shrinking supply of land and materials can prudently be expected only to accelerate the rise in cost of capital construction despite the miracles that need performing in labor costs, regulations and design.

Land-use policy for the guidelines of the future manager stems from the growing population that requires more land for living, domestic and foreign consumption, recreation, and energy sources. Future managers will be expected to create the equivalent of a new city for a million people about every four months during the remainder of the century. They will also be expected to produce for a per capita consumption of some 700 British thermal units of energy by the year 2000, in comparison with 377 in 1970, and at the same time protect the environment from water and air pollution and trash.

Proposed legislation in Congress (S. 1283) will create a new federal agency with authority to relieve the fuel shortage. The legislation will create five "government-industry" corporations to develop technology to turn coal into gas, extract oil from shale rock, and harness geothermal energy. Soon legislation may be passed for the control of trash pollution in addition to water and air pollution. Currently we are producing enough trash annually to fill the Panama Canal four times over with a disposal cost of some $5 billion a year. This cost is exceeded only by that for schools and roads in the public services. Our trash volume will triple in the next decade to harass the future manager as increased demands will be made for the discharge of his social responsibilities.

Although the land resource is considered fixed for the future manager, he will have an increasing supply of labor flowing from the enlarging population. However, this labor resource will be different from that of the past and will require a different style of managing. This style must recognize the consent of the managed with an orientation around results rather than activities in more viable organizations. The members of the labor force of the future will be the best educated in history with knowledge and skills that many managers will need but will not possess. Furthermore, employees' expectations and value systems will be different.

Over 80 percent will be high school and college graduates who will expect managers to utilize their talents and abilities in interesting and challenging work opportunities with a minimum of boredom and monotony. Their work styles and life styles may be as important to them as their pay scales. They will resist being used as impersonal "inputs" in complex organizations under authoritarian supervisors. They will be products of the new knowledge industry that may account for half of the GNP by the end of the century, and they will expect managers to fulfill their responsibilities for both economic and social objectives.

In the future labor force, some will be specialists, others technologists, and many humanists. Some will have broad preparation, such as the proposed "poly-socio-econo-politico-technolo-gist" background that has been conceived by Simon Ramo, vice-chairman of TRW, Inc. The manager of the future will be expected to utilize intelligently this highly competent labor force and avoid underemploying or wasting human resources. The wealth of the state and the nation will be measured more by the productivity of the labor force than by gold bullion, and future managers may be evaluated more on their abilities to skillfully utilize a growing labor force than to use capital equipment. The human asset will appear on the balance sheet of the future. Advancing technology will aid the future manager in his use of resources, but he will need to arrange a satisfactory combination of ethical human values with the flow of science and technology.

The capital resources available to managers in the future should be adequate if inflation can be controlled. National personal income in the United States has passed the lofty mark of a trillion dollars per annum for another historical first. No other nation has come close to this annual flow of personal income from wages, salaries (with fringe benefits), interest, rent, dividends, and social welfare, and the income to business proprietors and professional personnel. Reasonable savings and investment of a portion of this personal income can provide adequate capital resources for future managers to combine with land and labor resources for the maintenance of a healthy economy.

The public managers of the future will differ more in their values and attitudes than in their knowledge and skills. One can already discern in the United States that the line between public and private is narrowing because all private enterprise has some degree of public responsibility. The larger and more complex the enterprise, the more public responsibility it is expected to carry. Regardless of their personal values, more managers in private enterprise are serving more and more as public managers or executives.

If the manager of the future makes the transition from the firm-oriented professional manager of today to the public oriented manager, the business foundation of democracy and private enterprise can be maintained with managerial freedom to set objectives and policies for the best balanced interests of the economy. Furthermore, the future public manager can be recognized for making contributions to society as beneficial as those made by doctors, lawyers, ministers, engineers, educators, and scientists.

The public manager of the future can lessen the credibility gap in management that has widened since 1965. It is ironic today that our citizens want business to become more active in public leadership, yet believe that business is doing less than before, according to a recent Louis Harris survey. The future public manager will perform the essential managerial functions in society in a manner that will enhance his credibility. Alec Mackenzie, in his recent book *The Credibility Gap in Management,* states that "credibility is that quality, state, or condition that produces believability or trustworthiness." He comments that credibility depends more upon relationships with people than upon systems. Somehow, the public is inclined to believe that business is out of phase with current expectations and demands. It is not the capability and competence of business managers that are being questioned, it is their sense of priorities and good faith.

At a time when the public is crying for a new leadership style, some managers are retreating into fixed behavior patterns. They are charged with proclaiming a modern managerial theory but continuing to execute in antiquated managerial practices. Unless the manager of the future assumes a role similar to the public manager concept, there looms the possibility of the establishment of a public management commission because of the importance of managers in our economy and to prevent serious management failures in essential corporations that affect the public interest.

If governmental commissions are considered essential for the proper utilization of the resources of land, labor, and capital, it is not inconceivable that public pressures could develop for monitoring the application of the management resource in our society. Without the resource of management to utilize other resources, little is accomplished. Managers who learn to manage with a public orientation will obviate any need for a public management commission. Their value systems will embrace the service of multiple claimants in society by the setting and the achievement of both the economic and the social objectives of their firms.

The public manager of the future has the opportunity to achieve the prestige and the recognition that managers have earned but not received on the basis of contributions to society. Congress or a state legislature can recognize the importance of the future public managers by establishing a national or a state Management Day. For the contributions that managers make to economic and social progress, it would be suitable to have two holidays in one week, Labor Day on Monday and Management Day on Tuesday. This would focus attention on the relationship of both segments of our private enterprise society. Together they have produced the biggest national output, the highest personal income, and the highest standard of living in the world.

Conclusion/D
A final thought

67 On technological progress
John D. MacDonald

I remembered the time he had told me how he had researched the (project).
It seemed almost too easy. I asked why other people didn't do the same
thing he had done.

He had frowned, shaken his head slowly. "It's one of the great mys-
teries of the human condition. . . . Maybe we all think it is not worth doing
merely because it is so obvious it must have been done already. Fantastic
warehouses of knowledge rot away, untouched. The scholars seem to have
no interest. The adventurers have no research skills. They've found ancient
jewelry in tombs in the Middle East made of smelted platinum. It takes eighteen hundred degrees centigrade to melt it. Two thousand years ago, the
Chinese made aluminum ornaments. Getting aluminum from bauxite is a
sophisticated chemical-electrical procedure. In the Baghdad Museum you
can see the parts of a dry battery which worked on the galvanic principle
and generated electricity sixteen hundred years ago. More smelted platinum
has been found in Peru, in the high country. Knowledge fades away, and
some is rediscovered and some isn't. We never seem to take the trouble to
really find out—until too late. For several years the public baths at Alexandria
were heated by burning the old scrolls and documents carted over from the
great library. Are we so arrogant we believe that there was nothing that was
burned up that hasn't been rediscovered? I dug back only four hundred
years or so. That's easy. Yet I found journals which had turned to solid
blocks, as if all the pages had been glued together. I found old documents
so fragile I could not touch them without turning them into dust, and others
where the ink had faded until it was completely gone. Treasures are buried
on those pages, never to be found again except by the rarest accident. It's
the . . . contemporary arrogance that bothers me. The idiot idea that we are
the biggest, the greatest, the most powerful people who ever walked the
earth. Know something? Think this over. I could take you to the high country

Source: From John D. MacDonald, *The Turquoise Lament,* pp. 115–117, Greenwich,
Connecticut: Fawcett Publications, Inc., 1973. © John D. MacDonald 1974.

of Peru, to a quarry area near Sacsahuaman, and show you where a particular block of stone was quarried and dressed, and I could show you that block of stone half a mile away. It was transported there during the time of the Incas. If, on the basis of national emergency, this nation were to be required to devote all its technological skills, all its wealth, and all its people to moving that block back to the quarry, we would try and we would fail, my friend. It weighs twenty thousand tons! Forty million pounds! The only time we ever move that much weight is when we let a vessel as big as the MONTEREY or the MARIPOSA slide down the ways at the shipyard, into the harbor. We have no cranes, no engines, no levers to budge that much mass. Do you think the Incas knew something mankind has since forgotten? Bet on it. Knowledge is the most priceless and most perishable substance on earth."

68 See what we mean?
George A. Krimsky

Moscow—On the morning of June 30, 1908, an explosion lit up the already bright sky over central Siberia. The force was strong enough to knock horses to the ground more than 400 miles away.

Investigators later estimated that the blast was equal to the detonation of 300 million tons of TNT or the equivalent of 1,500 atomic bombs of the type that devasted Hiroshima.

Sixty-eight years after it happened, scientists are still unable to agree on the cause of the "Tunguska" phenomenon, named for the remote forest site where the explosion took place. The initial assumption was that a gigantic meteorite had smashed into the earth, but this idea was ultimately rejected when no crater and no meteor fragments could be found.

Every summer for the past 17 years, the Soviet Union has sent expeditions to the area where thousands of charred and flattened trees still lie over a vast expanse shaped like a butterfly, stretching 50 miles from wing to wing.

The Tunguska mystery has spawned numerous theories from both serious scientists and dreamy science fiction writers.

Continued interest in the Tunguska explosion has particular relevance in the nuclear age. More than once, scientists have posed the question: What if it happened today?

How, for example, would the nuclear powers react if an explosion of the Tunguska magnitude occurred again anywhere on Earth?

Source: Associated Press, October 28, 1976.

Here are the generally accepted data about the Tunguska phenomenon:

A space body of undetermined size penetrated the earth's atmosphere, traveling from east to west at a speed of more than 3,000 miles per hour. It exploded about four miles above the earth.

The blast leveled trees over a 1,250-square mile area, presumably killing all living things. But since the area was largely uninhabited, few human deaths were recorded. The explosion was followed by intense radiation, which ignited a massive fire.

For weeks after the explosion, the night sky glowed with extraordinary luminescence, seen as far away as Western Europe.

In addition, there were some particularly puzzling features. The trees at "ground zero," immediately beneath the blast, remained standing. Only their bark and branches were stripped clean.

Also, because of the radiation burns and the resemblance to a nuclear explosion, scientists expected to find heavy traces of radioactivity in the area. But they did not.

What they did find, however, was unusually lush vegetation which had grown in the area since the explosion. And examination of the growth rings of trees which survived outside the devastated zone showed that the wood had increased 10 to 12 times its normal rate since 1908.

Although no meteorite fragments were found, microscopic particles of melted silicate, or glass, were discovered several years ago in the peat bogs of Tunguska. These particles did not resemble other silicates found on earth.

They contained the rare elements selenium and ytterbium, which were thought to originate only in the depths of planets.

The most prevalent theories as to what happened:

- A comet head blew up. This notion supposes that the head of a comet, a huge "dirty snowball" of frozen gases, exploded from the heat generated by its clash with earth air. This would explain why there was neither a crater nor traces of meteorite iron found later.

Opponents of this theory ask why the "comet" was not seen approaching the earth.

Probably the most effective argument against this theory is that a comet head would likely have exploded as soon as it hit earth's atmosphere several hundred miles up.

- A rock of anti-matter, composed of atomic elements opposite to those making up the matter in this universe, traveled from another solar system and annihilated upon contact with earth's ordinary atoms. Modern astronomy has proposed the existence of anti-matter, and some have theorized that its collision with matter would produce a gamma ray fireball and blast similar to the Tunguska occurrence. This theory would explain the radiation burns, as well as the absence of a mushroom cloud.

The biggest drawback to this theory is that it is too much of just that—theory. Anti-matter remains a laboratory and blackboard calculation, not a known astronomical substance.

- Even more exotic is the "black hole" theory, which suggests that a collapsed star from another galaxy hit Siberia, passed through the earth and came out through the north Atlantic, continuing on its way out of the universe.

  This possibility was raised in a 1973 article by two University of Texas scientists, expanding on new assumptions that there are objects—"black holes"—in the sky so dense in gravity that even light is swallowed up by them. The two contended that a tiny black hole's penetration would explain most of the effects reported from Tunguska.

- A number of scientists here and abroad cling to the belief that Tunguska was a nuclear explosion. They arrive at this largely through a process of elimination of what Tunguska could not have been.

  If this theory is the most plausible so far, it raises the obvious question: Who or what was responsible for a nuclear explosion almost four decades before man harnessed nuclear fission?